Teach
Yourself
MICROSOFT ®
VISUAL
INTERDEV™

in 21 Days

Teach Yourself
MICROSOFT®
VISUAL
INTERDEV™
in 21 Days

Michael Van Hoozer

201 West 103rd Street
Indianapolis, Indiana 46290

To my wife, Gina, who complements, supplements, and completes my life; and to my sons, Drew and Will, who provide an inspiration for my life.

Copyright © 1997 by Sams.net Publishing
FIRST EDITION

International Standard Book Number: 1-57521-093-2

Library of Congress Catalog Card Number: 96-67211

2000 99 98 97   4 3 2

Interpretation of the printing code: the rightmost double-digit number is the year of the book's printing; the rightmost single-digit, the number of the book's printing. For example, a printing code of 97-1 shows that the first printing of the book occurred in 1997.

Composed in AGaramond and MCPdigital by Macmillan Computer Publishing

Printed in the United States of America

Trademarks

Publisher Richard K. Swadley
Publishing Manager Mark Taber
Director of Editorial Services Cindy Morrow
Director of Marketing Kelli Spencer
Assistant Marketing Managers Kristina Perry, Rachel Wolfe

Acquisitions Editor
Kelly Murdock

Software Development Specialist
Bob Correll

Production Editor
Howard A. Jones

Copy Editor
Lisa M. Lord

Indexers
Ginny Bess
Ben Slen

Technical Reviewer
BCI and Associates

Editorial Coordinator
Katie Wise

Technical Edit Coordinator
Lorraine Schaffer

Resource Coordinator
Deborah Frisby

Editorial Assistants
Carol Ackerman
Andi Richter
Rhonda Tinch-Mize

Cover Designer
Tim Amrhein

Book Designer
Gary Adair

Copy Writer
Peter Fuller

Production Team Supervisors
Brad Chinn
Charlotte Clapp

Production
Betsy Deeter
Brad Lenser
Paula Lowell
Andrew Stone

Overview

Week 3 in Review 663

Contents

Foreword

How do you ever untangle all the competing technologies for the Web? Better yet, how do you bring all of the technologies together for the good of your application? At times, it seems like an insurmountable task. With all of the excitement surrounding the Web, tools and technologies are growing at an ever-increasing pace. Organizations are seeking to capitalize on these new technologies to gain a competitive advantage, be it decreased costs, increased customer satisfaction, or even increased sales. However, the expertise to achieve these goals is locked within a few individuals, namely the software developers. It is definitely an exciting time for developers who can capitalize on the new technologies to deliver Web-based solutions.

There is, however, frustration and complexity associated with this new Web opportunity: which tool to use and when? Developers have spent several years accumulating their own favorite set of tools for traditional client/server development. Until now, the tools for the Web have been introduced in a sporadic and disjointed fashion. So, of the new tools coming into the market for Web-based development, which tools should developers put into their toolbox?

In designing Visual InterDev, we listened to the cries of the developers who wanted a comprehensive, integrated development tool that would give them the ease of use of Visual Basic, the extensibility of Visual C++, and the database functionality of Microsoft Access, while using a common development environment. As with our tools for traditional client-server development, Microsoft worked diligently to develop a tool that would enable the developer to build applications that are robust and extensible for the Web. We are very pleased with the functionality and potential of Visual InterDev.

With Visual InterDev, we have developed a tool that shares the same integrated development environment of our other tools, while at the same time giving developers the best and most advanced functionality for the Web. We envision robust, database-driven applications soon becoming the norm for the Internet and intranets.

Just as Visual InterDev provides you with the right tool for your Web-based development efforts, this book empowers you with the knowledge you need to take advantage of our new tool. Mike has been working with the product since the early alpha testing and has contributed to its progress along the way. I know that you will appreciate this book as the key to unlocking the power and capabilities of Visual InterDev. I am very proud of our product and this book and hope that you thoroughly enjoy them both.

Karen Anderson
Visual InterDev Product Manager
Microsoft Corporation
April 1997

Acknowledgments

I would like to thank all the great people at Sams.net for the opportunity to write about such a revolutionary product for the Internet. Specifically, I thank Kelly Murdock, my development editor, who gave me the opportunity to write this book and who worked with and encouraged me every step of the way to ensure its success. I also truly appreciate the efforts of Howard Jones, my production editor, along with the other team of editors who worked diligently to develop a quality product. Sams.net is an excellent publisher, and I sincerely enjoyed working with everyone associated with the Sams family.

I truly appreciate the willingness and support of Andersen Consulting, where I perform my day job, for giving me the chance to dedicate time away from clients and real work to write this book. I have truly benefited from my experiences and association with the best consulting firm in the world. I also appreciate the support, inspiration, and input from all of my colleagues at Andersen. I couldn't ask for a better group of co-workers. Specifically, I want to thank Terrence Gee, my mentor and friend, who has truly impacted my personal and professional life. Finally, I appreciate the diligent and persistent efforts of Debbie Goldstein, Addison Kuo, and others who provided the inspiration for the case study in the book.

On a personal note, thanks to all of my friends and colleagues who encouraged and prayed for me during the writing of this book. I would like to thank my eleventh grade English teacher, Carol Ramsey, who enriched and molded my writing abilities and taught me the importance of a good vocabulary. Carol, all of those ultra-marathon vocabulary tests paid off. I also would like to sincerely thank Dr. Jim King who taught me about systems analysis while I was at Baylor University and inspired me to pursue consulting as a career. Dr. King is one of those rare professors who transcends theory and allows you to truly learn.

Most importantly, I thank my wife, Gina, and our two boys, Drew and Will, who supported and encouraged me throughout this exciting journey. Thanks for the sacrifices that you made to allow me to pursue my dream of writing. I also appreciate my Mom and grandparents for their interest, support, and prayers along the way. I especially thank my Mom, a former English teacher, for raising me and inspiring me to write.

About the Author

L. Michael Van Hoozer, Jr. is a Senior Manager for Andersen Consulting and has over nine years of systems development experience. He has worked in three different areas of the Andersen Consulting practice, including business process, organizational and instructional design, and client-server technology. He began his career at Andersen designing and developing oil and gas trading systems for some of the major oil companies in Houston, TX, where he resides. For the last six years, Mike has focused solely on client-server and now Internet-related technologies. Mike has strong ties to Microsoft in that he has been very involved with the alpha and beta testing of products including Visual Basic and Visual InterDev. Mike also has implemented solutions for his clients based on these tools, using his strong application development and user interface design skills.

Mike was a contributing author for *Visual Basic 4 Unleashed* (Sams Publishing, 1995) and has written articles for Information Week. He also has developed and conducted several training courses for his clients as well as Andersen Consulting employees and is sought out as a speaker for organizations and businesses in the Houston area. He has a B.B.A. degree in Finance, Economics, and Information Systems from Baylor University. He has volunteered much of his time to Child Advocates, Inc., serving as an outspoken advocate for abused and neglected children. He has served in various capacities with Child Advocates since 1989, including Chairman of the Board of Directors in 1996. He currently serves as the Recruitment, Training, and Retention Committee Chair for Child Advocates, where he actively speaks to organizations, businesses, and civic groups about the issue of abuse and the need for quality volunteers. When he is not working or volunteering, Mike enjoys spending time with his wife Gina and their two children, Drew and Will.

Tell Us What You Think!

As a reader, you are the most important critic and commentator of our books. We value your opinion and want to know what we're doing right, what we could do better, what areas you'd like to see us publish in, and any other words of wisdom you're willing to pass our way. You can help us make strong books that meet your needs and give you the computer guidance you require.

Do you have access to CompuServe or the World Wide Web? Then check out our CompuServe forum by typing **GO SAMS** at any prompt. If you prefer the World Wide Web, check out our site at http://www.mcp.com.

 NOTE

> If you have a technical question about this book, call the technical support line at (317) 581-3833.

As the team leader of the group that created this book, I welcome your comments. You can fax, e-mail, or write me directly to let me know what you did or didn't like about this book—as well as what we can do to make our books stronger. Here's the information:

Fax: (317) 581-4669

E-mail: newtech_mgr@sams.mcp.com

Mail: Mark Taber
         Sams Publishing
         201 W. 103rd Street
         Indianapolis, IN 46290

Introduction

The technology community thought it would never get here. Competitors underestimated the ability of the company to make the necessary changes to adapt. Now we can celebrate the fact that Microsoft has made one of the most tremendous turnarounds in history. It sounds very funny to mention "turnaround" and "Microsoft," one of the most successful companies of modern times, in the same sentence. Yet, it is true. The Internet forced Microsoft to adapt and make revolutionary changes to all of their products and to develop new products as well. The public was demanding software to support their growing addiction to the World Wide Web (WWW), and Microsoft delivered.

The first products that Microsoft developed focused on the end-user and included Internet Explorer and Internet Assistant for the Microsoft Office applications. These products allowed functional users to browse the WWW and easily change their documents to the Hypertext Markup Language (HTML) format supported by the Web. Developers, on the other hand, had to piece a myriad of tools together to develop both high-end content and applications. Microsoft heard their cries and created Visual InterDev, a high-end development tool for building Web-based applications.

This tool addresses several major concerns of developers. First, Visual InterDev provides a robust, integrated development environment that includes all the necessary tools to develop and deploy applications for the Web. Developers no longer have to use multiple tools and environments to build their applications and distribute them to the world. Second, Visual InterDev provides tools to build dynamic Web-based applications through the use of Active Server pages. Active Server pages include components and scripts on the server machine that provide a dynamic experience for the user. The user can now maintain an interactive session with the server instead of passively viewing static information. Finally, Visual InterDev includes very powerful tools for building robust database applications that connect to desktop as well as high-end database management systems. The tools are graphical and provide an easy-to-use interface that significantly enhances a developer's productivity. Comprehensive site management tools also are included for the deployment of your completed applications.

The need for a tool like Visual InterDev has been great. Most developers have used a combination of HTML editors, tools specifically geared toward Java, and various database connectivity products to create their applications. The HTML Layout editor and the ActiveX Control Pad from Microsoft also have been included in a developer's toolbox. Someone must have asked the question, "Wouldn't it be nice if we could package support for all of these tools into one integrated environment?" Visual InterDev is the answer. The idea is to provide a comprehensive, integrated development environment that supports all the current Web technology. By using Visual InterDev, a developer can perform WYSIWYG HTML editing through the use of the FrontPage editor as well as use technology such as VBScript, JavaScript, ActiveX controls, Java applets, Active Server pages, and ODBC to build dynamic applications for the Web.

With the rapid growth of the WWW, companies are realizing the need to build a presence on the Internet. The WWW provides a platform for creating multitiered distributed applications. The next wave of client-server has hit, and it is the Internet. Organizations are realizing that they can use the Web for private intranet applications that enhance and/or replace such functions as Human Resources, Accounting, Electronic Commerce, and so on. In these applications, the browser becomes the universal client, and the server holds the key to unlocking corporate information. The use of a browser on the client machine reduces the administration time necessary to deploy proprietary client application software on every user's desktop. Visual InterDev is the perfect tool for riding the Internet wave of client-server. Visual InterDev allows for the creation of effective, multitiered applications by supporting the use of HTML, controls, components, and services.

Hopefully, you are already familiar with developing content for the Web. Maybe you have been juggling multiple tools while building applications for the Web. Regardless of your experience level, you have chosen this book to learn more about Visual InterDev and how you can create dynamic Web-based applications. This book will guide you through a step-by-step process of learning all of the powerful features of Visual InterDev. This book takes you on a journey and teaches you how to integrate HTML, scripting languages such as VBScript and JavaScript, ActiveX controls and Java applets, Active Server pages and components, and database connectivity to build rich and robust applications. Upon completion of this book, you will be able to unleash the power of Visual InterDev and take full advantage of its capabilities.

Who Should Read This Book?

You have chosen the right book if you are in one of the following categories:

☐ You have experienced the Web and now want to contribute.

☐ You are tired of using multiple tools to create a single application for the Web.

☐ You want to create dynamic applications for the Web instead of publishing static documentation.

☐ You want to enhance your productivity through the use of graphical database tools.

☐ You want to create a dynamic experience for your users.

☐ You have used FrontPage and now want to migrate to a higher-end development tool.

☐ You have used Java tools and now want to try a more comprehensive and integrated tool.

☐ You have developed client-server applications using tools such as Visual Basic and now want to try your hand at Web application development.

What This Book Contains

This book is intended to be completed in 21 days—a chapter each day. The book is designed in such a way that you determine the pace. Some readers will spend more time than this, based on their proficiency or schedule. Other readers may choose to approach the book at a more rapid pace.

This book is very similar to taking a self-paced course. I begin the book by talking about the basics and build upon these concepts as the weeks go on. By the end of the first week, you will have created your first Visual InterDev project. You will continue to build your skills through the second and third weeks and will develop more advanced applications. Throughout the book, I provide many examples and relevant exercises for you to try. Through reading and applying the material, you will become very proficient in using the tool. At the end of each chapter, I provide you with a chapter summary and a question and answer section based on topics covered in that chapter. Be sure to study hard during each chapter though, because you will be tested on the material with an end-of-chapter quiz. I don't know about you, but I always read the material more closely when I know I shall be tested on it.

☐ During Week 1, you get a general overview of the Internet and the World Wide Web, intranets, and a discussion of the features of Visual InterDev. I also discuss design and development considerations when building an application for the Web, and you create your first Visual InterDev project. Finally, you learn how to use the FrontPage Editor for Visual InterDev, how to add images and multimedia features into your applications, and how to extend your Web pages through the use of client-side script.

☐ During Week 2, you are introduced to database connectivity and communication. You learn all the aspects of using a database, from inserting a simple connection to using the Visual Data Tools in Visual InterDev to gain maximum productivity and features. You also take a journey through the world of server-side scripting and experience its capabilities. Finally, you get a chance to interact with objects including HTML objects, ActiveX controls and Java applets, and design-time controls.

☐ During Week 3, you learn how to integrate objects into your applications. You also learn how to implement some of the more advanced features of Visual InterDev into your application, like building your own design-time control and using Active Server components to create a mutlitiered application. You learn how to use Visual

InterDev to manage your web site files. You are exposed to other topics to consider when building a Web-based application, such as working in teams, source code control, and debugging your application. The culmination of the final week is a case study that builds upon all of the knowledge that you have gained in the first 20 days.

By reading, studying, and applying this book, you will become extremely proficient with Visual InterDev. You will instantly begin developing and deploying robust applications and will gain the confidence that you need to master the Web. Just think, if you start right now, you could be a webmaster in 21 days or less!

What You Need To Begin

Based on your purchase of this book, I assume that you already have Visual InterDev and have installed it on your PC. This book is a hands-on course, and you will need to try out the examples as you go along. Also, to get the full use out of the tool, you should have an ODBC-compliant database installed on either your desktop or a server machine to which you have access. Database connectivity is one of the key features for you to learn to provide dynamic applications for your users. My assumption is that you're familiar with HTML and have at least developed some kind of Web page or application. You don't need to be an expert in all the technologies supported by Visual InterDev; I'll introduce each of these in due time. If you're familiar with these technologies, the discussion can serve as a refresher—or you can skip to new or more advanced topics.

You're now ready to learn about a tool that is worth waiting for. I'm elated to present the newest member of the Microsoft Visual Tools family and its potential. Let's begin our exciting expedition.

WEEK 1

1
2
3
4
5
6
7

At a Glance

This book is intended to teach you how to use Visual InterDev to develop powerful applications for the Web. During this week, you will take a look at the features of Visual InterDev and discuss how it fits into the world of Internets and intranets. You also will be creating your first Visual InterDev project by the end of the week. You need to make sure that you have loaded Visual InterDev onto your PC so that you can take full advantage of the examples and instructions in this book.

Where You Are Going

Week 1 begins with a brief overview of the importance of the Internet, intranets, and the World Wide Web. You will get an introductory look at the features of Visual InterDev and how the tool fits into the big picture. I discuss design and development considerations you need to keep in mind when building your applications, including development and deployment platforms, browser features and extensions to HTML, and effective user interface design. You will be developing your first Visual InterDev project by mid-week and be exposed to some of the advanced features on the client machine, like multimedia and client-side script. The Workshops and Quizzes enable you to test your knowledge one chapter at a time. During this week, you will be introduced to the fundamentals that will provide the basis for learning more advanced features of Visual InterDev.

Day 1

Introducing Visual InterDev and the World Wide Web

Visual InterDev, the long-awaited Web application development tool from Microsoft, is finally here. Many developers are applauding its features and the application development needs that it addresses. Developers now have a tool similar to other application development tools like Visual Basic and Visual C++ that they can use to create their Web applications. No more downloading the latest beta copy of a single-focused tool from the Web. You now have a tool that integrates many of the popular components and technologies.

During the first day, the context for Visual InterDev will be set, and you'll be introduce to some of the latest developments concerning the Internet and the WWW. You will learn about the importance of the Internet. You also will learn about the rising number of intranets, or private internets, that are growing within many companies. You will see how the WWW has become ubiquitous and the implications that it has for individuals and businesses. In discussing the WWW, you will discover the differences between static and dynamic web pages and what you should focus on for the future. You will then be introduced to the reasons for having an application development tool for the Web. Finally, you will get a glimpse of Visual InterDev.

NOTE

In this book, the term *Web* and WWW are used synonymously to refer to the commercial collection of Web servers located on the World Wide Web. The term *web* is used to refer to pages and sites that are individual in nature. Most of the time, web refers to pages that you're developing to build your site.

The Importance of the Internet

You obviously realize the importance of the Internet or you wouldn't be reading this book. The Internet and the World Wide Web are everywhere. You can't read the newspaper or watch television without seeing some kind of reference to the Internet. "Cyberspace" and the "Information Superhighway" have become common vocabulary for a whole new audience. Virtually every television commercial and print ad contains a reference like the following:

"For more information, visit us at our Web site at www.whatever.com."

The Internet has come a long way since the old ARPANET days. Originally designed for research use by the Department of Defense, the Internet has become a haven for millions of people who have experienced the value of communicating with people around the world. Internet users have instant access to a plethora of knowledge supported by this network of networks.

Most people point to 1991 as the beginning of the Internet explosion. In the late 1980s, the academic community began to see the Internet as a valuable tool. Professors and students at universities around the world began using the Internet as a way to gain valuable research and knowledge about myriad subjects. Services such as electronic mail (e-mail), file transfer capability (ftp), and newsgroup discussions all contributed to the growth of the Internet audience. Then, in 1991, the National Science Foundation (NSF), which was the major funding group for the Internet, dropped most of its financial support and allowed commercial traffic onto the Internet. The door was now open for all types of individuals and businesses to take advantage of this vital communication network.

We are truly living in the Information Age, and the Internet has become the primary means for expanding our horizons. The Internet has opened up any number of possibilities for applications by providing a ready-made network for businesses to use. Growth in the Internet has also forced us to rethink the way we approach life. A student in California can communicate with his parents in Florida via e-mail instead of building up a hefty, long distance telephone bill. In fact, now most families can conduct conversations over the Internet, thereby skirting the phone companies.

With the growth of the WWW, businesses have been scrambling to gain a presence on the Internet. In 1995, corporate spending on Internet/intranet systems was $12 billion. This figure is expected to grow to $208 billion by the year 2000. Developers will play a huge role in helping organizations and businesses understand the importance of using the Internet from an application and communication standpoint.

The Rise in Intranets

Many companies are realizing the benefits of the Internet from within their companies. These organizations are creating intranets, which are private, or internal, internets. These intranets have been established initially as an internal communication tool. Employees can send e-mail to other employees within the company. Intranets enable private and sensitive corporate information to be distributed and shared within the organization. This new medium of communication has become a very cost-effective solution, especially for geographically dispersed businesses that have employees all over the world. The time to communicate new policies, procedures, and information is immediately reduced along with postage and paper costs.

An intranet also can be used for software distribution and for providing access to vital applications. Companies are now starting to put applications like survey forms and employee benefit registration forms on their intranets to simplify basic processes. Businesses also are starting to consider replacing or enhancing their mission-critical applications (like accounting, sales order entry, oil and gas trading, and so on) with applications that are secured within an intranet. Intranets are usually protected and secured by means of a firewall that prevents outside intruders from accessing the internal network. To the user, there is no difference between accessing the Internet and the company's intranet. Figure 1.1 depicts a typical configuration for an intranet.

Figure 1.1.

A high level view of an intranet.

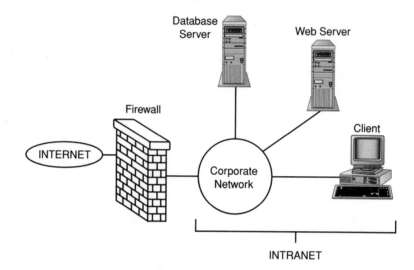

Sun Microsystems is a perfect example of how a company can save real money in terms of printing, processing, and mailing costs through the use of an intranet. Sun has used the Internet to communicate basic corporate information, such as organization charts and geographic office locations. Employees can access monthly updates from their CEO Scott McNealy which are presented in audio and video formats. Sun also provides information about its products by providing an online product catalog and updates on new products. Employee information regarding training, travel, and human resource policies is placed on the intranet. Sun even provides an "Applications Chest" that gives employees access to a variety of tools that enhance their productivity.

Internet performance has become a huge topic of conversation. Some individuals have even discussed totally redesigning the Internet infrastructure to support the growing number of users. Without entering this debate, I would like to point out that intranets provide a way to use the Internet while taking more control over performance of your applications. With an intranet, a company can use the Internet architecture model while providing the internal infrastructure to guarantee response time and security.

Intranet applications also are cost effective from an administration and deployment stand-point. The browser serves as the universal client for all desktops. The server makes the desktop come alive by providing information and database access. Deployment and administration costs are reduced, because you don't have to reinstall an updated application on everyone's desktops as you do when creating proprietary client-server applications. Electronic commerce is going to drastically grow in the next few years and with it will come a continued rise in the use of intranets.

This section has described intranets as being internal to an organization or business. Private intranets that focus on providing a reliable and secure infrastructure for groups of businesses also are emerging. Technology companies are beginning to prepare for this occurrence. Microsoft formed an alliance with British Telecommunications and MCI to provide private data networks for global companies and their customers.

Private intranets offer the same reliability, security, and guaranteed response time that a company's internal intranet provides. The difference between them is that a company's reach extends beyond the internal organization to external entities. The use of private intranets will continue to rise as application requirements exceed the current capabilities of the Internet infrastructure.

The Ubiquitous Web

The second explosion that propelled the Internet into national prominence was the creation of the World Wide Web. The Web has many origins, but most people point to the time period between 1989-1991 when the *Conseil European pour la Recherche Nucleaire* (CERN) European Laboratory for Particle Physics in Geneva, Switzerland, developed its first specifications. Tim Berners-Lee, a researcher for CERN, developed the basic concepts of sharing information through the use of a consistent, universal interface. Mark Andreessen is credited with developing the first browser (Mosaic) for the Web in 1993. The use of a browser to view the Internet turned attention away from the information stored on the server, focusing more on the user experience through the client machine. The browser provided a graphical, point-and-click interface for viewing Web content that made the Internet easier to access.

The Web is the primary service responsible for bringing the Internet into the homes of millions. The Web is the most popular and useable service. The hypertext links to a plethora of information allow the user to experience a "web" of knowledge. The user can choose the learning path instead of following a sequential or linear pattern.

The most recent numbers estimate that more than 45 million people have visited the Web at least once. When sports figures, music celebrities, and news anchors are touting the Web, you know it has become ubiquitous. The Web provides an alternate delivery channel for all types of information as well as graphically robust applications. Major software vendors are totally revamping their products to make them Internet-enabled. Banks are having to rethink their strategy of targeting and servicing their customers by providing online banking. Businesses are establishing a presence on the Web to offer products and services electronically. The Web is everywhere, and we must learn how to properly and constructively use its capabilities.

The first wave of Web development involved information publishing. Rudimentary tools were provided to convert documents created with common word processors to the HTML format of the Web. HTML editors also have provided a way to create original documents as well as Web pages and deploy them on the Web. As stated, the Internet and the Web have saved a lot of money for companies in terms of printing, processing, and mailing costs. The Web has extended the notion of textual documentation to provide graphical information as well. Graphics, 3D images, audio, and video can truly enhance the user's experience on the Web. Companies like Macromedia and RealAudio have contributed to the multimedia experience by providing enhanced and animated graphics and audio capability. The ESPNET SportsZone is one of the most popular sites on the Web largely due to the way the site employs multimedia. You can download ESPN commercials both in audio and video format as well as listen to press conferences and other sporting events. This site does owe some credit to the popularity of ESPN, but the people would not be visiting the site if it didn't provide a rich and rewarding experience.

The second wave of Web development has been the creation of functional applications. These applications extend the simple registration forms commonly seen on Web sites to become true interactive applications that include database accessibility. These applications can be classified as just another phase of client-server.

In taking a look at the architecture of the Web, many of the principles have been carried over from client-server architectures. Figure 1.2 illustrates a typical client-server architecture.

Figure 1.2.

A typical client-server architecture.

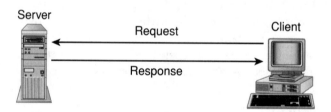

Client-server is a style of computing where the client machine makes a request of a server machine. The request is usually a request for information, as in a database request, or for processing, such as updating a database or running a batch process. The client machine makes the request, and the server machine fulfills this request. The benefit of client-server systems is that they take advantage of the strengths of each machine or platform. In a typical scenario, the client handles some application logic and the presentation to the user while the server provides the back-end processing and database functions.

In a typical Web application, the browser serves as the universal client that sends a request for a web page, interprets the HTML document, and displays it to the user. The web server receives the request through the HyperText Transport Protocol (HTTP) and returns the required information in HTML format that the client can understand. Similar to client-server, you can distribute the application processing and database management portions to varying degrees between the client and the server machine. Figure 1.3 depicts a typical Web-based architecture.

Figure 1.3.

A typical Web-based architecture.

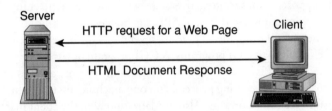

The main benefit to Web-based applications over client-server is found in the deployment. In a Web-based scenario, you don't have to deploy a new executable on each person's desktop with each new application feature or update. The browser serves as the universal client, providing access to the most current information on the server. Version control, software distribution, and systems management costs are significantly reduced for Web-based applications.

A more in-depth discussion concerning how the web client and server interact is warranted here. Historically, Web applications have been based on HTML and common gateway interface (CGI) programs on the server. The Web browser interprets the HTML tags and appropriately formats the page for the user. A web page can be a combination of formatted text, images and graphics, audio, and video. HTML also allows for the creation of basic forms that contain text fields, radio buttons, checkboxes, push buttons, and listboxes. These objects are discussed in more detail on Day 12, "Using Basic and Advanced HTML Form Controls."

CGI programs have typically been used for processing requests on the server and distributing information to the client machine. CGI programs, or scripts, are executable files that can be built using languages such as UNIX shell script, Perl, C, and so on. As information is updated on your database, the CGI script can handle accessing the data and passing the information back down to the client browser. The advantage is that you don't have to write new HTML code for every new document or database update. The CGI server program provides a reusable component that saves development time.

I mentioned the HTTP protocol earlier in this chapter. HTTP is the protocol that allows the browser to connect to a web server. HTTP is a stateless protocol; that is, the client and server don't maintain a persistent connection. The client makes a connection to the server and sends a request. The server receives the request, processes it, then terminates the connection. This process is repeated many times during a user session. This kind of communication would be like having a telephone conversation with a friend where you would say something, hang up the telephone, then dial again to say something else. This dialogue is very tedious. Interactive applications must have some way to maintain state with the user machine in order to provide for the needs of applications like sales order processing.

Microsoft and Netscape have led the charge to develop an effective server process that supports a more interactive state with the client machine. The creation of application programming interfaces, or APIs, has opened up all kinds of possibilities over the traditional use of CGI programs. There are several specific benefits to using APIs. First, APIs are more efficient than CGI programs. A CGI program opens up a process in memory for each client request. APIs execute processes in the same memory address space, eliminating the overhead of separate executing processes on one machine. By using this model, APIs use less memory for executing a process. Also, initialization with the client machine is performed once for all requests. Another benefit of APIs is their ability to maintain state. API programs permit a persistent connection between the client and server, which can be a huge benefit when developing an application with moderate to intensive database connectivity. Also, separate requests can share information about the client, because the programs remain resident in memory.

The main disadvantage to APIs is that they're proprietary in nature. Whereas CGI programs are server-independent, APIs are confined to their respective web server platforms. Table 1.1 presents the most common APIs and their supported server platforms.

Table 1.1. The most popular APIs, their respective vendors, and supported server platforms.

API	Vendor	Server Platform Supported
ISAPI	Microsoft	Microsoft Internet Information Server, Process Software Purveyor WebServer
NSAPI	Netscape	Netscape Commerce/Communication Server
WSAPI	O'Reilly & Associates	O'Reilly & Associates WebSite

To summarize, the Web has become popular for a variety of reasons. The Web provides graphically rich content on a variety of topics to many users. The Web also supports transaction-based services that enable businesses and consumers to come together in an electronic market. Examples include ordering books, making airline reservations, and trading stocks. Learning is also significantly enhanced by having access to all kinds of documents, white papers, and training materials. Name the subject, and you can become an expert on it in no time at all by accessing the Web.

The Difference Between Static and Dynamic Web Pages

Web-based applications have made the transition from solely publishing information to creating an interactive session with the user. Static web pages represent those pages that provide information that is nicely formatted in standard HTML. For example, a person might be able to request an employee benefit handbook to become familiar with the latest updates in benefits. Static pages are nice, but users want something more.

Dynamic web pages are those pages that provide true user interaction. In this model, users interact through the use of server-side programs that provide for an enhanced experience. Instead of just reading about the latest human resource benefits, employees can register and update their benefits. Dynamic web pages support the building of true interactive applications. Once you have read the published flight schedules, you can make airline reservations electronically over the Internet. Stock brokerage houses can publish the hottest stock tips and then enable you to capitalize on the investment through online stock trading. Dynamic web pages provide a world of new possibilities over static pages.

I briefly discussed the use of CGI and API programs in providing a gateway between your client and server machine in a Web-based application. Here, I will focus on the ability to use client- and server-side scripts to create dynamic HTML web pages.

Client-side script is usually associated with objects on the HTML page. These objects could be standard HTML controls or ActiveX controls. Client-side script is usually included to make up for the limited functionality of HTML. The script is included in the HTML page when it is downloaded from the server to the client machine. The script code executes on the client machine in response to user interaction and program events. By keeping the script in the HTML page on the server, a developer only has to make changes to centralized code located on the server. The browser downloads the revised web page simplifying the software distribution process. The goal in this model is to keep the code resident on the server leaving little or no code on the client machine. Some examples for using client-side script include user interface functions, entry verification, and standard programming functions.

Two of the most popular scripting languages are Netscape's JavaScript and Microsoft's VBScript. Visual InterDev supports both of these scripting engines, although Microsoft has implemented its own version of Netscape's JavaScript called JScript. There are no significant differences between the JScript and JavaScript implementation.

Another way to create a dynamic experience is through the use of ActiveX controls and Java applets. Visual InterDev includes and supports the use of both ActiveX controls and Java applets within your application. These controls provide many additional functions from multimedia to database connectivity. Both JavaScript and VBScript are used to interact with these controls extending the reach of the interface. Similar to the use of Visual Basic code with Visual Basic controls, VBScript and JavaScript serve as the glue between the browser and the particular control. The process is essentially the same as using a traditional client-server tool like Visual Basic. You add a control to your page, setting its methods and properties. Once you have established the basic properties, you add scripting code to handle the application logic. Visual InterDev incorporates a visual tool for creating client-side script for your ActiveX controls. The Script Wizard, first included in the ActiveX Control Pad from Microsoft, provides a visual interface that builds both VBScript and JavaScript.

Visual InterDev also supports the use of Active Server Pages. Active Server Pages are a new feature included with Internet Information Server 3.0; they provide a framework for creating dynamic Web pages.

Active Server Pages are based on the ActiveX Scripting engine and enable you to include server-side executable script directly into an HTML document. You can create Active Server Pages using any of the popular scripting languages, including VBScript, JavaScript, Perl, and so on. Figure 1.4 illustrates how an Active Server Page interacts with a client machine.

Figure 1.4.

This diagram shows how Active Server Pages interact in a Web-based application.

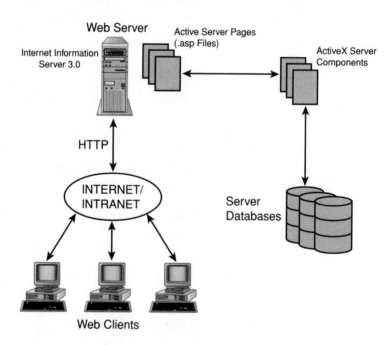

You will notice from the diagram that the web clients communicate with the web server through the HTTP protocol. The web server can be on the Internet or within an intranet. The web server is comprised of Internet Information Server 3.0, which includes the ActiveX Server Scripting engine. The diagram shows the Active Server pages, or .asp files, where the server-side script resides. These files are simply HTML pages that contain scripting code. This scripting code extends basic HTML and provides additional functionality for your application.

Visual InterDev enables you to create Active Server Pages. Some of the visual tools within Visual InterDev generate much of the server-side script for you. You have the ability to modify this code as well as create your own server-side script. You will get your chance to build Active Server Pages on Day 11, "Extending Your Application Through Active Server Script."

The Need for a New Kind of Tool

There are many extensive and powerful technologies for creating Web applications, but most tools only focus on a single, specific need. Other tools are being developed to address a few needs. Developers have been dreaming of the day when they can use a comprehensive, integrated development environment to build their applications. Why, you ask, do you need an integrated tool? Take a walk through a typical Web development effort and look at the many different types of tools that you can use to build a Web-based application.

First you need an HTML editor. Many people have created a new function for an old product and made Notepad the HTML editor of choice. Table 1.2 outlines some of the more robust and popular products on the market.

Table 1.2. Popular HTML editors.

HTML Editor	Vendor
Hot Dog Pro	Sausage Software
HoTMetaL Pro	SoftQuad
NaviPress	Navisoft
FrontPage	Microsoft

Microsoft also has created add-in products for its Office suite of products that enable HTML conversion. For example, a user who is familiar with Microsoft Word can use the Internet Assistant for Word to convert a document to HTML format for display in a browser.

NOTE

> The Office 97 suite of applications supports the ability to save files for HTML formatting for display on the Web.

Choosing an HTML editor is only the beginning. To build an application, you must consider the server-side products as well. You have two basic choices, as previously mentioned: CGI or APIs. If you choose to use CGI, you will need to find a programming environment based on the language you select. The possible languages include Perl and UNIX shell scripts, Visual Basic, C, and C++. If you choose an API, you need to select the appropriate API implementation for your application platform's web server. Refer to Table 1.1 for a listing of APIs and their supported web server platforms. API server programs are implemented as dynamic link libraries (DLLs) and built using either C or C++. Again, you will need to select the appropriate programming environment to support the selected language.

Java also can be used on the server to provide additional functionality for your Web-based application. Sun Microsystems built Java as an independent programming language. It can be implemented as an application program or as a Java applet. A Java application can interact with system resources and make calls to external programs. A Java applet is found embedded within a web page and cannot interact with system resources. Regardless of your Java implementation, an environment will be needed to support your Java development. Microsoft's Visual J++ and Symantec's Visual Café are some of the more popular tools for Java development.

You will invariably need to select a scripting language to support the functionality of your application. Whether it is VBScript or JavaScript, you will need an editor. Notepad, Visual Basic, and the ActiveX Control Pad from Microsoft all can support your VBScript needs to varying degrees. Netscape Navigator Gold and Notepad support JavaScript development.

If you're wondering about connecting your application to a database, many options exist for database connectivity, depending on how you want to implement your application. If you're building a Java-based application, you will select a tool that supports Java Database Connectivity, or JDBC. Most of the popular Java tools also support JDBC. Microsoft and Netscape also provide environments and tools for database connectivity based on their API specification.

The point in this example is that you could spend a lot of time and effort using a number of tools to implement a robust, Web-based application. Compatibility between the tools becomes a debugging nightmare. Also, you spend a lot of time switching between the development environments, thereby diminishing your productivity. Due to these limitations, Microsoft created Visual InterDev to address the many needs for today's Web-based application developer.

Presenting Visual InterDev

The emphasis in creating Visual InterDev was to provide a tool with a comprehensive, integrated development environment. Visual InterDev's creators wanted to provide a tool that enabled developers to utilize many technologies to create and deploy dynamic, Web-based applications. Microsoft also wanted to emphasize a visual tool. Many products have been created that enable you to code HTML or connect to a database; however, these tools typically haven't focused on the ease of use for the developer.

Developer productivity was a major design goal for Microsoft, and they have accomplished it by providing Visual InterDev with many wizards and visual tools, as well as database development features. Powerful database integration and connectivity were clearly of paramount importance for its design. Visual InterDev even supports developers in deploying their sites once they have been built by integrating comprehensive tools to create and maintain a web site into Visual InterDev.

Integrated Development Environment

Visual InterDev provides a robust, integrated development environment to address the many capabilities of the Web. You can integrate various technologies, like ActiveX controls and Active Server Components, to create a powerful application. The integrated development environment enables you to use scripting languages like VBScript and JavaScript to create dynamic applications and Web pages. You can work on simultaneous projects of different types all from within Visual InterDev's Developer Studio interface. In addition to Visual InterDev projects, you also can develop Visual C++ and Visual J++ projects.

Visual InterDev Features

Now that you have been introduced to the features and benefits of the integrated development environment, it's time for a brief look at some of the specific features of Visual InterDev. This discussion sets the context for Day 2, in which you will get to meet Visual InterDev up close and personal.

Visual InterDev includes a wide range of visual tools to augment an application developer's productivity. HTML editing is significantly enhanced through the use of the HTML Layout

Editor and a version of the FrontPage HTML editor. The HTML Layout Editor, introduced with the ActiveX Control Pad from Microsoft, enables you to precisely place your ActiveX controls onto your web page. It also enables you to control the x and y coordinates to ensure that the ActiveX controls are displayed in the proper manner. By using this tool, you're able to take more control of your user interface, and can ensure that the interface you build is an effective one.

Visual InterDev also provides WYSIWYG editing through its own FrontPage 97 HTML editor. FrontPage enables you to visually author your HTML page. Content authors can use FrontPage 97 to create files that are completely compatible with Visual InterDev's version of the FrontPage Editor. Visual InterDev also provides site management tools that are very similar to those tools provided in FrontPage 97.

The Script Wizard is another visual tool that greatly enhances a developer's productivity. The Script Wizard enables you to associate specific actions with associated ActiveX control events. By linking these events and actions, the Script Wizard generates all of the necessary script language for you. Once the language is generated, you have the ability to modify and add to the code. This process can save you considerable development time by generating the routine script and enabling you to focus on the more advanced code for your application.

Visual InterDev also includes two tools for spicing up your web pages. These tools focus on multimedia creation and management. The Microsoft Image Composer and Microsoft Music Producer enable you to create graphical images, music, and sounds for your web site. You can use the Microsoft Image Composer to create engaging images for your web pages. The Image Composer supports the Adobe Photoshop file format as well as GIF and JPG formats. The Image Composer is simple to use, and you don't have to be a graphic artist to master it. The Music Producer enables you to create music and sound effects for your web site. You pick from over 100 pre-defined styles of music and can modify the arrangement of instruments as well as the tempo.

Again, the goal of both of these products is to provide a rich and rewarding experience for the user. The Media Manager enables you to manage all of your multimedia files through the use of specialized folders. By using Media Manager, you can properly organize your images, sounds, video clips, and other multimedia files.

Now consider some of the key features for building robust server applications. Visual InterDev enables you to create dynamic web pages through the use of Active Server Pages. The concept of Active Server Pages was touched on earlier in the day. As a refresher, Active Server Pages are HTML pages that contain server-side script. The script code can be either VBScript, JavaScript, or some other scripting language. The Active Server Page, or .asp file, resides on the server machine and executes before being downloaded to the browser.

Active Server Components are a significant part of building distributed and powerful applications. Active Server Components are programs, DLLs, or executables (EXEs), that are built using the Component Object Model (COM) specification. Visual Basic, Visual C++, and Visual J++ all support the development of COM-based components. These programs can be called from Active Server Pages to provide robust application processing on the server machine.

For example, you might want to build an Active Server Component that uses the strength of the C++ language to perform financial analysis and return the results to the Web browser. You also can distribute the application processing load through the use of Distributed COM (DCOM). Active Server Components provide a method for building high transaction processing capability into your application. Visual InterDev provides an environment that is conducive to incorporating these components into your applications.

Database Integration

Visual InterDev provides some very robust database tools. The Visual Data Tools included with Visual InterDev are easy to use and significantly reduce the time and effort for adding database capability into your application. Some of the features include the following:

- [ ] **Data View.** Visual InterDev project window that enables you to view all of your database objects including tables, views, stored procedures, and triggers.
- [ ] **Query Designer.** A tool that enables you to visually build your SQL database queries and test the results.
- [ ] **Database Designer.** A tool that enables you to design, create, and maintain your SQL database.
- [ ] **Stored Procedure/Trigger Editor.** A tool for editing stored procedures and triggers for Microsoft SQL Server 6.x and Oracle 7.x.

The Query Designer and the Database Designer employ a user interface similar to Microsoft Access that's very easy to use. You can drag and drop objects into the workspace and automatically build your SQL queries. You also can use the Database Designer to populate the database and modify existing data.

Other database features include the following:

- [ ] **ActiveX Data Objects.** An object-based approach to accessing a database over the Web that uses ActiveX Scripting.
- [ ] **Database Design Time Controls.** Controls geared toward the automatic creation of database connectivity and generation of Active Server scripting.
- [ ] **Database Wizards.** Wizards that guide you through the creation of an HTML, data-bound form.

Database connectivity and integration is one of the best features of Visual InterDev. You will get a chance to use these features and tools beginning with Day 8.

Summary

Today you began a glorious journey to the land of Web-based application development. You started the day with a discussion of why the Internet is important and were introduced to the significance of learning how to properly use this communication vehicle from a business perspective. You then moved on to intranets and learned about the rise in these vital private networks. You learned how businesses use intranets for communication, software distribution, and applications now and in the future. You then read about the most popular service of the Internet: the World Wide Web. After reading a brief history of the Web, you learned about the different waves of Web development.

You also learned about the similarities and differences between Web-based applications and client-server applications. You found out about the difference between CGI and API programming. You received an overview of the differences between static and dynamic Web pages, then learned how client- and server-side script could be used to provide an interactive experience for the user.

Throughout the lesson, you got a feel for the need for a tool like Visual InterDev. You were walked through an example that showed the range of tools that could be used when building a Web-based application. At the end of the day, you were presented Visual InterDev for your approval. Finally, you got a taste of the features and tools that are included in the tool. What did you think? I bet that you can't wait until tomorrow to meet Visual InterDev up close and personal.

Q&A

Q What's the difference between client- and server-side script?

A Client-side script is included within the HTML page and executes on the client machine in response to events and user interaction. An example includes validating data entered into a field before the page is sent to the server. Server-side script is script that resides on the server machine and is processed on the server before a page is sent back to the client machine. Server-side script enables you to provide application processing that can call other application programs, such as an Active Server Component.

Q Does Visual InterDev support the development of scripts?

A Yes. In fact, Visual InterDev generates much of the scripting for you.

Q What databases does Visual InterDev support?

A Visual InterDev provides connectivity to any ODBC-compliant database including Microsoft SQL Server, Oracle, Sybase, Microsoft Access, Microsoft FoxPro, and IBM DB/2.

Workshop

Make sure you have installed Visual InterDev. Tomorrow, you will be taking an in-depth look at the tool and its development environment. It's important that you have the tool installed so you can follow along with the exploration of its features.

Quiz

1. What is an intranet?
2. What are the two waves or phases of Web development?
3. What are the two most popular scripting languages that help to create dynamic web pages?
4. Name two of the Visual Data Tools.

Quiz Answers

1. An intranet is a private, or internal network, that provides access to the Internet but is secured from external access through the use of a firewall. Intranets are used as an internal communication tool and as a medium to distribute software and provide access to internal applications.
2. The first wave of Web development was the publishing of information. The second wave of Web development has been application development.
3. VBScript and JavaScript.
4. Possible answers include:

    Data View

    Query Designer

    Database Designer

    Stored Procedure Trigger Editor

Day 2

Visual InterDev: Up Close and Personal

On Day 1, you learned about the need for a new kind of tool like Visual InterDev to address the urgent void of application development tools for the Web. Developers have been clamoring for an integrated development tool that provides comprehensive support for the various tools, languages, and technologies for creating Web applications. There has been a lot of press about Visual InterDev and how this tool finally addresses many of these concerns. Today, you will have an up close and personal tour of Visual InterDev, and see its fascinating features. You also will learn the answers to the following questions:

- [ ] What is Visual InterDev?
- [ ] Why use Visual InterDev?
- [ ] How should I use Visual InterDev?

Throughout the day, you will see application examples that have been built using Visual InterDev. Today's objective: exploring the integrated development environment of Visual InterDev and discovering how the tool can immediately begin enhancing your applications and productivity.

What Is Visual InterDev?

The World Wide Web (WWW) has made the Internet come alive for many new users. In the initial stages, users realized that they could view numerous documents on various topics from all over the world. Through the WWW, people have access to a plethora of knowledge. Not only can you read about many interesting topics on the Web, but you also can find information about your favorite products and services.

Once you have gained this knowledge, you will invariably want to act on it. Some companies have built Web-based applications, enabling you to buy their products and services electronically over the Internet. Other companies enable you to fill out registration information to begin receiving certain services. The point is, applications enable the user to act on the knowledge they have gained. Businesses can capitalize on opportunities sooner by becoming closer to the customer through a virtual marketplace. Visual InterDev provides all the necessary tools to build these vital applications for the Web.

Visual InterDev is a comprehensive, Web-based application development tool. Visual InterDev provides an integrated environment that brings together various technologies to work towards a common goal of building robust and dynamic applications for the Web. Visual InterDev achieves this integrated development environment through the use of the Developer Studio shell interface, first used in Microsoft's Visual C++. You can open and work on Visual C++ and Visual J++ projects while simultaneously creating your Visual InterDev project. This feature greatly enhances productivity, especially when you're building COM and DCOM components and incorporating these components into your Visual InterDev application.

Visual InterDev enables the developer to build applications that are dynamic and interactive. Yesterday you learned about the difference between static and dynamic web pages. Visual InterDev enables the developer to build dynamic web pages through the use of client- and server-side script. VBScript is the default scripting language, but JavaScript also can be used.

Database integration is vital to any application. Visual InterDev provides a rich and robust set of visual database tools to immediately enhance your productivity. Visual InterDev supports the major ODBC-compliant databases, both on the desktop and the server.

Managing your web site once it has been developed is a very crucial function. Visual InterDev provides a set of tools to view and maintain your site. These tools are similar and compatible with the site management tools found in Microsoft FrontPage.

Visual InterDev supports the major object-based technologies that exist for developing Web-based applications, including ActiveX controls and Java applets. Visual InterDev supports the use of third-party ActiveX controls and enables you to integrate your own custom ActiveX controls. Visual InterDev also provides Design-time Controls that enable you to set control properties when you're designing your application and then use this functionality at runtime without the overhead of a typical ActiveX control.

In a nutshell, Visual InterDev is an exciting new tool that significantly augments a Web developer's productivity. In this next section, you will learn why you need to use Visual InterDev instead of other development tools.

Why Visual InterDev?

The basic premise behind the creation of Visual InterDev was to provide a tool that enabled developers to build dynamic and interactive applications for the Web. On the first day, you read about some of the similarities and differences between client-server application development and application development for the Web. Essentially, these two modes of computing were the same in that they both used the client-server model. That is, client-server and Web applications both facilitate the client making a request of the server. The main difference is the degree to which they distribute the application logic between the client and the server. Figure 2.1 depicts the distribution of logic for a typical client-server application.

Figure 2.1.

A typical configuration for a client-server application.

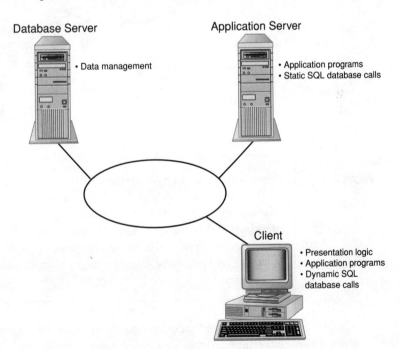

Database Server
• Data management

Application Server
• Application programs
• Static SQL database calls

Client
• Presentation logic
• Application programs
• Dynamic SQL database calls

While a client-server application distributes a mix of presentation, application, and database logic between the client and server, Web applications typically parcel almost all of the logic to the server. Using this mix, Web applications can provide the thinnest client of all, where the only component that's installed on the client machine is a browser. Figure 2.2 shows the configuration for a typical Web-based application.

Figure 2.2.

A typical configuration for a Web-based application.

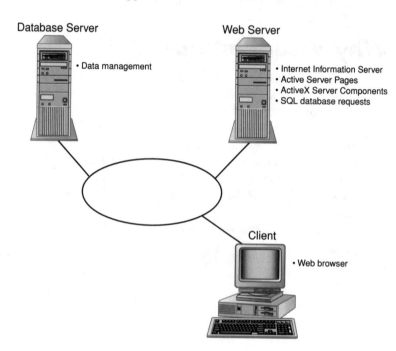

The previous architecture diagrams represent a typical configuration for both client-server and Web-based applications. You can distribute the presentation, application, and database logic to varying degrees between the client and the server in both computing models. This comparison is meant to show the benefit of the Web-based style of computing over client-server in terms of software distribution, version control, and administration.

The benefit of Web-based applications hinges on providing a universal client to all users that make requests of a centralized application stored on the server. This application is comprised of HTML pages, client- and server-side script, object-based controls, and other server-side components that provide robust application processing. With a client-server application, you still have a client component that you have to install with every new enhancement and change to your application. With a Web-based application, the browser and, hence, the client remain unchanged, and the application changes are made centrally, in one place at one time on the server. Administration, software distribution, and version control are significantly simplified under this model.

A problem occurs under the Web-based model in that the Internet doesn't inherently support interactive sessions with the user like the client-server model. Visual InterDev supports the use of server-side components to accomplish a persistent dialogue with the user and, thus, an interactive session.

Visual InterDev provides the tool to take advantage of the new Web-based model of computing. Some development tools focus on supporting a single Internet technology. Others support several technologies for Web-based development but don't provide visual tools to accomplish these tasks. Visual InterDev exceeds existing Web development tools by providing a way to integrate multiple technologies and supplies visual tools to greatly enhance a developer's productivity. Visual InterDev also surpasses and extends the reach of client-server tools to the Internet and the Web.

The Essence of Integration

The *American Heritage Dictionary* defines the word *integration* in the following manner:

"1. To make into a whole; unify. 2. To join with something else; unite."

Truly, Visual InterDev unifies and unites the technologies of the Web through its integrated development environment. You can use the environment to rapidly build a robust application. You have at your disposal all of the tools necessary for Web-based application development in one integrated package. In this sense, the whole really is greater than the sum of its parts.

Visual InterDev Development Environment

Visual InterDev provides an integrated container for a variety of visual tools. The integrated development environment is like a house with many rooms. Each of the rooms has its own specific function that contributes to the overall purpose of the house. Similar to the rooms of a house, each function contributes to the well-being of the developer or resident. No single tool is more important than the other, just as no room is more important than another. In a typical house, you can eat, sleep, and take care of your personal hygiene all under the same roof. With Visual InterDev, you can develop your web pages, connect them to a database, and deploy your web site all within the confines of the same development environment.

The Visual InterDev development environment utilizes an implementation of the Developer Studio shell that was first found in Microsoft's Visual C++. Microsoft's Visual J++ also incorporates this development environment. By using the Developer Studio workspace, multiple projects and tools can be supported. Microsoft is bringing its Visual Tools family together by using the same initial shell across products. Developers can open many types of projects created with Visual InterDev, Visual C++, and Visual J++.

The advantage of this integrated support is found in using multiple applications to provide a robust solution. You can build a Java applet using Visual J++, incorporate the applet into your Visual InterDev web application, and test and debug the application all within the same environment. The same holds true for building an ActiveX control using Visual C++. Again, "integration" is the key word. Figure 2.3 illustrates the ability to open multiple types of projects from within the Visual InterDev integrated development environment.

Figure 2.3.

Opening projects with Visual InterDev.

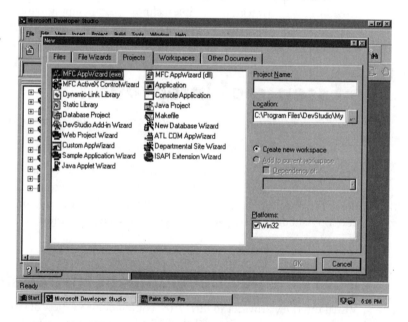

Figure 2.3 shows the Visual InterDev File Open Project dialog window. Notice the ability to open multiple types of projects from within the environment.

When you open your Visual InterDev project, you're viewing your actual web site. The Visual InterDev development environment uses the Explorer interface to view and manage your web site files and folders. This interface simplifies the task of creating and maintaining your web site files and folders. Also, the interface enables you to fully organize the construction of your Web-based application. The integrated development environment enables easy site creation through the use of wizards, and enables developers to reuse files from other sites.

Visual InterDev enables you to easily import existing files into your web site structure. The Explorer interface enables you to accomplish this task through a point-and-click metaphor, just as you copy and paste files and folders on your PC. Figure 2.4 shows a Visual InterDev project using File View.

Figure 2.4.

A typical Visual InterDev project.

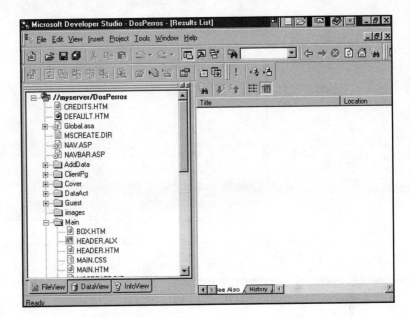

The File View is the default view for a typical Visual InterDev project. Notice the tabs at the bottom of the pane on the left-hand side of the workspace. File View enables you to see the structure of your web site including files and folders. This view displays the entire contents of your site, including HTML pages, images, controls, applets, and other files. The pane to the right of this workspace displays the object that is selected based upon its file type. For example, if you selected an HTML page from the list on the left, the HTML code would be displayed in the window on the right.

DataView is the other tab located next to the FileView tab. This view shows all of your database objects, including tables, views, stored procedures, and triggers. The Data View provides a direct connection to your ODBC datasource to enable remote configuration and maintenance as well as interaction. Figure 2.5 demonstrates the Data View showing a sample Access database.

Figure 2.5.

The Data View.

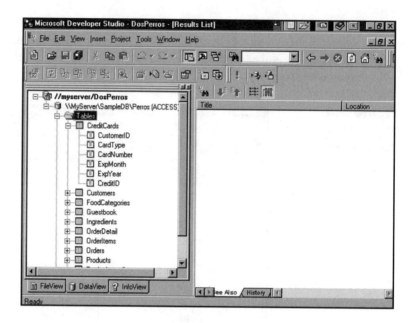

NOTE

> The Data View only appears as an option for web projects after you have inserted a database connection. The Data View also is displayed for Database Projects.

Visual SourceSafe Integration

Visual InterDev supports integration with Visual SourceSafe to provide version control capabilities like check-in/check-out. Similar to any application development effort, source code control becomes a big issue when you're building a site with multiple team members. Developers can check out their portion of the site, make the appropriate changes, and send the file back to the server to be incorporated with the other developers' files. Effective team development is covered in more detail on Day 19, "Working Effectively in Teams with Visual SourceSafe."

Browser Integration

Another feature of Visual InterDev is the integration of a browser within the development environment. Visual InterDev includes an implementation of the Microsoft Internet Explorer 3.0 browser. This implementation supports all of the same features of the commercial version of Internet Explorer, including Java applets, ActiveX controls, ActiveX documents, VBScript and JavaScript, style sheets, and HTML 3.x features such as frames and tables. By using the Preview in Browser feature, you don't have to use one tool to build the application and then open up your browser to view it. With Visual InterDev, you can build your Web-based application and view the results all from within one environment. This feature adds to the speed with which a developer can create and update applications and web sites.

You do have the capability to use the Browse With function to view your web site from within the browser's native window. For example, you could configure Internet Explorer or Netscape Navigator and view the site from within the production browser environment. You probably will want to use this feature during final testing of your web site. If you're deploying your site for use with the Netscape Navigator browser, you have to use this feature.

You can use either of these features by selecting an HTML file and right-clicking the mouse to display the shortcut menu. Figure 2.6 shows the Preview in Browser and Browse With menu options on the shortcut menu for an HTML file.

Figure 2.6.

Browser viewing options.

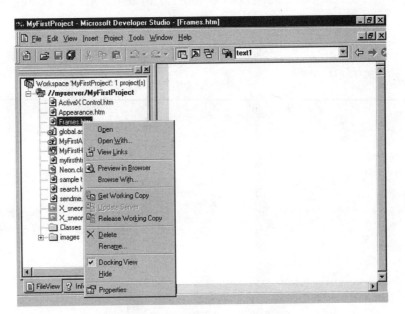

Taking a Closer Look at the Components

The previous section discussed how Visual InterDev provides an integrated development environment from which to work. You saw the basic Visual InterDev workspace and the different views that are available. In this section, you get a guided tour through each of the features and components that make up Visual InterDev.

Visual InterDev Editors

Visual InterDev provides several visual editors for designing and developing your HTML web pages. The following list outlines those that are available:

- ☐ HTML Source Editor
- ☐ FrontPage Editor for Visual InterDev
- ☐ HTML Layout Editor
- ☐ Object Editor

HTML Source Editor

Using this editor, you can create and edit your HTML code, which is color-coded, providing a visually appealing syntax. You can incorporate many objects and controls, such as HTML layouts and controls, ActiveX controls, and Design-time ActiveX controls. The editor also supports the use of script with your HTML web page. Figure 2.7 highlights standard HTML code using the HTML Source Editor.

Figure 2.7.

The HTML Source Editor.

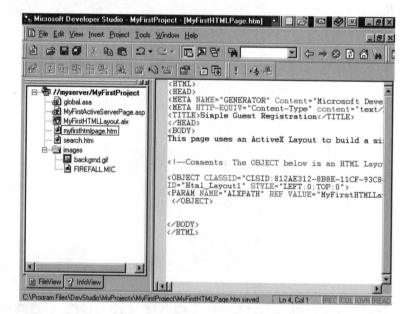

FrontPage Editor for Visual InterDev

This editor is an implementation of the Microsoft FrontPage Editor created for Visual InterDev. This editor is completely compatible with the full version of Microsoft FrontPage and provides a visual tool for developing HTML web pages. You may already be familiar with Microsoft FrontPage. The FrontPage Editor uses a WYSIWYG approach to develop HTML code. This approach enables you to add HTML features to your web page through a graphical, point-and-click metaphor. For example, to add a table, you select the Insert Table menu item from the Table menu and then visually set the parameters, such as number of rows and columns. With the FrontPage Editor, you can visually work with objects instead of the underlying HTML to construct your web pages. This method can substantially save development time. Once you have constructed a web page using the graphical editor, you can access and manipulate the generated HTML code and add your own custom HTML.

The FrontPage Editor also supports the incorporation of plug-ins, ActiveX controls, and Java applets. Figure 2.8 highlights the WYSIWYG features of the FrontPage Editor for Visual InterDev.

Figure 2.8.

The FrontPage Editor for Visual InterDev.

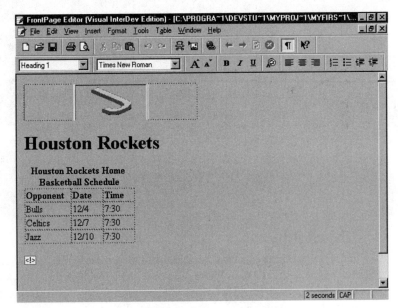

HTML Layout Editor

The HTML Layout Editor is the same editor that was first included with the ActiveX Control Pad from Microsoft. This editor provides a way to accurately position all of your ActiveX controls on your web page. The interface is very similar to tools like Visual Basic, which enable you to position your objects on forms. With this layout editor, you can drag and drop controls onto the layout and establish their properties and exact position within the web page. When the form is displayed by the browser at runtime, the controls are positioned at the exact coordinates that were specified at design time. The toolbox enables you to add and delete controls. You also can use the Script Wizard to automatically add scripting code for use with your controls. Figure 2.9 displays the HTML Layout Editor.

Figure 2.9.

The HTML Layout Editor.

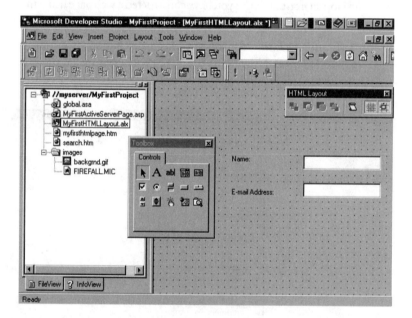

Object Editor

The Object Editor enables you to establish the properties for your ActiveX and Design-time ActiveX controls as well as Java applets and Netscape plug-ins. The Object Editor is activated after you insert an object into your HTML source code. For example, to position an ActiveX control on your web page, you would right-click the mouse where you wanted the object to be placed within your HTML code.

NOTE

> You must click between the <HTML> and </HTML> tags that signify the beginning and ending of your code.

You can then choose between regular and Design-time controls. Once you have chosen a control, the Object Editor is displayed, enabling you to set the properties for the given control. Figure 2.10 exhibits the Object Editor for a typical ActiveX control.

Figure 2.10.
The Object Editor.

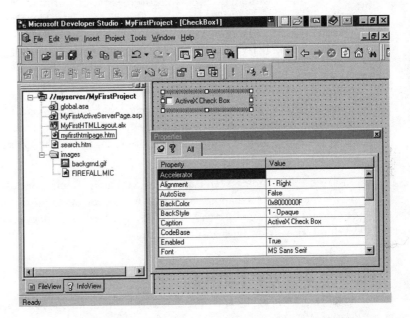

As you can see, there are several editors that you can choose, based on the task that you're trying to accomplish. These editors are covered in-depth later in the week. You also will get a chance to use each of these editors to experience their features during the first week.

ActiveX Controls and Java Applets

Visual InterDev includes and supports the use of ActiveX controls. ActiveX controls are the next generation of OLE controls, .OCX files. These controls use less overhead and memory and are perfect for transporting over the Internet. These controls also can be used with other client-server development tools, like Visual Basic and Visual C++. ActiveX controls extend the reach of HTML controls and enable you to create effective user interfaces. Using the editors mentioned in the previous section, you can visually set the properties for the ActiveX control.

Visual InterDev also supports the use of Java applets and Netscape plug-ins. You can work within the frame of either of these controls to visually establish their properties.

Design-Time ActiveX Controls

Visual InterDev uses Design-time ActiveX controls to provide similar functionality to regular ActiveX controls without the processing overhead. Design-time ActiveX controls enable you to visually set properties for the control at design time. The Design-time control then generates HTML and scripting code based on the properties that you select. Regular ActiveX controls differ in that they include a run-time component that executes within the context of the browser.

Design-time ActiveX controls have no run-time component. Their script is processed on the server, and the HTML and results are returned to the client. Visual InterDev provides many Design-time controls, including some very powerful controls for building database connectivity. You can also build your own design-time controls with tools such as Visual Basic and Visual C++.

On Day 14, "Extending Web Pages Through Design-Time Controls," you will see how to extend your Web-based applications through the use of design-time controls. On Day 16, "Building Design-Time ActiveX Controls," you will have the opportunity to design and develop your very own design-time control.

Active Server Pages

Visual InterDev enables you to add powerful processing for your application on the server through the use of Active Server Pages. If you remember from yesterday's lesson, Active Server Pages are a combination of HTML and scripting code that resides on the server. The script is processed before the page is returned to the client machine. Some common uses of Active Server Pages include interacting with a database and performing loop operations on a web page.

Active Server Pages seamlessly integrate with your HTML files. These pages remove the need to link separately compiled programs to accomplish robust application tasks. The other benefit to using Active Server Pages involves the use of ActiveX Server Components. You can build an ActiveX Server Component with tools like Visual Basic and Visual C++ to handle additional application processing.

In a distributed environment, ActiveX Server Components can be used to spread the processing across several application servers. Scripting code is very useful but has its limitations, like the inability to perform file I/O or provide access to system resources. ActiveX Server Components extend the limitations of scripting code by providing these features as well as other robust features. You should use a combination of Active Server Pages and ActiveX Server Components to provide the best solution for the server side of your application equation.

The Script Wizard

Once you have created your basic HTML page and included a few objects, you will want to make your objects come alive. The Script Wizard enables you to accomplish this task, providing a method for adding script to enhance your ActiveX controls. Those of you who have used the ActiveX Control Pad will be familiar with this wizard. You activate the Script Wizard by right-clicking the mouse in an HTML file that contains the object you want to add script for. The Script Wizard provides two basic views: List View and Code View. List View enables you to associate actions with the available events for that control. The script is automatically generated based on the actions that you choose. Code View enables you to directly modify the generated script code as well as add your own custom code. Although the default scripting language is VBScript, Visual InterDev also supports the use of JavaScript. Figure 2.11 shows the Script Wizard in List View.

Figure 2.11.

The Script Wizard as seen through the List View.

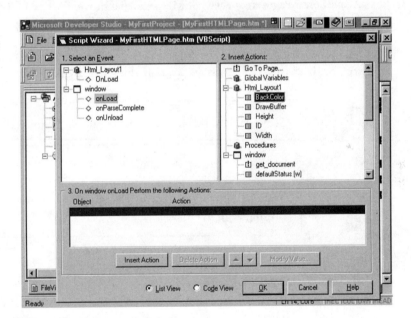

File Components

You will be working with various files when developing your Visual InterDev project. The following list outlines some of the most relevant files that you will be working with:

☐ HTML files

☐ Active Server Page files

☐ ActiveX Layout files

☐ Global files
☐ Multimedia files

HTML Files

HTML files are the most basic file created by Visual InterDev. These files are specified by the .htm extension and contain the HTML code for your web pages. I mentioned earlier today the Visual InterDev editors that are available to edit your HTML code. Visual InterDev supports the HTML 3.2 standards as well as some Microsoft Internet Explorer and Netscape Communicator browser extensions.

Active Server Page Files

Active Server Pages are special HTML pages that provide ActiveX scripting on the server. A few common uses of Active Server Pages include executing loops and connecting to a database. An Active Server Page is denoted by the .asp filename extension. These files reside and are processed on the server before the page is sent to the client machine. The script is never seen by the client. The results are the only thing that are passed back to the browser.

NOTE

> Script code is designated by the <% and %> delimiters.

TIP

> You can create an .asp file by changing the filename extension of an existing .htm file to .asp.

ActiveX Layout Files

These are files that are created and maintained by the HTML Layout Editor. This editor, as discussed earlier in the day, enables you to visually construct the layout of your web page and controls. An .alx file is created when you use this editor. Your HTML file references this file and incorporates the layout at runtime. You can edit these files by directly opening the file from within File View or by right-clicking the mouse within the <OBJECT> tag for the HTML layout and selecting Edit HTML Layout from the shortcut menu.

2

Global Files

These files are denoted with the .asa filename extension. A global file, by default, is constructed when you use the Web Project Wizard to create a new project. The global file is very useful for both application and session initialization and termination routines.

Multimedia Files

While enhancing your web page you will probably create images, sounds, music, and other multimedia files to enhance your web page. Some of the multimedia products included with Visual InterDev will be presented in detail later this week. For now, it's important to mention that you can incorporate these files within the context of your Visual InterDev project. Some of the more common image filename extensions include .jpg, .gif, .img, .mic, and .bmp. Some of the more common audio and video extensions include .mid, .mmp, .avi, and .wav. These file types will be explained on Day 6, "Spicing Up Your Interface with Images and Multimedia."

File Management Components

So far you have seen different components and files that make up a Visual InterDev project. The benefits of having an integrated tool to manage these components has been emphasized. Visual InterDev provides comprehensive site and file management tools to help maintain your components during every phase of development and deployment.

The File View enables you to view and manage all of the file types located in your project. The left-hand pane of the Visual InterDev workspace behaves just like the Windows Explorer, enabling you to drag and drop files. Full right-mouse button functionality is also provided. The shortcut menu makes it easy to change the names of files, to move files within your web site hierarchy, and to copy files to other Visual InterDev projects. You can create folders that represent the sub-directories for your web site. You can copy the sub-directories, including all of the files, to another web site. Another powerful feature is the Copy Web command. This feature enables you to copy an entire web site from one place to another. This can save time when preparing your site for deployment. By using this command, you can migrate your site from a development server to a testing server and, eventually, to a production server.

Visual InterDev automatically verifies links between pages and ensures that no links have been changed or broken. Upon detection of a broken link, Visual InterDev is able to repair these broken links. For example, if you changed the name of a file that was used by a web page in your project, Visual InterDev would detect the link and prompt you to update the web page reference to the file.

The Link View provides a powerful tool for viewing the entire structure of your web site. This tool enables you to graphically see the content of your web site, how each object is related, and filename and property information of each object. This view is similar to using an entity relationship diagram to graphically view a database. You can double-click on any item in the view to use the appropriate editor to manipulate the object. You also can select parameters to view only certain objects or files. Figure 2.12 illustrates the power of the Link View.

Figure 2.12.

The Link View.

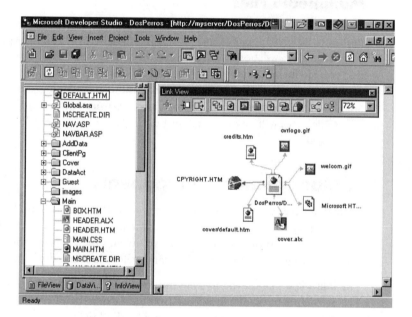

Visual InterDev incorporates many components to provide a very robust and powerful development platform. You will have a chance to use each of these components in due time. For now, though, it's time to discuss some of the multimedia tools that accompany Visual InterDev.

Multimedia Tools

Several multimedia tools are included with Visual InterDev. These tools are separate applications but can be initiated from within the Visual InterDev development environment. Each of these products also can be purchased separately from Microsoft. The multimedia tools include

☐ Image Composer

☐ Music Producer

☐ Media Manager

NOTE   The Image Composer and the Music Producer are covered in detail on Day 6.

Image Composer

The Microsoft Image Composer enables you to develop professional-looking graphics through an easy-to-use interface. The Image Composer is capable of many of the features of other graphics packages, but differs from them in that it supports images as objects, or sprites. Sprites are independent objects that have a defined shape. Sprites enable you to easily edit images by selecting, moving, and changing the individual sprites that make up the image. Figure 2.13 displays the Image Composer environment.

Figure 2.13.

The Image Composer.

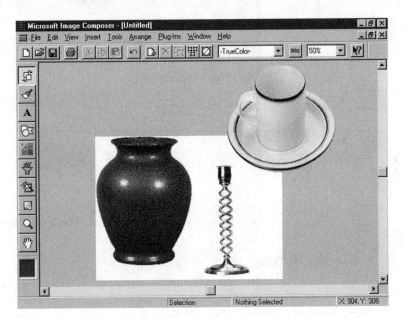

Music Producer

The Microsoft Music Producer enables you to create sounds and music for your web site. The Music Producer includes many musical styles for building creative and innovative musical compositions. Once you select a musical style, you can then choose the personality of the music as well as the band. A band can include up to six different musical instruments. You then compose the music based on your selections while modifying the tempo, timing, and key of the music. Sounds and music can definitely enliven the web page experience for your users. Figure 2.14 depicts the Music Producer workspace.

Figure 2.14.

The Music Producer.

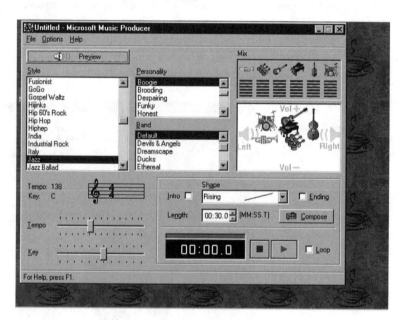

Media Manager

The Media Manager provides a tool to manage your multimedia files. This tool is incorporated into the Windows Explorer to enable proper file management of all your multimedia components. Special folders are created for each of your multimedia file types. You can create thumbnail sketches of your files based on the file type to see a quick view of the file without launching its host application. This feature is similar to the Quick View feature of the Windows Explorer. Figure 2.15 shows the Windows Explorer with the special folders for your multimedia files.

Figure 2.15.

The Media Manager.

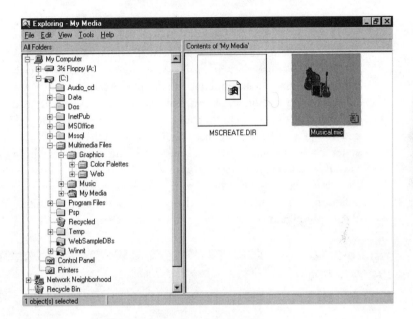

Finally!...Database Integration

There has usually been a tradeoff between the power of database tools and their ease of use. The development tools that have provided the most robust power in terms of features have not been very intuitive to use. Likewise, those tools that have been very easy to use haven't provided the most powerful features. With Visual InterDev, you now have both: powerful features and an intuitive, easy-to-use interface.

Another component that has been missing specifically in Web-based development tools has been database connectivity and integration. You typically have had to use one tool to develop your web site and another tool to provide the database connectivity. Connecting to a database is extremely important when building a Web-based application. Visual InterDev takes care of this aspect, as well, by incorporating the Visual Data Tools within the Visual InterDev development environment. These visual tools significantly augment a database programmer's capabilities and productivity.

Data View

The Data View is one of the main views available within Visual InterDev. This view enables you to see all of the database components contained in your project. These components include tables, fields, views, stored procedures, and triggers. Through this view, you can directly manipulate the objects in your database. By selecting an object, you can view detailed information about the object in the display area to the right of the Data View pane.

Query Designer

The Query Designer enables you to visually build SQL queries for your application. The Query Designer uses the Microsoft Access interface and significantly improves development time for building database interaction. Similar to the Access interface, you can drag and drop objects onto the design pane area. You can then construct your query by associating various tables and fields. As you build your query, the results are displayed in the design pane. You can view the SQL as it's constructed as well as the query criteria upon which the SQL statement is comprised. You can stack the different windows within the design pane display area. For example, you might want to view the tables, SQL statement, and results, all within the design pane. Using this layout, you could manipulate your SQL statement while validating the results, all within the confines of the design pane. Figure 2.16 demonstrates the graphical nature and power of the Query Designer.

Figure 2.16.

The Query Designer.

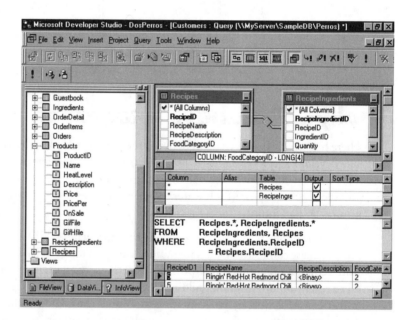

As you can see from Figure 2.16, the query designer visually displays your database objects. This picture illustrates how you can stack a diagram of the tables, the query criteria, the constructed SQL, and the query results all in the design pane display.

The Query Designer saves an inordinate amount of time in building your SQL statements. You may choose to manipulate the generated SQL or build SQL statements on your own. Visual InterDev enables you to easily accomplish all of these tasks.

2

Database Designer

Visual InterDev provides the Database Designer to help you design and implement your SQL database. This tool currently only supports Microsoft SQL Server. The Database Designer provides a visual tool for creating and maintaining your database. You can directly manipulate the properties of your database objects, or you can generate the necessary Data Definition Language (DDL) scripts to execute against the database. Figure 2.17 shows some related tables using the Database Designer.

Figure 2.17.

The Database Designer.

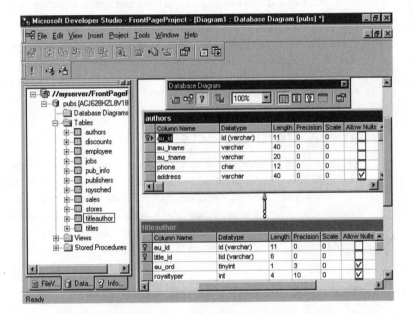

One of the most laborious tasks for database administrators (DBAs) is changing a field type for a table that has existing data. I remember how cumbersome this process was from my early Microsoft SQL Server DBA days. First, you had to back up the existing data. Then, you had to execute a DDL script that would drop the table and create a new table with the revised field type. Finally, you restored the data back into the revised table.

The Database Designer enables you to change field types for your database table by selecting the type from a drop-down combo box. The Database Designer handles the data type conversion for you. Again, the ease of the Microsoft Access interface has been used to make cumbersome administrative tasks relatively easy.

Stored Procedure/Trigger Editor

This tool enables you to create and maintain stored procedures and triggers for your application. Stored procedures are SQL statements that are precompiled in the database. You call a stored procedure by name from your application, passing it the appropriate parameters. Stored procedures are more efficient than dynamic SQL because they reduce the number of steps to execute the SQL call. A trigger is a special type of stored procedure that executes based on some event that occurs in the database. For example, you might create a trigger to execute whenever a row is deleted in an Order Header table, ensuring that referential integrity is maintained and no Order Detail records exist for the deleted Order Header.

Visual InterDev enables you to create, view, and maintain stored procedures for Microsoft SQL Server 6.x and Oracle 7.x databases. You also can establish who has permission to execute this stored procedure or trigger. You can debug your stored procedures through the use of the Visual InterDev debugger.

ActiveX Data Objects

Visual InterDev achieves database integration through the use of the ActiveX Data Objects model (ADO). The ADO model has been specifically designed for database connectivity over the Web. These database objects are more efficient than previous database controls used with existing client-server tools. Also, ADO easily accommodates the management of binary objects like images and other multimedia objects. The ADO model supports the use of stored procedures and cursors for robust database access.

Database Design-Time Controls

Visual InterDev includes several database Design-time controls. These controls enable you to easily establish database connections for your applications by setting database connection properties for the particular control. After you have set these properties, the Design-time control automatically generates all of the necessary scripting and connection information for you. Examples of database Design-time controls include the Data Command control and the Data Header and Data Footer control. These powerful controls enable you to construct a web page that interacts with a database and displays the results with little or no programming. You will get a chance to use these controls on Day 8.

Database Wizards

Visual InterDev provides several database wizards that significantly reduce the time for developing database connections for your web pages. These wizards guide you through the process of establishing connectivity with your database. Examples of Visual InterDev database wizards include the New Database Wizard and the Data Form Wizard. The New Database Wizard guides you through the process of creating a new SQL Server database. The Data Form Wizard enables you to create an ActiveX HTML form that is database-enabled. In other words, this form can execute all of the relevant database functions including inserting, selecting, updating, and deleting information.

NOTE   The Data Form Wizard creates an Active Server Page, or .asp, file to execute the database calls. This .asp file must reside on a server that supports the ActiveX Server framework.

How Should I Use Visual InterDev?

With all of the features introduced today, you may be wondering where to begin. Also, you may be asking questions about how to use these features when building your Web-based application. Visual InterDev should be used as a high-end development tool for building applications for the Web. The key words in the last sentence are "high-end" and "applications." If all you want to do is publish basic information on the Web, you might want to consider another tool like an HTML editor. Visual InterDev is too powerful for a menial task like document publishing. This prior example would be synonymous to having Charles Barkley, forward for the Houston Rockets, carry the suitcases for the team on all the road trips. He could do it, but there are people better suited for this task.

Visual InterDev is specifically designed to meet all of your application development needs while providing compatibility with other tools like FrontPage. In fact, for your development team, you may want to include functional members such as a marketing person to construct the content for the various web pages, using a tool like FrontPage. Then, application developers can incorporate that content into Visual InterDev and build a robust Web-based application. The different roles of development team members are discussed in more detail on Day 5.

The following is a checklist for deciding how to use each of the features of Visual InterDev:

1. Define what are you are trying to accomplish.
2. Identify the alternatives for accomplishing this task.
3. Assess the strengths of each method.
4. Choose the best alternative.
5. Implement to perfection.

Summary

As you can see, Visual InterDev is a very comprehensive and powerful tool. In today's lesson, you were taken on a guided tour of Visual InterDev. You have been given a taste of the features and components that make Visual InterDev such a powerful application development tool for the Web.

When the day began, Visual InterDev was described, and the question of why you should use this exciting new tool was answered. An in-depth discussion of its components and features followed. I talked about the powerful integrated development environment, which significantly enhances your productivity and makes Web programming fun again by enabling you to build your applications within the confines of a single tool. I then covered each of the major Visual InterDev components. In reading about the components, you saw how their features could be used to develop your application.

Database integration is one of the most significant features of Visual InterDev. For this reason, this topic was saved for the end of the day to keep your attention. Visual Data Tools that enable you to use an intuitive, visual environment while constructing and executing powerful database commands were discussed, as were database wizards, which can make your life easier by guiding you through complex processes.

Remember, this material is just scratching the surface of the power of this tool. Over the next few weeks, you will be exploring and learning about the power of Visual InterDev. You should set a goal to learn how to incorporate each of these features into building more robust and powerful Web-based applications. Your overall goal, however, should be to learn to use Visual InterDev to its fullest capacity. Your users will thank you for it when they interact with your applications.

You have already learned a lot so far. Yesterday, you learned about the relationship between applications, the Web, and Visual InterDev. Today, you went on a guided tour of the features and components of Visual InterDev. These two lessons have set the stage for tomorrow when you will learn the final component necessary for developing applications for the Web. On Day 3, you will learn about development and deployment considerations when designing, constructing, and promoting Web-based applications. After tomorrow's lesson, you will be ready to start building your first Visual InterDev project, which you will do on Day 4.

Q&A

Q **What is the difference between Visual InterDev and FrontPage?**

A Visual InterDev is a development tool for building Web-based applications and is a part of the Microsoft Visual Tools family. Other tools in this group include Visual C++, Visual Basic, and Visual J++. FrontPage is a Web authoring tool for non-programmers and is an extension of the Microsoft Office family. While FrontPage focuses on content and publishing, Visual InterDev focuses on application development. Visual InterDev and FrontPage are completely compatible. Visual InterDev also includes the FrontPage Editor for Visual InterDev, which is a special implementation of the editor included in the commercial version of FrontPage.

Q **Does Visual InterDev support Java?**

A Yes. Visual InterDev supports the incorporation of Java applets and Java components.

Q **How can I get ActiveX Controls for my applications?**

A Visual InterDev includes many ActiveX and Design-time ActiveX controls. You also can choose from over 1000 third-party controls on the market. Finally, you can create your own ActiveX and Design-time ActiveX controls with tools like Visual Basic and Visual C++.

Workshop

Think about previous client-server or Web-based application development that you may have done. Think about the tools that you used and the strength of their features. For those of you who have developed for the Web, I want you to specifically think about how many tools you have used in the past to develop and deploy your application. Compare that list to Visual InterDev and how you think it will make your life easier. For all developers, write down your expectations and anticipated benefits. Save this list for the third and final week and see if Visual InterDev exceeds your expectations.

You may want to have an HTML reference on hand as you venture on through the week. *HTML 3.2 and CGI Unleashed* by John December and Mark Ginsburg is a very good reference.

Quiz

1. What is the main benefit of Web-based applications over typical client-server applications?
2. What is the purpose of the HTML Layout Editor?

3. What is the difference between Active Server Pages and ActiveX Server Components?

4. What is the difference between an ActiveX control and a Design-time ActiveX control?

5. Name a multimedia tool that is included with Visual InterDev and its purpose.

Quiz Answers

1. The main benefit to Web-based applications is that code changes to the client are practically reduced, thereby simplifying software distribution, version control, and administration. The reason for this is the use of a browser as a universal client and the use of the server as the primary location of the presentation, application, and database logic. In a client-server configuration, an executable file resides on the client. When you make changes to your application, you have to re-deploy the application to each of the client machines. In the Web-based model, you make your changes in one place on the server.

2. Similar to the ActiveX Control Pad, the HTML Layout Editor enables you to accurately position ActiveX controls onto your web page.

3. Active Server Pages are a combination of HTML and scripting code that enable you to perform dynamic actions for your applications at the server. All of the script is processed on the server and the results are sent back to the client. Active Server Components are executable programs or dynamic link libraries that execute at the server to handle tasks such as file I/O and resource-intensive processes. The difference is that an Active Server Component is a compiled program. Active Server Pages are not compiled, and are typically used to call ActiveX Server Components.

4. ActiveX controls differ from Design-time ActiveX controls in that ActiveX controls include a run-time component that executes within the context of the browser. Design-time ActiveX controls provide a visual guide for establishing properties that are generated into HTML and scripting code. Design-time ActiveX controls don't incur processing overhead because they don't have a run-time component.

5. Possible answers include the following:

    Image Composer—Design and development of graphic images

    Music Producer—Creation of music and sounds

    Media Manager—Management of multimedia files

Day **3**

Design and Development Considerations

The design and development of a Web-based application is a very intricate process. The application can be implemented rapidly, but you should definitely spend adequate time planning the end result. With proper planning, you can create an application that is a success both in your eyes and in the eyes of your users.

Whether the topic is client-server or Web-based development tools, most programmers don't enjoy the discussion of planning and standards. The most popular books on the market are those that teach the intricacies of a specific tool, like the book you're currently reading. When was the last time you traveled to the local bookstore to buy the latest title on project planning, project management, or project standards and methodology?

The answer is probably never, and rest assured, today's lesson isn't about these topics either. This lesson focuses on the most important aspects to consider when developing your Web-based applications.

Language-specific coding references, such as HTML or VBScript, aren't mentioned in this chapter. There are plenty of good references for these topics. This chapter does, however, discuss how to use these languages to build the best applications. It also touches on how to avoid the difficulties of standards that continue to change with each new company innovation.

In today's lesson, you will learn about effective user interface design for your application. No matter how efficient your code is, you can't overlook the one aspect that is most apparent to your users. After that you will read about whether or not to use browser-specific extensions in your application. Available HTML standards and browser extensions are briefly touched on to demonstrate their capability.

During the middle part of the day, the lesson covers choosing the proper development and deployment platform for your application, along with several alternatives specific to Visual InterDev. After you have learned about the certain platforms, the concept of choosing the right database for your application will be discussed. Specifically, you will learn about the differences between desktop, or PC, databases versus client-server databases. At the end of the day, you will read about security issues and discover a considerations checklist that you can use when developing applications for the Web.

Effective User Interface Design

User interface design is one of the most important aspects of your application. You may personally prefer talking about the intricacies of ActiveX controls or C++ programming, and you may want to spend more time developing new components and class libraries that are fast and efficient.

No matter how much you enjoy other phases of development, however, you can't overlook the most important customer of the application: the user. If users don't want to experience your application, your miraculous code will be banished by your users and the Web community, and dissipate in a vast wasteland of despair.

I have been a student of user interface design since my COBOL mainframe days. Those are days that I would like to forget. We have come a long way, through advances in the Macintosh and OS/2 interfaces to all of the Windows interfaces, including Windows 3.1 and Windows 95. I have truly enjoyed studying as well as writing about each of these new developments and the promises that they exhibited.

3

Today developers have to contend with the Web interface. From a computing model, some say that we have gone back in time to the mainframe, dumb-terminal days. I personally think we have finally figured out a way to effectively use the client-server model of computing. Whatever the case, there is a new challenge: to use the browser to exploit the advantages of the World Wide Web.

Consider the power that the Web-based interface has given to today's technology companies. The Web has caused some of the technical giants in the industry to totally change their applications to be Web-enabled. Microsoft has completely revamped their current and new products to use aspects of this new interface. After building a brand-new way to explore files on your desktop, they made a conscious decision to revamp the Windows Explorer interface to be capable of exploring Web files as well. That's a lot of power!

The following list outlines some basic steps to consider when designing an effective user interface for your Web-based application:

1. Define a purpose for the interface.
2. Identify the users' expectations and needs.
3. Design the user interface.
4. Conduct usability testing.
5. Incorporate the feedback into your interface.

Define a Purpose for the Interface

The first step involved in creating an effective user interface is to define the purpose of your interface and how that purpose accomplishes the mission of your application. Why are the users here? Why should someone use your application? Defining a purpose sets the context for how you will present the information and application to the user. If you can't define why your pages exist, then why should users visit your application?

In defining a purpose for your interface, you should consider the following things:

- ☐ **Content**: What information should be included?
- ☐ **Audience**: Who is the target audience?
- ☐ **User benefits**: What benefit will the users gain from the application?

Identify the Users' Needs and Expectations

While building applications, developers often take an overbearing parent approach to programming. This method could also be called the "I know what's best approach." This approach is synonymous to a father or mother who takes action for their son or daughter based solely on their knowledge of the situation. The parent forms an opinion that is one-sided and then acts on that knowledge without seeking to understand the child's point of view. Likewise, developers design and build an application without consulting with the end user and are distraught when the users don't appreciate the finished product. Maybe, if developers talked to the users more, they could find out what users need and design and develop their applications accordingly.

This is the next step in designing an effective interface. Talk to the users. Find out their expectations for your application. Identify their specific needs. You can answer these questions by conducting user interviews or focus group sessions.

In facilitating these discussions, you need to make sure that you establish a specific agenda and that these meetings don't become gripe sessions about current applications. Keep the group focused on the issue at hand. The use of a white board can really facilitate good discussion during a meeting with your users. Using the white board, you can construct a flowchart of the web pages and outline specific implementation objectives for each page. You also can scope out the basic design of the web pages and application. Accomplishing these tasks can take several sessions but will save you much grief and sorrow in the long run.

Design the User Interface

Once you have defined the purpose and have identified the users' needs and expectations, you're ready to begin designing the interface for your application. In designing the interface, you need to choose a metaphor that is easy and intuitive to use and understand. You may be thinking that you don't have many choices in the matter because the browser is the metaphor. While the browser does serve as the universal client for all users, you have many choices concerning the design of your web pages. Just as with client-server applications and tools, you have many objects, designs, and tools to choose from. You need to make sure that you use the tools in your toolbox wisely. Don't consider everything a nail just because you have a hammer. Proper discernment and consideration is crucial in designing your interface.

Before you begin designing individual pages, you need to consider the overall flow of the application. A roadmap is very helpful for defining the links and possible paths that your users can take. The Web presents a greater challenge than client-server applications in that the users have more flexibility in choosing the route that they take. Users may enter a certain page in your hierarchy without passing through the default home page first. Your application must be able to account for this situation and present the user with choices for navigating through your application. Figure 3.1 illustrates a roadmap for a sample web site.

3

Figure 3.1.
Visualizing the final product.

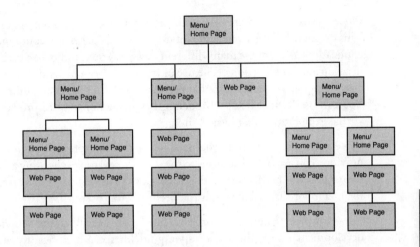

A roadmap for your Web-based application can help you visualize the final product. As shown in Figure 3.1, the menu structure is balanced and isn't too deep or shallow. Your application should provide relevant access to information within three levels of menus. If they don't receive the access to information or tasks within this range, don't expect them to become a return customer. A web site full of menus provides very tedious navigation for the user. Likewise, a web site that only contains a collection of pages with little or no coordination isn't very intuitive. You must be careful to design your application so that it balances logical organization with timely access to information and action. In diagramming your roadmap, you also need to make sure that there are no *dead ends*.

NEW TERM   A *dead end* is a web page that doesn't provide a path to any other pages within your web site. The only way to leave this page is to use the navigational buttons supplied by the browser.

Think about how you feel when you take a wrong turn down a dead-end street with no warning. You feel frustrated. You say to yourself that you will never come in this neighborhood again. Users react to your applications in the same way if they have no defined navigation path to other areas in your site. From every page, a user must be able to choose a course. You might be tempted to rely on browser menu or option buttons that provide back-and-forward scrolling options. Don't submit to this alluring temptation. You should take as much control of user choices as you can, so that you can guide their experience. Your users should receive the full benefit of your web site, and the best way to accomplish this is to present the user with options.

Once you have created a roadmap, the next step is to choose a metaphor for your application. This decision will drive the design of the individual pages and components that fit into your application. You can use many different designs. You can choose a basic web page, including heading and body sections. The use of frames also can be used. You can choose to provide a very graphical experience so that users can click on images and other multimedia options. You can use Virtual Reality Modeling Language (VRML) to provide a 3D metaphor for virtual exploration of a physical site.

Once you make a selection, you need to use this metaphor throughout your application to provide a consistent look and feel to the user. For example, choosing a frame-based metaphor means that you need to use frames for each of your web pages. The overall goal is to choose the metaphor that will best suit the needs of your users.

After you select the metaphor, you can begin designing the individual pages. On any development effort, the use of style guidelines can significantly augment programmer productivity and drastically eliminate design inconsistencies. You should create common templates for each of your developers, content authors, and graphic artists so that they can complete their specific piece of the application puzzle. The use of style sheets also can greatly enhance the team's productivity.

Other design considerations include the following:

- ☐ Aesthetics
- ☐ Page design and layout
- ☐ Semantics
- ☐ Navigation

Aesthetics

You need to design an interface that is aesthetically, or visually, pleasing to the user. The application should provide a rich and rewarding experience for the user. Most people interpret this point to mean that they need to go overboard on the use of images and graphics. Consider the hammer and nail discussion again. You must choose the tools that you use to create your interface carefully. Moderation is the best guideline to follow concerning any of the tools that you have available. Color should also be used properly. Use color to enhance, not overshadow, the content of your application.

Page Design and Layout

The design of your pages is paramount to the success of the application. Your pages should employ a common look and feel that is consistent across the application. You should present information in the same way where possible. You need to use the proper tool for presenting your information in the best way. Use color, where appropriate, to highlight useful information. Images and graphics can add a lot to your application. Be sure that you consider the placement and performance of these objects when designing your pages.

You also must logically organize the layout of your pages. Regardless of the metaphor that you choose, most pages will contain a header area, a body, and a footer area. The header area should include title and heading information for the page. The body section will contain the detailed information part of your application. The body section will be different based on the metaphor you choose. The key point is to make sure that your information is logically organized on the page. Remember that people read top to bottom and left to right. Design the layout of your application accordingly. The footer section usually includes copyright and usage information as well as the contact name and e-mail address for the web page.

Your web page design should be consistent with your application's purpose. The interface should facilitate the accomplishment of the application's mission and enable users to receive a rewarding experience.

Semantics

Semantics refers to how you present meaning to your user through the design of your web pages. You use different visual cues to convey this meaning. For example, you may use certain images to portray concepts about your application and web pages. Make sure that the image you choose is a good representation of the concept you're communicating. The user should clearly understand what the symbol means. If you feel there could be some confusion, use another visual cue.

Navigation

A user must be able to easily and properly navigate through your application. You can use the header and footer areas of your page to provide navigational cues to guide the users in their journey. Examples include toolbars, tabs, and textual hyperlinks to other pages in your application.

3

You should make sure that you inform the users where they are in the application. Don't assume that they know where they are or where they're going. You need to effectively present them with options about where to travel next. Remember the example of dead-end streets? Providing navigational links is one way to avoid a dead-end web page. You need to be cognizant of the fact that users may enter detailed pages in your web hierarchy through another web page. You should provide a technique for navigating to your home page, so that users receive the full experience of your web site. Search utilities also are nice for first time and experienced users. For first time users, a search engine can help overcome information overload by providing a utility to find their required information or action. For experienced users, the search utility provides a big time-saver for navigating to an exact location or service.

So far, the lesson has addressed basic considerations and techniques for effective user interface design. The next few sections discuss specific HTML standards and some of the proposed and incorporated browser standards.

Conduct Usability Testing

You should continue to evaluate the usefulness and usability of your Web-based application throughout the development process. Does the application achieve its mission and purpose? Does the application enable the user to achieve his or her needs? You need to designate time in your development plan for usability testing. This task should be performed by a team member as well as some of your end users. Monitor their effectiveness at using the application to accomplish their tasks. Note those areas in the application where there is confusion or concern.

You also should record the strengths of the interface for future reference for other applications. During this process, you need to involve development team members, including your programmers, content authors, and graphic artists. These team members will be able to gain firsthand insight and feedback from watching the users and can incorporate this knowledge into constructing a more user-friendly interface.

The best way to conduct usability testing is to develop a script for some of the most important tasks that a typical user would want to accomplish. For example, a task for a sales order entry application may be to place an order for an item. You should group these tasks into cycles. A cycle consists of a certain number of steps to carry out a specific task. In other words, the steps would be everything the user needed to accomplish to place an order for an item using your application. Figure 3.2 demonstrates a sample form for documenting a usability test.

3

Figure 3.2.

A sample usability testing form.

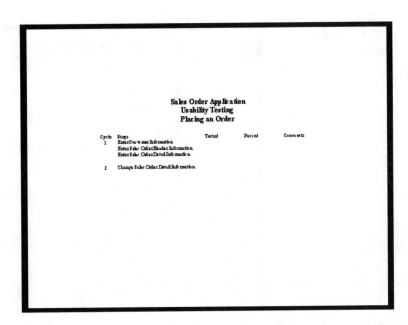

NOTE This document also is on the CD-ROM included with this book for your use when developing your applications.

This form is for scripting the user actions. Another form for documenting the results, strengths, and opportunities for improvement also is on the CD-ROM for you to use. Figure 3.3 shows the layout of this form.

NOTE These forms aren't rigid standards and can be adapted for a variety of purposes. Perhaps usability is a new concept to you, and you have never really considered performing these tests before you deploy your application. Whatever the case, usability is important, and you should consider the concepts that are mentioned in this section.

Figure 3.3.
Recording the results.

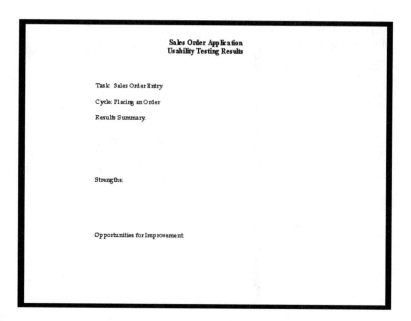

Usability is usually performed during the system testing stage of a development project. I overheard a conversation the other day in which a project manager was talking to one of his developers. The project manager asked the programmer if he was going to perform a system test on the application which would include a usability test. The programmer answered the project manager with a very confident response, "That's what users are for!" Don't wait until your application is deployed to absorb feedback from users. Be proactive.

Incorporate the Feedback into Your Interface

After you conduct the usability test and document the results, you should evaluate the strengths and possible opportunities for improvement in your application. You need to assess what the user felt comfortable with and where the user needed further assistance. The opportunities for improvements relate directly to possible changes to the application. You should prioritize each of these changes and analyze the time and effort needed to make each change. Does the benefit to the user outweigh the cost to make the change and delay deployment of your application? If the benefit is greater than the cost, make the change. If the cost is greater than the benefit, document the change for possible implementation later. You need to communicate to your users why the change wasn't made and that it will be considered in future releases.

3

Which Standards Should I Use?

There are several competing standards that define the structure and layout of documents. The HTML Working Group of the Internet Engineering Task Force has historically defined the standards for HTML.

The most current specification is HTML 3.2. You may be wondering what happened to HTML 3.0. The difference between the HTML 3.0 standards and the HTML 2.0 standards was enormous and proved to be an implementation nightmare. Also, the major software vendors like Netscape and Microsoft had already included extensions to their browsers that were becoming de facto standards. The World Wide Web Consortium (W3C) decided to compromise and include some of these extensions to create HTML 3.2.

This section provides an overview of the features of HTML 3.2, as well as Netscape and Microsoft browser extensions to these standards. In developing your application, you should try to find common ground between these competing standards. Which standards you use are determined in large part by answers to the following questions:

☐ What browsers reside in my user community?

☐ What features do I need to support my application?

☐ What standards do I need for future expansion of my application features?

Determining the Browser

First, you need to determine what browsers are going to be used to view your application. You may have control of setting the standard for which browser is used, as in the case of an intranet application where you are setting the standard for the company or organization. For external Internet applications, you may not know what browser a person is going to use to interact with your application, because users with all types of browsers can view it.

 TIP

You should feel relatively confident that most browsers support the use of the latest HTML standards. If you need to use extended features of a specific browser, implement the feature, but plan for an alternate route for those browsers that can't support the feature. An example would be using the Microsoft extension of a borderless frame for your page. If you use borderless frames for your application, you also need to provide a frame-based metaphor or textual explanation for those browsers that don't support this feature.

Selecting the Features

You need to decide which browser features you need to support your application needs. As you design your pages, you assess how you're going to accomplish the particular application requirement. You should develop a list of alternatives for each requirement. Once you have determined the possible alternatives, choose the extension that best supports your need and has the greatest reach. In other words, try to use features that accomplish your needs and that are supported by the most popular browsers.

Predicting the Future

Finally, you need to assess what future features you will be adding to your application. Based upon these features, you should determine if the standards that you have chosen will limit the expansion of your application. If you use the tip from the preceding section, you should have room for expansion in your applications.

The development of browsers is growing faster than the pace of any product on the market, including other software products, PCs, and cameras. Like these products, the browser you use today will be obsolete tomorrow, even if it is from the same company. As you begin using a browser, the next beta is available for downloading. Microsoft and Netscape have been leading the charge to develop these products to capture the hearts of the Web community. In 1996 alone, Microsoft has worked on three different versions of their browser.

You need to recognize this market phenomenon and plan accordingly. You should watch for features that you can use and employ them in your interface. Likewise, you should resist the temptation to use too much of a good thing. You need to provide some consistency for the user.

HTML 3.2

The latest specification by the W3C is the HTML 3.2 standard. This specification was previously code-named Wilbur. Before discussing HTML 3.2 specifications further, the context needs to be set by briefly mentioning the basic features of the previous HTML specifications.

HTML Levels 0 and 1 established the first standards for providing basic character formatting for documents to be displayed by browsers for the World Wide Web. Levels 0 and 1 provide the structure that enables the construction of a page, including a header, body, and footer section. Other features of 0 and 1 include the display of numerical and bulleted lists and the ability to insert graphical images. With HTML Levels 0 and 1, you can't insert movie files, display tables, or create multiple columns of text.

The biggest advancement in the HTML Level 2 specification was the addition of forms. A form enables you to place basic objects such as text boxes, push buttons, radio buttons, and checkboxes to collect user input. The form has been great for allowing organizations and companies to request and obtain information from their visitors. Based on this information, a company can tailor content, products, and services to the appropriate audience. This specification provided the first taste of true user interaction.

HTML 3.2 adopted many of the browser extensions that had been developed previously by Microsoft and Netscape. The HTML 3.2 specification supports the use of tables, applets, superscripts, and subscripts. The following sections introduce some of the specific features of the HTML 3.2 specification.

Tables

A table enables you to present information that consists of rows and columns. The table is especially useful when presenting a result set from a query against a database. The following code sample shows the structure for formatting data for a table that has three rows and three columns.

```
<TR>
<TD>Cell1</TD><TD>Cell2</TD>
<TD>Cell3</TD>
</TR>
```

In this code example, the tag `<TR>` stands for table row, and the tag `<TD>` indicates table data. A tag surrounded by `<>` denotes the beginning of the tag. The end tag is represented by `</>`. For example, `<TR>` indicates the start of the tag, and `</TR>` indicates the end of the tag. Listing 3.1 shows code for a sample table.

Listing 3.1. Formatting a table.

```
<table border="0">
    <caption align="top"><strong>Houston Rockets Home Basketball
    Schedule</strong></caption>
    <tr>
        <th align="left" width="75">Opponent</th>
        <th align="left" width="50">Date</th>
        <th align="left" width="50">Time</th>
    </tr>
    <tr>
        <td width="75">Bulls</td>
        <td width="50">12/4</td>
        <td width="50">7:30</td>
    </tr>
    <tr>
```

continues

Listing 3.1. continued

```
        <td width="75">Celtics</td>
        <td width="50">12/7</td>
        <td width="50">7:30</td>
    </tr>
    <tr>
        <td width="75">Jazz</td>
        <td width="50">12/10</td>
        <td width="50">7:30</td>
    </tr>
</table>
```

Figure 3.4 shows how this code sample would be displayed in Microsoft Internet Explorer 3.0.

Figure 3.4.

Browsing a table.

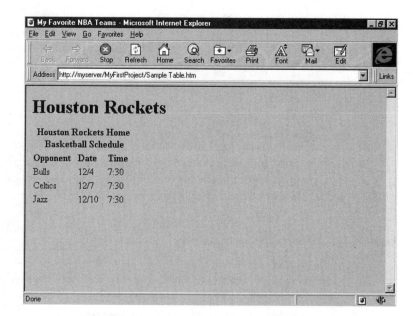

Other table features include inserting images into a table, nesting a table within a table, and providing a URL link to another page.

Applets

HTML 3.2 supports the use of Java applets. Java applets are executable programs created with the Java language from Sun Microsystems. These applets execute within the context of your web page and can provide various functionality from multimedia to spreadsheet applications.

The following code example shows an applet that has been embedded in a web page.

```
<h1><applet code="Neon.class" align="baseline" width="296"
height="61"><param name="picture1" value="X_sneon1.gif"><param
name="picture2" value="X_sneon2.gif">This is a neon coffee cup</applet></h1>
```

As you can see in the example, you can set the height and width of the applet display area. You also can pass specific parameters to the applet by using the <param> tag. Other customizable attributes include the alignment of the applet and the text to display if a browser can't execute Java applets. Figure 3.5 illustrates how a Java applet looks within a browser.

Figure 3.5.

A Java applet.

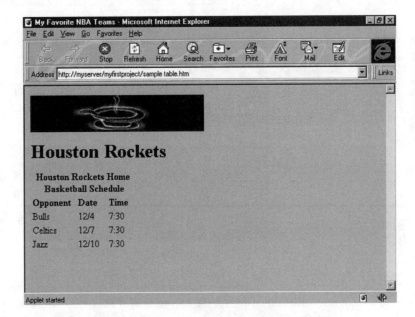

You will see a more in-depth discussion of Java applets, including information about how to use them in your applications on Day 15, "Integrating Objects into Your Applications."

Other Information Appearance Elements

HTML 3.2 provides a variety of new logical and physical elements to affect the appearance of text and information. The following code shows some of the available features.

```
This is <BIG>Big Print</BIG>
<BR><BR>
This is <SMALL>Small Print<SMALL/>
<BR><BR>
This is an example of <STRIKE>Strike Through</STRIKE>
<BR><BR>
This is a <SUB>Subscript</SUB>
```

```
<BR><BR>
This is a <SUP>Superscript</SUP>
<BR><BR>
This is <U>Underlined Text</U>
```

Figure 3.6 shows how these effects are displayed.

Figure 3.6.

Formatting the information.

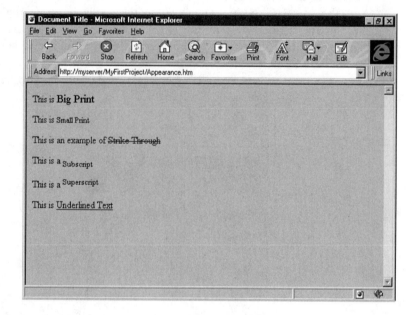

The HTML specifications continue to evolve, as companies like Netscape and Microsoft continue to push standardization and acceptance of their unique features and extensions. "Cougar" is the code name for the next version of HTML. Features that are being considered include client-side scripting, style sheets, and objects. Until then, you can access these features by using the extensions provided by the two leading developers of browsers: Netscape and Microsoft.

Netscape Extensions

Netscape has implemented several exceptional features in their browsers over the past couple of years. Some of these extensions are being proposed for future versions of the HTML standards. I will touch on a few of the more popular Netscape extensions.

Frames

Frames enable you to divide a page into separate scrollable panes. A common implementation of this feature is to provide a table of contents frame that remains static on the pane to the left of the display area while the dynamic body pane displays the contents of the different sections. You also can create static panes at the top and bottom sections to provide static header and footer information, like a title at the top and copyright information at the bottom. You should be careful not to go overboard when using frames. You can find a good example and implementation of frames at the following Web site:

```
www.netscape.com/comprod/products/navigator/version_2.0/frames/eye/
```

Netscape exhibits this page to demonstrate how web pages should be designed using frames. Other businesses and organizations are taking advantage of frames to disseminate information. The following is another Web site to check out:

```
www.childadvocates.org
```

Appearance

Netscape provides many options for customizing the look of your web pages. You use these elements with the <Body> tag to affect the appearance of the page. You can set the background image and background color for your page. You also can establish the color of your text and the color that indicates links to information within your web page. For links, you can further customize these colors to indicate those links that are active and those that have been previously visited. You can specify the font size and color of any text within the document.

You might want to add a horizontal line at the top and bottom of your page to separate these sections from the main body. This style can add a feeling of logical organization to your pages. Netscape provides a feature to place horizontal lines on your page and to set their parameters like size, width, and alignment.

Netscape also provides a way to further customize the look of your tables by specifying the width of table borders, the spacing around the cells, and the width of the actual data cells.

Another popular feature involves placing text around your images. Figure 3.7 demonstrates this feature.

Figure 3.7.

Placing text around an image.

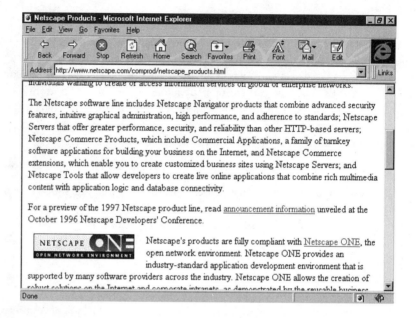

Microsoft Extensions

Microsoft has made significant enhancements to its Internet Explorer since the first version was released in 1995. With version 3.0, Internet Explorer regained the lead for features, surpassing some of the Netscape capabilities. The more unique extensions of Internet Explorer 3.0 are covered in the following sections.

Tables

Microsoft also supports the use of tables. Microsoft has developed some very nice features within Internet Explorer to enable you to create very graphical tables similar to the capabilities in Microsoft Word. You can set individual background colors and background images for each cell in the table.

Frames

Microsoft finally supports the use of frames. The addition of this feature allowed Microsoft to catch up with Netscape. Microsoft took this concept a step further, though, by providing the ability to create floating and borderless frames. Floating frames enable you to incorporate the frame concept into an area of your window without the frame consuming the page.

3

A floating frame can be sized and placed anywhere within the page. Borderless frames are frames that don't have a border. Figure 3.8 displays a floating frame, while Figure 3.9 shows the concept of a borderless frame.

Figure 3.8.
A floating frame.

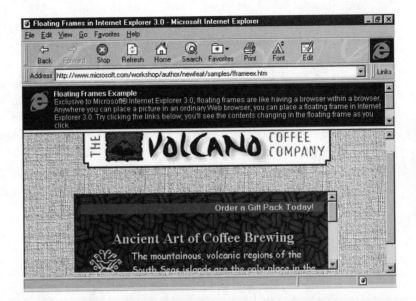

Figure 3.9.
A borderless frame.

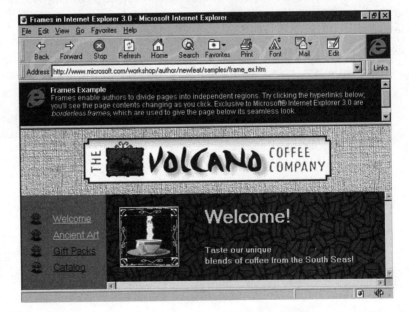

Cascading Style Sheets

A style sheet enables you to set formatting and appearance instructions for all your web pages. This is similar to using a formatting template in Word or a desktop publishing package. You construct the style sheet once to provide a common look and feel for your web pages. For example, you might want the title to be the same font and color for all your web pages. Instead of formatting the title for each web page, you could use a style sheet to handle this aspect for you.

Microsoft takes this feature a step further with cascading style sheets. You may establish a particular style sheet for your web pages while one of your users has developed a different, personal style sheet for all incoming pages to his browser. Cascading style sheets resolve the differences between the two styles and present the proper settings. You set the style for your web pages with the <STYLE> tag.

Cascading style sheets enable you to establish a consistent look and feel for your web pages. Common standards for web page development can be established while allowing room for creativity from your content authors and developers.

Other Extensions

Microsoft supports some other features for extending your web pages. The <MARQUEE> tag enables you to place a scrolling marquee of text on your web page. You can control the frequency, behavior, height, width, color, and other parameters for this tag.

Microsoft enables you to insert inline movies within the <IMG> tag. This feature supports the use of video clips for your users to see while using VCR-like controls. Microsoft also enables you to insert background sound and music in your web page. The sound or music plays in the background when your web page is displayed. You use the <BGSOUND> tag to accomplish this feature.

Many of these features are presented in detail in the coming days and weeks. As you learn to use Visual InterDev, you can apply examples from this book to build dynamic web pages for your applications.

Choosing a Development and Deployment Platform

Choosing a proper development architecture and platform is critical to the success of any project. This section focuses specifically on platform considerations for selecting the right development and deployment environment.

Visual InterDev can run on Windows 95, Windows NT Workstation, and Server. Each of these platforms offers a viable alternative. You also can use a combination of these operating systems to support your efforts. In selecting a development platform, you need to consider the following factors:

- [ ] Scalability
- [ ] Development tools
- [ ] Standards
- [ ] Architecture
- [ ] Database

Scalability

You need to think about the current and future needs of your application. You may be supporting 50 users currently, but the popularity of your application may grow and with that growth will come an increase in user count and the size of your database. Scalability refers to how well a platform can scale or move to handle an increase in the growth of your application needs. You may originally size your database and plan your application based on these current needs but allow no room for growth. When planning your application, you need to choose a platform and build an application that permits growth.

Development Tools

You also need to select the proper development tools to support the user requirements of your application. Before you select these tools, you will need to perform a proper analysis of what the user needs are and how your application is going to address these needs. These requirements will help you choose what tools you need to build the most effective application.

You should select these tools before you begin the development phase of your project. Integration is much harder when you incrementally add tools along the way. One of the best ways to proceed is to establish a toolset and provide the tools in it as an integrated package to the developers. This toolbox significantly increases the productivity of the programmers. Also, the chance for having development environment problems is drastically reduced, because the tools have already been selected and tested for interoperability.

Standards

Without standards, there is anarchy. Some would say that with standards, there is no room for creativity. In truth, though, you need to have standards and allow room for developer creativity. You can accomplish both.

You need to provide a set of standards that give your developers a consistent platform. If you're a project manager, you should assign a developer to set these standards. You need to get involvement from any and all members of the development team who have an interest in establishing the standards. Those members who don't help are saying that they can live with the standards that are set. You should establish these standards for all aspects of your development, including programming, testing, and documentation. Some of these standards will be how-to documents that define how to perform such operations as testing your application and promoting your application between the environments. You also should construct standard programming shells for your developers. These shells will augment the productivity of your developers and promote consistency within your application code. Style sheets for your HTML pages are an excellent example of this concept.

Standards aid in all phases of your development and help resolve conflicts when questions and issues arise.

Architecture

Establishing the right architecture is a critical step in your development effort. You need to create an architecture that supports your development both on the client and the server. If you create a standard architecture for connecting to the database and communicating with server-side programs and applications, you can be assured that every developer is performing these functions in the same manner. Also, this process enables you to build an architecture that effectively supports your application's needs.

Database

Choosing the right database is crucial to your application. I will talk about this process a little later in the day. For now, I wanted to mention what you need to focus on from a development perspective once you have selected a database.

First, you should logically design your database based on user requirements. These user requirements keep appearing, but they drive many aspects of your application development. Entity/Relationship (E/R) diagramming tools can definitely help with this task. Some of the more popular tools include Erwin from Logic Works and S-Designor from Sybase's Powersoft division. These tools are very robust and should handle all of your database administration needs. If you're using MS SQL Server as your database, you can use the Database Designer within Visual InterDev to create and maintain your database objects. You should assign a specific person to handle the database administration functions for your project if you have the luxury. This person can work with the users and translate their functional requirements into technical requirements for the database model.

3

Once you have logically designed the database, you will physically create the database. Most of the E/R tools on the market automatically create the physical database based on the logical model that you construct. You need to create a development, testing, and a production environment for each of your databases. Each environment should support the different phases of your project.

NOTE

> For big projects with many development team members and users, you may need to create a fourth database environment for training the users. You can use the testing environment for training, but problems will invariably occur due to the nature of the environment. Conflicts will happen between the testing by the development team and the training of the users. I have conducted many training sessions in which the system crashed and I wished I had a separate training environment. This can save an initial bad impression of your application in the long run.

You should perform regular backups of your database. You also should maintain a pristine copy of the database, especially when you begin the testing phases of your project. This copy will represent the initial set of test data. As developers run their tests, the actions will insert, change, and delete this data. Once they have completed their tests, you can restore the data back to its initial state. This process provides a controlled environment for your testing.

Now that you have learned about some general aspects and considerations for your application architecture, it's time to talk more specifically about Visual InterDev alternatives and their implications.

Using Windows 95 as Your Client and Server

Visual InterDev can run on a Windows 95 platform. You can use Visual InterDev to develop your application as well as deploy both your client and server portions on Windows 95. There are specific benefits and considerations you need to think about when developing and deploying on a Windows 95 platform. Each of these subjects is discussed within the context of the client-server model and the database model for your Windows 95 Web-based application.

NOTE

> The considerations discussed in this section apply to both Windows 95 and Windows NT Workstation. While Windows NT Workstation is a full 32-bit operating system and more robust than Windows 95, it is still a client platform. The ideal model for medium to large applications with high transaction volumes is a client-server platform that includes either Windows 95 or Windows NT Workstation on the client and Windows NT Server for your server.

Client-Server Model

You can develop and deploy your Visual InterDev applications solely on the Windows 95 platform. While this is not recommended from a scalability standpoint, there are some benefits to using this client-server model for development. Also, you could use Windows 95 as your client and server in low user/low volume applications.

The client side of this equation involves the use of a browser, such as Internet Explorer, Netscape Navigator, or another type of browser. The server involves the use of the Microsoft Personal Web Server for Windows 95. This web server was developed to compete with products such as Netscape's Fastrack Server, which also runs on Windows 95. The primary goal of this server is to provide a local server for those people developing on Windows 95 who don't have the luxury of a network connection.

Microsoft's Personal Web Server supports all of the server-side scripting functionality of Active Server Pages as well as other server features of Visual InterDev. The very name of the product suggests its scalability limitations. The Microsoft "Personal" Web Server was designed to be a personal, individual web server. The benefit is that you can develop your application on a single machine. The limitation is that you won't be able to support a high volume application with a large number of users.

Windows 95 is an ideal development environment for Visual InterDev. Deployment of your client-side components is also very viable on the Windows 95 operating system. Deployment of your application server components on a Windows 95 environment should be avoided if your application is going to be a medium to high-volume application.

Database

The robustness of your database options on a Windows 95 platform is somewhat limited. Some of the same scalability and transaction support questions arise concerning the database ingredient of the application equation on a Windows 95 platform. The robustness of your database is a function of the Windows 95 operating system and the type of products that are offered for this environment. Your choices of PC databases include Microsoft Access, Microsoft FoxPro, Sybase SQL Anywhere, and any other ODBC-compliant database for Windows 95. PC databases provide an easy-to-use environment to create the database for your applications. These databases provide an alternative for those applications that support a low number of users, have a database that is small to medium in size, and don't need the power of a traditional client-server database.

For the more robust applications, you can still use a PC database for part of your development effort. An example of this scenario involves the use of Microsoft Access. You can use a single Windows 95 machine to build a prototype of your application that uses the Personal Web Server as the server and Access as the local database.

Using this architecture, you can rapidly build your prototype application. During this development, you can conduct joint application design (JAD) sessions with your users to demo your application and record their feedback. Along the way, you construct the logical model and physical creation of your database in Microsoft Access.

Once you have refined the prototype and incorporated the user recommendations, you can upsize your application to a more traditional client-server platform. Microsoft provides an upsizing wizard that enables you to transform your Access database to a MS SQL Server database. I have used this method for both client-server and Web-based development projects to greatly reduce the development time of my projects.

Combining Windows 95 and Windows NT

You can use Visual InterDev to develop and deploy Web-based applications in a mixed environment like Windows 95 and Windows NT.

NOTE When I talk about mixed environments, I'm speaking specifically about platforms that support Visual InterDev features like ActiveX controls, Active Server Pages, and so on. You can build applications with Visual InterDev to inter-operate in a mixed environment with legacy applications and other custom-developed programs that run on platforms such as UNIX.

This platform is probably the preferred environment both from a development and deployment standpoint. You also can substitute Windows NT Workstation for Windows 95 in this model. The client considerations are practically the same.

Client-Server Model

In this model, the client machines run on Windows 95, and the server is Windows NT. From a development standpoint, you can support team development by using this networked environment to provide central source code management on the server. Also, you can adequately test your server components to see how these components perform in a robust client-server environment. Regarding deployment, Windows NT Server and Microsoft's Internet Information Server provide a very robust, industrial strength platform to serve the needs of your application.

Database

The database options in this model are more powerful. You can use true client-server databases that have a plethora of features and support a high volume application with a large number of users. Choices include Oracle, MS SQL Server, Sybase SQL Server, and other ODBC-compliant databases.

The benefits of using a SQL database for this model include more administrative control and a more robust environment to develop your applications. You can truly take advantage of the power of a database in this class to meet the more advanced needs of your application.

Choosing the Right Database for the Job

I talked previously about the different client-server models that you can use to develop and deploy your Visual InterDev applications. I also briefly touched on the database options in this model and their strengths and benefits. In this section, I want to cover specific aspects of PC databases versus SQL, client-server databases. This section also touches on factors to consider when choosing a database for your applications.

PC databases are designed to be intuitive and user-friendly. With a minimum knowledge of database techniques and concepts, you can create, maintain, and interact with most of the popular PC databases on the market. These PC databases include Microsoft Access, Microsoft FoxPro, Sybase SQL Anywhere, and others. On the other hand, client-server databases like MS SQL Server, Oracle, and Sybase offer a more powerful and robust solution. These databases have been designed to handle a large number of users and a high transaction volume. Most of the platforms that support these databases are traditional server platforms

3

like Windows NT and UNIX. You should consider the following factors when choosing between a PC database and a client-server database:

- [ ] Performance
- [ ] Database Size
- [ ] Reliability
- [ ] Systems Management

Performance

The performance of your application is critical to its acceptance by your users. Database performance is a big factor in determining the overall performance of the application. Client-server databases provide better performance for highly intensive, transaction-processing applications. Also, if your application executes queries that will return many rows of data, you should use a client-server database. PC databases usually support a more static environment in terms of the content of the data and usually support a low to medium number of users. You should use a PC database if you're not going to support a high number of users who are contending for the same information.

You also can scale a client-server database to multiple processors. This option enables you to spread the processing between multiple processors or machines. This kind of solution offers better fault tolerance and higher performance.

 Fault tolerance refers to the ability to handle the failure of a machine or system. A fault-tolerant system tolerates a crashing machine by switching over to another machine to process the application's need.

Database Size

Client-server databases usually support larger databases than PC databases. The design goals of client and server platforms are very different, and these goals translate into the objectives for the respective database. PC databases are usually supported by typical client platforms while the robust, SQL databases are supported by the traditional server platforms.

You should estimate the size of your database, and then select the database that is going to meet the needs of your application. Remember, the size of your database can rapidly grow. As the database becomes larger, you should consider moving to a client-server database. Predicting the size of your database is both an art and a science. Make sure that you choose the right database when considering and estimating its size.

Reliability

Your database and application must be reliable. Users must have faith that they can use the application without having the system go down. PC databases don't provide as much reliability as client-server databases. Most of the PC databases run a copy of the database engine on the client machine and don't have robust support for distributed transactions. In a networked environment, the client machine can crash and potentially corrupt the database. Client-server databases process the transactions centrally and insulate the databases from client machine failures.

Client-server databases also offer better locking features. These features can significantly enhance an application in which you have users who are contending for the same information. Data integrity is maintained, and you can use better strategies for ensuring that all users are viewing the most up-to-date information.

Systems Management

As the size and importance of your database grows, you will want to use effective tools to manage your database. Client-server databases offer better systems management tools for maintaining your database. The backup and recovery tools are significantly better. Some client-server databases even support hot, online backups of the data. These tools also offer other administrator features such as e-mail notification of system problems. PC databases don't offer the range or power of systems management tools.

Security Issues

Security is always a flamboyant topic, whether you're implementing a client-server application, developing a Web-based application, or living in your home. Everyone has the basic need to feel secure. Security has become a big topic on the Internet, because companies and users have pushed for the ability to conduct electronic commerce. Security has implications for the applications that you develop, whether these applications are for a company's intranet or an external Internet application. There are many good sources both in bookstores and on the Internet that cover security exhaustively. For the context of this lesson, I will attempt to point out some specific emerging initiatives that you may want to research further.

It's important to discuss some issues that are driving these security initiatives. Authentication is the first major concern and refers to verifying the identity of something or someone. The process of authentication could refer to verifying code to determine that the author is genuine. Another example of authentication involves electronic commerce in which a company would want to confirm a person's identity before enabling them to make a purchase.

Authorization is another major concern and refers to confirming that a person has the authority to perform an action. Returning to the electronic commerce example, once you have verified that the person is who he says he is, you need to determine that he has the authority to buy the selected items. The third issue is integrity, which involves the process of ensuring that the information that has been passed over the network hasn't been altered in any way. Now that I have defined three of the major issues surrounding security, it's time to take a look at several emerging initiatives that warrant discussion.

Netscape Secure Sockets Layer

Netscape designed the Secure Sockets Layer (SSL) to ensure secure communication between the client and server machines. SSL supports server authentication, data encryption, and message integrity. Outbound information is properly encrypted so that it can't be easily translated and read. Inbound information is decrypted and displayed to the user. SSL applies to the available Internet protocols like HTTP, FTP, and Telnet.

Microsoft Security Initiatives

Microsoft has developed several security initiatives that merit discussion. Each of them is discussed in the following sections.

Secure Electronic Transactions Framework

The Secure Electronic Transactions (SET) framework was designed to securely permit electronic bank-card payments over the Internet. SET is a joint project developed by MasterCard, VISA, Microsoft, Netscape, IBM, GTE, and others. This framework uses digital certificates to verify all of the major players involved in an online transaction: the buyer or cardholder, the merchant, and the merchant's financial institution.

Code-Signing

With the introduction of Internet Explorer 3.0, Microsoft developed a way to authenticate and qualify particular components of code like ActiveX controls. The code-signing specifications enable a developer to sign their application. A user can be assured that the code is authentic and reliable based on a digital signature from the author of the code. Authenticity refers to the origin of the code. A user can be assured that the person who signed the code is the original author. Integrity indicates that the code hasn't been altered since its inception.

CryptoAPI

Microsoft has developed the CryptoAPI to provide an interface to developers when designing security features into their applications or products. Many of Microsoft's specifications including SET and code-signing are based on the CryptoAPI. The CryptoAPI is derived from the word cryptography, which refers to the use of encryption and decryption to protect and read sensitive or secret information. The CryptoAPI provides a way to encrypt and decrypt information based on several popular methods of encryption, like RSA technology. The CryptoAPI also enables developers to digitally sign their code and provides a method for verifying signatures.

Security is an area in which the standards are continuing to emerge as the importance of the Internet rapidly grows. You should follow these technologies as well as other new and emerging initiatives as they develop.

Considerations Checklist

In closing the lesson for the day, I want to summarize the material that I have presented. The following list represents a considerations checklist that provides some general tips for Web-based development:

- ☐ Create a rich and rewarding experience for your users. Make them glad that they visited, and provide a reason for them to return.

- ☐ Design and develop an effective user interface. The interface should enable the user to be effective in accomplishing their tasks. Effectiveness has as much to do with the interface as the efficiency of your code.

- ☐ Provide a common and consistent look and feel across your application. Your pages should reflect a consistent font, color, page background, and page layout.

- ☐ Use an appropriate metaphor for the overall structure of your application. Also, use appropriate metaphors and symbols on your web pages that associate the correct meaning to the user.

- ☐ Give navigational cues to the user that provide the proper guidance.

- ☐ Provide the user with a path at all times. Do not create dead-end pages.

- ☐ Use graphics, multimedia, and advanced features to contribute to the overall mission and purpose of your application and web pages. Avoid the use of too many features. Resist the temptation to use advanced features just for the sake of using them.

- ☐ Avoid having the user scroll excessively either horizontally or vertically. Provide a table of contents for long documents that provide jumps to the individual sections.

- ☐ Provide textual cues for your images. These cues will inform the user about the hyperlink when images are being loaded initially or are turned off.

☐ Provide search features for your site that enable a user to find information easily.

☐ Take advantage of the different development and deployment platform options to enhance your productivity.

☐ Choose the right database for the job. Proactively plan your application needs, and select the proper database and tools to accomplish these requirements.

In summary, think about what you're trying to accomplish by developing your application. After you have considered the users' needs, devise a plan to design and develop the "killer app."

Summary

I hope today's lesson has been helpful and piqued your thinking about the application development process. Many of the things that were discussed today apply to both client-server and Web-based application development. Other concepts are only pertinent to Web-based development.

At the beginning of the day, you learned about effective user interface design. Hopefully, your interfaces are already effective and this section served as a review. You learned about specific steps to follow when designing your application interface. Important steps to follow involve defining a purpose for your application, identifying user needs, and conducting testing to ensure the usability of your application. You learned about specific factors that affect your interface, like aesthetics, page design and layout, and navigational cues.

You then learned about the ever-changing standards for developing web pages. You learned about the latest HTML standards and their implications for designing an effective web page. You then read about some of the more popular extensions to these standards from Netscape and Microsoft. This part of the lesson focused on why you would want to use these features to support your application needs. In later lessons, you will get a chance to implement these features. You were provided with some guidelines for choosing between the various browser standards.

Later in the day, you learned about the different alternative platforms for developing and deploying your application. In this section, the focus was on the benefits, strengths, and limitations of each alternative. You discovered how to use each alternative to enhance your productivity. The lesson also focused on how to choose the right database using specific guidelines for this process. You learned that there are strengths to both PC and client-server databases. You also learned how to take advantage of each class of database to support your development effort.

Toward the end of the day, the lesson introduced the topic of security. You learned about some of the initiatives that are in progress and why they are important.

3

At the close of the day, you were provided with a summary of the lesson's material in the form of a considerations checklist. This checklist should help to provide some general guidelines you can use when designing and developing your applications.

Q&A

Q Are there any problems with using frames as my application metaphor?

A Frames provide a structure method to divide your page, and are intended to provide an effective navigational technique. Unfortunately, frames can provide some navigational nightmares in a number of ways. Users can become confused with what pane they are interacting with. Also, printing can be complicated. Sometimes you request the printer to print one pane, and another pane is sent to the printer.

Sometimes frames can cause problems for users who are trying to add a particular page to their favorites or bookmark list. A user may add a bookmark only to find out that the page that was saved was not the intended page. A final problem with frames involves the interaction with the navigational buttons of the browser. The Back and Forward buttons do not always take you to the page that you expect. With all of these problems, frames can provide a good interface if implemented correctly. Microsoft's borderless frames may provide an answer to some of these problems. As always, use discernment when choosing this metaphor.

Q What are the main factors to consider when choosing a database?

A Database size, application type, and number of users are the main considerations when you pick a database for your application. A large database that supports a transaction-intensive application with a medium to large number of users will warrant a client-server database. A decision-support system with a small-to medium-sized database and a low to medium number of users can be supported by a PC database.

Workshop

Web-based development presents a new and interesting challenge. The proper design and development of a Web-based application is essential to its acceptance. You can choose from many metaphors, features, and standards to implement your web pages. For today's workshop, I want you to visit several of your favorite sites to determine the strengths and weaknesses of the web pages. Note the features that you like and those features that are unnerving. You should record some of these features to be able to use in later lessons and future applications. In addition to your favorite sites, take a look at these sites for additional ideas:

- ☐ ESPNET Sportszone (`espnet.sportszone.com`)
- ☐ Land's End (`www.landsend.com`)
- ☐ Virtual Vineyards (`www.virtualvin.com`)
- ☐ Microsoft (`www.microsoft.com`)
- ☐ Netscape (`www.netscape.com`)

Quiz

1. Name the five basic steps for designing an effective user interface.
2. What are dead ends?
3. What is the new feature in the HTML 3.2 standards that is geared toward displaying database result sets?
4. Name two of the Microsoft extensions to the HTML standards.
5. Name the four factors to consider when choosing a database for your Web-based application.

Quiz Answers

1. The following steps outline the five basic steps to designing an effective interface:
    1. Define a purpose for the interface.
    2. Identify the users' expectations and needs.
    3. Design the user interface.
    4. Conduct usability testing.
    5. Incorporate the feedback into your interface.

2. Dead ends are like dead-end streets—they leave you with no place to go. A dead-end page is a web page that provides no navigational path within the context of the application. The only way for a user to navigate out of a dead end is to use the browser navigational buttons of Back and Forward.

3. HTML 3.2 provides support for tables, which are a great way to show returned rows from a database query.

4. Possible answers include

>   Cascading Style Sheets
>
>   Frames (regular, floating, and borderless)
>
>   Background sound
>
>   Marquees
>
>   Movies
>
>   Formatted tables

5. Possible answers include

>   Performance
>
>   Database size
>
>   Reliability
>
>   Systems management

Day 4

Creating Your First Visual InterDev Project

Today is going to be an exciting day. You finally get to create your first project using Visual InterDev. You have learned about many features in the last few days, and in this lesson, you will finally have a chance to experience some of these features for the first time.

You will get the most out of this lesson if you practice using the tools as you go along. To begin the day, you will explore a standard Visual InterDev project, and take a look at its dissected components. This dissection won't be as dreadful as your experience with a frog was in high school biology, though.

In this section, you will learn the different components and parts of a project. This knowledge should build a foundation so that you can appropriately use all of the Visual InterDev features and technologies in developing your Web-based applications. After looking at each of the Visual InterDev project components, you will get a brief refresher on browser extensions and how they fit into the Visual InterDev scheme.

At the end of today's lesson, you will build your first Hello Web application. For C programmers, this application will be a little more sophisticated than the simple Hello World application that you built for your first C program. The Hello Web application will contain most of the main project components that are the focus of this lesson. While you won't be developing the whole application, you will be adding some code and interacting with the components and code provided for you. This lesson should be a very good introduction to the Visual InterDev development experience.

Get a refill on that cup of coffee, and let's begin.

Exploring a Standard Project

At this point, you have read a lot about the features of Visual InterDev as well as the various technologies that it supports. The focus of this lesson is on assimilating what you've read into a Visual InterDev project. If you have participated in any type of development effort, you are familiar with the concept of a project. You know that a project usually consists of various files that come together to build an application.

Developing an application is like making pancakes. When you're making pancakes, you have to add specific ingredients that include the pancake mix, eggs, oil, and milk, into a bowl. The ingredients symbolize the technologies such as HTML, ActiveX, and VBScript. The bowl symbolizes the project that provides a workspace for you to work with the ingredients. Once you have mixed the ingredients in a bowl, you cook the results to produce the finished product. Likewise, once you have finished cooking up your Web pages with Visual InterDev, you will deploy them for display on your Web server.

Understanding a Visual InterDev Project

A Visual InterDev project consists of multiple files that integrate to form your web site and Web-based application. During development, you can install both the client and server portions on the same machine. Yesterday, you learned about the advantages and disadvantages of this approach. A more typical configuration enables the Visual InterDev development environment on the client machine to access all of the files on a central web server. These files are downloaded from the server to your machine in a local working directory so you can make any changes to your code. Possible project files include HTML files, Active Server Pages, images, and other components that make up your web site.

When you create a new Visual InterDev project, Visual InterDev builds a sub-directory for your web within the root directory of your web server. Your project files will be stored within this sub-directory. The name of this sub-directory assumes the name of your project. For example, if you named your project MyFirstProject, a folder would be created within the root directory of your Web server called MyFirstProject.

You also can create sub-directory folders from within Visual InterDev to organize your files within your project directory. An example would be the Images sub-directory that's created by default when you create a Visual InterDev project. This directory structure contains all of the master copies of your files. A virtual root directory for your Web site also is created on your web server. This virtual root directory takes on the name of your project and points to the files within your project sub-directory.

The virtual root represents the directory that contains all of the files for a project on your Web server. The virtual root is comprised of the Web server name and the virtual root directory for your project. The Web server name also is referred to as the domain name. The following example shows a virtual root for a sample project.

```
Http://MyServer/MyFirstProject
```

In this example, you see how the name of the Web server, MyServer, and the name of a project, MyFirstProject, join together to form a virtual root for your application. You can see the virtual root for your application from within Visual InterDev, using FileView. Visual InterDev saves you time by handling the creation of this virtual directory structure.

The advantage of the virtual root is that users can access your files through a Uniform Resource Locator (URL) instead of having to search through your project file directory structure. Taking this example a step further, a sample URL for your project might consist of the following:

```
Http://MyServer/MyFirstProject/Default.htm
```

where Default.htm is the name of a web page in your project.

By default, a global file (global.asa) and a search file (search.htm) are created. These files are placed in the root of your web project directory. The global file enables you to place server-side script for initialization and termination routines for your session and application. The search file adds full text searching capabilities to your web pages. Visual InterDev also creates a local working directory on your client machine. This working directory serves as a placeholder for the server files as you access them.

Working with Files

The project workspace is the pane on the left-hand side of the Visual InterDev development environment workspace. The project workspace consists of three views: FileView, DataView, and InfoView. Each of these views appears as a tab at the bottom of the project workspace based on what you're currently working on within Visual InterDev.

Once you have created a project, you will begin to work with the files within that project. Some files will be created for you. You will add other files as you design and develop your application, and use the FileView to interact with your project files. The FileView provides a Windows Explorer-like interface, enabling you to effectively create and maintain your files and folders. The FileView uses most of the Explorer functions like drag-and-drop support for moving files and right mouse button support for accessing the shortcut menu for a particular file. You can add files and create new folders for existing files.

The DataView enables you to view all of your database objects from the database server. The DataView becomes accessible when you add a database connection to an Active Server Page within your project. You can interact with each object and display the results to the right of the project workspace pane. This view is very similar to the FileView. The only difference is that you are manipulating objects in your database as opposed to files on your web server.

The InfoView enables you to view the help files and topics regarding Developer and Visual InterDev. InfoView uses the book metaphor that became a standard for help files using the Windows 95 interface. You are presented topics and a table of contents for each topic. You can then probe deeper into the contents and display the contents to the right of this pane. When you open Visual InterDev, InfoView is displayed by default. The other views are available as you open a workspace and files and insert database connections into your applications.

Visual InterDev provides several methods for you to open your project. You can use the Open command from the File menu which concentrates on opening a specific file type like HTML files and images. You also can use the Open Workspace command from the File menu. This option focuses on a project and workspace. You will use the Open Workspace option most of the time.

> **TIP**
>
> Visual InterDev provides a feature that enables you to access your most recent files and workspaces. This feature is similar to Microsoft Word and Excel in that it provides a list of the most recent files or the most recent workspaces that you have opened. These two options are available at the bottom of the File menu.

You can open a file with its native editor by double-clicking on the file. You also can select the file and right-click the mouse to display the shortcut menu. Then, you can select the Open menu option to open the file with its default editor.

You also can choose the Open With menu option to open the file with another application, as long as the selected program supports the file type. When you open a file in your project, the client first attempts to get the file from the working directory on the client machine. If no working copy exists, the client machine requests a working copy from the server. The server machine sends a copy of the master file to the client and places the file in the working directory of the client machine.

Visual InterDev provides visual cues to indicate the status of the file. The icon for a file that has a working copy resident on the client machine is colored, and the icon for a file type that doesn't have a working copy resident on the client machine or that is read-only is grayed.

You can request a working copy from the server by selecting the file and choosing the Get Working Copy option from the shortcut menu. This command retrieves the file from the server.

If you have already retrieved a working copy and made changes to the file, a warning message is displayed, indicating that you already have a working copy of the file. The message asks whether you want to use the local file or the copy from the server as your working copy. The dialog window displays the file statistics for both the server master copy and the local file, including the name, date, and time of each. You then can choose to use the existing local file, use the master copy from the server, or cancel the action.

Figure 4.1 displays the Confirm Get dialog window for a sample project file that already has a local file on the client machine.

Figure 4.1.

The Confirm Get dialog window.

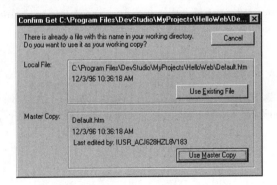

After you have made changes to a file, you choose the Save, Save As, or Save All option to save your changes. This action updates the master copy on the server. The Save command saves the current file, while the Save As command enables you to save the file with another name. The Save All option saves all the files in your project.

Visual InterDev won't inherently resolve conflicts between changes and updates to files. When you get a working copy of a file from the server, you don't place a lock on this file to keep others from retrieving and making changes to the file. Also, the server won't warn you that someone has checked out this file.

For big development teams, you should use a source code control package. Visual InterDev is fully compatible with Microsoft Visual SourceSafe and can be integrated to provide a robust option for managing your project source code. By using this combination, you can ensure that developers can exclusively check out files from the server. When the updates are made, a developer can send the file back to the server for others to access. On Day 19, "Working Effectively in Teams with Visual SourceSafe," you will learn how to use and integrate Visual SourceSafe with your Visual InterDev projects.

Visual InterDev uses a client-server model for development that's very effective. This model is similar to the interaction of a production web site. Your information is downloaded to the client upon request. You interact with the information, and the changes are sent back to the server.

Dissecting the Components of a Visual InterDev Project

A Visual InterDev can contain many individual files and components. In this section, you will be guided through this maze and introduced to the most common and relevant files that you will be working with.

Web Project Files

These files are the main ingredients of which your web site is comprised. The most typical files in this category include the following:

- [ ] HTML files
- [ ] Global file
- [ ] Image and multimedia files
- [ ] Active Server Pages
- [ ] ActiveX Layout files

HTML Files

HTML files contain your HTML code and are denoted with the .htm extension. These files also might contain objects such as ActiveX controls, Java applets, Netscape plug-ins, ActiveX

Layout files, and images and multimedia files. You can activate the appropriate editor for most of these objects by placing the cursor over the file reference in the HTML code and right-clicking on the mouse. This action displays a shortcut menu containing a menu item for editing the object. You can select the menu option, and the object will be opened in its native editor. For example, right-clicking the mouse while your cursor is on an ActiveX control reference in your HTML file opens the Object Editor. Your cursor must be placed between the <OBJECT> tags for that control.

On Day 2, "Visual InterDev: Up Close and Personal," you received a brief overview of the HTML editors that are provided with Visual InterDev. You have two main choices to create and edit your basic HTML code: the HTML Source Editor and the FrontPage Editor for Visual InterDev. The HTML Source Editor provides a specialized text editor that enables you to create and maintain your HTML code. This editor provides some specialized features over basic text editors in that the HTML Source Editor displays your HTML code in a color-coded fashion. This format enables you to distinguish the different types of text within the file. For example, HTML code is a different color than your comments within the code. The FrontPage Editor enables you to visually create your HTML web page. You select objects and choose properties for your web page, and this WYSIWYG editor generates the HTML for you. You still can access and manipulate the generated HTML. You also can add your own custom HTML.

If you're stubborn and want to stick with Notepad or some other editor, Visual InterDev also enables you to use other editors to create HTML code. You then can import this code into your Visual InterDev project.

You also can create client-side script to be included in your HTML files. This script will be downloaded from the server with the web page and will be executed on the client machine. An example of client-side script would be providing basic field validation for a form.

You can create client-side script by using the available HTML editors within Visual InterDev or another editor. The script code is denoted by the <% %> delimiters and is located between the <SCRIPT> and </SCRIPT> tags. Visual InterDev supports Microsoft's VBScript as the default scripting language, and you also can use Microsoft's implementation of JavaScript called JScript from within a Visual InterDev project.

Global File

This file is automatically generated when you create a new project and is denoted by the .asa file extension. The global.asa file enables you to use server-side script for initializing your application at start-up, handling your database connections, and cleaning up the application when the application is finished. You can add scripting code for the duration of both the application and the user sessions.

A user session enables you to maintain state with the client machine. An example of using the session events would be maintaining a database connection with the client machine. This persistent state can be very useful for tasks such as high-volume sales order entry applications where you need to make sure that the order is confirmed. Figure 4.2 shows an example of the global.asa file that is created by Visual InterDev when you begin a new project.

Figure 4.2.

The global.asa file as viewed through the HTML Source Editor.

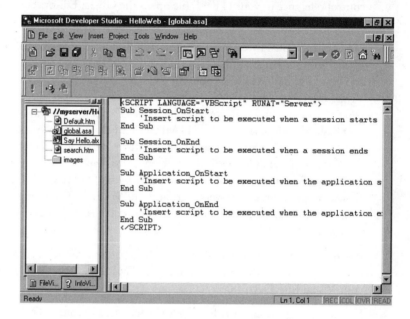

Figure 4.2 shows how Visual InterDev creates a shell for your scripting code. The scripting code is indicated at the top of the file. This example uses VBScript as its default scripting language. The RUNAT=Server command instructs Visual InterDev to execute this script at the server. Comments are included to show you where to put your application and session code. Notice the four sub-procedures that are created for your application within this file: Session_OnStart, Session_OnEnd, Application_OnStart, and Application_OnEnd.

The Application_OnStart event is initiated when the application is first accessed. Specifically, this code is executed when the first page of the application is requested. You use this event to make information available to all users of your applications. For example, if you wanted to set a variable or display a message for all client machines that requested your application, you would populate the variable or define the message in this event. Then, as

4

users accessed your application, the variable and message would be available to them. This information also is available to any of your web pages. You can use this event to reduce redundancy in your code.

The Application_OnEnd event executes when the web server is stopped. You should include termination and clean-up routines for ensuring that the application finishes cleanly and smoothly. Also, you might want to add checks for any unsaved data.

The Session_OnStart event is activated when the user requests a first page. When you add database connection to your application, the scripting code for that connection is placed in the Session_OnStart event. Each session is unique to a user and absorbs some server overhead. Use this event wisely, and resist the temptation to place too many objects in this event. Additional users can present a resource nightmare and burden. You can create objects at the page level to avoid the resource issue. A good use of the session event involves the use of Recordset variables to store database values across your web pages. In this way, you can avoid having to maintain access to those values across related web pages.

The Session_OnEnd event executes when the user session is over. A session can end in several ways. First, the session terminates if the user doesn't request a page within the time period specified by the Timeout property of the Session object. The default value for this property is 20 minutes. You can adjust this property based on your application needs. Also, you can specifically call the Abandon method of the Session object to end a session. Again, you would want to include any clean-up routines for the individual user session in this procedure. An example might include prompting for saving changes to data that was still being processed.

While adding a database connection to the Session event was touched on here, it will be discussed in detail on Day 8, "Communicating with a Database." For now, it's important that you see what a Session_OnStart procedure looks like for a database connection. Figure 4.3 depicts the Session_OnStart event that includes script for connecting to a Microsoft Access database.

Visual InterDev generated this scripting code when a database connection was selected to be inserted into the global.asa. Although you may be unfamiliar with the code, don't worry if you're scratching your head. The point of this illustration is to show you what scripting code in these four events looks like. You will become very comfortable interacting with a database during the second week.

4

Figure 4.3.

In this figure, the `Session_OnStart` *event displays scripting code for connecting to a database.*

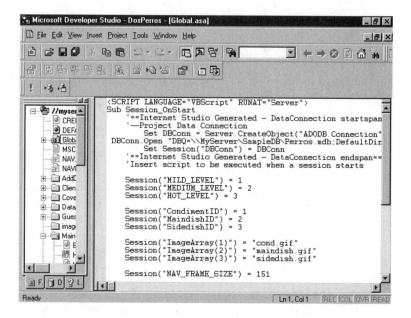

```
<SCRIPT LANGUAGE="VBScript" RUNAT="Server">
Sub Session_OnStart
    '==Internet Studio Generated - DataConnection startspan
    '--Project Data Connection
        Set DBConn = Server.CreateObject("ADODB.Connection"
DBConn.Open "DBQ=\\MyServer\SampleDB\Perros.mdb;DefaultDir
        Set Session("DBConn") = DBConn
    '==Internet Studio Generated - DataConnection endspan==
    'Insert script to be executed when a session starts

    Session("MILD_LEVEL") = 1
    Session("MEDIUM_LEVEL") = 2
    Session("HOT_LEVEL") = 3

    Session("CondimentID") = 1
    Session("MaindishID") = 2
    Session("SidedishID") = 3

    Session("ImageArray(1)") = "cond.gif"
    Session("ImageArray(2)") = "maindish.gif"
    Session("ImageArray(3)") = "sidedish.gif"

    Session("NAV_FRAME_SIZE") = 151
```

Image and Multimedia Files

Visual InterDev includes several additional applications that enable you to create and manage image and multimedia files. These files can be easily incorporated into your project to enhance the user experience. Microsoft Image Composer, Music Producer, and Media Manager are very robust products and are discussed in detail toward the end of this week on Day 6, "Spicing Up Your Interface with Images and Multimedia." You also can use other products to create your images and multimedia files. Visual InterDev supports practically all of the standard Internet file formats for these objects.

You can work with these files by double-clicking on the particular file. This action causes the file to be opened with its native application if there's a default application associated with the file type. If no default application has been linked with this file, you need to use the Open With dialog window to associate an application from the listbox with this file. From this window, you can select a program from the list and press the Default push button to make this application the default editor for this file. You also can add applications as well as remove them from the list. Figure 4.4 displays the Open With dialog window for a .gif image that has been selected.

You also can use the Open With dialog window to open files with a different application than the program that has been associated with that file. Both editors must support the specified file type. For example, you can use Image Composer to open a .gif file that had been created with another graphics application.

4

Figure 4.4.

The Open With dialog window.

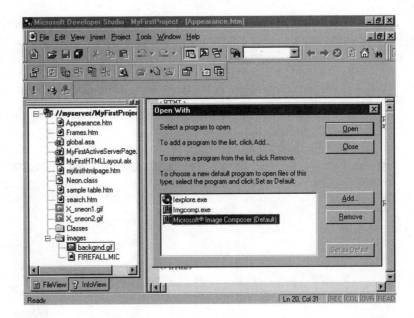

You also can open these files by selecting the file and right-clicking the mouse. The shortcut menu is displayed, and you can select either the Open or Open With menu option.

NOTE

Microsoft has developed a new standard file format for images and music compositions. Microsoft Image Composer defaults to the new .mic file extension. Image Composer also can save to file types such as CompuServe's Graphic Interchange Format (GIF) and other industry standards. Microsoft Music Producer saves compositions to the .mmp filename extension. Music Producer also can save to industry standard file formats such as the Musical Instrument Digital Interface (MIDI).

Active Server Pages

The first two days gave you an introduction to Active Server Pages, which are special HTML pages that contain server-side script and are denoted by the .asp file extension. These files process on the server before sending the resulting HTML page to the client machine. Your choices for scripting languages include VBScript, JScript, Perl, and other scripting languages. Active Server Pages enable you to interface with ActiveX Server Components and to interact with your database.

You can use the HTML Source Editor in Visual InterDev to create and maintain these pages. You can insert an Active Server Page by choosing the New menu item from the File menu. Select the Active Server Pages option from the list and enter a filename for this page. The Add to Project option is checked by default, and the current project is displayed. The project directory for your files also is displayed as the default location to place your new page.

Figure 4.5 shows a highlighted Active Server Page and the options for creating this file from the File New dialog window.

Figure 4.5.

Creating an Active Server Page.

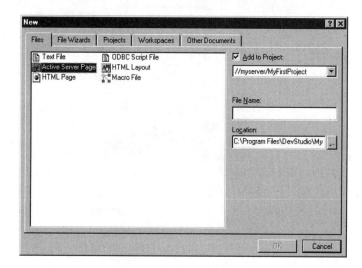

Figure 4.6 demonstrates the format of a newly created Active Server Page as seen through the HTML Source Editor.

The format of this page is practically the same as an HTML page. The scripting language is denoted at the top of the document. The page contains a Header, Title, and Body section. Comments are included so that you know where to place your HTML code. As a general guideline, you should place your scripting code at the bottom of this file before the </HTML> tag. You learn how to integrate Active Server Pages into your applications on Day 11, "Extending Your Application Through Active Server Script."

Figure 4.6.

A sample Active Server Page.

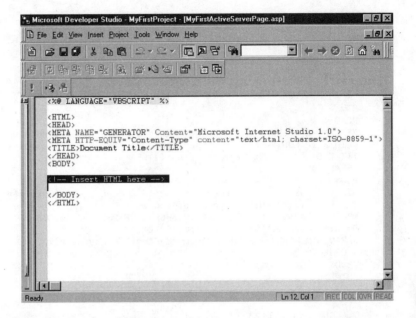

ActiveX Layout Files

ActiveX Layout files specify the exact placement of ActiveX controls onto your HTML pages. They are followed by an .alx extension. You can create these files with the Visual InterDev HTML Layout Editor, which provides you with a graphical environment to drag and drop controls in the layout and visually adjust their properties. Another feature enables you to place controls on top of other controls, which is similar to using a frame in Visual Basic to house a group of radio buttons or checkboxes. Once you have created your layout, you need to reference this .alx file within your HTML code. You can reference your layout files from either an Active Server Page (.asp file) or an HTML page (.htm file). A single layout file can be used by multiple web pages. A single HTML file or Active Server Page also can contain multiple layout files.

TIP

You should place multiple layouts included in a single HTML file in the order that you want them to appear on the page.

Listing 4.1 demonstrates how to reference an HTML Layout from within an HTML web page.

Listing 4.1. Referencing an HTML Layout.

```
<HTML>
<HEAD>
<META NAME="GENERATOR" Content="Microsoft Developer Studio">
<META HTTP-EQUIV="Content-Type" content="text/html; charset=ISO-8859-1">
<TITLE>Simple Guest Registration</TITLE>
</HEAD>
<BODY>
This page uses an HTML Layout to build a simple guest registration form
<!-- Here is the HTML Layout Reference -->
<OBJECT CLASSID="CLSID:812AE312-8B8E-11CF-93C8-00AA00C08FDF"
ID="Html_Layout1" STYLE="LEFT:0;TOP:0">
<PARAM NAME="ALXPATH" REF VALUE="MyFirstHTMLLayout.alx">
 </OBJECT>
</BODY>
</HTML>
```

The file MyFirstHTMLLayout.alx is a separate file in your project workspace and is referenced from the HTML file in Figure 4.6.

Figure 4.7 depicts a project that contains all of the files that have been discussed so far and how they're displayed in FileView.

Figure 4.7.

*A typical Visual
InterDev project.*

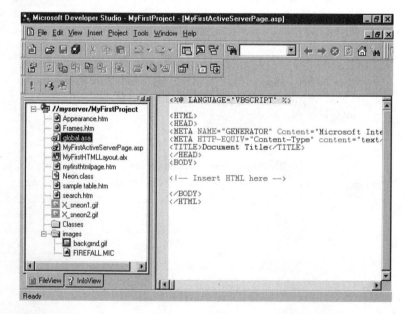

ActiveX Controls

During the first two days you were introduced to ActiveX controls, which are another component that you will want to use in your applications. Just as you would use graphical controls in a client-server development tool like Visual Basic, ActiveX controls are the next generation of objects built especially for the Internet.

You will use the Object Editor as well as the HTML Layout Editor to establish the properties, actions, and layout of these controls. Visual InterDev includes many ActiveX controls to handle functions like database connectivity as well as the objects that you have probably used in the past to build client-server interfaces. Examples of these controls include checkboxes, radio buttons, push buttons, and the listbox. More advanced controls built specifically for Web-based applications include the ActiveMovie control and the Marquee control. Figure 4.8 shows an HTML web page that uses the ListBox control.

Figure 4.8.

An ActiveX control as displayed within the HTML code.

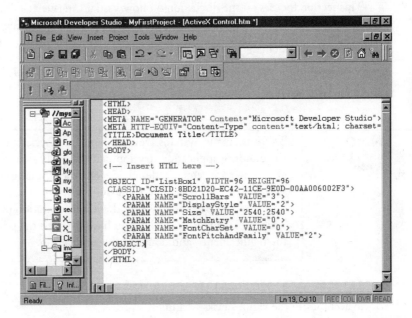

You should notice that the attributes for the control have been placed within the <OBJECT> and the </OBJECT> tags. To edit this control, you place your cursor somewhere between these two tags and right-click the mouse to display the shortcut menu. You then select Edit ActiveX control from the list of options. This action activates the Object Editor and enables you to establish or change the properties of this control.

You will interact with ActiveX controls on Day 13, "Interacting with Objects and ActiveX Controls," and you will learn how to truly integrate these objects into your applications for the best results on Day 15, "Integrating Objects into Your Applications."

Design-Time ActiveX Controls

You received a brief overview of Design-time ActiveX controls during the first two days, and should know that these controls enable you to automatically generate HTML and scripting code by visually setting properties while designing your application. You insert an ActiveX control for your application and set the properties and attributes for the control. HTML and scripting code is generated based on the values that you set. This code is then executed at run time without the overhead of an actual object. Design-time controls are placed within an Active Server Page to handle actions such as connecting to a database. Design-time controls are covered in detail on Day 14, "Extending Web Pages Through Design-Time Controls."

Understanding the Development Process

This section focuses on the discussion on how Visual InterDev facilitates the development process. You will see the three distinct phases of application building:

1. Development
2. Testing
3. Production

NOTE

> There are many Systems Development Life Cycles and methodologies surrounding application development. Most of them include planning, gathering requirements, design, development, training, testing, conversion, and production. This discussion simplifies the process and focuses on the main phases involved in the implementation of an application. This discussion assumes that you have planned the project, gathered the requirements, and designed the application.

Along the way, you'll learn what each phase is comprised of and how you use Visual InterDev to accomplish the various tasks within each phase.

Development

This phase focuses on building the application. So far, you have seen the most common files that you will use to design and develop your application. For a typical development project, you first create your web pages using HTML and a scripting language, possibly VBScript or JScript. Next, you develop an Active Server Page to handle your needs from the server, such as creating a dynamic web page or connecting to a database. You also might create an Active Server Page to control the flow of logic while interacting with an Active Server Component. You should insert a database connection into your application. For the sake of this example, the discussion is focused on using a server database such as MS SQL Server, although the basic tenets apply to desktop databases such as Microsoft Access, as well.

At the beginning of the day, you learned how to get your files from the web server and load them into a working directory on your local machine. As you create your files, save them on the web server machine. Use the Visual Data Tools to interact with your database through an ODBC connection to the database server. This connection is live, and enables you to create and maintain objects and manipulate the data. You also can design and test your SQL calls for inserting, selecting, updating, and deleting data in the database.

Figure 4.9 gives an overview of the development architecture and process and how Visual InterDev facilitates this process.

Figure 4.9.

The development process.

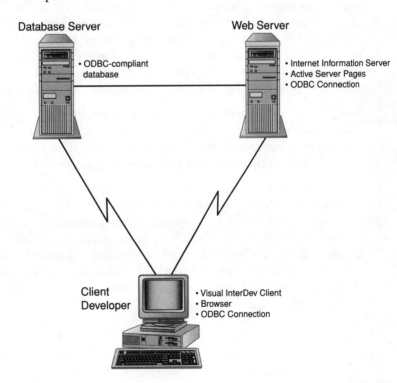

Note that you use Visual InterDev on your development client machine to design and build your application. You interface directly with the development web server machine as well as the development database server. These interactions are distinct in nature. In other words, you maintain a network connection to the web server and interact with files on the server. You can use the Preview in Browser menu option to view your web pages and test the look and feel of the interface. The use of this command enables rapid application development by enabling you to test the web pages within the confines of Visual InterDev.

You also can use a commercial release of a browser to view your web pages within the eventual production environment. For database access, you're connected through an ODBC connection over the network. This architecture assumes that your network contains separate database and web server machines and that these machines are on the same network.

Testing

Once you build your application, you need to test it. This phase involves previewing the web pages in the browser to make sure that they're visually correct. You also need to make sure that your scripting code reacts to user events properly and creates the dynamic effect for your web pages. You need to test your database connections to make sure that your users are able to retrieve the correct information. On Day 3, "Design and Development Considerations," it was suggested that you write scenarios of tasks that users would need to accomplish through your application. You should use these test cycles to test specific user tasks and actions.

You will use the development client machine to preview the web pages through a browser. You can use the Preview in Browser command during the development and testing phase to view the web pages, but during the testing phase, you should use the browsers that will be in the production environment to test the whole application.

As you view the web pages, you will be accessing the web server machine. You should migrate your application from a development area to a separate test area, as suggested on Day 3. By using separate and distinct development and testing areas, you can manage different releases, changes, and fixes more effectively. Your developers have an environment to test individual changes that then can be migrated and incorporated with other developer changes to create a new release. This new release then can be tested in an environment similar to the production environment. After the application has been fully tested, the web site can be migrated to a separate production environment.

NOTE

While having separate environments for development, testing, and production is recommended, don't think that all of these areas have to reside on separate machines. You can place your development web site and testing web site on the same machine with different directory structures. You should, however, have a separate machine for the production environment web server for your applications and web sites.

In the development phase, you connected directly to the database server. During the testing phase, the client-server model changes. The web server now connects to your database server to process your database requests. While you still can connect to the database server directly from your client machine, you will want to simulate the production environment process for database connectivity using the web server as the central hub for these requests. The web server maintains an ODBC connection to the database server and processes and database request from the client. The web server receives the results and returns the formatted data to the client machine browser. Figure 4.10 illustrates this process.

Figure 4.10.

The testing process.

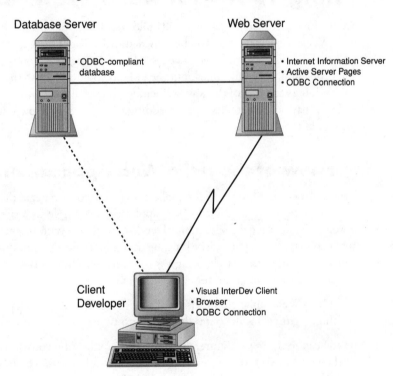

Database Server

- ODBC-compliant database

Web Server

- Internet Information Server
- Active Server Pages
- ODBC Connection

Client Developer

- Visual InterDev Client
- Browser
- ODBC Connection

Production

Once you have thoroughly tested your application, you will deploy the web site to a production environment. The user machine now becomes the client machine. A user requests web pages from the web server, and the web server processes the request by executing any server-side script and interacting with the database server to send the resulting pages back to the user's client machine browser. As the user interacts with a page, client-side script is executed on the client machine, based on certain user events and actions.

Visual InterDev contains some good tools for supporting these phases of developing and deploying a web site. Many of them will be discussed in detail on Day 18, "Managing Your Web Site Files with Visual InterDev."

Now that you have learned the Visual InterDev architecture and process, you're ready to develop your first application using Visual InterDev.

Creating Your First Hello Web Application

For the final lesson of the day, you will build your first application, a Hello Web application, using Visual InterDev. You will be provided with a list of tasks and steps to accomplish, as well as all the code examples you need to add. Make sure that you pay attention to the steps and code examples, and think about the tasks as you do them so that you understand what you're doing each step of the way. Remember, there will be a quiz at the end of the chapter, and you may be asked to accomplish additional tasks on your own during the workshop at the end of the day.

Overview of the Hello Web Application

You need to see an overview of the application before you can begin the development process. You are going to create a Hello Web application, a simple web site that will give you an introduction to using the Visual InterDev development environment. Although creating the application is simple, you will be learning the basic application building techniques and how best to accomplish those tasks using Visual InterDev. The tenets that you learn in this lesson will serve as the foundation for every other application that you construct.

The Hello Web application consists of a web page that displays a personalized Hello Web greeting. Figure 4.11 illustrates the main web page.

As you can see from this figure, the Hello Web application consists of a web page with two label controls, two text box controls, and two push buttons. The label controls are named First Name and Greeting. These controls define the contents of the text box controls to the right of each label. The push buttons are labeled Submit and Reset. The objective of this application is to provide the user with a personalized greeting when the user types in his or her name and presses the Say Hello push button. Figure 4.12 displays the results from typing Mike in the name field and pressing the Say Hello push button.

Figure 4.11.
The Hello Web application.

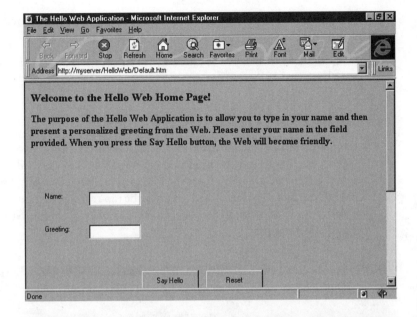

Figure 4.12.
Saying Hello Web.

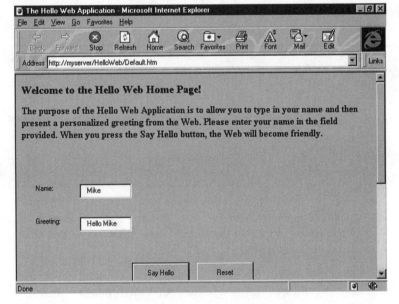

When the user presses the Reset push button, the greeting is cleared from the web page, enabling the user to start over and enter a new name.

This application enables you to interact with an HTML Page, an HTML Layout, an Active Server Page, and VBScript.

Creating the Hello Web Project

Now that you have a roadmap, you can begin construction. First, if you haven't already opened Visual InterDev, you need to do so now. The InfoView will be opened by default. Select the New menu option from the File menu. This action will display a tabbed dialog window with many choices. The five tabs at the top represent the categories of new files that you can create within Visual InterDev. Figure 4.13 displays the File New dialog window with the available categories.

Figure 4.13.

The File New dialog window.

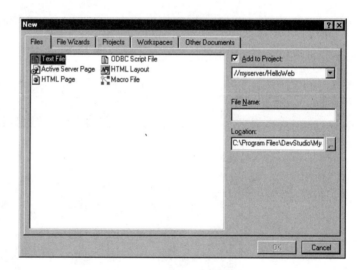

As you can see from Figure 4.13, the five categories are Files, File Wizards, Projects, Workspaces, and Other Documents. The following section briefly discusses what each of these categories represents.

The Files category represents individual files. By using the tab that refers to it, the Files tab, you can add specific file types to your Visual InterDev project. The available choices are displayed in Figure 4.13. This dialog window was mentioned earlier in this chapter during the discussion of the creation of Active Server Pages. If you don't have a project opened, all of the options are grayed out. This tab will be discussed further after you create the project.

The File Wizards tab is the next dialog window. The File Wizards dialog enables you to use wizards to create certain types of files for your project. These wizards help you create your file through a step-by-step process. The available types of wizards include the Data Form Wizard and the Template Page Wizard. The Data Form Wizard enables you to create an ActiveX HTML form that is bound to a database. The Template Page Wizard enables you to create a web page based on a predefined template.

Figure 4.14 shows the File Wizards tab and the wizards available for creating files for your projects.

Figure 4.14.

The File Wizards tab.

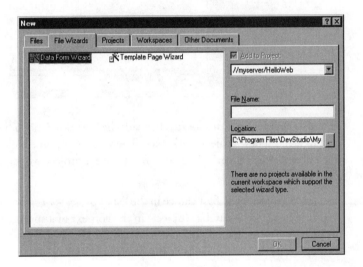

Visual InterDev enables you to create several types of projects with the Projects tab. Additionally, wizards are provided to create most of the different types of projects. Figure 4.15 displays the available types of projects that you can create.

Several fields are displayed to the right of the list in Figure 4.15, including Project Name and Location. You must enter a name for your project into the Project Name field.

The default location for your projects is the MyProjects sub-directory within the DevStudio directory. You can change this location if you want to place your projects in another directory.

NOTE

The project location that you select is your working directory, where all files that you retrieve from the server are placed. After you make changes to the local copy, these files are returned to update the master copy on the server.

Figure 4.15.

The Projects tab.

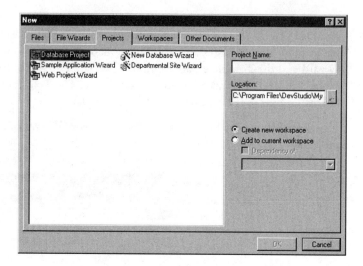

You also have two options located beneath the Location field. The first radio button enables you to create a new project workspace. The second option enables you to add the project to the current project workspace. You must have a project workspace open in order for this option to be enabled.

Database Project is the first choice in the list of projects to create. A database project enables you to manage your database objects in the context of a specific project. A live connection to the database is maintained, and you can use the Visual Data Tools to create, edit, and manage your data and objects in the database.

The Sample Application Wizard enables you to install sample applications on your web server and database server including data that is needed by the sample application. You have the option of installing a Visual InterDev application or a custom application.

The Web Project Wizard enables you to create a new Visual InterDev web project. You will become very familiar with this wizard and use it often to create your new projects. In a few moments, you will use this wizard to create the Hello Web project.

The New Database Wizard enables you to define and create a new MS SQL Server database. This wizard also automatically creates a new database project for you to administrate this new database.

The Departmental Site Wizard creates an entire web site for a typical department or workgroup, based on pre-defined templates. Web pages that are generated with the site include a What's New page, a Feedback Form page, a Projects page, a Products page, a Teams page, and a Department Overview page. You can select some or all of these pages to be included in the departmental web site.

The Workspaces tab is the next category of files that you can create from the File New dialog window. You can create a blank workspace from this tab by selecting the Blank Workspace from the list. You must enter a name for your workspace in the Workspace Name field to the right of the list. The default location is the MyProjects sub-directory within the DevStudio directory. You can change this field to another directory.

The Other Documents tab enables you to add other documents to your project, such as a Microsoft Word document. For example, you might want to include design specifications documented in Word within the confines of your Visual InterDev project. Another example would be a Word document that you want to insert into an HTML page.

Now that you have learned about all of the tabs on the File New dialog window, it's time to create that new project. You are going to create a new Visual InterDev project entitled Hello Web that will be created in the MyProjects sub-directory within the DevStudio directory. The following instructions will guide you through this process.

1. Choose the Projects tab and select the Web Project Wizard.
2. Press the Tab key to place your cursor in the Project Name field.
3. Type the words **HelloWeb** into the Project Name field.
4. Accept the defaults for the location and creating a new project workspace and click OK.

 NOTE

If you accepted the defaults during the installation of Visual InterDev, the location should default to C:\Program Files\DevStudio\MyProjects\. You may have changed the directory for your Visual InterDev to be something other than the Program Files directory. Whatever the case, for step 4, make sure that you create the new project in the DevStudio\MyProjects folder. This will make it easier to follow along with the instructions and examples.

The Web Project Wizard should now be displayed. There are two steps to creating a new web project. First, you must specify the target web server for the project. Figure 4.16 shows the first step in creating a new web project.

You must select or enter the name of your web server in the Server Name combo box. The name of the web server is also referred to as the domain name. If you're connected to a web server through a network, you should enter the name of that web server. If you're running a local configuration on a standalone machine, you should enter the name of the web server on your local machine.

Figure 4.16.

The Web Project Wizard—Step 1.

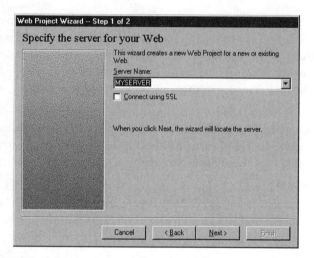

TIP

If you don't know the server name, you can discover it by identifying the computer name for the web server. For example, you can identify the computer name for a standalone web server configuration by right-clicking on the Network Neighborhood icon on the desktop and selecting Properties from the shortcut menu. Choose the Identification tab. This dialog window will then display the computer name for that computer, which is also the name of the web server.

You also have the option of selecting the Connect using SSL checkbox. SSL stands for Secure Sockets Layer from Netscape and enables you to connect to the server through this Netscape standard.

After you enter your server name, press the Next push button. The Web Project Wizard contacts the web server and retrieves a list of the current webs on the web server.

WARNING

You may get the Cannot Contact Server error message if the Web Project Wizard can't contact the web server. Click OK on this dialog window and you're taken back to the Web Project Wizard. Verify that you entered the correct server name. If the name is correct, verify that the server is running and then click Next to advance to step 2.

In step 2 of creating a new web project, the Web Project Wizard will prompt you to either create a new web for your project or connect to an existing web on the web server. Figure 4.17 shows that the Create New Web option is selected by default on the step 2 dialog window of the Web Project Wizard.

Figure 4.17.

The Web Project Wizard—Step 2.

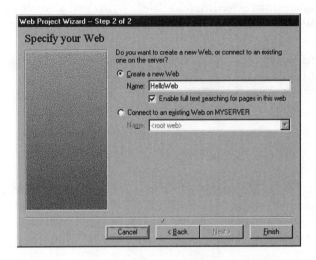

The Web Project Wizard displays a web name that is the same as your project name in the Name field under the Create New Web radio button. Your dialog window should look the same as the window in Figure 4.17. The checkbox to enable full text searching of the web pages within this site is selected by default.

The other option on this dialog window enables you to create a project as part of an existing web site. Use this option if you want to add new applications to your current web site. If you select this radio button, the Name combo box will enable you to choose from the list of web sites on your server. Choosing the root web option places the project in the root of your web server.

Make sure that the Create New Web radio button is selected and that the name of the web is HelloWeb. Accept the default to enable full text searching of the web site. Press the Finish push button and your new web project will be created.

Analyzing the Results

You should now be looking at your project within Visual InterDev. The next section helps you analyze the results of your actions.

Analyzing the Server

The Web Project Wizard created a new web with a directory (both named HelloWeb) for your project files on the server. Your project directory and project files are contained within the root directory for your web server. For example, if you're using Microsoft Internet Information Server, the folder HelloWeb is located within the wwwroot directory. Using the Windows Explorer, Figure 4.18 shows the file directory structure for the HelloWeb web site.

Figure 4.18.

The HelloWeb server files.

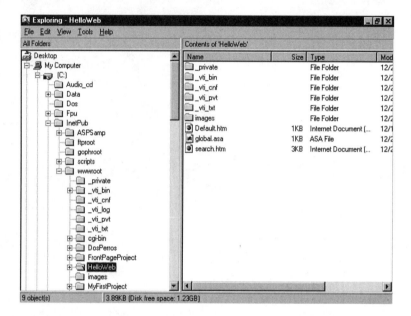

In the preceding figure, the global.asa and the search.htm files have been created in the root of your web directory. Also, an images folder has been created by default within the HelloWeb directory. You can create additional folders to further organize your files from within the Visual InterDev development environment.

Analyzing the Client

The Web Project Wizard also created a HelloWeb directory on your client machine. This working directory serves as the placeholder for server master files that you retrieve from your web project directory. When you retrieve these files, you're making a working copy to manipulate and then copy back to the server. This directory structure is the same as the directory structure on the web server. A copy of the global.asa is copied from the server. Also, several additional project files are generated in the client working directory. Figure 4.19 shows the HelloWeb file structure for a client machine.

Figure 4.19.

The HelloWeb client files.

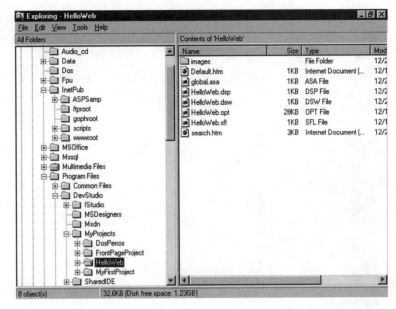

These are project files for your application. The two most notable files are HelloWeb.dsw and HelloWeb.dsp. The .dsw suffix denotes that the file is a project workspace. The .dsp extension indicates that the file is a project. Recall the discussion of the File New dialog window, in which one tab enabled you to create a blank workspace and another enabled you to create new projects.

A workspace can have multiple projects, but a project can have only one workspace. In other words, a workspace has a one-to-many relationship with a project, and a project has a many-to-one relationship with a workspace. For example, you could have a database project and a web project all contained within one workspace.

Analyzing Visual InterDev

Now that you know what the Web Project Wizard has created behind the scenes, it's time to take a look at these files through the eyes of Visual InterDev. Within the Visual InterDev development environment, you should see the HelloWeb project workspace. The HelloWeb project is displayed in File View by default. You can see that the FileView tab has been added to the project workspace area on the right-hand side of the Visual InterDev workspace. The virtual root for this project is displayed as the top node within the File View. Your virtual root should be similar to the one created in Figure 4.20.

Figure 4.20.

Visual InterDev displays the HelloWeb project.

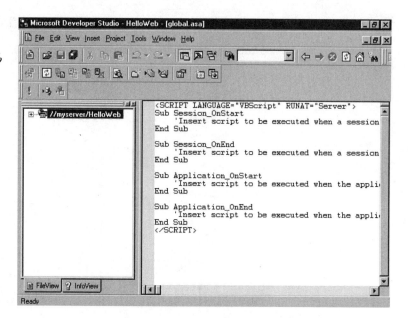

```
<SCRIPT LANGUAGE="VBScript" RUNAT="Server">
Sub Session_OnStart
    'Insert script to be executed when a session
End Sub

Sub Session_OnEnd
    'Insert script to be executed when a session
End Sub

Sub Application_OnStart
    'Insert script to be executed when the appli
End Sub

Sub Application_OnEnd
    'Insert script to be executed when the appli
End Sub
</SCRIPT>
```

Remember that the virtual root is the combination of your server name and the name of your web site. In this example, the name of the server is myserver and the name of the project is HelloWeb. These names combine to form the virtual root of //myserver/HelloWeb. The + sign to the left of the virtual root indicates that there are files and/or folders located within this directory. Double-click on the virtual root to expand the directory structure and view your project files.

You should now see the global.asa and the search.htm files as well as the images folder. The icon for the global and search files should be gray, which means that you don't have a working copy of the files. Double-click on the global.asa file to retrieve a working copy.

TIP

To get the working copy of a file, you also can select the file and right-click the mouse to display the shortcut menu. Choose the Get Working Copy menu option to get a working copy from the server. Selecting the Open menu item also retrieves a working copy of the file from the server. The Open command tries to open a copy of the file from your local working directory. If a working copy doesn't exist, this command executes the Get Working Copy command to retrieve the file from the server.

Two things happen as a result of this action. First, Visual InterDev will retrieve a working copy of the file from the web server into the local working directory of your client machine. A message is displayed beneath the tabs of the project workspace indicating that the working copy is being retrieved from the web server. Second, Visual InterDev displays the file's contents in the pane to the right of the project workspace.

You will be interacting with these two panes a lot, so it's important to understand how they work. When you open a file within your project, Visual InterDev uses the default editor for the file to display its contents. For example, when you opened the global.asa file, the contents were displayed using the HTML Source Editor, which is the default editor for HTML and script files.

Another good example involves ActiveX and Design-time ActiveX controls. For these controls, the Object Editor is activated to display the object's contents and settings. You learned how to change the default editor earlier today when working with images and multimedia files was discussed. You could change the default editor for an HTML file from the HTML Source Editor to the FrontPage Editor for Visual InterDev.

Constructing the Web Page

Now that you have examined the initial files for your project, it's time to construct the main web page using basic HTML. The following instructions will guide you through the process.

1. Select the virtual root and choose the New menu option from the File menu. The Files tab should be displayed.
2. Select the HTML Page option and type the name **Default.htm** in the Filename field.
3. Accept the defaults for the rest of the fields and press the OK button.

Visual InterDev creates a basic HTML page named Default.htm and adds this file to your project workspace.

 TIP

Visual InterDev automatically adds the correct file extension to the filename based on the file type that you have selected. In the preceding example, you chose to create an HTML file. Based on that selection, you could have just entered **Default**. Visual InterDev would then have added the .htm extension to your file.

Your Visual InterDev workspace should now look like Figure 4.21.

Figure 4.21.
The HTML shell.

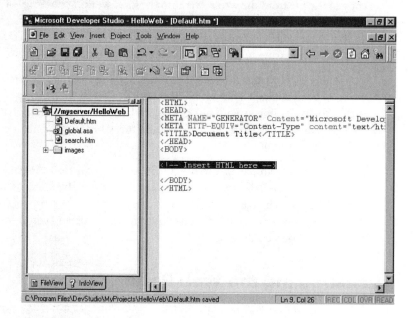

Visual InterDev created a basic template for you to use while constructing your HTML web page. Notice the format of the HTML template. You have a header section that includes space for a title for your web page. You also have a body section for you to place the main section of your web page. The other lines aren't important for the purposes of this lesson.

The following are your instructions for creating the content for the web page:

1. Highlight the words Document Title between the `<TITLE>` and `</TITLE>` tags.
2. Type the words **The Hello Web Application**.
3. Highlight the whole Insert HTML here comment line.
4. Type the following code:

```
<H3>Welcome to the Hello Web Home Page!</H3>
<P><B>
The purpose of the Hello Web Application is to allow you to type in your
name and present a personalized greeting from the Web. Please enter your
name in the field provided. When you press the Say Hello button, the Web
will become friendly.
</B></p>
<BR>
<HR>
```

Now that you have entered your HTML code, you're going to preview your results in a browser. You first need to save your project. To do this, choose the Save All menu item within the File menu. This option saves all of the files in your project.

To preview your web page, use the Preview in Browser function. Remember, this browser is an implementation of the Microsoft Internet Explorer browser. To use this browser, select the Default.htm file and right-click the mouse to display the shortcut menu. Choose the Preview in Browser option. Figure 4.22 shows what your web page should look like using this option.

Figure 4.22.

The Preview in Browser view.

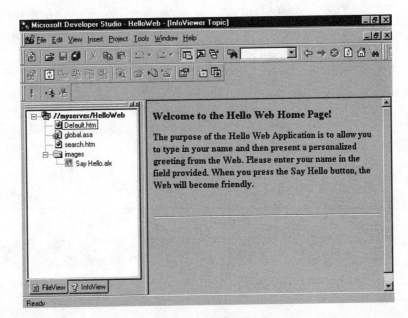

Now select your HTML file again and this time choose the Browse With option from the shortcut menu to see the difference between the two options.

Constructing the HTML Layout File

You are now going to construct the HTML Layout file to be included on your main web page. The HTML Layout enables you to precisely position your controls on the web page. The following are the instructions for constructing your HTML Layout:

1. To create a new HTML Layout, select the File menu and click New.
2. Select the HTML Layout option from the Files tab.

3. Type the name **Say Hello** in the Filename field.

4. Click the OK push button.

The HTML Layout is then created. The file Say Hello.alx should now be displayed in your project workspace, and the HTML Layout Editor should be active in your display pane. You also should have a floating toolbox containing multiple objects and controls and a floating HTML Layout toolbar that contains buttons that affect the appearance of these controls.

TIP

> You can place, or dock, the HTML Layout toolbar on the main Visual InterDev toolbar. Position your mouse over the title bar area of the toolbar, click the left mouse button, and simultaneously drag the HTML toolbar to the preferred area of the Visual InterDev toolbar. When you release the mouse, the HTML toolbar becomes part of the main Visual InterDev toolbar. To reverse this action, place your cursor over the double line area of the HTML toolbar and drag the toolbar into the Visual InterDev workspace. The HTML toolbar becomes a floating toolbar again.

Figure 4.23 illustrates the features of the HTML Layout Editor and the available controls and options.

Figure 4.23.

The HTML Layout Editor.

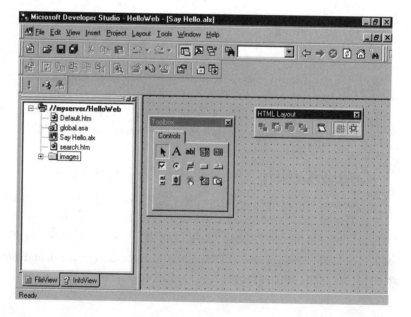

The HTML Layout Editor provides a form for you to place your controls in. The controls are located on the toolbox. As you can see from the preceding figure, you have several objects for creating a basic user interface.

If you're familiar with the ActiveX Control Pad or Visual Basic, you will be very comfortable using the HTML Layout Editor. The basic method of creating your interface is the same. The process consists of placing objects, or controls, onto the form, properly positioning these controls, and setting their properties.

A property defines how the controls look and behave. For example, you can set the property of a form to be a certain height, width, and background color. Every control has a distinct set of properties. These properties have default values that you can change.

The HTML Layout Editor is covered in detail on Day 13. For now, add the controls to your form and set their properties. To add a control to the form, select the object from the toolbar and then click your mouse on the area of the form where you want the control placed.

NOTE Similar to other application toolbars, the Tooltips message for each control displays as you rest your mouse over the control, indicating the type of control.

1. Click your mouse on the label control.
2. Place your mouse on an area of the form and click the left mouse button. For right now, where you place the control isn't important.
3. Repeat step 2.

You should now have two label controls painted on your form. The default names of these controls are Label1 and Label2. When using controls, you should always change the name and ID of the control to a distinct and descriptive name. Also, these labels were created using a default length, height, and width.

TIP To change the properties for a control, put your cursor in the field next to the property and enter the value or text for the property.

1. Double-click on the Label1 control. This displays the properties windows for this control.

2. Put your cursor in the field next to the Caption and change the name of the caption to `Name:`.

3. Change the value of the `ID` property to `lblName`.

4. Change the `Height` and `Width` properties to **17** and **50** respectively.

5. Change the `Left` property to **17** and the `Top` property to **33**.

6. Click the X in the top right-hand corner of the Properties dialog window to close the window.

Now you're going to change the properties for the second label control. On Day 13 you will learn more tips and shortcuts that will increase your productivity when painting controls.

1. Double-click the Label2 control.

2. Change the `Name` of the property to `Greeting:`.

3. Change the value of the `ID` to `lblGreeting`.

4. Change the `Height` and `Width` to **17** and **50** respectively.

5. Change the `Left` property to **17** and the `Top` property to **74**.

6. Click the X in the top right-hand corner of the Properties dialog window to close the window.

You are now going to paint the text box controls onto the window. Follow the same method that you just used to place the label controls on the form. The text box control is located next to the label control. After you paint the two text box controls onto the form, follow these instructions to set the properties of the controls:

1. Double-click the first text box.

2. Change the `ID` property to `txtName`.

3. Change the `Height` and `Width` to **18** and **66** respectively.

4. Change the `Left` property to **74** and the `Top` property to **33**.

5. Click the X in the top right-hand corner of the Properties dialog window to close the window.

Now change the properties for the second text box:

1. Double-click the second text box.

2. Change the `ID` property to `txtGreeting`.

3. Change the `Height` and `Width` to **18** and **66** respectively.

4. Change the `Left` property to **74** and the `Top` property to **74**.

5. Click the X in the top right-hand corner of the Properties dialog window to close the window.

4

Finally, you need to paint the command buttons onto your form. These buttons also are referred to as push buttons. Refer to the previous Note on Tooltips for help. After you have placed two push buttons on your form, change the following properties.

1. Double-click the first command button.
2. Change the Caption to **Say Hello**.
3. Change the ID property to **cmdSayHello**.
4. Change the Height and Width to **25** and **74** respectively.
5. Change the Left property to **140** and the Top property to **132**.
6. Click the X in the top right-hand corner of the Properties dialog window to close the window.

Now it's time to change the second push button.

1. Double-click the second command button.
2. Change the Caption to **Reset**.
3. Change the ID property to **cmdReset**.
4. Change the Height and Width to **25** and **74** respectively.
5. Change the Left property to **223** and the Top property to **132**.
6. Click the X in the top right-hand corner of the Properties dialog window to close the window.

You have one remaining task to complete. You need to set the properties for the form. To set the properties of a form, double-click the form itself. The following are the changes you need to make:

1. Change the ID property to **laySayHello**.
2. Change the Height and Width to **200** and **313** respectively.
3. Click the X in the top right-hand corner of the Properties dialog window to close the window.

You have now created an HTML Layout. This process may have been a review for some of you. The next section shows you the final stage of putting these components together.

Using the HTML Layout

Now that you have constructed your HTML Layout, you need to reference this layout form within your HTML web page. Open your HTML page from the project workspace and follow these instructions:

1. Place your cursor two lines below the <HR> tag.

2. Right-click the mouse to display the shortcut menu.

3. Choose the Insert HTML Layout option from the shortcut menu. This action displays the Select HTML Layout dialog window. This dialog should display your project as well as the contents of your project, which include the file SayHello.alx.

4. Select the file SayHello.alx and click the OK push button.

An HTML Layout is inserted into your HTML file. The layout is denoted by the <OBJECT> tags.

Adding the Code

The final step in this process is adding the logic for your application. You are going to use the Script Wizard to accomplish this function.

1. Place your cursor somewhere inside the <OBJECT> and </OBJECT> tags.

2. Right-click the mouse to display the shortcut menu.

3. Choose the Edit HTML Layout option from the shortcut menu. This action displays the HTML Layout Editor for you to edit your .alx file.

4. Select the Say Hello push button and click the right mouse button to display the shortcut menu.

5. Choose the Script Wizard option. This action displays the Script Wizard dialog window.

You should be looking at the same window that is shown in Figure 4.24.

Figure 4.24.

Adding code using the Script Wizard.

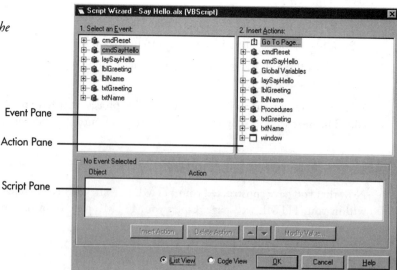

The Script Wizard enables you to choose controls and related events and associate actions for those events. The List View is the default view for this dialog window and enables you to build your code through a point-and-click metaphor.

As you can see from Figure 4.24, the first pane is the Event Pane, which displays your form's controls and their possible events. The pane to the right of the Event Pane is the Action Pane, which shows the actions for these controls. The bottom pane is the Script Pane and shows the results of your choices in the first two panes. As you build select control events and actions, your code is displayed in the Script Pane.

The Script Wizard is covered in detail on Day 15. For now, use the following instructions to build your application logic:

1. Double-click the cmdSayHello control in the Event Pane. This action expands the view to display all of the selected control's possible events.

2. Select the Click event.

3. Double-click on the txtGreeting control in the Action Pane. This action expands the view to display the available properties for the selected control.

4. Select the Text property. The Insert Action push button should now be enabled.

5. Press the Insert Action push button to insert your code. This action will display a dialog window for you to enter the text string property for this action. You can either enter some text or choose the Custom push button to enter a single value or a variable name.

6. Choose the Custom push button.

7. Type the words **txtName.Text**, which represents the text value that is contained in the Name text box, and click OK. You should now see the object and action within the List View of the Script Pane.

8. With the Script Pane line item selected, choose the Code View radio button located to the right of the List View option. This action changes the display of the Script Pane to Code View.

9. Modify your code to look like the following:

```
Sub cmdSayHello_Click()
txtGreeting.Text = "Hello " + txtName.Text
```

10. Press the OK push button to confirm the code modification.

11. From the Script Wizard dialog window, press OK again to confirm your application logic.

For the Reset push button, follow the same method that you used for the Say Hello push button:

1. Double-click the cmdReset control in the Event Pane. This action expands the view to display all of the selected control's possible events.

2. Select the Click event.

3. Double-click the txtGreeting control in the Action Pane. This action expands the view to display the available properties for the selected control.

4. Select the Text property. The Insert Action push button should now be enabled.

5. Press the Insert Action push button to insert your code. This action displays a dialog window for you to enter the text string property for this action.

6. Press the OK push button without entering any text. This action clears the value of the text. If you view the results in Code View, you will see that txtGreeting. Text is set to " ", or null.

7. Repeat steps 3-6 for the Text property of the txtName control.

8. From the Script Wizard dialog window, press OK again to confirm your application logic.

You are now ready to preview the results of your first project. Before moving on, you should choose the Save All menu from the File menu to save your work.

Interacting with the Final Product

You can either use the Preview in Browser or the Browse With function from the File menu to view your first web application. You should be able to enter your name and press the Say Hello push button to display the personalized greeting. When you press the Reset push button, the Name and the Greeting fields should be cleared, enabling you to enter another name.

Refer back to Figures 4.11 and 4.12 to verify your results. Does your application look the same? If not, check to make sure that you followed the steps correctly.

Summary

Today was a long but very productive day. You finally got a chance to interact with Visual InterDev and develop your first application. As you can tell, Visual InterDev is very easy to use once you get a feel for the features.

This morning, you explored a standard project, learning about the different files and components. You learned about the concept of a Visual InterDev project by comparing it to making pancakes, then about the virtual root and how Visual InterDev builds the virtual root based on your project name. Next, you read about working with Visual InterDev files and learned some of the more common files within a Visual InterDev project. During the middle part of the day, the Visual InterDev development process was discussed. You learned how Visual InterDev facilitates each phase of this process from development to deployment.

The final part of the day was spent developing your first project—the Hello Web application. You received a hands-on approach to development through each step involved in building this application. Throughout the day, you the saw Visual InterDev development environment, including pertinent dialog windows and menu options. The lessons you learned today will prove invaluable as you delve deeper into Visual InterDev's features and capabilities.

Q&A

Q What is the difference between a workspace and a project?

A A project is a collection of files that join together to accomplish some specified purpose. For example, a web project is made up of HTML files, Active Server Pages, and ActiveX Layout files that work together to build a web site and application. Another example is a database project, which is comprised of database objects that enable a programmer to manipulate a database. The project operates within the confines of a workspace. A workspace allows the project or projects to accomplish their mission. Going back to the pancake example, the kitchen or house is analogous to the workspace. A workspace can contain multiple projects.

Q How can I create additional folders for my project?

A You can create new folders for your project within the confines of the Visual InterDev development environment. Right-click the mouse on the virtual root in your project workspace to display the shortcut menu. Choose the New Folder option from the menu, enter a name for your folder, and click OK.

Q Can I configure my Netscape Navigator browser to work with Visual InterDev?

A Yes. Visual InterDev includes Microsoft Internet Explorer. You can, however, add another browser including Netscape Navigator or Communicator from the Browse With dialog window.

4

Workshop

In today's workshop, you create your own application. Use today's lesson as a guide to create your web page and HTML Layout. You should practice using the various components that you learned about today. Begin by starting a new project and walk through the whole process. Also, use the Windows Explorer to view the file structures and files as they are created. You should understand the basic building blocks by using Visual InterDev to produce your application. Practice makes perfect!

Quiz

1. What two components make up the virtual root?
2. What is the purpose of the virtual root?
3. How do I link my HTML Layout with my web page?
4. What are the two views of the Script Wizard?

Quiz Answers

1. The virtual root is comprised of the name of your web server and your project name.

2. The virtual root enables a user to logically access your web without knowing the physical location of your files and the file directory structure. By selecting the virtual root URL, a user can have access to all of the web page files within the application.

3. To link an HTML Layout with an HTML web page, you need to reference the layout from within the HTML file. To accomplish this, click within the <HTML> tags in your HTML file and choose the insert HTML Layout option. This dialog enables you to pick an HTML Layout to insert into your web page.

4. The two views of the Script Wizard are List View and Code View.

4

Day 5

WYSIWYG HTML
Editing with FrontPage

In yesterday's lesson, you created your first Visual InterDev project, using the HTML Source Editor to construct your Web page. In today's lesson, you learn about another HTML editor included with Visual InterDev. The FrontPage Editor for Visual InterDev is very intuitive and powerful and provides a visual alternative to the HTML Source Editor.

The first part of today's lesson introduces you to the FrontPage Editor for Visual InterDev. You then receive an overview of the benefits of a visual development environment. Toward the middle of the day, you will take a guided tour of the features of the FrontPage Editor. You will learn about all of the powerful features and how to use them to construct your web pages. Afterwards, you will learn how to use the FrontPage Editor and its features to create a web page. The end of the day covers the different team members and roles involved in a web development project. This part of the lesson focuses specifically on the different contributions to the development of a web site and how Visual InterDev and FrontPage can facilitate this process.

FrontPage Editor for Visual InterDev

Most HTML editors focus on supporting different HTML specification levels without providing an easy-to-use interface. Developers have faced the challenge of programming cryptic codes to format their web pages. After they create this code with an editor like Notepad, they hope and pray that the web page that's displayed in the browser is the one they envisioned. What they see in their mind is not always what they get.

Microsoft FrontPage provides an answer to this dilemma. FrontPage is a very robust and powerful HTML editor, combining the latest in HTML specification and browser extensions support with an interface that's intuitive and easy-to-use. The FrontPage Editor enables you to visually construct your HTML. Hard-core programmers, who are from the old school of HTML development, can still manipulate the generated code and add their own custom enhancements and modifications. FrontPage is a *WYSIWYG* editor.

 WYSIWYG stands for what you see is what you get. In the context of constructing web pages, WYSIWYG means that the web document's formatting that you see in the editor mirrors how the browser displays the web page.

The web page that you create and view within the editor is the same page that you see in the browser. This reduces a lot of guesswork when you design a web page. Visual InterDev provides an implementation of the FrontPage Editor that is completely compatible with the commercial version of FrontPage. The FrontPage Editor for Visual InterDev provides the same robust features and user-friendly interface as the commercial version of the product.

As stated before, the FrontPage Editor provides a WYSIWYG authoring environment with the same powerful features as the commercial version of FrontPage. If you have used FrontPage, you're familiar with its features. The FrontPage Editor for Visual InterDev provides basically the same robust features for constructing your web site.

The WYSIWYG authoring environment enhances your productivity by enabling you to construct your interface through a graphical tool. The FrontPage Editor enables you to visually choose the options and formats that you want for your web page. Then, based on the design formats that you select, the FrontPage Editor generates the proper HTML code to produce the desired web page. You have access to this code to make changes and extend its capabilities.

You might feel like you're giving up control of your design when you use a tool like FrontPage. On the contrary, by using the FrontPage Editor, you're gaining control of your design. By enabling the editor to generate the basic HTML for you, you have more time to focus on the overall design and look and feel of the web site. You also have more time to develop the more difficult application logic.

5

The FrontPage Editor provides support for all of the basic HTML features as well as some more advanced browser extensions. You can publish basic information using the editor. Also, you can create HTML forms and objects to elicit user input. One of the more robust features for constructing a web page is the Page Wizard. This wizard provides a step-by-step guide to construct several types of designs, including frames and tables. WebBots also greatly augment your productivity. A WebBot is a program that is a part of the web page and performs certain tasks as needed. The FrontPage Editor comes with several WebBots that are covered later in the day. WebBots provide a way to combine scripts with your HTML code to create a dynamic web page.

You can use images to enhance your web pages using the FrontPage Editor. The FrontPage Editor supports the standard GIF and JPEG file formats as well as other image formats. For these other image formats, the FrontPage Editor prompts you to convert them to either the GIF or JPEG file format. You can view your images as they will be displayed in the web page using the FrontPage Editor.

Once you begin to visualize the power of the FrontPage Editor, you will want to use this tool as your basic editor of choice. The good thing about Visual InterDev is that you don't have to decide between one tool or the other. You can combine many tools under one roof to meet all of your web and application development needs.

The Benefits of a Visual Environment

The pages that you design using the FrontPage Editor exemplify the final product. The visual editor is analogous to using Microsoft Word to format a document. You set the font type, font size, and character formatting such as bold and italics. When you print the document, the formats that you designed are printed exactly as you designed them. Likewise, when you design a web page using the FrontPage Editor, what you see is what you get. You don't have to guess about the layout or positioning of objects.

Also, the FrontPage Editor reduces the very iterative process of character formatting. With other non-visual editors, you have to code the format of your text and then test the results in the browser. For example, you specify your HTML code to format text to be bold and a certain font, then view the page in your browser to ensure that you used the right codes to produce the desired effect. With the FrontPage Editor, you can visually choose the proper formatting as you would in Microsoft Word. You also can see the results within the same environment.

The FrontPage Editor provides instant feedback about your design, saving valuable development and testing time. The benefit of a visual editor like the FrontPage Editor is that you select the choices and FrontPage does the work. If you want to insert a table, you select the

5

Insert Table option from the Table menu. You then can design the layout of the table, including the number of rows and columns. You don't have to code a series of HTML tags like <TH>, <TR>, and <TD>. The FrontPage Editor generates these tags for you.

Figure 5.1 illustrates the power of a visual environment to view your web pages.

Figure 5.1.

The FrontPage Editor.

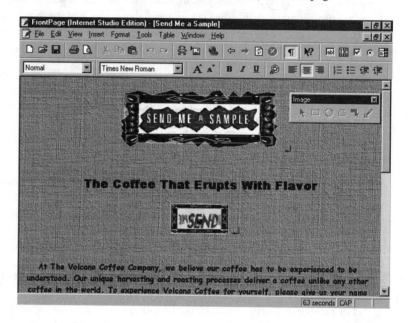

This figure shows the Volcano Coffee Company sample web site that's included with the Internet Information Server. This page enables you to order a sample of coffee. As you can see in this figure, the FrontPage Editor displays the images as well as formatted text and graphical controls. Try to use Notepad to rapidly construct this web page! The FrontPage Editor definitely provides the visual tool to construct graphical web pages. The need for this kind of tool becomes imperative as the industry continues to migrate from document publishing and move towards dynamic, interactive, and graphical web pages.

Now that the benefits of using a visual environment have been introduced, it's time to take a look at some of the specific features of the FrontPage Editor.

FrontPage Editor Features

The FrontPage Editor for Visual InterDev contains most of the same features of the released version of FrontPage. Some of the more pertinent features include the following:

- [ ] Basic character formatting
- [ ] Tables
- [ ] Forms
- [ ] Templates
- [ ] Images
- [ ] Advanced Controls
- [ ] WebBots

Basic Character Formatting

The FrontPage Editor supports all of your basic editing needs. You can visually set the font type and font size for your text as well as format the layout and style of your paragraphs. You also can easily create bulleted and numbered lists. The FrontPage Editor uses the same user interface method as Microsoft Word, making the process very intuitive. In fact, both tools use the same menu and menu items to accomplish these basic editing features.

The Format menu enables you to insert bullets and numbers and select options for the fonts of your text. You can format different types of headings in your document, as well as designate paragraph styles. This process is easy and enables you to focus on the page layout without worrying about the underlying HTML. You also can use the toolbar option to format your web page. The Format menu provides an option for setting the properties for the web page, including background color and images. You also can define the visual display and color of hyperlinks and text.

Tables

You can use the FrontPage Editor to create tables for your web page. Tables are very effective at displaying lists of data like rows from a database. FrontPage generates all of the underlying HTML to produce your table. To create a table, you select the Table menu and choose the Insert Table option. This action displays the Insert Table dialog window, which enables you to design the table layout. From this window, you can specify the number of rows and columns for your table. Also, you can indicate layout parameters, including the text alignment, border size, cell padding, and cell spacing. The FrontPage Editor supports many of the new HTML extensions and features, including the ability to include background colors and images for the table and individual cells. Figure 5.2 demonstrates the various attributes that you can set to enliven the look of your table.

5

Figure 5.2.

Creating a table.

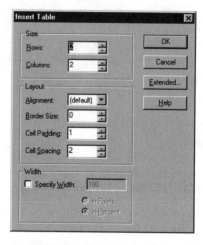

You can enter data directly into the table or use the variable names to represent data that will build the table's contents from another source, such as a database. When designing the table, you can enter data into the table just as you would enter information into a Word table.

Forms

The FrontPage Editor supports the use of HTML forms and provides a mechanism for constructing these forms for your web pages. You can choose the Form Field sub-menu option from the Insert menu to insert a control for your web page at the spot of your cursor. When you select the desired control, the FrontPage Editor creates a form containing the new control at the indicated spot. You can set properties for both the form and its controls. You also can choose several different types of event handlers to control your application logic for the form. The FrontPage Editor supports the following types of event handlers:

- [ ] ISAPI, NSAPI, or CGI script
- [ ] Internet Database Connector (IDC)
- [ ] WebBot programs

All of these event handlers provide a method for you to process user interaction between the client and the server. For example, you might use an API or CGI script program to gather input from a user and then store this information in a database. The lesson on Day 1, "Introducing Visual InterDev and the World Wide Web," talked about APIs and CGI script and the differences between the methods and their advantages. The Internet Database Connector (IDC) provides database connectivity to any ODBC-compliant database. The WebBot programs provide some specific solutions for unique forms, for example, a form and logic to handle user registration to your web site. Forms and form processing are discussed in more detail on Day 12, "Using Basic and Advanced HTML Form Controls."

Templates

The FrontPage Editor enables you to create standard templates for constructing your web pages. Templates can dramatically save you time during the design and development phases of your project. Also, templates ensure a common look and feel across the application. You can use templates to provide a consistent interface for the user.

The FrontPage Editor enables you to create templates for your web pages. Page templates provide standard design for an individual web page. You can construct a new page to be used as a template. You also can convert existing pages to serve as the templates for your web pages.

Images

Images are a big part of any dynamic web page. You can import a variety of them into your web pages using the FrontPage Editor.

To include images on your web page, simply place the mouse at the desired spot and select Image from the Insert menu. You can then choose to insert an image file located on your machine or a network. The image is imported into your web. In a sense, the image becomes a part of the project, enabling you to work with the original file. You also can insert an image from the Web. When you specify an image from the World Wide Web, you are referencing a URL for the location of the file. For this reason, these types of images can't be imported into your web page.

The FrontPage Editor supports the use of the standard GIF and JPEG Web file types as well as many other common image file types. The FrontPage Editor prompts you to convert any file that is not a .gif or .jpg to that format. The FrontPage Editor converts any image that uses up to 256 colors to the GIF format, and converts any image using more than 256 colors to the JPEG format.

Advanced Controls

The FrontPage Editor supports the use of advanced objects and features like ActiveX controls, Java applets, and plug-ins. These advanced features promote dynamic interaction with the user, and are very easy to include on your web page. Each of these control types are located on the Other Components sub-menu within the Insert menu. Figure 5.3 shows the components that you have available to enliven your web page.

5

Figure 5.3.
Inserting other components.

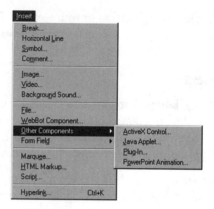

Once you choose the type of control that you want, a dialog window specific to that control is displayed. Figure 5.4 shows the results of selecting an ActiveX control.

Figure 5.4.
The ActiveX Control Properties dialog window.

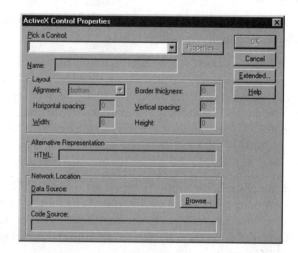

This dialog window enables you to set the properties for an ActiveX control. Once you pick the ActiveX control you want to insert, the other property fields become enabled, allowing you to further define the attributes of this control. These properties help you design the layout of the control relative to the web page. Also, you can establish properties that are specific to that control by pressing the Properties push button.

Java Applets

The process to insert a Java applet is basically the same as inserting an ActiveX control. Choose Java Applet from the Other Components sub-menu to insert a Java applet into your web page, and the Java Applet Properties dialog window is then displayed. This dialog window is more generic than the ActiveX Control Properties dialog, because Java doesn't inherently support a visual method for setting properties like ActiveX controls. You can set the properties for the applet and then press OK. Figure 5.5 displays the properties that you can configure for a Java applet.

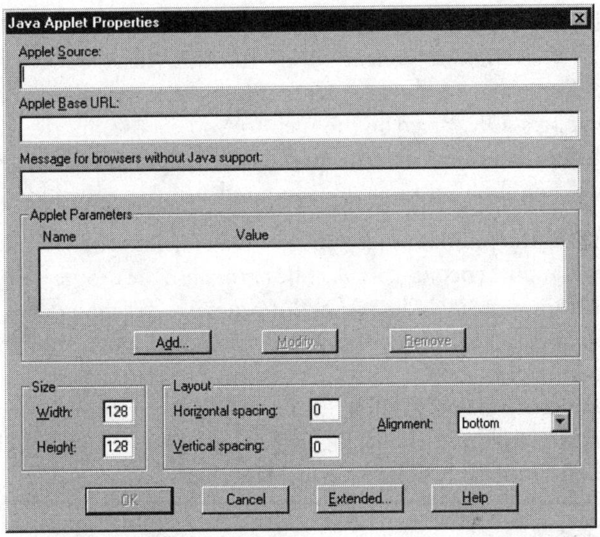

Figure 5.5.

The Java Applet Properties dialog window.

Plug-Ins

Plug-ins also enable you to extend the functionality of your web page. You can use plug-ins to view embedded files within the context of the browser. For example, you can use a plug-in to embed a video clip for the user to view within your web page. The FrontPage Editor supports the use of plug-ins with your web pages. The process of inserting a plug-in is similar to the process for the aforementioned objects. You choose the Other Components sub-menu from the Insert menu and select the Plug-In option and the Plug-in Properties dialog window is displayed. To complete the insertion process, set the properties for the plug-in and press the OK button.

PowerPoint Animation

You can use the FrontPage Editor to insert an animated Microsoft PowerPoint object into your web page. You have the option of inserting the object as an ActiveX control or a plug-in.

WebBots

WebBots are programs that combine HTML and script to perform routine administrative functions. These programs execute as needed and enable you to automate functions and reduce your custom development time. WebBot examples include gathering user results from a form and automating the user registration process for a web site.

To insert a WebBot, place your cursor at the desired location in your web page and choose the WebBot Component option from the Insert menu. The Insert WebBot Component dialog window is then displayed. From this window, you can choose a WebBot from the list and press OK. Based on the WebBot you choose, another dialog is displayed so that you can further set some properties for the WebBot program. After you select the properties and press OK, the WebBot program is inserted at the specified location on the page.

A WebBot program is visually denoted on your page by a distinct mouse indicator. Whenever your mouse encounters a WebBot program, the mouse pointer changes to a robot, indicating that this area includes a WebBot program. To change the WebBot component properties, place your mouse over the WebBot program and right-click the mouse. From the shortcut menu, select the WebBot Component Properties menu item. This option then displays the properties dialog window for the selected component, enabling you to change any of the settings for the WebBot. Figure 5.6 shows the available WebBot components included with the FrontPage Editor for Visual InterDev.

Figure 5.6.

The Insert WebBot Component dialog window.

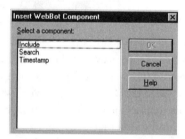

NOTE

This book is based on the Technical Beta 2 Release of Visual InterDev. In this release, the FrontPage Editor included the WebBot components that are pictured in Figure 5.6. More WebBots may be included in the final release.

Using the FrontPage Editor to Create Your Web Page

You have now learned about some of the more relevant features of the FrontPage Editor for Visual InterDev. This section guides you through the process of using the FrontPage Editor to create your web pages. Along the way, you will see the functions of the Editor and how to use them effectively for your Visual InterDev projects.

Visual InterDev Projects and the FrontPage Editor

When you use Visual InterDev to construct an HTML file, the newly created file is opened by the HTML Source Editor by default. As mentioned in yesterday's lesson, you can change the editor for the HTML file by selecting the Open With command from the shortcut menu. Once the Open With dialog window is displayed, you can open the file with an editor from the list as well as change the default editor for the file. You will probably want to change the default editor to FrontPage and use this editor for most of your initial HTML web page creation. This method enables you to quickly construct your web pages using the power of the FrontPage Editor. You can always switch back to the HTML Source Editor or another editor during the development process. Figures 5.7 and 5.8 illustrate the difference between viewing a page in the HTML Source Editor and working with that same page using the FrontPage Editor for Visual InterDev.

Figure 5.7.

Using the HTML Source Editor.

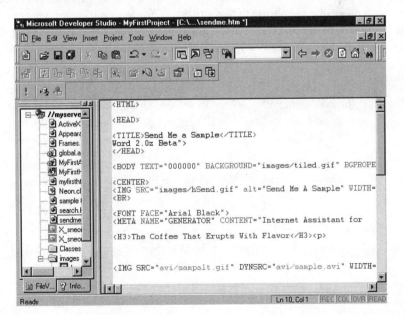

5

Figure 5.8.

Using the FrontPage Editor for Visual InterDev.

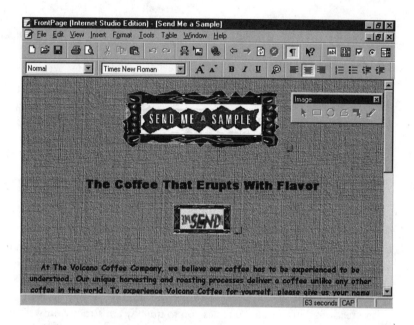

You may want to divide up your team into roles that take advantage of each environment. I will be talking more about these roles at the end of today's lesson. The point I want to make now is that Visual InterDev supports the use of both FrontPage as well as other editors to build your HTML web pages and include these pages in your Visual InterDev project. Whether people use the FrontPage Editor for Visual InterDev or the commercial release of FrontPage, the files will be compatible. Content developers can use either product to author their web pages. You can easily integrate these files into your Visual InterDev project.

There are two ways to integrate web pages into your project using the FrontPage Editor for Visual InterDev. The first method involves creating the web page using the New option from the File menu within Visual InterDev. This approach is the safest and most straightforward method for including HTML files into your project. Using this method, you create the new HTML file and then select the Open With command to open it using the FrontPage Editor.

After you press the Open push button, Visual InterDev activates the FrontPage Editor and opens the selected HTML file within the editor's environment.

NOTE

The FrontPage Editor isn't contained within the Visual InterDev environment. In other words, the FrontPage Editor is a separate executable program that can be called from within the Visual InterDev environment. While working on your web page, you operate within the FrontPage Editor's distinct environment. You can switch back and forth between the Visual InterDev and FrontPage environments.

The second approach to using the FrontPage Editor involves using FrontPage to create the HTML web page and then including the file in your project. Under this approach, you first create the HTML page using the FrontPage Editor. Next, you open Visual InterDev and add the HTML file to your project. To accomplish this task, right-click the mouse in the project workspace area to display the shortcut menu.

NOTE   Remember, the project workspace is defined as the pane on the right-hand side of the Visual InterDev workspace. The project workspace displays the list of files in your project.

Once the shortcut menu is displayed, you can select the Add Files menu item. This action displays the Insert Files into Project dialog window. This window enables you to insert the HTML file into your current Visual InterDev project.

NOTE   This dialog window also enables you to insert other types of files including images, Active Server Pages, Java CLASS files, and so on.

Now that you have seen the relationship between Visual InterDev and the FrontPage Editor, it's time to explore the FrontPage Editor in more detail. You have learned how to open HTML files with the FrontPage Editor. The next section focuses on how to use the FrontPage Editor features to construct your web page.

Exploring the File Menu

The File menu enables you to open, save, close, and print files. You also can distribute an HTML file via electronic mail. The File menu contains three options for saving files. The Save menu item saves the current file. The Save As option enables you to save the file under a different name or file type. The Save All menu item saves all of the files that are currently open within the FrontPage Editor. When you save a file that is a part of your Visual InterDev project, you are saving it within the context of that project. In other words, you use the FrontPage Editor to save the HTML page. You don't have to re-save it using Visual InterDev. You also can establish page properties, like specifying a background image and background sound for your web page from the File menu.

TIP

You also can access the properties for a web page by placing your mouse anywhere within the page and pressing the right mouse button. This action displays the shortcut menu for the page. Choose the Page Properties menu item to display the Page Properties dialog window.

You can use these same steps for any object, control, or character format. When you select the object and right-click the mouse, a properties menu item that pertains to that particular object is displayed in the list of menu items.

Another way to display the properties dialog window is to select the object and press Alt+Enter.

You can print your web page as well as preview the page in a browser. Selecting the Preview in Browser option from the File menu displays the Preview in Browser dialog window. From this window, you can indicate the browser that you would like to use to preview the page. If a browser that you want to use is not in the list, you can add the desired browser to the list. You also can designate the window size. This feature enables you to test what the page will look like on different size monitors. This type of testing is very important before you deploy your web site. You must be able to accommodate users with different monitor displays and sizes. This feature can help you in that testing effort. Figure 5.9 displays the various options from the File menu.

Figure 5.9.

The FrontPage Editor File menu.

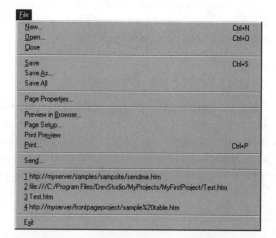

Exploring the Edit Menu

The Edit menu is very similar to the Edit menu in Microsoft Word and other word processing packages. This menu enables you to execute basic editing commands on the page. You can Cut, Copy, and Paste text as well as carry out other editing functions. You also can add bookmarks and hyperlinks to your web pages. Finally, this menu enables you to set the properties for WebBot components. Figure 5.10 shows the available options on the Edit menu.

Figure 5.10.

The Edit menu.

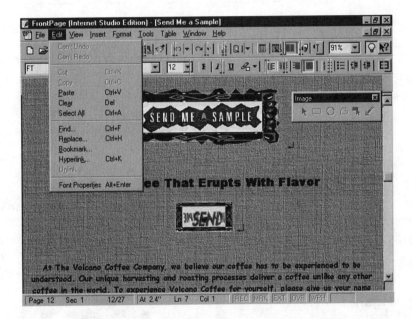

WebBots and hyperlinks are discussed in a later section, but I did want to briefly cover bookmarks here. You can use the FrontPage Editor to create bookmarks for different parts of your web page. Bookmarks enable the user to easily navigate and find different parts of your document. In the same way that you use bookmarks to navigate to your favorite web sites, a user can easily traverse your web sites through the creation of web page links to different sections.

To create a bookmark for your web page, execute the following steps:

1. Place your cursor within the bookmark text and choose the Bookmark option from the Edit menu. The Bookmark dialog window is displayed, enabling you to create a bookmark. You can either accept the default name for the bookmark or enter a new name.

2. Press OK to create the bookmark.

3. After you create a bookmark, you need to specify a link. Choose the Hyperlink option from the Edit menu. The Create Hyperlink dialog window is then displayed, enabling you to create a link to that bookmark on the web page.

4. Select the Open Pages tab and choose the web page from the list.

5. Choose the desired bookmark from the Bookmark combo box and press OK.

NOTE

You can create links to bookmarks on your web pages as well as pages on the World Wide Web. When you specify a link to a bookmark on the Web, use a # sign before the name of the bookmark. For example, to access the Overview bookmark for the sample web site below, you would enter:

```
http://www.nameofsite.com/default.htm#Overview.
```

Exploring the View Menu

The View menu enables you to customize the layout of the available toolbars. You can choose up to seven different toolbars to display on your title bar area. Some of the available toolbars include a formatting toolbar and a toolbar to include advanced controls like ActiveX controls and Java applets. Figure 5.11 illustrates the toolbars you can use to customize your development workspace.

Figure 5.11.

The View menu.

Exploring the Insert Menu

You will be using the Insert menu a lot to design your web page, because it has many useful options. Figure 5.12 shows the list of features and options that are available.

Figure 5.12.

The Insert menu.

Line Break

The first menu item is the Break command. This option enables you to insert a line break for the text in your web page. Selecting this menu item displays the Break Properties dialog window. Figure 5.13 shows the settings that are available for line breaks.

Figure 5.13.

Formatting line breaks.

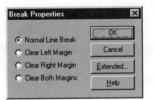

From this window, you can format a simple line break. There also are three other options enabling you to further customize the line break. If your web page contains images, you may want to consider these other options. The Clear Left Margin breaks the line and moves the text down to the first available line where there is no left margin, or the left margin is clear. If you don't choose this option, the text could be displayed to the right of an image instead of flush against the left margin.

The other two options are similar in nature. The Clear Right Margin provides a line break at the first clear right margin. The Clear Both Margins operates on both the left and the right margins. The Clear options can be useful, especially when dealing with floating images.

NOTE

Currently, only Microsoft and Netscape support the use of clear line breaks.

Horizontal Line

The Horizontal menu item enables you to place a horizontal line on your web page. Horizontal lines are very helpful in organizing your web page contents and bringing a sense and feeling of order to the user. To insert a horizontal line, place your cursor at the designated position on your web page and select the Horizontal option from the Insert menu. This action inserts a horizontal line. You can edit the properties by double-clicking the line. You also can choose the Horizontal Line Properties option from the shortcut menu for the line. Figure 5.14 shows the properties that you can choose to design the characteristics of a horizontal line.

Figure 5.14.

Designing a horizontal line.

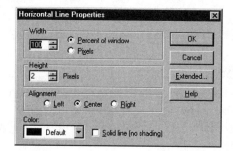

From this dialog window, you can set the Width, Height, and Alignment of the line, as well as the Color. You also can designate whether or not you want the line to be shaded (the default is a shaded line). A shaded line looks very good from a design perspective because the line appears to be engraved into the page.

Symbol

You can use the Symbol menu option to use special characters to create your web page. The Symbol option inserts the special character that you select from the list and can be used for HTML tag symbols such as <>.

Comments

The Comments menu item provides a way for you to easily insert comments for your HTML code. When you choose this menu option, a dialog window is displayed, enabling you to enter your comments in a multi-line text box. The FrontPage Editor formats your comments into the web page document. Comments provide an excellent way to document and explain your code. You should definitely use this feature when developing your web pages and applications.

NOTE

The Comments menu option actually uses the Annotation WebBot to format your comments. After you enter your text and press OK, you should notice a WebBot robot when you move your cursor over the text. All comments are displayed in purple.

Images

You can insert images into your web page by selecting the Image menu item from the Insert menu. You can choose to insert a local file or reference an image through a URL. To access the Image Properties dialog window, select the image and use the right mouse button to display the shortcut menu for the image. Once displayed, choose the Image Properties menu item. Figure 5.15 shows the available options related to image properties.

Figure 5.15.

Setting the image properties.

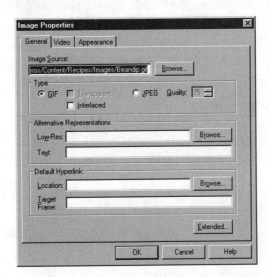

This window enables you to set the attributes for the image. The first field on the window displays the source for the image file. The next section displays the file type. If the image is a .gif file, you can set the attributes of the image to be interlaced and/or transparent. An interlaced GIF is an image that is displayed in stages on your web. This property is especially useful for really large files. The user receives a gradual picture of the image and can choose to wait for the full image to display or choose another action like navigating to another place on your site. The benefit is that the user won't have to wait for the full image to be displayed to get a picture of its purpose. Transparent GIFs are displayed with a clear, or transparent, background. The background color for the image is the same as the document background, so the image looks like part of the web page.

You also can convert GIF images to the JPEG format by clicking the JPEG radio button, enabling the Quality checkbox. You can use this checkbox to define the ratio of compression to use versus quality of the image. This setting defaults to 75 on a scale of 1 to 99. A higher number creates a better quality image at the cost of a larger file. You can choose alternative representations for your images. Examples include a lower resolution image or explanatory text for those browsers that can't display graphics.

The last section of this dialog window enables you to designate a hyperlink for the image. You can use this option if the user will click on the image to navigate to another location. You can establish a URL for the hyperlink in the Location field, and can specify a target frame if the user is traveling to a web page that uses frames.

The Appearance tab enables you to set layout and design properties for the image such as Height, Width, Alignment, Border Thickness, and Horizontal and Vertical Spacing.

Image Maps

You also can create image maps within the FrontPage Editor. Image maps enable you to define areas of the image that link to other documents, objects, and web pages. These areas are called hotspots. Each hotspot represents a portion of the image and is associated with a hyperlink to a URL or a target frame. The user can click on different hotspots to navigate to the pre-defined links that you have established. You can create polygonal, circular, and rectangular hotspots using the FrontPage Editor.

Figure 5.16 displays the Image toolbar, which you can use to create your image maps.

To create an image map, select the image and click on the type of hotspot that you want to create from the toolbar. You use the particular shape to define a specified region of the image for your hotspot. To create a rectangular hotspot, click the Rectangle object on the Image toolbar. As you move your mouse over to the image, you should notice that the mouse pointer becomes a pencil. This pencil enables you to draw your rectangular hotspot onto the image. Click and hold down the left mouse button to position the pencil where you want the first corner to be placed on the image (this corner is the anchor corner). Next, drag the rectangle to cover the portion of the image that you want defined for the hotspot and release the mouse button. This action creates the hotspot and instantly displays the Create Hyperlink dialog window. From this window, you can designate the target frame or URL hyperlink for the hotspot. You also can specify a link to a currently opened page.

Figure 5.16.

Exploring the Image toolbar.

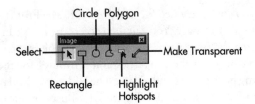

To create a circular hotspot, select the image and click on the Circle object on the Image toolbar. Position your cursor where you want the center of the circle to be placed and click and hold down the left mouse button. Next, drag the object to expand the circumference of the circle to the desired size of the hotspot. When you have designed the circle to be the correct size, release the left mouse button. This action creates the circular hotspot, and as with the rectangular hotspot, displays the Create Hyperlink dialog window, enabling you to specify the links for this hotspot.

To create a polygonal hotspot, select the image and click on the Polygon object on the Image toolbar. Position your cursor where you want the first point of the polygon to be placed and click the left mouse button. Next, drag the pencil to the next corner of the polygon and click the left mouse button again. Repeat this step until you're finished drawing the polygon. When you're finished, double-click the mouse. Again, the Create Hyperlink dialog window is displayed.

You can highlight the hotspots you have defined for an image by selecting the image and choosing the Highlight Hotspots object from the Image toolbar. This feature is very helpful when working with several hotspots for an image. When you use the Highlight Hotspots option, the image becomes clear and a colored outline is drawn around each of your hotspots. When you select a hotspot, the object looks black.

You also can use the Make Transparent object from the Image toolbar. This object enables you to make certain pixels in the image transparent. To use this tool, select the image and choose the Make Transparent object from the Image toolbar. Next, select the part of the image that you want to make transparent. As you move the mouse over to the image, you should notice that the mouse pointer changes to a pencil eraser. When you click on the desired area, the pixels become transparent.

Video

You also can insert video clips and background sound into your web pages. Choosing Video from the Insert menu displays the Video dialog window. This window enables you to enter a video clip file to use with your web page. You can either choose a local file or reference a file from the World Wide Web. The Browse push button enables you to search for the .avi file within your file directory structure.

After you choose a video file and press OK, the FrontPage Editor inserts a thumbnail of the file into the web page. You can then access the Image Properties dialog by selecting the video and using the right mouse button to access the shortcut menu. Select the Image Properties menu item to set the properties and attributes for the video clip. This dialog is used for inserting both images and videos. The Video tab displays, by default, enabling you to set the attributes for the video clip. Figure 5.17 illustrates the options that you can set for video clip files.

Figure 5.17.

Setting the properties for a video clip.

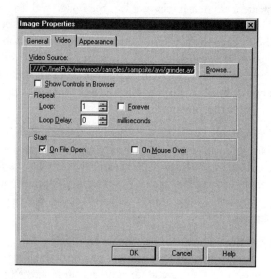

The first field on this window verifies the location of the source file. You can choose the Show Controls in Browser to display basic user controls for the video. These controls enable the user to play, rewind, fast forward, and stop the video. The Repeat section of the dialog window enables you to specify the number of times to replay the video. The Loop Delay defines the interval between each loop, or each time the video is replayed.

You can use the Start section to specify when the video begins to play. The options include after the file opens and when the user moves his mouse over the video within the web page. You can choose both of these options. An example of using both options would be if you wanted to play a video clip when your web page is initially opened. You may repeat the clip a couple of times and then enable the user to decide when the clip is played again. In this way the video doesn't dominate or interfere with the user experience. The Appearance tab enables you to set the layout and size attributes for the video frame.

5

NOTE The FrontPage Editor doesn't inherently provide a way to insert QuickTime video clips. You can, however, manually place these files into your web pages by using HTML tags.

Background Sound

You can add background sound or music to your web page by selecting Background Sound from the Insert menu, which displays the Background Sound dialog window. You can insert a local file or reference a file on the Web. For local files, the Browse push button enables you to explore files from different directories to which you have access. You can then choose a file and press OK. The background sound is then placed within the context of your web page.

To view the properties for the background sound, right-click the mouse anywhere on the web page and select the Page Properties option from the shortcut menu. The Page Properties dialog window is displayed, enabling you to view and edit the attributes for the current web page. The Background Sound section is displayed in the middle of this window. The source file that you insert is displayed in the Location field of this section.

One nice feature of Background Sound is that you can specify how many times to repeat the sound or music. The Forever checkbox enables you to continuously play the file until the web page is closed. Figure 5.18 demonstrates how to set the background sound for a web page, as well as other page properties.

Figure 5.18.

Setting the properties for background sound.

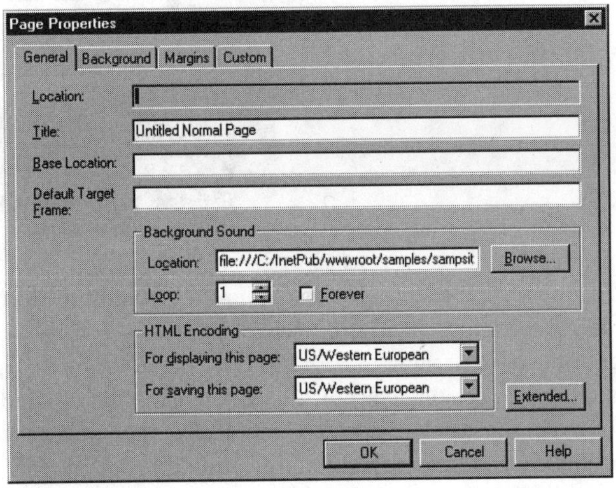

5

Page Properties dialog box:

General | Background | Margins | Custom

Location:
Title: Untitled Normal Page
Base Location:
Default Target Frame:

Background Sound
Location: file:///C:/InetPub/wwwroot/samples/sampsit   Browse...
Loop: 1   ☐ Forever

HTML Encoding
For displaying this page: US/Western European
For saving this page: US/Western European   Extended...

OK   Cancel   Help

WebBot Components

The Include WebBot automates the inclusion of other web pages into your existing page. For example, you could create a page that has a standard header and footer section for all of your pages. The Include WebBot enables you to merge this standard page with the page you're creating. These pages must exist within the same web.

When you select the Include WebBot component from the components list and press OK, the WebBot Include Component Properties dialog window is displayed. This window enables you to enter the URL reference to include on your web page. The FrontPage Editor retrieves this page from your web and inserts the page into your existing page. You will be able to view but not edit the contents of the inserted page. To edit the inserted page, you must open the original file.

The Search WebBot enables you to include full text searching for your web site. The Search WebBot component enables you to construct a custom Search form for your pages and web site. When you choose the Search WebBot from the components list, the WebBot Search Component Properties dialog window is displayed. This window enables you to design the layout of the Search form. Figure 5.19 illustrates the options that you can choose when designing this form.

Figure 5.19.

Setting the attributes for the Search form.

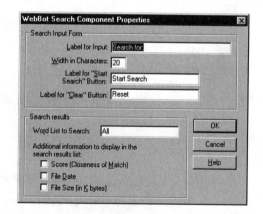

The top section enables you to design the layout of the form. You can specify the label text for the search input field and its character width. You also can enter the captions for the push buttons to begin the search and to clear the input field. These fields are set to Start Search and Reset by default. The bottom section of this dialog window enables you to customize the format of the search results. You can display the Score, or the closeness of the match, as well as the size and last creation/modification date for the file. The score is determined by the number of times that a search word is displayed on a page. After you select the properties and press OK, the Search form is inserted on your web page.

Remember, Visual InterDev also enables you to include full text search capability for your web site when you create a new project. The Search page that the New Project Wizard creates is more robust in that the page provides an explanation and specific instructions to the user about how to conduct the search. You will probably want to use the Visual InterDev Search.htm file when designing full text search features for your web site.

The TimeStamp WebBot enables you to indicate the last modification date and time of the web page. A timestamp can be very helpful to your users, letting them know the last time your web page information was updated. When you choose the TimeStamp WebBot from the components list, the WebBot TimeStamp Component Properties dialog window is displayed. From this window, you can choose to show either the last time the page was edited or the last time the page was automatically updated. The last time the page was edited refers to the last time you saved the file to the server. The last time the page was automatically updated consists of the previous event as well as when the page was last uploaded to the server and when the page's links were recalculated.

You can choose from many display formats to display the date and time. You can display none, one, or both of these fields. If you choose none for both the time and the date field, however, you negate the benefit and purpose of the timestamp. When you press OK, the timestamp is placed on your web page.

ActiveX Controls

The FrontPage Editor supports the use of ActiveX controls within your web page. Select the Other Components menu item to display a sub-menu list of other components. From the sub-menu, choose the ActiveX Controls item to display the ActiveX Controls Properties dialog window. Figure 5.20 displays the window for setting the attributes for your ActiveX control.

The top section of this window enables you to pick the ActiveX control and specify a name for this control. Once you have chosen the control, you can complete the other sections. The Layout section enables you to adjust properties for the control like the Alignment of the control, the Height and Width, the Horizontal and Vertical Spacing, and the thickness of the border for the control. The Alternative Representation field enables you to provide alternate HTML for those browsers that don't support ActiveX controls. You can use the Network Location field to specify a World Wide Web location for an ActiveX control and its associated data for controls that haven't been installed on the client machine.

WARNING

> ActiveX controls must be installed on the client machine in order for your web pages to use them.

Figure 5.20.

Choosing the ActiveX Control properties.

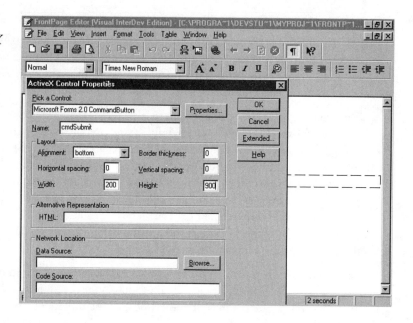

The Properties push button to the right of the Pick a Control combo box enables you to further establish attributes for the control. For example, the Common Dialog control has different features from the Data Command control. The Properties push button takes you to a dialog window specific to the properties of that control. Based on the ActiveX control you select, you should be able to set the proper attributes.

Java Applets

The method to insert Java applets is similar to that of ActiveX controls. To insert a Java applet, choose the Java Applet menu item from the list of other components. The Java Applet Properties dialog window is then displayed. Figure 5.21 displays the available properties for Java applets.

This dialog window is similar to the ActiveX Control Properties dialog in that you specify the size and layout settings for the applet. The top part of the window enables you to designate the name of the applet and the URL location. Also, you can establish parameter values to be used by the applet and a message for browsers that don't support Java applets. After you establish the properties for the Java applet and press OK, the FrontPage Editor places an icon on your web page to designate the position of the applet. You must use the Preview in Browser function to view the results. Figure 5.22 shows a web page that contains a Java applet using the FrontPage Editor.

Figure 5.21.

Setting the Java applet properties.

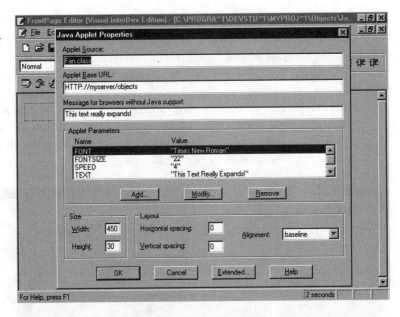

Figure 5.22.

The FrontPage Editor displays an icon as a reference to the Java applet.

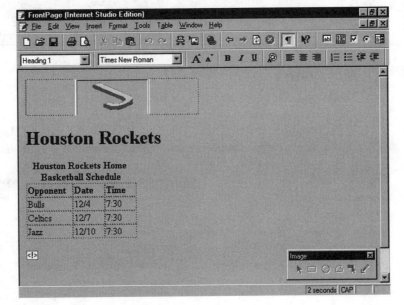

5

Plug-Ins

You can use plug-ins to support your web page. To insert a plug-in, choose the Plug-In option from the list of other components. This action displays the Plug-In Properties dialog window, enabling you to select the data file for the plug-in that you're going to use. From this dialog, you also can configure the size and layout as well as the message that will be displayed for browsers that don't support the use of plug-ins. You have the option of hiding the plug-in so that the plug-in is only displayed when it's activated. For example, you might want to show only a video player when the user chooses to view the video clip on your web page. Figure 5.23 displays the options for customizing plug-in objects.

Figure 5.23.

Setting the plug-in attributes.

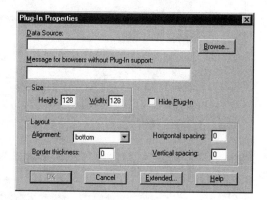

Marquee

The Marquee option enables you to display a marquee, or scrolling text, on your web page. This feature is a Microsoft extension to the HTML 3.x standards. When you select the Marquee option from the Insert menu, the Marquee Properties dialog window is displayed. Figure 5.24 highlights the options for adding a marquee to your web page.

Figure 5.24.

The Marquee Properties dialog window.

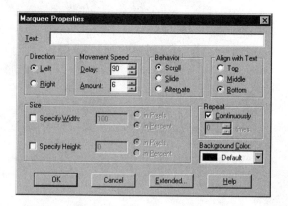

From this window, you can enter the marquee's contents in the Text field. Once you have specified the text that will be displayed, you can establish the marquee's behavior by configuring a variety of settings. The Direction section enables you to specify which way the text will scroll, while the Movement Speed indicates how fast the text will scroll. The Behavior section defines how the text will scroll. The Scroll option permits the characters to scroll across the page, and the Slide option causes the text to slide across the screen and stop. Finally, the Alternate option allows the text to slide back and forth across the page.

The middle section of this dialog window seen in Figure 5.24 enables you to define the size, including the height and width. Using the Repeat section, you can design the marquee to display continuously or to repeat a certain number of times. You also can set the background color of the marquee.

HTML Markup

The HTML Markup feature enables you to enter HTML tags and code that isn't directly supported by the FrontPage Editor. This code isn't validated by the FrontPage Editor and is denoted by the <?> tags. This command uses the HTML Markup WebBot to insert the non-supported HTML code.

Script

You can use the Script menu item to enter VBScript or JavaScript for your web page. When you select this option, you see the Script dialog window, from which you select the script language. The choices are VBScript, JavaScript, or Other. The VBScript option is selected by default. If you choose VBScript as the scripting language, you also can decide if you want to run the script on the server. The Script Wizard can be used for both VBScript and JavaScript. The FrontPage Editor Script Wizard is the same Script Wizard that is included with Visual InterDev.

Hyperlinks

You can use this option to create a hyperlink to another web page. The page destination could be a page within your web site or a page at another web site.

Both relative and direct links can be used between web pages. A relative link is used to access pages within your web server. With a relative link, you don't specify the full URL address, because you already know the protocol and have access to the web server's files. When you use a relative link, you're accessing the linked page in relation to the current page. There are several ways to specify a relative link. Table 5.1 illustrates different types of relative links and their meaning to the browser.

Table 5.1. Relative link options.

Relative Link	Browser Action
Page.htm	Link to a file in the current directory
../Page.htm	Link to a file in the parent directory
Within/Page.htm	Link to a file in the Within sub-directory
../../Page.htm	Link to a file two directories above current directory

A direct link indicates the full path name for the linked file. You don't have to specify the protocol for files that exist on local web servers. Table 5.2 illustrates two ways to designate a direct hyperlink.

Table 5.2. Direct link options.

Direct Link	Browser Action
http://www.AC.Com/	Link using the full URL
http://www.AC.Com/	Link using full path name and filename
/AC.Com/outlook/o_frintro.htm	Link without the protocol

To create a hyperlink, choose the Hyperlink menu item from the Insert menu. The Create Hyperlink dialog window is then displayed. The World Wide Web tab is the default display and enables you to specify the Hyperlink Type and URL address. You also can specify a Target Frame if you're linking to a page that uses frames.

An Overview of a Web Page Development Team

The final thoughts for the day surround an overview of a typical Web development team. The reason for discussing the topic in this lesson is to show how the FrontPage Editor and Visual InterDev work together to facilitate the development process. The following sections discuss possible development team member roles and tasks, and conclude with information about how the work can be integrated using Visual InterDev and its associated products.

Understanding the Roles of a Typical Development Team

Most Web development projects consist of the same types of team-member roles. The ratio of team member to role may not be a one-to-one correspondence. The same person might serve in multiple capacities due to the size of the project. Also, the scope of the project may determine that a role isn't needed. The following roles are typical for almost every Web-based application development effort:

- [ ] Designer
- [ ] Content Author
- [ ] Application Developer
- [ ] Graphic Artist
- [ ] Database Developer
- [ ] Architect
- [ ] Project Manager

Each of these roles is explained in detail in the following sections.

Designer

The main goal of a designer is to translate user requirements into the design of the Web application. This person is responsible for initially gathering the requirements from the users or target audience. The designer then takes these requirements and builds the design of the web site. Taking the technical competence of the users into consideration, the designer creates an effective user interface design and metaphor for the application. Finally, the designer works with all of the other roles to communicate the needs of the application's intended audience.

The designer should possess good communication and interpersonal skills because he or she has to communicate technical concepts to the users in simple terms. Similarly, this person should understand the technical implications of the design that is built and be able to communicate with the other, more technical members of the team about these issues. The designer is a key point person for ensuring the success of the application. You must begin with a good design for your web site. Permeating a bad design throughout the development process can be disastrous.

5

Content Author

The content author is usually a subject-matter expert about the business. This person also could be a marketing-type professional who knows how to effectively communicate the messages of the business. The person who fulfills this role will differ based on the type of Web-based application being built. In general, the content author participates in the development of the application by providing knowledge about the business or organization. This person also plays an active role in writing the content of the web pages.

Application Developer

The application developer is responsible for programming the logic of the application. This person translates the application design into technical specifications. An application developer should have a technical background and be very knowledgeable about the different technologies for developing Web-based applications. Application developers have different skill sets and backgrounds as well as levels of technical prowess. Roles for application developers can include developing the more advanced HTML code, programming the scripting and application processing logic, and developing advanced server programs like Active Server Components.

Graphic Artist

The graphic artist can make or break a web site. Your project may not have the luxury of including a professional graphic artist. This role, however, should be assigned to a person who understands basic concepts of graphics and the Web. This person should possess excellent user interface design skills. Also, this person should understand how to create and use effective images for your web site. The graphic artist also should understand the technical implications of implementing graphics on a web page. This person works with the designer, content author, application developer, and architect very closely.

Database Developer

The main role of the database developer is to translate the user and application requirements into technical requirements for the database. The ideal situation involves separating the role of database developer and database administrator. The database administrator creates the logical and physical design of the database and administers the database during the entire application development process. The true database developer focuses on programming the more extensive application code for interacting with the database. The database developer can create and test stored procedures and triggers for the database as well as dynamic SQL within the application. Some team members assume both the database developer and application developer roles if the individual is well-versed in both application- and database-programming.

Architect

The architect is responsible for ensuring the technical accuracy and quality of the architecture and infrastructure for the application and web site. This person should have deep technical knowledge and skills in the areas of networking and architecture concepts concerning the Internet and the World Wide Web. This person serves as the backbone to implementing a great application, and works closely with the database developer, application developer, and designer to understand the application goals. The architect then builds an architecture and infrastructure that can support the needs of the application.

Project Manager

I saved this role for last, and not because the project manager is not performing any work. On the contrary, this role is very critical to the success of any project. This person must work with all of the other team members to ensure that the application development project is a success. The project manager must possess good communication and interpersonal skills and be able to understand everything to some degree. The project manager must be able to communicate with all of the other team members on both a technical and functional level. This person must possess excellent decision-making and problem-solving skills and be able to resolve issues between competing application requirements and, sometimes, competing team members. Finally, the project manager must be able to properly plan the development effort and ensure that the project keeps on track.

Understanding the Role of Visual InterDev

Now that you have learned about the different roles of a development project, I want to focus specifically on how Visual InterDev can facilitate the efforts of the different team members.

As you have learned over the last few days, Visual InterDev provides several HTML editors for designing and developing the content of the web pages. The FrontPage Editor provides an excellent tool for the content author to generate the web pages for your site. Whether the content author uses the commercial version of FrontPage or the FrontPage Editor for Visual InterDev, the results can be used with your Visual InterDev project. An application developer can use Visual InterDev to integrate application logic in the form of client- and server-side scripts with these HTML web pages.

The database developer can use the Visual Data Tools to easily incorporate database interaction. The graphic artist can use the Image Composer to create professional-looking images and graphics for the web pages. Once created, these images can be included in your Visual InterDev project.

5

Visual InterDev is an excellent tool for both consolidating the various technologies of the Web and integrating the different roles of a development project.

Summary

Today's lesson has been packed with knowledge. You have learned about a very robust and powerful tool that can definitely enhance your productivity. The FrontPage Editor can be appreciated by both content authors and developers. Content authors can acknowledge the FrontPage Editor for its ease of use, and developers appreciate the time that the FrontPage Editor saves them in creating the routine HTML code.

This morning, the lesson introduced you to the FrontPage Editor for Visual InterDev. You learned about the benefits of the FrontPage Editor and its visual WYSIWYG environment. Next, you learned in detail about the features of the FrontPage Editor, discovering some of the more robust aspects of the editor, including character formatting, tables, forms, images, and advanced controls. Toward the middle of the day, you received a guided, in-depth tour of how to use the FrontPage Editor to construct your web pages. At the end of the day, you learned about some of the typical roles on a Web development project and how Visual InterDev and the FrontPage Editor can facilitate these roles.

So far, the topics have focused more on left-brain topics. Tomorrow, be prepared to use your creative right brain as you explore the world of images and multimedia.

Q&A

Q Is the FrontPage Editor exactly the same as FrontPage 97?

A The FrontPage Editor for Visual InterDev is an implementation of FrontPage 97. They aren't the same product. The FrontPage Editor and FrontPage 97 are completely compatible, however. The FrontPage Editor includes most of the functionality of FrontPage 97. You may notice some FrontPage 97 features that aren't included in the FrontPage Editor for Visual InterDev. The good thing is that you can use either product and integrate the results with Visual InterDev projects.

Q How do I view my HTML source code once I have constructed a web page using the FrontPage Editor?

A You can use either the FrontPage Editor or the Visual InterDev HTML Source Editor to view and manipulate your generated HTML code. Within the FrontPage Editor, you can choose the View menu and select the HTML menu item. The View or Edit HTML dialog window is then displayed. This window displays the generated HTML and, as the name suggests, enables you to view and edit the

5

HTML code. You also can choose to open the HTML page from within Visual InterDev using the HTML Source Editor. Select the file and choose the Open With item from the shortcut menu.

Q Does the FrontPage Editor support the use of other image formats besides GIF and JPEG?

A The FrontPage Editor enables you to choose other image formats besides the GIF and JPEG format. These other formats include BMP, TIFF, PCX, WMF, RAS, TGA, EPS, and PCX. The FrontPage Editor converts these images, however, to the GIF or JPEG format based on the number of colors in the image. The GIF format is used for images with 256 or less colors. The FrontPage Editor converts images with more than 256 colors to the JPEG format.

Workshop

Now that you have become familiar with the FrontPage Editor, you are going to create a web page using some of the techniques and features that you have learned so far. The objective of this lesson is to help you understand and learn how to use FrontPage in your development effort. You get to choose the idea and content for the web page. You should build several web pages that use the following features:

☐ A bulleted list

☐ Tables

☐ ActiveX controls

☐ Images with hotspots

☐ Horizontal lines

☐ Special character formatting like bold and centered text

Quiz

1. Name two types of advanced components that you can insert into your web page using the FrontPage Editor.

2. What are the three types of hotspots that you can create for your image maps?

3. What is the difference between an application developer and a content author?

4. What does WYSIWYG stand for?

5. What is the difference between a relative and a direct link?

5

Quiz Answers

1. Possible answers include:

   ActiveX controls

   Java applets

   Plug-ins

   PowerPoint animation

2. Rectangular, circular, and polygonal.

3. An application developer is responsible for coding the script and programming logic and components for the application. The content author usually generates and constructs the HTML content for the web pages.

4. WYSIWYG stands for What You See Is What You Get.

5. A relative link is used to view web pages that are local to a web server. You don't have to use the full path name with a relative link. A direct link is used to specify the full path filename for a file.

Day 6

Spicing Up Your Interface with Images and Multimedia

An effective user interface for your web site can mean the difference between a highly used web page and one that is banished to a desert to die a slow and painful death. Images and multimedia are important aspects of your web pages. Today's lesson concentrates on three specific tools that help you create and manage images and multimedia files. These products are included with Visual InterDev as separate applications. The images and multimedia files that you create can be integrated into your Visual InterDev projects.

A majority of today's lesson focuses on composing images. You will gain an understanding of Image Composer and learn how it uses sprites to enable you to interact with objects and images. You will then discover all of Image Composer's features. During this part of the day, you will discover how to use Image Composer to create professional and visually appealing images. You also will learn how to vitalize your images and make them come alive on your web pages.

Later in the day, the lesson teaches you how to compose music and sounds using Music Producer. In this section, you will receive a definition of Music Producer, an overview of its features, and a tour of how to use Music Producer to create sounds and musical compositions.

Once you have created multimedia and images, you need a way to manage these files. The Media Manager provides support for managing a range of multimedia files. Toward the end of the day, the lesson focuses on the Media Manager and how you can use this tool to properly organize your files.

The last section of the day is crucial, because it shows you how to integrate your results into your Visual InterDev applications.

What Is Image Composer?

Images are an extremely important part of your web page. Images help invigorate the web page and enhance the user experience. Image Composer provides the tool you need to create exciting and graphical images that enrich the look of your web pages.

Image Composer, first included as a part of the bonus pack with FrontPage 97, enables you to create and compose images as well as customize existing images for your web pages. You also can use your images for other uses like presentations. Image Composer provides a comprehensive environment in which to construct your images into *compositions*.

 A *composition* is comprised of an image or a group of images. When you work with images within the Image Composer environment, you save your workspace as a composition.

Image Composer is a separate application included with Visual InterDev. You can easily integrate the images that you create with Image Composer into your Visual InterDev project. Image Composer supports many of the industry file formats for images, including GIF, JPEG, TIFF, BMP, and Adobe Photoshop files. The major design aspects of Image Composer combine powerful features with ease of use.

You don't have to be a professional graphic artist to use the features of Image Composer. If you have used other graphics packages, you will be able to transfer that knowledge to the Image Composer environment. Many tool palettes are provided to help you during the creation of your images. Image Composer supplies many images and enables you to create your own. You can even use the Impressionist plug-in to apply special effects to your images. Image Composer also supports the use of Kai's Power Tools and Adobe Photoshop plug-ins.

Image Composer combines a non-intimidating, user-friendly editor with very robust features for composing images. Before you discover more about these powerful features, you need to understand the concept of sprites.

What Are Sprites?

Every image that you insert or create using Image Composer is considered a sprite.

 A *sprite* is an image that has a defined shape. In other words, the shape of the object is the image. Sprites have a transparent background; therefore, the shape of the sprite is defined by the part of the sprite that isn't transparent.

Image Composer differs from other graphical software tools by enabling you to interact with the actual shape of the object. With other tools, you work with the image and its standard rectangular background. Figure 6.1 depicts the shape of an image using a tool that doesn't support sprites.

Figure 6.1.

A standard image object.

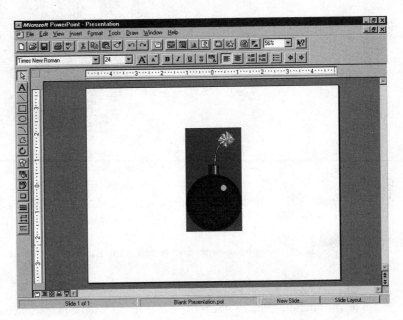

In contrast, a sprite has a transparent background. A sprite is represented by four *channels*: red, green, blue, and alpha.

 A *channel* provides the method for color to be transferred to a computer monitor display. Each pixel in an image is defined by a channel.

These four channels are sometimes called RGBA channels. The first three channels determine the mix of colors for your sprite. You can use the basic colors of red, green, and blue to adjust the color of your sprite, or combine these colors to produce a variety of others. The alpha channel defines the transparency of the sprite. You can adjust the alpha channel for a sprite on a scale of zero to 100 percent. A lower alpha channel percentage causes the sprite to become more transparent. An alpha channel of 100% makes the sprite completely opaque, or non-transparent.

Figure 6.2.

A sprite.

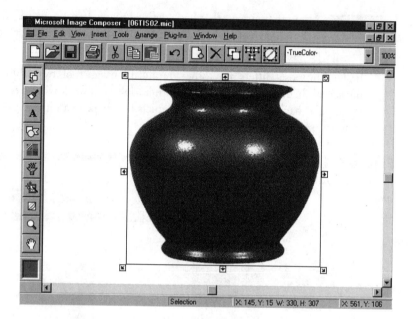

In Figure 6.2, notice that the sprite is selected and is surrounded by a box with many arrows. This box is called a *bounding box*.

NEW TERM   A *bounding box* defines and outlines the shape of the sprite.

The bounding box in Figure 6.2 contains handles indicated by arrows. Each of the arrows on the bounding box represent handles that you can use to manipulate the size and shape of the sprite. Based upon what you are doing, the bounding box may contain different types of handle indicators. For example, if you're painting the object, each handle is denoted by a paintbrush.

The *stack* determines the order in which the sprites appear in your composition.

NEW TERM   The *stack*, or z-order, refers to the numerical order of each sprite in a composition. The stack reflects the property of depth for a composition.

Spicing Up Your Interface with Images and Multimedia   165

Each sprite is designated by a stack number that determines where it displays in relation to other sprites within a composition. When you add or create a sprite to your composition, Image Composer places this object on the top of the stack. The stack is numbered from front to back, so the object assigned the number 1 is on top of the stack of objects. The sprite with the number 2 is displayed next, and so on. You can change the stack order of the sprites in your composition. The stack makes the process of moving images a lot more intuitive. Figure 6.3 illustrates the concept of the stack for a group of sprites.

Figure 6.3.
Visualizing the stack.

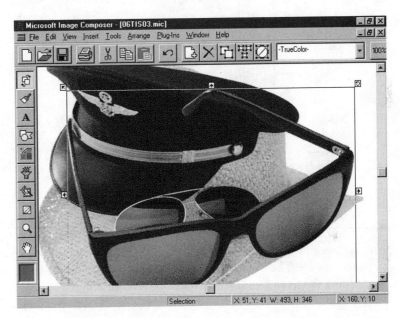

Sprites are a new and powerful concept. This new and intuitive approach to working with objects should make your life easier when you create images for your web pages.

Image Composer Features

Image Composer contains many robust and powerful features that enable you to manipulate your sprites and compositions. This section gives you an overview of those features and explains their potential.

Understanding the Workspace

Image Composer provides a new and flexible workspace in which you can interact with your images. Figure 6.4 displays the main workspace to construct your images.

Figure 6.4.

Image Composer's environment.

Toolbar Area

Composition Guide

Toolbox

Extended Workspace

Status Bar Area

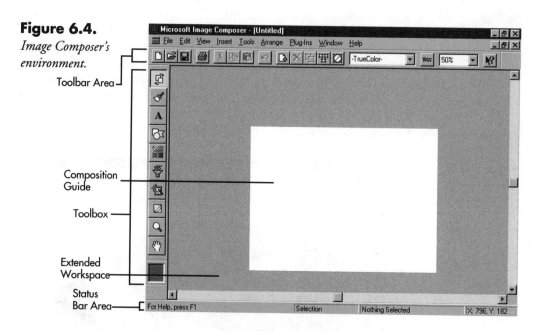

There are two distinct areas of the Image Composer environment: the Composition Guide and the Extended Workspace. The Composition Guide is the main working area of Image Composer workspace. The size of this working area can be easily adjusted. The images that are placed within the Composition Guide area are included in your composition when you save the file. The Extended Workspace serves as a scratch pad area. You can move different sprites to this area until you're ready to include them in your composition. Sprites that are in this area aren't included in the composition but are saved in the file.

You can use the Composition Guide and the Extended Workspace to develop your composition in stages and preview the results in your web page. For example, you could insert three images, placing two of the sprites in the Composition Guide and the other sprite in the Extended Workspace. All three files are included in the file when it is saved. When you integrate this composition in your web page, the only sprites that are displayed on the web page are the two sprites that were included in the Composition Guide. Later, when you're ready to include the third sprite in your composition, you can easily access it from the Extended Workspace and move it to the exact position within the Composition Guide. This process can help you rapidly develop your compositions and test them through an iterative process.

Another area on the workspace is the Toolbox, which is located to the left of the main workspace. You use these tools to change specific attributes related to a particular sprite.

The toolbar area at the top of the workspace displays standard tools that are available to interact with files. The toolbar also includes some options that relate to changing the properties of the objects and the workspace.

The status bar area at the bottom of the workspace indicates information about the workspace as well as the sprites that are located within the workspace. The left part of the status bar displays help information, including the names of tools as the mouse passes over them. The middle part of the window shows information about a selected sprite, including x and y coordinates, height, and width. The far right area of the status bar displays the x and y coordinates of the cursor.

Exploring the Toolbox

The Toolbox includes many tools for you to alter the different characteristics of sprites with, including the arrangement, shapes, colors, patterns, and effects. The Toolbox is displayed to the left of Image Composer's workspace. Figure 6.5 depicts the options that are available from Image Composer's Toolbox.

Figure 6.5.
Using the Toolbox.

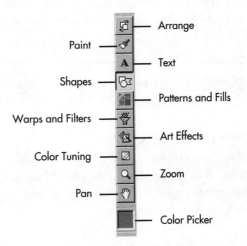

The first eight tools on the Toolbox focus on changing specific characteristics of a sprite. The next two, Zoom and Pan, enable you to change aspects of the workspace. The last option can be used with the other tools to pick various colors for your sprites. When you select most of the tools, a palette is displayed on the workspace. This palette represents features specific to the tool, which you can configure. The following section presents each of the available tools and their purpose.

Arrange

The Arrange tool enables you to arrange and resize the shape of a sprite. You also can rotate and flip the sprite. The Apply push button enables you to instantly view the desired effect. The Arrange Palette offers a feature to crop or extend the bounding box for the image. You can use buttons that enable you to establish a home position for the object, and once this position is established, you can move the sprites around and then return the sprite back to this default position. You also can lock the position of the sprite. An object that's locked can't be moved until it's unlocked.

Paint

The Paint option enables you to paint a particular color on the sprite using various tools including a paintbrush, an airbrush, a pencil, and other types of applicators. You can precisely paint the pixels as well as smear and spray the color onto the sprite.

Text

Using the Text option, you can create text sprites for your compositions. Image Composer provides many different fonts to choose from to format your text.

Shapes

The Shapes tool enables you to create both structured and free-form shapes. You also can extract the color and texture of a sprite and apply that to another sprite object.

Patterns and Fills

Using Patterns and Fills, you can add various patterns and fill colors to your sprites and can transfer colors from one sprite to the other. You also can use the Gradient Ramp to design a blended color to apply to your sprites. With this feature, you can choose a combination of up to four colors.

Warps and Filters

Warps and Filters enables you to add unique effects to your sprite. You can choose from different warping effects and outlines, including shadows and edges. Filters enable you to change the display of the sprite. For example, you can change the sprite to appear blurry. Color enhancements manipulate the color of the sprite. For instance, you can select Wash to cause the sprite to appear more transparent.

Art Effects

Art Effects provides very robust features to transform you into a graphic artist. You can apply these effects to your images to create professional-looking images. The artistic styles include three specific mediums to apply to your sprite:

1. The Paint option causes the sprite to make it look as though you painted it using a certain style.

2. The Sketch option applies to drawings and makes the sprite assume a specific drawing style like charcoal, pastel, or ink.

3. The Graphics option causes the sprite to look as though it was created from objects such as a piece of cloth or an ink stamp.

Color Tuning

You can use the Color Tuning option to alter the color attributes of the sprite like contrast, hue, and brightness. You also can adjust the four channels of the color of the sprite.

Zoom and Pan

The Zoom option pertains to the view of your composition in the workspace. You can place your cursor on a certain area of the Composition Guide to magnify, or zoom in on, the selected area. This feature can be very helpful when you want to view or change very fine details of a sprite. The Pan tool is in the shape of a hand and enables you to drag a sprite to different areas of the workspace.

Color Picker

The Color Picker displays a selected color for a sprite. You can choose from many different colors. You can drag the current color that is displayed on the Color Picker to the color swatches that are displayed on some of the tool palette options. For example, if you use the Warps and Filters tool and choose the shadow option from the tool palette, you can drag the color from the Color Picker to the Color box on the palette. Conversely, you can drag the color from the Color box on the palette to the Color Picker, thereby changing the color of this tool.

Exploring the Toolbar

The toolbar provides standard options for working and interacting with individual sprites and Image Composer workspace. Figure 6.6 displays a close-up of the available toolbar options.

6

Figure 6.6.
Image Composer toolbar.

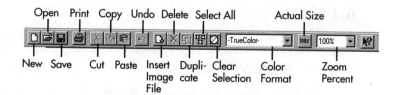

The first four toolbar options concern file operations. These items enable you to create a new composition as well as open, save, and print the current composition. The next four toolbar items provide standard editing features including Cut, Copy, Paste, and Undo.

The last five tools on the toolbar focus specifically on manipulating sprites in the workspace. The first icon enables you to insert an image file into the current composition. When you press this button, the Insert Image File dialog window display enables you to choose an image file to insert into the composition. The next icon deletes a selected sprite within the workspace. You can use the Duplicate tool to duplicate a sprite and its properties and copy it to the workspace.

TIP
You also can duplicate a sprite by pressing the Ctrl (Control) key and then clicking on the sprite to drag a duplicate of it to another area of the workspace.

This option saves a step from the traditional two-step process of copying an object to the clipboard and pasting it to the workspace. You can select all of the sprites in Image Composer workspace by pressing the Select All option. The next icon clears the current selection.

The Color Format combo box displays the available color palettes for the composition. Color palettes are covered in the section "Creating a Composition." The Actual Size button restores the size of the composition to its full size. You can use the combo box to the right of this button to increase or reduce the size of the current composition.

NOTE
The current composition refers to all of the sprites that are located within the Composition Guide area.

Working with Image Composer

As you can see, Image Composer provides a very robust set of features. This part of the lesson focuses on how to use some of the more relevant features to create your images. While this won't be an exhaustive tour of all of Image Composer's functions, the basics are covered to get you started. You can then venture out on your own and explore other Image Composer features based upon this foundation.

Working with Compositions

The first building block you need to learn involves working with compositions. Remember, the composition includes those sprites that are located within the Composition Guide. When you open Image Composer, a new workspace is displayed. This workspace consists of the Composition Guide and the Extended Workspace, which you learned about earlier.

The basic component of a composition is a sprite. You can insert an existing image into the composition or use Image Composer to create a new sprite. Existing images can be included in your composition in one of two ways. The first method involves using the Open menu item from the File menu. The second way to insert a sprite into your composition is to use the Insert menu. The following sections explore both of these alternatives.

Opening and Saving Images

Table 6.2 denotes the file formats that Image Composer enables you to open and save.

Table 6.2. Supported file types.

File Type	Description
.ACC	Altamira Composer
.BMP	Windows Bitmap
.GIF	CompuServe Graphics Interchange
.JPG	Joint Photographic Experts Group
.MIC	Microsoft Image Composer
.PSD	Adobe Photoshop
.TGA	Targa
.TIF	Tagged-Image Format File

6

You can open an image by selecting Open from the File menu. This action displays the Open dialog window. From this window, you can open any of the image file types specified in Table 6.2. Figure 6.7 demonstrates the capability of the Open dialog window.

Figure 6.7.

Opening an image.

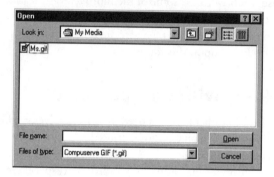

Once you have selected a file, Image Composer creates a new workspace for this image. To save a composition, you can choose Save from the File menu, which saves the file to the default format of the image. You also can save images to one of the other supported formats by using the Save As menu item.

 NOTE

When you save a file to a format other than the Microsoft Image Composer format, you lose any image that isn't contained within your Composition Guide. Image Composer flattens all Composition Guide sprites into one image and crops the rest of the images residing in the Extended Workspace. In other words, you lose the power of Image Composer to provide a flexible workspace for your images.

The Save Selection As menu option enables you to save the currently selected object. This object can reside anywhere within the Image Composer workspace, including the Composition Guide and the Extended Workspace. Figure 6.8 depicts the available options on the Save Selection As dialog window.

 TIP

You can use this option to save individual sprites as specific file types. This option can alleviate some of the problems mentioned in the preceding Note. For example, you can save all of your sprites as a Microsoft Image Composer file. Then, if you want to manipulate a certain sprite on your workspace and save it as GIF, you can use the Save Selection As option to accomplish this task.

Also, you can use the Save Copy As menu item to save a copy of the current composition to a specific file format. This action doesn't affect the original file format.

Figure 6.8.

Saving a selected sprite.

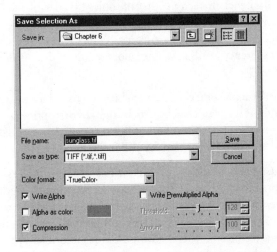

Figure 6.8 shows the many options available for saving a selected sprite. These options are enabled or disabled based on the file type that you select in the Save as type combo box. The top section of this dialog window is pretty self-explanatory. I will briefly describe the options in the bottom section, starting with the Color format combo box. This option indicates the color palette for the image file. The default is TrueColor, which represents a 24-bit color palette. Other choices for the color palette include Balanced Ramp, Gray Ramp, and Black and White. You also can create your own custom 8-bit color formats. Once you select a color palette, a description of this palette is displayed to the right of the Color format combo box.

NOTE

The difference between 24-bit true color and other 8-bit custom color palettes involves the number of available colors. When you use 24-bit color, you have all 16 million colors at your disposal. For monitors that can't display all of these colors, you may want to design an image using your own 8-bit custom color palette. 8-bit color limits your choices to 256 colors. Image Composer supports both 8-bit and 24-bit color for your images.

6

The Write Alpha checkbox preserves the alpha channel along with the other three channels in your image. Remember, the alpha channel depicts the amount of transparency that an object contains. When you select this option, the Write Premultiplied Alpha becomes enabled. Image Composer calculates a pre-multiplied alpha along with the other red, green, and blue channels. The Alpha as color checkbox enables you to assign a color for the transparency characteristics of the object. By default, an image that is transparent assumes the color of the background object. This object could be another sprite or the Composition Guide. If you select the Alpha as color option, you can establish a color for the image's transparency attributes. The color swatch to the left of this option enables you to choose a color.

The Compression checkbox enables you to reduce the size of the image file. You can use the Amount slider and edit box to the right of this option to adjust the compression ratio. A high number reduces the size of the file, but also lowers the quality of the image. The Amount slider and edit box are enabled for JPEG file formats.

The Threshold slider and edit box relate to the Alpha as color option. If you select a color for a sprite's alpha channel, you can specify the transparency threshold for all pixels on the image. The threshold determines what pixels will display the transparency color. A pixel that has a transparency level below the threshold amount displays the transparent color, and a pixel that has a transparency level above the threshold level appears opaque and doesn't display the transparency color.

Inserting Images into an Existing Composition

Another way to include sprites in your compositions involves the Insert menu. You have two options for inserting images using Image Composer. First, you can insert an image from a file. Choose the Insert menu and select the From File option. The Insert From File dialog window is displayed, enabling you to choose the desired image file. When you press the OK button, the image is inserted as a sprite into your composition.

TIP

> You can specify All Supported Formats from the Files of type combo box to look for all the file formats that Image Composer supports. This feature can save you time when you're looking for more than one image type.

The other option is to insert the image from a PhotoCD. This option is specifically designed for photographs that have been created using the Kodak PhotoCD discs. Other PhotoCD formats can be used by choosing the From File option.

Changing the Composition Properties

You can choose the Composition Properties menu item from the File menu to change the properties related to a composition. The Composition Properties dialog window enables you to view the properties for the composition as well as change the size and color of the composition. Figure 6.9 displays the properties for a sample composition.

Figure 6.9.

*The Composition
Properties dialog
window.*

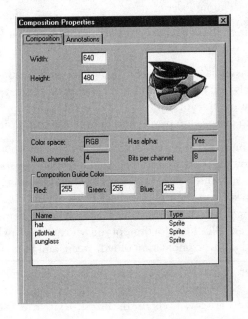

 TIP You also can access this window by right-clicking the mouse on the Composition Guide area and selecting Properties from the shortcut menu.

The Composition Properties dialog window has two tabs: Composition and Annotations. Composition is the default display tab. The first two fields in this view enable you to see and change the height and width of the composition. The picture to the right of these fields provides a thumbnail version of the composition. The next section on this tab displays the color properties of the composition. You can't alter these fields. The Color space field indicates the method for representing the colors of the sprite.

In Figure 6.9, the method for representing the colors is RGB, which means that a combination of red, green, and blue were used to achieve the desired color for the sprite.

Other available methods include HWB and HSV. HWB uses a mix of hue, whiteness, and blackness to achieve a color, while HSV uses hue, saturation, and value to produce the desired color.

NEW TERM *Hue* defines the frequency of light waves that pass through an object. The hue distinguishes one color from another. You can adjust the hue using the Color Tuning Palette.

NEW TERM *Saturation* refers to the amount of gray that is reflected in the color.

The Has alpha field indicates whether the sprite includes a transparency channel. The Num. channels field denotes the number of channels that are being used by the composition. The maximum value for this field is 4. The Bits per channel field shows the number of bits that are used per pixel to display the color of the composition.

The Composition Guide Color section enables you to view and alter the colors for the composition's background. The default is white, represented by the values of 255 in the Red, Green, and Blue fields. To change the background color of the composition, click on the color swatch to the right of these fields. The Color Picker dialog window is displayed, enabling you to choose the desired color. You also change the individual numbers of the Red, Green, and Blue fields for those of you who like to paint by numbers. The color swatch change is based on the combination of red, green, and blue that you choose.

The Sprites list enables you to see the individual sprites that make up the composition. You can view an individual sprite's properties by double-clicking on an item in the list. You also can select the item and choose the Properties item from the shortcut menu. Figure 6.10 shows the properties for an individual sprite within a composition.

From the Sprite Properties dialog window, you can view the properties for the selected sprite, including height, width, x and y coordinates, and color properties. You can change the name of the sprite from this window.

You can press the Apply push button at the bottom of the Composition Properties dialog window to see the effects of your changes. If you like the changes, press the OK button to confirm the modifications. Press the Cancel button to negate the proposed changes.

The Annotations tab enables you to view and document changes to the composition. You can record specific types of updates and changes including the person responsible and the date of the change. The Annotations database can help you organize your workgroup by documenting the composition process.

6

Figure 6.10.

The Sprite Properties dialog window.

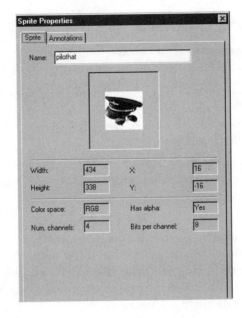

Scanning Images

Image Composer supports the use of scanning device and digital cameras that are based on the industry-standard TWAIN interface to insert sprites into a composition. To scan an image into a composition, select Scan from the File menu. A sub-menu is displayed, revealing two options. Choose the Select Scan Source menu item and pick the scanner that you're going to use. After confirming this choice, select the Acquire Scan item from the Scan sub-menu. Image Composer begins importing your image.

WARNING

> You must attach and configure a scanner for your computer to execute these commands.

Creating a Composition

So far, you have been introduced to the many features of Image Composer. You have learned about the different techniques to work with sprites to create a composition. In this section, you get a chance to create your own composition. Not every option and feature are covered, but you will discover how to use sprites and various colors and effects within Image Composer to construct dynamic compositions.

6

Creating a Sprite

The first step in building a composition is creating a sprite. The following instructions guide you through this process. Make sure that you set the Zoom Percent to 50%.

1. Click on the Color Picker icon on the Image Composer toolbar to change the color of your sprite. Select the True Color tab and enter 102, 102, 102 for the Red, Green, and Blue values, respectively. Press OK. The Color Picker should now reflect a dark gray color.

2. Click the Shapes icon on the Image Composer Toolbox. The Shapes Palette is displayed in the workspace.

3. Choose the Rectangle object.

4. Move your cursor to the Composition Guide. Notice that the mouse pointer has changed to a rectangle to indicate the type of shape that you have chosen. Click the mouse in the upper left-hand corner of the Composition Guide and drag the mouse to the lower right-hand corner to draw a rectangle the size of the Composition Guide. When you have properly sized the rectangle, release the mouse button, and the shape is drawn.

5. Click the Render push button to change the color of the rectangle to gray. You also can right-click the mouse on the rectangle and choose the Render Solid menu item to change the color.

6. Click the Rectangle object again and draw another rectangle that covers about 3/4 of the inside of the existing rectangle.

7. When you have drawn the inner rectangle, click the Erase option to erase the specified area of the rectangle.

Analyzing the Results

You have just created your first sprite. First, you selected a color for the sprite by using the Color Picker. You can use either the True Color tab or the Custom Palette for choosing colors. In the example, you entered values directly into the Red, Green, and Blue fields. The Custom Palette tab enables you to select from a choice of 256 colors. Figure 6.11 shows the Color Picker dialog window using the True Color display tab.

The Color Ramp shows the true color options and is located on the left-hand side of the dialog window. There are two handles that surround the Color Ramp. The top handle changes the hue, and the left handle adjusts the amount of blackness that is mixed with the hue.

The Whiteness Ramp is to the right of the Color Ramp. The right handle to the side manipulates the amount of whiteness that displays in the color.

6

Figure 6.11.

Choosing the true colors.

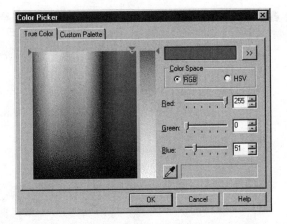

The New Color to use box appears in the upper right-hand corner of the dialog window, and depicts the original color of the swatch in the left half of the box, along with the new color that you create in the right half.

The sections below the New Color box enable you to choose and manipulate the Color Space model. You can choose either the RGB (Red, Green, and Blue) or the HSV (Hue, Saturation, and Value) model. The slider bars and edit boxes change, based on the model that you choose.

The eyedropper located below the Color Space sections enables you to pick a color from your desktop. In other words, you can choose colors outside of the Image Composer environment. To use this feature, click on the eyedropper button, choose a color on the desktop that you want, and click the mouse again. The selected color displays in the New Color to use box as you move the cursor over different colors on your desktop. As you move the cursor, the box to the right of the eyedropper shows the x and y coordinates of the eyedropper. You also can select an average of several colors by clicking the eyedropper and then drawing a rectangle around an area that contains the desired colors.

TIP

You can select the True Color tab and use the small circle that is displayed in the Color Ramp to adjust the color of the object. The selected color displays in the top right-hand corner of the Color Picker dialog window.

After designing the right color, you use the Shapes Palette to construct a rectangle, and you change the color of the rectangle to gray. You then cut out a portion of the rectangle by drawing a rectangle shape inside the existing rectangle and pressing the Erase button. Figure 6.12 depicts the Shapes Palette.

Figure 6.12.

Drawing a shape.

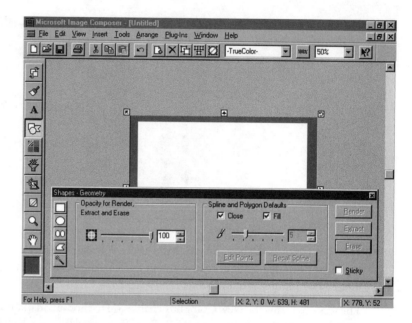

The Features of the Shapes Palette

The Shapes Palette contains several shapes located on the left-hand side of the window that you can construct. The first shape is the rectangle shape, which you used in the example. The other shapes include the oval, spline, and polygon.

NEW TERM The *spline* tool enables you to create a shape that consists of curved lines.

With each of the shapes, you can accomplish the following tasks:

☐ Create a sprite with the respective shape

☐ Create a duplicate section of an existing sprite that is in the form of the selected shape

☐ Erase a portion of an existing sprite that conforms to the desired shape

The Color Lift button is located below the polygon on the Shapes Palette. This button enables you to lift, or duplicate, the color of an existing sprite. You can use this feature by selecting a sprite and pressing the Color Lift button. The mouse cursor changes to a thin paintbrush. Position the cursor over the desired area and color within the currently selected sprite and click the paintbrush. Press the Render button on the Shapes Palette to create the duplicate sprite.

The next two sections on the Shapes Palette are used in conjunction with the shapes to the left and the three push buttons to the right of these sections. The first section enables you to set the opacity for rendering, extracting, and erasing sections of existing sprites. Remember, opacity refers to the amount of transparency the object contains. A value of 100 percent means that the sprite is completely opaque, or non-transparent. You can use the slider bar or edit box to change the opacity value. A good example of how to use this value involves duplicating an existing section of a sprite. You can create a copy of a section of an existing sprite by selecting a shape and drawing that shape over an area of the desired sprite. By adjusting the opacity value, you can adjust the amount of transparency that the new sprite picks up from the existing sprite.

The Spline and Polygon Defaults section contains options specifically for the spline and polygon tools.

The Close checkbox indicates whether spline curves will be opened or closed.

The Fill checkbox enables you to fill the spline or polygon with the current color in the Color Picker and the opacity value specified on the Shapes Palette. This option can only be checked when the Close checkbox is selected.

The next part of the Spline and Polygon Defaults section enables you to designate the width of a spline. You can use the Edit Points button to edit the points of a polygon or spline. The Recall Spline button recalls and enables the last spline that was drawn.

The Render button confirms an action for the Shapes Palette. The Extract button enables you to extract the shape and color of an existing sprite. The Erase button enables you to erase a designated section of an existing sprite based on the shape that you select. For example, during the previous exercise, you could have chosen a circle to erase part of the existing rectangle. This action would have formed the shape of a circle instead of a rectangle to display within the existing sprite. The Sticky checkbox preserves all of the custom settings for the shape tools.

Inserting Images

Earlier today, you learned how to insert an image into an existing composition. The next part of the lesson focuses on inserting several sprites from the Visual InterDev samples.

NOTE

The Help menu can assist you in locating all of the many sprites that are included with Image Composer. To find out about the sample sprites, choose the Help Menu and select Sample Sprites Catalog. Select the Sample Sprites option from the Help Topics dialog window to display the categories of sprites that are available. You can either choose digital stock photographs or Web art. After you choose a category, you can then navigate to a specific folder of interest within

6

the Help file and view the sprite. You also can find out the location of the sprite. If you installed the samples, the directory structure pertains to your file system. If you didn't install the sample sprites, the directory structure will relate to the Visual InterDev CD-ROM.

You need the CD-ROM during this portion of the lesson if you didn't install the sample sprites onto your file system.

1. Choose the From File option on the Insert menu.
2. Select the pltfrkkn.mic file from the \Client\Imgcomp\Mmfiles\Photos\Househld\ PhotoDsc folder and press OK. A plate with a fork and knife will be inserted into your existing composition.
3. Repeat step 1 to insert the following sprites:

   \Client\Imgcomp\Mmfiles\Photos\Plants\PhotoDsc\Brocoli.mic

   \Client\Imgcomp\Mmfiles\Photos\Plants\PhotoDsc\Pickles.mic

   \Client\Imgcomp\Mmfiles\Photos\Plants\Potato.mic

 TIP

You can insert multiple files from the Insert From File dialog window. To select multiple, non-contiguous files, use the right mouse button and the Ctrl (Control) key. To select files that are contiguous, use the Shift key with the right mouse button.

For example, in step 3 above, Brocoli.mic and Pickles.mic are non-contiguous files that are located in the same directory. After selecting the Brocoli.mic file, hold down the Ctrl key and move your mouse to select the Pickles.mic file. You should notice that both files appear selected and display in the File name field. When you press OK, both files are inserted into your composition.

4. Move the potato to the Extended Workspace.
5. Select the broccoli sprite.
6. Click on the Arrange button on the Toolbox. The Arrange Palette is displayed.
7. Change the Width and Height to 300 and 294, respectively, and press the Apply push button. This action changes the broccoli to a smaller size.
8. Move the broccoli to 222 and 26 on the x and y coordinates, respectively. You can use the status bar to help you verify the position of the sprite.

TIP

When an object is selected, you can move the object with the arrow keys to precisely position the sprite within your composition.

9. Select and move the plate sprite to the x and y coordinates of 126 and 28, respectively.

10. Select the pickle sprite and change the Width and Height to 200 and 205, respectively.

11. Move the pickle sprite to the x and y coordinates of 412 and 262, respectively.

12. Click on the Warps and Filters tool to display the Warps and Filters Palette.

13. Select Color Enhancement from the Wash and Filters group list combo box and choose Wash from the list of color enhancements.

14. Change the opacity value to 50 using either the Warp Opacity slider bar or edit box and press the Apply push button. This action causes the pickle to become transparent.

NOTE

You also can create a transparent sprite by choosing the Sprite to Sprite option in the listbox and selecting Transparency Map as the Sprite Texture Type. You should experiment with both types to determine which effect works for you.

Analyzing the Results

You have now learned how to insert and interact with multiple sprites. In this part of the lesson, you have discovered how to use the Shapes Palette to move and size your sprites as well as how to use the Patterns and Fills tool to create a transparent sprite. Your Image Composer workspace should look like the workspace pictured in Figure 6.13.

Producing the Desired Effect

In this section, you discover how to paint sprites and use art effects to enhance the look of your composition. The following instructions direct you through this process:

1. Use the Insert From File dialog window to insert the following sprites into your composition:

   \Client\Imgcomp\Mmfiles\Photos\Plants\Banana1.mic
   \Client\Imgcomp\Mmfiles\Photos\Plants\PhotoDsc\Purpfl1.mic

Figure 6.13.

A transparent sprite.

2. Move the purple flower to the upper left-hand corner of the Extended Workspace.

3. Select the banana sprite and click the Arrange tool on the Toolbox.

4. Type 90 in the Rotation edit box and press the Apply push button. The banana is rotated 90 degrees.

5. Enter 230 for the Width and 447 for the Height of the banana.

6. Move the banana to the x and y coordinates of 63 and 19, respectively.

7. Select the flower sprite and click the mouse on the Color Picker.

8. Change the Color Picker swatch by entering 255 for Red, 0 for Green, and 51 for Blue on the True Color tab display and pressing OK.

9. Click on the Paint tool to display the Paint Palette.

10. Choose the Colorize brush from the available options. This brush is directly below the pencil.

11. Position your cursor over the center of the flower. You should notice that the mouse cursor has become a paintbrush. Click on the left-mouse button to paint the center of the flower with the new color in the Color Picker swatch. If you paint over onto the edges of the leaves, you can erase this by choosing the Eraser from the Paint Palette and using your mouse in the same fashion as you did to paint the sprite.

12. Select the Arrange tool and change the Width to 150 and the Height to 160.

13. Move the flower to the x and y coordinates of 11 and 16.

14. Click the Art Effects tool to display the Art Effects Palette.

15. Select Exotic from the group list combo box and choose Glowing Edges from the listbox.

16. Press the Apply push button to view the effect.

Analyzing the Results

In this exercise, you were able to use the Paint and Art Effects tools to customize the look of your sprites. Both of these tool palettes offer many options to choose from. You can use the Paint Palette to alter the color of a sprite. The Paint Palette tools include a Paintbrush, an Airbrush, a Pencil, and an Eraser. Each of these tools enables you to paint a certain type of desired effect onto the sprite. For example, you can use the Pencil to draw very detailed lines around a sprite. Other tools on the Paint Palette provide painting effects, such as creating a smudged, impressionist look. You also can choose the size and opacity of the tool as well as create and use templates from this palette.

The Art Effects Palette enables you to use the effects of three different categories of art to produce a desired effect. The three categories include Paint, Sketch, and Graphic. The Paint category consists of various painting effects like watercolor and sponge painting. The Sketch category pertains to drawing and includes effects such as charcoal and pastel. You can use the Graphic category to produce an effect to make it look like a sprite was created from stained glass.

Two other Art Effects categories include Exotic and Utility. You used the Exotic art effect in the preceding exercise to create glowing edges for the flower. Other examples of Exotic effects include using plaster, glass, and chrome effects. You can add texture and 3D effects by using the Utility effects.

TIP   When you are using the Painting and Art Effects tools, you may find it easier to work with the sprite by increasing the Zoom Percent to a higher magnification.

To truly learn about all of these features, you should practice with different sprites and effects. Image Composer provides many options for designing professional-looking compositions.

6

Using the Impressionist Plug-In

Image Composer supports the use of third-party plug-ins like Kai's Power Tools to further enliven your compositions. In this section, you use the Impressionist plug-in included with Image Composer.

NOTE

You need to make sure that the Impressionist plug-in is installed. If not, you need to install this plug-in before you can complete the next part of the lesson.

1. Click on the rectangle sprite and select Impressionist from the Plug-Ins menu. The Impressionist dialog window is then displayed.
2. Click the Style button located at the top left corner of the Impressionist dialog window.
3. Choose the Paint item to display the list of sub-menu options.
4. Select Hot Swirl from the list. The style displays in the field to the right of the Style button.
5. Make sure that the Custom Color option is displayed in the Background combo box. Click the color swatch to the right of the combo box. This action displays the Color dialog window, enabling you to choose a color for the swatch.
6. Choose the last color swatch on the fourth row from the top. This color should be a medium purple color and have the following values: Hue = 180, Sat = 240, Lum = 120, Red = 128, Green = 0, and Blue = 255. Press the OK button to select the color.
7. Press the Preview button to view the desired effect on the Impressionist dialog window.
8. Press the OK button to confirm the effect.
9. Save the composition as a Microsoft Image Composer file with the name of **Food.mic**.

Analyzing the Results

The Impressionist plug-in enables you to produce some pretty creative and artistic styles. In this exercise, you used the Impressionist plug-in to change the color and style of the rectangle frame for your composition. You first chose the Style button to pick a specific style for the rectangle sprite. The Impressionist plug-in provides many style categories and options to choose from. Again, you need to experiment on your own with each of these styles to understand their potential.

TIP

You can press the Run Demo push button to discover the various effects of these styles on your sprite. The demo runs continuously and shows the result of a style in the preview box in the right corner of the Impressionist dialog window. To stop the demo, press the Esc key.

Next, you selected the background and color for the brush strokes. The Background combo box enables you to choose to which background you want the brush strokes applied. In the exercise, you selected Custom Color. This option enables you to apply the defined style to the custom color that you select. In other words, the Hot Swirl style was brushed onto the medium purple color. In contrast, you could have chosen Image from the Background combo box. This option applies the defined style to the original image.

The Impressionist dialog window enables you to save custom styles and colors that you define and create.

Animating Your Images with the GIF Animator

Animation has become an important part of images and web pages, and users have come to expect exciting pages that encourage participation and interaction. The Microsoft GIF Animator provides a great tool for creating animated images.

The GIF Animator is fully integrated with Image Composer. In fact, when you install the GIF Animator, a menu option is added to the Tools menu. You can use this menu option to start the GIF Animator from within the Image Composer workspace. Once you have started the GIF Animator, you can drag and drop your images from the Image Composer workspace to the GIF Animator environment.

The GIF Animator supports the GIF89a file format for animation. This format creates animation effects by storing timing information about the image.

6

Using the GIF Animator

You can start the GIF Animator by choosing the Tools menu from Image Composer and selecting GIF Animator from the list. Use the following instructions to guide you through a tour of the GIF Animator.

1. Click the potato sprite in your composition and choose the Arrange tool.

2. Change the Width and the Height of the sprite to 200 and 10, respectively, and press the Apply push button on the Arrange Palette.

3. Move the potato to an area of the Extended Workspace where you have some space to work with multiple copies of the sprite.

4. Press the Duplicate button on the Image Composer toolbar three times to create four duplicate potato sprites. Place the potatoes vertically on the Extended Workspace. Your workspace should look similar to Figure 6.14.

Figure 6.14.

Creating duplicate sprites.

5. Select the second potato sprite and click on the Arrange tool.

6. Enter 90 in the Rotation field and press Apply to rotate the sprite 90 degrees.

7. Select the third sprite and enter 180 in the Rotation field to rotate the sprite 180 degrees.

8. Select the fourth sprite and enter 270 in the Rotation field to rotate the sprite 270 degrees.

You are now ready to insert these sprites into the GIF Animator.

TIP

> You need to resize Image Composer to properly drag and drop sprites from Image Composer to the GIF Animator frames.

1. Resize and position the Image Composer application to be placed alongside the GIF Animator application. Your desktop should look like the one shown in Figure 6.15.

Figure 6.15.

Dragging images into the GIF Animator.

2. Click on the first potato sprite and drag it over to Frame #1 in the GIF Animator.
3. Repeat step 2 for the other three sprites. The order of each sprite corresponds to the GIF Animator frame number.

Now you're ready to customize the sprites using the features of the GIF Animator. The GIF Animator environment is pictured in Figure 6.16.

As you can see in Figure 6.16, the GIF Animator environment consists of a series of frames on the left-hand side and a tab display on the right. The potato sprites are positioned in each of the four frames. The tab display choices are Options, Animation, and Image. The Options tab enables you to set parameters regarding the management of your images. The Animation tab enables you to configure the animation settings including the size, duration, and transparency attributes. You can use the Image tab to set properties for an individual image.

6

Figure 6.16.

*Taking a closer look
at the GIF Animator.*

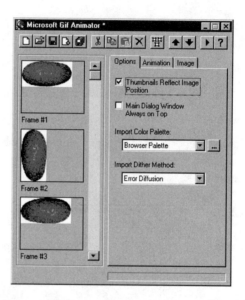

I want to point out some of the features on the Animation tab. The Height and Width fields enable you to set the size of the frame in which the animation is displayed. The GIF Animator presents a default display that can be changed. The Image Count field indicates the number of frames included in the current animation. You can use the Looping checkbox to repeat your animation. When you check the Looping option, the Repeat Count and the Repeat Forever fields become enabled. Repeat Count enables you to repeat your animation a specified number of times. Repeat Forever provides continuous animation. The Trailing Comment text box enables you to provide a comment for the animation. You can use the Image tab to configure settings for all of the images by selecting all of the frames and then using the options within this tab. To select all of the frames, click on the Select All button. This option is located next to the Move Up Arrow on the toolbar menu. You also can use the Shift key and the left mouse button to select the frames.

NOTE

A selected image is denoted by a thick, blue outline around the frame.

Follow these instructions to establish the animation settings.

1. Click on the Animation tab and change the Repeat Count field to 5.
2. Enter "This is a dancing potato!" for the Trailing Comment field.
3. Select all of the frame images.

4. Click the Image tab and change the Undraw Method to Restore Background. This option redraws the original background every time an image is displayed.

5. Enter 50 for the Duration field. This field designates the frequency of the animation in $1/100$ of a second increments.

6. Select the Transparency checkbox. This option enables you to pick a color within your animation that will be transparent.

7. Select each frame individually and set the Transparency Color by clicking on the color swatch next to the Transparency Color field. This action displays a color palette. Choose the white box from the color options and press OK.

8. Press the Preview button located to the right of the Move Down Arrow to see what the animation will look like.

9. Save your animation by pressing the Save button on the toolbar. You are then prompted to enter a name on the Save As dialog window. Name the file Dancing Potato.gif. Notice that you must save the file as a CompuServe GIF file.

10. From within the Image Composer workspace, insert this new animated GIF file by using the Insert From File dialog window. Choose the Dancing Potato.gif file from the location that you saved it and press OK.

11. Place the potato at the x and y coordinates of 226 and 328.

12. Save the composition.

Summarizing the Results

You have now learned the basics of using Image Composer to create professional looking graphics. You also discovered how to create animation for your sprites by using the Microsoft GIF Animator. This part of today's lesson has only touched the tip of the iceberg concerning the ability of these tools. I would encourage you to continue practicing and experimenting with the many features that these tools have to offer.

Integrating Music into Your Application Using Music Producer

Sounds and music also are a very important part of an interactive web site. Many web pages are using background sound and other types of music to provide an enjoyable experience for the user. This section switches gears and focuses on how to integrate music and sounds into your applications.

6

What Is Music Producer?

Now that you have had the chance to play the role of a graphic designer, you're ready for your next career in life. The Microsoft Music Producer makes you a musician in no time at all. Music Producer enables you to create compositions that consist of different keys, styles, tempo, personalities, and instruments. A composition also conforms to a specific *shape* that defines the instrument activity.

 Shape in the context of a musical composition refers to the overall pattern of the instruments and the music.

Music Producer uses the Microsoft Interactive Music Engine to translate your instructions to music and sounds. You can create MIDI compositions as well as Microsoft Music Producer (MMP) compositions. MIDI compositions are ideal for web pages because of the relatively smaller file size when compared to other audio compositions, like .wav files.

These compositions can be included in web pages and presentations. The best part about your Music Producer compositions is that they are royalty-free.

Creating a Composition

Music Producer contains many features for producing high quality music and sounds. The following sections focus on some of the main features that you will be using when creating compositions.

Previewing the Music

The first step to creating a composition involves understanding the available music options. The Preview button enables you to listen to your music choices and adjust the music as needed. Figure 6.17 shows the Preview button and illustrates the rest of the Music Producer environment.

The left side of the Music Producer environment displays a listbox of over 100 musical styles. The style defines the overriding theme of your composition. The key melodies and rhythm are portrayed through the style.

The middle part of the window contains the Personality and Band choices. The contents of each of these list boxes change based on the style that you select. The personality determines the mood of the music while the band consists of the musical instruments that will be used. A band is comprised of up to six musical instruments. When you select a band, the band's instruments display in the Mix pane on the right-hand side of the window.

Figure 6.17.

Using Music Producer.

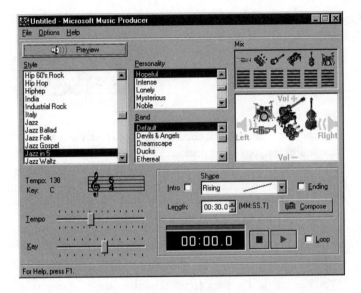

You can adjust both the balance and the volume of an instrument by dragging the musical instrument icon. The volume level is depicted vertically in the Mix pane. For example, if you wanted to increase the volume of an electric guitar, you would click on its icon and drag the guitar upward. To decrease the volume of the electric guitar, you drag the icon downward. The balance is defined horizontally. You can drag an icon to the left or right to adjust the speaker balance of an instrument. The Meters pane displays the volume level for each instrument and reflects any changes you make to a musical instrument's volume.

You also can adjust the tempo and key for the music. Each style has a default tempo and key. You can use the Tempo slider bar to adjust the speed of the music. If you move the slider to the right, the music becomes faster. You can adjust the slider to the left to create a slower tune. The value for the tempo can range from 10 to 350 beats per minute. The value that you choose using the slider bar is displayed in the Tempo field above the Tempo slider bar. The key defines the pitch or tone of the music, and is set by default to C. If you wish, you can adjust this value using the Key slider bar. The value that you choose is displayed in the Key field.

Composing the Music

After you have previewed and experimented with the various musical options, you need to create your own composition. The Compose area provides the tools you need to construct your composition. Figure 6.18 depicts the Compose area of Music Producer.

6

Figure 6.18.

Composing the music.

To create a composition, click on the Compose push button. You can then select different attributes for your composition. You can use the Intro and Ending checkboxes to create a distinct beginning and closing for your composition. The Shape combo box provides several options for defining the pattern and number of musical instruments that play throughout the composition. Available options include creating a rise or fall in the musical level as well as defining a peak in the middle of the composition.

You need to set a length for your composition by using the Length field. You must enter the length in terms of minutes, seconds, and tenths of a second, or MM:SS:T.

You can use the Playback controls to play, pause, or stop your composition before you save it. The Loop checkbox can be used to continuously repeat a composition during playback.

Saving the Composition

The final step in the creation of a composition is to save the file. You can save this file either as a MIDI or MMP composition. The default is the MMP format.

Integrating Your Results into Visual InterDev Applications

In this lesson, you have learned how to create images, sounds, and music to enhance the look of your web pages. You have discovered the power of Image Composer and Music Producer and gained a good understanding of the features of these applications.

The images that you create using Image Composer can easily be inserted into your Visual InterDev project. After you save an Image Composer composition, you can open your Visual InterDev project and add the file to the project. You can then insert the image into your HTML web page, or insert the image visually using the FrontPage Editor for Visual InterDev.

The process is similar for your musical compositions that you create using Music Producer. Typically, you create a musical composition and include the music as background sound for your web page. Again, you can include the file in your project and code the HTML using the Source Editor, or you can use a visual tool like the FrontPage Editor to insert the file into the page.

Summary

Visual InterDev includes some very robust tools for creating multimedia effects for your web pages. Image Composer provides an excellent environment for producing very artistic and graphical image compositions. Likewise, Music Producer enables you to create rich and exciting musical compositions to spice up your web pages.

During the first part of today's lesson, you gained an understanding of Image Composer and its features. You learned about the various tools and options that you can use to construct your compositions. You then took a guided tour of how to work with sprites to create an Image Composer composition. You inserted several sprites and used some of the painting and artistic palettes to produce a desired effect. You also learned how to use the Microsoft GIF Animator to make your images come alive.

The latter part of the day was spent learning how to use Music Producer. You learned about Music Producer's features and how to create a musical composition.

This lesson has provided you with just a taste of the power of Image Composer and Music Producer. The compositions that you create using each of these tools can easily be integrated into your Visual InterDev projects. You were able to put on a more creative and artistic hat for today's lesson. Tomorrow, you will put your developer hat back on as the lesson focuses on client-side script.

Q&A

Q What are the main advantages of sprites?

A Sprites are objects that have a defined shape. The main advantage to using sprites involves their appearance and nature. Sprites have depth and provide a 3D look and feel to your composition. Sprites also are easy to work with because you interact directly with the image object. With other tools, you manipulate a rectangular border for the object.

Q What is the difference between a MIDI and an MMP file?

A MIDI stands for Musical Instrument Digital Interface. MIDI files enable you to create a composition that contains musical instructions that tell your computer how to play the music. MIDI files are an industry standard and are ideal for the Web because of their relatively small file size and third-party support. MMP stands for Microsoft Music Producer and is the default file format for Music Producer. MMP files are smaller in file size than MIDI files. You can save files in this format to edit them later using Music Producer.

6

Workshop

In the lesson today, you created a composition using Image Composer and learned how to interact with sprites. In the following workshop, you experiment some more with both Image Composer and Music Producer. You can use the Image Composer composition that you created, or you can create a new composition. You should practice using each of the Image Composer tool palettes to really get a feel for their capability.

You also should practice using Music Producer to create some musical compositions. You should focus on using the various styles, personalities, and bands as well as adjusting the tempo and key.

Quiz

1. What is the Composition Guide?
2. What are the four color channels supported by Image Composer?
3. How many colors can you use with 8-bit color?

Quiz Answers

1. The Composition Guide is the central workspace for Image Composer. The Composition Guide defines the area of the composition for inserted sprites. Every sprite that is located in this area is included in the composition.
2. The four color channels are red, green, blue, and alpha.
3. 8-bit color supports the use of 256 colors.

Day 7

Extending Your Web Page Through Client-Side Script

Most of the focus for the week has been on the client. You have learned the basic building blocks of building a better client Web page. On this last day of the first week, you will learn a final piece to the client side of the application puzzle. Client-side scripting can provide a dynamic experience for the user if used in the right manner.

The first part of the day is an overview of how to successfully use scripting code on the client. You will gain an understanding of the power and pitfalls of executing script within the context of the user's browser. The lesson then defines VBScript and JavaScript. These two scripting languages are the most popular and widely used languages for coding client-side script. You also will learn how script code interacts and coexists with your HTML code.

The latter part of the day provides you with some VBScript basics. This section is not meant to be an exhaustive discourse on the topic of VBScript; however, it will give you a pretty detailed overview on the features and capabilities of the language. The last section teaches you how to use VBScript in your applications for the Web. In this section, specific examples of VBScript and web page interaction are covered.

Scripting for Success

HTML provides a standard method for Web browsers to render web pages but lacks the power to interact with the user. Scripting languages were created to provide a method for the user to interact with the web page. The user metaphor for the Web has gone from information gathering to true interaction. Web-based applications must have a way to interact with the user. HTML does a fairly good job of formatting documents for the Web but can't handle application processing.

The first applications for the Web used the server to execute special instructions and application logic. Program interfaces on the server like CGI have provided this processing in the past. This model is very inefficient in that the information and logic that could be verified and processed on the client is constantly passed back and forth between the client and the server. This situation creates more traffic across the network and additional processing for the server machine.

Client-side script can help alleviate this inefficient process. With the advent of scripting languages, the Web browser can process certain functions on the client through the use of script code embedded in the HTML. Script is normally used for user-initiated events like form activities or mouse events. For example, you can use client-side script to verify that a user entered the right type of information into a field on a form. A user that clicks the mouse or moves the mouse over a certain area of the web page could also trigger the execution of client-side script.

NOTE

> All references to script in this chapter pertain to the implementation of script within an HTML web page on a client machine unless noted otherwise. Day 11, "Extending Your Application Through Active Server Script," covers the concepts of implementing script on the server.

The advantages of using client-side script in your HTML web page include

- [ ] Increased interaction with the user
- [ ] Shared processing of simple tasks with the server
- [ ] Integration of multiple objects like ActiveX controls and HTML form controls
- [ ] More responsive web pages

There are some limitations to executing script on your client. First, security models are still being developed for the different scripting languages. Some people might argue that there is no definitive model. Most scripting languages were specifically designed with limitations that prevent the code from performing destructive actions on the client machine like destroying files. For instance, scripting languages cannot perform file I/O.

Another limitation to scripting languages is the lack of support for defining different data types. For example, VBScript only supports one data type. If you want to use a different data type, you have to change the type programmatically. The key point is that you must be careful in coding your client-side script. Both Microsoft and Netscape have attempted to implement security measures for their languages. You should, however, be cognizant of the fact that this code is still executing on an unsecured client machine.

You should definitely implement client-side script as a part of your Web-based application. The benefits far outweigh the limitations as long as you construct your code in the right manner. In this respect, a Web-based application is analogous to a movie. A movie must contain a good script no matter how good the actors are. Likewise, your applications must contain effective script to produce the desired results for your applications. You will learn how to implement effective script later in the day.

The Marriage of HTML and Scripting Languages

Scripting code is embedded within the confines of an HTML page. The <SCRIPT> and </SCRIPT> tags separate the script from the rest of the HTML. Listing 7.1 demonstrates the structure of an HTML document that contains scripting code.

Listing 7.1. VBScript code example.

```
<HTML>
<HEAD>
<TITLE>VBScript Page </TITLE>
</HEAD>
<BODY>
<P>HTML Paragraph Text
<SCRIPT LANGUAGE = "VBScript">
<!--
...VB Scripting Code is here
!-->
</SCRIPT>
</BODY>
</HTML>
```

7

In this example, the HTML document uses VBScript as its language. You can see the type of scripting language in the following line:

```
<SCRIPT LANGUAGE = "VBScript">.
```

The next line contains a comment tag that denotes the beginning of the scripting code. A comment tag is used for those browsers that can't execute script. Scripting code is hidden from these browsers and treated as if the code were comments. The next line contains the actual script. Your scripting code extends for multiple lines within your document. A closing comment tag is placed at the end of the script. This tag is followed by an ending `</SCRIPT>` tag.

> **NOTE**
>
> Script can be displayed in the `<HEAD>` and `<BODY>` sections. If the script is included in the `<HEAD>` section, the code is interpreted before the page is fully downloaded.

Scripting languages like VBScript and JavaScript are interpreted languages. An interpreted language must be translated by another program at runtime to be able to execute. This interpreter program performs the same duties as a person who acts as a translator between people who speak different languages. The interpreter listens to the speech of one person and translates those words into words that the second person can understand. In a similar fashion, an interpreter program must translate the language of a scripting program to a language that the client machine can understand. Given the code in Listing 7.1, the VBScript interpreter looks for the `<SCRIPT>` tags and processes all of the code in between.

For browsers that can read and support client script, the integration and marriage of HTML and script can be quite harmonious. You will definitely see the benefit of using scripting code on the client machine when you're building an application for the Web. Client-side script can significantly enhance the use of objects like Java applets, ActiveX controls, and HTML form controls.

You're probably wondering about the different scripting languages that are available. The next two sections provide a definition and overview of the two most widely used scripting languages.

What Is VBScript?

VBScript is a subset of the Visual Basic language and is Microsoft's entry into the Internet scripting languages arena. For developers who are familiar with Visual Basic, you will recognize much of the VBScript language and syntax. VBScript is very easy to learn and implement. Microsoft has created and optimized this scripting language specifically for the

Internet. Microsoft's Internet Explorer 3.0 supports the use of VBScript by providing the VBScript run-time interpreter.

VBScript uses procedures and functions to process your application needs.

What Is JavaScript?

JavaScript performs the same type of scripting extensions as VBScript. Netscape collaborated with Sun Microsystems to develop JavaScript as a scripting language to accentuate the Java programming language. Like VBScript, JavaScript is interpreted at runtime. You must use a browser that includes a JavaScript runtime interpreter.

Many publications use the terms JavaScript and Java interchangeably. JavaScript is not Java. The Java programming language enables you to create applets and applications. These programs are precompiled programs that execute specific functions. You can insert Java applets into your web page. You also can call Java programs on the server to process more extensive application logic.

JavaScript, on the other hand, is an interpreted scripting language that resides within the context of an HTML page. The browser, with the help of a JavaScript run-time interpreter, translates the script along with the rest of the HTML when the web page is downloaded from the server. JavaScript, by nature, doesn't possess the strength or robustness of the Java programming language. JavaScript borrows much of its syntax from the Java language. Listing 7.2 demonstrates the format for JavaScript code within an HTML document.

Listing 7.2. JavaScript code example.

```
<HTML>
<HEAD>
<TITLE>JavaScript Page </TITLE>
</HEAD>
<BODY>
<P>HTML Paragraph Text
<SCRIPT LANGUAGE = "JavaScript">
<!--
...JavaScript Scripting Code is here
// -->
</SCRIPT>
</BODY>
</HTML>
```

7

In Listing 7.2, notice the closing comment tag is different than the closing comment in the previous VBScript example. For JavaScript, a closing comment tag is denoted by two forward slashes. Also, the `<SCRIPT LANGUAGE>` tag set to `"JavaScript"` indicates that the scripting language is JavaScript.

VBScript and JavaScript are similar in coding structure. JavaScript, like VBScript, doesn't support specific type casting of variables. An integer is represented in the same way as a string. Also, JavaScript makes use of *functions*, *methods*, and *properties*, similar to VBScript, to accomplish its tasks. *Functions* are defined in the following section, "VBScript Basics." *Methods* and *properties* are defined on Day 13, "Interacting with Objects and ActiveX Controls."

NOTE

> At the time of the writing of this book, VBScript and JScript were only supported by Internet Explorer 3.0 and higher, while JavaScript was supported by both Internet Explorer and Netscape Navigator and Communicator.

Listing 7.3 shows a sample page implemented with VBScript.

Listing 7.3. Hello world with VBScript.

```
<HTML>
<HEAD>
<SCRIPT LANGUAGE="VBScript">
<!--
Sub DisplayHello_onClick()
MsgBox "Hello world!", 0, "VBScript"
end sub
-->
</SCRIPT>
<META NAME="GENERATOR" Content="Microsoft Developer Studio">
<META HTTP-EQUIV="Content-Type" content="text/html; charset=ISO-8859-1">
<TITLE>Sample VBScript Page</TITLE>
<H1>This is VBScript </H1>
</HEAD>
<BODY>
<CENTER>
<FORM>
<INPUT TYPE=BUTTON VALUE="Display VBScript" NAME="DisplayHello">
</FORM>
<BR><BR><BR>
</CENTER>
<a href="HelloWorld.htm">Hello World Home Page</a>
</BODY>
</HTML>
```

Listing 7.4 shows the same sample page implemented with JScript.

Listing 7.4. Hello world with JavaScript.

```
<HTML>
<HEAD>
<SCRIPT LANGUAGE="JScript">
<!--
function DisplayHello() {
alert("Hello world!");
}
//-->
</SCRIPT>
<META NAME="GENERATOR" Content="Microsoft Developer Studio">
<META HTTP-EQUIV="Content-Type" content="text/html; charset=ISO-8859-1">
<TITLE>Sample JavaScript Page</TITLE>
<H1>This is JavaScript</H1>
</HEAD>
<BODY>
<CENTER>
<FORM>
<INPUT TYPE=BUTTON VALUE="Display JavaScript" onclick="DisplayHello()">
</FORM>
<BR><BR><BR>
</CENTER>
<a href="HelloWorld.htm">Hello World Home Page</a>
</BODY>
</HTML>
```

These two code examples show some differences between VBScript and JavaScript. The first difference is the format of a JavaScript function. The syntax is very similar to the C++ language, which uses braces to organize a block of code statements and semicolons to signify the end of a statement.

Another difference is the method that is used to call a JavaScript function. Notice in the JavaScript example that the word onclick is used to call the function. In the VBScript code, the word NAME is used to activate the procedure. If you aren't familiar with C++ or Java, VBScript may seem like the more intuitive language. Both languages support your needs for providing robust, client-side functionality.

Microsoft has reverse engineered the JavaScript code into its own implementation called JScript. Both implementations are pretty much the same, although peculiarities do exist. Microsoft and Netscape agreed in November 1995 to define a single specification for JavaScript that will be managed by the European Computer Manufacturers Association (ECMA) standards body. This single specification hopefully avoids the problem that people have experienced with other "open" technologies, such as the UNIX operating system.

7

NOTE

Visual InterDev natively supports the use of JScript with its editors and tools. When you choose a scripting language for your projects, you must either choose VBScript or JScript. You can, however, create a web page containing JavaScript with another editor, such as Notepad, and insert this file into your project.

VBScript Basics

This part of the lesson teaches you the basic building blocks for creating VBScript code. In the section "Using VBScript to Extend Your Web Page," you apply these lessons and discover how to integrate VBScript into a web page.

Understanding Procedures

VBScript uses *procedures* to provide a home for its code. You're probably familiar with the concept of using procedures. Most programming environments, regardless of the language, use procedures as their basic foundation. Procedures provide a logical container for groups of related code.

 A *procedure* is a logical grouping of code statements that works together to complete a specific task. Procedures can be called from within your application and also can call other procedures.

VBScript contains three types of procedures:

1. Sub procedures
2. Functions
3. Event procedures

Sub Procedures

A sub procedure is a group of related VBScript code statements that complete a task but do not return a value to the calling program. I stated before that a procedure is called from your application or another procedure. When a program or procedure calls a sub procedure, the caller asks the procedure to perform a task. The calling program isn't interested in receiving anything in return. This process is analogous to a person calling a restaurant for carry-out food. The person calls the restaurant to prepare the food, and the person then drives to the restaurant to pick up the food. I will contrast this process with that of a function in the next section, so keep the food analogy fresh on your mind.

When a sub procedure is invoked, program control is temporarily passed to the called procedure. A sub procedure is denoted by the Sub and End Sub keywords. You can think of these keywords as tags that signify the beginning and ending of the procedure. They are similar in nature to HTML tags that mark the beginning and ending of an HTML element. The following code segment illustrates the basic structure of a sub procedure:

```
Sub CalculateTotal (A,B)
Total=A*B
MsgBox "The total is " & Total
End Sub
```

In this example, CalculateTotal is the name of the sub procedure. A and B refer to *arguments* that are passed by the calling program. These arguments are optional. You can pass up to *n* arguments to the called sub procedure. You also may develop procedures that don't need parameters to be passed. For those sub procedures, the parentheses are optional.

NEW TERM An *argument* is a variable that a procedure needs to complete its task. You can specify a number of arguments to be passed as long as they're in the correct order.

You can pass arguments *by value* to the procedure. You specify an argument to be passed by value by placing ByVal in front of the argument.

NEW TERM *By value* means that a copy of the variable's value is passed to the procedure. The procedure can use this value as well as make changes to it within the scope of the procedure. Because the variable is passed as a copy, changes that are made by the procedure to the value of the variable don't affect the original variable.

The following code segment demonstrates how to pass a variable by value:

```
Sub CalculateTotal(ByVal A, ByVal B).
```

Arguments also can be passed *by reference*. This method is the default method of passing a variable. This method differs from the traditional way that other development tools such as Visual Basic construe passing a variable by reference.

NEW TERM *By reference* in VBScript means that a variable's value is passed to the procedure as read-only. The procedure can read the value but can't make any changes to it.

In Visual Basic and other tools, passing a variable by reference enables you to access the storage of the original variable and changes the contents of the original variable. After the procedure has completed, the variable reflects the changes when the calling program tries to access its contents. VBScript doesn't enable you to alter the contents of the original variable.

You do not have to explicitly state that you're passing a variable by reference. The following code example shows how to pass a variable by reference:

```
Sub CalculateTotal(A, B).
```

7

You should develop descriptive names for your sub procedures so that anyone who uses the procedure will know what it does. I prefer to name my procedures using a verb-object nomenclature. For example, if I developed a procedure to format a date to display to the user, I would name that procedure `FormatDate`. `Format` is the verb that tells what the procedure is doing, and `Date` represents the object that is the object of the action. The preceding example multiplied two numbers to calculate a total, hence the name `CalculateTotal`. Valid characters to include in your procedure name include letters and numbers as long as the first character is not a number. You can't use symbols in your procedure name. VBScript performs error checking on your names to validate their syntax.

To call a sub procedure, you simply enter the name of the procedure. You also can use the optional `Call` keyword to activate a procedure. The following examples demonstrate how to call a sub procedure. The first example uses the `Call` keyword while the second example only states the name of the procedure. To call the `CalculateTotal` sub procedure, you can use

```
Call CalculateTotal(A, B)
```

or

```
CalculateTotal(A, B)
```

If the procedure that you're calling requires arguments, place the arguments within optional parentheses after the name of the procedure. To call the `FormatDate` procedure that doesn't require parameters, enter

```
FormatDate()
```

or

```
FormatDate
```

VBScript provides you with a lot of flexibility when calling a sub procedure. You may want to explicitly call procedures with the `Call` keyword so that you can distinguish the difference between a sub procedure and other elements within your code, such as variables.

Functions

The second type of procedure is a *function*. Similar to a procedure, a function is a collection of VBScript statements that work together to perform a task. The difference between a procedure and a function is that a function can return a value.

NEW TERM   A *function* is a group of code statements that collaborate to accomplish a task. A function is similar to a procedure in that a function can accept arguments and be called from the application and other procedures. A function can return a value to the calling program.

A function is denoted by the Function and End Function keywords. The following code example demonstrates the structure of a function.

```
Function Function Name(Argument 1, Argument 2,..., Argument n)
...Function Code
End Function
```

The structure of a function is very similar to the structure of a sub procedure. The same rules concerning sub procedure names and arguments apply to functions. I stated that the distinguishing factor concerning a function was the ability to return a value to the calling function.

When I explained the concept of a sub procedure, I used the analogy of calling a restaurant to order carry out. You call the restaurant, order the food, and pick it up from the restaurant. Extending the analogy, the function represents a person who calls and orders food to be delivered. You call the restaurant and ask for a mushroom pizza to be delivered to your house. The restaurant informs you that they need to cook the pizza, and it will be delivered in 30 minutes. The delivery person drives to your house and delivers the pizza. You can then use the pizza to feed yourself and your family. Similarly, a program makes a request of a function expecting to get something in return. When the function finishes executing its code, it sends a value back to the calling program. Listing 7.5 illustrates how a procedure can call a sample VBScript function and receive a value in return.

Listing 7.5. Returning a value.

```
<SCRIPT LANGUAGE="VBScript">
<!--
Sub ConvertTemp()
temp = InputBox("Please enter the temperature in degrees Fahrenheit:", 1)
MsgBox "The temperature is " & Celsius(temp) & " degrees C."
End Sub

Function Celsius(fDegrees)
Celsius = (fDegrees - 32) * 5 / 9
End Function
!-->
</SCRIPT>
```

In this code example, the sub procedure prompts the user to enter a temperature in degrees Fahrenheit. After the user enters the number, the function is called to convert the temperature to Celsius. Notice that the function variable, Celsius, which captures the converted temperature, is the same as the name of the function. In order to return a value back to the calling program, you must specify a variable to have the same name as the function. By design, the function returns a value through the use of its own name as the variable.

7

The function in Listing 7.5 contained only one line of code. Most of your functions will contain multiple lines of VBScript code. For this reason, you should make it a practice to populate the function variable in the last line of the function code. Listing 7.6 shows a sample function that contains multiple lines of code.

Listing 7.6. Formatting the function variable on the last line of code.

```
<SCRIPT LANGUAGE="VBScript">
<!--
Function CalculateAverage(A,B)
Dim Total
Total = (A*B)/2
CalculateAverage = Total
End Function
!-->
</SCRIPT>
```

In this example, a temporary variable, `Total`, is established to hold the value of the calculated average. On the last line of the function, `CalculateAverage` is set to the value that is stored within the `Total` variable. Although a simple example, I think you can extrapolate the significance if your function code has many lines. Using this standard can provide meaning to your functions. You will always know to look at the last line of the code for the value that is being returned to the calling program. Assigning the function variable on the last line of the function also prevents this statement from getting lost in the shuffle of your code.

Calling a function is different from calling a procedure. Because a function returns a value, you must be prepared to do something with the value when it returns from the function. The syntax for calling a function is

```
Return_Variable = Function Name(Argument 1, Argument 2,..., Argument n)
```

where `Return_Variable` is the name of the variable that will store the value that is returned from the function. To call the `CalculateAverage` function, you could enter either

```
Average = CalculateAverage(A,B)
```

or

```
Average = CalculateAverage A,B
```

Notice that the parentheses are optional. For a function that doesn't require arguments, you can enter either

```
Date1 = FormatDate()
```

or

```
Date1 = FormatDate
```

Notice again that the parentheses are optional.

Functions are very useful when you need to complete a task and then return the results back to the calling program.

Event Procedures

The first two procedures that you have learned about are procedures that you can create. The *event* procedure is different from sub procedures and functions in that it is constructed automatically for you by the objects and controls that you use to build your application. Event procedures also differ from sub procedures and functions in the manner that they are initiated. The browser calls event procedures automatically, based on user actions and requests. With sub procedures and functions, you must call them within the context of your program.

NEW TERM An *event procedure* is a group of code statements activated by a user-initiated event. This action could be the result of a user action such as clicking a button. An event procedure also could be triggered by a system action where the user has made a request of the system and the system needs to respond.

When you use objects such as ActiveX controls to create your application interface, standard events are associated with these controls. For example, a user can click a button; therefore, a standard event for a button is the On_Click event. This event is triggered and its code is executed any time the user clicks the button. The structure for your event procedure code is constructed automatically based on the controls that you select. You must fill in the blank with any code that you want processed when the event is initiated.

NOTE

On Day 4, "Creating Your First Visual InterDev Project," you received a glimpse of event procedures when you inserted some code for the Say Hello button. You used the Script Wizard to generate some of the code for you. You will learn more about using the Script Wizard to generate your scripting code for control events on Day 15, "Integrating Objects into Your Applications."

You don't have much choice in naming your event procedures. Most of the time this name is generated for you. The standard naming convention for an event procedure is as follows:

```
Sub ControlName_EventName()
```

7

ControlName is the name of the control and *EventName* refers to the name of the event. For example, an event procedure for a click event associated with the Submit button might be called

```
Sub cmdSubmit_OnClick
```

> **NOTE**
>
> The control name is based on the ID property value that you establish when you place the control within your application. In the preceding example, I placed a button on a web page and changed the value for the ID property to cmdSubmit. Naming conventions for controls are explained in more detail on Day 13.

Event procedures are preconstructed programming shells that a control provides for you. Each control will have a different set of events associated with it. Event procedures serve as a helpful reminder to think about the various user and system actions that can occur within your application. Based on these actions, you can then provide the logic process and handle the application requests.

Procedures and HTML

As you can see, procedures provide the foundation and residence for your VBScript code. Although you can place script outside the confines of a procedure, most of your application logic resides within a procedure. You should generally place your VBScript code within the <HEAD> section of an HTML document for readability. You may be tempted to separate your procedures into different script sections as in Listing 7.7.

Listing 7.7. Separating the script.

```
<SCRIPT LANGUAGE="VBScript">
<!--
Function CalculateTotal(A,B)
Total = A+B
CalculateTotal = Total
End Function
!-->
</SCRIPT>
<SCRIPT LANGUAGE="VBScript">
<!--
Function CalculateAverage(A,B)
```

```
Dim GradeAverage
GradeAverage = (A*B)/2
CalculateAverage = GradeAverage
End Function
!-->
</SCRIPT>
```

While VBScript enables you to divide your script into separate sections, as in Listing 7.7, it isn't a good habit to develop from a maintainability and readability standpoint. You should instead make it a habit to place all of your code into one script section. This practice enables you, as well as others who may use your code, to easily understand and locate your scripting code.

Summarizing Procedures

Although this section on procedures may have been refresher for some of you, I hope you have gained a better understanding of the basic building block for your code. VBScript procedures are very similar to Visual Basic and other development tools. Table 7.1 summarizes the three types of procedures and provides a description of each type.

Table 7.1. VBScript procedures.

Procedure	Description
Sub Procedure	Processes a group of related code statements
Function	Processes a group of related code statements and returns a value to the calling program
Event Procedure	Control-specific procedure that processes user or system events

Understanding Variables

I have mentioned the term *variable* several times today. I am sure that you have used variables to develop your applications, but I did want to define the term and outline how you can use variables within the context of VBScript.

NEW TERM A *variable* serves as a placeholder for some type of information.

You can use variables to store information that your application logic will need at some point in time. You can access the value of the variable as well as modify its contents.

7

Types of Variables

There is only one data type for a VBScript variable. The *variant* serves as the data type for all of the variables that you create within your VBScript code. A variant is very flexible in that it can hold almost any type of information.

 A *variant* is a special data type that can store all types of information, including strings, numbers, dates, and objects such as ActiveX controls.

When you define a variable, you don't have to state an explicit data type. In other programming languages, you have to specifically define a data type for the variable such as an integer or a date. All variables in VBScript are defined as variants.

You don't have to worry about specifying a data type for your variables. When you assign a value to a variable, VBScript stores additional subtype information about the data that's being held in the variable. This subtype, or category, information helps VBScript determine the usage of variants based on the variable's context. For instance, if you want to add two number variables that are stored as variants, VBScript assumes that the variables are numbers and treat them as such. Textual information is handled in a similar manner, based on the internal subtype of the variable. Table 7.2 describes the different subtypes for a variant data type.

Table 7.2. Variant subtypes.

Subtype	Description
Boolean	Contains a value of either True or False
Byte	Stores integers between 0 and 255
Integer	Contains a number between -32,768 and 32,768
Long	Contains an integer between -2,147,483,648 and 2,147,483,647
Single	Contains single precision, floating point data with a range from $-1.4E^{-45}$ to $-3.4E^{38}$ for negative numbers and $1.4E^{-45}$ to $3.4E^{38}$ for positive numbers
Double	Contains double precision, floating point, or decimal data with a range from $-4.9E^{-324}$ to $-1.8E^{308}$ for negative numbers and $4.9E^{-324}$ to $1.8E^{308}$ for positive numbers
Date/Time	Contains a date including time information between January 1, 100, and December 31, 9999
Empty	Contains 0 for numbers and "" for strings; represents a variable that hasn't been assigned a value

Subtype	Description
Error	Contains a VBScript error number
Null	Variable that contains no data; represents a variable that has been assigned a value of nothing
String	Contains alphanumeric information up to 2 million characters
Object	References an object like an ActiveX control

Exposing the Variable's Data Type

You can determine and change the subtype that VBScript selects for your variable. There are two ways to discover the subtype. First, you can use the VarType function. This function enables you to request the subtype of a variable. The syntax for this function is as follows:

```
VarType(VariableName)
```

VariableName is the name of the variable that you are inquiring about. Listing 7.8 illustrates the use of the VarType function:

Listing 7.8. Determining the subtype of a variant.

```
<SCRIPT LANGUAGE="VBScript">
<!--
Function DisplaySubtype(TestVariable)

Dim VariableSubtype

VariableSubtype = VarType(TestVariable) '
➥Determines the variable subtype
MsgBox "The subtype for the variable is " & VariableSubtype '
➥Displays the subtype
DisplaySubtype = VariableSubtype 'Assigns the value of the subtype
➥to the function variable

End Function
!-->
</SCRIPT>
```

Listing 7.8 is included on the CD-ROM with this book. You can use this function to determine the subtypes of variables within your application. This function requires that a variable be passed as an argument. The function determines the subtype for this variable and passes the value back to the calling program. I created it as a function that displays a message box as well as returns the value of the variant subtype.

7

The `VarType.htm` file on the CD-ROM contains the entire web page that calls the function. To test the function, I populate the argument `TestVariable` before it's passed to the function. When the web page is loaded, a message box displays the value of the subtype. I used the message box for testing purposes only as well as the hard-coding of the `TestVariable`. To use this function with your application code, you should copy the function code and insert it into your `<SCRIPT>` section. Also, if you want to use the return variable but not display the message box, remove the `MsgBox` line of code.

The second method to determine the subtype of a variant is to use some special functions provided with VBScript. These functions perform a check for a specific data type. After the check is performed, the functions return a value of `True` or `False`, indicating whether the variable matches the specific data type of the function. The following list shows the type of VBScript functions that are available:

- [ ] `IsArray`
- [ ] `IsDate`
- [ ] `IsEmpty`
- [ ] `IsNull`
- [ ] `IsNumeric`
- [ ] `IsObject`

The syntax for each of these functions is as follows:

FunctionName(VariableName)

For example, to call the `IsDate` function, you would enter

`IsDate(TestDate)`

Remember that these functions return a value of either `True` or `False`. For this reason, the most typical use of these functions is in the context of testing whether the return value of the function is `True` or `False`. This test can be performed using an `If...Then...Else` statement, which is covered in a later section, "Controlling the Flow of the Program."

NOTE

> Refer to Appendix D, "VBScript Language Reference" to discover more about these functions as well as other functions supplied by VBScript.

Changing the Variable's Data Type

VBScript also supplies functions to alter the internal data type of a variable. You can use these functions to specifically change the variable subtype that is assigned by VBScript for the variant. Table 7.3 displays the available VBScript functions to change a variant's subtype.

Table 7.3. VBScript subtype conversion functions.

Function Name	Description
CBool	Converts subtype to Boolean
CByte	Converts subtype to Byte
CDate	Converts subtype to Date
CDbl	Converts subtype to Double
CInt	Converts subtype to Integer
CLng	Converts subtype to Long
CSng	Converts subtype to Single
CStr	Converts subtype to String

The syntax for calling these functions is similar to the functions that determine the subtype for a variant. For example, to call the CInt function, you would enter

```
CInt(OriginalVariable)
```

This function converts the data to the integer format. For all of these functions, you need to assign the return value to a variable:

```
ChangedVariable = CInt(OriginalVariable)
```

NOTE Refer to the section entitled "Controlling the Flow of the Program" for a detailed code example outlining the use of these conversion functions.

Defining the Scope of a Variable

Variables can be used within the context of a procedure. You also can share variables across all of your procedures. The *scope* of a variable determines its availability to your code.

NEW TERM *Scope* refers to the ability of a code statement to access a certain variable's contents. The scope of a variable determines the context for usage by your application.

Variables consist of two types of scope—procedure-level and script-level. Procedure-level scope, sometimes called local scope, refers to variables that are declared within a procedure. Procedure-level variables can only be used and accessed within the context of that procedure.

7

Script-level scope refers to variables that are defined outside your procedures. Script-level variables can be recognized across all of your procedures. The lifetime of your variable signifies the length of time that the variable exists. Lifetime and scope are closely tied together. While scope determines what code statements have access to the variable, lifetime indicates how long the variable exists in memory. For procedure-level variables, the variable exists only for the life of the procedure. When the procedure ends, the variable no longer exists. Script-level variables exist until the script finishes processing.

You will constantly have a need to use variables. They are a powerful part of any programming language. As you progress through the next few weeks, the proper use of variables will become very evident.

Controlling the Flow of the Program

So far, you have learned about structuring your code through the use of procedures. You also have recognized that variables are a necessary component of any set of code statements. With all of this capability, how do you control your program's flow while unleashing the potential of your code? VBScript, like other programming languages, provides control structures that enable you to designate how your script is executed. Control structures are analogous to highway signs that direct you to the right place. You make decisions, based on these signs, about where to turn and which direction to drive. Similarly, control structures help your code make decisions about which logic to execute. This section covers the basic control structures that are available within VBScript. This section serves as a refresher for those experienced Visual Basic programmers.

If...Then...Else

This control structure is used to evaluate if a condition is `True` or `False` and compares the values of variables. The following code example demonstrates the use of this control structure:

```
If RoundWorld = True Then
MsgBox "Sail around the world!"
Else
MsgBox "Don't go! You'll fall off the earth!"
End If
```

Notice the structure of the If...Then...Else statement. You're basically telling your program to evaluate if a condition is true. If it is, you want to execute one piece of code. If the condition isn't true, you want to execute another piece of code. There are several variations to this control structure. The first variation involves only executing a piece of code if a situation is true. You don't care if the situation is false. For this situation, you would enter the following:

```
If RoundWorld = True Then MsgBox "Sail around the world"
```

Another variation that is similar to the preceding example is if you want to run multiple lines of code when a situation is true. For this scenario, you would enter

```
If RoundWorld = True Then
PackedBags = True
lblHouse.Caption = "Gone Sailing"
MsgBox "Sail around the world!"
End If
```

The End If statement is used in this example to signify the end of the code. You must include this statement when executing multiple lines of code within an If...Then statement.

You also can use this control structure to evaluate and compare the values of variables. For this kind of comparison, you need to use the VBScript comparison operators.

NOTE

VBScript contains comparison, arithmetic, and logical operators. Comparison operators, as the name states, enable you to compare variables. Arithmetic operators enable you to perform mathematical operations between numbers and variables. Logical operators assist you in testing the validity of one or more variables For a comprehensive reference concerning comparison operators, refer to Appendix D.

The following code example demonstrates the use of a comparison operator within an If...Then...Else statement:

```
If Age >12 Then
MsgBox "You are a teenager."
Else
MsgBox "You are not a teenager."
End If
```

A final variation includes the ability to construct multiple tests. You can use the ElseIf statement to construct another test within your If...Then...Else statement. The most common use of this structure is when you have multiple comparisons to perform. The following code example illustrates the use of this construct:

```
If Age <= 12 Then
MsgBox "You are a not a teenager."
ElseIf Age < 20 Then
MsgBox "You are a teenager."
ElseIf Age > 40 Then
MsgBox "It's all downhill from here."
End If
```

Notice from the previous example that you can construct multiple ElseIf statements within an If...Then...Else statement.

7

Select Case **Statements**

Select Case statements are similar in function to the If...Then...Else statement. Select Case statements enable you to execute code based on the value of an expression. You will want to replace an If...Then...Else statement with the Select Case statement when you have multiple conditions to test.

How many ElseIf statements are too much? I usually start to consider a Select Case statement after the third test of a variable. In other words, Listing 7.9 would be a good candidate for a Select Case statement.

Listing 7.9. Unwieldy If...Then...Else **statement.**

```
<SCRIPT LANGUAGE="VBScript">
<!--
Sub DisplayName(Name)

If Name = "Bob" Then
MsgBox "Your name is Bob."
ElseIf Name = "Mike"
MsgBox "Your name is Mike."
ElseIf Name = "Gina"
MsgBox "Your name is Gina"
ElseIf Name = "Steve"
MsgBox "Your name is Steve"
End If

End Sub
!-->
</SCRIPT>
```

Listing 7.10 shows what the previous listing would look like as a Select Case statement.

Listing 7.10. Providing structure through a Select Case **statement.**

```
<SCRIPT LANGUAGE="VBScript">
<!--
Sub DisplayName(Name)

Select Case Name
Case "Bob"
MsgBox "Your name is Bob."
Case "Mike"
MsgBox "Your name is Mike."
Case "Gina"
MsgBox "Your name is Gina"
Case "Steve"
```

```
MsgBox "Your name is Steve"
Case Else
MsgBox "You don't have a name"
End Select

End Sub
!-->
</SCRIPT>
```

The first statement in the `Select Case` statement provides the expression to be tested. This expression must have a distinct value. In other words, you can't use a `Select Case` statement to make comparisons between variables. The lines denoted by the `Case` statement signify the comparison value for each set of code statements. VBScript traverses the list of `Case` statements, comparing each value to the test expression. If it finds a match, the code for that `Case` statement is executed. If no match is found, the code within the `Case Else` statement is executed.

NOTE

It's a very good programming practice to use the `Case Else` statement even if you think you have covered all of the possible values in the `Case` statements. Your code will crash if you don't provide a parachute for the script to execute in case of emergency.

I have provided a function included on the CD-ROM with this book that determines the type of conversion that you want to perform and then converts the variable subtype. This function demonstrates the use of a `Case` statement in combination with some of the previous functions you learned about earlier today. Listing 7.11 displays the code for this function.

Listing 7.11. Changing a variant's data type.

```
<SCRIPT LANGUAGE="VBScript">
<!--
Function ConvertSubtype(ConversionType,OriginalVariable)

Dim ChangedVariable

Select Case ConversionType
Case "Boolean"
ChangedVariable = CBool(OriginalVariable)
Case "Byte"
ChangedVariable = CByte(OriginalVariable)
Case "Date"
ChangedVariable = CDate(OriginalVariable)
```

continues

7

Listing 7.11. continued

```
Case "Double"
ChangedVariable = CDbl(OriginalVariable)
Case "Integer"
ChangedVariable = CInt(OriginalVariable)
Case "Long"
ChangedVariable = CLng(OriginalVariable)
Case "Single"
ChangedVariable = CStr(OriginalVariable)
Case "String"
ChangedVariable = CStr(OriginalVariable)
Case Else
ChangedVariable = ""
End Select

ConvertSubtype = ChangedVariable

End Function
!-->
</SCRIPT>
```

For...Next **Loops**

The For...Next loop is a widely used method to control the flow of your code. You can use a For...Next loop to execute a group of code statements a specified number of times. A counter is used to control the number of times that the code is executed. By default, the counter is increased by one for each iteration of the loop. You can set the starting value of the counter as well as the value of the increment. You also can specify that the counter be decremented with each loop iteration. The format of a For...Next loop is as follows:

```
For counter = beginning to end Step increment
Execute Code segment
Next
```

counter represents the variable that is going to be incremented, beginning signifies the beginning number of the counter, end represents the ending value for the counter, and increment specifies how much to increase or decrease the counter after each iteration of the loop. The Step statement is optional.

Do **Loops**

The Do loop provides another popular way to execute your code multiple times. The Do loop can be implemented in a variety of ways. You can use the While keyword to execute a block of code as long as a condition is true. The behavior of the loop changes based on where the While keyword is placed in the loop. If the While keyword is placed in the opening line of the loop, VBScript first checks to see if the condition is true before executing the code segment.

The syntax for the `Do...While` loop is

```
Do While condition
...block of code statements
Loop
```

You also can place the `While` keyword at the end of the loop to execute the code at least once before exiting the loop. The syntax for the `Do...Loop...While` is

```
Do
...block of code statements
Loop While condition
```

You also can use the `Until` keyword to execute a block of code until a condition becomes true. The same rules for the `While` keyword concerning placement within the loop apply to the `Until` keyword.

Using VBScript to Extend Your Web Page

Now that you have learned some of the basics of VBScript, I want to walk you through two examples of using VBScript to extend and enhance the functionality of your web page. These examples are included on the CD-ROM with this book.

Validating User Input

The first example uses VBScript code to validate an input field for a form. The script validates that the user enters a numeric value between 1 and 10. The application displays a different message box based on a correct or incorrect entry. Listing 7.12 shows the web page and the VBScript code for this example.

Listing 7.12. Validating user input.

```
<HTML>
<HEAD>
<META NAME="GENERATOR" Content="Microsoft Developer Studio">
<META HTTP-EQUIV="Content-Type" content="text/html; charset=ISO-8859-1">
<TITLE>Validating User Input</TITLE>
<SCRIPT LANGUAGE="VBScript">
<!--
Sub Verify_OnClick
Dim MyForm
Set MyForm = Document.ValidForm
If IsNumeric(MyForm.txtEntry.Value) Then
If MyForm.txtEntry.Value < 1 Or MyForm.txtEntry.Value > 10 Then
MsgBox "Please enter a number between 1 and 10."
Else
```

continues

Listing 7.12. continued

```
MsgBox "Your entry was correct."
End If
Else
MsgBox "Please enter a numeric value."
End If
End Sub
-->
</SCRIPT>
</HEAD>
<BODY>
<H3> Validating the user input</H3><HR>
<FORM NAME="ValidForm" Action="">
Enter a value between 1 and 10:
<INPUT NAME="txtEntry" TYPE="TEXT" SIZE="2">
<INPUT NAME="Verify" TYPE="BUTTON" VALUE="Verify">
</FORM>
</BODY>
</HTML>
```

In Listing 7.12, I use an HTML form to provide the user interface. For the purposes of this
example, it isn't important that you understand how to implement an HTML form. I will
explain the use of HTML forms and controls on Day 12, "Using Basic and Advanced HTML
Form Controls." Figure 7.1 displays what happens when the user types in an incorrect entry.

Figure 7.1.

An invalid entry.

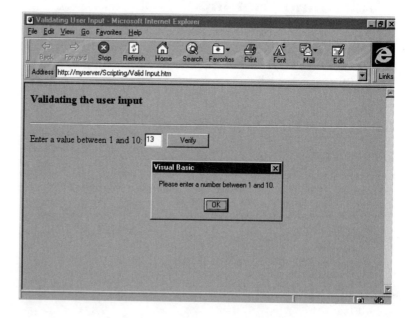

Although this example is simple in nature, you should be able to get a feel for how to integrate the power of VBScript into your HTML code. At the beginning of the day, I explained that user input validation was an important capability of client-side script. If you didn't use scripting code on the client, you would have to pass the entry and validate the information with a program on the server. If the input is wrong, you have to send a message back down to the client informing the user to enter the data again. This process could be repeated several times before the user enters a correct value for the field.

In Listing 7.12, you see the value of having the script resident within the web page on the client. Once the user enters a value and presses the Verify button, the input is instantly validated on the client machine. For the purposes of this example, a message box is displayed informing the user whether the entry was valid or not. Figure 7.2 shows the results of typing a correct value and pressing the Verify button.

Figure 7.2.

A valid entry.

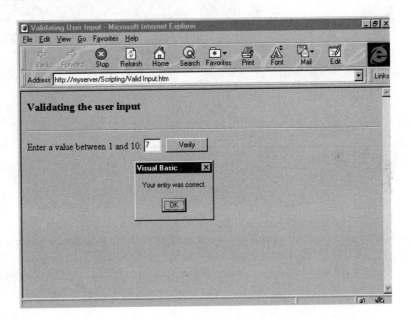

In the context of a more robust application, you might pass a valid entry on to the server for further processing.

Integrating VBScript with Controls

This next example illustrates how you can use client-side script to act as the "glue" between multiple objects and controls within your web page. In the example, I use an HTML Layout control to build the interface. You will learn how to construct an application with ActiveX controls and the Layout control on Day 13, "Interacting with Objects and ActiveX Controls," and on Day 15, "Integrating Objects into Your Applications." For the purposes of the example, focus on the way that VBScript interacts with the controls.

This application is a simple payment window that enables the user to enter the payment type for an order. If the user chooses Cash or Check, the Credit Card and Credit Card Number fields are disabled. Figure 7.3 demonstrates an example of selecting the Cash option button.

Figure 7.3.

Selecting to pay by cash.

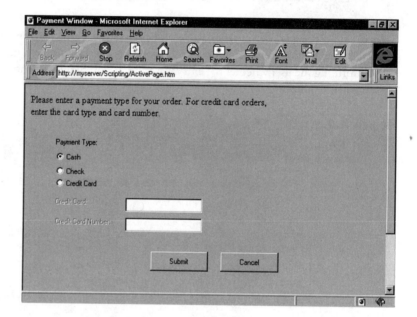

When the user clicks the Credit Card option button, the credit card information fields are enabled, allowing the user to enter the credit card type and number. The Submit button is enabled after the user enters information for both of these fields. Figure 7.4 illustrates how the page looks when the user selects to pay by credit card and enters the credit card information.

Listing 7.13 reveals the code that helps to integrate the activities of the different controls on this page.

Figure 7.4.

Entering credit card information.

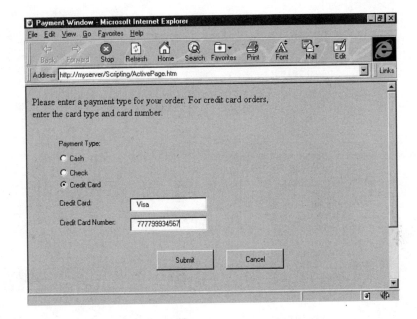

Listing 7.13. Selecting a payment type.

```
Sub Layout2_OnLoad()
cmdSubmit.Enabled = False
End Sub

Sub optCash_OnClick()
call DisableCard()
End Sub

Sub optCheck_OnClick()
call DisableCard()
End Sub

Sub DisableCard()
txtCreditCard.Enabled = False
txtCardNumber.Enabled = False
lblCreditCard.Enabled = False
lblCardNumber.Enabled = False
End Sub

Sub optCredit_OnClick()
txtCreditCard.Enabled = True
txtCardNumber.Enabled = True
```

continues

7

Listing 7.13. continued

```
lblCreditCard.Enabled = True
lblCardNumber.Enabled = True
Call CheckFields()
End Sub

Sub txtCreditCard_Change()
Call CheckFields()
End Sub

Sub txtCardNumber_Change()
Call CheckFields()
End Sub

Sub CheckFields()
If txtCreditCard.Text = "" Or txtCardNumber.Text = "" Then
cmdSubmit.Enabled = False
Else
cmdSubmit.Enabled = True
End If
End Sub
```

You can sample this application on the CD-ROM with this book. The code for an HTML Layout control is encompassed within the .alx file. You need to open this file and use the Script Wizard to view the script for the different control events and actions. You can see from the listing that user and system events trigger actions that you can process within your script. These tasks should not be passed to the server. For example, the credit card information fields are disabled when the user selects to pay by cash or check. This user interface function is ideal for the client to process.

Summary

You have ended the week on a very informative note. Hopefully, some of this information served as a refresher for you. If you have used Visual Basic before, you should notice the glaring similarities it has with VBScript. These similarities are only natural, because VBScript is a subset of the Visual Basic language. This lesson attempted to focus on the advantages of using a language like VBScript to enhance the functionality of your web page from a client perspective. As you enter the second week, you will discover the power that awaits on the server side of the equation.

Today you received an overview of how to use scripting code on the client, discovering both the power and some of the drawbacks of client-side script. Next, you learned about VBScript and JavaScript—two of the most widely used and popular scripting languages today. The lesson presented a brief introduction and definition for each of these languages. For further information on these languages, refer to Appendix D, "VBScript Language Reference," and Appendix E, "JavaScript Language Reference."

The latter part of the lesson provided you with some of the basics of VBScript. This part of the lesson taught you some of the more robust features and capabilities of the VBScript language. Finally, you saw some specific examples of VBScript and web page interaction. You can inspect these examples further by accessing them from the CD-ROM included with this book.

Q&A

Q Can I use JavaScript and VBScript within my web page?

A While Visual InterDev supports the both JavaScript and VBScript, you can only use one scripting language per page.

Q What is the difference between VBScript, VBA, and Visual Basic?

A Visual Basic is the parent language for both VBA and VBScript. Visual Basic provides both a robust language and development environment for client-server development. VBA and VBScript are subsets of Visual Basic. VBA stands for Visual Basic for Applications and is geared toward the power user. VBA is the programming language for the Microsoft Office suite of applications. VBScript is yet another derivative that is geared specifically for HTML web pages. VBScript can be used both on the client and the server side of a Web-based application. Refer to the Visual InterDev online help for a comprehensive list of VBA features that aren't included in VBScript.

Q What is a variant?

A A variant serves as the lone data type for all variables in VBScript. The variant can handle multiple data types, including numbers, text, dates, and objects. VBScript categorizes the data that is stored within a variant through the use of subtypes. These subtypes help VBScript to classify and perform operations on a variant.

Workshop

Using the code examples provided in today's lesson as well as the samples on the CD-ROM, practice using some of the VBScript principles that you used today. Specifically, you should become familiar with creating sub procedures and functions for your code. Also, develop a script that takes advantage of the program control structures. After developing this code, analyze the results to determine if the code acts the way you think it should. Be prepared to answer the questions of why or why not.

7

You also should make a list of additional uses of client-side script, besides the ones mentioned in this chapter. This list will help you better apply the concepts that you learned today when you begin putting all of the pieces together to build your application.

Quiz

1. What is the difference between Java and JavaScript?
2. What is the difference between a function and a sub procedure?
3. What is the difference between "Null" and "Empty"?
4. What does the ByVal statement do?
5. Given the following code segment, how many times will the code within the loop execute before the loop terminates?

```
Sub cmdCalculate_OnClick()
Dim A, B, C
A = 10
B = 20
Do While A > B
C = A - B
A = A - B
Loop
End Sub
```

Quiz Answers

1. Java is a programming language designed to create applications and applets, or "mini" applications. Java is a compiled language. JavaScript, on the other hand, is an interpreted language that resides within HTML on a web page. JavaScript is designed to provide scripting functionality to your web pages.

2. A sub procedure is a group of related code statements that work together to complete a task. A function is different from a sub procedure in its ability to actually return a value back to the program that called the function. A sub procedure cannot return a value back to the calling program. A sub procedure and a function are two types of procedures.

3. "Null" indicates that the variable has been intentionally set to equal nothing. "Empty" represents a variable whose contents have not been assigned a value.

4. The ByVal statement enables you to pass a variable by value to a procedure. Passing a variable by value makes a copy of the variable for the procedure to access and modify within the scope of that procedure. Any changes made to the variable within the procedure aren't reflected back to the calling program.

5. The answer is zero. The `Do...While` loop executes a block of code as long as a condition is true. The `Do...While` loop checks the condition first before executing the code. If the condition is false, as in this case, the code within the loop won't be executed.

7

In Review

The first week has been filled with information about Visual InterDev. You have discovered how this exciting new tool completes the application development puzzle. You learned about the features of Visual InterDev and had a chance to build your first project. The first week focused a lot of attention on the client side of the application equation. You should now have a good feel for how Visual InterDev addresses this piece of the puzzle.

Where You Have Been

At the beginning of the week, you received a brief overview of the importance of the Internet, intranets, and the World Wide Web. This introduction was followed by an in-depth look at the features and capabilities of Visual InterDev. You also learned about design and development considerations for your Web-based applications. You developed your first Visual InterDev project by the middle of the week. Next, you were introduced to the FrontPage Editor for Visual InterDev. During this part of the lesson you discovered the joys of visual editing. Toward the end of the week, you traded your developer hat for a creative artist's beret as you learned how to use the Image Composer and the Music Producer to spice up your web pages. The final day presented the dynamics of using client-side script to enhance your application.

Week 2

At a Glance

Week 1 provided you with a solid foundation upon which to build more advanced Visual InterDev topics. In Week 2, you will learn more about the server side of the application equation. A majority of the week focuses on integrating a database with your application. You also will learn about some more advanced client-side topics, such as how to use objects and controls to build your interface.

8

9

10

11

12

13

14

Where You Are Going

At the beginning of the week, you will learn how to communicate with a database. You will discover how to use the power of the Visual Data Tools included with Visual InterDev to provide true database interaction in your application. The lesson also teaches you how to administer and manage your database components. In the middle of the week, you discover how to create dynamic applications through the use of Active Server Pages.

The last few days of the week focus on using advanced controls and objects to construct your application interface. First, you learn about HTML forms and controls. Then you get a chance to interact with ActiveX controls and Java applets. The final day of the week teaches you how to extend the functionality of your web page using design-time controls. The topics covered during this week will adequately prepare you for the lessons in Week 3, in which you will assimilate all of the concepts to build an application.

Day 8

Communicating with a Database

The second week begins with a very exciting topic—database integration. Communicating with a database is an integral part of any application. For a Web-based application, it's essential to provide the users with a way to interact with data and information. This lesson begins a series of lessons on how to use the features of Visual InterDev to facilitate communication between the users and their data. Today's lesson provides an introduction to help you build database communication into your application. Day 9, "Using the Visual Data Tools for Maximum Productivity," extends the scope of today's lesson to show you how to use the Visual Data Tools to enhance your productivity. To round out the discussion of database integration, you will learn how to administer your database components on Day 10, "Managing Your Database Components."

Today you will receive an overview of how to leverage Visual InterDev to access your database information. In this overview, you are introduced to the benefits of database integration and how Visual InterDev seamlessly provides this essential component. The next part of the lesson explains the Active Data Object model. Visual InterDev uses this model to provide controls for communicating with the database. The lesson also explains the different types of datasources that you can establish based on the Open Database Connectivity (ODBC) standard.

The final sections introduce you to several database features of Visual InterDev. You will learn how to use the Data View to examine and interact with your database objects. The lesson also outlines the features of the Query Designer and how this tool can make your life easier. Lastly, you will see an introduction to special design-time ActiveX controls that are geared specifically at database integration.

Leveraging Visual InterDev to Access Your Data

Companies and organizations are jumping on board the Internet and intranet cruise liner at a rapid pace. Specifically, businesses are providing a way for people to take action. Electronic commerce is expanding at a rapid pace. You can visit your favorite retailer on the Internet and buy the gift that your family forgot to give you for your birthday. These retailers include new businesses where their only place of business is the online marketplace. Amazon.com Books is a good example of this kind of virtual business.

Corporations are discovering the power of the intranet to provide applications for their employees, and are using the power of private intranets to share applications and information with partnering companies. The thin-client model of a Web-based application provides a compelling reason to build new applications using this model as well as to convert existing systems to the Web.

All of the aforementioned developments require one central component to make them useful—data. Whether you're building an electronic commerce application for the Internet or constructing an intranet to provide applications for your employees, you must enable the users to interact with the information. The application must support creating, storing, modifying, and, if necessary, deleting information to be considered valuable.

A database provides the vehicle for storing the information for future use. But how do you develop applications that can access the database? Visual InterDev provides some very robust features for accessing the database from your application. You will be learning about a few of these features in today's lesson.

You can use Visual InterDev to rapidly build your application to include database connectivity. These features are intuitive, powerful, and easy to use. The word "leveraging" is used in the title for this section. The word leverage refers to the use of a lever to provide an advantage in the accomplishment of a task. For example, you might use a physical lever to help you move some heavy object. You might capitalize on a friendship to get you into the door at some organization or business. Similarly, Visual InterDev provides the lever to accelerate your development of an interactive, database application. You should realize the power of the database features over the next few days.

The Benefits of Database Integration

When I speak of database integration, I'm not only talking about being able to access a database from your Web page, but also using this connection to integrate the results to create a holistic application for the user. I also am referring to using a comprehensive development tool to produce these results.

Integrating the Data

A holistic application refers to an application that provides a complete experience for the user. If a user places an order for some items, the application should provide a way for that person to check the status of their order. Also, your application should integrate the use of the data to provide additional value to the different types of users.

The customer supplies some customer information along with the order. This data is stored in different tables within your database. You should be able to provide a way for the business user in the sales department to locate information about the customer and their order information. The sales manager may want to explore the past buying habits of this person and determine if he or she is a repeat customer. In other words, you should use the data and integrate this information throughout your application to satisfy the request of both external and internal users.

Your requirements will vary, however, depending on what type of application you're building. A public Internet site that provides electronic commerce will be dramatically different from a private intranet application. Integration of the data is still the key for both types of applications.

An example of an intranet application might be an oil and gas trading system that facilitates the exchange of oil and gas between energy companies. An energy company would consist of several departments that work together to complete a trade. First, an energy trader of company A makes a deal with company B to sell some oil or gas. Basic data about the deal is recorded, including the product, the price, and other company B information. Then, company A's contract administration workgroup uses the deal information to develop a formal contract.

The deal information is used as the core of the contract as well as for additional information concerning the terms and schedule of the contract. Next, the credit department uses the information to verify the credit history of company B. After the deal is consummated, company A's scheduling department schedules the transfer of the product along some medium such as a pipeline or barge. This information is linked to the transaction so that the accounting department can account for the movement of the product and send an invoice to company B. The accounting department would use all of the information that has been captured along the way to create the invoice as well as to maintain its books. Integration of data is essential to the completion of this cycle.

Comparing the Options

There are many options for providing database connectivity to your Web page. These options range from simple solutions that don't contain much robustness to the very powerful tools that are difficult to use. The matrix in Figure 8.1 compares some of the many options that are available for connecting a Web page to a database.

Figure 8.1.

Web-to-database connectivity comparison matrix.

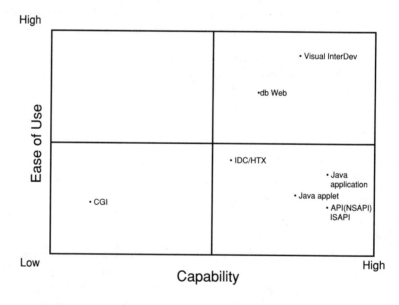

The matrix in Figure 8.1 consists of two axes. The horizontal axis measures the capability of the features of the tool and ranges on a scale from Low to High. The vertical axis describes the ease of use and again ranges from Low to High. I have rated each tool in the comparison on both of these scales to determine its position in the matrix. As you can see from the comparison, Visual InterDev is very robust and easy to use. Java applications and applets rate slightly higher than Visual InterDev on the capability scale due to their portability across platforms. These same tools rate lower on their ease of use due to the nature of the Java programming language.

Java is very similar to C++ and is, therefore, a more complex language when compared to a tool like Visual InterDev. The database tools in Visual InterDev are very intuitive and easy to use because you can visually build your SQL.

Visual InterDev also receives high marks for its ability to provide a single environment for constructing both the Web page and the database calls for your application. With earlier database solutions like Internet Database Connector (IDC), you had to create one file to handle your SQL information and calls and another file to process the formatted HTML page.

API programming receives a high rating on the capability scale but is more difficult to use than the other solutions. For those CGI pioneers, you're probably unhappy about the low rating of CGI in the comparison matrix. CGI will still be used as a solution for connecting to a database. With the advent of APIs that improve the performance of server connections as well as visual tools that significantly augment the time it takes to build your database application, CGI is now considered more of a legacy.

Visual InterDev Benefits

Now that I have illustrated where Visual InterDev compares with other database connectivity tools, I will outline some specific benefits of the database features included with Visual InterDev. The benefits of having an integrated development environment to create your application can't be understated. You may be familiar with some of the tools that were listed in the Web-to-database connectivity comparison matrix. With many of these solutions, you have to use separate development environments and tools to accomplish database connectivity. Visual InterDev provides a comprehensive and integrated development environment that offers the following features and benefits:

- [ ] Ease of use
- [ ] Visual environment
- [ ] Rapid application development
- [ ] Robustness

Ease of Use

Visual InterDev offers a seamless environment that includes several database tools under one integrated roof. For this reason, Visual InterDev is very easy to use. You don't have to migrate between separate tools and environments to build your database connection and SQL calls as well as your formatted HTML web pages. Also, the Visual InterDev development environment provides toolbar and menu options to guide you through the process of adding database functionality into your web page.

Visual Environment

Visual InterDev, as the name indicates, provides a visual environment with which to build your applications. This intuitive environment includes the Visual Data Tools, which you will learn more about tomorrow. These tools enable you to visually construct your SQL statements and immediately test the results. MS Access users love the interface of the tools because of the similarities between the two environments. You discovered the benefits of a visual tool to build your HTML web pages during the lesson on the FrontPage Editor for Visual InterDev in Week 1. The Visual Data Tools provide the same type of benefits to your database calls. You don't have to know the details of SQL to construct your queries. For power SQL programmers, the visual nature of the tools will save you time from programming the mundane and routine queries and enable you to spend time on the more complex SQL calls.

NOTE

Some people think of the term query to denote the execution of an inquiry, or a SELECT statement against a database. In this book, I use the term query to refer generically to any SQL statement that you can execute against a database. I will specifically use the word select or the keyword SELECT when I am describing an inquiry against a database.

Rapid Application Development

Visual InterDev provides an environment that enables you to rapidly build database connectivity and integration into your application. Our modern age requests, and sometimes demands, instantaneous information all the time. With Visual InterDev, you can use the database tools to help meet the desire of your users. Visual InterDev promotes the theory behind rapid application development by supporting both PC desktop and server databases.

You learned on Day 3, "Design and Development Considerations," how to use databases like MS Access and MS SQL Server at different stages of the development cycle to rapidly build your application. The method involves conducting joint application design (JAD) sessions with your users, using Visual InterDev and MS Access to build a working prototype of the application. The database tools enable you to construct actual ODBC-compliant SQL calls that can eventually be used when you migrate the application to a more robust production database like MS SQL Server. This method can facilitate a very iterative and rapid cycle for your development process.

Robustness

So far, I have talked a lot about the ease of use of the Visual InterDev database features. Some people seem to think that a product has to be difficult to offer powerful features, and that a product that is easy to use can't possibly be very robust. Visual InterDev provides the best of both worlds—robustness and ease of use. You can program complex SQL directly from within the Visual InterDev environment. For some databases, you also can edit and manage your database components. Visual InterDev supports all of the major ODBC-compliant databases including MS SQL Server, Oracle, Sybase, Informix, IBM DB2/2, MS Access, Microsoft FoxPro, and Borland Paradox.

The ActiveX Data Object

The ActiveX Data Object (ADO) provides database access for all of the Visual InterDev database tools. ADO serves as the central model for you to build database interaction within your web pages. ActiveX Data Objects can supply connections for your web pages to any ODBC-compliant database. Microsoft implemented ADO specifically to provide data access across the Web. The main benefits of the ADO model include low memory overhead and high speed, which are ideal for Web-based applications.

ADO enables you to use ActiveX scripting to establish a connection to your datasource. You also can use ActiveX scripting to customize the properties and methods of an ActiveX Data Object. ADO supports a variety of data types, including images and binary large objects (BLOBs). ADO supports transactions, cursors, error handling, and the use of stored procedures.

Exploring ADO

The following section provides a brief explanation of ADO. This overview provides a basic context for you to understand how Visual InterDev provides data access for your application through the use of ADO. This discussion isn't meant to be an exhaustive review of ADO and similar data access methods. For an in-depth discussion of these topics, I would suggest that you visit the Microsoft ADO Web site at

`www.microsoft.com/ado`

and the Microsoft OLE DB Web site at

`www.microsoft.com/oledb`

What Is ADO?

Microsoft designed ActiveX Data Objects, or ADO, to be language-independent objects for you to access a database from your Web pages. ADO is built on top of the OLE DB model from Microsoft. For Visual Basic programmers who are familiar with Data Access Objects (DAO) and Remote Data Objects (RDO), you may think that Microsoft is playing alphabet soup with so many standards and acronyms. ADO is the successor to both RDO and DAO. ADO combines the best of previous data access methods with an object-based standard, and includes the capability of RDO and DAO and extends their reach to provide data access for the Internet using the OLE model.

NOTE

Data Access Objects (DAO) were first introduced with previous versions of Microsoft Visual Basic and Microsoft Access. DAO was developed to encapsulate database functions and operations within the context of an object. DAO provides access to ODBC-compliant databases.

Remote Data Objects (RDO) were the successor to DAO and were included in Visual Basic 4.0. RDO provided a better solution for ODBC database access and extended the reach of these objects to the server.

The benefit of using ADO over these two methods is that you can independently create objects. With RDO and DAO, you had to create a hierarchy for your objects. Also, ADO is faster and more efficient.

The idea behind OLE DB is to provide an object-based interface that makes remote objects appear as if they were local. You can see how this model would help you in your development. The goal is to enable you to access your database through helpful objects that provide seamless access to your database, which could reside on a remote server or locally on your machine. Figure 8.2 illustrates how ADO and OLE DB work together to provide database access for a MS SQL Server database.

Figure 8.2 presents a configuration for a typical Web-based application built using Visual InterDev. You can see that the ActiveX Data Object resides within an Active Server Page on the web server. When the browser sends a request for database information, the Active Server Page is called, and ADO submits the request via OLE DB to the database server.

MSDA SQL is used to format the ODBC request for the database server. MSDA is an ODBC-specific SQL language, and both MS Access and MS SQL Server support the use of it to communicate with their respective datasources. The ODBC driver translates the MSDA SQL into a specific language for a particular database. The information is then passed back through this pipeline. The Active Server Page and ADO work together to format and send the results back to the browser.

Figure 8.2.
ADO and OLE DB.

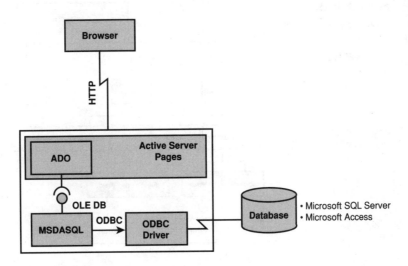

NOTE   The previous illustration contained some components that are specific to MS SQL Server and MS Access. ADO works with any ODBC-compliant database. This illustration is provided as an example to understand the communication links and path from the browser to the database and back. Other databases implementations of ADO may contain slightly different components, but the communication concepts will be the same.

Understanding ADO Objects

I have mentioned that ADO is an object-based solution. The ADO model includes seven major objects:

- ☐ Connection object
- ☐ Command object
- ☐ Recordset object
- ☐ Field object
- ☐ Parameter object
- ☐ Property object
- ☐ Error object

Figure 8.3 illustrates how each of these objects relate to each other.

Figure 8.3.
ADO model.

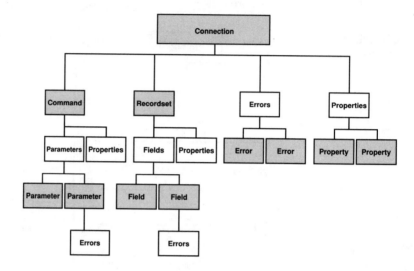

In this model, you see that the Connection object is the central object in the model. Every other object in the model is related to the Connection object. This hierarchy makes sense, because the other objects can't exist without a connection to the database. The ADO model isn't an autocratic hierarchy. In other words, you don't have to create the second tier of objects under a single Connection object. For example, you could create a Recordset object that is separate from a previously defined Connection object. The Recordset object that you define will exist under a newly created Connection object. Although you aren't confined to a strict hierarchy, you will typically use the structured nature of the ADO model to provide organization for your objects and code.

Before I explain each of these objects, I need to explain the concept of how objects, properties, and methods work together. Objects contain certain characteristics, or attributes. These attributes help to define their behavior and composition. Methods define certain commands that can be carried using these objects to accomplish some task. These terms are explained in detail on Day 13, "Interacting with Objects and ActiveX Controls."

The Connection **Object**

The Connection object controls your connection to the database. All of the information about your connection is established with this object. You can customize the behavior of the Connection object. For example, you can set the timeout properties and default database for the connection, and you also can specify to open and close the connection to the database and manage its transaction properties.

8

The Command Object

The Command object enables you to specify a specific command that you are going to execute on a database. For example, you could use the Command object to call a stored procedure. You can create a Command without associating the object with a previously defined Connection object. This feature is an example of where ADO differs from previous database access methods. You don't have to use a hierarchy of objects to carry out your commands. You will want to organize your objects into a hierarchy, however, when you execute multiple commands against the same database connection.

The Recordset Object

You can use the Recordset object to manipulate the records, or rows within your database tables. A recordset can contain all of the rows within a base table. A recordset also may consist of the result set from a specific query. The Recordset object supports both immediate and batch updates. Immediate updates are executed against the database instantaneously. With batch updates, the changes are saved and then sent as a batch to the database. Most of the time, you will probably be using immediate updates.

The Recordset object supports the use of four different types of cursors. These cursors indicate how the user will interact with the information in your database. The type of cursor that you can use depends on what cursors your database supports.

NEW TERM   A *cursor* establishes the navigation behavior for the data that is contained in a database. A cursor's relationship with a database is analogous to the mouse cursor's relationship with a document. The mouse cursor indicates where you are in a document and where you can go. Similarly, a cursor defines where you are in the database and where you can go.

Table 8.1 represents the four types of cursors that you can use with the Recordset object, along with a description of each.

Table 8.1. Recordset cursors.

Cursor Type	Description
Dynamic	View additions, changes, and deletions by other users
Keyset	View changes, but not additions and deletions
Static	View only a copy of the data; cannot view additions, changes, or deletions
Forward-only	Same as Static cursor but can only scroll forward through a table

The `Field` Object

The `Field` object pertains to a particular column within a recordset. You can use this object to retrieve specific information about the field as well as change the contents of a particular field.

The `Parameter` Object

You can use the `Parameter` object to specify parameters for executing a command against the database. For example, you could use this object to designate the values for the parameters that are passed to a stored procedure on the database. This object is typically used with the `Command` object.

The `Property` Object

The `Property` object captures specific properties that are defined by the service provider. The service provider performs the specific services that enable you to access and query your data. OLE DB service providers can choose to present additional characteristics, or properties, to the ActiveX Data Object. You can then use these properties to implement further capability within your application. For example, you could use the `Property` object to determine whether a service provider supported transactions.

The `Error` Object

The `Error` object collects error information that is generated from the database. Any errors that are encountered when attempting to perform a database function are captured within this object.

Understanding ADO Collections and Properties

ADO provides collections and properties for the objects within the ADO model. Collections consist of a group of properties for an object. You use properties to customize the behavior of your objects. Table 8.2 lists the types of collections that exist for ADO objects.

Table 8.2. ADO collections.

Collection	Description
Fields	Collection of `Field` objects for a `Recordset` object
Parameters	Collection of `Parameter` objects for a `Command` object
Properties	Collection of `Property` objects for an instance of an object
Errors	Collection of `Error` objects for an ADO operation

8

Each ADO consists of a distinct set of properties. Refer to the ADO help documentation within Visual InterDev for an alphabetical listing of all of the ADO properties.

Seeing Clearly with the Data View

Now that you have learned about the underlying data model used by Visual InterDev, you will get a chance to experience some of the Visual InterDev features that are supported by the model. The first feature that you will learn how to use is the Data View. You received an introduction to this feature during the first week. The Data View enables you to view all of the database objects within a database. These objects include tables, fields, views, stored procedures, and triggers. You can use the Data View to access all of these objects from your client machine. You also can use the Data View to examine detailed information about the database objects including field types, key structures, and table definitions.

Exploring the Data View

The Data View tab is displayed next to the File tab in the Visual InterDev project workspace when you connect your project to a datasource. You will learn how to use a wizard to walk you through this process in the next section entitled "Building a Connection with a Database Wizard." Visual InterDev uses a live connection to the database to present the Data View. This connection enables you to interact directly with the database objects. Figure 8.4 demonstrates the power of the Data View.

Figure 8.4.

Using the Data View to see your database.

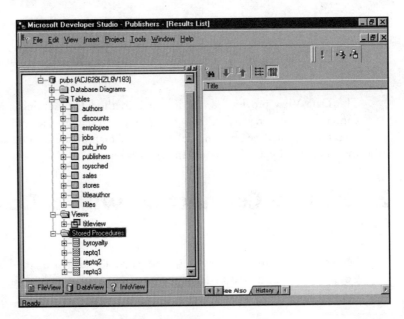

The best part about the Data View is that it provides a graphical tool for this interaction that is very intuitive. The Data View works in conjunction with the Query Designer and the Database Designer (which you learn more about tomorrow) to provide a robust set of database tools for a developer. The Data View enables you to connect to any ODBC-compliant database. You can establish multiple connections to different databases.

Table 8.3 examines the icons that are displayed within the Data View, as well as their meanings

Table 8.3. Data View icons.

Icon	Folder Name	Description
	Database Project	Project that contains database connection
	Data Source	Identifies a datasource connection
	Database Diagram	Indicates a database diagram
	Table	Represents a database table
	View	Represents a database view
	Stored Procedure	Indicates a stored procedure
	Parameter	Signifies a stored procedure parameter

The Data View provides a very intuitive method for examining your database and its contents. Moreover, you don't have to use a separate database administrator tool to view these objects. You can develop your application and manipulate your database objects all within the comforts of your own Visual InterDev home.

Building a Connection with a Database Wizard

You can connect to a database in several ways. The easiest method is to use the Database Connection Wizard to add a database connection to your project, and this section walks you through that very procedure.

Selecting the Datasource

To insert a database connection into your project, select the Project menu and choose the Add to Project menu item. The Add to Project submenu displays a list of choices for you to choose from. Select Data Connection from the list. This action displays the Select Data Source dialog window. Figure 8.5 illustrates the available options on the Select Data Source dialog window.

Figure 8.5.

Selecting a data-source.

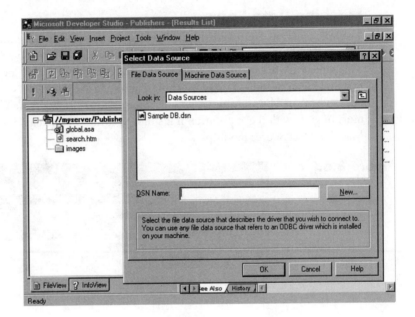

File Data Source

The File Data Source tab display is shown in Figure 8.5. This display enables you to configure a File datasource name (DSN) for your project. A File DSN enables you to set up a file-based connection that is local to a specific computer. This connection can be shared by multiple users.

A file-based connection means that the information to connect to the database is stored in a .dsn file. You must install an ODBC driver on this computer to communicate with the database. When the database connection is created for your project, the information in the .dsn file is inserted into the connect string within your global.asa file.

A File DSN is sometimes referred to a "DSN-less" connection, because connection information is stored within your project—not a separate file. A File DSN is recommended due to its portability. You don't have to copy or create a DSN file on the computer when you move the application.

The Look In combo box enables you to browse the file system for a datasource. This combo box defaults to the `ODBC\Data Sources\` directory on the computer. The File DSN listbox displays all of the available datasources within the specified directory. You can either double-click a datasource within the listbox or select the item and click OK to connect to the data-source. The New button enables you to create a new datasource.

Machine Data Source

The Machine Data Source tab display enables you to establish a machine datasource for your project. You can create two types of Machine datasources. The first type is called a User DSN. This type of DSN can only be used by the designated user and is specific to a machine. A System DSN is the other type of Machine datasource. A System DSN is specific to a machine but can be shared by multiple users. This information is stored in the Windows Registry and must migrate with the application if it's moved to another machine. Figure 8.6 depicts the Machine Data Source tab display.

Figure 8.6.

Specifying a Machine Data Source.

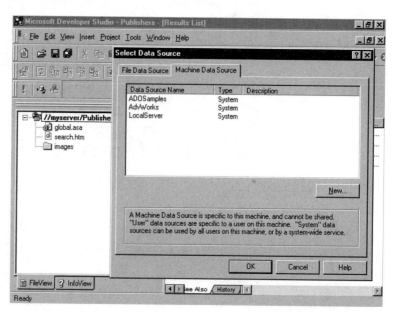

This window contains a list of machine datasources that are available. You can select an item from the list and click OK to create a connection to an existing Machine datasource. You also can create a new Machine datasource by pressing the New button. You will be prompted to indicate whether you're creating a User DSN or a System DSN.

Creating a New Datasource

I stated earlier that for both the File and Machine datasource you could choose an existing datasource to insert into your project. The datasource will create a connection, enabling you to interact with the database. This process is straightforward if you have already established the datasource. This section focuses on showing you how to create a new datasource. I will continue to walk you through the Database Connection Wizard windows to create a new File DSN. The process to set up a Machine datasource is very similar.

Selecting the Type of Datasource

When you click the New button from the Select Data Source window, the Create New Data Source dialog window is displayed. This window enables you to specify the database driver that will be used to create the new datasource. Figure 8.7 demonstrates an example of how to specify the datasource type.

Figure 8.7.

Selecting a new data-source type.

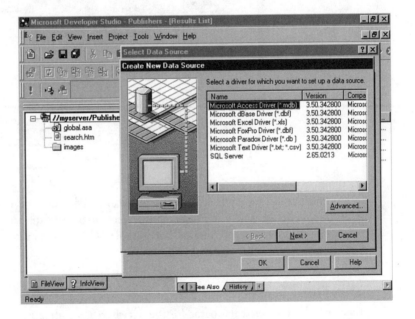

In Figure 8.7, a listbox displays the available drivers for the data type. These items vary depending on what database drivers you have installed on the machine. The Advanced button enables you to view the driver information that will be created for the datasource based on your selection. You can customize this information if you want to be very specific about the parameters that should be created for the datasource. You can use the Create New Data Source window to enter this information directly into the listbox. In this example, I'm going to select the SQL Server driver to create a new datasource connection to MS SQL Server. After you have made your selection, click the Next button to display the next dialog window.

The next step involves entering a name for your datasource. Figure 8.8 shows the window for entering this information.

Figure 8.8.

Naming the data-source.

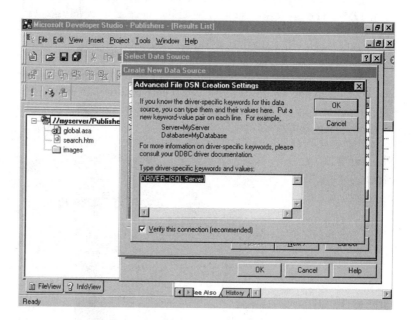

The name that you enter is used to represent the underlying datasource and database objects. You should choose a meaningful name that accurately indicates to the user what kind of information the datasource contains. For example, "Orders" is a more meaningful name than "MyData."

The Final Steps

Once you have entered the name for the datasource, a listbox is displayed, indicating the choices that you have made. This window specifies the datasource type, name, and driver. You can click the Back button to go back and change one of the parameters. Pressing Finish confirms the choices that you have made and creates the new datasource. You also can click the Cancel button to cancel this process. Figure 8.9 displays an example of a new File data-source named Publishers that will be created for a MS SQL Server database.

Figure 8.9.

*A new File
datasource.*

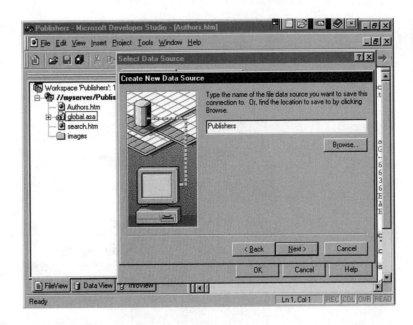

After you click Finish, a dialog window display prompts you to log in, if necessary, to the database that you have chosen. Figure 8.10 confirms your new datasource.

Figure 8.10.

*Confirming your new
datasource.*

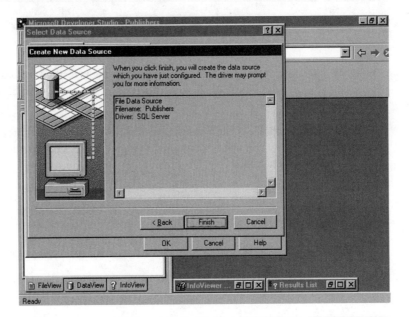

From this window, you enter the server, user ID, and password. The Options button enables you to enter specific datasource information like the name of the database and the application type. When you click OK, Visual InterDev logs in to the database and establishes the database connection. Figure 8.11 displays the additional options that are available from the SQL Server Login window.

Figure 8.11.

Logging in to the database.

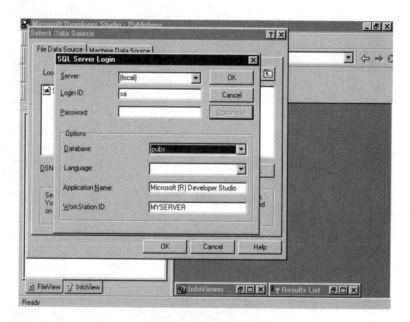

After you confirm the login parameters by pressing OK, the Database Connection Wizard creates the .dsn file. Figure 8.12 shows the resulting Publishers.dsn file that was created based on this example.

You can select the DSN file from the list and click OK to insert this datasource connection into your project. You will be prompted to log in, if necessary, to the server again. After you log in to the server, Visual InterDev creates the connection and the results are placed into your project.

Analyzing the Results

Figure 8.13 displays the datasource that was created from the preceding example.

Figure 8.12.

Selecting the newly created datasource.

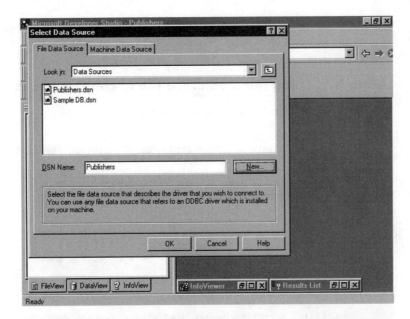

Figure 8.13.

Examining the results with the Data View.

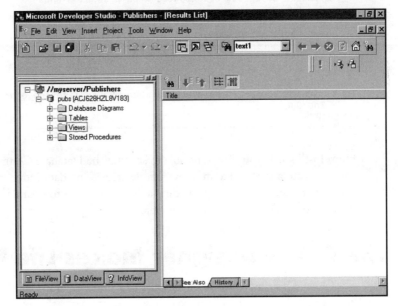

The datasource information is captured in the global.asa file. Listing 8.1 shows what happens to the global.asa file when a Microsoft SQL Server connection is inserted into a project.

Listing 8.1. Using the global.asa file to connect to a datasource.

```
<SCRIPT LANGUAGE="VBScript" RUNAT="Server">

Sub Session_OnStart
'==Visual InterDev Generated - DataConnection startspan==
'--Project Data Connection
Session("pubs_ConnectionString") = "DRIVER={SQL Server};
SERVER=MyServer;UID=sa;PWD=;APP=Microsoft (R) Developer
➥Studio;WSID=MYSERVER;DATABASE=pubs"
Session("pubs_ConnectionTimeout") = 15
Session("pubs_CommandTimeout") = 30
Session("pubs_RuntimeUserName") = ""
Session("pubs_RuntimePassword") = ""
'==Visual InterDev Generated - DataConnection endspan==

End Sub

Sub Session_OnEnd
'Insert script to be executed when a session ends
End Sub

Sub Application_OnStart
'Insert script to be executed when the application starts
End Sub

Sub Application_OnEnd
'Insert script to be executed when the application ends
End Sub
</SCRIPT>
```

From Listing 8.1, you should be able to see that the Database Connection Wizard enables you to create a datasource in a few simple steps. The datasource is placed in the Visual InterDev project workspace, providing a live connection to your database objects. You can then use the Data View to access the objects.

The Query Designer Makes Life Easier

The Query Designer is part of the Visual Data Tools included with Visual InterDev. These tools definitely make the life of a database programmer easier, providing graphical tools to access the database objects. You will learn how to use the Visual Data Tools tomorrow, but the following section introduces you to some of the Query Designer's features.

Understanding the Query Designer

Once you have created your datasource, you're ready to access the data. The Query Designer helps you accomplish this task by enabling you to visually specify your SQL statements. You build your statements by selecting the tables that you want to use as well as the fields within those tables. As you make your choices, the SQL statement is constructed. You can view the statement as it is built and make any changes to the native SQL. You also can test and view the results of your query within another pane in the Visual InterDev development environment. The Query Designer can significantly enhance your database development effort. You can use the Query Designer to drastically reduce your database programming and testing cycle.

Query Designer Features

To use the Query Designer, click the DataView tab within the Visual InterDev project workspace. The Data View display tab enables you to see and access all of the objects for the datasource. You can use the Query Designer to execute queries against the database, and to specify the tables, columns, and order of the query results. You can very easily create joins between multiple tables. In addition to queries, you also can insert, update, and delete data that is contained within the database. You also can use the Query Designer to execute stored procedures if you're using MS SQL Server as your database. The following section examines the features of the Query Designer in a little more detail.

Query Designer Workspace

The Query Designer contains four panes that you can use to interact with your data. The following list indicates the Query Designer panes:

- ☐ Diagram pane
- ☐ Grid pane
- ☐ SQL pane
- ☐ Results pane

Diagram Pane

The Diagram pane enables you to work with the database objects to construct a SQL statement. Using this pane, you can drag and drop tables and views into the workspace. Figure 8.14 depicts the layout of the Diagram pane.

Figure 8.14.

The Diagram pane.

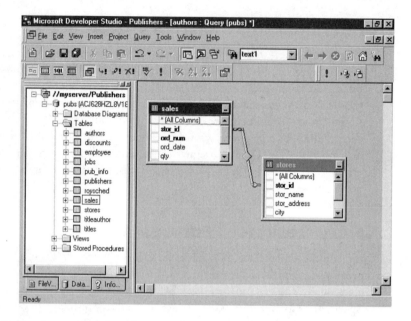

As you choose the tables, the Query Designer associates related tables and indicates table joins through the use of lines between the tables. You can select individual columns to be included in the SQL statement or select All Columns. For those SQL programmers, selecting the All Columns option performs a SELECT * to retrieve all of the columns within the table.

Grid Pane

The Grid pane provides a spreadsheet interface to customize the results of the query. You can designate which columns to show in the result set as well as how to order and group the results. Figure 8.15 shows the Grid pane for two sample tables.

SQL Pane

The SQL pane enables you to view the SQL statement for the tables and options that you have selected. You can use the SQL Pane to view a SQL statement as well as to modify the statement. You also can use this pane to create your own SQL statements. Figure 8.16 displays a SQL statement within the SQL pane.

Figure 8.15.

Customizing the results.

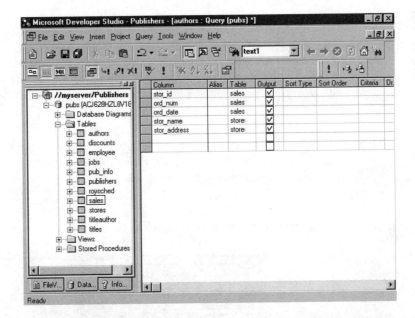

Figure 8.16.

The SQL pane.

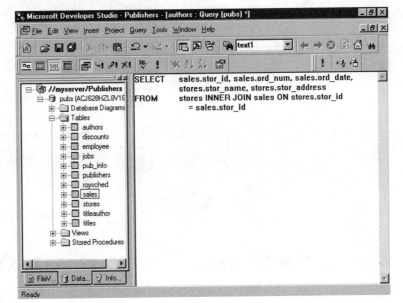

Results Pane

You can use the Results pane to view the data that is returned from the SQL statement. Based on the query that you construct, this pane displays the results set of the current query. You can use the Results pane to add, modify, and delete data in the database. The effects are immediate, because you're using a live connection to access the database.

 NOTE

> The actions that you can perform are limited to your access permissions on the database. Visual InterDev uses the access rights for your user ID and password to determine which commands you can execute.

Figure 8.17 shows the Results pane as well as the other three Query Designer panes.

Figure 8.17.

Displaying the Results pane.

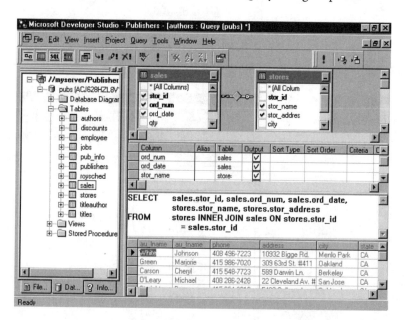

Database Design-Time ActiveX Controls

Visual InterDev includes several design-time controls for communicating with a database. You will see an in-depth lesson on these controls on Day 14, "Extending Web Pages Through Design-Time Controls." You received an introduction to design-time ActiveX controls during the first week. Design-time controls enable you to set properties and attributes at the time of design. At runtime, the properties that you set will perform robust functionality without the overhead of an ActiveX control.

The Database design-time controls that are included with Visual InterDev are built on top of the ADO model. These controls generate much of the script that is necessary for connecting and executing commands against a database. A good example of a database design-time control is the Data Command Control. You can insert this control into your application and then use the Query Designer to build your SQL statements. The Data Command Control will capture all of the scripting that is necessary to execute your SQL statements and insert this logic into an Active Server Page.

Database design-time controls can provide a lot of power to your application. You can use these controls to significantly reduce the time that it takes to build database integration into your application.

Summary

This lesson has provided you with an overview of how to communicate with a database from your Visual InterDev application, setting the stage for tomorrow when you discover how to use the Visual Data Tools.

First, the lesson centered on the benefits of database integration, explaining integration from a user's—as well as a developer's—point of view. Visual InterDev can serve as a powerful lever for building database integration into your application. Next, the lesson uncovered the mystery of the ActiveX Data Object (ADO) model. The ADO model was explained so that you could understand what Visual InterDev uses behind the scenes to connect and access the database. You then received an in-depth look at how to use the Data View to access your database objects. The Data View works in conjunction with the Visual Data Tools to provide some very robust features for interacting with the database.

Toward the end of today's lesson you learned how to build a database connection for your project using the Database Connection Wizard. The lesson provided a step-by-step tour of how to establish this connection. You also learned how to access your data using the Query Designer once the connection has been built. The lesson explained the basic Query Designer features and workspace. The final section of the day focused on Database design-time controls. The lesson presented an introduction to how these ActiveX controls can be used at design-time to provide robust functionality when your application is executed.

Q&A

Q **Are ActiveX Data Objects (ADO) just a renamed version of Remote Data Objects (RDO)?**

A ADO is the successor to RDO, but their models aren't identical. ADO extends the functionality of RDO to the Internet. ADO differs from RDO in that you don't have to create a hierarchy of objects to execute certain commands. All of the objects within the ADO model can be instantiated as individual objects.

Q **How does the Data View differ from the File View?**

A The Data View enables you to see the directory structure of your files within your Visual InterDev project. These files include everything from HTML web pages to images. The Data View is a special view that is inserted into the project workspace after a database connection has been made for the project. You use the Data View to specifically access and modify the objects within your database, including tables, fields, views, and stored procedures.

Q **When I use the Data View, do my changes affect the database or am I using a copy of the database?**

A When you insert a database connection into your project, Visual InterDev creates a live connection to the database. Therefore, when you use the Data View to view and modify the objects and data, you're interacting with the actual database. Your changes have an immediate effect on the database.

Workshop

For today's workshop, I want you to create the datasource that was presented in the lesson. If you're using a database other than MS SQL Server, create a datasource connection to your particular database. After you have established the connection, practice using the Data View and the Query Designer so that you will be familiar with these tools when you put them to the test during tomorrow's lesson. Try using all four of the Query Designer panes to produce the desired results from your SQL statements.

Quiz

1. What are the four panes of the Query Designer?
2. What is the difference between a File datasource and a Machine datasource?
3. Name the two types of Machine datasources.
4. In the ADO model, what is the Recordset object?

Quiz Answers

1. The four panes of the Query Designer include

   Diagram pane

   Grid pane

   SQL pane

   Results pane

2. A File datasource enables you to capture database connection information within a DSN file. Visual InterDev inserts the information contained in this file into an Active Server Page, thereby, creating a "DSN-less" connection. A File DSN is preferred, because you don't have to establish the datasource name on every user's machine.

   A Machine datasource creates a datasource connection that's specific to a machine. If you move the application to another machine, you also have to re-create the DSN for the new machine.

3. The two types of Machine datasources include a User DSN and a System DSN. The User DSN is tied to a specific user, while a System DSN can be shared among all users.

4. The `Recordset` object enables you to access the properties and values of a result set that is returned from your database. An example would be accessing the properties of a table and modifying the contents of the table or rows that are returned from a specific SQL call.

Day 9

Using the Visual Data Tools for Maximum Productivity

The Visual Data Tools provide a rewarding experience for the developer who is building an integrated database application. I bet you didn't know that "database programming" and "rewarding" could be found in the same sentence. Visual InterDev makes this possible through the use of visual tools that simplify the process of creating database functionality in your application. You received an overview of the Visual Data Tools during the first week. Yesterday, the lesson presented the Query Designer as one of the Visual Data Tools. Today's lesson provides an in-depth look at several members of the Visual Data Tools family. The lesson focuses on how to use the programming aspects of the tools to provide database interaction within your application.

To begin the day, you will learn how to use the Query Designer to build and construct your SQL statements. I will walk you through some examples of query construction within the context of a Web-based application. The lesson builds on the principles that you learned yesterday. Next, you learn how to use the Query Designer to modify the SQL statements that have been generated. This section targets those developers who need full control of their database code. You also will learn how to test the results of your SQL statements to verify that they produce the right results. The latter part of the day shows you how to integrate stored procedures and triggers into your application. You also will discover how to enter and manipulate the contents of your database. The final lesson for the day covers the Data Command Control and shows you how to use this database design-time control to communicate with the database.

Using the Query Designer to Generate Your SQL

On Day 8, "Communicating with a Database," the lesson walked you through an example of setting up a database connection. Today's lesson continues with that example to show you how to use the connection once it has been built. I hope that you had a chance to practice using the Query Designer on your own during yesterday's Workshop. In the following sections, you are guided through several examples of how to use the Query Designer to select, insert, modify, and delete your data. I will be using the data source that I established yesterday, which means the example will be using the sample Pubs database included with MS SQL Server.

NOTE

> If you're using Microsoft SQL Server and have installed this database, feel free to follow along with the example and execute the commands as they're presented in the lesson. If you're using another database, follow along with the example to understand the process. A good comprehension of the concepts enables you to apply the knowledge to other databases as well.

Query Designer Basics

The Query Designer works in conjunction with the Data View to enable you to access your data. To use the Query Designer, you must establish a connection to a data source. After you have established this connection, you're ready to begin communicating with your database.

I established a MS SQL Server connection to the Pubs database and named it Publishers. Figure 9.1 displays the tables, views, and stored procedures that are contained within this database.

Figure 9.1.

The Pubs database.

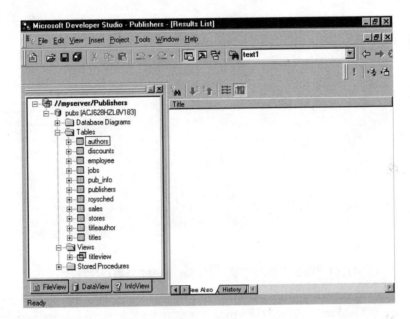

Opening a Table

Each type of database object is represented by a folder that describes its meaning. For example, the database tables are displayed in the Tables folder. You can open a table by selecting a table and pressing the right-mouse button to display the shortcut menu. You can then select the Open menu item. This action selects the entire contents of the table and presents the rows in the Results pane to the right of the project workspace. Figure 9.2 depicts the contents of the Authors table when it's opened using this method.

TIP You also can double-click an object to reveal its contents. In the previous example, you could have double-clicked on the Authors table to displays the rows contained within the table.

Once you have opened a table, you can use the Query Designer toolbar to create and view your queries, as well as to see the results.

Figure 9.2.
Opening the Authors table.

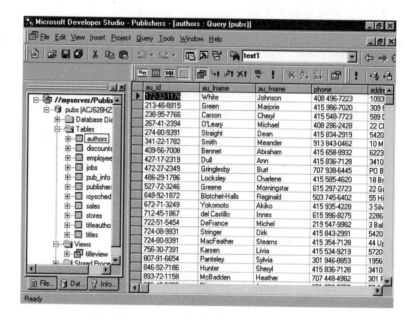

Using the Query Designer Toolbar

You learned about the four panes of the Query Designer during yesterday's lesson—the Diagram pane, the Grid pane, the SQL pane, and the Results pane. Each of these panes is represented by a toolbar icon that you can use to display a particular view. Figure 9.3 illustrates the available options of the Query Designer toolbar.

Figure 9.3.
The Query Designer toolbar.

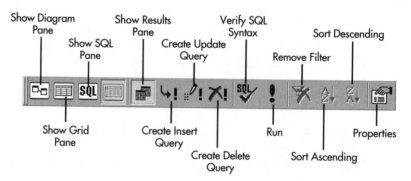

The next section provides a brief explanation of each of these icons.

Show Diagram Pane

You can use this option to display the Diagram pane. Remember, the Diagram pane enables you to work with specific tables and views to create your queries. This icon becomes enabled after you have opened a table or view. When you click this toolbar icon, the Diagram pane for that table or view is displayed. You can then work with that table, as well as drag and drop other tables into the Diagram pane.

Show Grid Pane

The Show Grid pane icon displays a view of the Grid pane, which enables you to customize the SQL statement. For example, you can choose the individual columns that you want to use in the query or select all of the columns within a table. The columns that are involved in the query display in the grid. The corresponding table for these columns also appears. You can enter search criteria for the query. For the rows that are returned from the database, you can designate ascending or descending order.

Show SQL Pane

You can use this icon to view the actual SQL statement for your query. From the SQL pane, you can modify the generated SQL statement, as well as create custom queries.

Show Results Pane

When you click this icon, the Results pane is displayed. This pane reveals the results from the database based on your query. From this pane, you can directly modify the database information. You also can add and delete database rows.

Create Insert Query

This icon enables you to create a new row for a table by copying data from an existing row within the table. You also can create a new row for a table by copying a row of data from one table into another table. If you use this feature, you generate an INSERT INTO SQL statement.

Create Update Query

This icon enables you to create an update query for a table. You can use this feature to update and change the values of a column or columns for one or more rows in a table. The resulting SQL statement will be an UPDATE statement.

Create Delete Query

You can use this icon to delete one or more rows from a table in your database. This query generates a DELETE SQL statement.

Verify SQL Syntax

This option enables you to test the validity of your SQL statement. You can use this option before you run your SQL statement to ensure that the syntax is correct. When you click this toolbar icon, the Query Designer tests your SQL statement against the data source. If the SQL syntax is accurate, you receive a confirmation message. If the SQL statement is incorrect, a message displays, indicating the syntax error as well as where the error is located.

Run

The Run toolbar icon enables you to execute your query against the database. You can view the results of the query using the Results pane.

Remove Filter

The Remove Filter option enables you to remove any special search criteria conditions that have been specified for the query. This option works in conjunction with the Diagram pane. After you select a field that contains a search criteria filter, the Remove Filter icon becomes enabled, allowing you to remove the conditions that have been created for this query.

Sort Ascending

You can click the icon to view your results in ascending order. The Sort Ascending toolbar option works in conjunction with the Diagram pane. This icon becomes enabled after you have selected a field within a table that is displayed in the Diagram pane. After you click this icon, an SQL statement is created, sorting the query in ascending order for the field that you select. You can choose multiple fields to help construct the sort.

Sort Descending

You can use this feature to view your results in descending order. The Sort Descending toolbar option works in conjunction with the Diagram pane. This icon becomes enabled after you have selected a field within a table that is displayed in the Diagram pane. You can choose multiple fields to help construct the sort.

Properties

When you click this toolbar option, you can view and change overall properties for the query. For example, you can select to display all of the columns for the tables within a query. You also can choose to view only distinct rows. This option enables you to avoid duplicate rows when you perform a query that joins two tables.

Using the Diagram Pane to Create a Query

Now that you have learned some of the basics about using the Query Designer, you're ready to create your first query. This part of the lesson covers how to combine features of the Query Designer panes and menu options to rapidly build queries for your applications. The main types of queries are discussed, including selecting, inserting, updating, and deleting data. You are shown how to perform each of these functions using the Query Designer.

Selecting the Tables

First, you need to select the tables that you're going to use to create the query. Earlier in the day, you learned how to open a table. You also discovered the Diagram Grid, which enables you to choose the tables that you want to use for your query. In this first example, I use two tables from the Publishers database to demonstrate the features of the Query Designer.

The first step involves selecting the table or view that you want to use in the Diagram pane. Using the Data View, click the left mouse button on the particular table or view. With the desired table highlighted, hold down the left mouse button and drag the mouse over to the Diagram pane. The mouse pointer displays the table icon when you have reached a valid spot to place the table. To drop the table into the Diagram pane, release the left mouse button. The selected table is positioned in the Diagram pane. Repeat these steps for each of the tables and views that you want to use to build your query. In my example, I have selected the Titles and Sales tables. Figure 9.4 shows these two tables within the Diagram pane.

As you can see, the name of the table is displayed along with the fields. You can use the shortcut menu to display only the name of the table. A join line also is displayed, defining the relationship between the two tables. The join line is composed of two components—the join type and the join relationship. Table 9.1 displays the possible types of joins and a definition of each type.

Figure 9.4.

Selecting the tables.

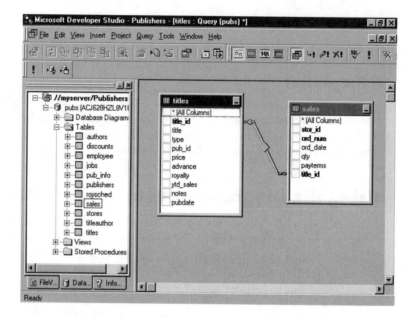

Table 9.1. Defining the types of joins.

Icon	Description
	Inner Join
	Inner Join using the greater than sign
	Left Outer Join
	Right Outer Join
	Full Outer Join

 NOTE

The join types illustrate how the tables are joined. A join based on the equal sign is the default type of join. For this reason, the equal sign does not display in the middle of the icon for joins of this type. If the join is based on another type, such as greater than or less than, the symbol displays in the middle of the icon.

Table 9.2 shows the possible join relationships and their meanings.

Table 9.2. Join relationships.

Icon	Description
	One-to-one relationship
	One-to-many relationship
	Many-to-one relationship
	Undefined relationship

Exploring Joins

A brief explanation of joins is warranted here. By default, the Query Designer creates an inner join between the tables, if possible. An inner join only returns a related set of rows between the tables. In the following example, the Titles and Sales tables were selected. The Query Designer created an inner join between these two tables and generated the following SQL statement:

```
SELECT titles.title, titles.price, titles.type, sales.ord_num, sales.ord_date,
sales.qty
FROM titles INNER JOIN sales ON titles.title_id = sales.title_id
```

Figure 9.5 shows the Diagram, SQL, and Results panes for an inner join between the Titles and Sales tables.

Notice that the inner join is based on the title ID field. If the title ID of the Titles table is equal to the title ID of the Sales table, the resulting row is displayed in the result set. Rows in either table that don't have the same title ID aren't returned from the database. In other words, sales information is displayed for each title that contains this information. If a particular title hasn't generated a sale, the title isn't displayed.

Figure 9.5.

An example of an inner join.

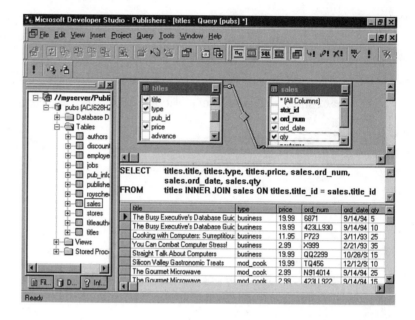

An outer join differs from an inner join in that an outer join can return rows that don't have related, or matched, rows in the joined table. The inner join only displays related rows between the tables. The outer join displays rows that fall outside the relationship based on the type of join. You can create three types of outer joins. The left outer join includes unmatched rows in the result set that are displayed in the left table, or the table that is specified first in the join statement. Figure 9.6 shows the Diagram, SQL, and Results panes for a left outer join between the Titles and Sales tables.

Right outer joins display all of the rows that are included in the right table, or the table that is listed second in the join statement. Figure 9.7 shows the Diagram, SQL, and Results panes for a right outer join between the Titles and Sales tables.

The third type of join is the full outer join, which displays all rows of all tables whether the rows have matching data or not. Figure 9.8 shows the Diagram, SQL, and Results panes for a full outer join between the Titles and Sales tables.

The Query Designer lives up to its visual nature by providing a way to easily designate the type of join you want to create. In fact, this visual feature enables you to create these joins without having to know the types of joins or their meanings. To change the type of join, click the mouse on the join line between the tables. The line becomes bold, indicating that this object has the focus of the mouse. You can then display the shortcut menu for the join line by pressing the right mouse button. Figure 9.9 displays the different options that you can select to change the type of join for the query.

Figure 9.6.

An example of a left outer join.

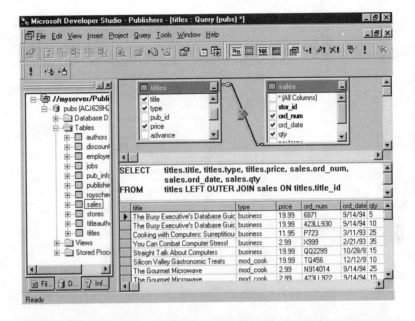

Figure 9.7.

An example of a right outer join.

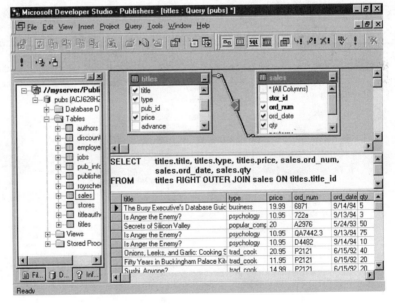

Figure 9.8.

An example of a full outer join.

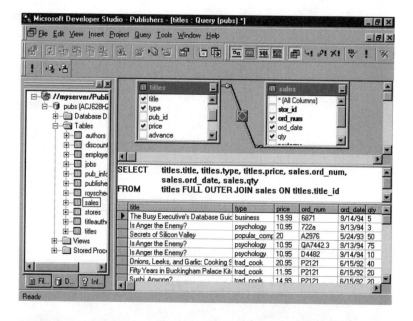

Figure 9.9.

Displaying the shortcut menu to create a join.

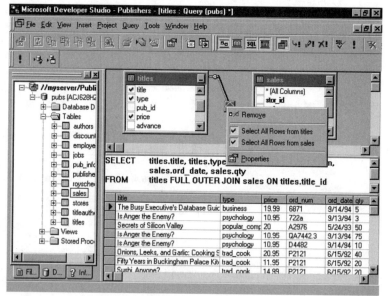

In Figure 9.9, you should notice that there is no mention of the word "join" in the list of menu items. The options are in plain English and describe the type of action that you are trying to accomplish. In this example, you can choose to display all of the rows from the Titles table (a left outer join). You also can choose to select all of the rows from the Sales table (a right outer join). Notice that these menu items are checkboxes, which means they aren't mutually exclusive. In other words, you can select both items at the same time, thereby creating a full outer join. This feature provides a very intuitive way to achieve the correct results for your queries.

Choosing the Columns for Your Query

After you have selected the tables for your query, you need to choose the columns of the tables that will have an effect on the query. You may use these columns to display the results of the query in addition to specifying the parameters for your query. You can choose individual columns by clicking the left mouse button in the box located to the left of the column name. Finally, you can select the All Columns option to include all of the table columns in the query.

All of the choices that you make in the Diagram pane are immediately reflected in the Grid and SQL panes. For example, if you choose three columns from the Titles table and two columns from the Sales table, these columns are reflected in the Grid pane and inserted into the SQL statement.

A symbol visually indicates how the column is being used in the query. In Figure 9.9, the columns contain a checkmark in the checkbox to the left. Figures 9.10 through 9.12 demonstrate the indicators for the other types of queries.

Figure 9.10.

Indicating an insert query column.

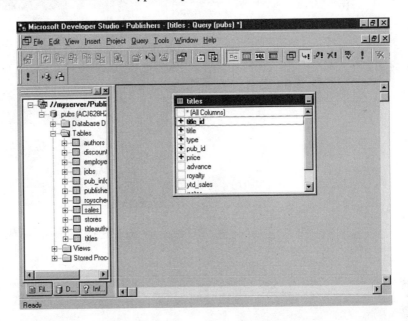

Figure 9.11.

*Indicating an update
query column.*

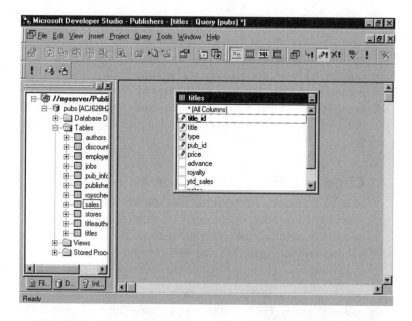

Figure 9.12.

*Indicating a delete
query column.*

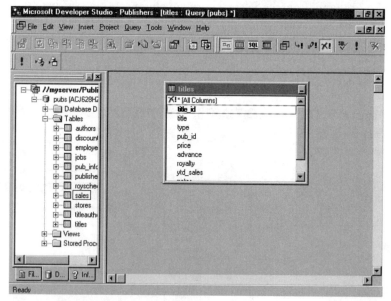

NOTE

The update query only pertains to one table. Also, the delete query relates to all columns of a particular table; therefore, this indicator only appears by the All Columns name in the table.

Several other symbols are displayed to the right of your column names. Table 9.3 illustrates these symbols and their meanings.

Table 9.3. Other column symbols.

Symbol	Meaning
A Z ↓	Sort column—Ascending (part of ORDER BY statement)
Z A ↓	Sort column—Descending (part of ORDER BY statement)
▼	Search criteria column (part of WHERE or HAVING statement)
[≡	Groups the results (part of GROUP BY statement)
Σ	Summary column (Used for aggregate functions like SUM and AVG)

Continuing with the example, I chose the Title, Type, and Price columns from the Titles table and the Ord_Num, Ord_Date, and Qty columns from the Sales table. Figure 9.13 displays these choices within the Diagram pane.

Figure 9.13.

Selecting the columns.

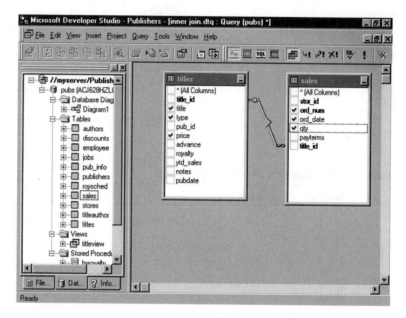

Executing the Query

So far, this lesson has taught you how to use the Diagram pane to construct a basic query. In the example, I chose to create a query that displays the title, price, type of book, order number, order date, and quantity of the order. The next step runs the query. Remember, to execute a query, click the Run icon from the Query Designer toolbar. You also can click the right mouse button in the Results pane. This action displays the shortcut menu for the Results pane, enabling you to choose Run from the menu item list. Figure 9.14 shows the rows that are returned from the database when I execute this query.

You can see from Figure 9.14 that several rows were returned from the database. The columns, however, aren't in the most intuitive order. For instance, the order number and order date fields are displayed too far to the right. A more useful way of organizing the data is to display these order information columns first and then the title information. You will discover in the next section how to further customize this initial query.

Figure 9.14.

Examining the results.

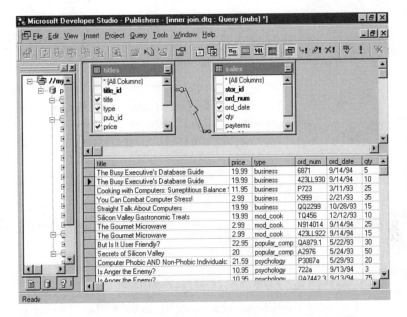

Using the Query Designer to Customize Your Queries

You received a brief introduction to the Grid pane yesterday. This pane enables you to work with the columns in the tables to further customize the query. Initial columns that you selected using the Diagram pane are displayed as rows within the grid. You can add to this list of columns as well as delete the columns that have been selected. To add a column to the query using the Grid pane, place the cursor in the column named Columns on an empty row. You can then choose a column from the tables you have selected from a drop-down listbox.

TIP

You also can drag and drop columns from the Diagram pane into the grid. Select a column from a table in the Diagram pane and hold down the left mouse button. Drag the field to the grid in the Grid pane. The mouse pointer changes to a plus sign, indicating that you're adding a column to the query. You can then insert the query anywhere in the list of columns. For instance, you can place the new column at the end of the list of columns. You also can choose to insert the new column before another column in the list.

To delete a row, click the box to the left of the Column name to select the row. The row is highlighted, enabling you to click the DEL (Delete) key or to choose Delete from the Edit menu to delete the row. Deleting a row removes the column from the query.

TIP You also can place your cursor in the Column name field and select the contents of the field. With the column name highlighted, delete the contents of the field. This action causes the column to be removed from the query.

Any changes that you make to the query using the Grid pane are instantly reflected in the Diagram and SQL panes. The next sections outline the Grid pane options that you can use to customize your queries.

Changing the Column Order

The order in which the columns appear in the grid on the Grid pane determines the order that the columns will be displayed in the results for your query. This order is determined by the order in which you selected your columns in the Diagram pane. You can change the order of these columns by selecting a row and moving it to the new location within the rows in the grid.

Changing the Names of the Columns

Many times, the name of the database column isn't a very user-friendly name. This is especially true if you have cryptic naming standards for defining your table columns that only a database administrator can understand. The Alias column within the Grid pane enables you to create an alias name for the column that is displayed with the result set. You can define a more intuitive name for the column that can be presented to the user. You also can use an alias for columns that are computed based on the values within your table columns. For example, you may want to create a query that displays the price and quantity for certain book orders. Because the order total changes frequently, this value isn't stored in the database. You could create an alias column that computes the total value of the order from the Price and Quantity columns and displays this total for each row.

To enter an alias, type the new name in the Alias field next to the column that you want to rename. The alias that you enter is then used to display the results. In the example, the column names for the order number, order date, and quantity aren't very intuitive. I changed the names of these fields by using the Alias column. Figure 9.15 shows the new names for the fields as they are displayed in the Grid pane.

Figure 9.15.

Providing more useful column names for the user.

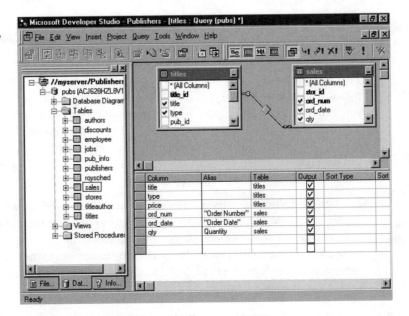

Specifying the Output

The Grid pane enables you to choose the results that you want the user to see when selecting information from the database. You can use the Output column to designate whether the column is displayed in the results for the query. This field is checked by default, meaning that the column is displayed in the query results. You may want to use columns in a table to construct a query but not display the columns in the query results. To change the Output column, click the mouse on the field and the checkmark is turned on or off, depending on its current status.

NOTE   The Output column pertains only to select queries. You use this column when you're inquiring on rows in a database and want to customize both the query and the results that are returned. This column is typically used with the Sort columns, which you will learn about next.

Customizing the Query

The next few columns in the Grid pane enable you to customize your query. The Sort Type field enables you to sort the query using that column. You can specify ascending or descending for the type of sort. To choose the sort type, place your cursor in the Sort Type field for a particular column. A drop-down listbox is displayed, enabling you to pick a sort type from the list.

The Sort Order indicates the priority of the columns to be sorted. This column is in conjunction with the Sort Type field. While the Sort Type field indicates the type of sort that you want to use, the Sort Order field determines the order in which columns will be sorted. The first field that you select to sort is indicated by the number 1. The second field contains the number 2, and so on. For example, you may want to sort the sales data by order date and then order number. To create this sort, you choose a sort type for the Ord_Date column first and then for the Ord_Num column.

The Criteria column enables you to enter special search conditions for the query. You can use this column to specify that you want the query to find only those columns that meet your search criteria. The default criteria condition is based on the = (equal) sign. If you enter a value into the Criteria field for a column, the Grid pane formats the condition using the equal sign. Figure 9.16 shows the Grid, SQL, and Results panes using an example of searching for a value that is equal to a column value.

Figure 9.16.

Searching for books that cost $19.99.

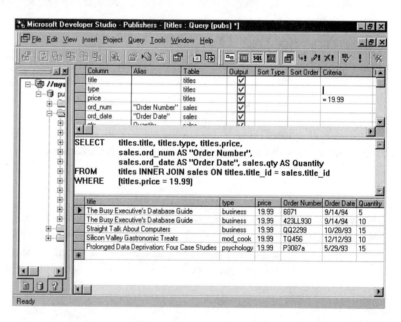

In this example, I entered the value into the field, and the Grid pane automatically inserted the = sign into the Criteria field. If you want to enter other types of search conditions, such as greater than or less than, you can manually enter these conditions, along with the search condition value. As you enter search condition criteria for multiple columns, these conditions are linked using the AND statement.

The Or column enables you to specify additional search conditions to a particular column. These conditions are linked together using the OR statement.

> **TIP**
>
> When you add a search condition value for the last Or column that is displayed for a column, the Grid pane inserts an additional Or column. You also can add additional Or columns by pressing the TAB or right arrow key in the rightmost Or column.

You also can enter the logical operators directly into the Criteria column. Figure 9.17 shows an example of this method.

Figure 9.17.

Using logical operators to create a query.

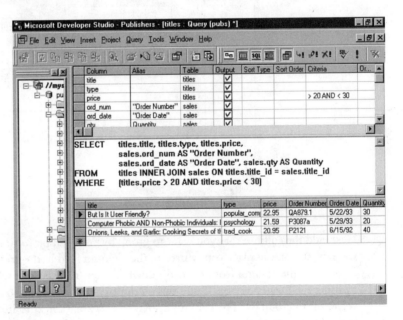

Notice in this example that the SQL pane creates the appropriate SQL statement, using the AND logical operator statement based on the choices made in the Grid pane. The Results pane displays the rows from the database based on this query. This example demonstrates the interactive nature of working with the Query Designer to create and construct queries that produce the desired results for your application.

Grouping the Results

You can use the GROUP BY statement to organize your rows into specific groups. For example, you may want to create a query that returns the average book price for a certain publisher. To create a query based on the GROUP BY statement, drag and drop the table that you want to work with into the Diagram pane. For this example, I use the Titles table. Make sure that you have the Grid pane activated as well. You also can group the results by selecting Group By from the Query menu. This adds a Group By column to the grid in the Grid pane. Figure 9.18 shows what your Query Designer workspace should look like so far.

Figure 9.18.

Selecting the table to group.

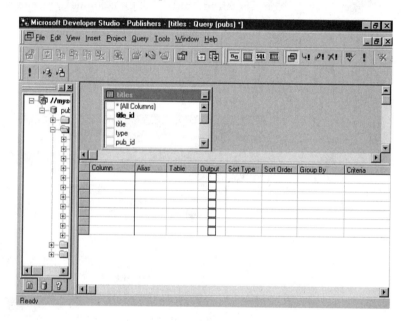

Next, add the column that you want to group by. You can perform this step in one of two ways. First, you can place your cursor in the Column field in the grid within the Grid pane and choose the column from the drop-down listbox. You also can select the group by field by using the Diagram pane. Using this method, click the box to the left of the column that you want to group by. The column displays a checkmark next to its name in the Diagram pane. The Query Designer also inserts this column into the grid in the Grid pane and selects the Group By value for the Group By column. Figure 9.19 shows what the Diagram, Grid, and SQL panes look like as a result of choosing the Pub_id column to group the results.

Figure 9.19.

Choosing the column to group the results.

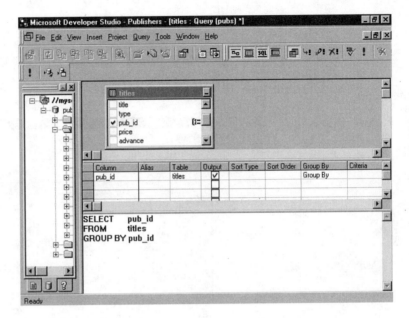

After you have chosen the column to group the results, you need to add the column that will average the prices of all the books for the publishers. This column will be a computed column that calculates the average, based on information in the database. It displays the average price in the query results.

You can add the column in one of two ways. First, you can add the column to the Grid pane from the drop-down listbox in the Column field. Place your cursor in the Column field for an empty row in the Grid pane. Choose the column that will supply the data for the computed column. Second, you can use the Diagram pane to add this column, similar to the method you used to add the Group By column in the preceding example. Click the column that you want to use. A checkmark is placed next to the name in the Diagram pane, and the field is added to the Grid pane.

TIP

You should always create an alias for computed columns. The alias name helps provide a useful and meaningful name for the column. If you don't supply an alias, the computed column's name is displayed as a generic name, such as Column 2. The reason for this generic name is that a computed column isn't stored in the database and, therefore, doesn't have a column name.

For purposes of this example, Average Price is used for the alias name of the computed column. After selecting the column that will be calculated, you need to select the computation method. In this example, I select the AVG function. This function calculates the average price for a particular publisher's books, based on the individual book prices for that publisher. Figure 9.20 depicts the choices I have made so far within the Query Designer workspace.

Figure 9.20.

Choosing the calculation method.

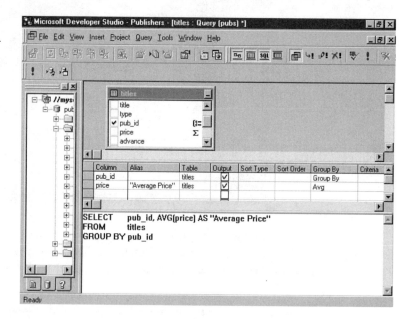

You can now run the query to discover the results. Figure 9.21 displays the results of this query example, using all four panes of the Query Designer.

In the previous example, you learned how to group your results and use the AVG function to calculate an average. You can use the Query Designer to build other aggregate functions. Table 9.4 lists all of the available aggregate functions and their descriptions.

Table 9.4. Group By aggregate functions.

Function	Description
AVG	Calculates the average of numeric values in a column
MAX	Finds highest value for a numeric column, last value for an alphanumeric column; ignores null values
MIN	Finds lowest value for a numeric column, first value for an alphanumeric column; ignores null values

Function	Description
SUM	Calculates the total of numeric values in a column
COUNT	Counts the number of values in a column if column name is specified; ignores null values
COUNT(*)	Counts the number of rows in a table; includes null values

Figure 9.21.

Showing results of average price query.

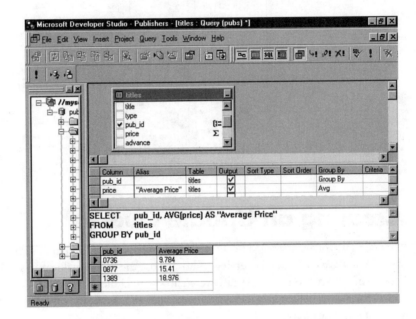

You also can use the WHERE and HAVING clauses to create specific criteria for your queries. You also can use expressions within your queries. For example, you might want to calculate the price of a book by a specific discount percentage. You could create an expression that multiplied the price times the discount percentage number to calculate the discount price. Figure 9.22 shows an example of calculating a discount of 20 percent on all the books in the Titles table.

You can choose the WHERE clause and the Expression options from the drop-down listbox for the Group By column in the Grid pane.

Figure 9.22.

Using an expression to discount the price.

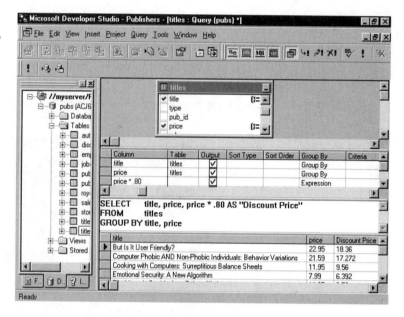

Creating an Update Query

So far, you have learned how to use the Diagram and Grid panes to construct a select query. You have received an overview of how to use the individual features of both panes to create your query. You also have discovered how your choices in the Diagram and Grid panes affect the SQL and Results panes. In this section, you learn how to apply those techniques to create an update query.

An update query enables you to change the value of a column or columns in a row. You also can create an update query to make changes to multiple rows. The update query uses the UPDATE SQL statement to execute against a database. The update query can be very useful when you don't want to manually update individual rows within a database.

Selecting the Table to Update

To create an update query, you first need to select the table that you want to update. This step can be accomplished using the same method that you performed to create a select query. Select the table from the Data View that you want to work with to create your update query. Hold down the left mouse button and drag the table over to the Diagram pane; then release the left mouse button to drop the table into the Diagram pane.

Next, you need to choose the type of query that you're constructing. To create an update query, click the Create Update Query icon on the Query Designer toolbar. You also can select Change Type from the Query menu. You can then choose Update to change the query type to an update query.

Selecting the Columns to Update

You're now ready to choose the columns that you want to update. Click the box to the left of each column that you want to use to create the update query. As in the previous example, these fields are displayed in the Grid pane in the order that you select them. A pencil indicator is displayed in the Diagram pane next to each column that you select.

For this example, I used the Titles table and have selected several of the fields to use in the update query. Figure 9.23 displays the Diagram, Grid, and SQL panes for this update query.

Figure 9.23.

Selecting the fields for the update query.

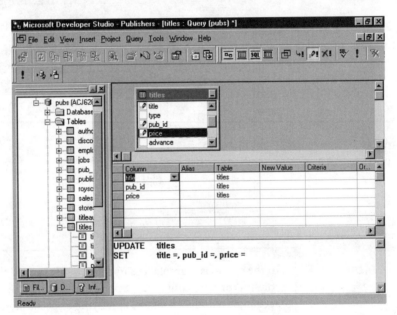

Next, you need to use the Grid pane to enter the new values for the columns that you want to change. The grid for an update query differs from the select query grid in that the update query grid contains a New Value column. You use this column to enter the new value for the column you're going to change. You can enter a value, a column name, or an expression in the New Value column.

After you enter the update value for the column, you need to specify any special search criteria for the update query. For example, you could create a query that discounts the price for all books for a certain publisher by 10 percent. You need to enter an expression into the New Value column for this type of update. You also need to include a special search condition that only updates the rows for that particular publisher ID. You can enter the search conditions in the Criteria column. The same search condition rules that apply to the select query also apply to update queries. In this example, a condition is entered to discount the price by 10 percent for all books that have a publisher ID number equal to 1389. Figure 9.24 demonstrates how this is displayed in the Query Designer workspace.

Figure 9.24.

Selecting the fields for the update query.

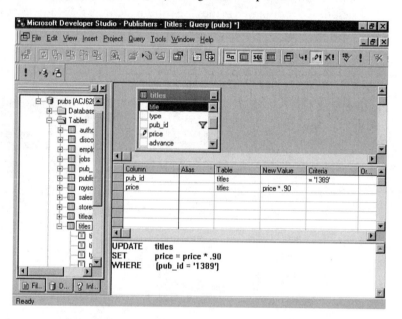

NOTE

In the previous example, the update query changed the value of a column for rows containing a publisher ID equal to 1389. The example accomplished this update by specifying a special search condition for the pub_id column. If you don't enter a condition in the Criteria field, all rows are updated with the new value for the column or columns that you select.

After you have entered the new values for the columns and specified a search condition, you can execute the query to update the database with new values. Figure 9.25 shows the results of the update query.

Figure 9.25.

Updating the database.

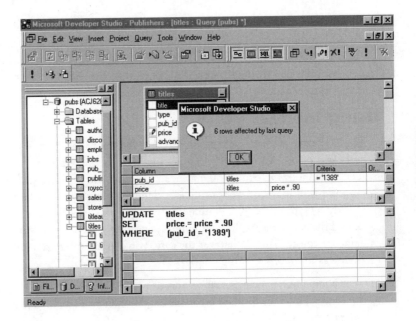

When you run an update query, the Results pane doesn't display any rows. Instead, a confirmation message indicates how many rows were affected by the update.

> **NOTE**
>
> Creating a delete query is similar to creating an update query. The delete query differs in function from the update query in that the delete query deletes all of the rows for the conditions that you specify. Like the update query, a confirmation message displays after you execute the query, indicating how many rows were affected by the delete query.

The update query is useful when you need to perform routine updates for multiple rows in a database. You can save a lot of time by creating an update query to handle this task instead of manually updating the rows.

Modifying the Generated SQL

This lesson has focused a lot of attention on how to use the Diagram and Grid panes to construct your queries. These two panes exemplify the intuitiveness of the Visual Data Tools. You have seen how quick and easy it is to build your SQL queries. This section is for those database programmers who want to take control of their SQL.

The Query Designer generates the SQL statements that you need, based on your input. You can add to and extend these statements by using the SQL pane. This pane shows you the SQL statements that are created and enables you to modify the statements directly. The following section walks you through an example of how to use the SQL pane.

Using the SQL Pane

The SQL pane automatically builds the SQL statement based on your choices in the Diagram and Grid panes. Any changes that are made to the Diagram and Grid panes are instantly reflected in the SQL pane. You may need to modify the SQL statement that is generated. For example, you may be a very proficient database programmer who can create a new query quickly by typing the SQL statement directly into the SQL pane. You might also want to extend the generated SQL statement to take advantage of some feature that's specific to the database you're using. Whatever the case, you can use the SQL pane to create new queries, as well as to modify existing queries.

The Query Designer verifies the syntax of your SQL. Figure 9.26 shows an example of how the Query Designer displays error messages when you have made a mistake in your SQL syntax.

Figure 9.26.

An erroneous custom SQL statement.

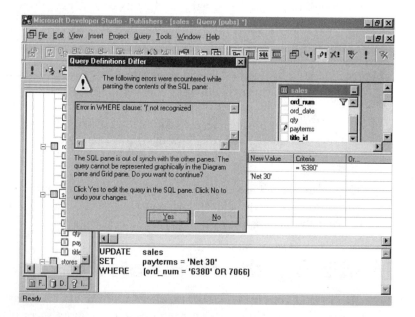

You can see from the preceding example that the Query Designer has found an error in the SQL statement. A description of the error is displayed in the listbox in the Query Definitions Differ dialog window. A message indicates that the query in the SQL pane differs from the query in the Diagram and Grid panes.

You can revert back to the last correct SQL statement, or you can correct the custom query that you are developing. If you choose to continue developing your custom query, the Diagram and Grid panes become disabled, signifying that you are creating a custom query. Pressing Yes on the Query Definitions Differ dialog window enables you to continue correcting your custom SQL statement, while pressing No cancels the changes that you have made to the generated SQL statement. Figure 9.27 displays an example of correcting the custom SQL statement.

Figure 9.27.

A correct custom SQL statement.

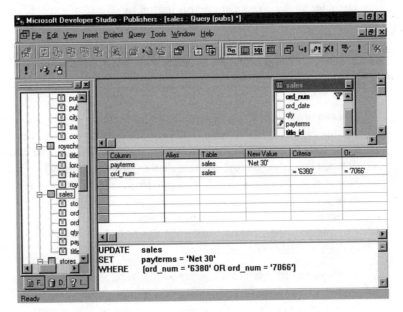

For this example, I pressed the Yes button on the Query Definitions Differ dialog window to correct the custom SQL statement. Notice that the Diagram and Grid panes are disabled. The second value for the WHERE clause needed to be enclosed in single quotes. Also, the table column needed to be specified. After you correct the error, the Diagram and Grid panes become enabled and reflect the changes you have made. You can then execute the query to update the database.

NOTE

> The Query Designer attempts to reflect any custom queries that you create by using the SQL pane in the Diagram and SQL panes. If the Query Designer can't duplicate the query, the Diagram and Grid panes remain disabled.

In this example, you saw how the Query Designer verified the SQL syntax. This verification is performed instantly when you use the SQL pane to construct the statement. As soon as you click another part of the workspace, the Query Designer verifies the syntax of your custom SQL query. You also can use the Verify SQL Syntax button to perform this function. You learned earlier today about the Verify SQL Syntax button, which is located on the Query Designer toolbar. You can use this button to validate the syntax of your SQL statement.

Interacting with Stored Procedures and Triggers

You can use the Query Designer to create and execute stored procedures for MS SQL Server 6.x and higher, and Oracle 7.x and higher. Stored procedures were defined during the first week. Remember, a stored procedure is a precompiled database call on the server database. A stored procedure is more efficient than embedding your SQL call within your application. Stored procedures are already compiled and, therefore, take fewer steps to perform the database query than SQL statements that you pass from your application to the database. A trigger is a special form of stored procedure that executes automatically, based on some event. For example, you could use a trigger to delete all detail sales line items for a book if the book in the Titles table is deleted.

While you gain a performance increase by using stored procedures, you give up portability of your application. Each database vendor implements stored procedures in a different and proprietary manner. For this reason, you won't be able to port your application from one database vendor to another if you use stored procedures and triggers. You need to weigh the costs and benefits of stored procedures to determine if they are right for your application.

This section shows you how to use the Query Designer to execute stored procedures. There are two ways to call a stored procedure: The first method involves the Data View, and the second way is to use the SQL pane in the Query Designer. Both methods are outlined in the following sections.

Using the Data View to Execute a Stored Procedure

The first way you can call a stored procedure is by using the Data View. The result is displayed in the Output pane located at the bottom of the Visual InterDev development workspace. Both the result set and the return value will be displayed. The return value indicates an error number. A return value of 0 means that the stored procedure executed successfully.

You can use the Data View to call existing stored procedures. These procedures will most likely be displayed in the stored procedures folder in the Data View. To execute a stored procedure using the Data View, open the stored procedures folder to see the list of available procedures. Select the stored procedure that you want to call and click the right mouse button to display the shortcut menu. Choose Run from the list of menu items. Many times, a stored procedure will need certain parameters to be able to execute. If the stored procedure requires parameters, the Run Stored Procedure dialog window displays, enabling you to enter the necessary values for the procedure. Figure 9.28 displays the window to enable you to enter the parameters for a stored procedure.

Figure 9.28.

Entering the parameters for a stored procedure.

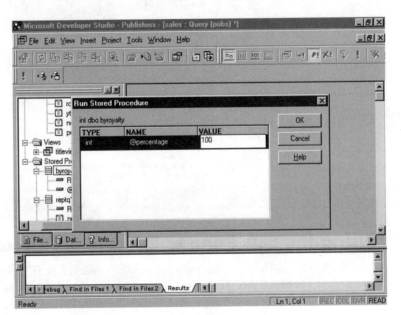

The Run Stored Procedure dialog window shown in Figure 9.28 is using the ByRoyalty stored procedure included with the Pubs database. This stored procedure requires that you enter a percentage number as its lone parameter. The procedure then returns the author IDs that match the specified royalty percentage.

The Run Stored Procedure dialog window enables you to enter a percentage for the stored procedure. Enter the value and then click OK. The Query Designer passes the parameter to the stored procedure to execute on the database. The results are displayed in the Output pane, along with the number of rows returned and the return value. Figure 9.29 illustrates the results of entering 100 for the percentage parameter and running the stored procedure.

Figure 9.29.

Executing the stored procedure using the Data View.

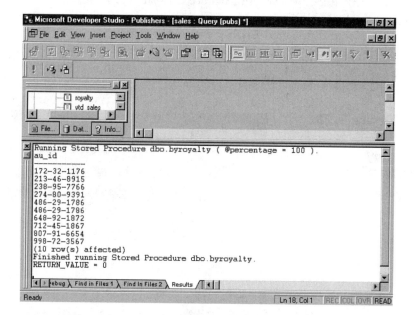

Using the SQL Pane to Execute a Stored Procedure

You also can use the SQL pane to call a stored procedure. The SQL pane enables you to enter the SQL for stored procedures as well as to specify the parameters to pass to the procedure. The proper syntax for calling a stored procedure is as follows:

```
EXECUTE procedure name parameter, parameter,..., parameter n
```

procedure name is the name of the procedure and *parameter* is the parameter to pass to the procedure. After you have entered the stored procedure name and the required parameters, click the Run button on the Query Designer toolbar to execute the stored procedure.

TIP

You also can click the mouse in the Results pane and right-click the mouse button to display the shortcut menu. Choose Run from the list of menu items to execute the stored procedure in the SQL pane.

This method isn't limited to stored procedures. You can use this shortcut to execute any SQL statement.

The Query Designer verifies the syntax of your stored procedure call and displays an error message if there's a problem with your syntax. The results are displayed in the Results pane, as shown in Figure 9.30.

Figure 9.30.

Executing the stored procedure using the SQL pane.

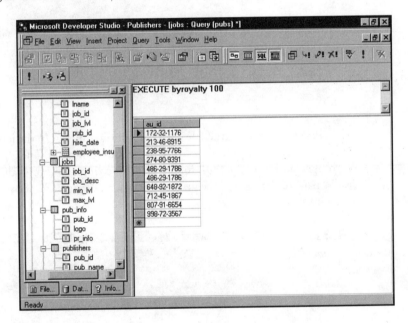

When you use the SQL pane to execute a stored procedure, neither the number of rows returned nor the return value is displayed in the Results pane. Remember, the Data View returns these values when you execute a stored procedure.

Working with Stored Procedures

You can use the Data View to see the stored procedures and triggers for your database. You may want to verify the SQL for the stored procedure before you execute it. To open a stored procedure, select the procedure and click the right mouse button to display the shortcut menu. Figure 9.31 displays the list of menu items for the Stored Procedure shortcut menu.

Figure 9.31.

Opening the Stored Procedure shortcut menu.

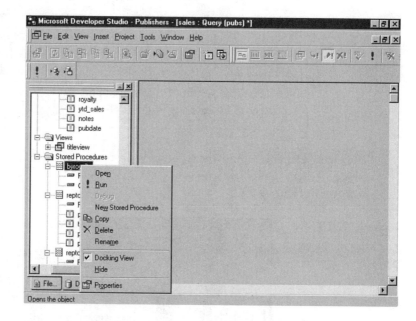

There are several options available from this shortcut menu. In the last section, you learned how to execute a stored procedure by using the Run command. The Open menu item enables you to open and view the SQL for a stored procedure. The procedure is displayed in the Display pane to the right of the project workspace. Figure 9.32 shows the ByRoyalty stored procedure.

Figure 9.32.

Viewing the stored procedure.

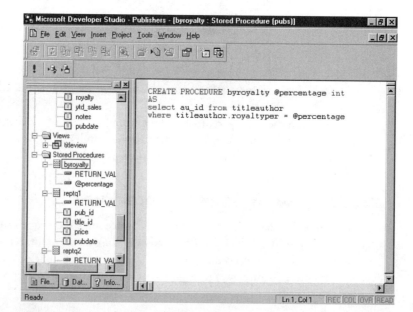

You will learn how to create and edit stored procedures in tomorrow's lesson.

Entering and Modifying Data

You can use the Query Designer to manually add, change, and delete data. You discovered in yesterday's lesson that the connection in your Visual InterDev project is a live connection to the database. Changes that you make manually or through your queries have an immediate impact on the information stored in the database. You can use the Results pane to manually update the database. Your ability to make updates to the database depends on your database permissions and any triggers that have been established to enforce referential integrity for the database.

Adding New Data

To add new data to a table, place your cursor in the first empty row in the Results pane. This row is denoted with an * (asterisk) in the box to the left of the Column field. When you begin to enter data for the row, the asterisk changes to a pencil indicator, signifying that you are editing the row. After you have finished entering the data for the last column, the Query Designer commits the information to the database. Figure 9.33 depicts a row that is being added to the Authors table in the Pubs database.

Figure 9.33.

Using the Results pane to add data.

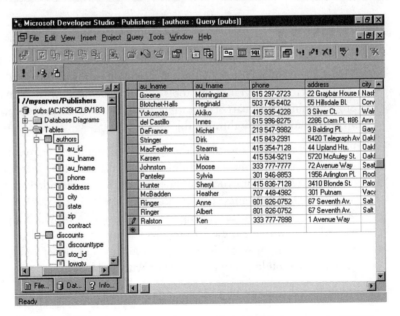

Changing the Data

To change the information stored in a database, place your cursor in the field you want to change and make the appropriate update. The change is confirmed when you exit the field. You can press the ESC (Escape) key before you move the cursor to cancel changes for a field. To cancel changes made to a row, press the ESC key while the cursor is in a field that hasn't been changed.

Eventually you may have to update a row that has already been updated by another user. In these situations, the Query Definitions Differ dialog window will display, indicating the conflict. You can choose to overwrite the other user's changes, cancel your changes, or return to the Results pane and run the query again to view the other person's changes.

Deleting the Data

You also can use the Results pane to delete rows within a database. Again, this ability is based on the permissions that have been established in the database concerning data deletion. To delete a row, select the entire row that you want to delete by clicking the left mouse button on the box to the left of the Column field. Once the row is highlighted, press the DEL (Delete) key. You also can select Delete from the Edit menu to delete the row. For deletes, a warning message is displayed, enabling you to confirm your delete.

Summary

The lesson for today has provided a wealth of knowledge and instruction concerning the Visual Data Tools. You have learned how to maximize your productivity by using these robust database programming tools that are included with Visual InterDev. Database programming is a big part of your application. You now can probably see the benefit to having visual aids to help you through this process.

First, you discovered how to use the Query Designer to generate your SQL statements. You spent the majority of the day learning how to work with the Query Designer workspace and features to visually construct your queries. The lesson provided an in-depth look at each of the Query Designer panes. You learned about the features of each pane and how to use these features to your advantage. Along the way, the lesson provided a guided tour through an example of how to use these features in a real-world situation. You should now have a very good understanding of the four panes of the Query Designer and feel comfortable in using these panes to build queries and interact with the database.

You also learned how to manipulate the SQL statements that are generated by the Query Designer. For this part of the lesson, you used the SQL pane of the Query Designer to build custom SQL statements.

The next part of the lesson focused on how to use the Query Designer to interact with stored procedures and triggers. During this section, you learned the different methods of executing a stored procedure and how to pass parameters to a stored procedure. The final lesson for the day taught you how to enter and modify information in the database, using the Results pane of the Query Designer.

You should feel very confident about using the Visual Data Tools to interact with the database. The Visual Data Tools can significantly boost your productivity and provide a great tool for working with the database.

Q&A

Q Do I have to use the Query Designer Diagram and Grid panes to construct my queries?

A No, you can develop your custom queries using the SQL pane. You may feel more comfortable typing in the SQL statement yourself. The Diagram and Grid panes serve as visual tools to help you quickly construct your queries. After you enter your custom query using the SQL pane, the Query Designer attempts to construct the query in the Diagram and Grid panes.

Q What is an alias?

A An alias serves as an alternative name for a column that is displayed in the results for a query. You can use an alias to provide a more intuitive name for a database column or to indicate a computed column.

Q How do the Query Designer panes relate to each other?

A The Query Designer consists of four panes—the Diagram, Grid, SQL, and Results panes. The Diagram pane enables you to choose your tables and provides a starting point to construct your query. The Grid pane enables you to extend the construction of the query by defining search criteria and update values. The SQL pane shows the SQL as it is constructed and enables you to modify this statement. These panes work together to help you build your query. Any changes that you make in one pane are reflected in the other panes. The Results pane displays the results of your query. All four panes work together to help you create a query and instantly verify the results.

Workshop

For today's Workshop, I want you to apply the concepts you learned today against a real database. You may be using MS SQL Server as your database. If this is the case, you can practice using some of the examples that were covered today. If you are using a different database, establish a connection with the database and practice using the Query Designer features and panes to build some queries. Practice makes perfect, and this Workshop should enable you to perfect your knowledge of the Visual Data Tools.

Quiz

1. What is an update query?
2. What is a stored procedure?
3. What is a computed column?

Quiz Answers

1. An update query enables you to update columns within a single row or multiple rows of data. The update query creates an UPDATE SQL statement to execute the command. The update query provides a very effective method for updating multiple rows of data rather than manually updating each row.

2. A stored procedure is a precompiled procedure that executes SQL statements on the server database. Stored procedures are more efficient and take fewer steps to execute than dynamic SQL, which is passed to a database to be processed.

3. A computed column is a virtual column that is created based on another column's values. A computed column isn't stored in the database, but is calculated and displayed in the query results as if it were a database column.

9

Day 10

Managing Your Database Components

The proper administration and management of objects in your database is not a rudimentary exercise. Yesterday, you discovered some of the Visual Data Tools that facilitate interaction with the database. Today's lesson demonstrates how you can create, organize, and maintain all of the components within your database. Visual InterDev, again, is true to its name by providing visual tools that remove the difficulty from database administration.

The first part of today's lesson introduces you to the type of objects that are contained in a database. Once you understand the different types of database objects, the lesson teaches you how to use the Database Designer to manage your database components. You will receive a detailed tour of the Database Designer features and learn how to apply these features to your database environment. Next, you will discover how to create and maintain database objects such as fields and tables. You also will learn how to create diagrams of your database. Visual InterDev provides a tool that helps you create a visual picture of your database. These diagrams help you understand how the various objects relate to each other.

Toward the end of the day, the lesson focuses on the creation and maintenance of stored procedures and triggers. Yesterday's lesson taught you how to execute a stored procedure. Today, you will learn how to create your own stored procedures for use in your applications. The lesson also teaches you how to save SQL scripts for creating your database objects.

You may be thinking that this lesson is targeted at database administrators (DBAs) and not developers. Actually, the lesson is targeted at both. As a developer, you need to understand the principles of database administration so you can communicate your application needs to your DBA.

You may be a part of a development team that does not have the luxury of allocating a dedicated person to assume the role of DBA. This chapter reveals how the Visual Data Tools enable you to properly manage and administrate your database. You do not have to be a DBA to use these tools. The Database Designer is very intuitive and powerful. For DBAs, the Database Designer provides yet another set of tools to add to your toolbox. You may find that you like them much better than the typical database administration tools. Whether you are a developer or a DBA, this chapter is very important. The lesson helps you understand how you can use Visual InterDev to create and maintain the right type of database for your application.

Using the Database Designer to Manage Your Database

The Database Designer enables you to manage and administrate your database objects. Using the Database Designer, you can build SQL databases without having a detailed knowledge of SQL or database administration. Visual InterDev provides a very intuitive and easy-to-use interface to manage your database components. You also can create diagrams that visually depict your database and the relationships between the objects. The first part of the lesson defines the types of objects that you can use with the Database Designer.

NOTE The Database Designer only supports the use of MS SQL Server 6.5 and higher. Most of the lesson today is based on the use of MS SQL Server as your database. Later in the day, you will learn about the creation and maintenance of stored procedures. The stored procedure editor supports the use of MS SQL Server 6.0 and higher and Oracle 7.0 and higher.

In future versions of Visual InterDev, Microsoft may support the use of other databases with the Database Designer.

Introduction to Database Objects

A database is composed of objects that define its behavior and use. You may be familiar with a lot of the terms in this section. By using the Database Designer, you can create and manage the following objects:

- ☐ Tables
- ☐ Relationships
- ☐ Constraints
- ☐ Indexes

10

Tables

Tables are the basic object contained in a database. You use tables to store your information in the database. Tables are composed of columns that help further define the attributes of the data. Each table must contain at least one column to be saved in the Database Designer. When you define a column for a table, you must specify the column name, length, and data type.

Relationships

After you construct your database tables, you must define how they will interact, or their relationship to each other. Relationships help avoid redundant data by enabling you to relate two tables together instead of storing the same information in both tables. For example, you can create an order header table that contains basic order information and then relate an order detail table that contains multiple line items for each order header. Each order detail line item represents an item that has been ordered. By relating these two tables, you avoid having to store the order header information for each detail line item. For each order detail line item, you only need to store the order number from the order header table.

Relationships also help to enforce referential integrity. The data contained in the database must be accurate and correct. *Referential integrity* means that everywhere the data is referenced in the database, the integrity of that data is maintained. Referring back to the order header and order detail example, an order detail line cannot exist without having an order header row. Conversely, an order header row that references order detail lines cannot be deleted without first deleting the order detail lines.

You define a relationship through the use of keys. A primary key is a column or set of columns that uniquely identifies a row in the table. For example, the order number is the primary key for the order header table in the preceding example. Likewise, the combination of the order number and order detail line number serves as the primary key combination for the order detail table. A foreign key is a column or set of columns that matches the primary key of another table. The order number that resides in the order detail table is referred to as a foreign key, because its value matches the value of a column in the order header table.

There are three basic types of table relationships: one-to-many, many-to-many, and one-to-one.

One-to-many is the most common type of relationship. A one-to-many relationship consists of a table with one row that relates to many rows in another table. Each order header row can consist of many order detail lines. Figure 10.1 conceptually depicts this relationship.

Figure 10.1.

A one-to-many relationship.

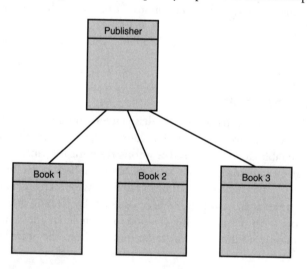

Many-to-many is the second type of relationship. A many-to-many relationship consists of many rows of one table that relate to many rows in another table. This association is achieved through the use of a junction table, which helps to relate the two tables. An example of this relationship can be found in the sample Publishers database that was referenced in yesterday's lesson.

The Titles table has a many-to-many relationship with the Authors table. A title can have multiple authors, and an author can write multiple titles. The junction table for the Titles and Authors tables is the TitleAuthor table. This table primary key contains the primary key from the Titles table as well as the primary key from the Authors table. Figure 10.2 shows a diagram of these three tables.

Figure 10.2.

A many-to-many relationship.

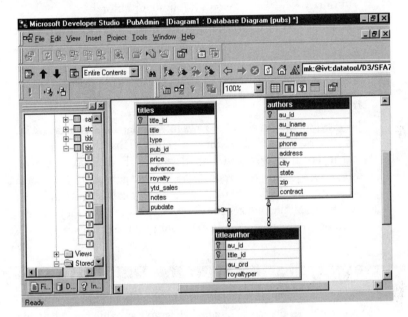

The third type of relationship is one-to-one. In a one-to-one relationship, a row from one table relates to a single row of another table. This relationship really defeats the purpose of the relational model and isn't used very often.

Constraints

You will want to enforce certain rules concerning the columns within your database. Constraints enable you to define the rules for the values of the columns in your tables. Table 10.1 displays the five types of constraints provided by MS SQL Server and their descriptions.

Table 10.1. MS SQL Server constraints.

Type	Description
Check	Enforces valid data values for one or more columns
Default	Provides a default value for a column
Primary Key	Avoids duplicate or null values
Foreign Key	Enforces referential integrity foreign key relationships
Unique	Ensures a unique value for a column or set of columns

Indexes

Indexes provide fast access to rows in your database. A database index is very similar to the index in this book. You use the book index to find the page for a certain topic and then turn to that page number to read about the topic. The database index works in much the same way by storing a pointer to certain data in your database. The index consists of a column or set of columns within the table. You should only establish indexes for data that the user will access frequently. While indexes provide fast access to data, they absorb disk space and slow the speed of inserts, changes, and deletions into the database.

Getting Started with the Database Designer

The Database Designer provides a very flexible and intuitive environment for working with your database objects. Database diagrams provide the main interface for creating and maintaining your database objects. A database diagram visually depicts the columns, tables, and the relationships of the tables within your database. I will talk about diagrams in the next section, "Visualizing Your Database."

I prefer to use Visual InterDev to create a database project for the specific purposes of administering my database. In this way, you can separate the development tasks from the database administration tasks. You can determine what is best for your project based on personal preference.

To create a database project, select New from the File menu. The New tabbed dialog window is then displayed. Choose the Projects tab and select Database Project from the list. Type a name for the new database project and click OK. You will be prompted to add or select a database connection similar to the database connection that you added during Day 8, "Communicating with a Database." For purposes of this example, I selected the Publishers datasource that I established earlier. This data connection creates a live connection to your database that you can then use to manage your database.

10

NOTE

You can choose to add the database connection after you have created the project by choosing Add Data Connection from the shortcut menu.

Figure 10.3 shows the database project for the Publishers database.

Figure 10.3.

A sample database project.

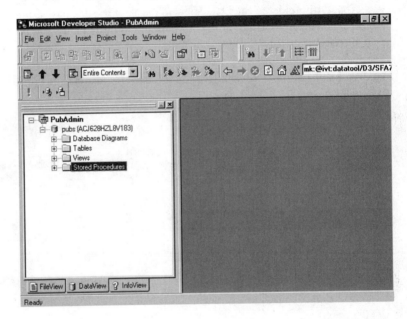

Once you have created a database project, you are ready to get started. The next section provides an overview of database diagrams and their relevance to managing your database.

Visualizing Your Database

The Database Designer uses diagrams to graphically depict the objects in your database including tables, columns, constraints, and indexes. The database diagram will also show the relationship between tables in your database. You can make modifications to these objects as well as the table relationships by using the database diagram. Your changes won't affect the database until you save them, enabling you to create what-if scenarios for the database.

When you're finished with your modifications, you can choose to either update the database, save the changes to execute later, or cancel the changes. If you choose to save the changes for later use, the modifications will be saved in a Transact-SQL script. I will provide more detail on the use of these scripts at the end of today's lesson, in the section "Utilizing SQL Scripts."

Exploring a Database Diagram

Database diagrams are saved in the Database Diagram folder within your project. You can expand this folder in the Data View to see all of the database diagrams for your database. A database diagram will typically contain one or more tables. Figure 10.4 displays a diagram for the Authors and TitleAuthor tables.

Figure 10.4.

A database diagram.

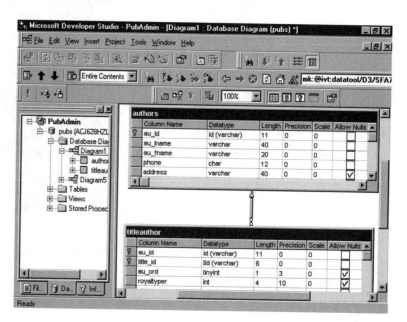

As you can see from the picture, the Authors table has a one-to-many relationship with the TitleAuthor table. You learned about the relationship symbols during yesterday's lesson. Each table is represented by a grid that contains its columns. A key symbol in the box next to a column designates the keys for each table. In the Authors table, there is a key beside the au_id (Author ID) column. The key for the TitleAuthor table is a combination of the au_id and the title_id columns.

Table 10.2 defines each of the columns within the database diagram grid.

10

Table 10.2. Database column properties.

Column Property	Description
Column Name	Name of the column
Datatype	Type of data to be stored
Length	Length of the column (determined by data type)
Precision	Maximum number of digits used or maximum length of column for alphanumeric columns
Scale	Maximum number of digits to the right of the decimal
Allow Nulls	Specifies whether null values can be allowed
Default Value	Sets a default value for the column
Identity	Column that will contain a system-generated value
Identity Seed	Initial value for the system-generated column
Identity Increment	Increment for the system-generated value

NOTE

The length is defined automatically when you assign a data type for a column. You can change the length of some fields, including binary, char, varbinary, and varchar.

Understanding Database Diagram Properties

You can access and change the properties for the tables, indexes, and relationships for your diagrams by using the Properties dialog window. This window is a tabbed display dialog window that contains the properties for each of these objects. The following section explains the property fields for each of these database objects.

Table Properties

You can access the properties for your tables by selecting the table and clicking the right mouse button to display the shortcut menu. Choose Properties from the list of menu items. Figure 10.5 demonstrates the available properties for a sample table.

Figure 10.5.

*Setting the table
properties.*

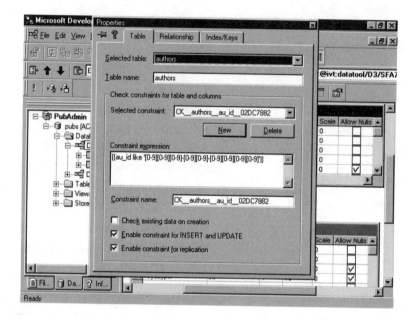

This window enables you to view and change the properties for a particular table. The
Selected table drop-down listbox enables you to choose another table from the list and view
its properties. This listbox only displays tables that are included in the current database
diagram that you are working in. The Table name field enables you to view and change the
name of the selected table. The bottom half of this window enables you to see the selected
check constraints for the table and its columns. The Selected constraint drop-down listbox
enables you to choose a column that contains a check constraint. See Table 10.3 for details.

Table 10.3. The Selected constraint drop-down listbox.

Property	Description
New push button	Enables you to create a new check constraint for the table
Delete push button	Deletes the currently selected check constraint from the database
Constraint expression field	Use it to enter the Transact-SQL syntax for the check constraint
Constraint Name	Enables you to view and change the name of the check constraint
Check existing data on creation	Applies the constraint to existing data in the database if the checkbox is enabled

10

You can check the Enable constraint for INSERT or UPDATE to apply the constraint to all insertions and updates into the database. The Enable constraint for replication enables you to use the constraint for replicating the table to a different database.

Relationship Properties

The Relationship Properties dialog window enables you to change the properties of the relationships of the tables contained in your database diagrams. Figure 10.6 shows the fields that are contained on this window.

Figure 10.6.

Setting the relationship properties.

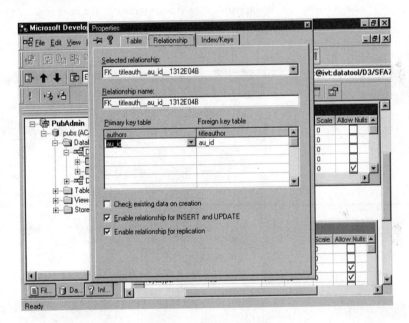

The first field on this page displays the Selected relationship. You can choose another relationship from the drop-down listbox.

The Relationship name field enables you to change the name of the currently selected relationship.

The Primary key table shows the name of the primary key table in the relationship and the columns that make up the primary key.

The Foreign key table displays the name of the foreign key table in the relationship and the columns that make up the foreign key.

The next three checkboxes are similar in meaning to the checkboxes contained on the Table Properties window. These checkboxes apply to the foreign key in the table relationship. If the

Check existing data on creation is enabled, the constraint is applied to existing data in the database when the relationship is added to the Foreign key table. You can check the Enable constraint for INSERT or UPDATE to apply the constraint to all insertions and updates into the Foreign key table. Enabling this checkbox also prevents a deletion of a row in the Primary table if a related row in the Foreign key table exists. The Enable constraint for replication enables you to use the constraint for replicating the Foreign key table to a different database.

Index/Keys Properties

You can use this dialog window to view and change the keys and indexes for the tables within your database diagrams. Figure 10.7 shows the options that are available in this dialog window.

Figure 10.7.

Setting the properties for the indexes and keys.

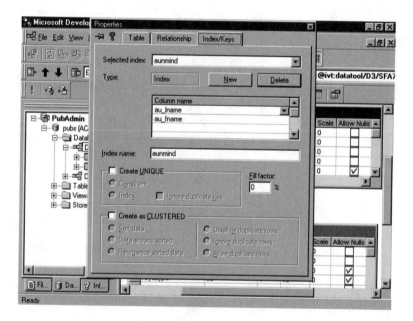

As you can see from Figure 10.7, the Selected index field displays the indexes and keys for the selected table. The Type display box located below the Selected index field denotes whether you're viewing a primary key, unique key, or index for the selected table. The Column name grid displays the column names that are included in the index or key. You can add, change, or delete columns from the list by using the New and Delete push buttons. The Index name enables you to establish a name for the index.

10

The Create UNIQUE checkbox enables you to create a unique constraint or index for the table. If you create a unique index, you can choose to ignore duplicate keys. You can use the Fill Factor field to specify how full to make the index page within the database. This field is used by database administrators to fine-tune performance of the database. The Create as CLUSTERED field enables you to create a *clustered index*. A clustered index provides faster access to data than non-clustered indexes.

 A *clustered index* is a type of index in which the logical order of the key values of the index is the same as the physical order of the rows containing the keys.

The remaining checkboxes on the Index/Keys dialog window enable you to further specify attributes of the clustered index, and are pretty self-explanatory.

Creating and Editing SQL Server Objects

So far, you have learned about the types of database objects that you can manipulate as well as how database diagrams provide the main method for working with these objects. In this section, you are guided through the process of creating and saving a database diagram. The lesson also teaches you how to create and maintain the database objects within your diagrams.

Creating a Database Diagram

Before you can work with the database objects, you need to create a database diagram. You can create a diagram in one of two ways. First, you can select a table and click the right mouse button to display the shortcut menu. Choose Design from the list of menu items to create a database diagram with the selected table. This diagram will be a single table diagram for the selected table.

The second method involves selecting the Insert menu and choosing Insert Database Item from the menu items. Select Database Diagram from the list of choices, and a blank database diagram will be created. You can then drag and drop tables from the Data View to add additional tables into the diagram. Once you drop the table into the diagram, the relationship between the tables will be automatically depicted. Figure 10.8 shows a database diagram for the Titles and Sales tables in the Publishers database.

Figure 10.8.

A sample database diagram.

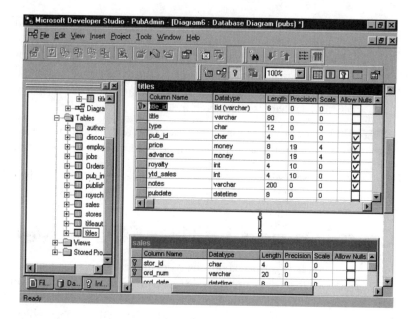

Creating a New Database Table

You can click the New Table icon on the Database Diagram toolbar to insert a new table into your database diagram. This icon is the icon furthest to the left on the toolbar. After you click this icon, a blank table is displayed, enabling you to enter the column names and properties into the grid, as displayed in Figure 10.9.

To enter a name for the table, select the table and click the right mouse button to display the shortcut menu. Choose Properties from the list of menu items to display the Properties dialog window. Select the Table tab and enter a new name for the table in the Table name field. When you change the name of the table using this field, the Selected name drop-down list-box changes to reflect the new name of the table that you enter. Figure 10.10 displays the Table Properties window with a newly created table that has been renamed.

 TIP

> There are several other methods for creating a new database table. First, you can right-click the mouse and choose New Table from the shortcut menu. Another method involves selecting the New Database Item from the Insert menu and choosing Table from the list of database items. You also can right-click the Tables folder in the Data View and choose Insert New Table from the shortcut menu.

10

Figure 10.9.

Creating a new table.

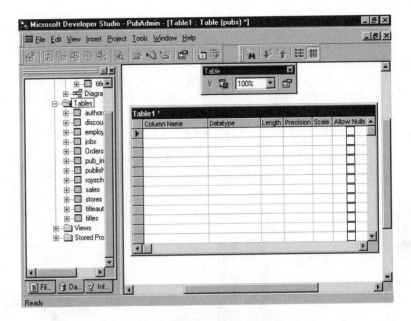

Figure 10.10.

Renaming the table.

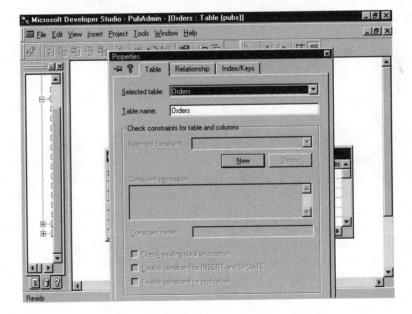

10

Defining the Column Properties

Once you have created the table and given it a meaningful name, you can enter the column names and properties. You can use the Tab and arrow keys to navigate within the fields in the grid. An arrow in the box to the left of the column name denotes the current row that you are inserting within the grid. Once you enter a column name, you can choose a data type from the drop-down listbox in the Datatype field for the column. Figure 10.11 shows an example of some of the available data types using the Database Designer.

Figure 10.11.

Setting the data type.

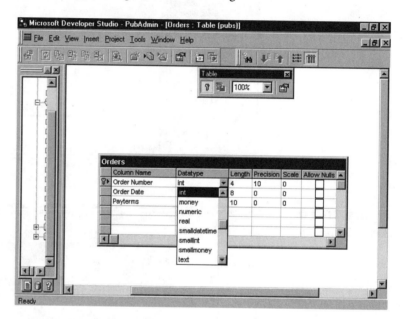

After you enter the columns for the table, you need to set the key values for the table. Select the row that you want to be the primary key and click the Set Primary Key icon on the Database Diagram toolbar. If the primary key of the table is a combination of columns, you need to select all of the columns that are a part of the key and then click the Set Primary Key icon. To select multiple rows in the grid, click the mouse in the box to the left of the Column name field to highlight the first column row. Then click the Shift+Down Arrow key combination to highlight the next column row. Repeat this step until you have highlighted all of the column rows for the primary key and then click the Set Primary Key icon from the Database Diagram toolbar. A key indicator is displayed next to the columns that you designate as the primary key.

Saving Your Database Changes

The final step to creating your new database table involves saving the changes to the database. You have learned over the last couple of days that the database connection that you establish is a live connection. In other words, the actions that you perform have an immediate effect on the database. The Database Diagram gives you the option of directly updating the database or saving the changes for later. To save a newly created table, you have several available options. First, you can choose Save from the File menu. You will be prompted to enter a name for the diagram you used to create the new tables. Once you enter the name and click OK, the Database Designer inserts the new table or tables into the database.

NOTE

The Save All command from the File menu has the same effect as the Save option. Both of these menu commands will perform immediate updates against the database.

You also can choose Save Change Script from the File menu, which saves the SQL script to a text file that you can execute against the database at a later time.

Figure 10.12 shows the results of saving the Orders table against the Publishers database.

Figure 10.12.

Saving the new table.

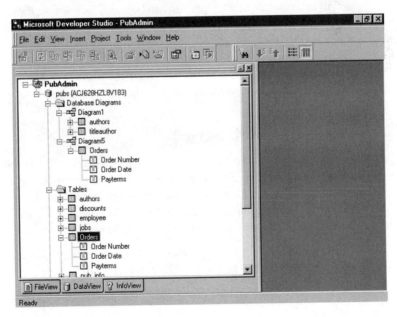

Working with Diagrams and Tables

You can use the Database Designer to view the relationships of the tables in your database. You also can use the Database Designer to modify existing table relationships and properties. To open an existing database diagram, right-click the mouse on the selected diagram from within the Data View and choose Open from the list of menu items. This action opens the database diagram, enabling you to work with the tables contained in the diagram. You can make changes to the column properties as well as the relationships between the tables. You also can add new tables to the diagram, as explained in the previous section. Once you have made your modifications, you need to save your changes to the database. You can either save these changes immediately to the database or save the changes to a text file for later use.

Utilizing SQL Scripts

In the previous section, you discovered that you can execute immediate updates against the database. You also learned that you can save these changes in a text file to be executed at a later time. These files contain Transact-SQL commands that perform administrative functions against the database.

SQL scripts can be useful, especially if you have to execute the same commands repeatedly against a database. These scripts also can be useful for creating the same databases and tables for separate development, testing, and production database environments. You learned about the benefits and use of these environments on Day 3, "Design and Development Considerations." A good DBA learns the benefit of SQL scripts very quickly in life. It only takes having to delete a table and re-create it manually one time to see the benefit of an automated script that performs this function for you.

Saving the SQL Script

Earlier today, you learned how to create and modify tables. The last step involves saving those changes. The previous example showed you how to immediately update the database with the changes. To save the changes to a SQL script instead, choose Save SQL Script from the File menu. The Save Change Script dialog window displays. Figure 10.13 shows a SQL script for a change to the column data type of an existing table.

The Save Change Script dialog window displays the actual Transact-SQL that will be saved to the text file. Listing 10.1 shows the complete code sample for Figure 10.13.

Figure 10.13.

Examining the SQL Script.

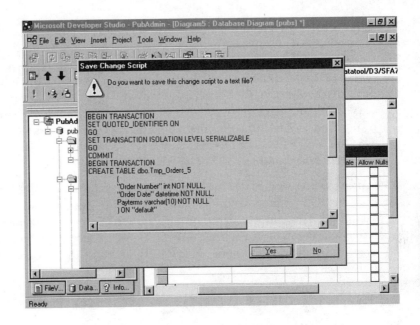

Listing 10.1. Changing the data type of a database column.

```
BEGIN TRANSACTION
SET QUOTED_IDENTIFIER ON
GO
SET TRANSACTION ISOLATION LEVEL SERIALIZABLE
GO
COMMIT
BEGIN TRANSACTION
CREATE TABLE dbo.Tmp_Orders_4
(
"Order Number" int NOT NULL,
"Order Date" datetime NOT NULL,
Payterms varchar(10) NOT NULL
) ON "default"
GO
IF EXISTS(SELECT * FROM dbo.Orders)
EXEC('INSERT INTO dbo.Tmp_Orders_4("Order Number", "Order Date", Payterms)
SELECT "Order Number", "Order Date", CONVERT(varchar(10), Payterms)
➥FROM dbo.Orders TABLOCKX')
GO
DROP TABLE dbo.Orders
GO
EXECUTE sp_rename 'dbo.Tmp_Orders_4', 'Orders'
GO
ALTER TABLE dbo.Orders ADD CONSTRAINT
PK_Orders PRIMARY KEY NONCLUSTERED
(
"Order Number"
) ON "default"
GO
COMMIT
```

I'm not going to examine the entire code listing, but I did want to outline a very robust feature of the Database Designer. You can use the Database Designer to change the column data types of tables that contain existing data. This code listing shows the Transact-SQL that creates a temporary table named Tmp_Orders_4. This temporary table is used to insert any data that resides in the Orders table and convert it to the new data type. The original Orders table with the old data type for the Payterms column is then deleted. Finally, the Tmp_Orders_4 table that contains the order information with the new data type is renamed to Orders. The Database Designer creates all this logic for you, which should make DBAs appreciate the robustness of the Database Designer even more.

After you have verified that the SQL syntax is correct, you can click Yes to save the changes for the SQL script. A confirmation message with a default name for the script is then displayed. The name is assigned by the Database Designer and contains the .sql extension. You can edit this file using Visual InterDev as well as any text editor. You also may want to rename the file to conform to any standards that you have established for your project.

Creating and Editing Stored Procedures

The stored procedure editor provides a very intuitive tool for creating and maintaining stored procedures for your applications. Visual InterDev supports the use of the stored procedure editor with MS SQL Server 6.0 and higher and Oracle 7.0 and higher. If you're using MS SQL Server 6.5 or higher, you also can also debug your stored procedures.

Creating a Stored Procedure

To create a new stored procedure, select the Stored Procedures folder and right-click the mouse to display the shortcut menu. Choose New Stored Procedure from the list of menu items. The stored procedure editor opens and presents a template for creating your new stored procedure. Figure 10.14 displays a sample template for creating a new stored procedure.

The template includes the Transact-SQL key words CREATE PROCEDURE that signify all stored procedures. Also, the template provides a place for you to enter the name of the new procedure. You can then enter the SQL for your procedure after the AS key word. The stored procedure template also provides a placeholder at the end of the procedure for capturing the return code. After you have developed your stored procedure, you can save it by choosing Save or Save As from the File menu. The Save As option enables you to save the file in a separate text file that is denoted with the .tsq filename extension. Figure 10.15 shows an example of a stored procedure.

Figure 10.14.

Creating a new stored procedure.

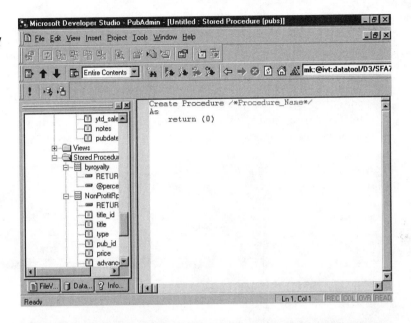

Figure 10.15.

A sample stored procedure.

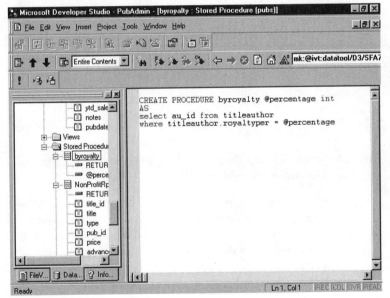

Executing a Stored Procedure

You learned during yesterday's lesson how to execute a stored procedure. Once you have created and saved your stored procedure, you should test the procedure to ensure that it produces the desired results. You can execute the procedure from within the stored procedure editor by right-clicking the mouse anywhere within the stored procedure. Choose Run from the list of menu items. If there is an error in your procedure, the stored procedure debugger displays an error message indicating the mistake, as shown in Figure 10.16.

Figure 10.16.

An erroneous stored procedure.

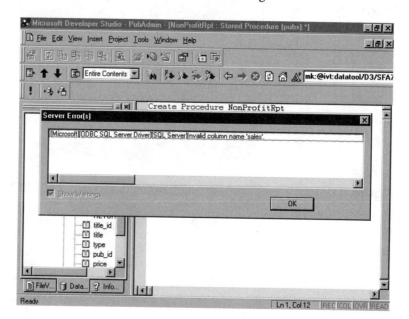

If no errors are found, the result is displayed in the Output window at the bottom of the Visual InterDev project workspace, as depicted in Figure 10.17.

You still need to make sure that the stored procedure returned the results that you expected. A bug-free procedure does not mean that the stored procedure is accurate. You need to test the procedure to make sure that it meets your application requirements both now and in the future. A stored procedure is usually shared among the developers. Develop these procedures in a manner that can be universally applied across the application. This doesn't mean that you should have one stored procedure that meets everyone's needs. You should, however, create procedures that are targeted to the needs of more than a single developer.

Figure 10.17.

Executing a successful stored procedure.

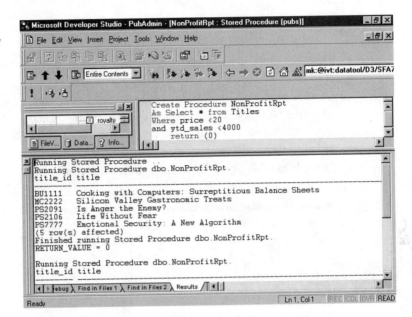

Summary

Today's lesson concludes the last section focused solely on the database part of your application. You should be able to apply the database principles that you have learned over the last three days toward the other lessons this week and next week. Database administration isn't an exciting pastime, but a good DBA is worth his or her salt. You can use the Database Designer to perform routine database administration and management functions without becoming a full-fledged DBA. The Database Designer provides a visual tool that removes a lot of the mundane chores of managing your database components.

Today's lesson first provided you with an introduction to the Database Designer. You learned about the types of database objects that you can create and manipulate using the Database Designer. Next, you learned how to use database diagrams to create and maintain your database objects. You discovered the usefulness of database diagrams in providing a visual picture of your database as well as a visual tool to manage the database tables and objects.

Toward the end of the day, the lesson focused on the use of SQL scripts. You learned about how the different Save options have an impact on the database and how you can use SQL scripts for database updates in the future. The final lesson for the day taught you to how to create and edit a stored procedure.

Q&A

Q **Does the Database Designer replace my existing database administration tools?**

A The Database Designer is meant to complement your other DBA tools. The Database Designer enables you to administrate and manage database objects once you have created a database. You can use the Database Designer as yet another tool in your DBA toolbox.

Q **What is the difference between an index and a primary key?**

A A primary key is used to uniquely define a row in a table. A primary key can consist of a single column or a combination of multiple columns. An index consists of a key value and a pointer to the data contained in the table. An index provides an additional method for accessing data in your tables.

Workshop

Today's workshop focuses on the use of database diagrams. Use the Publishers database included with MS SQL Server to create some database diagrams of your own. Create some new tables to add to the database and practice defining column properties for these tables. Use the examples provided in this lesson as a guide to walk you through these steps.

You also should practice developing a few stored procedures for the Publishers database. This database includes a few examples to get you started.

Quiz

1. What is a foreign key?
2. What is the Default Value column property used for?
3. Name three types of column constraints.

10

Quiz Answers

1. A foreign key is a column or set of columns whose value matches the primary key value of another table.

2. The Default Value property enables you to specify a default value for a column. This property can be used in situations when you want to populate the value of the column if the user doesn't enter a value for the field within the context of your application.

3. Possible answers include

    Check

    Default

    Primary Key

    Foreign Key

    Unique

10

Day 11

Extending Your Application Through Active Server Script

A key design goal of Visual InterDev is to provide a tool that facilitates the construction of dynamic, Web-based applications. Visual InterDev accomplishes this objective through the use of Active Server Pages.

During the last few days, you have learned about server side topics such as integrating a database into your application. This lesson continues with that theme and introduces you to another component that resides on the server: Active Server Pages. Active Server Pages enable you to combine HTML and script code on the server to build dynamic and highly interactive web pages. On Day 7, "Extending Your Web Page Through Client-Side Script," you learned about the use of scripting languages within the context of the browser on the client machine. For today's lesson, you will learn how to apply the power of script code on the server.

First, you receive a brief introduction to making the server an active part of your Web-based application. Next, you will discover what makes Active Server Pages so dynamic and powerful. The lesson provides a closer look at the client-server picture. In exploring the conceptual architecture for a Web-based application, the lesson explains how Active Server Pages fit into the big picture, helping you understand how to use Active Server Pages within the scope of your application. At the end of the day, you will create your first Active Server Page.

Throughout the day, I will provide examples of Active Server Pages and dissect the meaning of the code. You learned during the first week that Active Server Pages support the use of scripting languages such as VBScript and JScript. VBScript code examples are used throughout the lesson. The principles that you will learn, though, apply to either scripting language.

Making the Server Come Alive

The Web has been transformed into a place of interaction. Users don't just want to browse a web page; they want to experience a web site. Using the server to provide this exciting experience for your users is a very important concept to master. Active Server Pages enable you to easily integrate server-side logic into your application. You may have used CGI or APIs in the past to provide this logic. With both of these methods, you have to create an executable program on the server that involves a development process different from your web page development.

Active Server Pages add an intriguing alternative to your choices for server-side development. You can design and develop Active Server Pages in a way similar to the process that you use for your web page development. Active Server Pages consist of HTML and script that reside on the server. The same popular scripting languages that you use on the client, including VBScript and JScript, are supported by Active Server Pages. The main benefit is that you can leverage the investment you make learning HTML and a scripting language on the client to your development for the server.

What Makes Active Server Pages So Dynamic?

Active Server Pages can be used as the main hub to control your server activity. You can code application-specific logic directly into an Active Server Page. This logic could be HTML as well as script code that changes the format of your web pages.

Within an Active Server Page you also can include ActiveX and Design-time ActiveX controls that are built specifically to execute on the server. Active Server Pages can be integrated with Active Server Components to provide robust application processing on the server. For example, you could build an Active Server Component with Visual Basic or Visual C++ that processes financial data and then returns the results through the Active Server Page. You also can place your database connections in Active Server Pages.

The development paradigm for Active Server Pages differs slightly from programming script on the client. If you remember from the lesson on client-side script during the first week, the script that you develop for the client is embedded within the web page that is sent to the browser. This script is then executed by the browser based on system and user events. The browser must support the use of the particular scripting language to execute the code. If the browser doesn't recognize the script language, it will ignore the code. With Active Server Pages, all of the script is processed on the server by the ActiveX Server scripting engine. The results are returned to the client in a standard HTML format that is universally recognized by the browser.

Taking a Closer Look at the Process

This section explores how a browser interacts with an Active Server Page. First, the web page references an Active Server Page (ASP) within the context of the application. Active Server Pages contain the file name extension of .asp. The following line of code demonstrates an example of calling an Active Server Page:

```
<FORM METHOD= "POST" ACTION="ProcessForm.asp">
```

When the browser requests the ASP, the file is first processed by the server. The ASP may contain both HTML and scripting code. Any HTML code is passed directly to the browser as well as any client-side script. The server then searches for any server-side script. Similar to script on the client, server-side script is denoted by the symbols <% and %>. Upon locating the server-side code, the server processes the script and returns the results to the browser in the form of HTML. The server processes the script based on the current conditions and events. This model gives your application its unique and dynamic nature. The web page that is formatted is based on conditions that are dynamic and changing, instead of a static HTML file that resides on the server. These conditions could be based on user input as well as information that is contained in a database.

Exploring the Client-Server Picture

Active Server Pages are an important part of your application. You can use Active Server Pages to create more intelligent server processing that handles the needs of your application. Active

Server Pages are a central figure in the client-server model for your application. Figure 11.1 demonstrates the role of an Active Server Page in the overall scheme of your application.

Figure 11.1.

Playing an active part of the client-server picture.

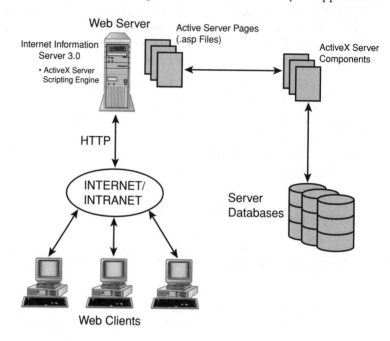

As you can see, Active Server Pages reside on the web server and play an active part in the functionality of your application. Active Server Pages are based on the ActiveX Server scripting engine first introduced with Internet Information Server 3.0. First, you can return dynamic web pages to the client based on the preferences entered by the user. The ASP also can interface through the Component Object Model (COM) with Active Server Components. These components are applications that you develop using a more robust language such as Visual Basic or Visual C++. These components are compiled as executable (EXE) or dynamic link library (DLL) programs that handle the detailed processing of the application. You learn more about working with and developing these components on Day 17, "Using Active Server Components to Create Multitier Applications."

In Figure 11.1, you should also notice the database component of the application. You can use Active Server Pages to directly interface with the database. The other alternative is to use an Active Server Component that is called from an ASP to handle the database processing. For database-intensive processes and transaction processing, you will probably want to use the power of a language like Visual Basic or Visual C++ for these activities.

Understanding Active Server Pages

Active Server Pages can contain both script and HTML. Visual InterDev supports the use of VBScript, JScript, JavaScript, and LiveScript. The scripting engines for VBScript and JScript are included with Visual InterDev. You can choose the scripting language by selecting the Tools menu and choosing Options from the list of menu items. The Options dialog window displays, enabling you to specify a default scripting language for your Active Server Pages. Figure 11.2 depicts the Options dialog window.

Figure 11.2.

Choosing a default scripting language.

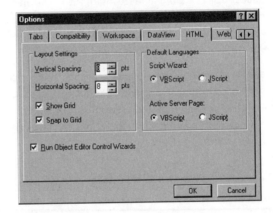

Once you specify a default scripting language, the chosen language is used when you create new Active Server Pages. Visual InterDev formats a line of your ASP to denote the type of scripting language that is being used, similar to the way that client-side script is recognized in an HTML file. The following code example demonstrates an ASP that uses VBScript for the scripting language:

```
<%@LANGUAGE="VBSCRIPT"%>
```

You can include both client- and server-side script in an Active Server Page. The client-side script is passed to the client along with the HTML and executes within the context of the browser. The HTML also may contain references to intrinsic controls as well as ActiveX controls.

The Active Server Page Object Model

Active Server Pages use a robust object model that enables you to develop the correct logic to handle your application needs. This object model resembles object models that are used in Visual Basic. The following list outlines the five basic objects that are available in an ASP:

1. `Request` object
2. `Response` object

3. `Session` object
4. `Application` object
5. `Server` object

Each of these objects is covered in detail in the following sections.

The `Request` Object

The `Request` object enables you to obtain information from a user. This object is useful when you're trying to discover preferences specified by the user. Also, you can use this object to retrieve information that is entered on a form. A Guest Book is a good example where the user enters information into an initial form that is then later used by the application.

The `Request` object consists of five collections. The concept of collections was first mentioned on Day 8, "Communicating with a Database." A collection is a set of related objects that are accessed using the same method. An object uses a collection to access variables that define certain attributes and characteristics about the object. Table 11.1 lists the types of `Request` collections and their purposes.

Table 11.1. The `Request` collections.

Collection	Purpose
ClientCertificate	Retrieves certification fields from the browser request
Cookies	Retrieves the value of cookies in the request
Form	Retrieves the values of a form using `POST` command
QueryString	Retrieves the values of a query string
ServerVariables	Retrieves the value of environment variables

You can access the information contained in a collection using the following syntax:

`Request.CollectionName("variable name")`

`CollectionName` is the name of the collection and `variable name` is the name of the collection variable containing the desired information. You can use the following method as an alternative:

`Request.("variable name")`

11

NOTE

> If you use the alternate method, you must ensure that different collections contain unique variable names. You should explicitly use the collection name method to access a variable if you have collection variables with the same name.

As indicated previously, the `Request` object can be used to get information from the user. The following sections demonstrate how to use this object to accomplish this task.

Using the Cookies Collection

You have probably used cookies in developing previous Web-based applications. A cookie represents information about the user session that is stored on a client machine. You can use cookies to maintain information about the user across the scope of your application. A cookie can be sent by the browser to the server or from the server to the client machine. You can use Active Server Pages to both populate and retrieve values for your cookies. The syntax for the Cookies collection is as follows:

```
Request.Cookies(cookie)[(key)].attribute]
```

`cookie` specifies the value of the cookie to be retrieved, `key` indicates an optional parameter that is used to retrieve sub key values of the cookie, and `attribute` contains information about the cookie. The `attribute` parameter can be used to determine if a cookie contains multiple key values as in the following code example:

```
<%Request.Cookies("MyCookie").HasKeys%>
```

If `MyCookie` contains multiple key values, the preceding code statement returns a value of `True`. A value of `False` is returned if the cookie only contains a single value.

The following code sample shows how to retrieve the value of a cookie named User that contains only one value of `Male`:

```
<%Request.Cookies("User")%>
```

If the HTTP request from the browser contains multiple key values for the `User` cookie, as in

```
Gender=Male&Age=30
```

then the code to return the value of this cookie is

```
<%Request.Cookies("User")("Age")%>
```

This code statement returns the value of 30. As you can see from the examples, key values are used to contain type and subtype information about the user.

The Cookies collection can be used as an alternate method to store information about the user. This method is sometimes disputed, because information about the user is being stored on the local machine and distributed to the server without the user's knowledge. You should be careful not to store sensitive information within a cookie to ensure the security of your application and your users.

Using the Form Collection

The Form collection contains the values of a form that are submitted via the POST method. The syntax for using the Form collection is

```
Request.Form(parameter)[(index)].Count]
```

where *parameter* is the name of the form element that contains a value. The optional *index* attribute enables you to access the specific value of a parameter that can contain multiple values. The Count attribute denotes the number of possible values for a parameter in the form. The value of the index can be an integer between one and the value of the Count attribute.

The following examples exhibit how you can use the Form collection in an ASP file to retrieve information from the user. Both examples use HTML forms as the basic user interface. You may already be familiar with working with HTML forms. You learn about developing HTML forms during tomorrow's lesson (Day 12, "Using Basic and Advanced HTML Form Controls"). It isn't important to understand the development of the form for purposes of these examples. For now, focus on the logic contained in the ASP and how the ASP is used to process the needs of the application.

The first example involves a basic HTML form that retrieves the user name and favorite type of coffee drink. Figure 11.3 illustrates the layout of this form.

The HTML form in this example contains a text field for the user name, along with a drop-down listbox that contains a list of choices of different coffee drinks. The form also contains a Submit button for the user to click the preferences have been entered. When the users enter their preferences and press the Submit button, the form is submitted to the Active Server Page. Listing 11.1 displays the code for the HTML file that contains the layout of the form.

Figure 11.3.

Retrieving the user preferences.

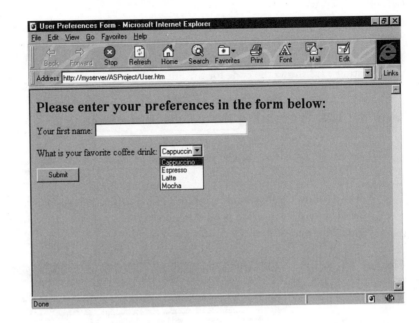

Listing 11.1. User Preferences Form.

```
<HTML>
<HEAD>
<TITLE>User Preferences Form</TITLE>
<H2>Please enter your preferences in the form below: </H2>
</HEAD>
<BODY>
<form action="/ASProject/scripts/submit.asp" method="post">
<p>Your first name: <input name="firstname" size=48>
<p>What is your favorite coffee drink: <select name="drink">
<option>Cappuccino <option>Espresso <option>Latte <option>Mocha
</select>
<p><input type=submit>
</form>
</BODY>
</HTML>
```

As you can see from Listing 11.1, an ASP file is referenced in the form action line. Those of you familiar with CGI scripts should notice that this line is different from the typical way you have processed your forms in the past. You're probably used to specifying a CGI script in this line of code. This method is a basic difference with Active Server Pages. The ASP file is used to process the form instead of the CGI script. The Submit.asp file retrieves the information that is entered and displays the preferences in a new page to the user with a welcome message. Listing 11.2 shows the code for the Submit ASP.

Listing 11.2. Processing the user's preference.

```
Welcome, <%= Request.Form("firstname")%>.
Your favorite coffee drink is <%= Request.Form("drink")%>!
```

This ASP shows how you can combine HTML with script code to construct a dynamic web page. The Form collection is used to obtain the firstname as well as the drink parameter. Figure 11.4 demonstrates a sample user entry.

Figure 11.4.

Entering the user preference.

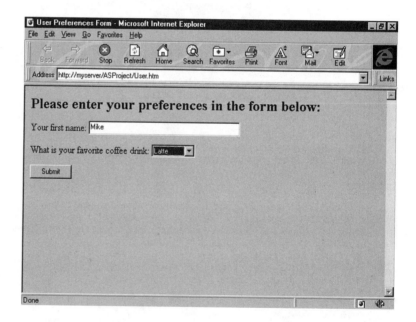

Based on the user preference entered above, Figure 11.5 depicts how the new page will be formatted by the Submit ASP.

11

In this example, the ASP used the Form collection to process the user preference and create a new web page based on these values. You may have a need to send results back to the same form that submitted the user preference. For example, you may need to confirm that the user entered a valid character in a field before the value can be stored in the database. If the form parameter value is incorrect, the server needs to send the message to the user within the context of the user form, so that the user can correct the mistake on that form.

Figure 11.5.

Displaying the user's preference.

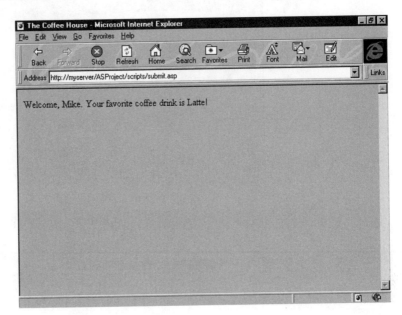

The other alternative is to send a message to the user on a new page indicating that a field was incorrect on the form. The user would then have to navigate to the form and correct the field. The better alternative is to develop an ASP that both creates and processes a form to handle this case and present the message within the proper context of your application.

The following example illustrates the use of an ASP to create this dynamic form. Figure 11.6 shows a sample form to obtain a user name and e-mail address.

Figure 11.6.

Entering an e-mail address.

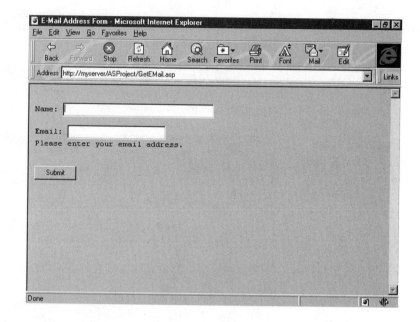

This form is constructed using the ASP file that is shown in Listing 11.3.

Listing 11.3. Creating a dynamic web page.

```
<HTML>
<!-- This is GetEmail.asp -->
<%
If IsEmpty(Request("Email")) Then
Msg = "Please enter your email address."
ElseIf InStr(Request("Email"), "@") = 0 Then
Msg = "Please enter an email address" & _
" in the form username@location."
Else
Msg = "This script could process the " & _
"valid Email address now."
End If
%><FORM METHOD="POST" ACTION="GetEmail.asp">
<PRE>
<p>Name: <input name="firstname" size=48 VALUE= "<%=Request("firstname")
%>">
<p>Email: <INPUT TYPE="TEXT" NAME="Email" SIZE=30 VALUE= "<%= Request("Email")
%>">
<%= Msg %><P>
<INPUT TYPE="SUBMIT" VALUE="Submit">
</PRE>
</FORM>
</HTML>
```

This code listing demonstrates the effective combination of HTML and script to construct a dynamic web page. Also, this example shows how you can properly handle the needs of your application. You learned earlier today that HTML contained in an ASP file is initially sent to the browser. The HTML form contained in the GetEmail.asp file is, therefore, created first. After the user submits the information, the ASP script processes the form using the Request object and Form collection. The e-mail field is validated to ensure that an @ sign was included in the e-mail address. If this character isn't in the e-mail address, the ASP sends an error message and the original form to the browser, so that the user can correct the mistake. Figure 11.7 shows the page that is formatted by the ASP.

Figure 11.7.

Displaying the form and a message.

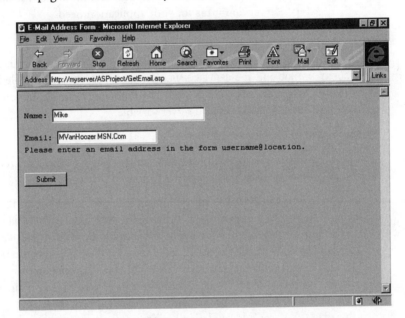

As you can see, this method provides an effective way to process user input. The Form collection is an invaluable tool for handling the values of the form.

Using the `ServerVariables` Collection

You can use the `ServerVariables` collection to retrieve environment variables that pertain to the browser request. The syntax for this collection is

```
Request.ServerVariables(variable)
```

where *variable* references the name of the server environment variable to retrieve.

NOTE There are many variables that exist for the ServerVariables collection. It is beyond the scope of this lesson to exhaustively cover each of the variables that you can access. Refer to the Visual InterDev documentation for a comprehensive list and description of each of the possible variables for the ServerVariables collection.

I am going to cover two of the more useful variables for the ServerVariables collection in the following section. These examples should provide you with a good idea of how to use other ServerVariables for your application needs.

Two of the more useful server variables that you can access with this collection include the REQUEST_METHOD and the SERVER_NAME. The REQUEST_METHOD variable indicates the method with which a page has been requested. The following example demonstrates how to capture the value of the REQUEST_METHOD server variable:

```
RequestMethod = Request.ServerVariables("REQUEST_METHOD")
```

The value of this variable will be POST when the page has been referenced by another form and GET when the user has specifically requested the form.

In the previous section, you learned about the use of Active Server Pages to process HTML forms. The ACTION parameter was formatted with a value of POST when the user submitted the form. If the page is called by any other method, the REQUEST_METHOD value is equal to GET. You can use this variable to provide validation for the page based on the access method. For the form example, if a user refreshes an Active Server Page or enters the URL directly without completing the user preferences form, the page may not contain the proper values to dynamically format the page. For both of these requests, the REQUEST_METHOD is equal to the value of GET. You can add validation logic to confirm the access method for the page and then process the page based on this value. Listing 11.4 displays sample validation logic for the user preferences form.

Listing 11.4. Verifying the request method for a page.

```
<HTML>
<HEAD>
<TITLE>Your Personal Preferences </TITLE>
</HEAD>
<BODY>
<%
DIM RequestMethod
' Captures the request method for the page
RequestMethod = Request.ServerVariables("REQUEST_METHOD")
```

```
' Validate the value of the request method
If RequestMethod = "GET" then
' The user has refreshed the ASP - Display error message
%>
<P>You have chosen to refresh this page. If you want to change the value of
your preferences to display on this page, go back to the User Preferences form
and enter your choices. After you change your preferences and click Submit,
this page will display the results of your new preferences.
<%
Else
%>
Welcome, <%= Request.Form("firstname")%>.
Your favorite coffee drink is <%= Request.Form("drink")%>
<%
End If
%>
</BODY>
</HTML>
```

In the code listing, the script uses an If...Then...Else statement to determine the value of the REQUEST_METHOD. Based on the value of this variable, the appropriate code block is executed. Within an ASP, you will see a combination of HTML and script. Many times, the HTML and script will be intermingled, as shown in Listing 11.4. This coding standard is different from the method that you learned concerning client-side script. With client-side script, the recommendation is to use a strict split between the HTML and script code. The dynamic nature of Active Server Pages dictates that a combination coding convention be used instead of a strict split between HTML and script. Figure 11.8 demonstrates what happens when a user refreshes an Active Server Page using the new validation logic.

Figure 11.8.

Displaying an error message.

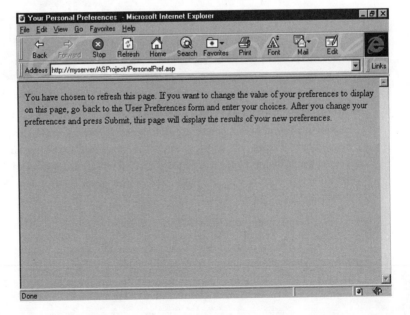

The SERVER_NAME is another server variable that can be used to provide valuable information to your application. The SERVER_NAME variable contains the server's host name, DNS alias, or IP address that is used in self-referencing URL addresses. This variable can be used to format a URL link to another page in your application. The following code sample demonstrates the use of this variable:

```
<A HREF = "http://<%= Request.ServerVariables("SERVER_NAME") %>
/ASProject/scripts/MyPage.asp">Link to MyPage.asp</A>
```

In this example, the ServerVariables collection is used to retrieve the value of the host server name. This value is used to format the prefix of the URL link to an Active Server Page. Figure 11.9 illustrates the results of executing this code sample.

Figure 11.9.

Creating a dynamic link.

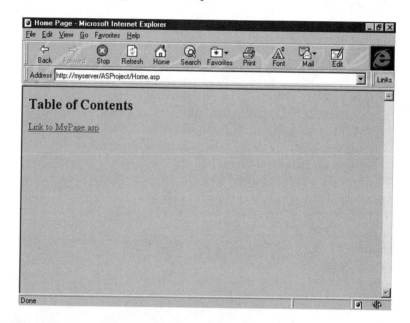

Using the QueryString Collection

The QueryString collection enables you to access the values of the variables in an HTTP query string. These values are located after the question mark in an HTTP request. The QueryString collection provides an easy method to access the value of these variables, because you can reference the variables by name. The syntax for the QueryString collection is as follows:

```
Request.QueryString(variable)[(index)].Count
```

variable is the name of the desired variable in the HTTP query string and *index* is an optional parameter that enables you to retrieve the value of a variable that contains multiple values. The index can contain an integer between one and the value of the Count attribute.

Take a look at the User Preferences Form again. You could use an ASP that contains the `QueryString` collection to process the user input. Listing 11.5 demonstrates an example of using the `QueryString` to display the name and coffee drink preference for a particular user.

Listing 11.5. Using the `QueryString` collection to process the user's preference.

```
Welcome, <%= Request.QueryString("firstname")%>.
Your favorite coffee drink is <%= Request.QueryString("drink")%>
```

Figure 11.10 displays the page that is produced from the ASP code.

Figure 11.10.
The results of the
QueryString.

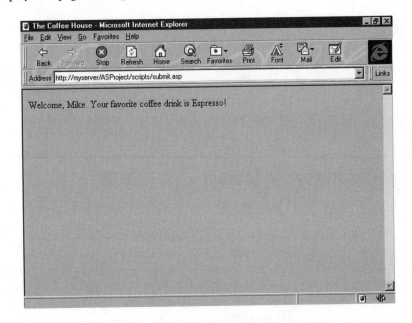

For variables that contain multiple values, the `QueryString` collection creates a new collection instance with the number of values that are passed to the ASP. For example, if the User Preferences form is changed to allow multiple names to be passed to the server, the `QueryString` creates a new collection instance called `firstname`. If three names are passed to the ASP, `firstname` contains three values. The `index` attribute can be used to reference each value within the `firstname` variable. The following example illustrates how the `firstname` values would be accessed by the `QueryString`. For the sake of example, suppose that the following values are passed to the ASP from a client request:

```
/scripts/submit.asp?firstname=Mike&firstname=Matt&firstname=Chris
```

The following `QueryString` statements

```
Request.QueryString("firstname")(1)
Request.QueryString("firstname")(2)
Request.QueryString("firstname")(3)
```

would produce the values of

```
Mike
Matt
Chris
```

respectively. The `Count` attribute would be three for the `firstname` collection instance. You also could reference the `firstname` collection using the following statement:

```
Request.QueryString("firstname")
```

This statement would produce a comma-delimited value of

```
Mike,Matt,Chris
```

The `QueryString` can be used with forms that use both the `GET` and `POST` action commands. If you use the `QueryString` collection with a form that uses `GET`, the collection will contain all of the information contained on the form. If the ASP is requested using the `POST` statement, the `QueryString` collection will contain all of the information that is passed as a parameter to the ASP.

The `Response` Object

You can use the `Response` object to send information to the user. You can format HTML to be sent to the client as well as manipulate state and session information. Some examples include redirecting the user to another URL address and formatting the value of a cookie on the server. The `Response` object supplies several properties and methods needed to accomplish these tasks. A property defines characteristics about the object that it represents, and a method indicates an action that the object can execute. Properties and methods are thoroughly explored during the lessons on Day 13, "Interacting with Objects and ActiveX Controls," and Day 15, "Integrating Objects into Your Applications."

The Cookies collection is the single collection of the `Response` object. You can use this collection to set the values of cookies. Table 11.2 defines the properties that are available for the `Response` object.

Table 11.2. The Response properties.

Property	Description
Buffer	Indicates whether the page is buffered
ContentType	Defines the content type for the response
Expires	Indicates the length of time before the expiration of a page that has been cached by the browser
ExpiresAbsolute	Indicates date and time of the expiration of a page that has been cached by the browser
Status	Indicates the status line value returned by the server

These properties can be used with the Response object methods to send the proper information to the user. Table 11.3 lists the methods that are available for the Response object.

Table 11.3. The Response methods.

Method	Description
AddHeader	Defines a name for the HTML header
AppendToLog	Adds a string of text to the web server log
BinaryWrite	Writes the output to the HTTP response without converting the characters
Clear	Erases all HTML output that has been buffered
End	Terminates ASP processing and returns the result
Flush	Sends buffered output immediately to the client
Redirect	Redirects the user to another URL address
Write	Writes the output to the HTTP response as a string

The next few sections explore some of the more powerful properties and methods of the Response object that you can use to enhance the functionality of your Active Server Pages.

Using the Cookies Collection

The Cookies collection for the Response object provides a way to set the value of a cookie on the server. You can create new cookies as well as change the value of existing cookies. The syntax for using the Cookies collection for the Response object is similar to the format that you used for the Request object. To use the Cookies collection for the Response object, type the following:

```
Response.Cookies(cookie)[(key).attribute] = value
```

cookie is the name of the cookie. The key is an optional parameter used to define a cookie that contains multiple key values. The attribute parameter describes information about the cookie. The value parameter can be used to set the values of the key and attribute parameters. You also can use the HasKeys attribute to determine if the cookie contains key values. Table 11.4 provides a complete listing of the attributes for the Cookies collection.

Table 11.4. The Cookies collection attributes.

Attribute	Description
HasKeys	Determines if the cookie contains key values
Expires	Indicates expiration date for the cookie
Domain	Defines the domain for which cookies are distributed
Path	Defines the path for which cookies are distributed
Secure	Indicates whether the cookie is secure

You can update the value for all of the attributes of the Cookies collection except HasKeys, which is read-only. The HasKeys attribute evaluates to a value of True to indicate that the cookie contains key values or False to specify that the cookie does not contain key values.

Listing 11.6 demonstrates several methods for populating the value of cookies.

Listing 11.6. Setting the value of cookies.

```
<%
'Sets the value of cookie
Response.Cookies("Name") = "Mike"
'Sets the value of cookie with key values
Response.Cookies("MyCookie")("FirstName") = "Mike"
Response.Cookies("MyCookie")("LastName") = "Van Hoozer"
'Changes the cookie to a non-key value cookie and sets the new value
Response.Cookies("MyCookie") = "Mike"
'Sets the value of a cookie and its attributes
Response.Cookies("StdCookie") = "User"
Response.Cookies("StdCookie").Expires = "December 31, 1997"
Response.Cookies("StdCookie").Domain = "mydomain.com"
Response.Cookies("StdCookie").Path = "/www/home/"
Response.Cookies("StdCookie").Secure = "TRUE"
%>
```

The code example in Listing 11.6 sets the value of the Name cookie to Mike. The next example creates a cookie called MyCookie and sets the key values of FirstName and LastName. The third code example demonstrates how you can change the type for the cookie as well as its value. This example changes MyCookie to a non-key value cookie. The values that were previously stored in this cookie are discarded, and the new value of Mike is assigned to MyCookie. The final code example shows how to set both the value of a cookie as well as its attributes.

Using the Buffer Property to Process Your Script

You were introduced to the properties of the Response object. The properties help describe the characteristics for an object. The basic syntax to reference a Response object property is

```
Response.PropertyName
```

PropertyName is the name of the property.

The Buffer property defines whether the page results are buffered. You can use the Buffer property to process all of the script code in your ASP before the results are sent to the client. The syntax for the Buffer property is as follows:

```
Response.Buffer = flag
```

flag contains the value of True or False to indicate whether or not to buffer the page output. If you set the value of the flag parameter to True, the page output is buffered, and the script code is processed before distributing the results to the browser. The default value for the flag parameter is False.

You cannot set the value of the Buffer property if your ASP has previously sent output to the client. If you are going to process your script before sending the results to the client, you should assign the value of the Buffer property in the first line of your ASP to prevent this situation from happening.

There are two methods that can be used to halt the processing of the script code in your ASP. You can use either the Flush or the End method to stop the script processing and send the results to the client. The syntax for these two methods is

```
Response.Flush
```

and

```
Response.End
```

You should balance the need to process your script versus the length of time that it takes to process your script. For long scripts, you may want to send intermediate results to the user while your script continues to process. In these situations, you won't want to set the value of the Buffer property to True.

11

Using the `Write` Method to Send Output to the User

You can use the `Write` method to format a string of text to send to the user. The syntax for the `Write` method is

```
Response.Write variant
```

variant represents the data to be written. The *variant* parameter can contain any value that is supported by the VBScript variant data type, including characters, strings, and integers.

The `Write` method is commonly used to format HTML to be sent to the client browser. The following code example shows how to use the `Write` method to format the User Preferences Form:

```
Welcome, <% Response.Write Request.Form("firstname")%>.
Your favorite coffee drink is <% Response.Write Request.Form("drink")%>
```

Notice that this example differs from the previous ASP code that was used to format the User Preferences Form. Instead of using the `= Request.Form` statement, the equal sign is replaced by the `Response.Write` method. Figure 11.11 displays the results of using the `Write` method.

Figure 11.11.

Using the `Write` *method to format the page.*

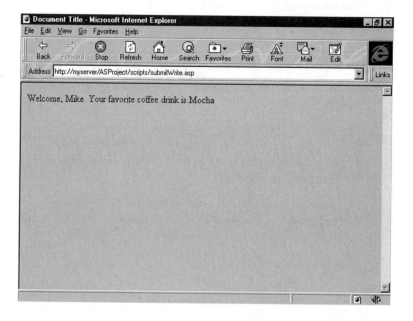

You also could use the `Write` method to create a dynamic header for your web page, based on the user ID that is entered. For new users, you could display an initial greeting that is different from the greeting for return visitors to your site. Listing 11.7 demonstrates the use of the `Write` method in an Active Server Page to create this type of greeting.

Listing 11.7. Creating a dynamic greeting.

```
<%
If NewUser Then
Response.Write "<H3 ALIGN=CENTER>Welcome to the Overview Page</H3>"
Else
Response.Write "<H3 ALIGN=CENTER>Welcome Back to the Overview Page</H3>"
End If
%>
```

In this code listing, the NewUser variable is used to designate whether the ID represents a new or existing user. If NewUser is True, the initial welcome message is displayed. If this user is a return visitor, the welcome back message is displayed. Notice that the text is formatted using the header HTML tags. You could use this code with a procedure that verifies user IDs against those IDs stored in your database.

Using the Redirect Method

The Redirect method can be used to redirect the user to another URL address. The syntax for using the Redirect method is as follows:

```
Response.Redirect URL
```

URL is the URL address location to redirect the browser.

NOTE   You cannot use this method from an ASP if results have already been distributed to the client.

This method is helpful for ensuring that users follow a specific path when using your application. For example, an order entry application may require that a user enter basic order header information like name and address before selecting the items that will be ordered. If a user attempts to access the order detail page to order an item, you can use the following code sample in Listing 11.9 to redirect them to the initial page of your application.

Listing 11.9. Guiding the user's path.

```
<%
If NOT Session("OrderHeaderPage") Then
Response.Redirect "OrderHeader.asp"
End If
%>
```

This code example uses the Session object, which will be covered in a later section. You can use this object to store variables for a user session. In this example, a variable is used to verify that the user has entered the application from the Order Header page. If this variable isn't true, the browser will be redirected to the ASP to process the Order Header page.

Specifying the Type of Content

You can use the ContentType property to designate the type of content that is located in the response for the page. The syntax for this property is

```
Response.ContentType = content type
```

content type represents the type of content for the page. This value is a string that conforms to the MIME standards for a web page. The content type defines the type and subtype of information that's contained in the response that is sent to the client. The type describes the general category of the information, while the subtype specifically defines the content type. The default value for the ContentType property is "text/HTML". This value defines the content type for a response as text and the content subtype as HTML. The following code samples demonstrate how to use this property:

```
Response.ContentType = "text/HTML"
Response.ContentType = "image/GIF"
Response.ContentType = "text/plain"
```

The Session Object

You can use the Session object to store and retrieve information during a specific session for a user. The information contained in the Session object persists for the entire time that the user interacts with your application. You can use and access this information across the web pages in your application.

A Session object is automatically created by the web server when a user accesses a web page in your application. The user session persists until the user leaves the application, the session times out, or the session is explicitly abandoned. To access the Session properties, the syntax for referencing the Session object is

```
Session.property
```

and it is

```
Session.method
```

to access the Session methods. The Session object consists of two defined properties and one defined method.

The SessionID property returns the Session ID for a user. The web server creates a unique identifier as it creates each user session. The value of this identifier is a LONG data type. The syntax to reference the SessionID property is

```
Session.SessionID
```

NOTE

The Session ID that is generated is stored as a Session cookie. If the user's browser doesn't support the use of cookies, the Active Server engine examines the URL references on the page. The Active Server Engine determines which URL links reference another page in your application and append the Session ID to each of these references. In this way, the Session ID remains available within the user session scope of the application.

The other property of the Session object is the Timeout property. You can use the Timeout property to identify the maximum length of time before the session will end, or time out, for a user. This property is measured in minutes. If there is no user activity such as refreshing or requesting a page before the timeout period, the session terminates. The syntax for using this property is

```
Session.Timeout = nMinutes
```

nMinutes indicates the number of minutes for the timeout period. The default value for the timeout period is 20 minutes.

The Abandon method is the sole method for the Session object. You can use the Abandon method to explicitly terminate a session and destroy all of the information stored in the session object. The syntax for calling the Abandon method is

```
Session.Abandon
```

After you call the Abandon method, the page processes any remaining script and then terminates the session.

Working with the Session Object

You can create additional properties and variables for the Session object to store information about a user session. Examples include user preferences as well as global information to be shared between the pages for a particular user session. Another example would involve storing data to be used to calculate the grand total for an order. The following example shows how to store variables in the Session object:

```
Session("UserName") = "John Smith"
Session("Email") = "JSmith@msn.com"
Session("CoffeeDrink") = "Latte"
Session("Age") = 32
```

These examples show how you can store various types of information using the Session object. The information contained in these variables can then be accessed and referenced throughout the scope of this user's session.

You also can use the pre-defined properties and methods of the Session object. For example, if you want to change the timeout period for a user session, you can alter the value in the Timeout property. The following code sample changes the timeout period from the default of 20 minutes to 30 minutes:

```
Session.Timeout = 30
```

Listing 11.10 demonstrates how to use a Session object variable to dynamically format a page based on the user preferences that were entered on an initial User Preferences Form.

Listing 11.10. Using a new variable in the Session object.

```
<HTML>
<% If Session("CoffeeDrink") = "Latte" Then %>
<IMG SRC="/MyApp/images/latte.GIF" WIDTH="85"
<% Else %>
<IMG SRC="/MyApp/images/Cappuccino.GIF" WIDTH="85"
<%End If%>
</HTML>
```

In this code example, the ASP checks the value of the user's coffee drink preference, which is stored in the Session object. If the preference is a Latte, then the page is formatted with an image of a Cafe Latte. If the user specified something other than a Latte, the page is formatted with an image of a Cappuccino. This code again demonstrates the dynamic nature of Active Server Pages.

Working with the Session Events

The Session object is related to two events that are unique to an Active Server Page. The Session_OnStart and Session_OnEnd events can be used to execute script when a session is initially created and when the session is terminated. These events are contained in the global.asa file. You were first introduced to the global.asa and these events during Day 4, "Creating Your First Visual InterDev Project."

The `Session_OnStart` event is triggered when the server creates the new session. The `Session_OnStart` script is the initial code that is processed for a new user session. In other words, the script that you place in the procedure for this event is processed before the request for the page is executed. You can access all of the objects for an ASP, including the `Application`, `Session`, `Server`, `Request`, and `Response` objects during this event. The `Session_OnEnd` event occurs when the user session is abandoned or times out. The only ASP objects available during the `Session_OnEnd` event include the `Application`, `Server`, and `Session` objects.

An example of using the `Session_OnStart` event involves the `Redirect` method for the `Response` object that you learned earlier today. I used the example of redirecting a user to a defined start page for the application. Listing 11.11 demonstrates an expansion of this example used within the context of the `Session_OnStart` event.

Listing 11.11. Starting the user off right.

```
<SCRIPT RUNAT=Server Language=VBScript>
Sub Session_OnStart
' Sets the value of the Order Header start page
OrderHeaderPage = "/MyApp/OrderHeader.asp"
' Sets the value of the current user page
CurrentPage = Request.ServerVariables("SCRIPT_NAME")
' Do a case-insensitive compare on the pages. If they
' don't match, send the user to the Order Header page.
If strcomp(currentPage,OrderHeaderPage,1) then
Response.Redirect(OrderHeaderPage)
End If
End Sub
</SCRIPT>
```

Because the code in the listing executes when a user session is initiated, the `Session_OnStart` is a perfect place to verify that the user is beginning with the proper page in your application. This code example combines several of the concepts that you have learned today to demonstrate their value within the context of an application.

The `Application` Object

The `Application` object enables you to share information across all users of the ASP-based application. While the `Session` object is limited to a single user, this information is globally available for all users of the application. The `Application` object is created when the application is initiated. Upon initial creation, the `Application` object is then available to each additional user who accesses your application. The syntax for accessing the Application object is as follows:

```
Application.method
```

method is the name of the method for the Application object. The Application object supports two defined methods. The Lock and Unlock methods provide a way to prevent contention between multiple users. The Lock method enables you to prevent other users from modifying an Application object that has been accessed by a user. The Unlock method enables you to then unlock the Application object once it has been released by the user. When you use the Unlock method, other users are then able to modify the Application object's properties and variable information.

A great example of using the Application object involves calculating the number of visits to your web site. Almost all web sites track this information. For commercial sites, the number of people that visit a web site continues to be a very important number. This number is used to justify the existence of the web site as well as to determine how much to charge advertisers that place a banner on the web page. The code in Listing 11.12 demonstrates how to use the Application object to determine the number of hits for a web site.

Listing 11.12. Determining the number of web site visitors.

```
<%
' Locks the Application object
Application.Lock
' Increments the number of visits by one
Application("NumVisits") = Application("NumVisits") + 1
' Unlocks the Application object
Application.Unlock
%>
' Displays the number of visitors for the application
This application page has been visited
<%= Application("NumVisits") %>   times!
```

In this code example, the NumVisits variable is created the first time the code is executed. The variable is initialized to zero. The NumVisits is then incremented each additional time the code is executed, and the value is stored in the Application object.

The values that are stored in the Application object are contained in persistent storage. For this reason, you can access the values of these variables even if you have to stop and restart your server. You can, therefore, create and use variables for your application that need to be consistently maintained. You want to use good judgment about the kind of values that you store in the Application object. You should store simple rather than complex information.

Working with the Application Events

The Application object has two associated events that are contained in the global.asa. You were first introduced to the global.asa and these Application events during Day 4.

The Application_OnStart event is triggered when the first user accesses a web page within the application. This event occurs before the Session_OnStart event. The Application_OnEnd event is activated when the application terminates. The Application_OnEnd occurs after the Session_OnEnd event. The Server and the Application objects are the only objects that are available during both the Application_OnStart and the Application_OnEnd events.

The Server Object

The Server object enables you to interface with Active Server Components, also called OLE Automation Components. These components provide robust application processing on the server. Active Server Pages include the following five Active Server Components:

1. Database Access Component
2. AdRotator Component
3. Browser Capabilities Component
4. File Access Component
5. Content Linking Component

These components are included with Visual InterDev and enable you to accomplish certain tasks within the context of an ASP. You also can create custom Active Server Components for your Active Server Pages. You learn how to interact with these components as well as build your own custom Active Server Component on Day 17.

The syntax for referencing the Server object is as follows:

Server.*method*

method is the name of the method for the Server object. The methods for the Server object are outlined in Table 11.5.

Table 11.5. The Server object methods.

Method	Description
CreateObject	Creates an instance of an object
HTMLEncode	Applies HTML encoding to a string
MapPath	Maps the virtual path to a physical path
URLEncode	Applies URL encoding to a string

The `Server` object also contains one property that can be accessed. The `ScriptTimeout` property defines the length of time for a script to be able to run. The syntax for this property is as follows:

```
Server.ScriptTimeout = NumofSeconds
```

`NumofSeconds` represents the number of seconds before the script times out and terminates its processing. The default value for this property is `90` seconds. The `ScriptTimeout` property only applies to the processing of the script code. A script won't time out based on this property while a server component is processing. You set the value of this property as well as retrieve its value to store in a variable within your application. For example, if you wanted to find out the `timeout` period for the server script, you could execute the following code:

```
<% TimeoutForScript = Server.ScriptTimeout %>
```

This code sample would retrieve the value of the `timeout` period for the server script and store the value in the variable `TimeoutForScript`.

You will typically interact with the `Server` object by using the pre-defined server components for Active Server Pages as well as your own custom ActiveX Server Components. The following sections explain how to create and work with an instance of an object.

Creating a `Server` Object Instance

The `CreateObject` method is the most widely used method for the `Server` object. You can use this method to create an instance of a particular object that can then be used by your application. The syntax for calling this method is as follows:

```
Server.CreateObject progID
```

`progID` indicates the type of object to create. The syntax for the `progID` parameter is

```
Vendor.Component.Version
```

`Vendor` is the author of the component, `Component` is the name of the component, and `Version` is the version number of the component.

When you use this method to create an instance of an object, the scope of the object exists for the lifetime of the ASP. For example, if you execute this method in a typical ASP within your application, the component only exists while your ASP script is processed. The object is destroyed when the ASP completes its processing. Listing 11.13 demonstrates an object that is created for the lifetime of an ASP.

Listing 11.13. An object with limited existence.

```
<%
' Creates an instance of the Browser Capabilities object
Set bc = Server.CreateObject("MSWC.BrowserType")
' Check to see if the browser supports VBScript
If bc.vbscript = "True" Then %>
' Format a friendly confirmation message
Your Browser supports VBScript!
<%Else %>
' Format another message
Your Browser is very limited!?!
```

In this code example, the object that is created can only be referenced for the lifetime of the ASP. After the script executes the last line of code to format a message to display on the browser page, the object is destroyed. Any references to the object after the ASP has completed result in a runtime error, as shown in Figure 11.12.

Figure 11.12.

Referencing an object that has died.

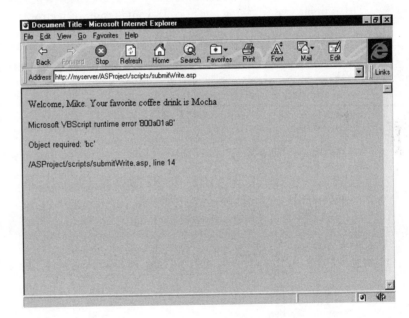

You can extend the life of your objects by calling the CreateObject method and storing its value in a Session or Application object variable. For example, you could execute the following line of code to store an object in an Application object variable:

```
<% Set Application("BrowserCapabilities") =
Server.CreateObject("MSWC.BrowserType") %>
```

In this example, an instance of the BrowserType object is created and stored in an Application object variable named BrowserCapabilities. The BrowserType object, also referred to as the Browser Capabilities component, enables you to determine the capabilities of the current browser. Because an Application object variable is used to store this object, the object and its methods and properties can be referenced for the lifetime of the application.

NOTE

> In the previous code example, notice the Set statement used to store the component in the Application object variable. The use of this word differs from the normal convention that you learned earlier. You must use the Set keyword to store object variables.

You have now learned two methods for storing an instance of an object. When naming a variable to store an instance of the object, you cannot choose a name of a pre-defined object. For example, the following line of code would result in an error.

```
<% Set Application = Server.CreateObject("Application") %>
```

You also can use the <OBJECT> declaration to create an instance of an object in the global.asa file. You must declare these objects to contain either Application or Session scope. The syntax for using the <OBJECT> tag is as follows:

```
<OBJECT RUNAT=Server SCOPE=Scope ID=Identifier
{PROGID=ProgID¦CLASSID=ClassID}>
```

Scope indicates the scope of the object. This value of this parameter will be either Session or Application. The *Identifier* parameter designates a name for the object. The *ProgID* parameter was discussed previously. The *ClassID* parameter represents a unique class identifier for an OLE class object. You must enter either the *ProgID* or the *ClassID* parameter. Listing 11.14 demonstrates a global.asa file that declares an object with Session scope.

Listing 11.14. Using the <OBJECT> tag to extend the life of an object.

```
<SCRIPT LANGUAGE="VBScript" RUNAT="Server">
<%
If ProgramID Then
' Declare an object with Session scope using the PROGID
<OBJECT RUNAT=Server SCOPE=Session ID=MyConnection
PROGID="ADODB.Connection">
Else
' Declare an object with Session scope using the CLASSID
<OBJECT RUNAT=Server SCOPE=Session ID=MyConnection
CLASSID="Clsid:8AD3067A-B3FC-11CF-A560-00A0C9081C21">
</OBJECT>
```

Both the PROGID and CLASSID formats are used in this code example for the purpose of illustration. You will typically use either one format or the other, depending on the object that is being declared. This code listing shows an example of a database connection that is declared in a global.asa file. You could then reference characteristics about this connection object throughout the lifetime of a user session.

TIP

> The lesson has outlined the different lifetimes of an object based on when and where it is created. If you're ruthless and want to kill the object yourself, you can accomplish this task by using the Nothing keyword. To destroy an object, set the object variable equal to Nothing. For example, to destroy the bc object instance, execute (pardon the pun) the code: <%Set bc = Nothing %>. This code will destroy the instance of the BrowserType object that has been stored in the variable bc.
>
> This is the only tip that you get on how to destroy something. The lesson will not provide any tips on how to destroy your coworker's house or property.

Creating Your First Active Server Page

Now that you have learned about all of the benefits and features of Active Server Pages, you're probably wondering how to create an ASP. As you would expect, Microsoft has included a template within Visual InterDev to make this process easy.

From the File menu, select the New menu item. You are probably very familiar with the New tabbed dialog window by now. Figure 11.13 displays the Files tab within the New dialog window.

From this window, you can select the Active Server Page option from the list. You need to enter a name for the ASP and click OK. The ASP is created with the name that you specify and added to the current project. Figure 11.14 shows a newly created ASP.

Notice that the scripting language is denoted at the top of the ASP. This language is based on the default scripting language that you selected for your ASP. You learned how to change the default scripting language earlier in today's lesson.

Figure 11.13.
Creating an Active Server Page.

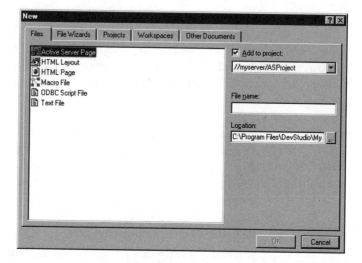

Figure 11.14.
A sample Active Server Page.

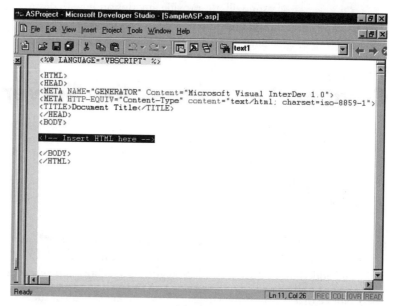

You're now ready to add processing logic to your ASP. An ASP is very similar to the HTML files that you created with Visual InterDev during the first week. The Active Server Page contains a place to put your HTML. You also can add your scripting code to the ASP. You can use most of the same options that are available for creating an HTML page, including

HTML layouts and ActiveX and Design-time ActiveX controls. To add these features to your ASP, right-click the mouse in the ASP to display the shortcut menu for the ASP, as seen in Figure 11.15.

Figure 11.15.

Adding additional features to your ASP.

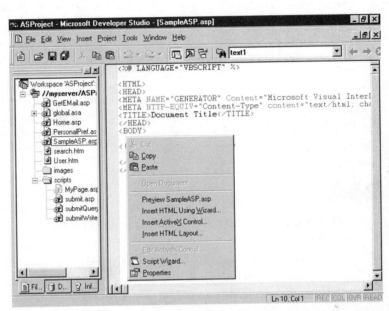

You can then choose an option to insert into your ASP.

Summary

Active Server Pages provide an excellent method for constructing interactive applications. Today's lesson has provided you with a thorough overview of Active Server Pages. Visual InterDev enables you to easily implement Active Server Pages within your application. You now understand how Active Server Pages derived their name—an ASP represents the difference between a passive, dull site and a site that truly comes alive, thereby providing a rich and rewarding experience for the user.

During today's lesson, you first received an explanation of a server that is alive and active, then learned about the features and benefits of Active Server Pages. During this part of the lesson, you learned the characteristics of Active Server Pages that give them their dynamic nature. The lesson then provided an overview of the client-server picture of a Web-based application. The role of an Active Server Page was outlined within the context of the application components.

You learned about the types of scripting languages that are used within an Active Server Page. You also learned how Visual InterDev assigns the scripting language for an ASP and how you can change the default language for your Active Server Pages. A majority of the lesson covered the various objects that can be used with Active Server Pages. You learned about the five types of ASP objects. You also received an exhaustive discourse on the collections, methods, and properties of these objects. The lesson provided detailed examples of how to access and reference these objects. Throughout the lesson, you received relevant examples of scripting logic that can be used to meet the needs of your application.

At the end of the day, you received an overview of how to create your first Active Server Page. You were able to view the format of an ASP. Finally, you learned about the Active Server Page's additional features such as ActiveX controls and Design-time ActiveX controls that can be added to an ASP.

Q&A

Q What is the main difference between an HTML web page and an Active Server Page?

A An HTML web page consists of HTML, limited client-side script, ActiveX controls, and other objects that help to format the look of the web page. All of the logic included within an HTML file is executed within the context of the client browser. An ASP, on the other hand, can include all of the aforementioned items as well as robust server-side script. This server-side script executes on the server and can interact with Active Server Components that are also on the server. An ASP can dynamically generate formatted HTML back to the client, based on both client and server conditions. The dynamic nature of an ASP is what distinguishes it from a regular HTML web page.

Q Can I use an Active Server Page instead of an HTML file to create my web pages?

A Definitely, yes. In fact, I think you will appreciate the dynamic nature of Active Server Pages so much that you won't want to go back to using HTML files. Of course, there still may be situations where you need to use an HTML web page instead of an Active Server Page.

Workshop

Today's workshop will enable you to explore the development of an Active Server Page. You're going to use the template that you created during the last section of the lesson to add your application logic. Choose some of your favorite objects and examples from today's lesson, and experiment using these objects and the examples that were provided to create a sample application of your own. This application should use Active Server Pages to create a dynamic experience for the user. You should also extend the functionality of the examples to include your own ideas. For example, you may want to extend the functionality of the User Preferences Form to include other preferences besides name and favorite type of coffee drink.

You should practice using the ASP concepts explained in today's lesson to develop your application. You also should experiment using different scenarios for your ASP and your application. An example would be to experiment creating your objects in different places, including creating an object in a regular ASP as well as in the global.asa file. Finally, you should practice using variables that contain different scopes, such as `Application` versus `Session` versus `Page`.

Quiz

1. Name the five types of ASP objects.
2. Which object supports a method to write HTML back to the client?
3. Which object contains a collection which enables you to access the object values on a form?
4. Explain the difference between `Session` and `Application` scope.
5. Given the following code for an Active Server Page, what is displayed as the value of the `NumofVisits` variable for user C after users A and B access the application?

```
<%
Session("NumofVisits") = Application("NumofVisits") + 1
%>
This application page has been visited
<%= Session("NumofVisits") %> times!
```

Quiz Answers

1. The five types of ASP objects are:

      `Request` object

      `Response` object

      `Session` object

      `Application` object

      `Server` object

2. The Response object

3. The Request object

4. Session scope of a variable extends for the lifetime of a user session, and information stored in a Session variable is only available to the specified user. As long as the user interacts with your application, this information is available to the user. Application scope refers to a variable that is available to all users of your application.

5. The answer is 1. A Session variable was used instead of an Application variable. The developer of this code was attempting to track the number of visitors to the web site application. As you discovered from correctly answering Quiz question number 4, the Application variable would have provided access to all users of the application. If an Application variable had been used, the code would have reflected the accurate number of people who had visited the site—3.

Day 12

Using Basic and Advanced HTML Form Controls

This lesson is the first in a series about constructing a user interface for your application. You were introduced to design considerations and HTML and browser extensions on Day 3, "Design and Development Considerations." Today's lesson focuses on intrinsic objects and controls available with HTML 3.x. These HTML objects and controls enable you to build an interface for your application that lets the user interact with the information in your web site and make use of your application's features.

The objects and controls described in this lesson are *intrinsic* to HTML—that is, an inherent part of the language. You can use these controls right out of the HTML box.

NEW TERM *Intrinsic* defines a control as part of a native language. In the context of the Web and this lesson, the term *intrinsic* defines those objects and controls that are part of HTML. In other words, these controls are internal to, or included with, HTML.

You will learn about other objects and controls over the next few days that are *extrinsic*, or external, to HTML. In tomorrow's lesson, Day 13, "Interacting with Objects and ActiveX Controls," you will explore the ActiveX controls included with Visual InterDev. You will also get an overview of how to use these objects and Java applets to extend your application's user interface. On Day 14, "Extending Web Pages Through Design-Time Controls," you will learn about using Design-time ActiveX controls in your Visual InterDev application. Finally, on Day 15, "Integrating Objects into Your Applications," you will learn how to integrate extrinsic objects and controls into your application and extend the objects' functionality with scripting code.

NEW TERM *Extrinsic* defines a control as external to the native language. In the context of the Web and this lesson, the term *extrinsic* defines those objects and controls that are external to HTML. In other words, these controls are separate from HTML. Extrinsic controls are developed by third-party software providers and can be integrated into a web page by inserting the object or control into the HTML document.

Today's lesson covers these topics: First, it examines HTML forms and their controls. The majority of today's lesson is spent covering the basic and advanced elements of HTML forms. You learn about HTML controls that you can integrate into your application interface, including the text control, the textarea control, the button control, the radio button and checkbox controls, and the password control. You get instructions on how to use these controls to design the perfect interface. The lesson also introduces you to some of the more advanced HTML controls that are available.

Next, you learn how to use these controls to develop an HTML form. The lesson also reviews some basic concepts of HTML form design and effective design tips for your forms. At the end of the day, the lesson combines all the concepts and methods you've learned to create a form-based application.

NOTE

> Today's lesson may be a review for some of you. HTML form design is still used as a viable user interface for Web-based applications. This lesson gives you the basic building blocks to understand the power of the more robust extrinsic objects and controls. Once you gain an understanding of basic form design, you will appreciate controls like ActiveX controls, which extend the functionality of the basic user interface to a new, exciting level.

Exploring HTML Forms

A form provides the house for a control. Just as a house consists of rooms, an HTML form consists of HTML controls. Rooms can't be useful unless they're constructed within the house. You don't, for example, build a kitchen as a separate structure (not these days, anyway); a kitchen becomes useful when it combines with other rooms to form a house. Similarly, a control or group of controls get their meaning, or purpose, within the context of a form. The form gives function to the control.

The Form and Its Function

The basic function of a form is to provide an interface for the user to perform a task or set of tasks. The *American Heritage Dictionary* defines *interface* as "the point of interaction or communication between a computer and another entity, such as a person."

The form enables a person to interact with the computer and, more important, your application. You can create forms to supply many functions for your applications, including the following:

- [ ] Letting a user enter user preferences for your web site
- [ ] Allowing a user to enter parameters to search for information in your database
- [ ] Enabling a user to enter guest book information to be tracked in the application
- [ ] Giving a user a way to enter online order information for products and services

HTML forms are easy to construct in a short time by using simple HTML tags and attributes. Developing HTML forms is iterative and quick, and you can preview their layout in the Visual InterDev environment to assess the strength and effectiveness of their design.

As with other graphical tools, such as Visual Basic, you must be careful how you use them. You don't want to throw your interface together without any thought just because the process and tools are quick and easy. Also, you don't need to use each and every control on a form just because you have so many to choose from. Form design considerations are discussed in more detail in the section entitled "Reviewing HTML Form Design."

How Does a Form Take Its Function?

A form is placed in a web page document by using the start tag `<FORM>` and end tag `</FORM>`. All the form tags, attributes, and controls must be placed inside the start and end tags. The start tag consists of two associated attributes: `METHOD` and `ACTION`. These attributes help define the form's behavior.

12

The METHOD attribute specifies the data format of the information submitted from the form to the server program. It has two valid values: GET and POST. The default value, GET, is used for a few simple values to be sent to the server. These values are added to the end of the URL that's passed to the server. The GET value limits the amount of information that can be passed to the server. You can also use the POST value to pass information for multiple form elements to the server; use this if your form has more than a couple of fields.

The ACTION attribute indicates the location and name of the server script that processes the form. You can specify the script's URL or use a relative path to set the value of the ACTION attribute. Many of the examples in yesterday's lesson on Active Server Pages used forms as the main user interface. The value of the ACTION attribute in those examples referred to an ASP that contained the server script. You can use any type of scripting code to process a form's request, including CGI, ASP, and native APIs, such as ISAPI or NSAPI. The following code line demonstrates how to use the attributes of the <FORM> tag:

```
<FORM METHOD="POST" ACTION="/MYProject/Scripts/Submit.asp">
```

This code example uses the POST method to send the data to a server script program called Submit.asp that's located in the relative path of /MyProject/Scripts. By using the POST method, the server script has access to all the data elements contained on the form.

Now that you understand the purpose of the form, you can go on to learn about the HTML controls that make the form come alive.

Exploring HTML Intrinsic Controls

If you have developed an application that used a graphical user interface, you're probably already familiar with *controls*, which give you the basic tools for constructing your application's user interface. Controls serve as the intermediary between users and applications. You can use controls to enable the user to enter information, designate preferences, and select items from a list. In other words, the controls on your form make it possible for users to interact with your application to perform certain tasks.

HTML forms support the use of certain intrinsic controls that offer specific functions based on their design. The following sections describe the form controls offered by HTML.

Using Tags to Create a Control

You create controls by using certain sub-element tags within a form's start and end tags. Table 12.1 lists the types of form sub-element tags and their functions.

Table 12.1. Form sub-element tags.

Tag	Function
<INPUT>	Creates user input controls
<OPTION>	Constructs options in a selection list
<SELECT>	Creates a selection list
<TEXTAREA>	Creates a multiline text entry field

These sub-element tags help you specify the type of control you want to construct. For a selection list, you can use the <SELECT> tag to create the options to populate the list. These tags must be placed inside the starting <FORM> and ending </FORM> tags. The next sections explain the syntax for using these tags.

Using the <INPUT> Tag

The <INPUT> tag is the most common type of sub-element tag, probably because it can be used to create several of the most common controls you define for a form. The controls created by the <INPUT> tag give you a way to collect information from the user. They include text controls, radio buttons, checkboxes, images, and push buttons. The syntax for using the <INPUT> tag is as follows:

```
<INPUT TYPE="Type" NAME="Name" VALUE="Value"¦SIZE="nChars"
¦MAXLENGTH="nChars"¦CHECKED >
```

Type is the type of control you want to create, Name defines the name of the control, and Value represents the initial value displayed for the control. The nChars value, when related to the SIZE attribute, defines the text control's width in number of characters; when it's related to the MAXLENGTH attribute, it defines the maximum number of characters that can be entered in a text control. Use the CHECKED attribute to allow a checkbox or radio button to appear selected.

Using the <SELECT> Tag

You can use the <SELECT> tag to create a selection list control, which enables the user to choose an item from a list of options. You have probably used this type of control with other development tools and referred to it as a *drop-down listbox* or a *scrollable listbox*.

The <SELECT> tag is used with the <OPTION> tag, which is used to specify the list of available options. This is the basic syntax for the <SELECT> tag:

```
<SELECT NAME="Name" SIZE="Number"¦MULTIPLE>
<OPTION VALUE="Value">NameofValue</OPTION>
</SELECT>
```

12

In this code example, Name is the name of the selection list control, Number specifies the number of items in the list that are visible to the user, Value is the value to be sent to the server when the value option is selected, and NameofValue is the formatted name of the option that's displayed to the user. You can use the MULTIPLE attribute to enable the user to select multiple items from the list.

A typical selection list has many items, so you usually construct a selection list with the following syntax:

```
<SELECT NAME="Name">
<OPTION VALUE="Value1">NameofValue1</OPTION>
<OPTION VALUE="Value2">NameofValue2</OPTION>
<OPTION VALUE="Value3">NameofValue3</OPTION>
...
<OPTION VALUE="Valuen">NameofValuen</OPTION>
</SELECT>
```

Listing 12.1 demonstrates how to use the selection list control.

Listing 12.1. Constructing a selection list.

```
<HTML>
<HEAD>
<TITLE>Selection List</TITLE>
</HEAD>
<BODY>
<H2>Scrollable Selection List</H2>
<HR>
<P>
<FORM METHOD="POST" ACTION=" " >
<H3>Choose Your Favorite NBA Basketball Team:</H3>
<P>
<SELECT NAME="lstTeams" SIZE="7">
<OPTION VALUE="Bulls">Bulls</OPTION>
<OPTION VALUE="Cavaliers">Cavaliers</OPTION>
<OPTION VALUE="Celtics">Celtics</OPTION>
<OPTION VALUE="Heat">Heat</OPTION>
<OPTION VALUE="Jazz">Jazz</OPTION>
<OPTION VALUE="Lakers">Lakers</OPTION>
<OPTION VALUE="Magic">Magic</OPTION>
<OPTION VALUE="Mavericks">Mavericks</OPTION>
<OPTION VALUE="Pistons">Pistons</OPTION>
<OPTION VALUE="Raptors">Raptors</OPTION>
<OPTION VALUE="Rockets">Rockets</OPTION>
<OPTION VALUE="Suns">Suns</OPTION>
</SELECT>
</FORM>
</BODY>
</HTML>
```

12

NOTE

For the purpose of this example, the ACTION attribute is set to " ", which means the form won't do anything. I'm trying to emphasize the control, not the script that processes the information. You learn more about script processing later in the day in the section entitled "Using Client-Side Script with HTML Forms."

This code example, which displays a list of basketball teams, constructs a scrollable selection list that displays seven items at a time, as shown in Figure 12.1.

Figure 12.1.

Viewing items in the list.

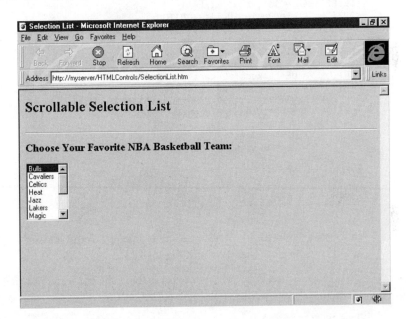

In addition to creating a scrollable listbox, you can also create a drop-down listbox by manipulating the SIZE attribute of the <SELECT> tag. A drop-down listbox displays only one item at a time, but the user can see the rest of the items by clicking the down-arrow key. The drop-down listbox is also referred to as a *pop-up selection list*. Listing 12.2 shows how to make a simple change to the previous code example to create a drop-down listbox.

Listing 12.2. Constructing a drop-down listbox.

```html
<HTML>
<HEAD>
<TITLE>Selection List</TITLE>
</HEAD>
<BODY>
<H2>Pop-up Selection List</H2>
<HR>
<P>
<FORM METHOD="POST" ACTION=" " >
<H3>Choose Your Favorite NBA Basketball Team:</H3>
<P>
<SELECT NAME="lstTeams" SIZE="1">
<OPTION VALUE="Bulls">Bulls</OPTION>
<OPTION VALUE="Cavaliers">Cavaliers</OPTION>
<OPTION VALUE="Celtics">Celtics</OPTION>
<OPTION VALUE="Heat">Heat</OPTION>
<OPTION VALUE="Jazz">Jazz</OPTION>
<OPTION VALUE="Lakers">Lakers</OPTION>
<OPTION VALUE="Magic">Magic</OPTION>
<OPTION VALUE="Mavericks">Mavericks</OPTION>
<OPTION VALUE="Pistons">Pistons</OPTION>
<OPTION VALUE="Raptors">Raptors</OPTION>
<OPTION VALUE="Rockets">Rockets</OPTION>
<OPTION VALUE="Suns">Suns</OPTION>
</SELECT>
</FORM>
</BODY>
</HTML>
```

In this code example, the SIZE attribute is changed to the value of 1, which means one item at a time is displayed, as shown in Figure 12.2.

To display the items in the drop-down listbox, the user can click the down-arrow to make the items pop up, as shown in Figure 12.3.

The SELECTED attribute can be used with the <OPTION> tag to define an initial, or default, selection in the list. If you specify this attribute for an item in the list, that item is selected when the form opens. For example, you could choose the Rockets as the default selection for your favorite team when the form first opens, as shown in Figure 12.4.

Figure 12.2.

Viewing one item at a time.

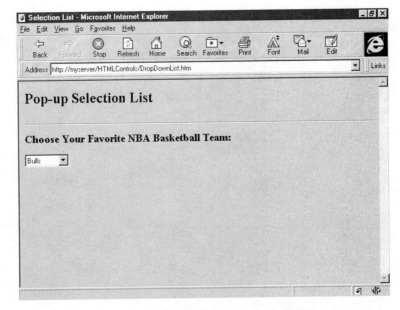

Figure 12.3.

Seeing the rest of the items in a drop-down list.

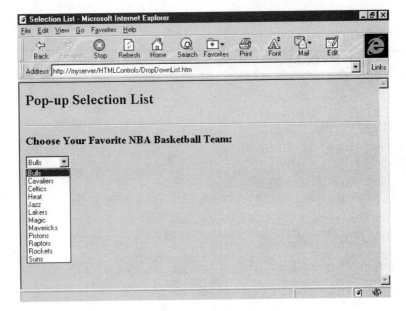

12

Figure 12.4.

Choosing a default selection.

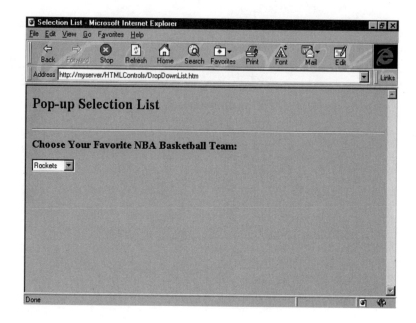

Listing 12.3 gives you the code for defining a default selection for the list.

Listing 12.3. Specifying a default selection.

```
<HTML>
<HEAD>
<TITLE>Selection List</TITLE>
</HEAD>
<BODY>
<H2>Pop-up Selection List</H2>
<HR>
<P>
<FORM METHOD="POST" ACTION=" " >
<H3>Choose Your Favorite NBA Basketball Team:</H3>
<P>
<SELECT NAME="lstTeams" SIZE="1">
<OPTION VALUE="Bulls">Bulls</OPTION>
<OPTION VALUE="Cavaliers">Cavaliers</OPTION>
<OPTION VALUE="Celtics">Celtics</OPTION>
<OPTION VALUE="Heat">Heat</OPTION>
<OPTION VALUE="Jazz">Jazz</OPTION>
<OPTION VALUE="Lakers">Lakers</OPTION>
<OPTION VALUE="Magic">Magic</OPTION>
<OPTION VALUE="Mavericks">Mavericks</OPTION>
<OPTION VALUE="Pistons">Pistons</OPTION>
```

```
<OPTION VALUE="Raptors">Raptors</OPTION>
<OPTION VALUE="Rockets" SELECTED>Rockets</OPTION>
<OPTION VALUE="Suns">Suns</OPTION>
</SELECT>
</FORM>
</BODY>
</HTML>
```

In this example, the <OPTION> tag for the Rockets item uses the SELECTED attribute to specify this item as the default selection in the list.

The next few sections cover the types of form controls you can build by using HTML and the <INPUT> tag.

The Text Control

The text control enables you to create a single-line entry field that can handle alphanumeric data, including numbers and strings. You can create a text control by using the <INPUT> tag; its syntax was explained earlier in today's lesson. Here's an example of using the <INPUT> tag to develop a text control:

```
<INPUT TYPE="TEXT" NAME="txtName" SIZE="20">
```

The TYPE attribute is set to "TEXT", which is also the default value for the <INPUT> tag. If you don't define a value for the TYPE attribute, a text control is created; however, you should always assign an explicit value for your attributes so that your code is easily understood by other developers. The NAME attribute contains the value of "txtName" in this example. Text controls should have the prefix *txt*. The SIZE attribute of 20 defines the text control as approximately 20 characters long. If you don't specify a value for the SIZE attribute, a text control is created with the default size. Figure 12.5 shows the text control created from this line of code.

 NOTE

I'll introduce the naming standard for each control as it's discussed. A summary table that outlines the naming standard for each HTML form control is supplied later in the section "Reviewing HTML Form Design."

Figure 12.5.

Creating a text control.

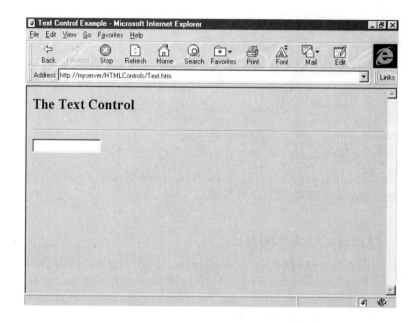

The VALUE attribute, defined earlier, can also be used with the text control. This attribute enables you to indicate an initial value that's displayed in the text field. Another attribute that can be used with the text control is the MAXLENGTH attribute, which is used to specify the maximum number of characters that can be entered in the text field.

The Button Control

The button control is used to create a push button for the form. Push buttons were first introduced during the lesson on Day 7, "Extending Your Web Page Through Client-Side Script." Most of the scripting examples covered during that lesson used a push button to carry out an action, which is exactly what a button control is for; it enables the user to perform or complete a task. The button's caption should describe the action to be performed. For example, a Submit button tells the user it's the button to click to submit the form to the server.

The following example demonstrates the syntax for defining a button control for your form:

```
<INPUT TYPE="SUBMIT" NAME="cmdSubmit" VALUE="Submit">
```

This line of code creates a push button named Submit. The TYPE attribute is assigned the value of "SUBMIT", which means a button control will be placed on the form. This type of button control submits the form for processing by the script specified in the form's ACTION attribute. Another value of the TYPE attribute is RESET, which creates a button to clear the contents of the form elements and reset any default values for the controls. The VALUE attribute is used

12

to define the caption on the push button. Also, notice that the NAME attribute has the value of "cmdSubmit". The naming standard for the button control uses the *cmd* prefix. The caption for the push button should accurately describe its function; however, don't use too many words for the text. For example, if a button saves information to a database, use the caption of Save rather than Save the Record to the Database. For HTML button controls, the button's size is determined by the caption you specify for the control. The browser uses the length of the caption and font size to determine the button's appropriate size.

NOTE

> The inability to define a size for an HTML button control is one of its limitations. You learn about more robust ActiveX controls you can use to define a control's size during Day 13.

Using the Button Control

You can use the button control to send and retrieve information to the server. The push button is typically used with other controls on a form to enable the user to perform some action. In the previous section, you learned about setting the TYPE attribute to a value of SUBMIT, which constructs a push button that sends data on the form to the server. This form is processed by the script you specify in the ACTION attribute of the <FORM> tag. Listing 12.4 demonstrates how to use this attribute, along with the other controls you've learned about so far, to create a form that submits information to be processed by the server.

Listing 12.4. Submitting the form's information to the server.

```
<HTML>
<HEAD>
<TITLE>The Button Control</TITLE>
</HEAD>
<BODY>
<H2>The Power of the Button Control</H2>
<HR>
<P>
<FORM METHOD="POST" ACTION="/HTMLControls/scripts/Submit.asp" >
<INPUT TYPE="TEXT" NAME="txtName" SIZE="20">
<P>
<H3>Choose Your Favorite NBA Basketball Team:</H3>
<P>
<SELECT NAME="lstTeams" SIZE="1">
<OPTION VALUE="Bulls">Bulls</OPTION>
<OPTION VALUE="Cavaliers">Cavaliers</OPTION>
```

continues

12

Listing 12.4. continued

```
<OPTION VALUE="Celtics">Celtics</OPTION>
<OPTION VALUE="Heat">Heat</OPTION>
<OPTION VALUE="Jazz">Jazz</OPTION>
<OPTION VALUE="Lakers">Lakers</OPTION>
<OPTION VALUE="Magic">Magic</OPTION>
<OPTION VALUE="Mavericks">Mavericks</OPTION>
<OPTION VALUE="Pistons">Pistons</OPTION>
<OPTION VALUE="Raptors">Raptors</OPTION>
<OPTION VALUE="Rockets" SELECTED>Rockets</OPTION>
<OPTION VALUE="Suns">Suns</OPTION>
</SELECT>
<INPUT TYPE="SUBMIT" NAME="cmdSubmit" VALUE="Submit">
</FORM>
</BODY>
</HTML>
```

This code example combines the text control, the selection list, and the button control to create a useful form. Users can enter their name, select their favorite NBA team, and then submit this information to the server by clicking the Submit button. The user information is processed by an Active Server Page called Submit.asp. This script formats a page with the user's name and his or her favorite NBA team. Figure 12.6 shows the form that the user sees.

Figure 12.6.

Selecting your favorite team.

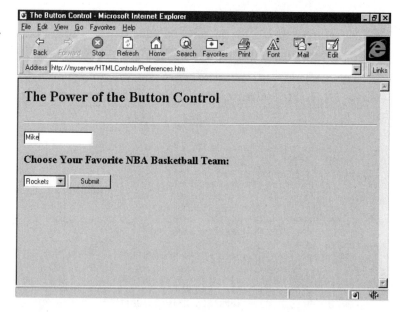

Figure 12.7 demonstrates the results returned to the user based on the information that was entered.

Figure 12.7.

Displaying the results.

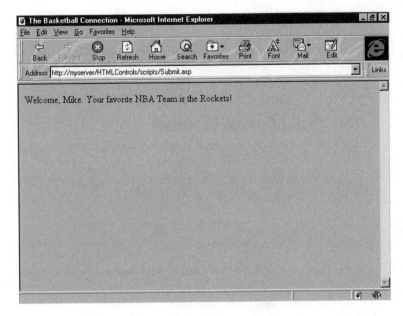

NOTE

You can also set the value of the TYPE attribute to BUTTON and use client-side script to provide logic for the control. As mentioned, SUBMIT is the only value of the TYPE attribute that can send the form's data to the server. You can, however, create event procedures for the BUTTON TYPE attribute and use a scripting language such as VBScript to process the events.

This topic is covered in more detail in the section "Developing HTML Forms."

The location of the button control is determined by where you place its definition in the HTML document. In the previous example, the Submit button is placed next to the selection list control. You could have moved the push button to a new line in the web page by using a <P> or <BR> tag to specify a new paragraph or a line break. You can also use the alignment tags to change the placement of the button control. For example, the following line of code places a push button in the center of a web page:

```
<CENTER><INPUT TYPE="SUBMIT" NAME="cmdSubmit" VALUE="Submit"></CENTER>
```

12

Option Buttons

Option buttons enable a user to choose from a small list of options. There are two kinds of option buttons: radio buttons and checkboxes. HTML supplies both of these controls to display on your forms.

The Radio Button Control

The radio button control is used for mutually exclusive options. In other words, the user can choose only one of the options. Choosing from a list of credit cards to confirm a payment method is a good example of using mutually exclusive choices. Radio buttons should be used only when the number of choices is six or less.

This is the syntax for creating a radio button control:

```
<INPUT TYPE="RADIO" NAME="Name" VALUE="Value">
```

Name is the name of the radio button, and Value is an optional parameter that indicates the value for the option passed to the server. For example, the following lines of code create two radio buttons to enable users to specify their gender:

```
<INPUT TYPE="RADIO" NAME="optGender" VALUE="Male"> Male <BR>
<INPUT TYPE="RADIO" NAME="optGender" VALUE="Female"> Female
```

Figure 12.8 illustrates how these options are displayed on the form.

Figure 12.8.

Specifying your gender.

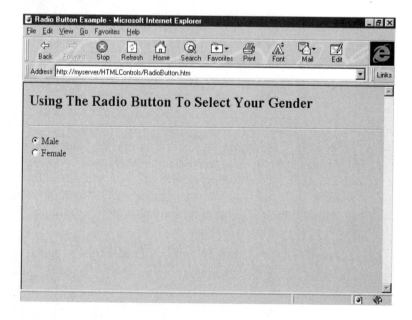

12

When the user specifies a gender, a dark circle covering most of the center of the radio button indicates that the item has been selected.

The previous code example uses the prefix naming standard of *opt* for radio buttons. Notice, too, that the names are identical for both options. You must use the same name for radio buttons that are grouped together. If you didn't assign the same names for these controls, the form would treat the options as independent controls, and the user could then select both options, as shown in Figure 12.9.

Figure 12.9.

A lack of proper grouping.

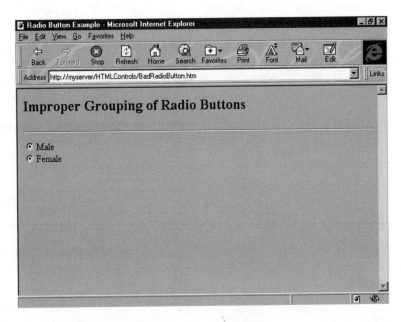

You can also use the CHECKED attribute to select a default option for the user. The following lines of code make Female the default selection:

```
<INPUT TYPE="RADIO" NAME="optGender" VALUE="Male"> Male <BR>
<INPUT TYPE="RADIO" NAME="optGender" VALUE="Female" CHECKED> Female
```

Notice that the CHECKED attribute is placed as the last parameter in the <INPUT> tag.

The Checkbox Control

The checkbox control enables the user to select more than one option from available choices. Indicating your completed levels of education is a good example of using checkboxes. As with radio buttons, you should use checkboxes only when the number of choices is six or less.

This is the syntax for creating the checkbox control:

```
<INPUT TYPE="CHECKBOX" NAME="Name" VALUE="Value" >
```

Name is the name of the checkbox, and Value is an optional parameter that indicates the value for the option passed to the server. The following lines of code create checkbox options for users to indicate their completed levels of education:

```
<INPUT TYPE="CHECKBOX" NAME="chkHighSchool" VALUE="High School"> High School
➥<BR>
<INPUT TYPE="CHECKBOX" NAME="chkCollege" VALUE="College"> College <BR>
<INPUT TYPE="CHECKBOX" NAME="chkGrad" VALUE="Graduate"> Graduate
```

Notice that the naming standard for checkboxes uses the *chk* prefix. Also, the options in a checkbox have different names. As opposed to selecting only one item with radio buttons, users can select several items with checkboxes. For this reason, you must supply different names for the individual options. Figure 12.10 shows the results of this code example.

Figure 12.10.

Selecting multiple items.

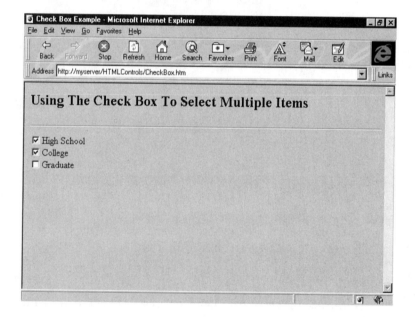

The user can select all the education levels that apply from the list of choices. Notice that a check mark indicates selected items.

As with the radio button control, you can use the CHECKED attribute to specify an option as the default selection. The code to carry out this task is similar to that for the radio button control:

```
<INPUT TYPE="CHECKBOX" NAME="chkHighSchool" VALUE="High School" CHECKED> High
➡School <BR>
<INPUT TYPE="CHECKBOX" NAME="chkCollege" VALUE="College"> College <BR>
<INPUT TYPE="CHECKBOX" NAME="chkGrad" VALUE="Graduate"> Graduate
```

In this example, High School is the default selection.

Exploring the Behavior of Option Buttons

The radio button control and the checkbox control differ slightly in their behavior because they have different purposes. The process of actually selecting a radio button or a checkbox is the same—the user simply clicks the item he or she wants.

The difference is in how items are deselected. For radio buttons, the currently selected item is deselected when the user chooses another radio button in the list. That new item, then, is selected. For the checkbox control, the user can select multiple items. To deselect an item, the user must click a currently selected item. The check mark disappears, indicating that the item is no longer selected.

The Password Control

The password control is a special version of the text control. Essentially, the two controls are the same, but the password control displays asterisks, not text, as the user enters his or her text. You can use the password control for "sensitive" information, such as a user's password; that's why it's called the password control. The asterisks mask the characters from displaying in the field.

The syntax for this control is almost identical to the text control, except that the value of the TYPE attribute changes, as shown in this example:

```
<INPUT TYPE="PASSWORD" NAME="txtPassword" SIZE="10">
```

What you specify for the TYPE attribute is the biggest difference between defining a password control and a text control. In this example, the TYPE attribute has been assigned the value of "PASSWORD", which means the control is a password control. The naming standard for the password control is the same as the text control's; both use *txt* as the prefix.

The SIZE attribute of 10 defines the password control as approximately 10 characters long. If you don't specify a value for the SIZE attribute, then the password control is created with the default size.

The VALUE attribute can be used to indicate a default selection that's displayed in the password text field when you open the form. Another attribute that can be used with the password control is MAXLENGTH, which enables you to specify the maximum number of characters that can be entered in the password text field.

12

Listing 12.5 shows how to use the password control in an application.

Listing 12.5. Constructing a password control.

```
<HTML>
<HEAD>
<TITLE>Logging On</TITLE>
</HEAD>
<BODY>
<H2>The Killer App</H2>
<HR>
<P>
<FORM METHOD="POST" ACTION="../scripts/Signon.asp" >
<H3>Please enter your user name and password to experience the Killer App:</H3>
<P>
User Name: <INPUT TYPE="TEXT" NAME="txtName" SIZE="20">
<P>
Password: <INPUT TYPE="PASSWORD" NAME="txtPassword" SIZE="10">
<P><P>
<INPUT TYPE="SUBMIT" NAME="cmdSignon" VALUE="Sign On">
</FORM>
</BODY>
</HTML>
```

This code example gives the user a way to log onto your killer application. A text box control is used for the user name, and a password control is used for entering his or her password. This information is then passed to an Active Server Page that verifies the user name and password. Figure 12.11 shows the form that's displayed as a result of this code example.

Figure 12.11.

Logging onto the killer application.

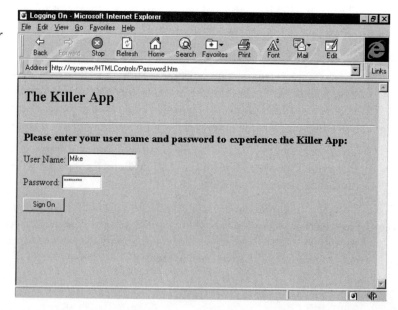

12

The Textarea Control

The textarea control enables you to construct a multiline text box that lets the user enter multiple lines of text. This is the basic syntax for the textarea control:

```
<TEXTAREA NAME="Name" ROWS="nRows" COLS="nCols"></TEXTAREA>
```

Name is the name of the control, nRows defines the number of rows, or height, for the textarea control, and nCols specifies the number of columns, or width, for the control. The number of rows defining the control's height equates to a specified number of lines; the number of columns defining the control's width is measured in number of characters.

The browser determines to some degree the behavior of the multiline text box. Some browsers automatically word wrap the text to the next line. With others, you can enter text past the control's display area and use a scroll bar to view the text.

The following line of code shows how to use the textarea control:

```
<TEXTAREA NAME="txaAddress" ROWS="5" COLS="40"></TEXTAREA>
```

This line of code creates a multline text box that enables the user to enter an address, which is a common use for this control. It's often used for entering e-mail messages and memos, too. Notice that the naming standard of the textarea control uses the prefix *txa*. The control in this example is 5 lines long and 40 characters wide.

The textarea control doesn't support using the VALUE attribute to assign a default selection for the control. As an alternative, you can specify text to be placed in the control by placing it inside the textarea tags. The following line of code demonstrates this method:

```
<TEXTAREA NAME="txaAddress" ROWS="5" COLS="40">Houston, Texas</TEXTAREA>
```

This code formats the text Houston, Texas as the control's initial value when the form opens.

12

Using Client-Side Script with HTML Forms

So far, you have learned about a form's characteristics and how to construct one. You have also learned about the HTML form controls and seen how to use them on a form. In the following sections, you learn how to develop functional HTML forms that use client-side script. The lesson gives you some examples of integrating VBScript with forms and form controls.

Creating Event Procedures for Your Controls

You learned about client-side script on Day 7. Today's lesson and the lessons for the next couple of days teach you how to apply the concepts you learned.

You can create event procedures for your controls. For a button control, there are two types of event procedures: implicit procedures and explicit procedures.

Creating an Implicit Procedure

The first type of procedure, called an *implicit event procedure*, is tied to the control. Here's the syntax for creating an implicit event procedure:

```
Sub ButtonName_OnClick()
... event procedure code
End Sub
```

`ButtonName` refers to the name of the button control on the form, and the event procedure's name must be the same as the name assigned to the button control. Listing 12.6 shows how to use an implicit procedure and client-side script to process a button click.

Listing 12.6. Creating an implicit event procedure.

```
<HTML>
<HEAD>
<TITLE>An Implicit Procedure</TITLE>
</HEAD>
<BODY>
<H2>The Killer App</H2>
<HR>
<P>
<FORM NAME="MyForm" >
<H3>Please enter your user name and password to experience the Killer App:</H3>
<P>
User Name: <INPUT TYPE="TEXT" NAME="txtName" SIZE="20">
<P>
Password: <INPUT TYPE="PASSWORD" NAME="txtPassword" SIZE="10">
<P><P>
<INPUT TYPE="BUTTON" NAME="cmdSignon" VALUE="Sign On">
</FORM>
<SCRIPT LANGUAGE="VBSCRIPT" >
<!--
Sub CmdSignon_OnClick
Dim Password
Password = Document.MyForm.txtPassword.Value
If Len(Password) < 6 Then
MsgBox "You must enter a password that is at least 6 characters long."
Document.MyForm.txtPassword = " "
End If
End Sub
-->
</SCRIPT>
</BODY>
</HTML>
```

12

This code example extends the form created in Listing 12.5 that allowed the user to sign onto your killer application. The `<FORM>` tag is used to assign `MyForm` as the form's name. The form name is used to access the value of the text control for the user name. Notice that the name of the event procedure is the same as the name of the button control; that's why the procedure is referred to as "implicit."

The `Password` variable is created and assigned the value entered by the user in the form's password control. The `VALUE` attribute contains the text entered in this field. For HTML form controls, you must prefix the control's name with the name of the form and the name of the web page. In this case, `Document` refers to the entire web page. The method for referring to a value for a form control is easy to figure out because the controls are contained on the form that's part of the document or web page.

Next, the `Len` statement is used to verify that the length of the password is six characters or more. If not, a message box is displayed informing the user that the password must be at least six characters, as shown in Figure 12.12.

Figure 12.12.

Reminding the user that the password must be at least six characters long.

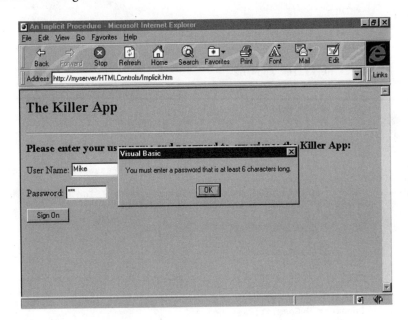

Creating an Explicit Procedure

The second type of event procedure, called an *explicit procedure*, enables you to process script code for a button control. The "explicit" in the term *explicit procedure* means you can give the procedure a name. Remember that an implicit procedure must assume the name of the button control. With an explicit procedure, however, you're free to customize the name of the procedure so you can supply a more descriptive name. You can also share this procedure across controls on your form because it isn't implicitly tied to the button control.

The following lines of code create an explicit event procedure:

```
<INPUT TYPE="BUTTON" NAME="cmdSignon" VALUE="Sign On"
LANGUAGE="VBSCRIPT" ONCLICK=" ValidatePassword"
```

In this example, the ONCLICK attribute enables you to specify which procedure to execute when the push button is clicked. Here, the procedure is named ValidatePassword. The LANGUAGE attribute is used to indicate the scripting language for the event procedure; this example uses VBScript. Listing 12.7 shows an example of using an explicit event procedure to process the user sign-on form.

Listing 12.7. Creating an explicit procedure.

```
<HTML>
<HEAD>
<TITLE>An Explicit Procedure</TITLE>
</HEAD>
<BODY>
<H2>The Killer App</H2>
<HR>
<P>
<FORM NAME="MyForm" >
<H3>Please enter your user name and password to experience the Killer App:</H3>
<P>
User Name: <INPUT TYPE="TEXT" NAME="txtName" SIZE="20">
<P>
Password: <INPUT TYPE="PASSWORD" NAME="txtPassword" SIZE="10">
<P><P>
<INPUT TYPE="BUTTON" NAME="cmdSignon" VALUE="Sign On"
LANGUAGE="VBSCRIPT" ONCLICK=" ValidatePassword">
</FORM>
<SCRIPT LANGUAGE="VBSCRIPT" >
<!--
Sub ValidatePassword
Dim Password
Password = Document.MyForm.txtPassword.Value
If Len(Password) < 6 Then
MsgBox "You must enter a password that is at least 6 characters long."
Document.MyForm.txtPassword = " "
End If
End Sub
-->
</SCRIPT>
</BODY>
</HTML>
```

12

This example uses an explicit event procedure to validate the length of the password. Notice that the procedure name is customized to reflect what the procedure does. Also, the tag to create the button control includes the LANGUAGE and ONCLICK attributes. The ONCLICK attribute gives control to the ValidatePassword procedure when the user clicks the Sign On button.

Reviewing HTML Form Design

The form's design of the user interface is crucial to your application's success. Using the house analogy again, if you hired a builder to build a new house, you wouldn't want him to suddenly grab a hammer and nails one day and decide to build the house. You hope that the builder spends some time designing the house first, and you want him to follow blueprint designs and approved standards for constructing the rooms. You have asked for the rooms to be built in a particular way because you want living in the house to be a rich, rewarding experience—a place you look forward to returning to.

Form design might not be as important as providing a roof over your head, but this analogy shows you the importance of form design. You should definitely spend time contemplating your form's design. Ask yourself: "What is the user trying to do by using my application? How does this form help her perform certain tasks? Which controls should I use to make performing those tasks easier?" As a developer, the task of choosing the right control to perform the task is a vital part of constructing the user interface. Choosing the right tool is a required skill when you're designing and developing an application.

The next section outlines some design tips for HTML forms.

Designing an Effective Form

You should design your form with effectiveness in mind. In other words, you should design and develop an interface that lets the user be effective in performing the necessary tasks. Here are some tips to remember for designing an effective form:

- ☐ Group your controls in a logical, related manner on your form.
- ☐ Design forms that are consistent across your application.
- ☐ Use consistent fonts, colors, and backgrounds for your forms.
- ☐ Place the controls on your form in a logical order.
- ☐ Use the right control for the job.
- ☐ Supply default selections, when possible, for radio buttons, checkboxes, and selection lists.

12

Using the Proper Name

During today's lesson, I have given you standard naming conventions for each control. These standards make it easier to distinguish each control and its type. A summary of these naming standards is given in Table 12.2.

Table 12.2. Naming conventions for HTML form controls.

Control	Prefix	Example
Button	cmd	cmdSubmit
Checkbox	chk	chkHighSchool
Password	txt	txtPassword
Radio Button	opt	optCreditCard
Selection List	lst	lstVacationSpots
Text	txt	txtName
Textarea	txa	txaMemo

Putting It All Together to Build an Application

This section shows you how to build a sample application using the concepts you've learned about forms and form controls. The application uses forms, form controls, and some client-side script. The server-side process isn't covered in this lesson, so refer to yesterday's lesson on Active Server Pages for a refresher on server processing. You get a chance to integrate both the client and server side of an application during the lesson on Day 21, "Putting It All Together: The Publishers' Paradise Case Study."

Creating Functional Forms

This sample application demonstrates how to use each of the controls you've learned about today to build an effective user interface. The first form enables users to log onto the application. After they sign on, they can enter their name and address information and choose their favorite NBA teams to order a game schedule, roster, and a catalog of team items for the current season.

12

Building the User Sign-On Form

The first form uses a previous code example to create a form that enables the user to log onto the application. Listing 12.8 contains the code to create this form.

Listing 12.8. Creating the Log On form.

```
<HTML>
<HEAD>
<TITLE>Log On</TITLE>
</HEAD>
<BODY>
<H2>The Killer App</H2>
<HR>
<P>
<FORM NAME="MyForm" >
<H3>Please enter your user name and password to experience the Killer App:</H3>
<P>
User Name: <INPUT TYPE="TEXT" NAME="txtName" SIZE="20">
<P>
Password: <INPUT TYPE="PASSWORD" NAME="txtPassword" SIZE="10">
<P><P>
<INPUT TYPE="BUTTON" NAME="cmdSignon" VALUE="Sign On"
LANGUAGE="VBSCRIPT" ONCLICK=" ValidatePassword">
</FORM>
<SCRIPT LANGUAGE="VBSCRIPT" >
<!--
Sub ValidatePassword
Dim Password
Password = Document.MyForm.txtPassword.Value
If Len(Password) < 6 Then
MsgBox "You must enter a password that is at least 6 characters long."
Document.MyForm.txtPassword.Value = " "
Else
location.href = "order.htm"
End If
End Sub
-->
</SCRIPT>
</BODY>
</HTML>
```

You studied this code example earlier today. As a reminder, the code uses an explicit event procedure containing client-side script to validate that the password entered is the appropriate length. This code doesn't verify the user ID against a database, but you could easily add this feature by using an Active Server Page. Figure 12.13 shows the first form users see when using this application.

12

Figure 12.13.

Logging onto the application.

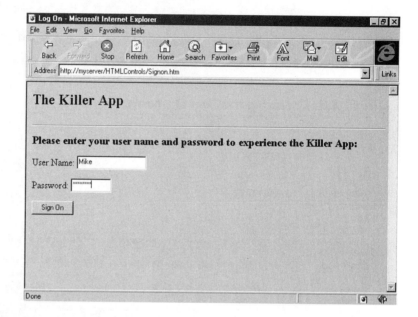

Building the Order Form

Next, you need to construct the order form used to order the roster, game schedule, and a catalog of team items, such as jerseys, hats, and so on. Listing 12.9 shows the code for creating the order form.

Listing 12.9. Creating the order form.

```
<HTML>
<HEAD>
<TITLE>The B-Ball Source</TITLE>
</HEAD>
<BODY>
<H3>Your Guide to Basketball Heaven</H3>
Welcome to our web site! You can order a schedule of your favorite<BR>
NBA team's game schedule along with a current year roster and a<BR>
catalog of your favorite team's apparel all for the cost of $5.95<BR>
to cover shipping costs.
<HR>
<FORM METHOD= "POST" ACTION="/HTMLControls/scripts/Submit.asp" >
<PRE>Name:           <INPUT TYPE="TEXT" NAME="txtName" SIZE="20"></PRE>
<PRE>Address:        <TEXTAREA NAME="txaAddress" ROWS="5" COLS="40">
</TEXTAREA></PRE>
<P>
<SELECT NAME="lstTeams" SIZE="1">
```

12

```
<OPTION VALUE="Bulls">Bulls</OPTION>
<OPTION VALUE="Cavaliers">Cavaliers</OPTION>
<OPTION VALUE="Celtics">Celtics</OPTION>
<OPTION VALUE="Heat">Heat</OPTION>
<OPTION VALUE="Jazz">Jazz</OPTION>
<OPTION VALUE="Lakers">Lakers</OPTION>
<OPTION VALUE="Magic">Magic</OPTION>
<OPTION VALUE="Mavericks">Mavericks</OPTION>
<OPTION VALUE="Pistons">Pistons</OPTION>
<OPTION VALUE="Raptors">Raptors</OPTION>
<OPTION VALUE="Rockets" SELECTED>Rockets</OPTION>
<OPTION VALUE="Suns">Suns</OPTION>
</SELECT>
<P>
<PRE>Items:          <INPUT TYPE="CHECKBOX" NAME="chkSchedule"
VALUE="Sched">Schedule </PRE><BR>
<PRE>                <INPUT TYPE="CHECKBOX" NAME="chkRoster"
VALUE="Ros">Roster </PRE><BR>
<PRE>                <INPUT TYPE="CHECKBOX" NAME="chkItmCatalog"
VALUE= "Cat">Catalog</PRE>
<P>
<PRE>Credit Card:   <INPUT TYPE="RADIO" NAME="optCreditCard"
VALUE= "AMEX"> American Express <BR></PRE>
<PRE>                <INPUT TYPE="RADIO" NAME="optCreditCard"
VALUE="MC" CHECKED> Master Card <BR></PRE>
<PRE>                <INPUT TYPE="RADIO" NAME="optCreditCard"
VALUE="V"> Visa </PRE>
<P>
<PRE>Card Number:   <INPUT TYPE="TEXT" NAME="txtCardNumber"
SIZE="20"></PRE><BR>
<INPUT TYPE="SUBMIT" NAME="cmdSubmit" VALUE="Submit">
</FORM>
</BODY>

</HTML>
```

12

This code example creates an order form that uses many of the controls explained in today's lesson. The <PRE> tag is used to define explicit formatting for the controls on the form. The form uses the text control for the name and credit card number fields. Checkboxes are used to enable users to select the items they want to order. Since all the items can be chosen, the proper control is the checkbox. Radio buttons are used for the type of credit card to be used for payment. Figure 12.14 demonstrates the results of this code example.

The user has entered a name and address, chosen a favorite NBA team, and selected several items to be ordered. When the user enters the credit card information and clicks the Submit button, the order information is sent to the ASP to be processed.

Figure 12.14.

Ordering information about your favorite team.

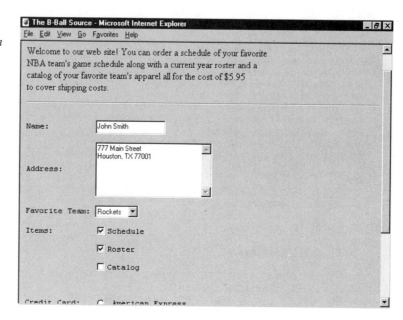

This example demonstrates how to effectively design and develop a form for your application. Over the next few days, you will learn to distinguish the differences between using HTML form controls and using other controls and objects to process information for your application.

Summary

You have learned a lot about forms and controls and their purpose. HTML forms aren't the most robust, powerful user interfaces, but they do have their purpose. Over the next few days, you will learn about some more robust tools that can be used to build the user interface. The concepts you've learned today, however, can be applied to other types of controls. The forms and controls described today enable the user to supply input to the application. These forms can also be used to display information found in a database. All of the controls explained in today's lesson are intrinsic to HTML. The controls covered in the next few lessons are considered extrinsic controls; they must be inserted into the web page document.

In the first part of today's lesson, you learned about the purposes of a form and how a form can be useful to both the user and your application. You also learned the basic tags and attributes used to create a form. Next, you learned about the different intrinsic controls found in HTML forms, including the selection list control, the text control, the button control, the radio button control, the checkbox control, the textarea control, and the password control.

12

For each control, you learned how to create it and what its naming convention and attributes are. Several examples showed you how to design an effective form.

The lesson then showed you how to use client-side script with HTML forms. Several examples were given to demonstrate how to use the power of a scripting language with your forms. The lesson also reviewed some design tips for your forms and gave you a summary of the naming conventions for your form controls. The final lesson of the day showed you how to integrate controls on a form to construct a user interface for your application.

Q&A

Q Should I use forms for my application's interface?

A Forms offer a useful interface for supplying basic functions to your application. Forms can be used with CGI scripts and Active Server Pages to submit information to, and get information from, the server. The next few days of lessons will introduce other controls and objects that offer more functions and features for your application's interface. After learning about the different tools available, you can decide which tool offers the best features for your application.

Q How much text can I enter in the textarea control?

A The limit for the textarea control is approximately 65,000 characters.

Q Why should I adhere to standard naming conventions for my controls?

A Without standards, there would be chaos. Seriously, though, standard naming conventions help provide descriptive names for your controls. The most important advantage to using standard prefixes for your control names is that they enable you to easily identify the type of control being used. The prefix also makes it easier to read and understand your code.

For example, the control name CreditCard doesn't tell you what type of control is being used. It could be a text field, a radio button, or some other type of control. The nonstandard name relies on your memory of the control type to properly use it in your code. If you use the standard name optCreditCard, then you know that the control is a radio button, so you can use the correct tags, attributes, and code for a radio button control.

Workshop

In the workshop for today's lesson, you can have some fun with the concepts you have learned today. I want you to design and develop an application using the controls you learned about today. The application can consist of several web pages. You must properly use every form control that has been discussed. As you develop the forms for your application, think about the proper uses of each control, and figure out why the control you're using meets the needs for your application. You should also think about additional uses for these controls.

You might also want to create some Active Server Pages and client-side script to handle the processing of your application. You can consider this part extra credit. The benefit for you is that you will begin to see how each of the application components work together for the good of the application.

Quiz

1. What's the difference between a radio button and a checkbox?

2. What value of the TYPE attribute for a button enables you to send information to the server based on the ACTION method defined for your form?

3. What are the advantages of an explicit event procedure?

Quiz Answers

1. With a radio button, the user can select between mutually exclusive choices; in other words, he or she can choose only one option from the list of items. However, with a checkbox, the user can select more than one item from the list of options. These controls also look different. The radio button is circular and contains a dark circle for the selection indicator. The checkbox is square and uses a check mark for its selection indicator.

2. Use the value of SUBMIT to send information to the server for processing.

3. An explicit event procedure isn't tied to a single event. You can share this procedure among several controls. Also, you can supply the name for the procedure, which lets you accurately describe its function.

12

Day 13

Interacting with Objects and ActiveX Controls

Yesterday's lesson covered HTML forms and the intrinsic controls that give the form its usefulness. For some of you, the lesson may have been a refresher; for others, it may have served as an introduction. Whatever the case, you now have a foundation with which to explore more advanced objects and controls. In a continuing effort to design the killer app, I think you will find these advanced objects a perfect addition to your Web toolbox. The objects and controls that are discussed in this lesson enable you to build a more effective and interactive interface for the user. By using these objects in your application, you can design an application that truly accomplishes its purpose while providing a rich and rewarding experience for the user.

The first part of the lesson provides an overview of objects. The lesson explains the concept of objects and provides a basic definition to serve as a foundation for the rest of the day. You then receive an introduction to Java applets. This introduction will focus mainly on the purpose of Java applets and how they can be incorporated into your Visual InterDev application.

Next, you are introduced to ActiveX controls. Because Visual InterDev includes many ActiveX controls, most of the lesson focuses on ActiveX controls and technology. The lesson first provides an ActiveX overview. Then you are given an in-depth tour of the HTML Layout Editor. You discovered this editor when you built an application on Day 4, "Creating Your First Visual InterDev Application." In today's lesson, you learn how to use the HTML Layout Editor to construct an interface based on ActiveX controls. The final treatise for the day unveils some of the more common ActiveX controls that can be used with Visual InterDev. This section introduces you to the controls that are included with Visual InterDev. On Day 15, "Integrating Objects into Your Applications," you learn how to use these objects and controls in your applications.

Object Overview

Yesterday, you learned about HTML forms. You discovered that a form is comprised of intrinsic controls that are an inherent part of HTML. These controls provide basic functionality for your application. Today's lesson extends the discourse to extrinsic controls and objects, which also were defined yesterday. Extrinsic controls are external to HTML and can be used to provide additional functionality to your application.

You will recognize some of the extrinsic objects and controls because they're similar in name and purpose to HTML intrinsic controls. You also will discover new and exciting controls that enable you to enhance the look and feel of your application. All the extrinsic controls usually provide more functionality than their intrinsic control brethren. Today's lesson begins by declaring a definition of objects to provide a good starting point for this lesson.

Defining Objects

The *American Heritage Dictionary* defines the word *object* in the following manner:

1. Something perceptible by the senses; a material thing.
2. A focus of attention or action.
3. The purpose of a specific action.
4. A noun that receives or is affected by the action of a verb or that follows and is governed by a preposition.

Objects definitely provide a sensory experience for the user. You may not be able to smell objects, but you can definitely see and hear them. The second and third definitions of an object mention that objects are the "focus" and "purpose" of "attention or action." While the author of the dictionary might not have considered Java applets or ActiveX controls when scripting this definition, it can certainly be applied to these objects. The objects that you integrate into your application become the "object" of the user's attention and actions. Objects facilitate interaction between the user and your application. You can use objects and controls to complement, supplement, and complete your application interface.

NOTE   During today's lesson as well as future lessons, I use the terms objects and controls almost synonymously to refer to items that are placed on a web page to enable the user to perform some function. Where necessary, I explicitly cite where an item is referred to solely as an object or a control.

Now that you understand the definition of an object, it's time to examine two of the most common types of objects—Java applets and ActiveX controls.

Introduction to Java Applets

Java applets are an integral component of the Internet both in name and in function. Java applets are derived from the Java programming language developed by Sun Microsystems, Inc. The biggest benefit of the Java language is its support for cross-platform development. You can develop an applet or application with Java to support different client platforms. The Java program will, in theory, execute in the same manner on both the Windows 95 platform and an Apple Macintosh, for example.

I mentioned that you can develop both applets and applications with Java. You received an explanation about the difference between a Java applet and application during the first week. As a reminder, applets are embedded in a web page and execute within the context of a browser. The browser must support Java to be able to execute the program. Java applications are executable programs that run independently of any browser or other program. Because the theme for today centers on using objects in your web pages, this section focuses on Java applets.

NOTE   Today's lesson as well as Day 15 focuses on the explanation, use, and integration of objects such as Java applets and ActiveX controls into your Visual InterDev application. It is beyond the scope of this book to teach you how to build a Java applet. You will, however, learn how to build an ActiveX control during the lesson on Day 16, "Building Design-Time ActiveX Controls."

13

How Do Java Applets Work?

I mentioned that Java applets execute within the context of a browser. It's high time you knew a little more about the interaction between the browser and a Java applet. First, a user requests a certain web page. The HTML document is sent from the web server to the browser on the client machine. If the browser detects a Java applet embedded in the document, the browser requests the individual applet. The browser detects the applet by discovering the <APPLET> tag within the HTML document. The <APPLET> tag is covered in the next section. The applet is distributed to the client machine in the form of bytecodes. The browser interprets these bytecodes with the help of a Java runtime interpreter and executes the applet program. Figure 13.1 visually depicts this process.

Figure 13.1.

Executing a Java applet.

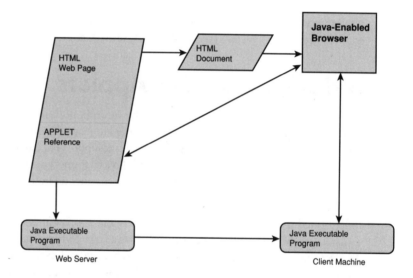

As you can see, the process of using a Java applet is highly interactive. Good communication between the client browser and the web server is paramount. The next section explains how to define an applet and explain its basic attributes.

Understanding Java Applets

The basic tag to define an applet is the <APPLET> tag. This tag is supported by the HTML 3.2 standard and enables you to insert an applet into an HTML document. The syntax for using the <APPLET> tag is as follows:

```
<APPLET [CODEBASE="URL"] CODE="applet" [ALT="alternate text"]
[NAME="appletInstanceName"] WIDTH="nPixels" HEIGHT="nPixels"
[ALIGN="alignment"] [VSPACE="nPixels"] [HSPACE="nPixels"]>
```

As you can tell from the syntax, the only parameters required for inserting an applet into a web page are the CODE, WIDTH, and HEIGHT attributes. The following sections explain each of these parameters.

NOTE
> The <APPLET> tag is the HTML standard for referencing Java applets. Microsoft's browser, Internet Explorer, supports the use of the <OBJECT> tag for inserting Java applets into a web page. The <OBJECT> tag is covered in a later section entitled "ActiveX Overview." Keep in mind that you can use either tag to insert a Java applet into a web page.

CODEBASE

The CODEBASE attribute is an optional parameter that enables you to specify the URL location of the applet code. The browser uses the web page document's URL by default if this parameter isn't included. The browser uses this parameter to locate the code for the applet after it realizes that the web page document contains an applet.

CODE

The CODE attribute indicates the name of the compiled applet program to be used with the web page. The syntax for referencing the applet is as follows:

```
<APPLET CODE="Applet.class">
```

Notice that the applet has a suffix of .class. This suffix is the standard naming convention for Java applets. In this example, "Applet.class" represents the applet code that will be executed within the context of the browser. The file must be located either in the same directory as the HTML document or in the URL directory that you specify using the CODEBASE attribute.

ALT

The ALT attribute enables you to provide alternate text to display for browsers that cannot execute Java applets. This attribute is an optional parameter for the <APPLET> tag. In these cases, the browser understands the <APPLET> tag and recognizes its inability to process the applet code. Given this scenario, the browser uses the ALT attribute to present the alternate text to the user. The value of this attribute is a string of text enclosed within quotes, as shown in the following line of code:

```
<APPLET CODE="Applet.class" ALT="I'm sorry. I don't do JAVA!">
```

13

NAME

The NAME attribute is an optional parameter that enables you to specify an instance name for the applet. This attribute is useful for web pages that include multiple applets on the same page. These applets use the instance name to communicate with each other. Also, the instance name is used by scripting code to reference the web page applet and its attributes.

A brief discussion about instances is warranted here. As you probably can tell from some of the examples in this book, I am a huge sports fan. I think sports can be applied to any subject, even object-oriented programming. Without going into great detail about Java and object-oriented concepts, I would like to give a sports analogy to help explain a class instance.

Basketball is one of my favorite sports. When I think of the word basketball, I form a mental picture of its color, shape, form, and function. In other words, I recognize its attributes, purpose, and capabilities. I cannot take advantage of the basketball or use it simply by contemplating its value. I must do something with it.

A basketball at the local sporting goods store could be used to describe a Java applet class. You and I both know the purpose of the basketball as it sits on the shelf. I can't do something with the basketball until I go down to the store and purchase it. Then, when I refer to my basketball, I can do something with it, like shoot a three-point shot or perform a slam dunk. Just like the basketball, a Java applet that has been developed has a defined purpose. It is not until I create an instance of the applet in my web page that I can truly enjoy the benefits of the program. The NAME attribute enables me to provide an instance name for referencing the applet within the context of my application. For example, I could use script code to extend the functionality of the applet. In my script code, I would use the instance name to reference the applet.

WIDTH and HEIGHT

The WIDTH attribute is used to specify the width of the display area for the applet measured in number of pixels. The HEIGHT attribute indicates the height of the applet display area and also is measured in number of pixels. These parameters are required. The following line of code provides an example of specifying the width and height for an applet:

```
<APPLET CODE="Applet.class" WIDTH=250 HEIGHT=200>
```

ALIGN

You can use the ALIGN attribute to indicate the alignment for the applet. This attribute is an optional parameter of the <APPLET> tag. The valid values for this attribute include left, right, middle, absmiddle, texttop, baseline, bottom, and absbottom. The ALIGN attribute and its

13

alignment values are similar in nature to that of images. You can use the ALIGN attribute to specify the layout and alignment of the applet in relation to the rest of the content for the web page.

VSPACE and HSPACE

The VSPACE attribute defines spacing in terms of pixels above and below the applet. The HSPACE attribute defines spacing to the left and right of the applet. The HSPACE attribute also is measured in terms of pixels. These attributes are similar to their <IMG> tag brethren.

Using Parameters with Java Applets

Most applets use parameters to establish values for the applet's properties and attributes. You can supply these parameters when the applet is loaded into the web page. The syntax for supplying applet parameters is as follows:

```
<PARAM NAME="appletParamName" VALUE="appletParamValue">
```

appletParamName is the name of a parameter for the applet, and appletParamValue is the value to be supplied to the applet. The following code sample demonstrates an example of using parameters with an applet.

```
<APPLET CODE="NervousText.class WIDTH=400 HEIGHT=100>
<PARAM NAME="Text" VALUE="This text shakes!">
```

This example uses the Nervous Text applet and defines the width and height to 400 and 100 pixels respectively. The Nervous Text applet contains the Text parameter which is set to "This text shakes!" in the example. You should notice that the parameter name is specified, as well as the value for the parameter.

ActiveX Overview

The other day I was recalling the first time I used a Visual Basic control, which was the Grid control included with Visual Basic 1.0. Controls have progressed tremendously since the old VBX days. Microsoft now provides users with a new kind of control—the ActiveX control. In an effort to keep up with this fast-paced world, Microsoft has built all their products to be active—Active Server, Active Documents, Active Server Pages, and ActiveX controls, just to name a few. Just as OLE controls replaced the VBX controls, ActiveX controls are currently the new kid on the block.

You can use ActiveX controls to build a dynamic and interactive interface for your client-server or Web-based application. The ability to integrate ActiveX controls into a web page

13

without a lot of overhead gives these controls their new and improved name. These controls are ideal for using over the Internet and the Web. ActiveX controls basically enable you to provide a dynamic interface for a user to interact with your application. ActiveX controls are similar in purpose to Java applets and HTML form controls. In fact, some ActiveX controls have the same name as the HTML form controls that you learned about yesterday. ActiveX controls are much more robust, as you will discover on Day 15.

Understanding ActiveX Controls

Many ActiveX controls exist on the market. These controls have been developed by Microsoft as well as third-party software vendors. Independent developers such as yourself also have developed their own custom ActiveX controls and made them available for use by Web and client-server developers. ActiveX controls can be inserted into a web page using the <OBJECT> tag. The attributes and parameters to include an ActiveX control into a web page differ slightly for each control, but Table 13.1 outlines the basic attributes that can be used to define all ActiveX controls.

Table 13.1. The <OBJECT> tag attributes for ActiveX controls.

Attribute	Description
CLASSID	Unique identifier for the ActiveX control
ID	Instance name of the ActiveX control
HEIGHT	Specifies the height of the control
WIDTH	Specifies the width of the control
ALIGN	Specifies the alignment and placement of the control
HSPACE	Defines the left and right margin around the control
VSPACE	Defines the top and bottom margin around the control

The following sections explain each of the attributes for the <OBJECT> tag.

CLASSID

The CLASSID attribute represents the key to unlock the power of an ActiveX control. The CLASSID, or class identifier, explains the implementation of the control to the browser. In other words, the CLASSID helps the browser identify the type of control contained within the web page. Once the ActiveX control has been identified, the browser realizes the characteristics and behavior of the control.

Every ActiveX control contains a unique class identifier. The CLASSID consists of characters and numbers. The following example displays the class identifier for a command button:

```
CLASSID="CLSID:D7053240-CE69-11CD-A777-00DD01143C57">
```

You may be wondering how the browser can interpret these characters. The CLASSID is linked to an entry in the Windows registration database. The entry in the Registry, in turn, points to the code for the ActiveX control.

TIP

You can locate the CLASSID by its filename in the Windows Registry under HKEY_CLASSES_ROOT. You also can look in the CLSID section of HKEY_CLASSES_ROOT in the Registry.

You also could use the CODEBASE attribute that was discussed in the previous section concerning Java applets to specify the location of an ActiveX control. Remember, this attribute enables you to indicate a URL address location for the object. In the case of ActiveX controls, the browser downloads the ActiveX control to the web page. As the browser downloads the ActiveX control, the control automatically registers itself on the client machine.

NOTE

The more popular browsers enable you to designate what kind of controls and content can be executed on the client machine. These browser security options control the ability of an ActiveX control to register itself and run on the client machine.

ID

The ID attribute basically refers to the instance of the object. You use the ID attribute to refer to and access the properties and methods of the control within your code. The ID provides a name for you to use when communicating with the control. For example, *man* could be analogous to an object. When you hear the word *man*, you instantly think of the basic characteristics of a man. You wouldn't refer to a male friend of yours as *man*. You would communicate with him by using his first name. In my case, you would refer to me as Mike. I am an instance of the *man* object; therefore, my ID attribute is equal to Mike. Likewise, the ID helps you identify the instance of the ActiveX control within your code.

13

HEIGHT and WIDTH

These attributes are similar to the HEIGHT and WIDTH attributes that are used with the <APPLET> tag. The HEIGHT and WIDTH attributes for the <OBJECT> tag enable you to specify the size for the ActiveX control. The area that you specify basically defines the size of the placeholder for the control on the web page. You can designate the value of both the HEIGHT and WIDTH attributes in number of pixels as depicted in the following example:

```
WIDTH=240 HEIGHT=240
```

You also can specify the attributes as a percentage of the screen size, as denoted in the following example:

```
WIDTH=50% HEIGHT=50%
```

ALIGN

The ALIGN attribute enables you to design the alignment of the control in relation to the rest of the content on the page. You can use most of the same values that you used for the similar Java applet attribute.

HSPACE and VSPACE

The VSPACE attribute defines spacing in terms of pixels above and below the ActiveX control. The HSPACE attribute defines spacing to the left and right of the control. The HSPACE attribute also is measured in terms of pixels. These attributes are similar in nature to their applet counterparts. You can specify the values for these attributes in terms of a percentage of the screen.

Using Parameters with ActiveX Controls

Just like Java applets, you can use parameters to specify certain values for an ActiveX control. The format for the PARAM attribute is the same as the syntax for the <APPLET> tag. The syntax for setting the value of ActiveX control parameters is as follows:

```
<PARAM NAME="objectParamName" VALUE="objectParamValue">
```

objectParamName is the name of the parameter, and *objectParamValue* specifies the value for the parameter.

Using the Attributes to Define an ActiveX Control

Now that you have learned about the attributes for an ActiveX control, it's time to look at an example of a command button. The following example shows the definition for a command button:

```
<OBJECT ID="cmdSubmit" WIDTH=96 HEIGHT=32
CLASSID="CLSID:D7053240-CE69-11CD-A777-00DD01143C57">
<PARAM NAME="Size" VALUE="2540;846">
<PARAM NAME="FontCharSet" VALUE="0">
<PARAM NAME="FontPitchAndFamily" VALUE="2">
<PARAM NAME="ParagraphAlign" VALUE="3">
</OBJECT>
```

This example demonstrates an object declaration for a command button, or push button. You can see that the ID attribute is set to cmdSubmit. The cmd prefix adheres to the naming standard for command buttons. The WIDTH and HEIGHT also are specified for the control. The second line of the declaration depicts the CLASSID for the command button. I think you will agree that cmdSubmit is a lot more intuitive than CLSID:D7053240-CE69-11CD-A777-00DD01143C57. In this example, four parameters also are depicted for the command button. ActiveX controls can consist of a variety of parameters. You can assign values to these parameters, which supply attributes and characteristics that help define the appearance and behavior of a control.

Visualizing ActiveX Controls

So far, you have learned about the tags and attributes that enable you to define Java applets and ActiveX controls. The previous example demonstrated how to use the <OBJECT> tag to define an ActiveX control. You might be thinking, "Visual InterDev should provide an easier way to define a control rather than using tags and attributes. After all, the name of the tool is *VISUAL* InterDev." Don't worry, Visual InterDev lives up to its name regarding the integration of controls into your web pages. Visual InterDev provides two robust editors to accomplish this task. These editors provide very visual and intuitive methods for placing controls on your web page.

The following sections introduce and explain the HTML Layout Editor. Visual InterDev includes this tool to provide a better and easier way to integrate your controls into your web page. This editor removes you from the process of having to remember tags and attributes to define a control. The knowledge that you have gained concerning object tags and attributes is still very valuable. It is always better to know what is taking place behind the scenes. You also will be able to use your knowledge of tags and attributes to interpret the HTML file once you have used one of the visual editors to insert ActiveX controls into your web page.

The other editor is the Object Editor. You can use this editor to insert ActiveX controls directly into your web page. The Object Editor should be used for placing no more than a few controls on a web page. There are some limitations that will be explored concerning the use of this editor when designing an elaborate interface that uses many controls.

Both of these Visual InterDev editors provide an intuitive way to work with objects. Both editors support the use of client-side script to access and extend the power of ActiveX controls. The following sections teach you how to use the features of both the HTML Layout Editor and the Object Editor.

13

The HTML Layout Editor

You were introduced to the HTML Layout Editor during the first week, and you used it to create a layout consisting of ActiveX controls during the lesson on Day 4. Yesterday, you learned that a form provides a house for your HTML controls. The lesson made the point that HTML controls derive their meaning and usefulness in the context of a form. In a similar manner, you can use an HTML layout to integrate multiple ActiveX controls into your web page. The layout provides purpose and order to the controls. The HTML Layout Editor also makes it easier for you to develop and work with the various controls on your web page. This section explains the basic features of the HTML Layout Editor.

 NOTE
> As you learn how to use ActiveX controls and the Layout Editor, reflect on yesterday's lesson and how HTML forms and controls compare to ActiveX controls. You also should consider the development process for each.

Exploring the Process

If you have used the Microsoft ActiveX Control Pad, you are already familiar with this editor. The HTML Layout Editor provides a tool to build form layouts that contain ActiveX controls. The editor is similar to other visual tools that you may have used in the past to build a graphical user interface. The method for building your interface uses the same process as tools such as Visual Basic. You select the controls that you want to use from a toolbox and place them onto a form. Once you accurately position these objects onto your form, you set their *properties* to define their behavior and characteristics. You can then use *methods* specific to a control to perform certain tasks. Every ActiveX control contains unique properties and methods. You can use the HTML Layout Editor to define the value of the control's properties. The methods for a control enable you to affect the behavior of a control.

 Properties define the appearance and behavior of a control. Every control has a unique set of properties that pertains to the control.

 Methods enable you to perform a specific function on the object. Every object has a defined set of methods that relate to the control. A method is a pre-defined procedure for the object that you can use in your code.

13

An ActiveX control also contains certain events that are specific to the control. You can associate script code with the events for the controls in your interface. When an event occurs for the control, the script executes.

Using the HTML Layout Editor

This section explores how to use the HTML Layout Editor to create a user interface for your web page. To create an HTML layout, select the File menu and choose New from the list of menu items. Select HTML Layout from the list of items in the File tab of the New dialog window. You also will need to enter a name for your HTML layout, as shown in Figure 13.2.

Figure 13.2.

Creating an HTML layout.

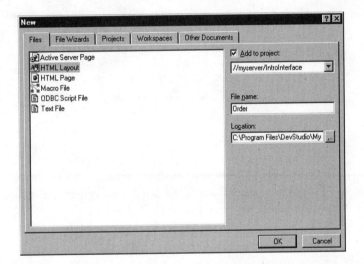

You can see that the Add to project checkbox is selected, and the project name defaults to the currently opened project. The location defaults to the directory for the default project.

NOTE

> You can deselect the Add to project checkbox to create an independent HTML layout. You also can change the project name and directory for the HTML layout.

When you click the OK push button, an HTML layout file is created, and the HTML Layout Editor is activated and displayed as illustrated in Figure 13.3.

Figure 13.3.

The HTML Layout Editor.

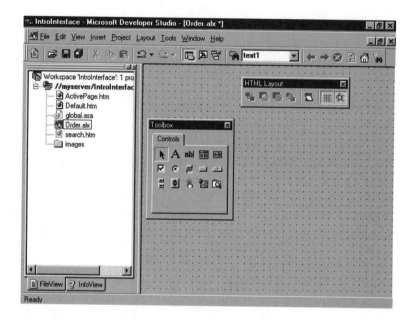

As you can see from the example, the HTML Layout Editor provides a form to place your controls as well as a toolbox that contains basic ActiveX controls. You also can see the HTML Layout toolbar. This floating toolbar can be docked on the main Visual InterDev toolbar. You will notice that a file called Order.alx has been created in the project workspace. The .alx extension identifies the file as an HTML layout.

You can adjust the properties for the HTML layout by clicking the right mouse button anywhere on the layout to display the shortcut menu. Choose the Properties menu item to adjust the ID, height, width, and background color of the layout. Figure 13.4 shows the properties window for a sample HTML layout.

Notice that the BackColor property contains a cryptic code for its value as well as three small dots to the right of this code. The code defines the background color for the layout. The three dots save you from having to memorize all the codes for the possible colors. When you click the dots, the Color dialog window displays, as shown in Figure 13.5.

As you can see, you are presented with a color palette from which you can choose a defined color for the layout. You also can create a custom color for the layout background. The ID defines a name for the layout that you can use to reference the layout within your code.

Figure 13.4.

Setting the properties for an HTML layout.

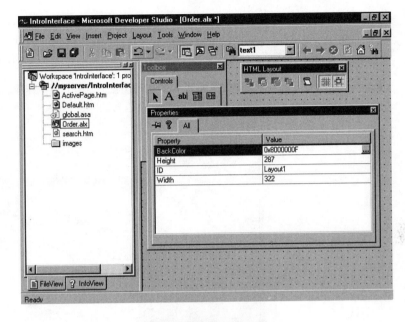

Figure 13.5.

The Color dialog window.

13

Adding ActiveX Controls to Your Layout

Once you have created an HTML layout, you can add ActiveX controls to build the interface. Click a control in the toolbox and move your mouse to the desired position for the control on the form. Click the left mouse button on the form to create a control with a default size. You also can hold down the left mouse button and drag the mouse to define a custom size for the control. You were first introduced to this process on Day 4.

Once you have placed the control on the form, you can customize the properties for the control. For example, you could place a label onto a form and edit its properties, as shown in Figure 13.6.

Figure 13.6.

Setting the properties for a label.

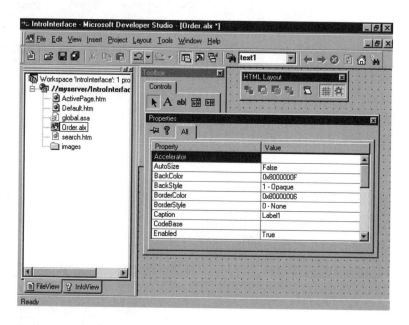

As you can see, there are a lot more properties for a label than for a layout. You can set the height, width, top and left alignment, caption, font size, and so on. You also will want to define a descriptive name to reference the control. The ID property is used for defining this attribute. The naming convention for a label control contains the lbl prefix. For example, the ID for a label for the name text box should be called lblName.

You can easily move the controls on the layout to ensure their proper placement. You also can graphically drag the corners of a control to alter its size. If you need to move multiple controls, you can click the first control and then hold down the Shift key and click the other controls. This method enables you to select multiple controls at a time and move the controls as a group. You also can select multiple controls at a time and set the correlating properties for the controls. For instance, you could select three labels that were placed vertically on a form and set the Left property for the controls to be the same. To do this, you use the method presented previously to select the three controls. With the three controls selected, click the right mouse button and choose Properties from the shortcut menu. A Properties window is displayed for the controls. You can then set the value of the Left property for the controls. Figure 13.7 depicts this dialog window.

13

Figure 13.7.

Setting the properties for multiple controls.

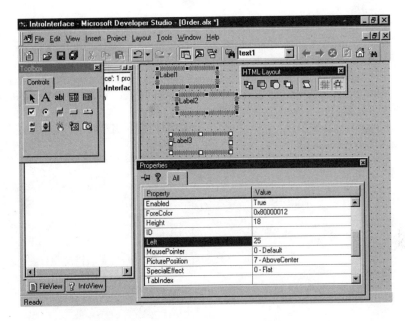

Notice that the value that you enter applies to all three controls. The label controls are then displayed and aligned, as seen in Figure 13.8.

Figure 13.8.

Aligning the labels on a form.

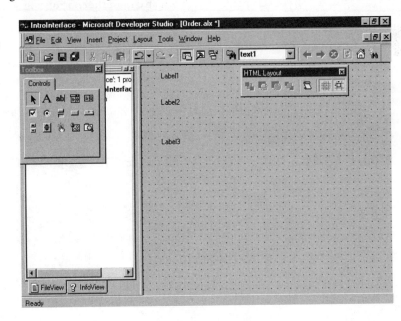

13

Customizing the Toolbox

You were introduced to the HTML Layout Editor toolbox in Figure 13.3. This example displayed the default controls for the toolbox. You can add more controls to the toolbox by clicking the right mouse button on the toolbox. Choose Additional Controls from the shortcut menu to display a list of additional controls, as illustrated in Figure 13.9.

Figure 13.9.

Adding controls to your toolbox.

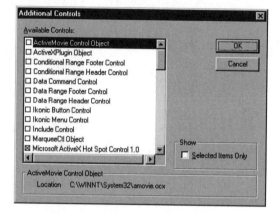

The Additional Controls dialog window displays all the ActiveX controls that have been registered on your client machine. You can choose the controls you want to add to the toolbox by clicking the checkbox to the right of the desired controls and clicking OK.

You can delete controls from the toolbox as well as customize the configuration of current controls on the toolbox. To delete a control from the toolbox, right-click the mouse on the control and choose the Delete option from the list of menu items. To alter the display of a control on the toolbox, right-click the mouse on the control and select the Customize menu item. Figure 13.10 demonstrates how you can alter the way a control is displayed on the toolbox.

Figure 13.10.

The Customize Control dialog window.

You can alter the Tool Tip text for the control and the picture that is displayed in the toolbox. You can edit the current image as well as load a new image for the control.

You also can create new tabs, or pages, for the toolbox. Click the right mouse button on the Controls tab to display the toolbox shortcut menu. Figure 13.11 displays the list of options for the toolbox.

Figure 13.11.

Managing the tabs in the toolbox.

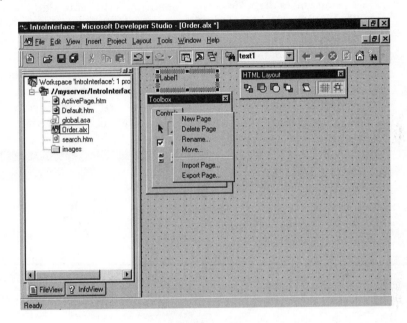

Each of these options has a different function. You can use these options to further organize your ActiveX controls. Table 13.2 defines each of the menu items for managing the tabs in your toolbox.

Table 13.2. Shortcut menu options for the HTML toolbox.

Menu Item	Function
New Page	Creates a new tab for the toolbox
Delete Page	Deletes the current tab in the toolbox
Rename	Enables you to rename the current tab
Move	Moves the order of the tabs
Import Page	Imports a pre-defined tab page from a file
Export Page	Saves a tab page to a file

13

Once you create the HTML layout, you can save the layout by selecting Save from the File menu. After you have saved the layout, you are ready to insert it into your HTML page.

Inserting a Layout into a Web Page

You must insert the HTML layout file into the web page to use the layout in your application. The HTML web page document uses the ALX file to refer to the layout. The ALX file contains all the information concerning the placement and characteristics of the controls as well as any script that has been included for the layout. To insert a layout into a web page, right-click the mouse button at the location in your web page document where you want the layout and choose Insert HTML Layout from the shortcut menu. A dialog window that enables you to choose the HTML layout to insert is then displayed. Figure 13.12 demonstrates an example of the Select HTML Layout dialog window.

Figure 13.12.

Selecting an HTML layout.

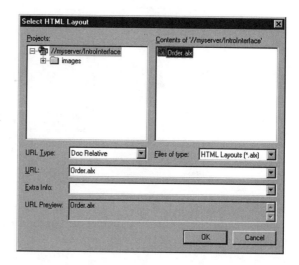

You can choose an HTML layout from the list in the dialog window and click OK to insert the HTML layout. Figure 13.13 depicts an example of an HTML layout as it is displayed in a web page.

To edit this layout, right-click the mouse in between the object tags for the layout and choose Edit HTML Layout from the list of menu items. The HTML Layout Editor becomes activated and opens the layout. You can then visually manipulate the properties and characteristics of your layout. Save your changes to the layout. The updates are communicated to the web page that contains the HTML layout.

13

Figure 13.13.

A non-visual view of the HTML layout.

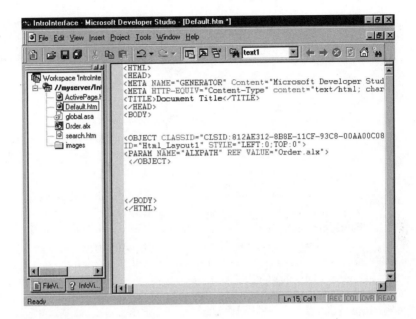

The Object Editor

The Object Editor provides the other visual editor for inserting ActiveX controls into your web page. The Object Editor is best used for individual controls that you want to include on your web page. Whereas the HTML Layout Editor enables you to manage multiple controls on a form, the object editor is used for managing one control at a time. You cannot place controls on top of controls with the Object Editor as you can with the HTML Layout Editor. For example, you might need to place a set of radio buttons on a frame for a form. Because the radio buttons are placed on top of the form, or layered, you must use the HTML Layout Editor to achieve this. The Object Editor doesn't support this kind of interface.

The Object Editor does, however, provide a robust visual editor for manipulating the properties of individual controls on a web page. The following sections outline how to insert an ActiveX control into a web page and use the Object Editor to set its properties.

Inserting an ActiveX Control into a Web Page

You can insert an ActiveX control into a web page by right-clicking the mouse at the location in the web page where you want to place the ActiveX control. Select Insert ActiveX Control from the shortcut menu. A dialog window will be displayed, enabling you to insert ActiveX and Design-time ActiveX controls. This window is displayed in Figure 13.14.

13

Figure 13.14.

Inserting an ActiveX control.

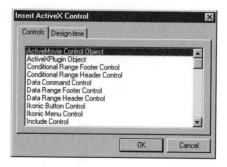

You then can choose a control from the Controls tab. You also can click the Design-time tab to insert a Design-time control. These controls are covered during Day 14, "Extending Web Pages Through Design-Time Controls." The controls that are listed in this dialog window are ones that have been registered for use on your client machine. Once you choose a control and click OK, the Object Editor is displayed along with the control that you have selected. Figure 13.15 displays a command button as it appears in the Object Editor.

Figure 13.15.

The Object Editor.

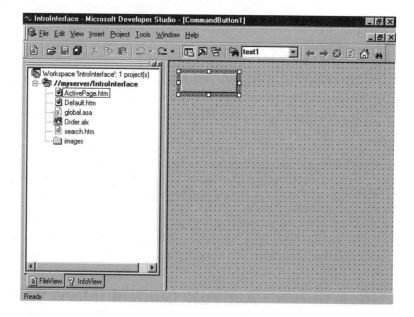

You can set the properties for this control by right-clicking the control and choosing Properties from the shortcut menu. Figure 13.16 depicts the Properties window for the command button.

Figure 13.16.

Setting the properties for the command button.

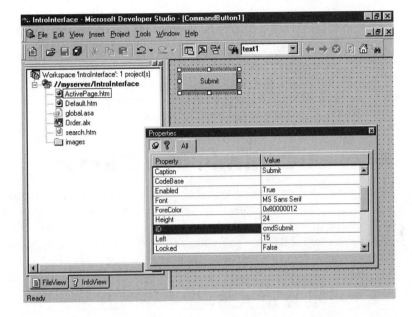

Once you have defined the properties for the control and saved the object, the ActiveX control is inserted into your web page. Figure 13.17 depicts the presence of the command button in a sample web page.

Figure 13.17.

An ActiveX control as it appears in a web page document.

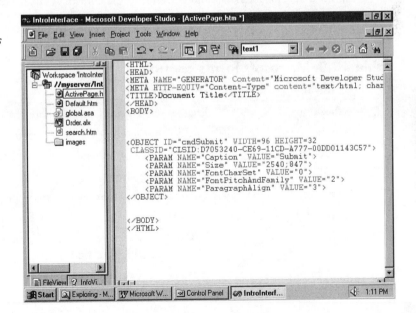

Editing an ActiveX Control

To edit the ActiveX control, open the web page document and right-click the mouse within the object tags for the control that you want to edit. Select Edit ActiveX Control from the shortcut menu to display the Object Editor for the control. You can then change the properties for the control as described in the preceding section and save the updates. The changes that you make will be reflected in the web page.

ActiveX Controls at a Glance

Visual InterDev supports the use of ActiveX controls in your web pages. Many powerful and exciting ActiveX controls are included with Visual InterDev. The previous sections provided an overview of the visual editors that you can use to work with these controls. This final section for the day briefly introduces you to some of the ActiveX controls that are available within the Visual InterDev environment.

A Preview of ActiveX Controls

Visual InterDev includes several controls for you to use when designing the interface for your application. These controls provide basic functionality similar to the forms controls that you discovered yesterday. ActiveX controls, however, offer more properties that you can set to customize the characteristics and behavior of the control. You also can use a robust set of methods and events for the controls to enliven your application. Table 13.3 outlines some of the basic controls that are available with Visual InterDev.

Table 13.3. Microsoft forms controls.

Control	Description
Check Box	Enables user to select one or more choices
Combo Box	Enables user to enter text or select item from a list
Command Button	Push button that user can press to initiate an event
Label	Text typically used to describe other controls
List Box	Enables user to choose one or more items from a list
Radio Button	Enables user to select one choice from a group of items
Scroll Bar	Enables the user to set the value of another control by scrolling in some direction
Spin Button	Enables user to change a number by clicking one of the arrows

13

Control	Description
Tab Strip	Presents a tabbed dialog window to the user that groups related controls
Text Box	Enables the user to enter a single line of text
Toggle Button	Displays whether a control is selected

There also are some very specific ActiveX controls that have been developed especially for the Internet. These controls are relatively new and enable you to build an interface for your application that is truly tailored to the Web. Table 13.4 depicts some ActiveX controls that are specifically geared to the Web.

Table 13.4. Web-based controls.

Control	Description
Hot Spot	Represents an area on a page that can trigger an event
Image	Displays an image to the user
Marquee	Enables you to place scrolling text onto a web page
New Item	Enables you to denote new items on a page
Preloader	Enables you to load a control's URL into the client computer's cache and download the control when necessary
Stock Ticker	Provides a stock ticker for the web page that downloads dynamic data

ActiveX controls are displayed in the Visual InterDev environment if they have been downloaded and registered for use on your machine. You will get a chance to use these controls during the first part of next week.

Summary

Today's lesson extends the knowledge that you gained yesterday concerning form controls to the wonderful world of ActiveX controls and Java applets. These advanced objects can be used to truly enrich the look and feel of your Web-based application. This lesson has served as a primer for the lesson on Day 15, when you will be able to apply this knowledge to building an interface for your application.

13

The first part of today's lesson presented an overview of objects. The lesson provided a definition of an object to set the context for the day. Then, you were introduced to Java applets. During this part of the lesson, you gained an understanding of the <APPLET> tag. The lesson taught you how to use this tag to insert a Java applet into your web page. You also discovered some of the attributes and parameters associated with the <APPLET> tag to define its basic characteristics. The lesson then moved on to a discussion of ActiveX controls. You received a basic overview of ActiveX controls. You also learned about the typical attributes for an ActiveX control.

The latter part of the day focused on the visual editors for ActiveX controls included with Visual InterDev. The HTML Layout Editor enables you to relate, organize, and work with multiple ActiveX controls. You can create a robust form interface for your application through the use of this editor. The Object Editor is another visual editor that enables you to insert individual ActiveX controls into a web page. The final part of the lesson presented an introduction to some of the more common ActiveX controls.

Q&A

Q How can I use ActiveX controls?

A ActiveX controls provide a robust solution for creating an interface for your application. You can use some of the more basic controls like text boxes, radio buttons, list boxes, and push buttons to create intuitive forms for your users. You also can use some of the newer controls that have been built specifically for the Web to create dynamic web pages.

Q Is ActiveX Microsoft's answer to Java?

A It is a common mistake to compare ActiveX and Java. They are complementary, not competing, standards. Java is a programming language that supports multi-platform development. ActiveX differs in that it provides objects written in a variety of languages that you can use to integrate into your application. ActiveX controls can be used with Java applets to provide rich functionality for your application.

Workshop

For today's workshop, you need to visit two web sites on the Internet. These sites provide pertinent information on the use of Java applets and ActiveX controls. The first site is www.gamelan.com. This site provides one of the best web sites for discovering more

13

information on Java programming and Java applets. The second web site is www.microsoft.com/activex/controls/. This site provides extensive information on ActiveX controls, including a gallery of many ActiveX controls from third-party providers.

Quiz

1. What is the tag that can be used to insert Java applets as well as ActiveX controls into a web page?
2. Name the two visual editors for objects provided by Visual InterDev.
3. What is a property?

Quiz Answers

1. The <OBJECT> tag.
2. The HTML Layout Editor and the Object Editor.
3. A property defines the characteristics and behavior of a control. Every control has a unique set of properties that can be customized.

13

Day 14

Extending Web Pages Through Design-Time Controls

If you are a developer, you recognize the importance of an application's design. Throughout this book, I have tried to emphasize the design as the crux of your application. A design can make or break an application. You also probably realize the importance of the design stage of a development project. It is imperative that you spend the proper time contemplating the aspects of the application design so that the system will execute successfully when the user runs the application.

These design aspects can be applied to the use of design-time controls. Microsoft has introduced a new kind of control to enable you to design specific functionality into your application that will execute when the system is run. In the same way that your application exhibits its characteristics and design concepts when it is run, design-time controls reveal their behavior at runtime. These controls enable you to focus on designing robust functionality into your application.

Today's lesson focuses on the use of design-time controls within your Web-based applications. First, the lesson explains and defines the concept of a design-time control, teaching you what a design-time control is and how it can be used within your web pages. Next, the lesson explains the difference between design-time controls and regular ActiveX controls.

The middle part of the day presents one of the more robust design-time controls that can be used in your web pages. The Data Command control can be used to provide rich database integration for your applications. You learn how to insert and use design-time controls like the Data Command control. You also discover the remnants of a design-time control placed within your web page document.

The final lesson for the day outlines how to truly use and integrate these exciting new controls into your applications. You will discover how to extend the power and functionality of your application through the use of design-time controls.

Defining Design-Time ActiveX Controls

Based on yesterday's lesson, you should now understand the concept of an ActiveX control. You realize that you can use these controls to build the interface for your application. You also know that ActiveX controls exhibit their presence and functionality when the user initiates the application. But, what is a design-time control? Does this mean that I can use this control when I design my application, but not when I run it? This section answers these questions and more, and provides a basic definition for a *design-time control.*

A design-time control is an important new control, developed specifically for the Web, that enables you to place rich functionality in your application without additional overhead. Design-time controls are the Diet Coke of the computer interface—same great taste with half the calories!

Design-time controls enable you to take advantage of the same benefits as ActiveX controls during the time of application design. This means that you can visually set the properties and characteristics of the control, similar to ActiveX controls. The distinguishing factor is that design-time controls don't incur the overhead cost at runtime. When you insert a design-time control into your web page, you establish the characteristics of the control. These property attributes are saved as text within the context of the document. The text contains special instructions based on properties that you have designed for the control. When the user runs the application, the actual control that you used to develop these instructions is disabled, and the instructions execute the designed functionality. In other words, you receive the same powerful functionality with a lower overhead cost, hence the Diet Coke analogy.

14

NEW TERM A *design-time control* is a special type of ActiveX control that enables you to integrate specific properties and behavior characteristics when designing your applications. These controls insert instructions into your documents instead of an actual control, thereby reducing the amount of processing overhead in your application.

Design-Time ActiveX Controls Versus ActiveX Controls

While the ActiveX control is typically a graphical object that is used to construct a user interface for your application, the design-time control provides a visual helper at the time of design. This visual aid then works behind the scenes to execute the desired functionality.

With a few exceptions, ActiveX controls are usually visible to you when you're designing your application. You have learned about several controls that enable you to build a graphical user interface. These ActiveX controls include the command button, the radio button, the checkbox, the listbox, the marquee, and so on. You have used some of these controls during the first two weeks. Once you insert the controls on your web page, you establish the property values for the controls to affect their appearance and behavior. At runtime, these controls appear in your web page and provide specific functionality. Runtime refers to the period of time that the user is running the application and executing the code. ActiveX controls contain a binary runtime component that provides additional functionality when the application runs. You incur the overhead of the control being alive during application runtime to receive the additional functionality.

Design-time controls, on the other hand, don't contain a runtime component. Design-time controls aren't visible when the user runs the application. You can use these controls while designing your web pages to provide powerful functionality to your application. These controls are like wizards that facilitate the construction of your application during the design phase of your development effort. When the user executes the application, the functionality is exhibited in the application without the appearance of the design-time control. It's control might not be visible at runtime, but its effects are evident to the user.

Design-Time Controls Make Effective Parents

A design-time control has a similar relationship and responsibility to the application as a parent has to a child. A parent is charged with raising children. This task includes providing the proper guidance and instruction, so that the child can thrive when he or she becomes an

14

adult. The parent serves as a counselor and coach who visually provides an example in his or her actions and his or her speech. When the child becomes an adult, he or she will exhibit behaviors, values, and characteristics that have been taught by the parents. As a parent, I can already see the effects of this relationship in my two small children.

A design-time control provides a similar guide to the web pages and application. The design-time control affects your application by the properties and characteristics that are set for the control. This information is stored in the context of the web page documents. In a sense, the web page is affected by the instruction, or "teaching," of the design-time control. The control tells the web page what behaviors to exhibit.

You can think of the runtime environment as adulthood for the web page that includes the code produced by the design-time control. During runtime, the control is no longer around to help. This is analogous to the parent who is no longer around to instruct the child, now an adult, what to do. The newly independent adult must live his or her own life, using the characteristics and values that the parents taught him or her as a child. Similarly, the runtime text code that was created in the web page must execute independently of the design-time control when the application is executed. Although the design-time control parent is no longer visibly around, this code exhibits the properties and characteristics that were instilled during design-time. Figure 14.1 illustrates both the parent/child and the design-time control/run-time code relationship.

Figure 14.1.

The design-time control—an effective parent.

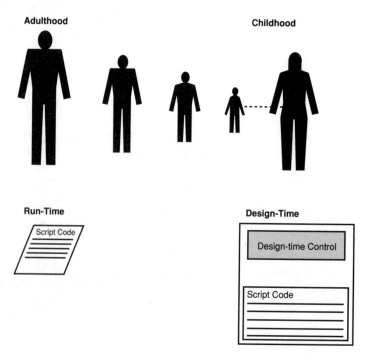

The Origin of Design-Time Controls

Visual InterDev is one of the first tools to use design-time controls as a part of the development environment. Design-time controls, like regular ActiveX controls, are based on Microsoft's Component Object Model (COM). This model provides a standard definition and structure for all design-time controls. Because a design-time control is constructed based on COM, applications can access its functionality through a standard method. You can build a design-time control with hard-core languages like C and C++, as well as more intuitive languages such as Visual Basic. You also can build design-time controls with the Java programming language.

NOTE

> You must use Visual Basic version 5 or higher to build a design-time or ActiveX control. Microsoft also offers a trimmed down version of Visual Basic 5.0 called the Visual Basic Control Creation Edition. This product is specifically targeted at developers who want to build design-time and ActiveX controls. You will get a chance to learn about this product and how to use it to build a design-time control on Day 16, "Building Design-Time ActiveX Controls."

Once you become familiar with using design-time controls, I think you will want to rush out and build your controls. You will realize their benefit and structure and recognize the importance of their reusability across your development team. You might even begin by developing reusable design-time controls across your development team.

After you become appreciated internally, you could expand your reach by authoring controls that can be used commercially by a plethora of developers. Whatever the case, I think you will see how easy it is to use and develop design-time controls. You will also appreciate their power and capability.

Visual InterDev provides many design-time controls that you can integrate into your application. The controls generate both HTML and scripting code that can be used in a variety of ways, including the creation of the following items:

- ☐ HTML content
- ☐ Client-side scripting
- ☐ ActiveX controls
- ☐ Java applets
- ☐ Server-side scripting
- ☐ Active Server Components

14

Within your Visual InterDev application, you can integrate design-time controls in your client- and server-side components. Some of the more powerful Visual InterDev design-time controls enable you to integrate rich and robust database functionality into your application. The next few sections explain and explore these exciting new controls.

Understanding Design-Time Controls

This section is for those intrigued minds who wonder how a design-time control can achieve its purpose without visibly appearing in the application at runtime. This part of the lesson explains how to insert a design-time control into your application. Once you understand the process, I will review the inner workings of the design-time control, then explain how these controls accomplish their tasks.

Inserting a Design-Time Control

Design-time controls are typically placed within a web page or an Active Server Page. The design-time control must be installed and registered on the machine where it is used. This requirement is the same as regular ActiveX controls. Once registered, the design-time control can be used within the context of your application.

To insert a design-time control, open the ASP or HTML file and right-click the mouse at the desired position in the file. Select Insert ActiveX Control from the shortcut menu. When the Insert ActiveX Control tabbed dialog window is displayed, click the Design-time tab. You will then be presented with a list of all of the registered design-time controls. Figure 14.2 depicts a list of available design-time controls that are included with Visual InterDev.

Figure 14.2.

Selecting a design-time control.

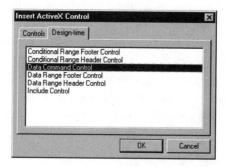

You can pick the design-time control from the list and click OK. The Object Editor that you learned about yesterday will then be activated. You can use this visual editor to set the properties of the design-time control. Figure 14.3 depicts the Data Command control, a powerful database design-time control, as seen through the eyes of the Object Editor.

14

Figure 14.3.

Setting the properties for a design-time control.

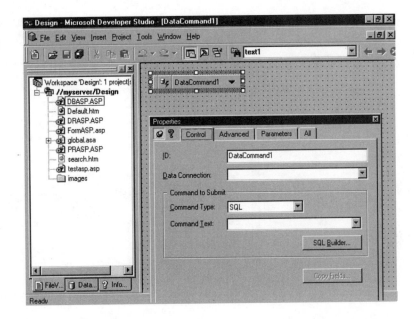

The Object Editor was covered in yesterday's lesson. You can use the Object Editor to configure the properties and characteristics of the control. After you set the properties of the design-time control, it is inserted into your web page document. Later in the day the lesson teaches you how to set the properties of some of the more robust design-time controls. For now, you should focus on learning the basic structure of all design-time controls. The next section teaches you how to recognize the presence of a design-time control within a web page. The lesson also defines the general attributes of a design-time control.

Reviewing the Remnants of a Design-Time Control

Just exactly what does a design-time control look like? What magic is going on behind the scenes to enable such elaborate behavior? How does a design-time control affect my application? This section answers these questions, walks you through a review of the remnants of a design-time control, and explains the basic structure for all design-time controls as seen within an HTML or ASP document. Figure 14.4 depicts a design-time control as seen within the confines of an ASP file.

14

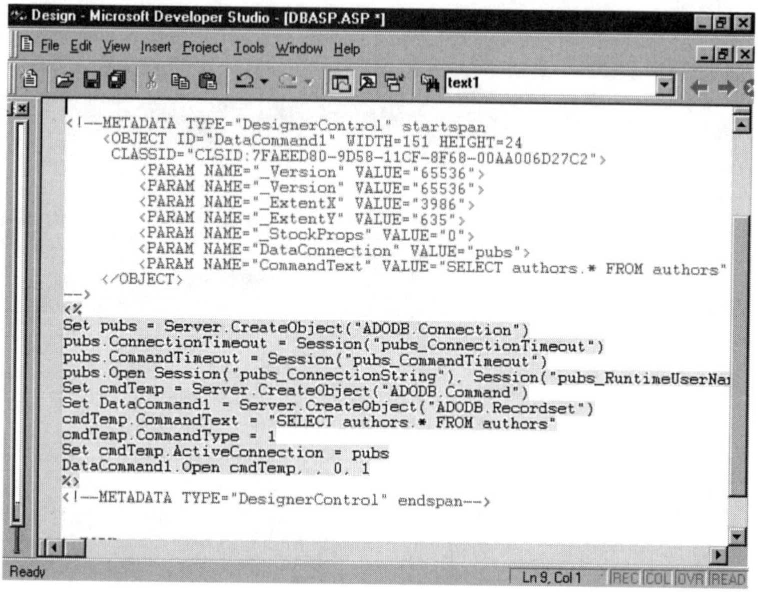
Design - Microsoft Developer Studio - [DBASP.ASP *]
File Edit View Insert Project Tools Window Help
text1
<!--METADATA TYPE="DesignerControl" startspan
<OBJECT ID="DataCommand1" WIDTH=151 HEIGHT=24
CLASSID="CLSID:7FAEED80-9D58-11CF-8F68-00AA006D27C2">
<PARAM NAME="_Version" VALUE="65536">
<PARAM NAME="_Version" VALUE="65536">
<PARAM NAME="_ExtentX" VALUE="3986">
<PARAM NAME="_ExtentY" VALUE="635">
<PARAM NAME="_StockProps" VALUE="0">
<PARAM NAME="DataConnection" VALUE="pubs">
<PARAM NAME="CommandText" VALUE="SELECT authors.* FROM authors"
</OBJECT>
-->
<%
Set pubs = Server.CreateObject("ADODB.Connection")
pubs.ConnectionTimeout = Session("pubs_ConnectionTimeout")
pubs.CommandTimeout = Session("pubs_CommandTimeout")
pubs.Open Session("pubs_ConnectionString"), Session("pubs_RuntimeUserNa
Set cmdTemp = Server.CreateObject("ADODB.Command")
Set DataCommand1 = Server.CreateObject("ADODB.Recordset")
cmdTemp.CommandText = "SELECT authors.* FROM authors"
cmdTemp.CommandType = 1
Set cmdTemp.ActiveConnection = pubs
DataCommand1.Open cmdTemp, , 0, 1
%>
<!--METADATA TYPE="DesignerControl" endspan-->
Ready
Ln 9, Col 1
REC COL OVR READ

Figure 14.4.
The markings of a design-time control.

As you can see from Figure 14.4, the design-time control somewhat resembles an ActiveX control. The control is denoted by the `<OBJECT>` tag and contains an `ID`, `CLASSID`, and some parameters similar to an ActiveX control. The design-time control differs from an ActiveX control in that it is initially denoted with the `METADATA` comment. The design-time control also visually appears in green within the ASP document. The runtime text for the control is highlighted and displays below the ending `<OBJECT>` tag. The next few sections examine the appearance and structure of a design-time control.

Examining the Structure of a Design-Time Control

The `METADATA` comment is used to denote the start of the design-time control. The `TYPE` attribute is equal to the value of `Designer Control`, which is true of all design-time controls. The `startspan` attribute indicates the beginning of the `METADATA` comment and causes this line of the comment to be passed over. Another reason for using the `METADATA` comments to surround a design-time control is to prevent instantiation of the object.

One of the key points and benefits about design-time controls that has been noted in this lesson is that these controls don't incur the overhead of regular ActiveX controls. Because the object is surrounded by comments, it won't be instantiated. Only the runtime text will persist, thereby reducing the overhead incurred by the application.

The <OBJECT> tag enables you to work with the control and visually sets the properties of the control. In a sense, the <OBJECT> tag informs Visual InterDev that the control is an object. This information enables you to easily edit the properties of the design-time control. You can right-click the mouse within the <OBJECT> tags to display the shortcut menu, as seen in Figure 14.5.

Figure 14.5.

Editing the properties of the design-time control.

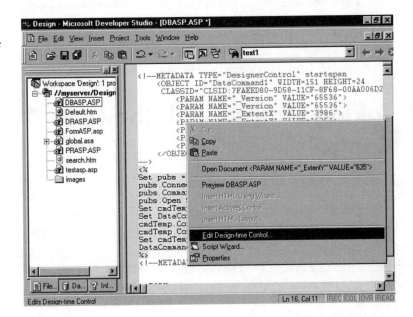

The option to edit a design-time control differs slightly from an ActiveX control. As you can see from Figure 14.5, you select Edit Design-time Control from the list of menu items to alter the properties of your control. This action activates the Object Editor and displays your design-time control.

The attributes and parameters contained within the <OBJECT> tags for the design-time control help to generally define the runtime code for the control. The code in this example is displayed as script and explicitly defines the behavior of the control. This scripting code is what the application and browser are going to execute at runtime. The object declaration is passed over, and the runtime text is the only thing that is noticed and processed. The ending METADATA comment contains the endspan attribute, which signifies to the browser the end of the runtime text for the design-time control.

14

Editing the Script for a Design-Time Control

In the previous example, the runtime script that was displayed was automatically generated based on properties defined in the Object Editor. You may be wondering whether Visual InterDev enables you to extend and customize this scripting logic. The answer is yes. There might be cases in which you need to customize the generated logic for the control. The only thing you need to be aware of concerns the METADATA comment tags. When these comment tags are present, opening the control after you have made changes to the script replaces your customized code with the generated scripting logic defined by the control's properties. To avoid this situation, remove the METADATA comment tags.

Taking Charge with the Data Command Control

Now that you understand the basic structure of a design-time control, the lesson explores some of the more robust design-time controls. Visual InterDev includes several design-time controls that provide rich database functionality for your application. This section covers the Data Command control, which you received a preview of in the previous section.

The Data Command design-time control uses a database connection to perform a basic query against a database. The Data Command control creates a Recordset object that you can use to perform your queries. You learned about the Recordset object on Day 8, "Communicating with a Database." As a refresher, the Recordset object represents all of the records in a specified table. You can use the Recordset object to retrieve the individual rows within a designated table.

NOTE

> The rest of the lesson assumes that you have a valid database connection for your project. To use the database design-time controls, you must first add a database connection to your project. Refer to the lesson on Day 8 for a refresher on how to accomplish this task. The examples that are used rely on the Publishers database connection that was created earlier in the week.

The Data Command design-time control should be used for retrieving and modifying a single row within a table. You will discover other design-time controls in the next section that enable you to work with multiple rows of a table. You can specify command text properties

14

for the Data Command control that indicate the type of command to execute against the database. This information is used with the Recordset object to perform the specified type of database action against the desired row within a table.

Inserting a Data Command Control

To insert the Data Command design-time control into your application, open the file that will contain the control. Click the right mouse button at the desired position within the document and select Insert ActiveX Control from the shortcut menu. Click the Design-time tab and choose Data Command Control from the list, as seen in Figure 14.6.

Figure 14.6.

Selecting the Data Command design-time control.

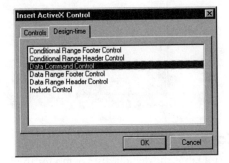

TIP
You should use Active Server Pages to handle your database logic. When inserting a database design-time control, choose an ASP file instead of an HTML file.

After you have chosen the Data Command control, click the OK button. You will then be able to edit the properties of the control using the Object Editor. Figure 14.7 displays the Data Command control and its property window.

The Data Command Properties window consists of the following tabs:

☐ Control tab
☐ Advanced tab
☐ Parameters tab
☐ All tab

Each of these tabs is explained in the next few sections.

14

Figure 14.7.

The Data Command control Properties window.

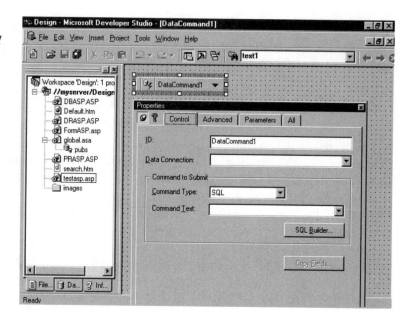

The Control Tab

The Control tab is the default display tab for the Properties window. You saw a preview of this window in Figure 14.7. The first field on the window is the ID field, which enables you to define a name for the control. You use this ID to reference the control within your code.

The Data Connection drop-down listbox enables you to specify the data connection for the control. Any active data connections for the project will be displayed in the list. For this example, I chose the database connection to the Pubs database that was defined at the first part of this week's lesson. The Command to Submit frame contains several options that enable you to specify the type of SQL command to execute.

The first drop-down listbox on the frame is the Command Type, which enables you to indicate the type of command to send to the database. Table 14.1 displays the available choices for the Command Type.

Table 14.1. Command types for the Data Command control.

Type	Description
SQL	Enables you to format an SQL statement
Stored Procedure	Specifies the use of a stored procedure
Table	Specifies the use of a database table
View	Specifies the use of a database view

The Command Text drop-down listbox indicates the command that will be sent to the database. The Command Type that you choose affects the contents of the Command Text drop-down listbox as well as the behavior of the other controls in this frame. For example, if you select Stored Procedure for the Command Type, the contents of the Command Text drop-down listbox display the available stored procedures in the database. Also, the SQL Builder push button is disabled because you're choosing to use a pre-defined SQL procedure that already exists. The SQL Builder push button enables you to use the Query Designer within Visual InterDev to create and construct an SQL database call.

If you choose SQL for the Command Type, the SQL Builder push button is enabled, allowing you to construct your SQL statement. You also can choose to directly enter the SQL statement in the Command Text field. A Command Type of Table will disable the SQL Builder push button and display a list of the available tables within the database in the Command Type drop-down listbox. Similarly, you can select View for the Command Type, which will disable the SQL Builder push button and populate the Command Text drop-down listbox with the views that are contained within the database. Finally, the Copy Fields push button enables you to copy the fields from the database table for insertion into your web page document. When you click this button, the Copy Fields dialog window displays as shown in Figure 14.8.

Figure 14.8.

Copying fields from a database table.

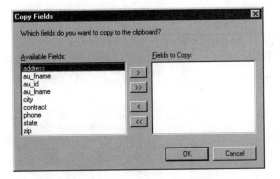

The Copy Fields dialog window displays the available column fields contained within a database table in the list box on the left-hand side of the window. You can double-click a field to move it to the Fields to Copy listbox. You also can select the available field and click the single arrow button that points to the right to place the field into the Fields to Copy listbox.

Pressing the double-arrow button that points to the right moves all of the available fields into the Fields to Copy listbox. You can remove fields that have been selected to be copied in a similar manner. You can either double-click the item within the Fields to Copy listbox or select the item and click the single arrow button that points to the left. To deselect all of the fields to be copied, click the double-arrow button that points in the direction of the Available

14

Fields listbox. The fields that you choose are copied to the clipboard. You can then insert them into your web page document using the text editor of your choice. This feature provides an easy way to access the values of the columns within a row in your table.

The Advanced Tab

The Advanced tab enables you to customize your database commands. In many cases, you can accept the defaults for this tab. Advanced database developers typically use this dialog to fine-tune the performance of the application. For example, you can specify the type of cursor to use with a query.

You also can choose the type of locking scheme that you want to use for database requests among different users. This option can be used with applications and databases that support high-volume transaction processing. For instance, if your application will have users contending for the same data, you may want to use a locking scheme that prevents users from overwriting changes to the same data. You can choose from among several database locking schemes within the Advanced tab to meet the needs of your application. You also can set the numbers of records to cache into local memory. The Advanced tab enables you to prepare, or compile, an SQL statement when it's initially executed. After the first user executes the SQL, performance will increase for additional users, because the statement has already been compiled against the database. Figure 14.9 displays the options on the Advanced tabbed dialog window.

Figure 14.9.

The Advanced tab.

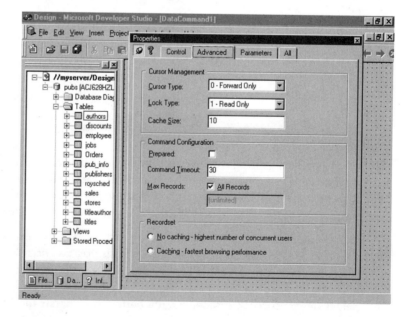

14

The Parameters Tab

The Parameters tab is specifically used with stored procedures. If you choose Stored Procedure for your Command Type on the Control property page, you can then input values for the parameters for the stored procedure, if necessary.

The All Tab

You can use this property page to view all of the properties for the Data Command design-time control. Figure 14.10 displays the properties for a sample Data Command control.

Figure 14.10.

Viewing all of the properties for the control.

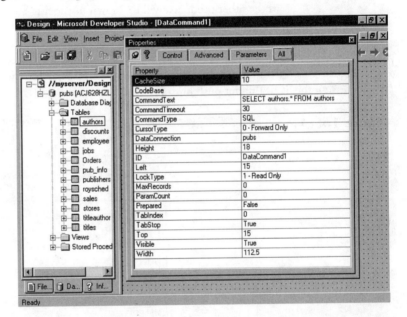

As you can see from Figure 14.10, this view is similar to the Properties dialog window for ActiveX controls. All of the properties are listed along with their values. This view maintains all of the values that are assigned on the individual property pages for the control. You can use the All tab to get a comprehensive view of the available properties and to assign their values at one time instead of tabbing through the individual pages.

Building an SQL Statement with the Query Designer

I stated that you could use the SQL Builder push button on the Control tab to construct an SQL statement for your Data Command design-time control. Remember, you must select

a Command Type of SQL to enable the SQL Builder push button. When you click the SQL
Builder push button, the Query Designer will, by default, be activated.

NOTE

> The Query Designer is automatically displayed if it's the sole SQL
> builder installed on your machine. You can use other commercially
> available SQL builders with this button. If another type of SQL builder
> is installed on your system, you will be presented with a list of the
> available SQL builders on your machine. The Query Designer, as well
> as the other products, will be shown in the list. You can then select a
> tool from the list and build your SQL statement.

Figure 14.11 demonstrates an example of choosing SQL for the Command Type and
pressing the SQL Builder push button.

Figure 14.11.

*Using the Query
Designer to build your
query.*

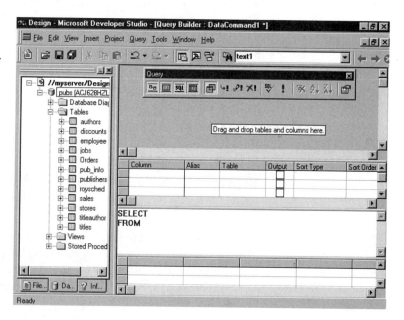

You can then use the Query Designer to construct your SQL statement. You learned how to
use the Query Designer and all of its panes on Day 9, "Using the Visual Data Tools for
Maximum Productivity." First, you need to drag and drop the tables that you want to use
into the Query Designer workspace. This example uses the Authors table, and uses the
Diagram pane to build an SQL query that selects all of the columns from the Authors table,
as shown in Figure 14.12.

14

Figure 14.12.

Constructing the SQL statement.

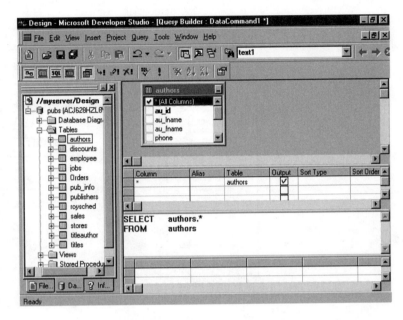

Once the query is built, you can save the query by selecting Save from the File menu. This option saves the query within the context of the Data Command control. In other words, you won't be prompted to provide a name for the query, as you were in the previous lesson when you were creating an independent query against the database. The Query Designer knows that you're creating this query for a database design-time control and saves the SQL statement in the Command Text for the Data Command control. When you close the Query Designer window, you should notice that the SQL statement that is built is displayed in the Command Text drop-down listbox on the Control property page, as shown in Figure 14.13.

NOTE

You can use all of the features of the Query Designer while building your SQL statement. You might want to test the results of your SQL statement before you save it, for example. You can execute the statement and view the results in the Results pane, just as you did during the lesson on Day 9. I will illustrate this process when I discuss the Data Range design-time controls.

14

Figure 14.13.

A newly created SQL statement.

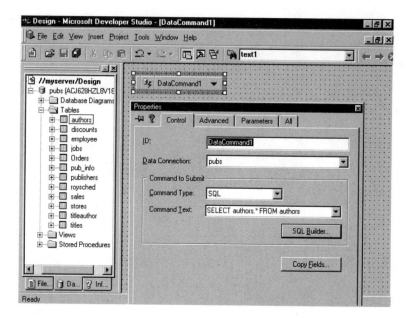

Examining the Results

Once you have finished setting the properties for the Data Command control, you can return to the ASP document to view the results. The <OBJECT> tag attributes as well as the runtime text are based on the properties that you define for the control. Listing 14.1 displays the code that was placed in the ASP file based on the previous example.

Listing 14.1. The ASP representation of the Data Command design-time control.

```
<!--METADATA TYPE="DesignerControl" startspan
<OBJECT ID="DataCommand1" WIDTH=151 HEIGHT=24
CLASSID="CLSID:7FAEED80-9D58-11CF-8F68-00AA006D27C2">
<PARAM NAME="_Version" VALUE="65536">
<PARAM NAME="_Version" VALUE="65536">
<PARAM NAME="_ExtentX" VALUE="3986">
<PARAM NAME="_ExtentY" VALUE="635">
<PARAM NAME="_StockProps" VALUE="0">
<PARAM NAME="DataConnection" VALUE="pubs">
<PARAM NAME="CommandText" VALUE="SELECT authors.* FROM authors">
</OBJECT>
-->
<%
Set pubs = Server.CreateObject("ADODB.Connection")
pubs.ConnectionTimeout = Session("pubs_ConnectionTimeout")
pubs.CommandTimeout = Session("pubs_CommandTimeout")
```

14

```
pubs.Open Session("pubs_ConnectionString"), Session("pubs_RuntimeUserName"),
Session("pubs_RuntimePassword")
Set cmdTemp = Server.CreateObject("ADODB.Command")
Set DataCommand1 = Server.CreateObject("ADODB.Recordset")
cmdTemp.CommandText = "SELECT authors.* FROM authors"
cmdTemp.CommandType = 1
Set cmdTemp.ActiveConnection = pubs
DataCommand1.Open cmdTemp, , 0, 1
%>
<!--METADATA TYPE="DesignerControl" endspan-->
```

In this listing, you can see both the object declaration and the runtime text. As stated before, the object declaration is enclosed in comments and won't be interpreted by the browser. The runtime text is the only item that will persist when the application is executed.

The first line of the runtime text creates a database connection object and stores the instance of this object in the pubs variable. The next line exhibits how the global.asa file and the ASP file that contains the database control work together to connect to the database. Using the pubs object that was created in the first line of this runtime text, the ConnectionTimeout and CommandTimeout properties are established, based on the database connection that was created for the project. The connection information can be found in the Session_OnStart procedure within the global.asa file. The information in the global.asa file stores general property information about the database connection. This information is used to help the ASP create the connection dynamically when it's needed. The ConnectionTimeout property defines the maximum length of time for the connection, while the CommandTimeout property specifies the maximum duration for execution of the SQL command.

Next, a session is opened for the pubs object, again, based on information contained in the Session_OnStart procedure in the global.asa file. The user name and password are used to connect to the database. The cmdTemp variable is used to create a Command object. This object is used later in the code to capture the SQL command to execute against the database. The DataCommand1 variable is used to create the Recordset object. After this object is created, the Recordset object is opened, using the SQL statement as a parameter. In this case, the CommandText object that is contained in the cmdTemp variable selects all of the columns from the Authors table.

The Data Range Controls

The Data Range Header and Footer controls provide two very robust design-time controls. These controls enable you to retrieve multiple records from a database. You can use the Data Range Header control to create the Recordset object and query and to begin retrieving rows from the database table. The Data Range Footer control works in conjunction with the Data Range Header control and enables you to page through the records in the database.

14

The Data Range Header Control

The process of inserting a Data Range Header design-time control is very similar to that of inserting the Data Command design-time control. Open the ASP file and right-click the mouse at the desired position for the control. Select Insert ActiveX Control from the shortcut menu and click the Design-time tab. Choose Data Range Header Control and click OK. The Object Editor activates, and the control and its property window are displayed as shown in Figure 14.14.

Figure 14.14.

The Data Range Header design-time control.

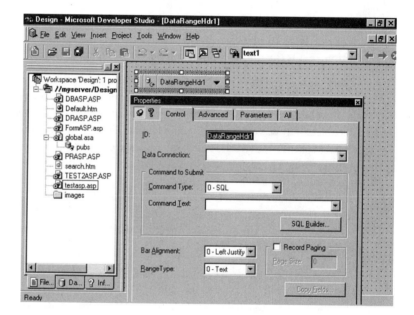

The fields in the top section of the Control property page are identical in meaning to the Data Command control.

There are some new fields that pertain to the Data Range Header control. The Bar Alignment enables you to align the database navigation bar on a web page. This bar provide navigation controls for the user to traverse the records in the database. The Range Type enables you to specify what type of fields will be used to display the data. You can specify either Text, Form, or Table format.

In the example pictured in Figure 14.14, I chose Text for the Range Type. The Record Paging checkbox and Page Size field are used together to define the number of rows that will be displayed on a page. If Record Paging is checked, you can indicate the number of rows that are displayed on your web page in the Page Size field. When the Page Size field is greater than zero, the navigation bar is also displayed on the page. If you don't select the Record Paging checkbox, all of the records for the query are displayed on one page.

NOTE To use Record Paging, you must set the Cursor Type on the Advanced property page to either Keyset or Static. These values are explained below.

The Advanced and Parameters property pages for the Data Range Header control contain the same fields as the Data Command control. Because the Data Range control pertains more to multiple rows of data, an explanation of the various cursor types is covered in this section. Table 14.2 explains the types of cursors that you can set using the Advanced property page.

Table 14.2. Available cursor types.

Type	Description
Forward Only	Enables you to move only to the next record
Keyset	Enables you to scroll through data in any direction; reflects up-to-date information concerning the database except for additions by new users
Dynamic	Enables you to scroll through data in any direction; reflects the most up-to-date information including additions by other users
Static	Enables you to scroll through data in any direction; contains a snapshot of the data at a certain point in time

As with the Data Command design-time control, you can use the Query Designer to build a query for the Data Range Header design-time control. After selecting Save from the File menu, you can view the design-time control within the ASP. For this example, I have chosen to build an SQL statement that selects the first and last name, phone number, and contract indicator from the Authors table. Listing 14.2 displays the Data Range Header design-time control within the context of an ASP.

14

Listing 14.2. The ASP representation of the Data Range Header design-time control.

```
<!--METADATA TYPE="DesignerControl" startspan
<OBJECT ID="DataRangeHdr1" WIDTH=151 HEIGHT=24
CLASSID="CLSID:F602E721-A281-11CF-A5B7-0080C73AAC7E">
<PARAM NAME="_Version" VALUE="65536">
<PARAM NAME="_Version" VALUE="65536">
<PARAM NAME="_ExtentX" VALUE="3986">
<PARAM NAME="_ExtentY" VALUE="635">
<PARAM NAME="_StockProps" VALUE="0">
<PARAM NAME="DataConnection" VALUE="pubs">
<PARAM NAME="CommandText" VALUE="SELECT au_fname, au_lname, phone, contract
FROM authors">
<PARAM NAME="CursorType" VALUE="1">
<PARAM NAME="PageSize" VALUE="10">
</OBJECT>
-->
<%
fHideNavBar = False
fHideNumber = False
fHideRequery = False
fHideRule = False
stQueryString = ""
fEmptyRecordset = False
fFirstPass = True
fNeedRecordset = False
fNoRecordset = False
tBarAlignment = "Left"
tHeaderName = "DataRangeHdr1"
tPageSize = 10
tPagingMove = ""
tRangeType = "Text"
tRecordsProcessed = 0
If Not IsEmpty(Request("DataRangeHdr1_PagingMove")) Then
tPagingMove = Trim(Request("DataRangeHdr1_PagingMove"))
End If
If IsEmpty(Session("DataRangeHdr1_Recordset")) Then
fNeedRecordset = True
Else
If Session("DataRangeHdr1_Recordset") Is Nothing Then
fNeedRecordset = True
Else
Set DataRangeHdr1 = Session("DataRangeHdr1_Recordset")
End If
End If
If fNeedRecordset Then
Set pubs = Server.CreateObject("ADODB.Connection")
pubs.ConnectionTimeout = Session("pubs_ConnectionTimeout")
pubs.CommandTimeout = Session("pubs_CommandTimeout")
pubs.Open Session("pubs_ConnectionString"), Session("pubs_RuntimeUserName"),
Session("pubs_RuntimePassword")
Set cmdTemp = Server.CreateObject("ADODB.Command")
```

14

```
Set DataRangeHdr1 = Server.CreateObject("ADODB.Recordset")
cmdTemp.CommandText = "SELECT au_fname, au_lname, phone, contract FROM authors"
cmdTemp.CommandType = 1
Set cmdTemp.ActiveConnection = pubs
DataRangeHdr1.Open cmdTemp, , 1, 1
End If
On Error Resume Next
If DataRangeHdr1.BOF And DataRangeHdr1.EOF Then fEmptyRecordset = True
On Error Goto 0
If Err Then fEmptyRecordset = True
DataRangeHdr1.PageSize = tPageSize
If Not IsEmpty(Session("DataRangeHdr1_Filter")) And Not fEmptyRecordset Then
DataRangeHdr1.Filter = Session("DataRangeHdr1_Filter")
If DataRangeHdr1.BOF And DataRangeHdr1.EOF Then fEmptyRecordset = True
End If
If IsEmpty(Session("DataRangeHdr1_PageSize")) Then Session("DataRangeHdr1_
PageSize") = tPageSize
If IsEmpty(Session("DataRangeHdr1_AbsolutePage")) Then Session("DataRangeHdr1_
AbsolutePage") = 1
If Session("DataRangeHdr1_PageSize") <> tPageSize Then
tCurRec = ((Session("DataRangeHdr1_AbsolutePage") - 1) * Session("DataRangeHdr1_
PageSize")) + 1
tNewPage = Int(tCurRec / tPageSize)
If tCurRec Mod tPageSize <> 0 Then
tNewPage = tNewPage + 1
End If
If tNewPage = 0 Then tNewPage = 1
Session("DataRangeHdr1_PageSize") = tPageSize
Session("DataRangeHdr1_AbsolutePage") = tNewPage
End If
If fEmptyRecordset Then
fHideNavBar = True
fHideRule = True
Else
Select Case tPagingMove
Case "Requery"
DataRangeHdr1.Requery
Case "<<"
Session("DataRangeHdr1_AbsolutePage") = 1
Case "<"
If Session("DataRangeHdr1_AbsolutePage") > 1 Then
Session("DataRangeHdr1_AbsolutePage") = Session
➥("DataRangeHdr1_AbsolutePage") - 1
End If
Case ">"
If Not DataRangeHdr1.EOF Then
Session("DataRangeHdr1_AbsolutePage") = Session
➥("DataRangeHdr1_AbsolutePage") + 1
End If
Case ">>"
Session("DataRangeHdr1_AbsolutePage") = DataRangeHdr1.PageCount
End Select
DataRangeHdr1.AbsolutePage = Session("DataRangeHdr1_AbsolutePage")
If DataRangeHdr1.EOF Then
```

continues

14

Listing 14.2. continued

```
Session("DataRangeHdr1_AbsolutePage") = Session
➥("DataRangeHdr1_AbsolutePage") - 1
DataRangeHdr1.AbsolutePage = Session("DataRangeHdr1_AbsolutePage")
End If
End If
Do
If fEmptyRecordset Then Exit Do
If tRecordsProcessed = tPageSize Then Exit Do
If Not fFirstPass Then
DataRangeHdr1.MoveNext
Else
fFirstPass = False
End If
If DataRangeHdr1.EOF Then Exit Do
tRecordsProcessed = tRecordsProcessed + 1
'WHERE IS THE REST OF THE DO LOOP???
%>
<!--METADATA TYPE="DesignerControl" endspan-->
```

As you can see, the Data Range Header control generated a plethora of code from just a few simple clicks of the mouse. I bet you can think of a million ways to spend the time that can be saved by using a visual control such as the Data Range Header control. The logic that is created basically creates the database connection and opens the Recordset object using the SQL statement that I constructed with the Query Designer. The other logic that is generated facilitates the ability to page through the database records.

I stated previously that the Data Range Header and Footer controls are used together. There is an error in Listing 14.2, because I haven't inserted the Data Range Footer control. Can you pick out the error? My comments within the code provide a significant visual aid to help you locate the error. The Data Range Footer design-time control must be inserted into the ASP to complete the logic for the Data Range Header design-time control.

The Data Range Footer Control

The process to insert the Data Range Footer design-time control is identical to the process for inserting the Data Range Header design-time control. Select the Data Range Footer Control from the list in the Insert ActiveX Control dialog window. The Data Range Footer control will be displayed in the Object Editor, as shown in Figure 14.15.

The property page for the Data Range Footer control contains one page that enables you to set all of the properties for the control at one time. After you set the properties, you can select Save from the File menu to save the control. You then can view the remnants of the Data Range Footer control within the ASP file. Listing 14.3 displays a more complete ASP file that includes the Data Range Footer design-time control.

Figure 14.15.

The Data Range Footer design-time control.

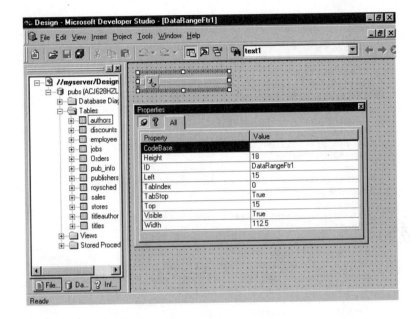

Listing 14.3. Completing the set.

```
<!--METADATA TYPE="DesignerControl" startspan
<OBJECT ID="DataRangeHdr1" WIDTH=151 HEIGHT=24
CLASSID="CLSID:F602E721-A281-11CF-A5B7-0080C73AAC7E">
<PARAM NAME="_Version" VALUE="65536">
<PARAM NAME="_Version" VALUE="65536">
<PARAM NAME="_ExtentX" VALUE="3986">
<PARAM NAME="_ExtentY" VALUE="635">
<PARAM NAME="_StockProps" VALUE="0">
<PARAM NAME="DataConnection" VALUE="pubs">
<PARAM NAME="CommandText" VALUE="SELECT au_fname, au_lname, phone, contract
FROM authors">
<PARAM NAME="CursorType" VALUE="1">
<PARAM NAME="PageSize" VALUE="10">
</OBJECT>
-->
<%
fHideNavBar = False
fHideNumber = False
fHideRequery = False
fHideRule = False
stQueryString = ""
fEmptyRecordset = False
fFirstPass = True
fNeedRecordset = False
fNoRecordset = False
tBarAlignment = "Left"
```

continues

14

Listing 14.3. continued

```
tHeaderName = "DataRangeHdr1"
tPageSize = 10
tPagingMove = ""
tRangeType = "Text"
tRecordsProcessed = 0
If Not IsEmpty(Request("DataRangeHdr1_PagingMove")) Then
tPagingMove = Trim(Request("DataRangeHdr1_PagingMove"))
End If
If IsEmpty(Session("DataRangeHdr1_Recordset")) Then
fNeedRecordset = True
Else
If Session("DataRangeHdr1_Recordset") Is Nothing Then
fNeedRecordset = True
Else
Set DataRangeHdr1 = Session("DataRangeHdr1_Recordset")
End If
End If
If fNeedRecordset Then
Set pubs = Server.CreateObject("ADODB.Connection")
pubs.ConnectionTimeout = Session("pubs_ConnectionTimeout")
pubs.CommandTimeout = Session("pubs_CommandTimeout")
pubs.Open Session("pubs_ConnectionString"), Session("pubs_RuntimeUserName"),
Session("pubs_RuntimePassword")
Set cmdTemp = Server.CreateObject("ADODB.Command")
Set DataRangeHdr1 = Server.CreateObject("ADODB.Recordset")
cmdTemp.CommandText = "SELECT au_fname, au_lname, phone, contract FROM authors"
cmdTemp.CommandType = 1
Set cmdTemp.ActiveConnection = pubs
DataRangeHdr1.Open cmdTemp, , 1, 1
End If
On Error Resume Next
If DataRangeHdr1.BOF And DataRangeHdr1.EOF Then fEmptyRecordset = True
On Error Goto 0
If Err Then fEmptyRecordset = True
DataRangeHdr1.PageSize = tPageSize
If Not IsEmpty(Session("DataRangeHdr1_Filter")) And Not fEmptyRecordset Then
DataRangeHdr1.Filter = Session("DataRangeHdr1_Filter")
If DataRangeHdr1.BOF And DataRangeHdr1.EOF Then fEmptyRecordset = True
End If
If IsEmpty(Session("DataRangeHdr1_PageSize")) Then Session("DataRangeHdr1_
PageSize") = tPageSize
If IsEmpty(Session("DataRangeHdr1_AbsolutePage")) Then Session("DataRangeHdr1_
AbsolutePage") = 1
If Session("DataRangeHdr1_PageSize") <> tPageSize Then
tCurRec = ((Session("DataRangeHdr1_AbsolutePage") - 1) * Session("DataRangeHdr1_
PageSize")) + 1
tNewPage = Int(tCurRec / tPageSize)
If tCurRec Mod tPageSize <> 0 Then
tNewPage = tNewPage + 1
End If
If tNewPage = 0 Then tNewPage = 1
Session("DataRangeHdr1_PageSize") = tPageSize
Session("DataRangeHdr1_AbsolutePage") = tNewPage
End If
```

```
If fEmptyRecordset Then
fHideNavBar = True
fHideRule = True
Else
Select Case tPagingMove
Case "Requery"
DataRangeHdr1.Requery
Case "<<"
Session("DataRangeHdr1_AbsolutePage") = 1
Case "<"
If Session("DataRangeHdr1_AbsolutePage") > 1 Then
Session("DataRangeHdr1_AbsolutePage") = Session
➥("DataRangeHdr1_AbsolutePage") - 1
End If
Case ">"
If Not DataRangeHdr1.EOF Then
Session("DataRangeHdr1_AbsolutePage") = Session
➥("DataRangeHdr1_AbsolutePage") + 1
End If
Case ">>"
Session("DataRangeHdr1_AbsolutePage") = DataRangeHdr1.PageCount
End Select
DataRangeHdr1.AbsolutePage = Session("DataRangeHdr1_AbsolutePage")
If DataRangeHdr1.EOF Then
Session("DataRangeHdr1_AbsolutePage") = Session
➥("DataRangeHdr1_AbsolutePage") - 1
DataRangeHdr1.AbsolutePage = Session("DataRangeHdr1_AbsolutePage")
End If
End If
Do
If fEmptyRecordset Then Exit Do
If tRecordsProcessed = tPageSize Then Exit Do
If Not fFirstPass Then
DataRangeHdr1.MoveNext
Else
fFirstPass = False
End If
If DataRangeHdr1.EOF Then Exit Do
tRecordsProcessed = tRecordsProcessed + 1
%>
<!--METADATA TYPE="DesignerControl" endspan-->
<!--METADATA TYPE="DesignerControl" startspan
<OBJECT ID="DataRangeFtr1" WIDTH=151 HEIGHT=24
CLASSID="CLSID:F602E722-A281-11CF-A5B7-0080C73AAC7E">
<PARAM NAME="_Version" VALUE="65536">
<PARAM NAME="_ExtentX" VALUE="3969">
<PARAM NAME="_ExtentY" VALUE="635">
<PARAM NAME="_StockProps" VALUE="0">
</OBJECT>
-->
<%
Loop
If tRangeType = "Table" Then Response.Write "</TABLE>"
If tPageSize > 0 Then
```

14

continues

Listing 14.3. continued

```
If Not fHideRule Then Response.Write "<HR>"
If Not fHideNavBar Then
%>
<TABLE WIDTH=100% >
<TR>
<TD WIDTH=100% >
<P ALIGN=<%= tBarAlignment %> >
<FORM ACTION="<%= Request.ServerVariables("PATH_INFO") & stQueryString %>"
METHOD="POST">
<INPUT TYPE="Submit" NAME="<%= tHeaderName & "_PagingMove" %>"
VALUE="   &lt;&lt;   ">
<INPUT TYPE="Submit" NAME="<%= tHeaderName & "_PagingMove" %>"
VALUE="   &lt;      ">
<INPUT TYPE="Submit" NAME="<%= tHeaderName & "_PagingMove" %>"
VALUE="   &gt;      ">
<INPUT TYPE="Submit" NAME="<%= tHeaderName & "_PagingMove" %>"
VALUE="   &gt;&gt;    ">
<% If Not fHideRequery Then %>
<INPUT TYPE="Submit" NAME="<% =tHeaderName & "_PagingMove" %>"
VALUE=" Requery ">
<% End If %>
</FORM>
</P>
</TD>
<TD VALIGN=MIDDLE ALIGN=RIGHT>
<FONT SIZE=2>
<%
If Not fHideNumber Then
If tPageSize > 1 Then
Response.Write "<NOBR>Page: " & Session(tHeaderName & "_AbsolutePage") &
"</NOBR>"
Else
Response.Write "<NOBR>Record: " & Session(tHeaderName & "_AbsolutePage") &
"</NOBR>"
End If
End If
%>
</FONT>
</TD>
</TR>
</TABLE>
<%
End If
End If
%>
<!--METADATA TYPE="DesignerControl" endspan-->
```

Notice that in this code example the Data Range Footer control nicely completes the Do Loop. The Data Range Footer control does a lot more, though, than simply add the word *Loop* to the end of the Do Loop. The Data Range Footer control adds complex logic to format the records with the database. Remember, I selected Text as the Range Type for the Data Range Header control. Based on this value, the Data Range Footer control builds the necessary code to format the data in a table. Also, the Data Range Footer control creates the logic for the user to traverse through the database records.

There is one thing left to do to make this code functional. So far, the structure has been developed to execute a query and display the results within a table. The code is useless for an application, because the fields haven't yet been inserted into the code. The following code sample can be inserted before the Data Range Header control in the ASP file to create column names for the table:

```
<TABLE WIDTH=100% BORDER=1>
<TR><TH>Name</TH><TH>Phone</TH></TR>
```

This code sample creates two table header columns for the name and phone number. To populate the rows of the table with the database information, you can insert the following lines of code between the Data Range Header and Footer controls in the ASP file:

```
<TR>
<TD> <%Response.Write DataRangeHdr1("au_fname") & " " &
DataRangeHdr1("au_lname") %> </TD>
<TD> <%Response.Write DataRangeHdr1("phone")%> </TD>
</TR>
```

This code sample formats the rows of the table with the names and phone numbers of the people found in the Authors table. In this example, the first name and the last name fields are concatenated together. Listing 14.4 displays the complete code listing for the Author Contact List web page.

Listing 14.4. The Author Contact List.

```
<%@ LANGUAGE="VBSCRIPT" %>
<HTML>
<HEAD>
<META NAME="GENERATOR" Content="Microsoft Visual InterDev 1.0">
<META HTTP-EQUIV="Content-Type" content="text/html; charset=iso-8859-1">
<TITLE>Contact List</TITLE>
<H3>Author Contact List</H3>
</HEAD>
<BODY>
<TABLE WIDTH=100% BORDER=1>
<TR><TH>Name</TH><TH>Phone</TH></TR>
<!--METADATA TYPE="DesignerControl" startspan
<OBJECT ID="DataRangeHdr1" WIDTH=151 HEIGHT=24
CLASSID="CLSID:F602E721-A281-11CF-A5B7-0080C73AAC7E">
<PARAM NAME="_Version" VALUE="65536">
<PARAM NAME="_Version" VALUE="65536">
```

continues

14

Listing 14.4. continued

```
<PARAM NAME="_ExtentX" VALUE="3986">
<PARAM NAME="_ExtentY" VALUE="635">
<PARAM NAME="_StockProps" VALUE="0">
<PARAM NAME="DataConnection" VALUE="pubs">
<PARAM NAME="CommandText" VALUE="SELECT au_fname, au_lname, phone, contract
FROM authors">
<PARAM NAME="CursorType" VALUE="1">
<PARAM NAME="PageSize" VALUE="10">
</OBJECT>
-->
<%
fHideNavBar = False
fHideNumber = False
fHideRequery = False
fHideRule = False
stQueryString = ""
fEmptyRecordset = False
fFirstPass = True
fNeedRecordset = False
fNoRecordset = False
tBarAlignment = "Left"
tHeaderName = "DataRangeHdr1"
tPageSize = 10
tPagingMove = ""
tRangeType = "Text"
tRecordsProcessed = 0
If Not IsEmpty(Request("DataRangeHdr1_PagingMove")) Then
tPagingMove = Trim(Request("DataRangeHdr1_PagingMove"))
End If
If IsEmpty(Session("DataRangeHdr1_Recordset")) Then
fNeedRecordset = True
Else
If Session("DataRangeHdr1_Recordset") Is Nothing Then
fNeedRecordset = True
Else
Set DataRangeHdr1 = Session("DataRangeHdr1_Recordset")
End If
End If
If fNeedRecordset Then
Set pubs = Server.CreateObject("ADODB.Connection")
pubs.ConnectionTimeout = Session("pubs_ConnectionTimeout")
pubs.CommandTimeout = Session("pubs_CommandTimeout")
pubs.Open Session("pubs_ConnectionString"), Session("pubs_RuntimeUserName"),
Session("pubs_RuntimePassword")
Set cmdTemp = Server.CreateObject("ADODB.Command")
Set DataRangeHdr1 = Server.CreateObject("ADODB.Recordset")
cmdTemp.CommandText = "SELECT au_fname, au_lname, phone, contract FROM authors"
cmdTemp.CommandType = 1
Set cmdTemp.ActiveConnection = pubs
DataRangeHdr1.Open cmdTemp, , 1, 1
End If
```

```
On Error Resume Next
If DataRangeHdr1.BOF And DataRangeHdr1.EOF Then fEmptyRecordset = True
On Error Goto 0
If Err Then fEmptyRecordset = True
DataRangeHdr1.PageSize = tPageSize
If Not IsEmpty(Session("DataRangeHdr1_Filter")) And Not fEmptyRecordset Then
DataRangeHdr1.Filter = Session("DataRangeHdr1_Filter")
If DataRangeHdr1.BOF And DataRangeHdr1.EOF Then fEmptyRecordset = True
End If
If IsEmpty(Session("DataRangeHdr1_PageSize")) Then Session("DataRangeHdr1_
PageSize") = tPageSize
If IsEmpty(Session("DataRangeHdr1_AbsolutePage")) Then Session("DataRangeHdr1_
AbsolutePage") = 1
If Session("DataRangeHdr1_PageSize") <> tPageSize Then
tCurRec = ((Session("DataRangeHdr1_AbsolutePage") - 1) * Session("DataRangeHdr1_
PageSize")) + 1
tNewPage = Int(tCurRec / tPageSize)
If tCurRec Mod tPageSize <> 0 Then
tNewPage = tNewPage + 1
End If
If tNewPage = 0 Then tNewPage = 1
Session("DataRangeHdr1_PageSize") = tPageSize
Session("DataRangeHdr1_AbsolutePage") = tNewPage
End If
If fEmptyRecordset Then
fHideNavBar = True
fHideRule = True
Else
Select Case tPagingMove
Case "Requery"
DataRangeHdr1.Requery
Case "<<"
Session("DataRangeHdr1_AbsolutePage") = 1
Case "<"
If Session("DataRangeHdr1_AbsolutePage") > 1 Then
Session("DataRangeHdr1_AbsolutePage") = Session
➥("DataRangeHdr1_AbsolutePage") - 1
End If
Case ">"
If Not DataRangeHdr1.EOF Then
Session("DataRangeHdr1_AbsolutePage") = Session
➥("DataRangeHdr1_AbsolutePage") + 1
End If
Case ">>"
Session("DataRangeHdr1_AbsolutePage") = DataRangeHdr1.PageCount
End Select
DataRangeHdr1.AbsolutePage = Session("DataRangeHdr1_AbsolutePage")
If DataRangeHdr1.EOF Then
Session("DataRangeHdr1_AbsolutePage") = Session
➥("DataRangeHdr1_AbsolutePage") - 1
DataRangeHdr1.AbsolutePage = Session("DataRangeHdr1_AbsolutePage")
End If
End If
```

continues

14

Listing 14.4. continued

```
Do
If fEmptyRecordset Then Exit Do
If tRecordsProcessed = tPageSize Then Exit Do
If Not fFirstPass Then
DataRangeHdr1.MoveNext
Else
fFirstPass = False
End If
If DataRangeHdr1.EOF Then Exit Do
tRecordsProcessed = tRecordsProcessed + 1
%>
<!--METADATA TYPE="DesignerControl" endspan-->
<TR>
<TD> <%Response.Write DataRangeHdr1("au_fname") & " " &
DataRangeHdr1("au_lname") %> </TD>
<TD> <%Response.Write DataRangeHdr1("phone")%> </TD>
</TR>
<!--METADATA TYPE="DesignerControl" startspan
<OBJECT ID="DataRangeFtr1" WIDTH=151 HEIGHT=24
CLASSID="CLSID:F602E722-A281-11CF-A5B7-0080C73AAC7E">
<PARAM NAME="_Version" VALUE="65536">
<PARAM NAME="_ExtentX" VALUE="3969">
<PARAM NAME="_ExtentY" VALUE="635">
<PARAM NAME="_StockProps" VALUE="0">
</OBJECT>
-->
<%
Loop
If tRangeType = "Table" Then Response.Write "</TABLE>"
If tPageSize > 0 Then
If Not fHideRule Then Response.Write "<HR>"
If Not fHideNavBar Then
%>
<TABLE WIDTH=100% >
<TR>
<TD WIDTH=100% >
<P ALIGN=<%= tBarAlignment %> >
<FORM ACTION="<%= Request.ServerVariables("PATH_INFO") & stQueryString %>"
METHOD="POST">
<INPUT TYPE="Submit" NAME="<%= tHeaderName & "_PagingMove" %>"
VALUE="   &lt;&lt;   ">
<INPUT TYPE="Submit" NAME="<%= tHeaderName & "_PagingMove" %>"
VALUE="   &lt;      ">
<INPUT TYPE="Submit" NAME="<%= tHeaderName & "_PagingMove" %>"
VALUE="    &gt;    ">
<INPUT TYPE="Submit" NAME="<%= tHeaderName & "_PagingMove" %>"
VALUE="   &gt;&gt;   ">
<% If Not fHideRequery Then %>
<INPUT TYPE="Submit" NAME="<% =tHeaderName & "_PagingMove" %>"
VALUE=" Requery ">
<% End If %>
</FORM>
</P>
</TD>
```

14

```
<TD VALIGN=MIDDLE ALIGN=RIGHT>
<FONT SIZE=2>
<%
If Not fHideNumber Then
If tPageSize > 1 Then
Response.Write "<NOBR>Page: " & Session(tHeaderName & "_AbsolutePage") &
"</NOBR>"
Else
Response.Write "<NOBR>Record: " & Session(tHeaderName & "_AbsolutePage") &
"</NOBR>"
End If
End If
%>
</FONT>
</TD>
</TR>
</TABLE>
<%
End If
End If
%>
<!--METADATA TYPE="DesignerControl" endspan-->
</BODY>
</HTML>
```

Figure 14.16 depicts the web page that is created from this code example.

Figure 14.16.

Viewing the authors.

The web page displays a table which contains a list of authors and their phone numbers. You can use the database navigation bar at the bottom of the page to traverse the database records. From this example, I think you can understand the functions of the Data Range Header and Data Range Footer controls. Basically, the Data Range Header control opens the database connection and executes the initial SQL statement.

The Data Range Footer control completes the Data Range Header logic and processes additional records through the use of the navigation bar. These controls are somewhat analogous to a header and footer that you design for your web pages. In Listing 14.4, you learned how to display the database information by inserting the logic to populate the table between the Data Range Header and Footer controls. Similarly, you design a web page to display the main content within the body of the document. In both of these cases, the header and footer provide necessary logic and structure to properly format the data.

Using the Data Range Builder

Now that you have learned how to individually insert the Data Range Header and Footer controls, I bet you would like to discover an easier way to place these controls in your web pages. Visual InterDev, again, lives up to its name by providing a visual wizard to construct and insert both the Data Range Header and Footer controls into your web page document. The Data Range Builder is a special type of wizard called an HTML Builder. You can use HTML Builder to combine HTML and design-time controls or to create pairs of design-time controls.

You can use the Data Range Builder to create a Data Range Header and Data Range Footer control. Open the ASP file and right-click the mouse to display the shortcut menu. Select Insert HTML Using Wizard, as shown in Figure 14.17.

After you select this menu item, the Choose Builder dialog window is displayed. Select the Data Range Wizard from the list. The Data Range Builder Wizard displays, as shown in Figure 14.18.

The Data Range Builder Wizard guides you through the process of creating the Data Range Header and Footer controls. The first window enables you to select how many records to display. You can choose to display all of the records on one page, or you can specify the number of records to display per page. This window also enables you to designate the alignment of the database navigation bar. After you complete your selections, click the Next button to advance to the next window. The second window of the wizard enables you to choose a name for your data range. Figure 14.19 shows the layout of this window.

Figure 14.17.

Selecting Insert HTML Using Wizard.

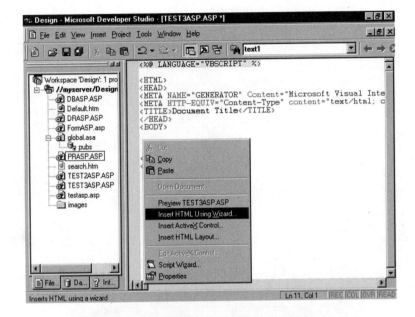

Figure 14.18.

Specifying the display options.

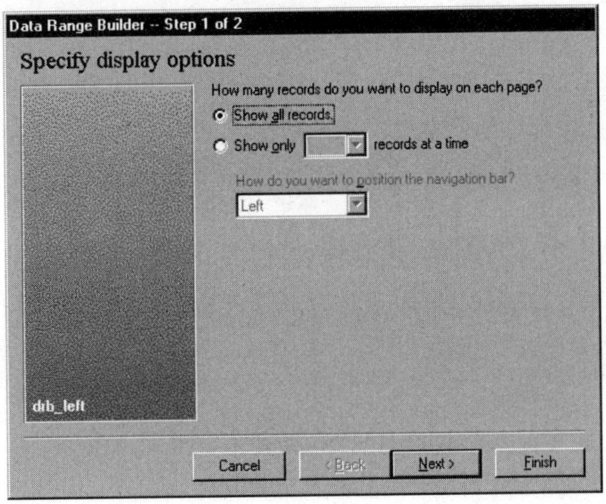

Figure 14.19.

Naming the data range.

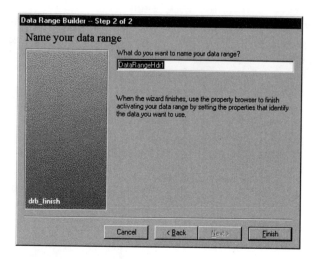

After you click Finish, the Object Editor activates, enabling you to further customize the properties of the Data Range Header control. You can choose the data connection and use the Query Designer to construct your SQL statement. Once you complete this process and close the Object Editor, the Data Range Header and Footer controls are displayed in your ASP file. The Data Range Builder provides a very intuitive and straightforward approach for creating the Data Range Header and Data Range Footer controls.

Integrating Design-Time Controls into Your Application

So far, you have learned how to use the Data Command, Data Range Header, and Data Range Footer design-time controls. The lesson has presented several examples of how to use these controls within your application. In the sections on the Data Range Header and Footer controls, you learned how to format a table with database information. This section explores another use of these controls to create a display form for your data.

Exploring Other Uses of Design-Time Controls

I am going to use the same example that was covered in the previous section and show you how a few minor changes can affect the application that you create. Using a new ASP file, I will cover how to create a Data Range Header and Footer again. Refer to the previous sections on this topic for a refresher. This example starts at the point of defining the Data Range Header control using the Object Editor.

In Listing 14.4, the application displayed the data in a table. I designed this functionality by choosing Text as the Range Type. Other available values include Form and Table. You can pick Form for the Range Type to display data within a form on your web page. Also, for form data, you should choose to display only one record at a time. You can select Record Paging and enter the value of 1 for the Page Size. Remember, you must set the Cursor Type on the Advanced property page to either Keyset or Static to be able to enter a value for the Page Size. Figure 14.20 displays these choices for the Data Range Header control as it appears in the Object Editor.

Figure 14.20.

Setting the control properties.

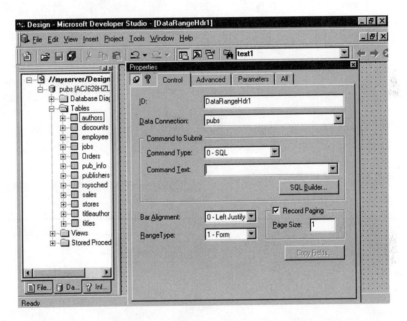

Next, you need to build a query for the control. I have chosen to build a query that selects the first name, last name, address, city, state, and ZIP code for all rows contained in the Authors table. Figure 14.21 displays this query on the Control property page.

The final task that needs to be completed is to copy the fields to the clipboard. You can click the Copy Fields push button and select the fields that you want to copy. These fields are inserted later into the ASP file to enable you to display the database information on the form. Figure 14.22 displays the fields to be inserted into the ASP file.

14

Figure 14.21.
Displaying the query for the control.

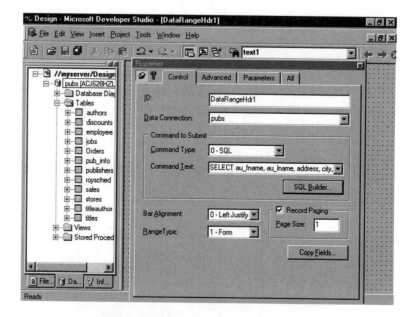

Figure 14.22.
Copying the fields.

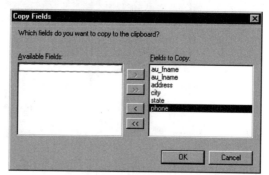

After you close the Object Editor, the Data Range Header design-time control is displayed in the ASP file. You then can create the Data Range Footer design-time control. The final step is to paste the copied fields in your ASP file between the Data Range Header and Data Range Footer controls. Listing 14.5 displays the resulting ASP file that is created from the previous steps.

Listing 14.5. The Author Contact display form.

```
<%@ LANGUAGE="VBSCRIPT" %>
<HTML>
<HEAD>
```

```
<META NAME="GENERATOR" Content="Microsoft Visual InterDev 1.0">
<META HTTP-EQUIV="Content-Type" content="text/html; charset=iso-8859-1">
<TITLE>Author Form</TITLE>
<H3>Author Contact Display Form</H3>
</HEAD>
<BODY>
<!--METADATA TYPE="DesignerControl" startspan
<OBJECT ID="DataRangeHdr1" WIDTH=151 HEIGHT=24
CLASSID="CLSID:F602E721-A281-11CF-A5B7-0080C73AAC7E">
<PARAM NAME="_Version" VALUE="65536">
<PARAM NAME="_Version" VALUE="65536">
<PARAM NAME="_ExtentX" VALUE="3986">
<PARAM NAME="_ExtentY" VALUE="635">
<PARAM NAME="_StockProps" VALUE="0">
<PARAM NAME="DataConnection" VALUE="pubs">
<PARAM NAME="CommandText" VALUE="SELECT au_fname, au_lname, phone, address,
city, state, zip FROM authors">
<PARAM NAME="CursorType" VALUE="1">
<PARAM NAME="RangeType" VALUE="1">
<PARAM NAME="PageSize" VALUE="1">
</OBJECT>
-->
<%
fHideNavBar = False
fHideNumber = False
fHideRequery = False
fHideRule = False
stQueryString = ""
fEmptyRecordset = False
fFirstPass = True
fNeedRecordset = False
fNoRecordset = False
tBarAlignment = "Left"
tHeaderName = "DataRangeHdr1"
tPageSize = 1
tPagingMove = ""
tRangeType = "Form"
tRecordsProcessed = 0

If Not IsEmpty(Request("DataRangeHdr1_PagingMove")) Then
tPagingMove = Trim(Request("DataRangeHdr1_PagingMove"))
End If
If IsEmpty(Session("DataRangeHdr1_Recordset")) Then
fNeedRecordset = True
Else
If Session("DataRangeHdr1_Recordset") Is Nothing Then
fNeedRecordset = True
Else
Set DataRangeHdr1 = Session("DataRangeHdr1_Recordset")
End If
End If
If fNeedRecordset Then
Set pubs = Server.CreateObject("ADODB.Connection")
pubs.ConnectionTimeout = Session("pubs_ConnectionTimeout")
```

continues

14

Listing 14.5. continued

```
pubs.CommandTimeout = Session("pubs_CommandTimeout")
pubs.Open Session("pubs_ConnectionString"), Session("pubs_RuntimeUserName"),
Session("pubs_RuntimePassword")
Set cmdTemp = Server.CreateObject("ADODB.Command")
Set DataRangeHdr1 = Server.CreateObject("ADODB.Recordset")
cmdTemp.CommandText = "SELECT au_fname, au_lname, phone, address, city, state,
zip FROM authors"
cmdTemp.CommandType = 1
Set cmdTemp.ActiveConnection = pubs
DataRangeHdr1.Open cmdTemp, , 1, 1
End If
On Error Resume Next
If DataRangeHdr1.BOF And DataRangeHdr1.EOF Then fEmptyRecordset = True
On Error Goto 0
If Err Then fEmptyRecordset = True
DataRangeHdr1.PageSize = tPageSize
If Not IsEmpty(Session("DataRangeHdr1_Filter")) And Not fEmptyRecordset Then
DataRangeHdr1.Filter = Session("DataRangeHdr1_Filter")
If DataRangeHdr1.BOF And DataRangeHdr1.EOF Then fEmptyRecordset = True
End If
If IsEmpty(Session("DataRangeHdr1_PageSize")) Then Session("DataRangeHdr1_
PageSize") = tPageSize
If IsEmpty(Session("DataRangeHdr1_AbsolutePage")) Then Session("DataRangeHdr1_
AbsolutePage") = 1
If Session("DataRangeHdr1_PageSize") <> tPageSize Then
tCurRec = ((Session("DataRangeHdr1_AbsolutePage") - 1) * Session("DataRangeHdr1_
PageSize")) + 1
tNewPage = Int(tCurRec / tPageSize)
If tCurRec Mod tPageSize <> 0 Then
tNewPage = tNewPage + 1
End If
If tNewPage = 0 Then tNewPage = 1
Session("DataRangeHdr1_PageSize") = tPageSize
Session("DataRangeHdr1_AbsolutePage") = tNewPage
End If
If fEmptyRecordset Then
fHideNavBar = True
fHideRule = True
Else
Select Case tPagingMove
Case "Requery"
DataRangeHdr1.Requery
Case "<<"
Session("DataRangeHdr1_AbsolutePage") = 1
Case "<"
If Session("DataRangeHdr1_AbsolutePage") > 1 Then
Session("DataRangeHdr1_AbsolutePage") = Session
➥("DataRangeHdr1_AbsolutePage") - 1
End If
Case ">"
If Not DataRangeHdr1.EOF Then
Session("DataRangeHdr1_AbsolutePage") = Session
➥("DataRangeHdr1_AbsolutePage") + 1
End If
```

```
Case ">>"
Session("DataRangeHdr1_AbsolutePage") = DataRangeHdr1.PageCount
End Select
DataRangeHdr1.AbsolutePage = Session("DataRangeHdr1_AbsolutePage")
If DataRangeHdr1.EOF Then
Session("DataRangeHdr1_AbsolutePage") = Session
➥("DataRangeHdr1_AbsolutePage") - 1
DataRangeHdr1.AbsolutePage = Session("DataRangeHdr1_AbsolutePage")
End If
End If
Do
If fEmptyRecordset Then Exit Do
If tRecordsProcessed = tPageSize Then Exit Do
If Not fFirstPass Then
DataRangeHdr1.MoveNext
Else
fFirstPass = False
End If
If DataRangeHdr1.EOF Then Exit Do
tRecordsProcessed = tRecordsProcessed + 1
%>
<!--METADATA TYPE="DesignerControl" endspan-->
<INPUT TYPE="Text" SIZE=25 MAXLENGTH=20 NAME=au_fname
VALUE="<%= DataRangeHdr1("au_fname") %>"><br>
<INPUT TYPE="Text" SIZE=25 MAXLENGTH=40 NAME=au_lname
VALUE="<%= DataRangeHdr1("au_lname") %>"><br>
<INPUT TYPE="Text" SIZE=25 MAXLENGTH=40 NAME=address
VALUE="<%= DataRangeHdr1("address") %>"><br>
<INPUT TYPE="Text" SIZE=25 MAXLENGTH=20 NAME=city
VALUE="<%= DataRangeHdr1("city") %>"><br>
<INPUT TYPE="Text" SIZE=25 MAXLENGTH=2 NAME=state
VALUE="<%= DataRangeHdr1("state") %>"><br>
<INPUT TYPE="Text" SIZE=25 MAXLENGTH=5 NAME=zip
VALUE="<%= DataRangeHdr1("zip") %>"><br>
<INPUT TYPE="Text" SIZE=25 MAXLENGTH=12 NAME=phone
VALUE="<%= DataRangeHdr1("phone") %>"><br>
<!--METADATA TYPE="DesignerControl" startspan
<OBJECT ID="DataRangeFtr1" WIDTH=151 HEIGHT=24
CLASSID="CLSID:F602E722-A281-11CF-A5B7-0080C73AAC7E">
<PARAM NAME="_Version" VALUE="65536">
<PARAM NAME="_ExtentX" VALUE="3969">
<PARAM NAME="_ExtentY" VALUE="635">
<PARAM NAME="_StockProps" VALUE="0">
</OBJECT>
-->
<%
Loop
If tRangeType = "Table" Then Response.Write "</TABLE>"
If tPageSize > 0 Then
If Not fHideRule Then Response.Write "<HR>"
If Not fHideNavBar Then
%>
<TABLE WIDTH=100% >
<TR>
```

14

continues

Listing 14.5. continued

```
<TD WIDTH=100% >
<P ALIGN=<%= tBarAlignment %> >
<FORM ACTION="<%= Request.ServerVariables("PATH_INFO") &
stQueryString %>" METHOD="POST">
<INPUT TYPE="Submit" NAME="<%= tHeaderName & "_PagingMove" %>"
VALUE="    &lt;&lt;    ">
<INPUT TYPE="Submit" NAME="<%= tHeaderName & "_PagingMove" %>"
VALUE="    &lt;      ">
<INPUT TYPE="Submit" NAME="<%= tHeaderName & "_PagingMove" %>"
VALUE="    &gt;      ">
<INPUT TYPE="Submit" NAME="<%= tHeaderName & "_PagingMove" %>"
VALUE="    &gt;&gt;    ">
<% If Not fHideRequery Then %>
<INPUT TYPE="Submit" NAME="<% =tHeaderName & "_PagingMove" %>"
VALUE=" Requery ">
<% End If %>
</FORM>
</P>
</TD>
<TD VALIGN=MIDDLE ALIGN=RIGHT>
<FONT SIZE=2>
<%
If Not fHideNumber Then
If tPageSize > 1 Then
Response.Write "<NOBR>Page: " & Session(tHeaderName & "_AbsolutePage") &
"</NOBR>"
Else
Response.Write "<NOBR>Record: " & Session(tHeaderName & "_AbsolutePage") &
"</NOBR>"
End If
End If
%>
</FONT>
</TD>
</TR>
</TABLE>
<%
End If
End If
%>
<!--METADATA TYPE="DesignerControl" endspan-->
</BODY>
</HTML>
```

Notice that the fields that are copied into the ASP file use the <INPUT> tags to create the display fields for the database information. The Data Range Header design-time control handles this formatting for you based on the Range Type that you select. This feature saves you precious development time. Figure 14.23 displays the form that is created from Listing 14.5.

Figure 14.23.

Displaying a form.

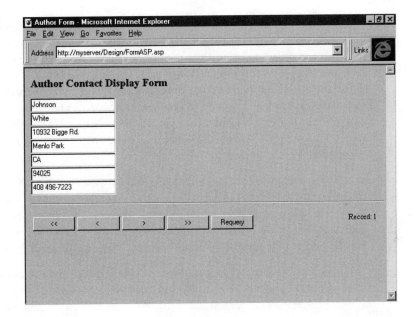

You could enhance the look of the form by adding additional line breaks or moving the fields around on the form. Listing 14.5, as well as the previous listings, demonstrates how you can rapidly build an application that interacts with your database information. Through the use of design-time controls, Visual InterDev takes care of the routine programming. The time that you save can be spent on enhancing the design of the web page and fine-tuning the programming logic.

Summary

Today's lesson has introduced you to the exciting new world of design-time controls. These new controls combine raw power with ease-of-use to become a true friend of the developer. Design-time controls can truly augment your productivity. You can use design-time controls to provide rich and robust functionality in your application while reducing the overhead costs of your application.

In today's lesson you first learned the definition of a design-time control. You should now be able to describe the basic concept of a design-time control, and be able to distinguish between a Design-time ActiveX control and a regular ActiveX control.

14

The lesson provided you with an overview of the origins of design-time controls and described some common functions of these controls. The lesson then guided you through the process of inserting a design-time control into your web pages. You learned about three specific design-time controls that are included with Visual InterDev. First, you learned how to use the Data Command design-time control. The lesson explained each of the property pages for this control and how to set these properties. The lesson also taught you about common uses of this control. Next, you learned about the Data Range Header and Data Range Footer controls. You discovered how these two controls complement and complete each other.

You also learned how the Query Designer can be used with all of the database design-time controls. Toward the end of the day, the lesson explained how to use the Data Range Builder Wizard. You can use this wizard to easily insert pairs of design-time controls into your web page documents at one time. The final lesson for the day focused on using the Data Range Header and Footer controls to create a display form for your database information.

You have just completed the second week of your Visual InterDev training. How do you feel so far about the product? Hopefully, the first two weeks have given you a good overall look at using the features of Visual InterDev. You should now possess a solid foundation with which to build robust applications with Visual InterDev. The final week teaches you some additional advanced concepts that you can use to build your applications.

Q&A

Q Can I build my own custom design-time controls?

A Yes. In fact, you will learn how to build a design-time control on Day 16, "Building Design-Time ActiveX Controls."

Q How does the design-time control hide its object instantiation at run-time?

A A design-time control is created at the time of design, using the <OBJECT> tags. These tags primarily exist to enable you to edit the properties for the control using the visual Object Editor. The <OBJECT> tags are enclosed in comments, however, which prevents the browser from viewing or recognizing the object. For this reason, the object is never instantiated at runtime.

Q If the object is never instantiated, how does the design-time control accomplish its functionality?

A The properties that you define for the design-time control generate runtime code, which persists when the application is run. This code can be a combination of both

HTML and scripting code and represents all of the logic for the design-time control. When the user runs the application, this code is recognized and executed, thereby providing the functionality of the design-time control.

Workshop

I want you to extend the examples that were provided in today's lesson. The goal is to gain extra practice using design-time controls within your application. Using the table example and the display form, develop an application that integrates the two forms. You also should develop additional functionality that enables you to submit updates and additions of new authors to the database. Draw on all of the knowledge that you have gained in the first two weeks to complete this workshop. If you aren't using MS SQL Server as your database, you can still plug in your specific database and apply the concepts to build an application.

Quiz

1. What is the difference between Design-time and regular ActiveX controls?
2. Explain the difference between the Data Command and the Data Range controls.
3. Which feature enables you to easily format the values of the database fields into a web page document?
4. Name the three types of data ranges that can be created for a Data Range Header design-time control.

Quiz Answers

1. A design-time control is a special type of ActiveX control that provides code that persists and executes at runtime without incurring the overhead of a control object at runtime. Regular ActiveX controls exist both at design-time as well as at runtime. ActiveX controls are typically used to construct a user interface for your application. An ActiveX control object is instantiated at runtime.
2. The Data Command design-time control enables you to create a database connection and a Recordset object which you can use to query the database. The Data Command control is typically used for selecting and updating one database row at a time. The Data Range design-time controls are similar to the Data Command control in that they also create a database connection and Recordset object. The

14

Data Range controls differ in that they typically are used for publishing and modifying multiple rows of data. The Data Range controls enable you to traverse through multiple records in the database.

3. You can use the Copy Fields dialog window to select database fields to insert into the web page document. This feature enables you to display the information contained in your database.

4. The three Range Types for the Data Range Header design-time control include:

Text

Form

Table

WEEK 2

In Review

You have now completed the second week toward your goal of learning Visual InterDev. During the first week, you learned how to use Visual InterDev to build the client portion of your application. This second week provided you with the knowledge to perfect the server side of the application equation. The lessons taught you how to integrate both the client and the server to build a better Web-based application. You now have a good handle on all of the components that you can use to create the killer app! You also understand how Visual InterDev provides the tools for completing the client and the server side of the application equation.

Where You Have Been

Much of this second week has focused on database integration. At the beginning of the week, you learned how to use Visual InterDev to communicate with a database. Next, you discovered the Visual Data Tools included with Visual InterDev. The lessons focused on how to develop a closer relationship with your database through the use of these tools. You learned how each of the Visual Data Tools combine pure power with ease of use. The topic of managing your database components also was covered during the second week. This lesson taught you how to use the Database Designer to manage and create components within your database.

After spending several lessons covering database integration, the second week switched gears to focus on other advanced topics. You received an in-depth lesson about integrating Active Server Pages within your application. The next two days focused on objects and controls that you can use to construct the user interface for your application. First, you learned about HTML controls and forms. Next, you learned about advanced objects, including Java applets and ActiveX controls. The final day of the second week taught you how to use the power of design-time controls to meet the needs of your application. You discovered how these exciting new controls can make your development life easier.

WEEK 3

At a Glance

During the first two weeks, you gained a better understanding of how Visual InterDev enables you to build Web-based applications. The third and final week covers some advanced topics and considerations concerning your applications. This week provides you with the knowledge that you need to put the finishing touches on your applications. The culmination of this week is an in-depth case study that will enable you to develop a Web-based application. You will be provided with a chance to demonstrate the knowledge that you have gained about Visual InterDev and the supporting technologies through the use of this book.

15

16

17

18

19

20

21

Where You Are Going

The first part of the week resumes the discussion about ActiveX controls. This lesson teaches you how to truly integrate ActiveX controls within your application. You then are taught how to build a design-time control using the Visual Basic Control Creation Edition. You also will learn how to integrate robust Active Server Components into your application mix. During the middle part of the week, you will receive an overview of how to use Visual InterDev to manage your web site files. You also will gain an understanding of how to handle team application development issues. Visual InterDev can be integrated with source code control products such as Visual SourceSafe to facilitate effective team development. You also will receive an overview of how to debug your Web-based application. The climax of the week is the final day. During this exciting day, you will test how much knowledge you have retained by developing a comprehensive application that uses all of the concepts you have learned.

Day **15**

Integrating Objects into Your Applications

The first day of the third week begins with a lesson packed with information and hands-on development. On Day 13, "Interacting with Objects and ActiveX Controls," you got an in-depth overview of objects and controls. Today's lesson continues with that topic and teaches you how to apply the concepts you learned on Day 13.

Java applets and ActiveX controls are two of the most exciting and popular object types on the Internet market today. You can use Java applets to extend your application's functionality, and you can either use pre-defined Java applets or build your own custom applets. With ActiveX controls, you can improve your application's appearance and performance and make user interaction and communication much easier. This lesson covers both Java and ActiveX objects and demonstrates how to integrate Java applets and ActiveX controls into your applications. After today's lesson, you should understand how to take advantage of the power and capabilities of these objects.

First, the lesson compares the strengths, benefits, weaknesses, and differences of Java applets and ActiveX controls. You should get a feel for when and why to use each object. The next two sections demonstrate how to insert Java applets and ActiveX controls into your applications. Most of today's lesson is focused on ActiveX controls and VBScript examples, but the concepts apply to Java applets, too. You learn how to manipulate the properties and methods of ActiveX controls to affect their behavior. The final lesson for the day explains how the Visual InterDev Script Wizard can make your development efforts easier. You can use the Script Wizard to easily incorporate scripting logic into your application and extend the functionality of your objects and controls.

By the third week of this book, you're probably recognizing a pattern to these lessons. Each lesson is designed to teach you the hard way to perform some task. After you persevere and learn the nuts and bolts of the process, the lesson teaches you an easier way to get the task done by using a key Visual InterDev feature. That doesn't mean you can take the easy road and immediately skip to the end of the lesson. In my experience, it's better to understand the inner workings of something before you move on to a more simplified approach. Using that training approach in this book helps you understand and appreciate what the Visual InterDev feature does behind the scenes. You will then have the knowledge you need to customize and extend the feature.

ActiveX Versus Java

The title of this section began gracing the covers of many magazines during 1996. The Internet community has also been engaged in this discussion. On the one hand, you have a faction who thinks of Microsoft as the evil empire, referring to ActiveX as "CaptiveX" because it supposedly imprisons people in the "Wintel" dungeon. There is another group who denies these accusations and speaks of Java with demeaning names, such as "ReactiveX." This community of dissenters feels that Sun Microsystems is trying to revise Java as a reaction to the power of ActiveX technology.

I imagine the debate will continue over the next few years, and the battle won't stop until some writer declares victory. Who wins in this relentless pursuit for the prize? Actually, it's the developer. Although pitting these technologies against each other makes for nice headlines and supplies topics for water cooler debates, you will probably use both of these technologies to develop your Web-based application. Both Java applets and ActiveX controls have a place and purpose in your application. Each technology offers important benefits that I'll highlight in today's lesson.

15

15

Exploring the Qualities of ActiveX

ActiveX controls, which enable you to construct interactive Web-based applications, have two main strengths. First, there are many different types of ActiveX controls that give you unique, effective ways to distribute and gather information from the user. These controls range from standard GUI controls, such as the push button and entry field, to the more robust Web-based controls, such as the Marquee control. You can use these ActiveX controls to create an effective user interface and metaphor for your application. ActiveX controls offer more robust objects and features than intrinsic HTML controls, which are somewhat limited in capabilities.

The second main advantage of ActiveX controls is their ability to integrate with other components on the desktop and the server. This feature can also be a disadvantage, as I will discuss in the next section, "Examining the Drawbacks of ActiveX." Since ActiveX controls are built by using Microsoft's Component Object Model (COM), you can integrate the controls with other components, such as a Microsoft Word document, Excel spreadsheet, or any other component that supports COM. This feature opens up new possibilities when you're designing your Web-based application.

Many people are converting their document information produced with proprietary software to the open HTML format for publishing on the Web. With ActiveX controls, you can integrate these documents into your application and avoid the conversion process. Much as you can embed a spreadsheet into a Word document by using Object Linking and Embedding (OLE), ActiveX controls give you a new model with less overhead to do the same task. You don't have to convert all the proprietary information. Instead, you can use ActiveX to embed this information into your Web-based application. The browser remains the universal client for your application. Your application interface incorporates the COM object into the web page, enabling the user to interact with the spreadsheet, graph, or document within the browser. These features also apply to the server, as you will discover in the lesson on Day 17, "Using Active Server Components to Create Multitier Applications."

Examining the Drawbacks of ActiveX

As already stated, one of the main benefits of ActiveX is also a potential disadvantage. The ability of ActiveX controls to interact with the file system and other components on the client and server machines is a potential security hazard for untrustworthy controls. You probably thought the concept of trust could be shared only among animate objects, but ActiveX controls can and do incorporate trust into their relationship with an application.

ActiveX controls rely on services that verify the reliability, or trustworthiness, of the control. Trust verification services make sure the control can be trusted to provide certain functions, which are verified by a neutral third-party trust administrator, based on the "blessing" of a trust authority. Trust authorities maintain policies for authenticating a control. For example, a trust administrator verifies that a company's ActiveX control can be trusted to perform a certain function. Based on this blessing, the browser can download the ActiveX control with the assurance that it won't engage in some harmful activity, such as corrupting your file system.

With Microsoft's Internet Explorer, you can set specific levels of Internet security for downloading ActiveX controls as an additional safeguard. Trust verification is a fairly reliable safeguard to ensure the reliability of ActiveX controls; however, it's not airtight and could result in a corrupt ActiveX control being downloaded to your system. If an untrustworthy ActiveX control masks its way through the process, the potential damage can be disastrous, but the reliability of the verification process makes the chance of this happening very slim.

Another drawback of using ActiveX controls is that they're targeted toward the Microsoft Windows platform, which can be a disadvantage if your application is going to be used across multiple platforms. Microsoft has transferred the ActiveX specifications to the Open Group in an effort to make the technology more acceptable and compatible across multiple platforms. The Open Group will provide an impartial consortium of vendors to oversee the expansion of the ActiveX technology and help address the cross-platform issues surrounding ActiveX controls.

Exploring the Qualities of Java

Java offers the promise of a true cross-platform development language, and to some, Java even represents a way of life. Developers have embraced Java as the Holy Grail and become as dependent on it as their morning cup of coffee. Some are going so far as to say that Java should be the universal language for everything, including your operating system, your spreadsheet and word processing software, and your car's engine. Two main advantages of Java are its support for multiple platforms and its security. Java's multiple-platform support includes Microsoft Windows, Apple Macintosh, and Sun Solaris, to name just a few; this support is built into the language. In theory, Java executes the same way across all the supported platforms because of its *implementation-neutral design.* This approach means that programs such as Java applets and applications behave in the same manner regardless of the platform. With this feature, you can create Web-based applications that use Java applets and applications and not worry about different end-user machines.

Another advantage of Java is its security, which Sun claims is better than ActiveX's. Supporters say that Java applets are more secure than ActiveX controls because applets can't access the local file system without specific permission. You can use the Security Manager to manipulate the level of file access an applet can have, and you can even choose to provide no file access at all. Also, the Java Virtual Machine (JVM) offers a systematic bytecode verification process. The JVM makes sure that the language adheres to Java standards and that the program hasn't been altered since its compilation. These security measures help ensure the safety of your Java-based application.

Examining the Limitations of Java

Although Java touts itself as being more secure, it's definitely more limited than ActiveX controls in desktop integration. Java doesn't offer the same robust features that ActiveX does when it comes to integrating desktop applications such as Excel or Word. Java's security model contributes to its limited file system access.

Java's cross-platform support prevents it from taking advantage of platform-specific features in your applications. For instance, Java applets don't offer the same choices as ActiveX controls do for your application interface. In some ways, Java sacrifices capabilities for portability. You have to decide what's more important to you. If you want to build an application that can be easily executed across multiple platforms, you might want to use Java throughout your application. However, if you've decided that Windows will be your deployment platform of choice, you can then consider a more heavy dose of ActiveX. You will probably use both technologies to construct your "killer" application.

Integrating Java Applets into Your Application

Now that I have explained the debate over ActiveX versus Java, I can cover subjects like how to integrate these exciting technologies into your applications. The lesson on Day 13, "Interacting with Objects and ActiveX Controls," explained the <APPLET> tag and its attributes, as well as how a Java applet works with your browser. The following sections teach you how to use the power of a Java applet in your application.

Inserting a Java Applet into Your Web Page

There are two basic ways to insert a Java applet into a web page with Visual InterDev. First, you can use the <APPLET> tag to define and declare the Java applet. This method was covered in the previous lesson on Day 13. For this lesson, I'm explaining the second method of inserting a Java applet into your web page, which is using the FrontPage Editor for Visual InterDev. This editor was covered on Day 5, "WYSIWYG HTML Editing with FrontPage."

First, you need to create a new web page or choose an existing one for the Java applet. Figure 15.1 shows a newly created web page.

Figure 15.1.

A sample web page.

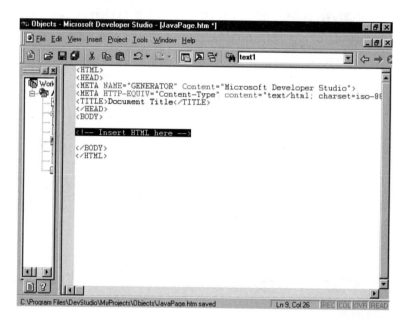

Next, you need to open the web page file, using the FrontPage Editor for Visual InterDev. As a refresher, select the HTML file in the project workspace and right-click to display the shortcut menu. Choose Open With from the list of menu items to display the list of available editors. You can then select the FrontPage Editor from the list, as shown in Figure 15.2.

The FrontPage Editor opens so you can use it to design the web page. Figure 15.3 illustrates the sample web page as it looks in the FrontPage Editor.

Figure 15.2.

Opening the file with the FrontPage Editor for Visual InterDev.

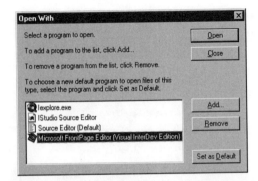

Figure 15.3.

Viewing the web page through the eyes of the FrontPage Editor.

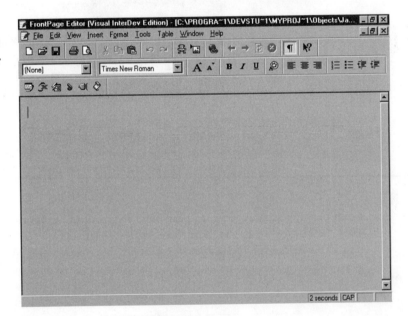

Now you're ready to insert the Java applet into the web page. To do this, choose Other Components from the Insert menu and select Java Applet from the list. The Java Applet Properties dialog box opens, as shown in Figure 15.4.

Figure 15.4.

Setting the properties for the applet.

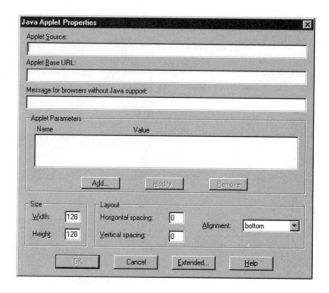

You can also click the Insert Java Applet icon on the Advanced toolbar to display the Java Applet Properties window. This icon is denoted by the letter *J* displayed in green.

From the properties window, you can enter the name of the Java applet class and the base URL address for the applet. The name of the applet source code typically has a suffix of "class." As far as the URL address, you can provide a path to your Visual InterDev project or an address on the Internet. Figure 15.5 demonstrates an example of selecting an applet and its properties.

This example assumes that the Fan.class file was previously added to your Visual InterDev project.

The applet in this example has text that gradually expands. You can see that the name of the applet code has been supplied, along with the Visual InterDev project path. Also, a message has been entered along with the width and height of the applet to be used for browsers that don't support Java. Once all the properties have been supplied, the final task is to specify any parameters required by the applet. You can do this by clicking the Add button in the Applet Parameters frame. You then see two entry fields where you can enter the name of the parameter and the value. Figure 15.6 demonstrates this process.

Figure 15.5.

Configuring an applet for your web page.

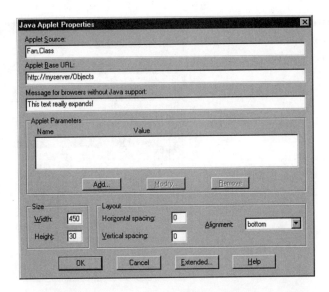

Figure 15.6.

Entering parameter values for the applet.

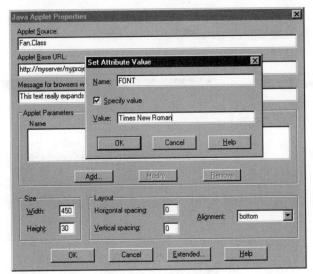

When you click OK, the name and value you enter appear in the listbox. You can repeat these steps for each additional parameter. Use the Modify button to change the value of a parameter and the Remove button to remove the parameter from the list. Figure 15.7 shows the parameters and their values for the Fan.class applet.

Figure 15.7.

Confirming the parameter values.

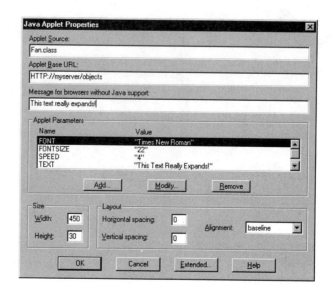

After you have confirmed the properties and parameters, click OK to insert the applet into the web page. Figure 15.8 shows how the FrontPage Editor represents Java applets in a web page.

Figure 15.8.

The presence of a Java applet in a web page.

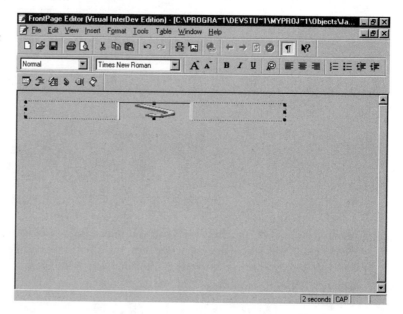

To edit the Java applet's properties, you can either double-click the applet or right-click the applet and choose Java Applet Properties from the shortcut menu. On Day 13, you learned how to use the `<APPLET>` tag to insert a Java applet into your web page. The FrontPage Editor improves this process by enabling you to insert the applet through a visual, user-friendly means. Instead of typing text and tags, you can supply answers and assignments and let the FrontPage Editor do the real work. Listing 15.1 contains the HTML code created by the FrontPage Editor based on this example.

Listing 15.1. Looking at the generated applet code.

```
<p><applet code="Fan.class" codebase="HTTP://myserver/objects"
width="450" height="30"><param name="FONT"
value="Times New Roman"><param name="FONTSIZE" value="22"><param
name="SPEED" value="4"><param name="TEXT"
value="This Text Really Expands!"><param name="VSPACING"
value="20">This text really expands!</applet></p>
```

Figures 15.9 through 15.11 illustrate the results of accessing this web page through Internet Explorer.

Figure 15.9.

Beginning to expand.

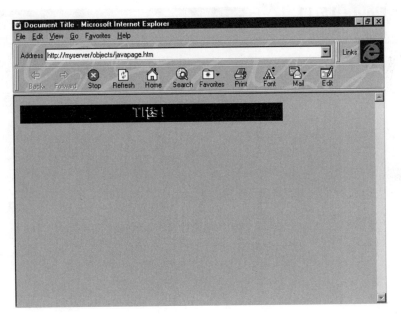

Figure 15.10.
More expansion.

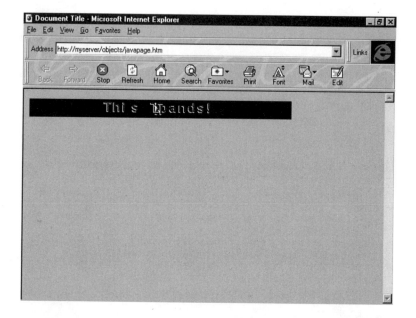

Figure 15.11.
Finally, the text is displayed.

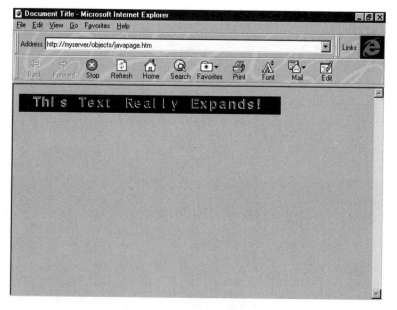

As you can tell, this process is very simple. By using the FrontPage Editor, you can rapidly integrate Java applets into your applications, which can be used to create dynamic and interactive web pages.

Integrating ActiveX Controls into Your Application

From today's lesson and the lesson on Day 13, you have discovered that ActiveX controls can enhance the look and performance of your application interface. Whether you're constructing an online entry form or publishing information about your products, ActiveX controls can make it much easier to develop an interactive application.

You had an overview of ActiveX controls during the second week, and previous lessons have explained how to insert ActiveX controls into your web pages. The rest of today's lesson explores how to integrate ActiveX controls into your applications. This lesson spends less time on the process of inserting ActiveX controls and more time on what you can do once the control has been placed in the HTML layout.

The example in this lesson shows you how to integrate several ActiveX controls to create an online order entry form for ordering book summaries electronically. The section "Customizing Properties for ActiveX Controls" explains how to extend the default values for the controls to meet the application's needs. Finally, you learn how to enhance the form's behavior with custom script in the sections "Making Objects Come Alive with Script" and "Using the Script Wizard with ActiveX Controls."

Creating an HTML Layout

So far, this lesson on ActiveX controls has focused on their strengths, benefits, and possible drawbacks. This section covers different types of ActiveX controls and teaches you how to use them in your application. The lesson gives you examples using the HTML Layout Editor as the main delivery vehicle for the layout of these controls.

You were introduced to the HTML Layout Editor during the first two weeks of lessons. The main benefit of an HTML layout is its ability to effectively handle multiple ActiveX controls. You can precisely place and position ActiveX controls in an HTML layout to design an effective user interface. The layout offers a great place for you to take full advantage of the power of ActiveX controls.

To create an HTML layout, choose New from the File menu and select HTML Layout from the list of items in the New dialog box. Enter a name for your HTML layout and click OK to create the HTML layout. The newly created layout is displayed in the HTML Layout Editor, enabling you to construct your interface with ActiveX controls.

Using Controls to Create an Order Entry Form

The next step is to construct the user interface using the newly created HTML layout. To give you an idea of what the end result looks like, Figure 15.12 shows the application in its final form.

Figure 15.12.

The Book Summaries application.

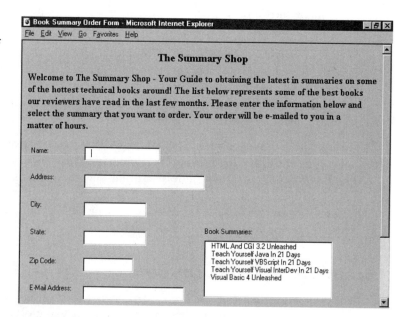

First, the entry fields need to be created so users can enter their information. The TextBox control is similar in purpose to the HTML Text control and can be used to provide this function. You also need to identify the purpose of the fields by using the Label control. You have already learned how to combine HTML text with the HTML Text control to describe an entry field. With ActiveX, you can use the Label control, which can be used to identify the contents of the text box as well as provide extra features, such as a heading on a web page. You learned how to insert controls with the HTML Layout Editor toolbox on Day 4, "Creating Your First Visual InterDev Project." As a reminder, click the control in the HTML Layout Editor toolbox, and then move your mouse over to the control's desired position in the HTML layout. Hold down the left mouse button and drag the mouse until you get the height and width you want for the control.

15

TIP You can easily insert multiple controls into an HTML layout by double-clicking the control in the toolbox. Then, you can move your mouse over to the HTML layout and click in the desired location for the control, which creates a control with a default size. You can then click to insert multiple controls of this type into the web page. When you're done inserting the controls, click the arrow key in the toolbox to go back to the default mode for editing the controls.

You can place your mouse over a tool in the toolbox to see the tooltips; they help you discover the identity of the control. Figure 15.13 shows how to discover the TextBox control with the help of tooltips.

Figure 15.13.

Using tooltips to discover a control's identity.

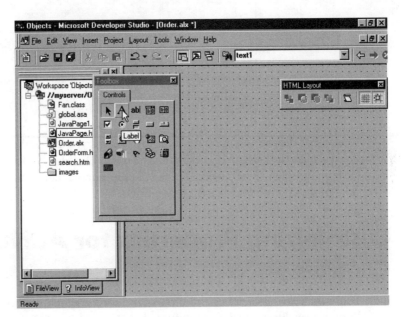

Table 15.1 lists the controls you need for this application.

Table 15.1. ActiveX controls used in the Book Summaries application.

Control	Quantity
Label	7
TextBox	6
ListBox	1
Command Button	1

Figure 15.14 shows the layout after the ActiveX controls have been placed.

Figure 15.14.

A layout with generic controls.

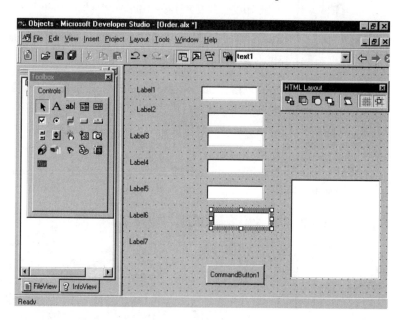

Notice that the controls don't resemble the controls you saw in the completed application. For instance, the labels are generically named Label1, Label2, Label3, and so on. Also, the push buttons don't have names. The next lesson demonstrates how to define the characteristics of the controls and give them identities.

Customizing Properties for ActiveX Controls

You learned about methods and properties during the first and second weeks of lessons. Properties enable you to define a control's behavior and characteristics, and methods are predefined procedures that enable you to perform some action that usually affects a control's behavior. In the following sections, you learn how to define the controls' properties for the Book Summaries application. The lesson entitled "Manipulating Methods to Achieve the Right Behavior" that follows this section teaches you to how to use the pre-defined methods for the controls.

Setting Properties for the Label Control

You can open the Properties window for a control by double-clicking on the control or by selecting the control, right-clicking, and choosing Properties from the control's shortcut menu. Figure 15.15 displays the Properties window for the first label control.

Figure 15.15.

Setting the properties for a label.

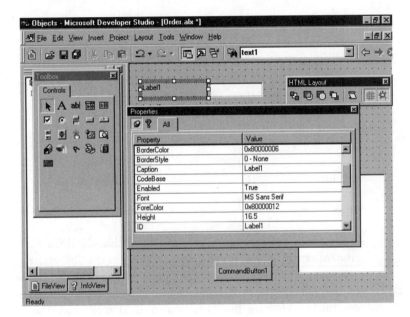

In this window, you can customize the label's characteristics by entering a value in the blank next to the property. Most property value fields are text entry fields where you can enter text or numeric values. Some properties display a combo box when you place your cursor in the field so you can select an item from a pre-defined list of options. Other property value fields display a button with an ellipsis. When you click the button for these properties, another dialog box opens in which you can enter or choose a value for the property. For this application, the main properties that need to be changed are the ID and the caption. Table 15.2 defines the IDs and captions for all the Label controls in the layout.

Table 15.2. Label properties and their values.

Control	Property	Value
Label1	ID	lblName
	Caption	Name:

continues

Table 15.2. continued

Control	Property	Value
Label2	ID	lblAddress
	Caption	Address:
Label3	ID	lblCity
	Caption	City:
Label4	ID	lblState
	Caption	State:
Label5	ID	lblZip
	Caption	Zip Code:
Label6	ID	lblEMail
	Caption	E-Mail Address:
Label7	ID	lblSummaries
	Caption	Book Summaries:

As you can see from the Value column of the table, the IDs are changed to conform to the standard naming convention for labels, which uses the "lbl" prefix. Also, the Name properties, or captions, are changed to more descriptive names to identify the contents of their associated text entry fields. The final design consideration is the alignment of the Label controls. To construct an effective interface, you need to make sure the layout is consistent and aesthetically pleasing.

The HTML Layout Editor enables you to select multiple controls and set the property values that are common for all the controls. To align the label controls, select the lblName control and then use the Ctrl (Control) key plus the left mouse button to select the other Label controls. As you select the other controls, you will notice that the previously chosen controls remain selected. You can then display the Properties window by using one of the two methods described earlier. Figure 15.16 shows the Properties window for the Label controls.

NOTE The example in the preceding paragraph demonstrated selecting similar controls that share the same properties. You can also select and enter property values for dissimilar controls. When you select different types of controls, the Properties window displays the properties that are shared between the controls. For example, you could select a label and a push button and set the properties that are common for both.

15

Figure 15.16.

Align multiple controls.

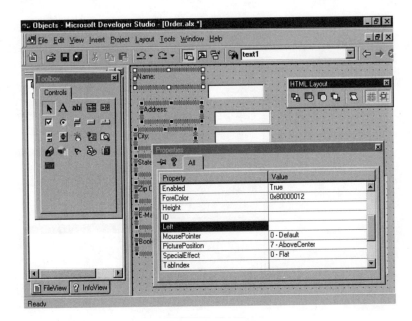

From the Properties window, you can then establish the controls' placement and alignment on the layout. Use the Left property to enter a numeric value that defines the control's placement on the layout. This value corresponds to the control's x coordinate. However, Visual InterDev has another method for aligning controls that's quicker and easier. When you open a layout with the HTML Layout Editor, a new menu—the Layout menu—is created in the Visual InterDev development environment. Use the Layout menu to perform certain functions for controls and the entire layout. Figure 15.17 shows the options available from this menu.

Using the Layout menu, you can determine the alignment, sizing, and spacing of controls on your layout. You can also alter the layering of controls. This unique feature of the HTML Layout Editor is useful when, for example, you want to place radio buttons on top of a frame to organize the controls. To align multiple controls, select all the controls and choose Align from the Layout menu. You can then choose the proper alignment from the list of choices, as shown in Figure 15.18.

Figure 15.17.
The Layout menu's options.

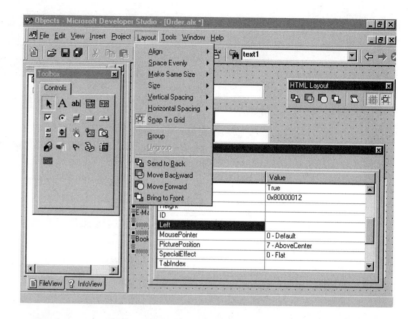

Figure 15.18.
Choosing the proper alignment for your controls.

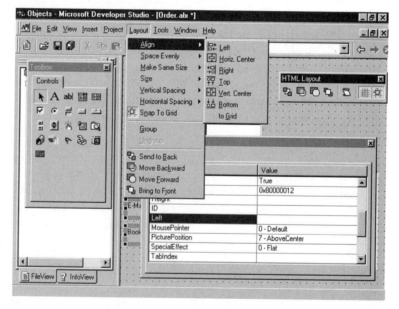

NOTE When discussing the first method for aligning controls, I said you could directly affect the placement and alignment of the controls. In covering the second method, which uses the Layout menu, I mentioned you can affect only the alignment. The first method offers an advantage because you specify the x coordinate for all the controls. In this way, you indicate not only the alignment of the controls, but also their exact horizontal placement.

You can also choose Space Evenly from the Layout menu to equally position multiple controls on the layout. You can choose to evenly space the controls both horizontally and vertically. This feature helps facilitate logical design and order on your layout.

Setting Properties for the TextBox Control

The next step of constructing the interface is to set the properties for the TextBox controls. The main properties that need to be entered for these controls are the ID, alignment, and placement. Table 15.3 outlines the properties and values for the TextBox controls on the layout.

Table 15.3. Text box properties and their values.

Control	Property	Value
TextBox1	ID	txtName
TextBox2	ID	txtAddress
TextBox3	ID	txtCity
TextBox4	ID	txtState
TextBox5	ID	txtZip
TextBox6	ID	txtEMail

Next, the TextBox controls need to be aligned horizontally and vertically with their respective labels.

Setting Properties for the ListBox Control

You can use the ListBox control to display multiple items so the user can select an item from the list. In this application, the ListBox control is used to display the available book summaries that can be ordered. Figure 15.19 shows the ListBox control and its Properties window.

Figure 15.19.

*Setting the properties
for the ListBox
control.*

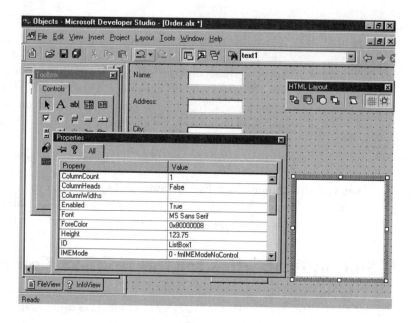

As you can see, the listbox has many properties you can customize to create several different types of ListBox controls. For example, you can design the listbox to have multiple columns and column headings. A multicolumn listbox can be created to display tabular information by entering the number of columns in the `ColumnCount` property and changing the `ColumnHeads` property to `True`. The default style is a single column listbox, as indicated by the `ColumnCount` property value of 1.

NOTE

Although the ListBox control supports creating a multicolumn listbox, there are better third-party controls that support the multiple column feature. Microsoft's grid control and Farpoint Technologies' spreadsheet control are two examples of controls you can use to display and interact with multiple columns of data.

You can adjust the size of the listbox by manually changing the width and height in the Properties window, or you can select the control and drag its handles to adjust the listbox's size. The standard naming convention for the ListBox control uses the prefix of "lst." For the ListBox control in this application, the ID property is set to the value of `lstSummaries`.

The remaining Label control is used to describe the ListBox control, as shown in Figure 15.20.

Figure 15.20.

*Viewing the resulting
listbox.*

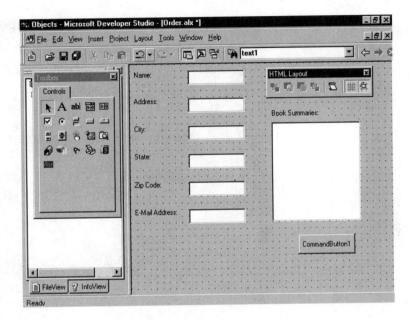

Setting Properties for the Push Button Control

The push button, or command button, is very similar to the command button you learned
about on Day 12, "Using Basic and Advanced HTML Form Controls." You can define the
size, caption, and font properties, among others, for the push button control. This button
is used by the application to submit the order for the book summary. Figure 15.21 displays
the Properties window for the command button.

The ID for this control uses the "cmd" prefix and is named cmdSubmit. The Caption property
has also been changed to the value of Submit. Figure 15.22 shows the user interface that's
created, based on the controls and properties set so far.

TIP

It's a good idea to supply accelerator keys for push buttons used in your
layout. Accelerator keys offer quick keyboard access to activate controls
in the application. Notice in Figure 15.22 that the letter *S* on the push
button is underlined, meaning that *S* is the accelerator key for the
Submit push button. You can use the accelerator key for this control by
pressing the Alt+S key combination. To create an accelerator key, enter
the letter in the Accelerator property found in the control's Properties
window.

Figure 15.21.

Setting the properties for the push button control.

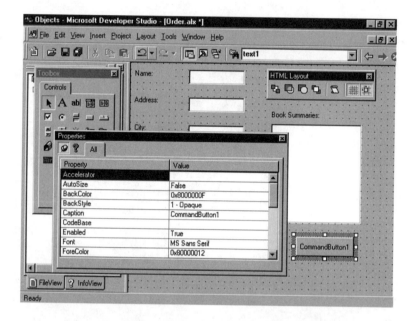

Figure 15.22.

The Book Summaries user interface.

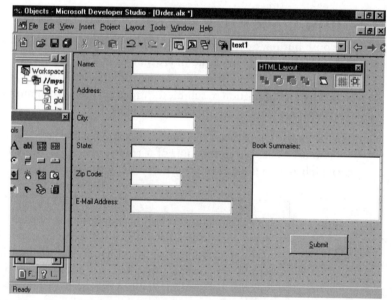

Manipulating Methods to Achieve the Right Behavior

A *method* is a pre-defined procedure you can call to execute a specific function on or by your control. Each control consists of associated methods inherent to the control that you can use in your application. The method contains prepackaged code that enables you to extend the control's power. Methods also save precious development time because you don't have to custom-develop the code carried out by the method.

This is the syntax for calling a control's method:

```
ControlID.MethodName
```

In this code line, `ControlID` is the ID for the control and `MethodName` is the name of the method you're calling. For example, one of the methods for the push button control is `Click`. The following line of code demonstrates how to call this method for a push button called `cmdSubmit`:

```
cmdSubmit.Click
```

If an application executes the `Click` method, the `Click` event is triggered, executing any code in the procedure for that event. Remember, the `Click` event is typically initiated by the user. For example, the user can activate the `Click` event by clicking a push button. This example demonstrates how you can use a pre-defined method for the push button control to simulate the same behavior in your application code.

NOTE

> The purpose of this part of the lesson is to teach you how to use methods in your application, but it's beyond the scope of this lesson to cover each and every method for all the different types of controls. You will, however, learn the purpose and basic concepts of using methods that you can apply to any control you integrate into your application. After you understand these concepts, you can research the product documentation for the ActiveX controls you're using to learn about their explicit methods.

Mastering Methods for Your Controls

So far, the lesson has explained how to construct a basic user interface for the Book Summaries application by using an HTML layout and ActiveX controls. In this section, you learn how to use some of the methods associated with the controls to create intelligent logic for your application.

The purpose of the Book Summaries application is to let users order a book summary, using an inventory list of available summaries. You might have noticed that although the basic ListBox control has been constructed, there are no items in the list. The ListBox control has a pre-defined method called AddItem that you can use to populate its contents. This is the syntax for the AddItem method:

```
ListBoxControlID.AddItem Item ¦varIndex
```

ListBoxControlID is the ID, or name, of the control, *Item* is the information to be added to a row in the listbox, and *varIndex* specifies the row in the listbox to add the data. Both the *Item* and *varIndex* attributes are optional. You can enter a variable or a value enclosed in quotes for the *Item* attribute. If you don't specify a value for *varIndex*, the item is added to the last row of the listbox. The *varIndex* attribute for the beginning row of the listbox has a value of 0.

NOTE

You can't assign a value to *varIndex* that's greater than the number of rows in the listbox. For example, if the listbox has ten rows, specifying a value of 11 for *varIndex* would cause an error.

Listing 15.2 gives you the code used by the Book Summaries application to fill the contents of the listbox.

Listing 15.2. Populating the items in the listbox.

```
Sub Layout1_OnLoad ()
lstSummaries.AddItem "HTML And CGI 3.2 Unleashed"
lstSummaries.AddItem "Teach Yourself Java In 21 Days"
lstSummaries.AddItem "Teach Yourself VBScript In 21 Days"
lstSummaries.AddItem "Teach Yourself Visual InterDev In 21 Days"
lstSummaries.AddItem "Visual Basic 4 Unleashed"
End Sub
```

This code example is placed within the procedure that executes when the layout is initially loaded. In this way, the user sees a list of items when the application opens, as shown in Figure 15.23.

Figure 15.23.

Giving the user choices.

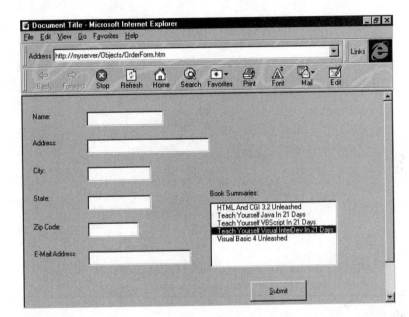

In this example, an item is highlighted when the user selects a particular book summary in the list. The listbox has been defined with the default values of Single and Plain for the MultiSelect and ListStyle properties, respectively. The MultiSelect property indicates whether the user can select multiple items from the list. Its default value of Single specifies that only one selection can be made at a time, but you can let the user select multiple items in the list by entering a value of Multi for the MultiSelect property.

By using the ListStyle property, you can place an option indicator next to the items in the list. Plain, the default value for this property, specifies that the items are displayed in the list without a visual indicator to their left. If you enter the value of Option for the ListStyle property, an indicator appears next to the items in the list. What this indicator looks like depends on the value you enter for the MultiSelect property. If the control is defined as a single-selection listbox, the indicator is a circle placed to the left of the items. When a user selects an item, a dark round circle, similar to a radio button, is placed next to the item, which is also highlighted, as shown in Figure 15.24.

Figure 15.24.

Using an indicator for a single selection.

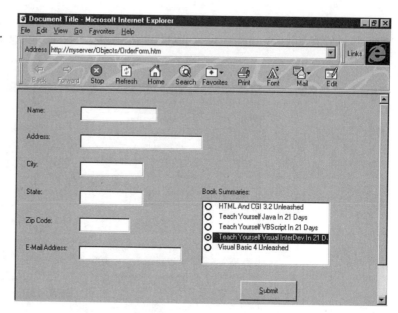

If you have entered a value of `Multi` for the `MultiSelect` property, however, the indicator is a checkbox. This indicator, which is placed to the left of the selected items, means you can select multiple items in the list. The checkmark indicator is shown in Figure 15.25.

Figure 15.25.

Using an indicator for multiple selections.

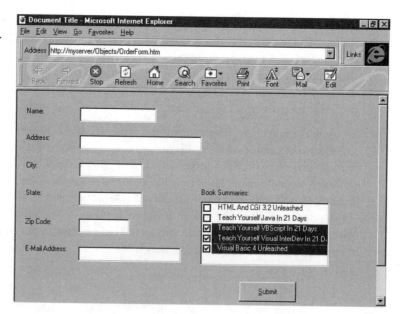

NOTE

> You could also create an Active Server Page that creates the web page and HTML layout and populates the contents of the listbox from rows in a database table.

Making Objects Come Alive with Script

Now that the HTML layout has been given a designated form, scripting code must be added to give the layout its function. As you have learned over the past two weeks, you can add scripting logic to both the client and server to meet your application's needs. Client-side logic can be used to provide user input validation and respond to user-initiated events. With Active Server Pages, you can extend the power of script code to the server to construct dynamic, interactive web pages. You can develop Active Server Pages that not only construct the user interface, including the web page and HTML layout, but also offer database and server interaction for your application.

Associating Script Logic with Your Controls

For purposes of this application, client-side script is used to validate the user input and to display a confirmation message to the user once the order has been placed. When you place an ActiveX control directly in a web page, you can also enter the client-side script in that file. When you use an HTML layout in your web page, the client-side script is associated with the actual HTML layout, or ALX, file. This means you need to use the HTML Layout Editor to actually view the code instead of seeing the script in the HTML web page file. The code still executes in the layout contained in the web page.

Using the Script Wizard with ActiveX Controls

So far, you have learned how to construct a user interface by using an HTML layout and ActiveX controls, design the characteristics and behavior of the controls by adjusting their properties, and affect the control's behavior by manipulating control-specific methods. The final lesson for the day teaches you how to add more functions and features to the application by using client-side script. The Script Wizard gives you a visual helper to implement scripting logic for your application. You can use the power of the Script Wizard to develop routine script logic through a point-and-click interface and then customize the generated code.

Reviewing the Script Wizard

For the purposes of the Book Summaries application, client-side script needs to be added to supply user entry validation and the code to display a confirmation message to the user. As you learned on Day 4, you can activate the Script Wizard by selecting a specific control or the layout and right-clicking to open the shortcut menu. Next, choose Script Wizard from the list of menu items, as shown in Figure 15.26.

Figure 15.26.

Seeking help from the Script Wizard.

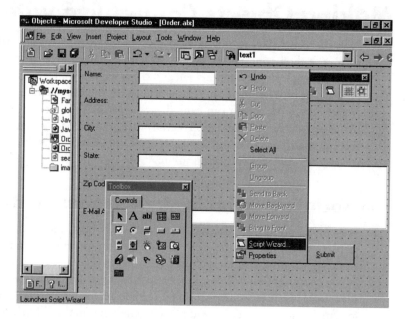

Figure 15.27 shows the options for the HTML layout, using the Script Wizard.

The List View displays the controls, events, and actions for the order form layout. You probably recall from the first week that the List View enables you to create the script code for your application by selecting the options and actions for the controls. The Code View enables you to manually enter the script logic for the controls and their actions.

15

Figure 15.27.

The List View of the Script Wizard.

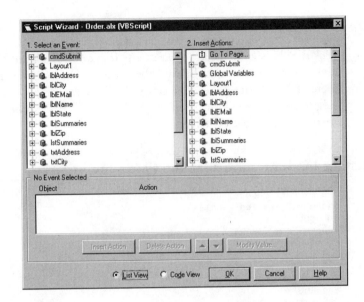

15

Adding the Finishing Touch to the Application

In this section, you use the Code View to add the scripting logic for this application. You can open this view by clicking on the Code View radio button at the bottom of the Script Wizard dialog box. Several functions need to be added to the Book Summaries application. First, the E-Mail Address field needs to be validated to make sure the user enters a valid address. Second, the application needs to verify that information has been entered for all of the fields and that an item has been selected from the list before the push button can be clicked for the user to submit the order. Finally, scripting logic needs to be added to display a confirmation message when the user clicks the Submit push button. Listing 15.3 displays the code for the Submit push button's Click event.

Listing 15.3. Validating the e-mail address.

```
Sub cmdSubmit_Click ()
If (InStr(EMail, "@") = 0) Then
MsgBox "Please enter an email address in the form username@location."
Else
MsgBox "Thanks! Your order will be sent to you shortly."
End If
End Sub
```

This code validates the information entered for the E-Mail Address field and displays a message if the address doesn't have an @ symbol. To enter this code using the Script Wizard, click the plus sign to the left of cmdSubmit in the Script Wizard's Event pane to expand the events for the Submit push button. Next, select Click to display the procedure for the Click event in the Script pane. You can then enter the script code in Listing 15.3 for the subprocedure. Listing 15.4 shows the individual procedure code to validate that all the order entry fields have been entered.

Listing 15.4. Making sure the fields are entered.

```
Sub Layout1_OnLoad()
cmdSubmit.Enabled = False
End Sub
Sub txtName_Change()
call CheckFields()
End Sub
Sub txtAddress_Change()
Call CheckFields()
End Sub
Sub txtCity_Change()
Call CheckFields()
End Sub
Sub txtState_Change()
Call CheckFields()
End Sub
Sub txtZip_Change()
Call CheckFields()
End Sub
Sub txtEMail_Change()
Call CheckFields()
End Sub
Sub lstSummaries_Change()
Call CheckFields()
End Sub
Sub CheckFields()
If txtName.Text = "" or txtAddress.Text = "" or txtCity.Text = ""
or txtState.Text = "" or txtZip.Text = "" or
txtEMail.Text = "" or lstSummaries.Value = "" Then
cmdSubmit.Enabled = False
Else
cmdSubmit.Enabled = True
End If
End Sub
```

These procedures are interspersed throughout the individual events for the controls. You can
add the code for specific events in the same manner that the code for the Submit push button
code was added. For example, to enter the code for the txtName field's Change event, click
Change in the Script Wizard's Event pane. You can then add your script for the event
procedure in the Script pane. The last procedure in this code listing is a common procedure
found in the Procedures section of the Action pane. You can create a common procedure to
be used throughout your code by selecting Procedures in the Script Wizard's Action pane and
right-clicking to display the shortcut menu. Figure 15.28 demonstrates how to create a new
common procedure for your code.

Figure 15.28.

*Creating a new
procedure.*

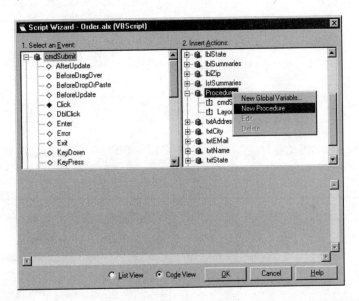

After you choose New Procedure from the shortcut menu, a subprocedure template is created
in the Script pane in which you can supply the name and scripting logic. Figure 15.29 shows
the CheckFields subprocedure in the Script Wizard's Code View.

After you have entered all the scripting logic for the individual procedures, you're ready to
run the application, as shown in Figure 15.30.

In this example, the user ordered a summary for a really good book!

Figure 15.29.

A sample procedure.

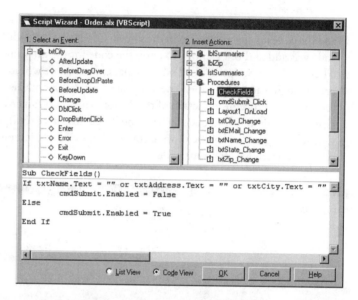

Figure 15.30.

Ordering the book summary.

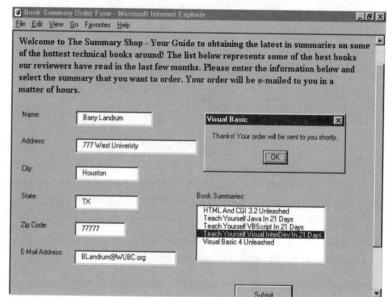

15

Summary

The Book Summaries application demonstrates how to integrate ActiveX controls into your application. Today's lesson has focused on building an application with the power of ActiveX controls. You should now understand the basic concepts and steps for developing an HTML layout, integrating specific ActiveX controls to construct the interface, and using control methods and script to extend the power of these controls. You should also understand how to integrate and use a Java applet to construct a dynamic application. Although the debate will continue to rage over Java and ActiveX, the central premise of this lesson is that you should use both of these robust objects in your application as complementary technologies.

The first part of today's lesson outlined the basic strengths, differences, and weaknesses of ActiveX controls and Java applets. Next, you learned how to use Visual InterDev to integrate a Java applet into your Web-based application. The lesson also gave you an overview of creating an HTML layout and inserting ActiveX controls into your web pages. The Book Summaries application is a good example of how to build an application based on ActiveX controls. The lesson guided you through inserting and positioning basic ActiveX controls into your layout and manipulating controls' properties and methods to get the behavior you want for your interface. Finally, you learned how to extend the reach of your controls by using client-side script.

Now that you have finished today's lesson, you should have a thorough understanding of building the front-end of a Web-based application. This knowledge, combined with your comprehension of server topics, such as database integration and Active Server Pages, learned during the second week, will enable you to use Visual InterDev to create a "killer" application for the Web.

Q&A

Q With security concerns on the rise and the potential risks of using objects, should I use Java applets and ActiveX controls in my web pages?

A Both Java and ActiveX have tried to define tight security standards for the implementation and use of objects. Moreover, browsers from Netscape and Microsoft have also implemented security controls for downloading these controls and objects. Finally, third-party vendors are building software to specifically monitor the activities of Java applets and ActiveX controls. One such company is Finjan Software, Ltd., who has developed a software product called SurfinGate that helps to keep these objects in check. This product is representative of some of the newer products being developed to further protect your Internet and intranet applications from the activity of rogue objects. The SurfinGate software analyzes and verifies the safety of Java applets and ActiveX controls and then provides a digital certificate of authenticity. Based on these safety measures, you should feel confident and secure about using ActiveX controls and Java applets in your Web-based applications. Remember, use only those objects and controls that have been digitally signed and authenticated.

Q What tools are available to build Java applets?

A Many tools already exist, or are being developed, to help you create Java applets and applications. Some of the more popular tools are Microsoft Visual J++ and Symantec Visual Café. If you're thinking of building your own custom Java applet, you should seriously consider Visual J++ because of its strong integration with Visual InterDev. The Developer Studio shell enables you to simultaneously open Visual J++ and Visual InterDev projects, reducing your development time and making it easier to integrate applets into your Web-based applications.

Q What tools can I use to develop ActiveX controls?

A You have several options for developing ActiveX controls, including Microsoft Visual C++, Visual Basic, and Borland Delphi. You will learn how to build ActiveX controls by using the Visual Basic Control Creation Edition during tomorrow's lesson.

Workshop

During today's workshop, you get a chance to extend the functionality of the Book Summaries application. You're going to use an ASP to create the HTML layout on a web page and populate the contents of the listbox from a database table. Feel free to use the layout, controls, code, and examples presented in the lesson. You can find them on the CD-ROM included with this book. You can choose to create a table using your database of choice to contain book summaries, or you can use an existing table in your database to present some other type of information. You need to change the application's functionality to match the information you decide to present. The goal of this workshop is to teach you how to integrate client and server components to build a robust application.

15

15

Quiz

1. What is a method?
2. What method do you use to add items to a listbox?
3. What property enables you to define the text for the label control?
4. What exciting Visual InterDev feature automatically generates script code based on your input?

Quiz Answers

1. A method is a pre-defined procedure associated with a control that performs a specific action to affect its behavior. You can use a control's method to further change its behavior and characteristics in your application.
2. Use the `AddItem` method to add items to a listbox.
3. The `Caption` property is used to set the text for the label control.
4. The Script Wizard enables you to visually choose controls, actions, and events to automatically generate script code for your application.

Day **16**

Building Design-Time ActiveX Controls

During the past couple of days, you have had a steady diet of ActiveX and Design-time ActiveX controls. By now, you understand the benefits of these objects and know how to incorporate them into your applications. Today's lesson is the breakthrough lesson that lets you try your hand at building a Design-time ActiveX control. You get a guided tour to teach you the whys and hows of developing these controls. Who knows: This lesson could offer a springboard to a new career of constructing commercially available controls for developers.

The first part of today's lesson centers on why you should build custom controls. Next, the lesson describes some of the available tools that enable you to construct these controls. The middle portion of the lesson walks you through the steps of creating a Design-time ActiveX control with the user-friendly, powerful Visual Basic 5 Control Creation Edition (VBCCE). During this tutorial, the lesson also explores the VBCCE development environment, explaining its features and functions. You also learn how to test the control in the VBCCE environment. Once your control has been built, the lesson explains how to integrate it into your Web-based application. Controls must have a purpose, which usually revolves around meeting the needs of your Web-based or client-server application. The final lesson for the day demonstrates how to review and test the results in your Visual InterDev project.

Why Should You Build a Design-Time Control?

As a developer, you have probably experienced the joys of using custom controls in your client-server and Web-based applications. Using third-party controls has become common-place among developers. Magazines, such as *Visual Basic Programmers' Journal*, are devoting at least a third of their pages to advertising and reviewing the latest controls that can be used in your application. With each new revision of products such as Visual Basic, developers check out the product's new features, especially the custom controls included as part of the tool. Next, they thoroughly review the book of supplemental controls that come with the product to discover other commercially available controls. Finally, they build their application with a set of robust controls, only to realize sometimes that the vendor didn't include all the necessary functionality.

Does this sound like an adventure ride you have been on before? No control is going to please everyone or do all you need it to, so you develop workaround solutions in your application to compensate for the function you want. Until recently, the thought of creating your own custom control probably frightened you because of the time involved and the availability of tools. In the past, you had to be a C++, object-oriented disciple to develop a custom control because the only products available to create custom controls were development tools—such as Visual C++ and Borland C++—that supported the C or C++ programming language.

With the advent of new tools such as the Visual Basic Control Creation Edition from Microsoft, you can no longer claim control technophobia: the fear of creating custom controls. Tools such as VBCCE simplify the process of developing custom controls while reducing the time it takes to construct a control. Now, you can create your own custom controls and have no one but yourself to blame if the control doesn't do everything you want it to. Why should you build a custom control, you ask? There are two main reasons for attempting this feat. First, you want to meet your application's needs. I'm sure you have been on a development project with two developers who needed to execute the same block of code within their individual code. Instead of putting the identical code in both places, someone created a common function or module that both developers could access from their program. The concept of a custom control is the same. Since you already know that no control is going to totally satisfy your development needs, at some point you will probably need to develop a custom control tailored to fulfill your application's requirements.

Second, you should try to develop a custom control because the process isn't as difficult as it once was. Now that you have new tools to make the process easier, there's no excuse not to build these exciting new controls. Remember, technology has come a long way since the days of VBX controls. ActiveX and Design-time ActiveX controls are now the hot new objects that can spice up both your client-server and Web-based applications. There are basically three types, or categories, of controls you can build; here are the three approaches for building these types of controls:

1. The Nestle Tollhouse approach
2. The Pillsbury slice-and-bake approach
3. The M&M cookie approach

You're probably wondering what baking cookies has to do with creating ActiveX controls, but the following sections outline each approach and explain the correlation.

The Nestle Tollhouse Approach

The Nestle Tollhouse approach means building a new, custom ActiveX control from scratch, much like the process of baking Nestle Tollhouse cookies. My grandmother used to buy Nestle Tollhouse chocolate chips and mix the necessary ingredients to bake the best chocolate chip cookies you could ever imagine. Although mixing the cookie dough from scratch and baking the cookies took a long time, they were definitely worth the wait. Similarly, you can construct a brand-new control from scratch by using the features (ingredients) of a tool such as VBCCE or Visual C++. These tools give you the basic core elements you need to build your control.

This approach offers the most flexibility because you're not confined to the limitations of another control. You design and develop the control from the ground up, including setting the control's properties, methods, events, and appearance. You have the ability and freedom to include the functions and features needed to address your application's needs. The drawback is that you must construct everything yourself because with freedom comes responsibility. You're responsible for designing all the control's features and functions, including its appearance, which can be a laborious process. The end product might be worth the wait, but you may be interested in using one of the other two approaches for creating custom controls.

The Pillsbury Slice-and-Bake Approach

Since my grandmother's days of baking, the process of creating cookies has made big strides. In this fast-paced world, the need for better and faster methods of delivering these tasty morsels grew. Pillsbury was one of the first companies to invent slice-and-bake cookies. These cookies are ready to bake—all you have to do is slice the dough into the number of cookies you want, put the slices on a cookie sheet, and bake them for 10 to 15 minutes. The slice-and-bake approach has revolutionized cookie baking because you no longer have to buy and mix the ingredients, which reduces the time spent making cookies. The main responsibility of the cook is to define characteristics about the cookie, such as size and amount, and put them in the oven.

This approach is similar to the second method of developing an ActiveX control, which is creating an ActiveX control based on an existing control. The existing control supplies certain features and functions you can use, enhance, and extend. You also can add your own custom properties, methods, and events to the control's predefined list. The slice-and-bake approach is faster than the Tollhouse approach because it gives you a starting point for your development efforts.

The M&M Cookie Approach

The M&M cookie approach is very similar to the slice-and-bake approach. After the invention of slice-and-bake chocolate chip cookies, people grew tired of eating the same type of cookie. This quandary was probably caused by the shorter cookie-making time, which led to people eating more cookies. Pillsbury decided to make a different type of cookie based on existing delicacies and created the M&M cookie. The makers of this cookie used two existing sweets that people loved—M&Ms and chocolate chip cookies—to create this new-and-improved cookie.

This revolutionary approach is similar to the third method for building controls, which makes use of several existing controls to build a new one. Using this approach, you can synergize the best features and functions of several controls to create an even better control. This approach is very similar to the slice-and-bake approach because both approaches take advantage of the power of existing controls. The difference is that the M&M approach uses the power of multiple controls, not just individual ones. Just as you can with the slice-and-bake approach, you can use the existing properties, methods, and events as you develop new ones. The M&M approach also reduces your development time.

16

What Tools Are Available?

Now that you're familiar with the different approaches to constructing ActiveX and Design-time ActiveX controls, the lesson describes some of the tools you can use to build these controls. These tools include Microsoft Visual Basic version 5.0 and the VBCCE, Microsoft Visual C++, Borland C++ and Delphi, and Symantec C++, to name just a few. The tools from Microsoft are probably the most popular, so they're covered in this section of the lesson.

16

Using the Microsoft Visual Basic Family

Of all the tools you can use to build an ActiveX control, Microsoft Visual Basic version 5.0 and the Microsoft VBCCE are the simplest and most user-friendly. Microsoft included the ability to create ActiveX and Design-time ActiveX controls in version 5.0 of the Visual Basic Enterprise Edition. This feature and the ability to natively compile the Visual Basic code are two of the best features in this version of the tool. Microsoft also extracted the control creation feature and marketed it as its own stripped-down version of the tool called the Visual Basic Control Creation Edition (VBCCE). You can get the VBCCE, a subset of the Visual Basic 5.0 Enterprise Edition, as a separate product. Microsoft targets the VBCCE at those developers who want to create custom controls rather than client-server applications. By doing so, Microsoft offers developers a choice in their selection of tools, making it possible for you to use the control creation capabilities without having to buy the full-blown Visual Basic product. Figure 16.1 illustrates the relationship between Visual Basic 5.0 Enterprise Edition and VBCCE.

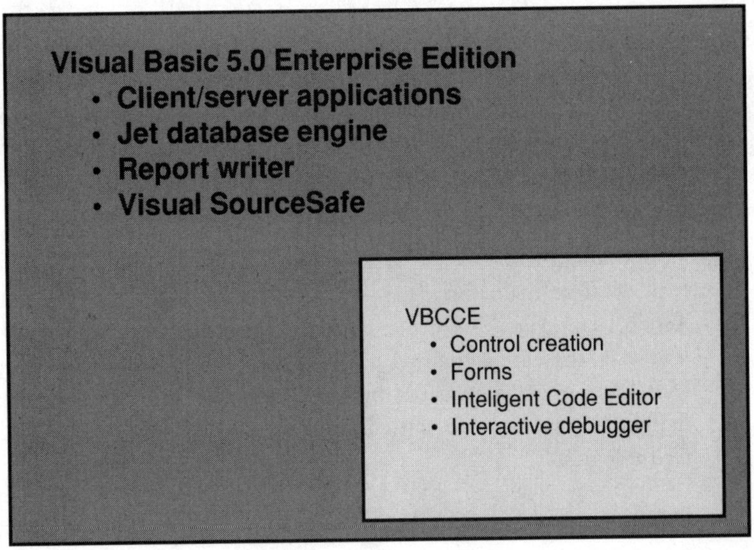

Figure 16.1.

Visual Basic 5.0 Enterprise Edition and one of its offspring: VBCCE.

Visual Basic 5.0 Enterprise Edition
- **Client/server applications**
- **Jet database engine**
- **Report writer**
- **Visual SourceSafe**

VBCCE
- Control creation
- Forms
- Inteligent Code Editor
- Interactive debugger

Regardless of which Visual Basic product is used, the features and functions are the same. Those of you who have used Visual Basic before know that it's the easiest control creation tool to learn. For those who haven't, you have some familiarity with this language from the lessons that have taught VBScript, a subset of the Visual Basic language. Visual Basic can now natively compile the fourth-generation language, so this feature should resolve some of the doubts you have about developing a control with Visual Basic and sacrificing performance for ease of use.

You can use Visual Basic to create ActiveX and Design-time ActiveX controls that can be used in your client-server and Web-based applications. Visual Basic offers a user-friendly, powerful *integrated development environment* (*IDE*). This robust IDE enables you to both code and test your control to ensure its quality.

Using Microsoft Visual C++

For hard-core developers, Visual C++ also offers the ability to develop ActiveX and Design-time ActiveX controls. As someone who has developed extensively with both Visual Basic and C, I can tell you that C and C++ aren't very user-friendly and are much harder to learn and comprehend than Visual Basic. The main advantage to using Visual C++, however, is better performance in your control's speed. This performance improvement results from C and C++ being third-generation languages, as opposed to Visual Basic, a fourth-generation language. Even with Visual Basic's advance in native compiling, applications and controls built with Visual C++ still tend to outperform those written in Visual Basic.

There are three different methods for developing a control with Visual C++. First, you can use the powerful features of the Microsoft Foundation Classes (MFC) packaged as part of the Visual C++ product. This method is the easiest one. Using the MFC means you don't have to know the intricacies of the Microsoft Component Object Model (COM) that all controls are founded on. Although you can create small controls that download relatively quickly, the drawback to this approach is that you must also install the control's MFC library on the user's machine. This DLL file is approximately 1M.

The second method uses the BASECTL samples that were first introduced in the ActiveX Development Kit. BASECTL includes three main components that help you develop ActiveX controls. The first component—called FRAMEWRK—gives you the framework for constructing ActiveX controls. The other two components included with BASECTL are TODOSVR and WEBIMAGE; they are actually ActiveX control samples built by using the FRAMEWRK method. Using this method, you can build the smallest and fastest ActiveX controls of the three methods; however, you must have a thorough knowledge of OLE, COM, and ActiveX technologies.

The final method uses the ActiveX Template Library (ATL), which is a library of C++ templates that enables you to quickly create small, fast ActiveX controls. These templates let you avoid some of the details of OLE, but you still need to know COM and ActiveX technology.

Regardless of which method you use, Visual C++ offers a challenging, powerful tool for constructing your ActiveX controls.

Introducing the Latest Member of the VB Family

Visual Basic had a recent addition to its family that makes creating ActiveX and Design-time ActiveX controls a breeze. The Visual Basic Control Creation Edition (VBCCE) simplifies the process of building your own custom controls. The objects you create can then be used in your client-server and Web-based applications. With the invention of VBCCE, you have a robust tool that encourages and facilitates both productivity and reusability. In this section, you get a tour of the Visual Basic Control Creation Edition and its features. Since entire books are written about this tool, this overview isn't an exhaustive discussion on the subject. You will, however, understand the basic methods of using the tool to create your controls. After this overview, you get to try your hand at creating an ActiveX and a Design-time ActiveX control.

VBCCE: The New Kid on the Block

This section isn't about some child prodigy music group that fizzled out. Instead, this part of the lesson takes you on a guided tour of the features and functions of the Visual Basic Control Creation Edition. This tour serves only as an introduction to the wonderful world of VBCCE.

As stated, VBCCE is a trimmed-down version of Visual Basic 5.0 Enterprise Edition. As you might expect, the integrated development environment (IDE) looks the same for both tools. VBCCE offers a very user-friendly workspace, whether you've worked with Visual Basic before or not. All the tools and features are just a mouse click away. Figure 16.2 shows Visual Basic's developer-friendly environment.

As you can tell, VBCCE's IDE is analogous to a cockpit, where everything you need to construct your control is right at your fingertips. The following sections briefly explain the VBCCE features.

Figure 16.2.
*The VBCCE inte-
grated development
environment.*

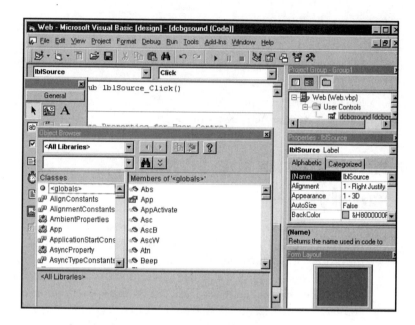

The Toolbox

The VBCCE toolbox is similar in purpose to other toolboxes, such as the HTML Layout
Editor toolbox found in Visual InterDev. All the controls that are registered on your machine
show up in the VBCCE. The ActiveX controls in the toolbox make it easier to develop your
own custom controls. You can click any of the controls and insert it into your Visual Basic
container form. You can customize the toolbox's look by creating additional tabs for
organizing your controls. To do this, right-click the toolbox to display the shortcut menu and
choose Add Tab. You can then type the name of the new tab in the dialog window, as shown
in Figure 16.3.

You also can add or remove controls on the toolbox by selecting Components from the
toolbox shortcut menu. You then see the Components dialog window, which allows you to
include or remove toolbox controls, as shown in Figure 16.4.

From this dialog window, you can select or deselect controls by clicking the checkbox to the
left of the control. After you have finished making your selections, click OK and the toolbox
then reflects your changes.

16

Figure 16.3.

Adding a new tab to organize your controls.

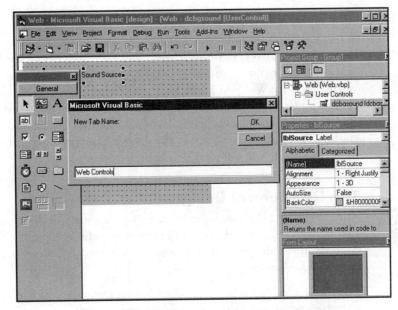

Figure 16.4.

The Components dialog window.

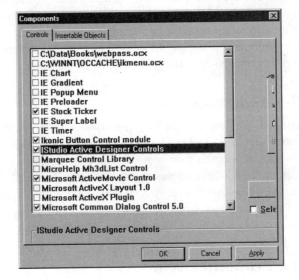

16

The Project Explorer

When you begin working with VBCCE, you initiate a project just as you do with Visual InterDev, Visual Basic, and other related tools. This project provides a house for your control, as well as its container, attributes, properties, methods, and events. The Project Explorer works much like Windows Explorer; it enables you to view all the objects and files in your project. You can move and resize the Project Explorer to get a clearer view of your project files. The Project Explorer organizes the files into folders that contain items such as forms and user controls. You can open folders in the Project Explorer to view their contents and open individual files to work in the VBCCE project environment.

The UserControl Designer

The UserControl Designer is the container for the control during design-time, enabling you to work with and define the control's properties and characteristics. You can insert ActiveX controls into the designer and then assign their properties and get instant feedback about the control's appearance.

You can set the properties for the UserControl Designer, which affects the appearance and characteristics of controls in the designer. In other words, you can affect some of the attributes of the control you're creating by setting the properties of the designer container, in addition to the control's properties. For example, you can set the background color for the designer and let the control assume this color. From the UserControl Designer, you also can double-click a control to open the code window.

The Code Window

The code window displays the Visual Basic code for your project. When you're creating a control, the code in this window represents all the logic needed to make your ActiveX or Design-time ActiveX control work. You can double-click a control on the form or double-click the form itself to activate the code window and display the entire set of code procedures and declarations for the project. If you double-click a specific control, you're taken to the procedure in the project code block for that control. The code window enables you to enter the necessary Visual Basic logic for your control and declare any objects or variables.

The Properties Window

The properties window is similar to the other property windows you have worked with during the first two weeks of lessons. The VBCCE properties window displays all the properties for the control you're constructing, for the container form, and for existing controls you're using to create your custom control. You can view the properties in alphabetical order, which is the default, or you can click the Categorized tab to display the properties by category.

Other IDE Features

The form layout window appears below the properties window; use it to determine the proper placement of forms used in your project. This window displays a computer monitor as a visual guide to help you position your form. You also can view the monitor size for your layout design by using the Resolution Guides found on the form's layout shortcut menu.

VBCCE has several toolbars you can use to create, compile, and test your controls. It also contains an integrated debugger that enables you to step through your code and monitor project variables.

With the Object Browser, you can find out which functions can be used with your ActiveX controls. You can open the Object Browser and view all the ActiveX controls that have been registered on your machine and that you have chosen to display in the VBCCE environment. This list can include any custom controls you have created. Figure 16.5 displays the enhanced Object Browser found in VBCCE and Visual Basic 5.0.

Figure 16.5.

The Object Browser.

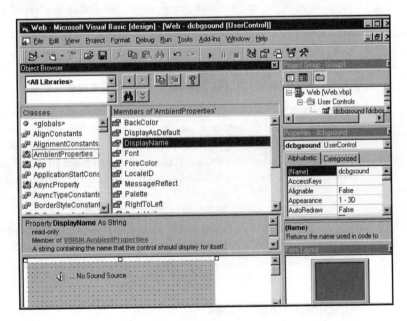

The Object Browser is an excellent tool that lists the methods, properties, and functions for a certain control. The left side of the Object Browser displays the classes, and the right side of the window reveals the class members, or functions, associated with the control class. The bottom portion of the window displays the syntax for a selected function, which gives you a helpful guide for correctly implementing or using a property or function. Another feature includes the Find icon that enables you to search for specific text in your class libraries.

Exploring the `UserControl` Object

The `UserControl` object is the basis for all ActiveX controls. Earlier in the lesson, you learned the three approaches to building an ActiveX control, which involved either creating a brand-new control from scratch or combining and customizing the power of existing controls. Regardless of the method you choose, your custom ActiveX control will always consist of the `UserControl` object.

The `UserControl` object is analogous to a form in Visual Basic. For those of you who aren't VB programmers, a form object is included with every project you create in Visual Basic. The form supplies a visual interface for your controls to reside in. For GUI applications, the form represents the window that's displayed to the user at runtime. For ActiveX controls, the `UserControl` object serves this basic purpose. Similar to the Visual Basic form object, the `UserControl` object contains many properties, methods, and events that you can customize. Later in today's lesson, you learn how to create the `UserControl` object.

Understanding ActiveX Properties

ActiveX controls consist of three basic properties: ambient, extender, and custom. Ambient properties contain information about the characteristics of the control's container, and extender properties are supplied by the container at runtime and result from a combination of the control and the container. Custom properties are those properties you design and implement. The following sections explain each of these types of properties in more detail.

 NOTE

Because of their visual nature, the properties covered in the following sections pertain mainly to regular ActiveX controls.

Ambient Properties

Ambient properties are supplied by the container so that the control fits into its environment more easily. The first time I visited the Microsoft campus, I wore a suit. Those of you who

16

have toured the campus or are familiar with the Microsoft environment know that suits aren't the norm. Obviously, I looked out of place. Based on my discovery of the Microsoft environment's characteristics, I adapted my attire to blend in with my environment. Ambient properties can be used similarly by your control. A container "publicizes" its ambient properties to the control so that the control can blend in with its environment and not look out of place. For example, a container's `BackColor` property is an ambient property that can be used to set the background color of the ActiveX control. In this way, the user won't see the ActiveX control as separate from its container. The key factors in ambient properties are information and communication. The container communicates information about its properties, and the ActiveX control receives the information and adapts accordingly. As a developer, you facilitate this communication by using the container's properties in the ActiveX control as it's designed and created.

You can find a container's ambient properties by using the `AmbientProperties` object, which is accessed through the `UserControl` object's ambient property. This is the syntax for finding ambient properties:

```
UserControl.Ambient.AmbientPropertyName
```

In this code line, `AmbientPropertyName` is the name of the ambient property you want to find. These properties are unique to the control and can only be accessed by using the `UserControl` object.

Ambient properties are used primarily during design-time. What if the ActiveX container's properties change at runtime? You can call the `UserControl_AmbientChanged` event procedure to adapt the control's property at runtime to match that of the container. Table 16.1 lists some of the more common ambient properties.

Table 16.1. Common ambient properties.

Property	Description
`DisplayAsDefault`	Indicates whether the control is the default control for the container
`DisplayName`	Specifies the control's instance name
`BackColor`	Identifies the container's background color
`ForeColor`	Identifies the container's foreground color
`Font`	Specifies the preferred font for the control's text
`TextAlign`	Specifies the preferred alignment of the control's text
`UserMode`	Indicates whether the control is in design mode or run mode

Extender Properties

The extender properties are a direct result of combining a control with a container. These properties are associated with the Extender object, which is typically created by integrating a control with a container. By using the UserControl object, you can access the Extender object and its properties from within your ActiveX control. Common examples of extender properties include size, placement, tab order sequence, and whether a control is enabled.

> **NOTE**
>
> Seasoned Visual C++ and Control Development Kit (CDK) developers might already be familiar with the extender properties but know them as *extended properties*, as they're called in the CDK.

Custom Properties

You determine how this category of properties is implemented. Custom properties enable you to design those features that never go any further than a third-party feature wish list. You have a lot of freedom in designing custom properties for your ActiveX control. In the following section, you learn how to implement custom properties.

Constructing a Control with Visual Basic Control Creation Edition

The ActiveX categories and approaches mentioned, along with the tools outlined in the lesson so far, should have convinced you why you should build ActiveX and Design-time ActiveX controls. The process is as easy as baking cookies! Seriously, you need to devote some time to building your controls, but the process has been simplified with the advent of new methods and tools, such as Visual Basic Control Creation Edition, to create ActiveX and Design-time ActiveX controls.

The lesson now shifts into high gear and leads you through the cookie-cutter approach to building ActiveX controls. During this part of the lesson, you learn how to construct a Design-time ActiveX control and integrate the control into your application.

> **NOTE**
>
> This part of the lesson assumes you're running Visual Basic Control Creation Edition. If you don't have VBCCE loaded on your machine, please do so now before you go on. You can install VBCCE from the

16

CD-ROM included with this book. This part of the lesson is very hands-on, so you will get more out of it if you perform the tasks explained in this lesson as you go along.

Examining the End Result

The first step is constructing the Design-time ActiveX control. You're going to build a custom control that enables you to design a background sound for your HTML web page. Figure 16.6 shows what this Design-time control looks like.

Figure 16.6.

The end result.

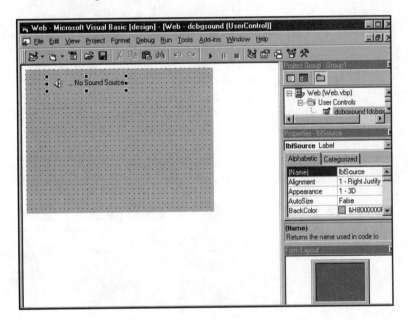

The main purpose of this control is to enable you to specify the location of a sound file. Based on a developer's specifications, the Design-time control creates the runtime text to do this. Now that you have a picture of where you're going, it's time to start VBCCE and design the control's appearance.

Creating the Custom Control

When you initially start VBCCE, you see the New Project dialog window, shown in Figure 16.7.

Figure 16.7.

Creating a project.

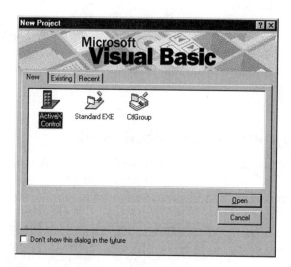

In this dialog window, you can create a Visual Basic project for your control. Here, you can choose to create an ActiveX control project, a standard Visual Basic project, or a control group project. This dialog window has New, Existing, and Recent tabs. The Existing tab enables you to open an existing project, and the Recent tab gives you an easy way to find your most recently opened projects. Select ActiveX Control project from the New tab and click the Open button. VBCCE then creates an ActiveX control project, inserting the UserControl object and displaying its visual designer in the VBCCE workspace, as shown in Figure 16.8.

Figure 16.8.

The UserControl Designer.

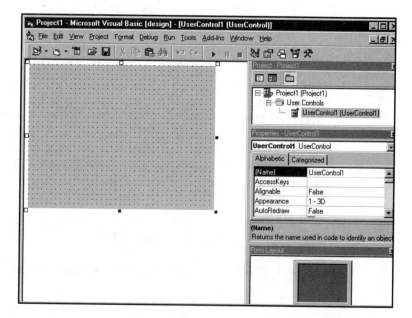

Next, you need to insert the existing controls that will be used to construct this new custom control. Click the mouse on the label control in the toolbox and insert it into the UserControl Designer. Select the label control and insert an image control on the left side of the label, as shown in Figure 16.9.

Figure 16.9.

Designing the look of a control.

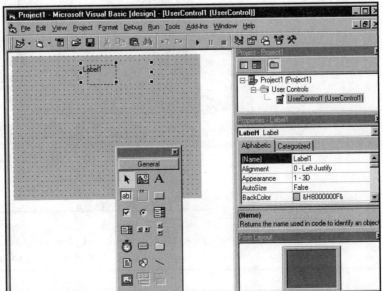

As you can tell, the label's caption is now covered up by the image, so you need to change the label's Alignment property to the value of Right Justify. Also, you need to change the label's Name property to lblSource and the label's Caption property to ... No Source Specified.

Next, click the image control to select the image for the control. After you have selected the image control, click the ellipsis displayed for the value of the Picture property in the control's properties window. The Load Picture dialog window opens so you can choose an image to insert into the image control. You need to select the bgsound.bmp file, which is on this book's CD-ROM, and click the Open button.

The next step is to name the Design-time control and the project. You can change the name of the Design-time control by choosing the UserControl object in the Project Explorer window. The properties window then displays the properties for the UserControl, enabling you to change the text of the Name property to dcbgsound. After you enter the new name, it shows up in the Project Explorer window. Next, select the project file in the Project Explorer window, and change the Name property in the properties window to Web. Your custom control should now look like the control illustrated in Figure 16.10.

Figure 16.10.

The background sound Design-time control.

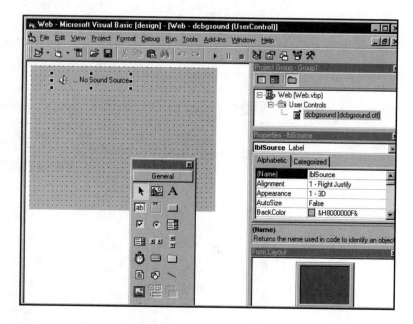

You should save your work now. You can do this by choosing Save Project Group from the File menu. You're prompted to save both the control and the project. To confirm the save, click Save for all these files.

Developing the Control's Interface

Now you're ready to build an interface for your control that enables developers to interact with your Design-time control. Choose ActiveX Control Interface Wizard from the Add-Ins menu. This wizard offers a visual guide to help you construct the properties and characteristics of the control that are available to the developer. Figure 16.11 shows the wizard's first dialog window.

This first dialog window gives you a brief overview and explanation of the interface creation process for your control. For future uses of the wizard, you can choose to ignore this window. Click the Next button to start the process. You then see a dialog window where you can select the interface members for your control. All the properties for the controls you have used to design your custom control appear as selected, as shown in Figure 16.12.

16

Figure 16.11.

The ActiveX Control Interface Wizard.

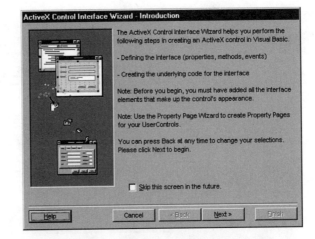

Figure 16.12.

Choosing the properties, methods, and events.

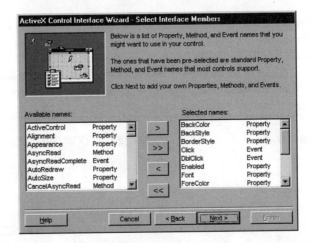

This dialog window displays a listbox on the left side that displays all the properties, methods, and events for the two controls you have chosen to use in your design. The listbox on the right side displays the properties, methods, and events that have been selected for your custom control. Use the buttons between the listboxes to insert or remove these items, either individually or all at once. For this example, remove all the selected items by clicking the button with the double arrows pointing toward the Available names listbox. When you're done, click the Next button to go to the next dialog window and create your own custom interface members. Click the New button to add a custom property for your control, as shown in Figure 16.13.

Figure 16.13.

*Creating a custom
control property.*

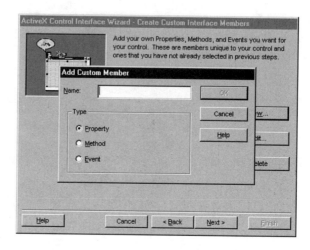

From the dialog window pictured in Figure 16.13, you can create custom properties, methods, and events for your Design-time control. Make sure that the Property radio button is selected and enter SoundSource for the name of the custom property. A developer can use this property to choose the source of the background sound file. After you confirm your entries and click OK, the newly created property appears in the Create Custom Interface Members dialog window, as shown in Figure 16.14.

Figure 16.14.

*The Create Custom
Interface Members
dialog window.*

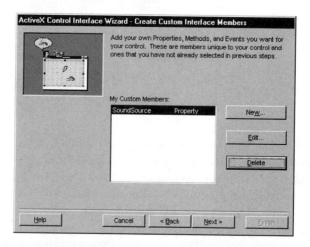

The listbox in this dialog window displays all the custom properties, methods, and events for your control. From here, you can add, edit, and delete any of the entries in the list. Click the New button and create another custom property named Repeat. This property is used to indicate the number of times the sound file is repeated.

16

After you have created the custom properties for your control, click the Next button to go to the Set Mapping dialog window. You can use this dialog window to associate the custom properties, methods, and events you have designed for your control to those of the *constituent controls*, which represent the existing controls you used to construct your custom control.

For this example, choose the SoundSource property in the Public Names listbox and select lblSource from the Control drop-down listbox. Once you have selected the lblSource control, all of its pre-defined members appear in the Member drop-down listbox. Choose Caption from the list of member items. This two-step process associates the caption on the label with the SoundSource property, which is used to enter a directory path and filename for the background sound. The association needs to be made so that the control can display the source of the background sound to the developer at design time. Figure 16.15 shows the end result of this mapping.

Figure 16.15.

Mapping a custom property.

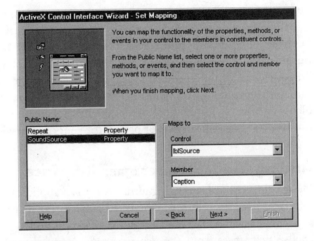

After you have mapped the SoundSource property, click the Next button to set the attributes for the Repeat property. The Set Attributes dialog window is displayed, where you set the attributes for any members you haven't mapped to a constituent control. From this dialog window, you can choose a member and set its data type and default value. You also can design its runtime and design-time controls and any arguments it should have. You should define arguments for members such as methods and events. You also can give a description for the member that tells a developer about its function and purpose. For the Repeat property, choose a data type of Integer and set its default value to -1.

Then click Next to complete the process and create the interface members you have defined for the control. The ActiveX Control Interface Wizard creates a summary report that outlines the remaining tasks you need to perform to finish developing and testing your control. You can choose to save this report and refer to it later, as shown in Figure 16.16.

Figure 16.16.

Reviewing the to-do list.

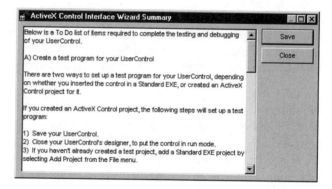

Implementing the Runtime Text

One of the key differences between an ActiveX control and a Design-time ActiveX control is that a Design-time ActiveX control doesn't have a visual interface at runtime. Instead, a Design-time control supplies text that can consist of HTML and script code that persists at runtime. This runtime text provides the smart logic for your application, based on the properties and attributes you set for the control at runtime. So far, the lesson has guided you through constructing your control's appearance and establishing the available properties. Now you're ready for the final step of the control creation process, which is providing the runtime text that will survive, or persist, for your control when the application is executed.

Adding the IActiveDesigner Interface

Design-time controls provide runtime text to an application by using the IActiveDesigner interface. You can use this interface to publish text that a container can access when an application is running, even though the control is no longer "alive." To add this interface, choose References from the Project menu. Next, choose Microsoft Web Design-Time Control Type Library from the list of items shown in Figure 16.17.

NOTE

If the name of this library isn't in the list, you can click the Browse button to search for and select the file that supports the Design-Time Control Type Library. The name of this file is webdc.tlb and is on this book's CD-ROM. Once you add this file, you can then select the library from the list.

16

Figure 16.17.
Adding the
`IActiveDesigner`
reference.

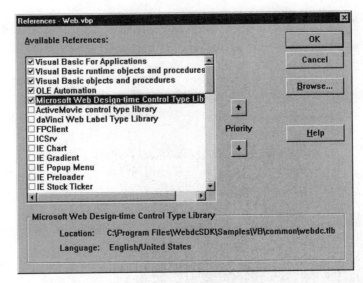

16

After you add the `IActiveDesigner` reference to your project, you need to provide the HTML and script code for the runtime text. This process requires two major steps. First, add a declaration for the `IRunTimeText` interface by double-clicking on the UserControl Designer to display the control's code procedures. Listing 16.1 shows the code that has been generated so far for the background sound Design-time control.

Listing 16.1. Reviewing the generated code.

```
'Default Property Values:
Const m_def_Repeat = -1
'Property Variables:
Dim m_Repeat As Integer

Private Sub Picture1_Click()

End Sub
'WARNING! DO NOT REMOVE OR MODIFY THE FOLLOWING COMMENTED LINES!
'MappingInfo=lblSource,lblSource,-1,Caption
Public Property Get SoundSource() As String
SoundSource = lblSource.Caption
End Property

Public Property Let SoundSource(ByVal New_SoundSource As String)
lblSource.Caption() = New_SoundSource
PropertyChanged "SoundSource"
End Property
```

continues

Listing 16.1. continued

```
Public Property Get Repeat() As Integer
Repeat = m_Repeat
End Property

Public Property Let Repeat(ByVal New_Repeat As Integer)
m_Repeat = New_Repeat
PropertyChanged "Repeat"
End Property

'Initialize Properties for User Control
Private Sub UserControl_InitProperties()
m_Repeat = m_def_Repeat
End Sub

'Load property values from storage
Private Sub UserControl_ReadProperties(PropBag As PropertyBag)

lblSource.Caption = PropBag.ReadProperty("SoundSource", "... No Sound Source")
m_Repeat = PropBag.ReadProperty("Repeat", m_def_Repeat)
End Sub

'Write property values to storage
Private Sub UserControl_WriteProperties(PropBag As PropertyBag)

Call PropBag.WriteProperty("SoundSource", lblSource.Caption,
"... No Sound Source")
Call PropBag.WriteProperty("Repeat", m_Repeat, m_def_Repeat)
End Sub
```

Figure 16.18 shows the code window containing the procedure code from Listing 16.1 for the Design-time control.

From this window, you can move through the different procedures for the control and add the necessary logic. The beginning of this file contains the general declarations for the control. Add the following definition for the `IProvideRuntimeText` interface to the declarations section:

```
Option Explicit
Implements IProvideRuntimeText
```

NOTE

One of VBCCE's exciting features is the `Auto List Members` function, which gives you a pop-up list of choices as you type in your code. When you enter the preceding lines of code, notice what happens after you type the word `Implements` and as you type `IProvideRuntimeText`.

> You get a list of choices that reacts and changes as you type the letters. You can select the item from the list at any time during this process and it's inserted into your code.
>
> This feature is a good time-saver and helps you avoid typing mistakes. VBCCE has the intelligent code editor that makes this feature and other smart editing features possible.

16

Figure 16.18.

Viewing the proce-dures.

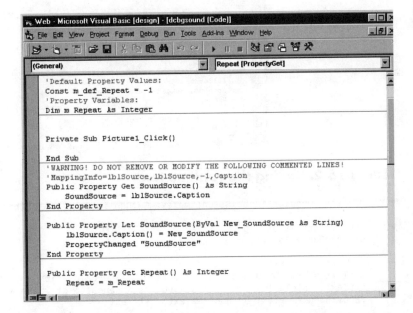

Once you define the interface definition, you're ready for the second step: selecting the IProvideRuntimeText object from the drop-down listbox in the code window, as seen in Figure 16.19.

After you select this object, the GetRuntimeText function is created, and you can add the code in Listing 16.2.

Figure 16.19.

Implementing the procedure.

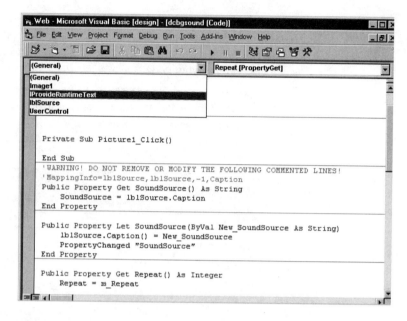

Listing 16.2. Coding the runtime text.

```
Private Function IProvideRuntimeText_GetRuntimeText() As String

Dim strText As String
Dim strQuote As String

strQuote = Chr$(34)
strText = "<BGSOUND SRC=" & strQuote & lblSource.Caption & strQuote
strText = strText & " LOOP=" & strQuote & Repeat & strQuote & ">"
IProvideRuntimeText_GetRuntimeText = strText

End Function
```

The code in this example declares two variables used to format the runtime text, which must be sent to the container as a string. The strQuote variable stores the ASCII character for a quotation and is used to enclose the values that appear in the runtime text in quotes. The strText variable is used to store the runtime text for the control, which includes the <BGSOUND> tag, the label's caption, the LOOP attribute, and the value of the Repeat property. The last statement of the code block sets the function name equal to the strText variable. Do you know why a function is used instead of a subprocedure? Refer back to the section on functions and subprocedures in the lesson on Day 7, "Extending Your Web Page Through Client-Side Script," if you need help answering this question.

16

After you include the code for the runtime text procedure, you're ready to compile the Design-time control and test the results. Choose Make Web.ocx from the File menu to create your Design-time control. This action compiles the code for your control to create an OCX file and, when done, automatically registers the control on your machine. You can then integrate and use the control in your applications.

Integrating the Control into Your Application

In the preceding section, you developed and compiled the code to build the OCX Design-time control. This section shows you how to integrate the control into your application and test its functionality. You can create a Visual InterDev project and insert the control into a web page. The control appears in the Insert ActiveX dialog window so you can select it from the list. Next, design the properties for your control by using the Object Editor, as shown in Figure 16.20.

Figure 16.20.

Inserting the Design-time control.

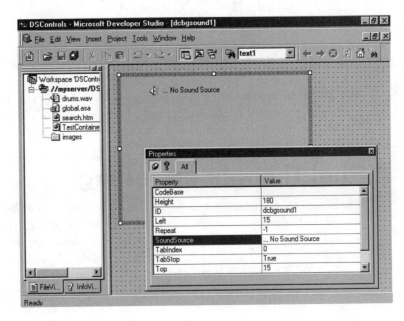

Using the Object Editor, you can set the Repeat and SoundSource properties and close the editor. The object and its runtime text are inserted into the web page, as shown in Figure 16.21.

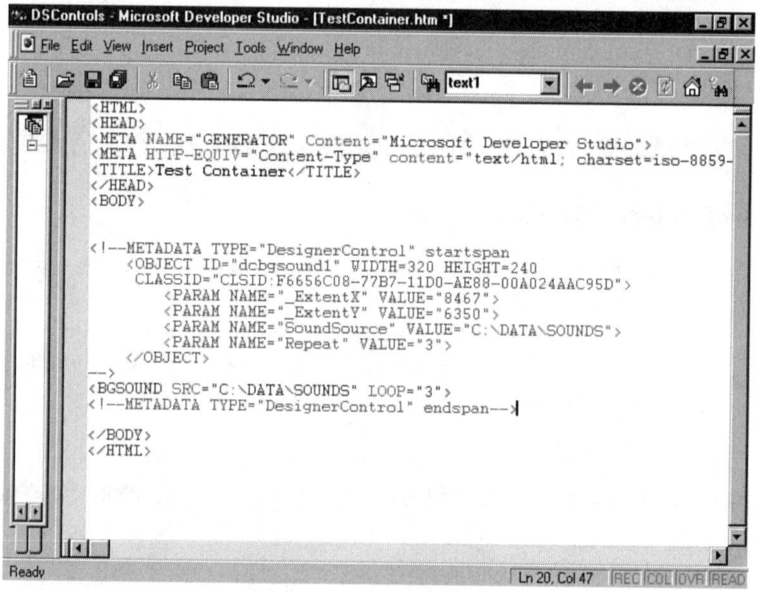

Figure 16.21.

Viewing the results.

Notice that the runtime text is formatted properly, as though you had entered the code in the web page yourself. This simple example shows how easy it is to construct a Design-time control. You can create powerful, useful controls in a short time with a tool like the VBCCE.

A Final Thought on Testing

The example in this lesson taught you how to design and build a Design-time control. The control you built was targeted specifically for a Web-based application, which is why you used Visual InterDev to integrate and test the control. Also, because the control was a Design-time control, you needed to actually see how the control worked. You can use the VBCCE to create regular ActiveX controls, which do have visual components that persist at runtime. You can create standard Visual Basic projects, as mentioned earlier, to test the implementation of your controls. These projects enable you to construct a form, insert the ActiveX control into the form, and then build an executable application to test the results. You also can save this test application project with the ActiveX control project as a VBCCE group project. This feature enables you to bundle a related group of projects, thereby associating the control project and its test application.

16

Summary

The lesson today has given you many reasons for creating your own custom ActiveX and Design-time ActiveX controls. The simplified process and tools, plus the ability to meet your application's needs, are compelling reasons to develop your own custom controls. It's easy to see why Visual Basic is continuing to take the development world by storm. Its straightfoward, user-friendly environment makes developers' jobs much easier.

Now review what you learned today. First, the lesson explained why you should build Design-time controls. You discovered that developing ActiveX and Design-time ActiveX controls is as easy as baking cookies. Next, you learned about the tools available to build these controls. Specifically, the lesson gave you an overview of two of the more popular tools for ActiveX control development: Visual C++ and Visual Basic Control Creation Edition. Next, you got an introductory tour into the world of VBCCE. You learned about its features and functions and how they can help you to construct ActiveX controls.

The latter part of the day's lesson focused on constructing and testing a Design-time ActiveX control. You learned step by step how to build a Design-time control. The lesson covered everything from designing the control's appearance to implementing the runtime text for the control. Next, you learned how to integrate the control into an application. The last section gave you a final thought on testing an ActiveX control.

Q&A

Q How does an ActiveX control created with Visual Basic work?

A ActiveX controls developed with Visual Basic work much like Java applets because these controls are interpreted by the virtual machine on the client computer. The virtual machine (MSVBVM5.DLL) is automatically downloaded and installed when a user accesses a web page containing a Visual Basic ActiveX control. Controls that use a newer version of the virtual machine also cause the virtual machine to be downloaded and installed to the user's client machine.

Q What are the main differences between VBCCE and Visual Basic Enterprise Edition?

A Visual Basic Control Creation Edition includes the new intelligent code editor, the ability to create forms, an interactive debugger, and the ability to create ActiveX and Design-time ActiveX controls. The full version of Visual Basic 5.0 has these features as well as other features not found in the VBCCE. These additional VB features include the JET database engine, report writing, and version control through Visual SourceSafe. VBCCE is included as part of the Visual Basic product but is also available as a separate product.

16

Workshop

Today's lesson gave you an opportunity to develop a Design-time ActiveX control. For today's workshop, you get a chance to build an ActiveX control so you can see what it's like to design a visual control that persists at runtime. This workshop helps you understand the differences between constructing an ActiveX control and a Design-time ActiveX control. The advantage to this workshop is that you get to design the ActiveX control of your choice. You should take this opportunity to implement and extend the features of an existing ActiveX control. Think about the new super control you want to develop and then use VBCCE to design and develop it.

Quiz

1. What interface enables your Design-time control's text to persist at runtime?
2. What unique VBCCE feature do you use to create custom properties for your control?
3. What is the UserControl object?

Quiz Answers

1. IActiveDesigner.
2. The ActiveX Control Interface Wizard.
3. Every ActiveX control created with Visual Basic consists of the UserControl object, which provides a visual designer for creating your control and a code shell to include your control's functionality.

16

Day 17

Using Active Server Components to Create Multitier Applications

As technology continues to change rapidly, new developments keep improving the lives of both producers (developers) and consumers (end-users). You have discovered many of the new developments for Web-based application development through the lessons in this book. Today's lesson continues exploring new developments by introducing you to the world of Active Server Components, previously known as OLE Automation Servers. Visual Basic developers are probably familiar with the concept of OLE Automation Servers, which were introduced in Visual Basic 4.0. Just as ActiveX replaced OLE controls, Active Server Components have become the new and improved version of OLE Automation Servers. These new and powerful components can be integrated into your Active Server Pages, enabling you to create robust applications that handle your users' processing needs. At the beginning of the first week, the lesson's main premise was that the Web had moved from a publishing metaphor to one of true interaction. Active Server Components help streamline this activity by giving your application robust functionality.

Today's lesson gives you insight into many topics. First, you gain an understanding of the Component Object Model and the Distributed Component Object Model from Microsoft. Next, you learn how to define and explain Active Server Components; you also learn about their main benefits and strengths for use in your application. The lesson then teaches you how to include and integrate Active Server Components into your Active Server Pages. This part of the lesson explains how to capitalize on these components' power to meet the needs of your application.

An Architecture Review: COM and DCOM

Microsoft developed the *Component Object Model* (COM) to supply a common method for communication between objects. COM's roots can be traced back to OLE technology, also developed by Microsoft. COM enables objects to communicate with each other through effective dialogue, thereby forming a synergistic relationship. With true dialogue, each object can understand the other object's interfaces, methods, and services so that they can work together for the good of the end-user. Two terms concerning COM technology are used throughout this part of the lesson: producer and consumer. The *producer* represents the object that provides the basic interfaces, methods, and services to another object; the *consumer* is the object or application that uses, or consumes, the services of the producer object. Some objects alternate being the producer and consumer, based on their capabilities and the relationship established between the two objects. An example of this kind of relationship is a project team consisting of many different team members who have certain unique skills. Each team member knows the strengths and roles of the other people on the team. Also, standard communication methods—e-mail, meetings, and telephone conversations—have been established to facilitate sharing knowledge. The team members communicate and share their abilities and services to create an application.

Other communication is strictly one-way in nature, such as communication in a relationship between a coffee shop and its customers. The coffee shop has communicated its message, advertising itself as the place to buy superb coffee drinks. Customers, including myself, realize the service it provides and consume drinks such as cafe mochas in large quantities. This kind of communication is similar to a COM object that advertises, or publishes, its unique services, while the client application consumes, or uses, these services.

NEW TERM A *producer* is an object that implements and provides certain methods and services through standard interfaces. COM is used to make these services available to other objects.

A *consumer* is an object that uses the services of a producer object. This type of object can also be referred to as a *client* or *container object*.

Objects use COM on the same machine. However, Microsoft has extended COM's reaches by creating the Distributed Component Object Model, or DCOM, which enables you to communicate with a COM object on another machine. The following sections explain COM and DCOM in more depth and cover the benefits of each technology.

 This discussion on COM and DCOM is meant to briefly introduce these exciting and robust technologies. It only begins to scratch the surface on these topics. This section gives you a foundation for the rest of today's lesson, which focuses on Active Server Components. For more information on ActiveX, COM, and DCOM, I highly recommend *Understanding ActiveX and OLE* by David Chappell.

Understanding COM

In the previous section, you learned that COM objects operate on the same machine and can be used as in-process servers or local servers. In-process server objects provide their code in a dynamic link library (DLL) that executes in the same process as the consumer object. Figure 17.1 demonstrates the communication between a consumer and a producer that has been implemented as an in-process server.

Figure 17.1.

An in-process server.

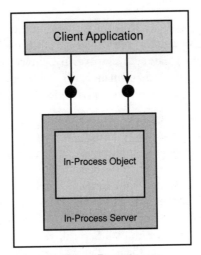

Client Process

Because an in-process server is implemented as a DLL, the objects in Figure 17.1 operate within the same address space in memory, so they can share information more easily.

You can also use a COM object as a local server that resides as a separate process running on the same machine as the consumer or client application. Figure 17.2 illustrates the communication process for a local server object.

Figure 17.2.

A local server.

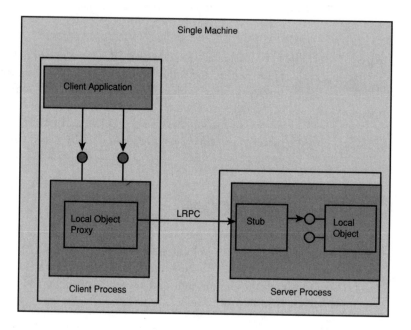

As you can see, the COM objects communicate through a special type of remote procedure call: *LRPC,* or *local/lightweight remote procedure call.* LRPCs offer a way for COM objects executing in separate address spaces in memory to communicate with each other. The LRPC communication mechanism indicates that the communication is local to the machine. In the next section, you learn another name for communication across multiple machines.

COM offers several benefits to a developer. First, COM enables you to create reusable components for your application. You can use COM's power to create separate software components that your application can access when necessary, thereby avoiding redundancy and duplication in individual code modules. In this way, the processing logic in the COM component is isolated from the application code, so you can change the component without affecting the application. This process has two main implications. First, you can separate the true business and database logic from your presentation logic, which takes advantage of a three-tier application model. Second, you don't have to recompile and redistribute your application whenever the logic in the component changes. In other words, the component centralizes the process for software updates, giving you a simpler approach to version control.

Another benefit of COM is that it offers a consistent method for objects to converse with each other. Using a standard form of communication means you know an object's message is received, understood, and incorporated into the life of the other object. Also, since COM objects implement a binary runtime interface, you can develop a COM object with one language and consume its services with an object or application created with another language. This benefit shows you that COM is a language-independent model for application and component development.

Understanding DCOM

Microsoft's DCOM is founded on the same principles as COM but extends these principles across multiple machines; its main design goal is to make use of the same powerful characteristics of COM across machines in your network. DCOM enables objects on different machines to communicate, thereby integrating COM's communications strengths and the network.

DCOM also opens up new possibilities for robust application processing. The first uses of OLE and COM were embedding a spreadsheet into a word processing document. Once users got over the novelty of this feature, they wanted the technology to deliver more functionality. DCOM capitalizes on the strengths of COM so you can offer the robust functionality your users have been clamoring for. You can integrate DCOM objects and components on a server machine to give your applications powerful server programs. Later in today's lesson, you learn how to integrate DCOM components into an application.

DCOM components are considered remote servers because they're implemented remotely on a different machine from the client consumer machine. You can implement a DCOM object as a DLL or a separate executable process.

DCOM uses *Object Remote Procedure Calls*, or *ORPCs*, as the communication vehicle for different machine objects, as shown in Figure 17.3. By using ORPCs, you can make communication between objects easier and cause the producer object to seem as though it's local to the consumer. This process is like virtual shopping, where you electronically move through a store, picking out the items you want to buy; this simulated shopping makes it seem as though you're actually in the store selecting items. DCOM provides tight security to make sure only authorized users can activate a specified DCOM component.

Microsoft has recently included DCOM with its Windows NT Server operating system, which should rapidly increase the number of DCOM applications being developed. You can make use of DCOM's strengths to integrate your Web-based applications with existing client-server and legacy systems. The following sections cover the capabilities of Active Server Components and Active Server Pages.

17

Figure 17.3.
The art of DCOM.

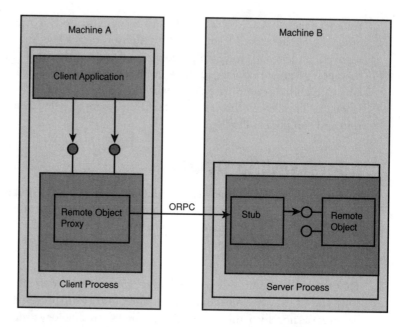

What Is an Active Server Component?

Now that you understand the basic concepts of COM and DCOM, you can go on to learn about Active Server Components. Today's lesson also describes the basic types of objects and components included as part of the Active Server Scripting model.

Active Server Components are objects or components implemented as part of your Web-based application with an Active Server Page. You can develop Active Server Components to exist as in-process DLLs or out-of-process executable programs, in addition to local or remote servers. A common example of a local server component is a DLL that executes within an Active Server Page (ASP). You might also want to create an Active Server Component that uses DCOM to integrate your Web-based application with a legacy application, such as an accounting system. In this case, the Active Server Component resides on a separate machine from the web server.

Visual InterDev includes several intrinsic and extrinsic objects included as part of the Active Server Pages model, previously code-named *Denali*. The intrinsic objects, covered previously on Day 11, "Extending Your Application Through Active Server Script," include the `Request`, `Response`, `Server`, `Application`, and `Session` objects. The Active Server Pages model also includes several extrinsic objects that can be used in your application. These extrinsic objects, or components, give you prepackaged functionality, such as checking a client browser's capabilities, providing database access, and rotating the display of ads. The following sections outline the uses and features of these extrinsic objects.

The Ad Rotator Component

The AdRotator object enables you to rotate the display of advertising images on a web page. The object name of this component is MSWC.AdRotator. This feature has probably been implemented on many of the sites you have visited, such as the Microsoft home site at this URL:

```
http://www.microsoft.com
```

You can specify the images in a text file and use the GetAdvertisement method to display a specific advertising image. You can also designate a URL link for the image so the user can travel to the web site indicated by the ad. The GetAdvertisement method uses the information in the text file, called an *ad schedule file*, to generate the HTML needed to display the ad image. A new ad is displayed every time the user opens or refreshes the web page.

The Browser Capabilities Component

The Browser Capabilities object enables you to determine the capabilities of a user's browser from within your application. This object is helpful when users with different browsers are accessing your web pages. You can use this object to determine the browser's capabilities and then take the appropriate actions with the application to give the user the best possible experience. The object name of this component is MSWC.BrowserType.

The Browser Capabilities object uses the HTTP User Agent header to determine which browser is being used. This header is sent by the browser when it connects to your web server. Based on the browser's name, this object then identifies the capabilities based on entries in the BrowsCap.INI file. The capability entries in the INI file become properties of the instance of the BrowserType object in your application. After you declare the instance of this object, you can access its properties to determine what capabilities the browser has. For example, you could create an instance of the browser object and then check to see whether the browser supports VBScript, as demonstrated in the following example:

```
<% Set bc = CreateObject("MSWC.BrowserType")

<% If (bc.vbscript = "True") Then
MsgBox "Your browser supports VBScript."
Else
MsgBox "I can't believe your browser does not support VBScript!"
End if %>
```

The Database Access Component

You can use the Database Access component to connect to a database from within your application. This component uses the Active Data Object (ADO) model to enable you to connect and interact with the database tables and information. Refer to the lesson on Day 8, "Communicating with a Database," for an overview of the ADO model and its objects, methods, properties, and attributes.

The Content Linking Component

The Content Linking component enables you to set up user-friendly page navigation in your application. You can design the flow of your Active Server Pages, include the hierarchy in a text file, and then use this component and its methods to determine the links between the ASPs. The text file lists URL addresses for your application and an optional description for each link. You can create a text file and specify one URL link per line in the order you want to design the page navigation. Once you have created the link file, you can see its contents by using the GetNthURL method, as demonstrated in Listing 17.1.

Listing 17.1. Retrieving the links.

```
<%
'Declares object instance of the Content Linking component
Set NextLink=Server.CreateObject("MSWC.NextLink")
'Determines how many links are included in the text file
count=NextLink.GetListCount("/Vroot/Nextlink.txt")
%>
<UL>
'Loops through the links displaying the URL address and its description
<% For i = 1 to count %>
<li><a href="<%=NextLink.GetNthUrl("/Vroot/Nextlink.txt",i) %>">
<%=NextLink.GetNthDescription("/Vroot/Nextlink.txt",i) %></a>
<% Next %></UL>
```

The Text Stream Component

The Text Stream component enables you to access the server machine's file system. Its object name is MSWC.TextStream. Using this component, you can perform all file access functions, including opening, reading, writing, saving, and closing a file. This component is useful for storing and accessing information you want to use frequently in your application but don't want to store in a database. You could, for example, store application state information as well as a listing of thoughts of the day.

Creating Custom Active Server Components

In addition to the standard ASP components, you can build your own custom Active Server Components to tailor the component to the needs of your application. As mentioned, Active Server Components are the successors to OLE Automation Servers, which you might have created with Visual Basic 4.0. Server components consist of robust application logic that gives your application functionality without requiring a user interface. You can develop an Active Server Component for your application with a variety of languages and tools, including Visual Basic 4.0 and higher, Visual C++, Visual J++, and other development tools that support building COM components.

The Benefits of Active Server Components

17

Using Active Server Components in your application offers many benefits. First, the tools that support creating these components enable you to incorporate robust and powerful functionality into your application. You no longer have to supply workaround solutions in your HTML and scripting code to meet the needs of your application. Tools such as Visual Basic and Visual C++ extend your application's capabilities. You can use the power of these tools to process sophisticated logic, thus improving the overall performance of your Web-based application. For example, you could convert the financial calculation routine you created with JavaScript into a powerful Visual Basic or Visual C++ Active Server Component. Your users will appreciate the extra time they gain because of this performance improvement.

Another advantage of Active Server Components is the integration of existing client-server and legacy systems. You may already have existing systems you want to integrate into your new Web-based applications. Active Server Components give you an excellent medium for tapping into the functionality of these applications without having to rewrite entire legacy applications. You can create Active Server Components to serve as the "glue" between your Web-based application and existing systems. The custom component you develop provides a gateway into the existing system's functionality and enables your Web-based application to make use of its capabilities. With custom components, you can preserve the investment in your legacy systems while incorporating new technologies into your applications.

Active Server Components offer another benefit: providing reusability for your development team and other applications. Instead of duplicating similar functions in every application module, you can create an Active Server Component that's accessible from all your ASPs.

Your developers benefit because they don't have to code the logic into their ASP module, and you eliminate redundancy in your application, which can improve its performance. Although you may create an Active Server Component with a single application in mind, the component might serve other applications you develop, too. This reusability feature can help reduce your development time.

Integrating Active Server Components and Active Server Pages

This section of today's lesson teaches you how to integrate and use Active Server Components in your Web-based applications. It also offers several examples of using the pre-defined Active Server Components that were previously described.

> **NOTE**
>
> You typically call an Active Server Component from within an ASP. You can, however, invoke an Active Server Component from other Active Server Components, as well as from ISAPI and Java applications.

Creating Dynamic Advertisements

This example uses the Ad Rotator component to demonstrate creating a dynamic web page. The lesson guides you through the process of declaring an instance of this object and then using it within an ASP to display rotating ads on a web page. The GIF files and code used in this example are on the book's CD-ROM.

You learned how to create and use ASPs in your application on Day 11. From the ASP lesson, you know that an ASP enables you to combine both HTML and script to construct a dynamic web page. In a newly created web page, you can use the Ad Rotator component to display alternating advertisements. The first step is to create an instance of the AdRotator object by entering the following line in the ASP file:

```
<% Set MyAd = Server.CreateObject("MSWC.Adrotator") %>
```

This code creates an instance of the AdRotator object and sets it equal to the MyAd variable. Once this declaration is made, you can then use the MyAd object in the ASP to access its properties and methods. Another way to create this object is to declare an instance of the object within the Session_OnStart event. Remember, this event begins whenever a user first opens your application. The scope of the object is then established for the entire time the user interacts with the application. The following code example shows how to declare an instance of the AdRotator object in the Session_OnStart event procedure:

```
Sub Session_OnStart ()
<% Set MyAd = Server.CreateObject("MSWC.Adrotator") %>
End Sub
```

You can also declare the object as a session object from within the ASP to accomplish the same purpose, as shown in the following code line:

```
<OBJECT RUNAT=Server SCOPE=Session ID=MyAd PROGID="MSWC.Adrotator">
</OBJECT>
```

In this example, a page-level instance is used for the AdRotator object. Once an instance of the object has been declared, you can access its properties and methods to make it functional. Use the GetAdvertisement method to retrieve and display advertising images on your web page. Here's the syntax to call this method:

```
AdObjectName.GetAdvertisement("FileName.txt")
```

In this code, AdObjectName is the object's instance name, and FileName is the name of the text file containing the image filenames. To retrieve the names of the image files in AdData.txt, for example, you would enter this code:

```
<% MyAd.GetAdvertisement("AdData.txt") %>
```

Listing 17.2 shows you the full code example for a sample ASP file that uses the AdRotator object.

Listing 17.2. Using the AdRotator object.

```
<%@ LANGUAGE="VBSCRIPT" %>

<HTML>
<HEAD>
<META NAME="GENERATOR" Content="Microsoft Visual InterDev 1.0">
<META HTTP-EQUIV="Content-Type" content="text/html; charset=iso-8859-1">
<TITLE>Ad Rotator</TITLE>
<H3>This Page contains dynamic ads!</H3>
</HEAD>
<BODY>

<%
'Declares an instance of the Ad Rotator object
Set MyAd = Server.CreateObject("MSWC.Adrotator")
'Writes the necessary logic to display the GIF on the Web page
Response.Write(MyAd.GetAdvertisement("/components/AdData.txt"))
%>

</BODY>
</HTML>
```

17

Based on the logic in this code listing, the advertisements in the AdData.txt file are displayed on the web page, as seen in Figures 17.4 and 17.5.

Figure 17.4.

Viewing the initial ad.

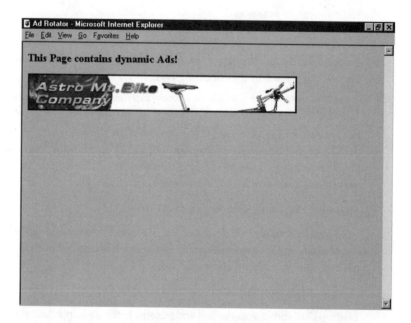

Figure 17.5.

Rotating the ads.

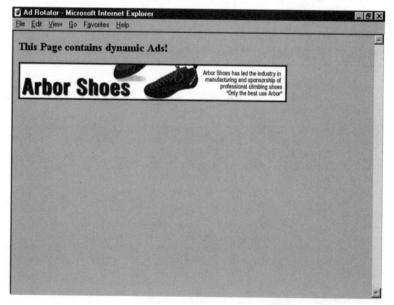

The advertisement images used in this example are some of the same ads used in the Adventure Works sample found on Microsoft's home site and included with Visual InterDev. Listing 17.3 displays the contents of the AdData.txt file.

Listing 17.3. Specifying the ad images.

```
redirect /AdvWorks/adredir.asp
width 460
height 60
border 1
*
/components/images/ad_1.gif
http://www.microsoft.com
Astro Mt. Bike Company
20

/components/images/ad_2.gif
http://www.microsoft.com
Arbor Shoes
20

/components/images/ad_3.gif
http://www.microsoft.com
Clocktower Sporting Goods
30

/components/images/ad_4.gif
http://www.microsoft.com
GG&G
30
```

As you can tell from this example, the ads are listed in the text file in the order they will rotate on the web page. The width and height are specified for the ad image container, along with a URL address and description for each of the images. The Redirect statement actually redirects the user back to a web page in the Adventure Works site. If you have installed the sample Adventure Works application, you can run the previous web page example and click an image to go to the Adventure Works site.

Displaying a Browser's Capabilities

This section demonstrates how to use the Browser Capabilities component in an ASP file. The example used in this part of the lesson displays an HTML table listing the capabilities of the user's browser. To use the Browser Capabilities component, you must first declare an instance of the BrowserType object, as shown in the following code line:

```
<% Set bc = Server.CreateObject("MSWC.BrowserType") %>
```

You can then use the bc instance of the object to determine and display the browser's capabilities. Listing 17.4 shows the code used to create this table.

Listing 17.4. Creating the Capabilities table.

```
<% Set bc = Server.CreateObject("MSWC.BrowserType") %>

<TABLE BORDER=1>
<TR><TD>Browser</TD><TD><%= bc.browser %></TD></TR>
<TR><TD>Version</TD><TD><%= bc.version %></TD></TR>
<TR><TD>Frames</TD><TD>

<% If (bc.frames = "True") Then %>TRUE
<% Else %>FALSE
<% End If %>

</TD></TR>
<TR><TD>Tables</TD><TD>

<% If (bc.tables = "True") Then %>TRUE
<% Else %>FALSE
<% End If %>

</TD></TR>
<TR><TD>BackgroundSounds</TD><TD>

<% If (bc.BackgroundSounds = "True") Then %>TRUE
<% Else %>FALSE
<% End If %>

</TD></TR>
<TR><TD>VBScript</TD><TD>

<% If (bc.vbscript = "True") Then %>TRUE
<% Else %>FALSE
<% End If %>

</TD></TR>
<TR><TD>JavaScript</TD><TD>

<% If (bc.javascript = "True") Then %>TRUE
<% Else %>FALSE
<% End If %>
</TD></TR>
</TABLE>
```

In this code example, an instance of the BrowserType object is created, and then the object is used to reference the browser's capabilities. A series of checks are made to determine what the browser supports. Based on these checks, the table is formatted with the browser's capabilities for the specified feature. Figure 17.6 displays the results of accessing the ASP with a sample browser.

17

Figure 17.6.

Discovering the browser's capabilities.

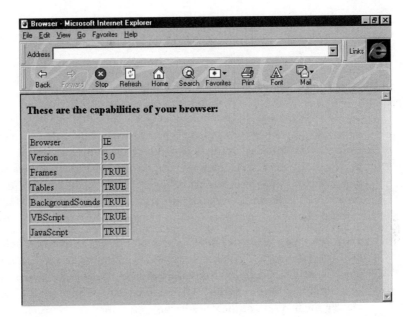

These are the capabilities of your browser:

Browser	IE
Version	3.0
Frames	TRUE
Tables	TRUE
BackgroundSounds	TRUE
VBScript	TRUE
JavaScript	TRUE

A Call to Action

Active Server Components are crucial to your Web-based applications. As technology continues to develop in this area, developers and users alike are realizing the importance of building a robust architecture for your application. Web-based applications offer a new challenge because the thin client model places even more of a burden on the server. New products, such as the Microsoft Transaction Server and other middleware products, that meet your application's needs are continuing to be developed. As a developer, you must be aware of the challenges in developing robust Internet and intranet applications.

Several years ago, client-server technology lulled developers into thinking they could paint a few screens with a RAD tool and implement a system. Developers soon found out there was more to implementing a system than inserting a few controls on a window and calling the application done. For some developers, it took users screaming about application response time to realize the importance of the system's architecture. Likewise, Web-based applications are now rolling out all over the world.

To avoid making the same mistake they made with client-server technology, developers should become knowledgeable about both the client and server sides of a Web-based application. They should study the application's requirements and design an architecture for it that adequately addresses these needs. Active Server Components can help keep your server from becoming overburdened, so as developers, you should learn more about Active Server Components. Analyze your application and identify whether you need to integrate a component into your application. Next, determine whether you need to build a custom server component and then act accordingly.

Summary

Today's lesson should have opened your eyes to the world of Active Server Components. The server side of your Web-based application needs all the help it can get, and Active Server Components are just what you need to do the job. In the future, you will see companies, such as Microsoft, integrating more robust features into their servers to meet the needs of organizations' applications. Active Server Components are just one part of the server equation. Middleware and transaction-processing software will become increasingly important for your Web-based applications, just as they have for client-server technology.

To review what you learned in today's lesson, you got an overview of Microsoft's COM and DCOM technologies. The lesson explained each of these models, their benefits, and how they can be used. Next, you learned about Active Server Components. The lesson gave you a definition, as well as examples of intrinsic and extrinsic ASP objects and components. During the first part of the day's lesson, you gained an appreciation of how Active Server Components serve as the glue between your Web-based application and other new and existing client-server and legacy applications. Next, the lesson demonstrated how to integrate Active Server Components into your application. You learned how to use some of the predefined Active Server Components included as part of the ASP model to meet your application's needs. Finally, I urged you to learn more about Active Server Components and how they can be used to develop effective applications.

Q&A

Q What's the difference between Active Server Pages and Active Server Components?

A Active Server Pages combine HTML with client- and server-side script to create dynamic web pages for your application. An ASP can be created with a text editor. Active Server Components, on the other hand, are executable programs or dynamic link libraries that can be called from your ASP. Active Server Components are constructed by using a robust development tool, such as Visual Basic or Visual C++.

Q Can I use Java applications with Active Server Components?

A The short answer is yes. Java applications are welcome in Microsoft's world of COM components. Using Microsoft's implementation of the Java virtual machine

(VM), Java applications appear as COM objects to Active Server Components. Likewise, COM objects appear as Java objects to Java applets and applications. This process is transparent to the components involved because Microsoft's Java VM performs all the necessary translations.

Workshop

Today's workshop presents a challenge to learn a language or development tool that will enable you to develop a custom Active Server Component. Your choices include Visual Basic, Visual C++, or a Java development tool, such as Symantec's Visual Café. Learn the tool of your choice, and then design and develop an Active Server Component to integrate into a Visual InterDev application. You will be glad you did!

Quiz

1. Name the five extrinsic components included with the ASP model.
2. What's the basic difference between COM and DCOM?
3. What method can be used to retrieve and display rotating advertisement images to the browser?
4. What's the vehicle or mechanism that enables DCOM objects to communicate with each other?

Quiz Answers

1. Ad Rotator

   Browser Capabilities

   Content Linking

   Database Access

   Text Stream
2. DCOM facilitates the communication of objects located on different machines. COM is used for objects and components residing on the same machine.
3. `GetAdvertisement`.
4. Object Remote Procedure Call (ORPC).

Day **18**

Managing Your Web Site Files with Visual InterDev

During the last three weeks, you have absorbed a lot of information about the creation of web pages and components to include in your Web-based application. You should now possess the knowledge to be able to create a variety of essential items to build the killer app. Given this newfound ability, how in the world are you going to manage the plethora of files that you develop for your application?

This lesson answers that question by presenting the robust site management tools that are included with Visual InterDev. These tools contain some highly integrated features that can help you organize your site and create order out of chaos.

The first lesson for the day teaches you about the Link View. You will learn how to use the powerful view to get a handle on all of the files contained in your web site. Next, you will learn how to leverage your web site development to other Web-based applications and sites that you create. Visual InterDev provides some powerful features for copying portions of all of your web site to other directories or web servers. The lesson then demonstrates the proper management of the different files contained in your web site, including web pages, databases, images and multimedia, and other objects and components. The final lesson for the day teaches you how to use the features of Visual InterDev to repair broken links within your web site.

Getting a Handle with the Link View

The Link View presents a new way to look at your web. This exciting and powerful feature enables you to truly get a handle on all of the files that are contained in your Web-based application. The Link View provides a graphical tool that enables you to visually examine the files within your web site and their relationships. You have the ability to expand or contract the view to explore different aspects of your site. For example, you may want to focus solely on a certain section or group of web pages or objects. The Link View gives you the power to pick the right view for your needs. In addition to viewing the relationships, you also can use the Link View to identify the file types for each of the items in your application. This feature includes everything from HTML web pages to Java applets. In short, the Link View provides a rich, graphical tool to help you conceptualize the design of your web site.

Exploring the Link View Features

The Link View not only presents a comprehensive picture of your web site, it also enables you to interact with your web site objects from within its view. Figure 18.1 illustrates the power of the Link View as it graphically displays a sample web site.

This illustration depicts a highly robust web site that includes just about every type of file imaginable for a Web-based application. You can see that graphical icons depict the file type for each item in the view, while lines and arrows indicate the relationship between the files. The arrows and circles located at the ends of the lines serve as visual indicators that describe the nature of the relationship. A circle next to an object indicates that it is the parent, and the arrow next to an object signifies that it is the child.

From Figure 18.1, you can determine that the HTML web page named internal.htm is the parent of all of the surrounding files. You can describe the relationship another way by stating that the global.asp. file is the child of the internal.htm web page. In other words, the ASP file is a part of the web page. As with every relationship, you will have times when the communication link is broken. The Link View graphically displays these broken links in red, indicating that there is a problem. You can use the Link View to see both links to objects within your web site as well as links to external sites such as a news server or a site on the Web.

Figure 18.1.

Getting a clearer picture with the Link View.

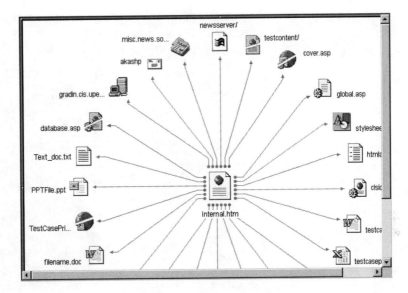

The Link View enables you to see a multitude of files, including HTML web pages, images and sound files, ActiveX controls, Java applets, and HTML layout files. You can basically examine any file that is a part of your web site using the Link View. From the Link View, you can then select and edit an object using its default editor. You also can choose to browse a web page from within this view and filter the Link View to see only the files of a certain type. This filter enables you to work with a discrete number of files contained in your web site, thereby simplifying the site management process.

The object contained in the middle of Figure 18.1 appears with a large icon, while all of the surrounding items display with smaller icons. The large icon signifies that the developer opened a Link View for this object. You will learn more about opening a Link View in the next section.

Opening a Link View

You can view a web site object using the Link View by selecting the file in the Visual InterDev project workspace and clicking the right mouse button to display the shortcut menu, as shown in Figure 18.2.

You can then select View Links from the shortcut menu to display a Link View for the file. Figure 18.3 depicts the Link View for the default web page used in the Dos Perros sample application included with Visual InterDev.

Figure 18.2.

Opening a file with Link View.

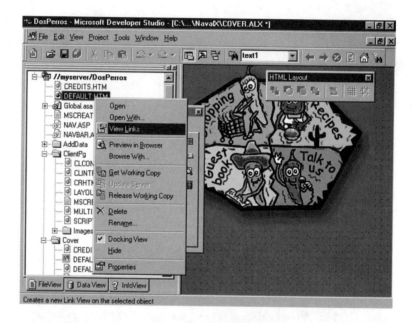

Figure 18.3.

Viewing the links.

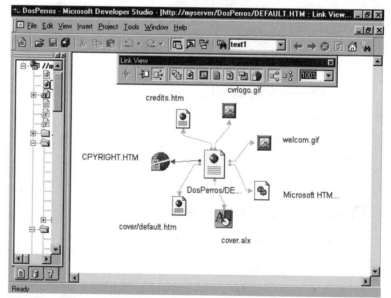

As you can see, the Default.htm consists of several GIF images, an HTML layout file (cover.alx), and several additional HTML files. The link to the CPYRIGHT.HTM file appears in red, indicating that the link to this file is broken. You should notice that the icon for this file is red and appears broken. When you open a file to view its links, the Link View initiates a verification process that gathers information on all of the object's associated files, including their file type and the nature of their relationship to the selected object. Figure 18.4 demonstrates the state and appearance of the associated files as they progress through the verification process.

Figure 18.4.

The visual progression of an object.

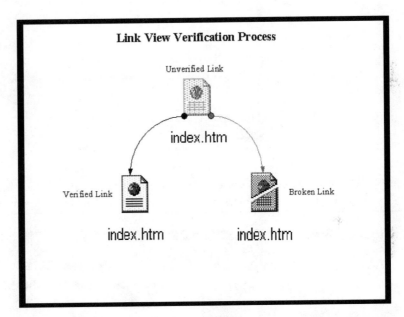

The file located at the top of the illustration represents a file whose relationship link hasn't been determined. Notice that it looks grayed out. After the Link View verifies the relationship, the icon is either displayed in its natural color, indicating that the link has been verified and established, or the icon appears red and broken, signifying that the link relationship has been broken.

You can open a Link View on any object that appears within the Link View diagram. This feature enables you to drill down to obtain a picture of your web site's hierarchy. To accomplish this task, select the desired object within the Link View diagram and right-click the mouse button. The shortcut menu will be displayed for the object, enabling you to select View Links, as shown in Figure 18.5.

Figure 18.5.
Drilling down on your web site.

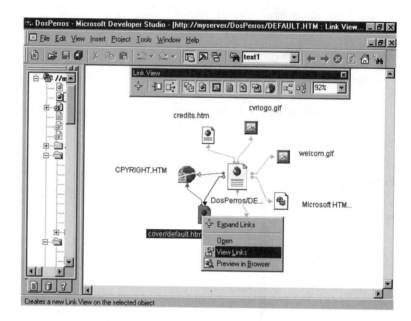

Once you select the View Links menu item, a Link View diagram is created, enabling you to view the selected object and its related files, as depicted in Figure 18.6.

Figure 18.6.
Viewing another object's links.

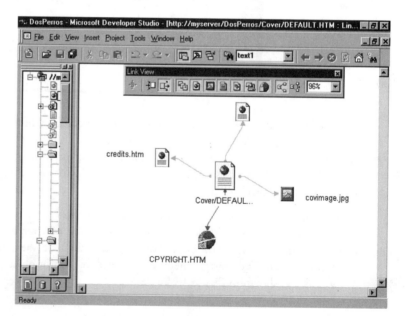

18

You also can view the links for any URL address by choosing the Tools menu and selecting View Links on WWW. You are then prompted to enter a URL address for the web page that you want to see in the Link View. This feature is helpful when you want to examine the structure of a web site without having to open the project within Visual InterDev. You can use this feature for your own internal intranet addresses as well as for external Internet URL addresses. Figure 18.7 depicts a Link View diagram for the Microsoft home page.

Figure 18.7.

Viewing the links for a URL on the Web.

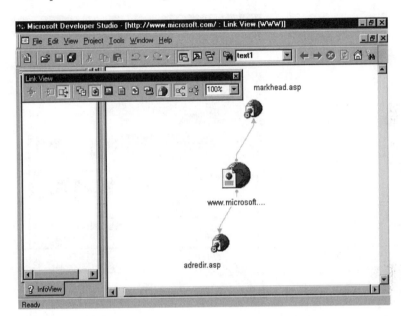

TIP

Once a Link View diagram has been created, you can choose the appropriate display size for the diagram by using the Zoom Link View icon on the View Link toolbar. This tool enables you to choose different percentages for the diagram display, which means that you can zoom in and zoom out on the objects. You can select a default value or enter a custom value for the zoom percentage. You also can select Fit from the drop-down listbox, which fits the Link View diagram into the Link View display area.

Filtering Your Link View

The Link View enables you to filter the amount and type of information displayed in your diagram, so you can more easily decipher and understand your web site structure. You can choose Filters from the View menu to display a menu list of available filter choices as depicted in Figure 18.8.

Figure 18.8.

Selecting a filter for your Link View.

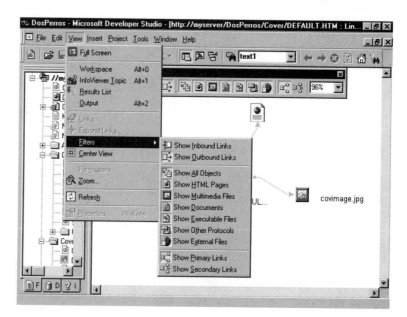

As you can see, Visual InterDev provides many choices to filter the objects that are displayed within your Link View diagram. Table 18.1 provides an explanation for each of the filter options that are available.

Table 18.1. Filter categories.

Icon	Category	Description
	Show Inbound Links	Displays the inbound links; in other words, the children of the parent object
	Show Outbound Links	Displays the outbound links; in other words, the objects that the parent links into (the parent's parent)

18

Icon	Category	Description
	Show All Objects	Displays all objects
	Show HTML Pages	Displays HTML web pages
	Show Multimedia Files	Displays images and multimedia files
	Show Documents	Displays documents files (MS Word, PowerPoint, and so on)
	Show Executable Files	Displays program files such as EXEs and DLLs
	Show Other Protocols	Displays links to non-HTTP objects, such as news servers, Mail, and Telnet
	Show External Files	Displays objects external to the project

18

You can use any of these filters to limit the types of files that are displayed in your Link View diagram. Initially, all of the available items will be enabled. Selecting a filter option from the list toggles the choice on and off. For example, in order to show only images and multimedia files in your diagram, you would need to turn off all of the other filter choices by selecting them. Figure 18.9 depicts the decision to display only multimedia files and how that affects the view of the default page for the Dos Perros application.

 TIP

Each of these menu items is displayed and can be executed from the View Link toolbar.

 NOTE

The process of toggling options on and off to filter the items on your diagram is counterintuitive to the captions that are displayed for these menu items. You would think that selecting Show Multimedia Files

> would limit the display to only images and other multimedia items. Instead, selecting this option when it's enabled hides your multimedia files. This behavior was exhibited in the Release Candidate 2 of the product. Hopefully, the final version or the next revision will address this usability issue.

Figure 18.9.

Viewing the images.

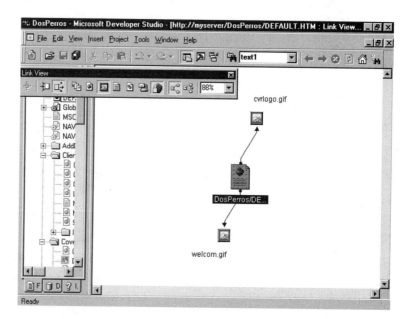

Working with Links

The default Link View diagram displays all of the *primary* links for the selected, or expanded, object. Primary links consist of those objects that are directly related to the expanded object. You also can choose to view the *secondary* links within your diagram. These links identify the relationships that exist between the objects that are displayed in the diagram. For example, several web pages may share the use of an image that is displayed on all of the pages.

For the sake of example, call the web pages Page1, Page2, and Page3 and the image Shared.gif. Page1 is the default page for the web site and contains the Shared.gif image and links to Page2 and Page3. If you opened a Link View diagram for Page1, the primary relationships for Page1 would exist with Page2, Page3, and Shared.gif. The secondary links would exist between Page2 and Shared.gif and between Page3 and Shared.gif. Figure 18.10 logically depicts these relationships.

18

Figure 18.10.

Conceptualizing primary and secondary links.

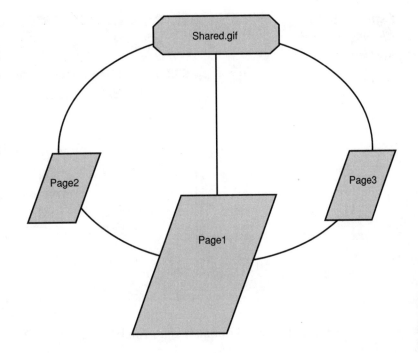

 NEW TERM   A *primary* link represents a direct relationship between an expanded object and one of its associated objects.

NEW TERM   A *secondary* link indicates a relationship between two or more of the associated objects for an expanded object.

Now that you understand the concept of primary and secondary links, it's time to look at a live example in the Link View. You can display the secondary links for an expanded object by clicking the Show Secondary Links icon on the Link View toolbar, as shown in Figure 18.11.

After you have selected this option, the secondary links for the expanded object are displayed in the diagram.

TIP   The Show Secondary Links icon serves as a toggle button. To turn off the display of secondary links, click the Show Secondary Links button again.

Figure 18.11.

Choosing to view the secondary links.

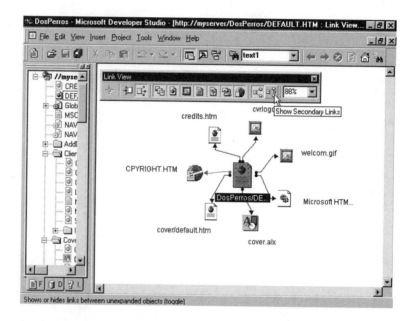

Figure 18.12 illustrates the primary and secondary links for the Dos Perros default page.

Figure 18.12.

Viewing the primary and secondary links.

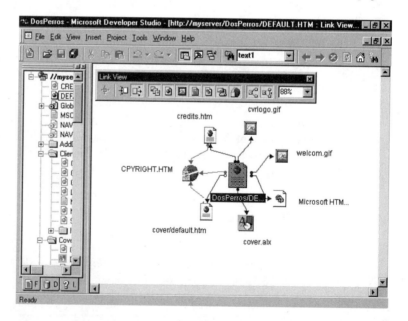

The common denominator in this diagram is the copyright page, which is shared among the three web pages. As you can tell, the link to this page is still broken. You learn how to repair this link during the final lesson for the day.

NOTE

> You can click the Show Primary Links icon on the View Link toolbar to toggle the display of the primary links for the expanded object. Although it defeats the purpose of expanding the object in the first place, you can click this icon to hide the display of the primary links. Clicking the button again reveals the primary links for the expanded object in the diagram.

Working with Objects

The purpose of opening a Link View for your objects is to examine and understand the structure and relationships that exist within the web site. Upon further review of your site, you may want to interact with the objects contained in the diagram. The Link View enables you to directly access the object and activate the default editor for one or more objects. When you select an object in the diagram, the diagram changes to reflect the link relationships for this object, in addition to the originally expanded object, as shown in Figure 18.13.

Figure 18.13.

Selecting an object.

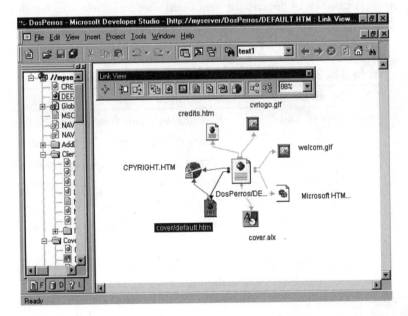

Once the object is selected, you can click the right mouse button to display the shortcut menu. For example, Figure 18.14 depicts the shortcut menu for an HTML Layout file.

Figure 18.14.

Opening the object from within the Link View.

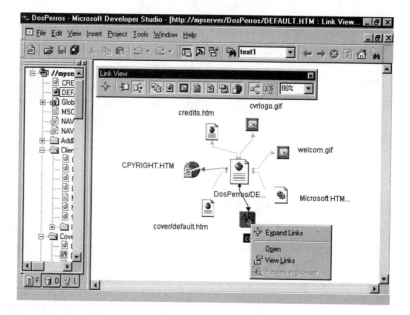

Figure 18.14 displays the menu options that are available for all Link View objects. The Preview in Browser option is disabled, because you can't view HTML Layout files in a browser. Table 18.2 lists and describes each of these options.

Table 18.2. Object shortcut menu options.

Menu Item	Description
Expand Links	Expands the diagram to include the links of the selected object
Open	Opens the object using its default editor
View Links	Creates a new Link View diagram for the object
Preview in Browser	Enables you to preview the web page using the default browser

Figure 18.15 demonstrates the results of choosing to open the .alx file from the shortcut menu in the Link View.

As you can see from the illustration, the selected .alx file is opened using the HTML Layout Editor, enabling you to make changes to the layout.

18

Figure 18.15.

Editing the object.

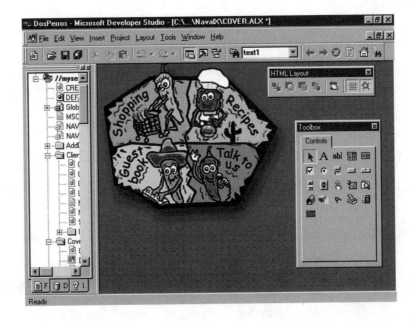

You have just learned how to select and edit a single object. You can also select multiple objects in the Link View diagram by holding down the Ctrl (Control) key and clicking the left mouse button on each object that you want to select. After you have made all of your selections, you can click the right mouse button to choose an action. For example, you may want to open and work with an image and a web page at the same time. You can select both the image and the HTML web page file from within the Link View and choose Open. Both of these objects are opened with their respective default editors, enabling you to make any necessary changes.

Another example involves expanding the links for your objects. You may want to expand the links for a portion or all of your web site to gain a comprehensive look at its structure. In this case, you could individually select the objects using the previously described method, or you can choose Select All from the Edit menu to select all of the items in the diagram. Then, you can select Expand Links from the shortcut menu to display the links for all of the selected objects.

NOTE

The order in which the files are opened is determined by the order in which they are selected.

18

TIP

> You also can select multiple files by dragging the mouse cursor over the objects that you want to select in the diagram. To accomplish this task, click the mouse in the diagram and drag it across the objects that you want to select. A rectangle will display as you drag the mouse to guide you through the selection. When the rectangle encloses all of the desired objects, release the mouse button. All of the objects contained in the rectangle will then be selected.

The ability to interact instantly with your objects from within the Link View provides a significant time-saver to your development effort. Whether you want to preview the design of a web page or directly modify an image file, Visual InterDev truly promotes the idea of an integrated development environment through the implementation of this feature.

Leveraging Your Web Site for the Future

One of the biggest challenges that businesses and IT departments face is how to leverage their current investment. Executives want to capitalize on the investments that are made in people, knowledge, or technology. A project isn't worth investing in if there's no return on the investment (ROI).

For those of you who see dollar signs as the only rate of return, let me be quick to point out that there are other investment returns that can be just as valuable as financial returns. The kind of return that I am talking about includes financial gain but also includes return on people, knowledge, and technology. You can apply this measure to any type of project. Certainly the project should translate into financial gain for the company or organization, but the people who work on the project should be better equipped at the end of the project than when they started. Also, the individuals and the company or organization should possess a richer knowledge base after completing the project. Finally, you should be able to leverage the technology for future endeavors. This technology return is what this part of the lesson focuses on.

Now, you may ask what this has to do with Visual InterDev. Well, Visual InterDev helps you leverage your technology investment in two significant ways. First, you can use the power of Visual InterDev to augment your productivity for a single Web-based application development effort. Second, you can leverage the functionality of your applications across multiple Web-based projects. Both of these methods involve the ability within Visual InterDev to copy an entire web site. The lesson describes the two methods and then demonstrates how to use this powerful feature.

Reaping the Benefits Within a Project

Visual InterDev contains a powerful feature that enables you to copy an entire web site to another location. This section describes how you can capitalize on this feature to facilitate and streamline your application development process. The lesson on Day 3, "Design and Development Considerations," explained the concepts of a development, testing, and production environment. You learned how these three environments can be used to make your project team more effective. The basic premise behind creating these environments involves the staging of your application. As you progress through your development effort, you need to provide separate environments that represent the different stages of your application. These concepts apply whether your development team consists of the well-known, three-person team of me, myself, and I, or a team of 50 people.

First, you need to create a development environment that supports the initial design and development of your Web-based application. Next, you need to create a testing area that reflects individually tested modules. This testing environment supports the integration testing of all of the components within your application.

This development stage is the final checkpoint before the application is released to the users. By having a separate testing environment, you can separate modules that are still being worked on versus those that have been adequately tested. In this way, you can ensure that individual developers don't hinder the work of their cohorts. The third stage is represented by the production environment. This environment supports the use of your web site by its constituents. This environment contains your fully tested Web-based application and separates the work of the developers from the users. Modules that are still being developed won't cause the user's version of the application to crash, because they operate in separate worlds. Figure 18.16 illustrates the concept of these three environments.

Visual InterDev supports the use of these environments by enabling you to copy your entire web site across the different environments. Given that you have established a unique directory structure for each site, you can use Visual InterDev to promote your site between each stage of development. You also could copy the web site to a different machine. In this way, you can ensure that all of the components in your web site are migrated properly without your having to identify and copy the individual files contained in your site. You will learn how to take advantage of this feature in one of the following sections, "Copying a Web Site."

Reaping the Benefits Across Multiple Projects

You also can use the copying feature across multiple projects. Invariably, you will want to use prior web sites as a starting point for future development efforts. By so doing, you don't have to reinvent the wheel every time you develop a Web-based application. You can use the Copy Web feature to copy the web site to a new location and then begin tailoring the components

to meet the needs of your new application. Again, Visual InterDev enables you to leverage
your prior investment in technology for the future by providing a starting point for new
projects.

Figure 18.16.

*The three phases of
development.*

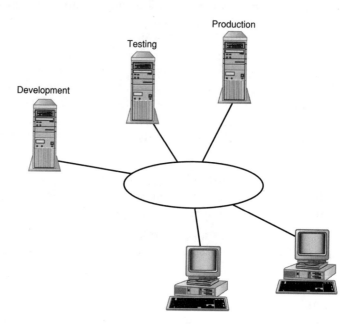

Copying a Web Site

Now that you understand the context of this feature, you can learn how to actually execute
this feature. The Copy Web feature enables you to copy an entire web site to another server
or to the same server with a new name.

NOTE

You must have administrator privileges on the destination server to
execute the Copy Web command. This security restriction is a function
of the server operating system, not Visual InterDev. Visual InterDev
attempts to execute the command on the destination server using your
user ID and password. If you have the correct administrator privileges,
the web site will be copied.

To copy a web site, select Copy Web from the Project menu to display the Copy Web dialog
window. Figure 18.17 illustrates the options that are available on this window.

Figure 18.17.

Copying a web site.

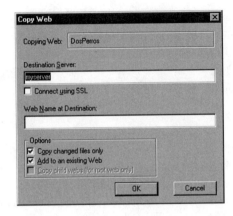

The name of the web site that is being copied displays in the top portion of this dialog window. From this window, you can enter the name of the destination server as well as a name for the web site that you are copying. You can enable a Secure Sockets Layer (SSL) connection by clicking the checkbox next to this option.

The options at the bottom of this window enable you to customize what is being copied. First, you can choose to copy only the changed files. This option is useful when you have initially copied a web site to the destination and you are copying an updated version to the destination. This option can be applied to the three stages of application development, when you are constantly migrating updated versions of your application from development to testing and from testing to production. You save a lot of time during the application promotion process by selecting this option, because only the files that have changed are copied to the destination location.

The Add to an existing Web option is similar to the one that you have used to create new projects. You can choose to add this web to an existing site or create a new web for this site.

 NOTE

Remember from the lesson on Day 4, "Creating Your First Visual InterDev Project," if you don't select the Add to an existing Web option, the name of the project is combined with the name of the web server to form the virtual root name for the web site.

The Copy child webs option is enabled only if you are copying the root web. In this case, you can check this option to copy all of the child webs that exist within the root web.

After you confirm your entries and click OK, the web is copied to the new destination, and you receive a friendly confirmation notice like the one shown in Figure 18.18.

Figure 18.18.

A successful copy.

The newly copied web site assumes the security settings of the root web on the destination server machine. You must create a Visual InterDev project to access the copied web site. To do this, begin the Web Project Wizard and enter a name for your new project. After you click OK, the Web Project Wizard is initiated, enabling you to enter a server name for your web, as shown in Figure 18.19.

Figure 18.19.

Specifying a server.

After you have chosen the server, you can click the Next button to proceed to the second step in the process. You will see the name of the project that you are creating as well as an option to connect to an existing server. Click this radio button and choose the name of the web that you entered during the Copy Web phase of this process. Figure 18.20 demonstrates this process for a web that was copied as a new web called TestComponents.

You can then click Finish to complete the process and create a new Visual InterDev project for the copied web as shown in Figure 18.21.

Figure 18.20.

Connecting to a newly copied web site.

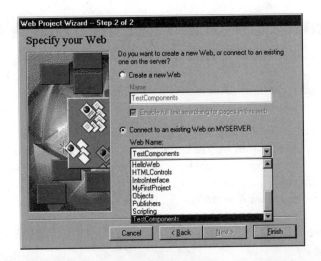

Figure 18.21.

Reviewing the results: New project, old web.

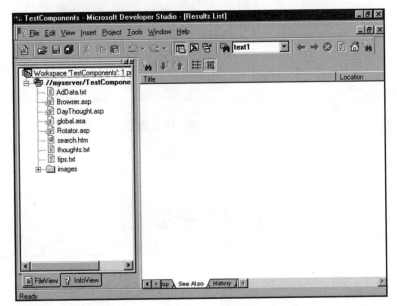

This process is very intuitive and straightforward. In a nutshell, it involves two major steps—copying the web site, and creating a new project for the newly copied web site. This feature definitely removes the headache of migrating your Web-based applications as well as helps to increase your ROI.

Managing the Files in Your Web Site

Visual InterDev supports many of the same Windows Explorer functions manipulating files and folders within your project. The File View resembles the Explorer and enables you to interact with all of the folders and files in your project. Using the File View, you can add, edit, copy, delete, or rename any file or folder that is displayed in the project workspace.

In the previous section, you learned how to copy an entire web site. Eventually you will have to add files from an existing project to a new project that you are working on. The File View makes this process easy by enabling you to copy these files into the new Visual InterDev project. To add files to the root directory of the project, select the root directory and click the right mouse button to display the shortcut menu, as demonstrated in Figure 18.22.

Figure 18.22.

Adding a file to your project.

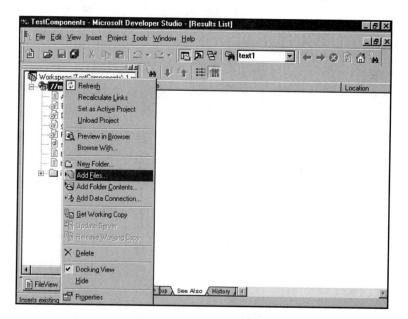

Next, choose Add Files from the list of menu options. The Insert Files into Project dialog window displays, enabling you to search for and select the file that you want to add to the project, as illustrated in Figure 18.23.

Once you select the file to add and click OK, it becomes a part of the project. Any changes that you make to the file occur within the context of the project. The changes don't affect the existing project, because you have made a copy of this file and saved it in a different project. You also can import a folder's contents into a project, which is helpful for copying multiple files into the project at the same time.

18

Figure 18.23.

Choosing the new addition.

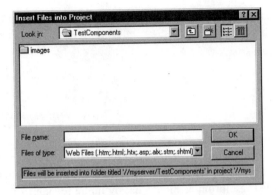

TIP

You can drag and drop files and folders from the Windows Explorer into the File View.

Another file- and folder-management function is adding a new folder to your project to properly organize your files. For example, you may want to create folders to organize items such as images, Java applets, sound files, and ASP files. You can right-click the root directory in the project workspace and choose Add New Folder from the shortcut menu. You will then be able to enter the name for your new folder.

To rename a file or folder, select the item in the File View and right-click the mouse to display the shortcut menu for the item. Choose Rename from the list of menu items and enter the new name for the file or folder.

To delete an item, right-click the mouse on the file or folder and choose Delete from the list of menu items. A message will display, confirming that you want to delete the file or folder. For folders that consist of multiple items, a confirmation is displayed, enabling you to either delete all of the files at one time, or confirm the deletion of each file contained in the folder.

The right mouse button functionality and features included with Visual InterDev tremendously simplify the process of managing and manipulating the files contained in your project. This functionality is accomplished through the File View, which borrows a page from the Windows Explorer and provides a highly intuitive approach to working with your files.

Repairing the Links

The final lesson for the day teaches you how to resolve broken relationships within your diagram. Visual InterDev consists of an automatic tracking system that monitors the links between the objects and files in your project. For example, when you rename a file in your project, you receive a warning message similar to the one displayed in Figure 18.24.

Figure 18.24.

Resolving a conflict:
the proactive
approach.

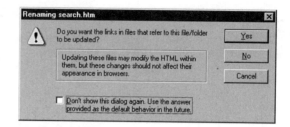

This dialog window enables you to update the links in files that refer to this object so that a conflict won't arise when you try to run your application. This proactive approach to conflict resolution ensures a happy home for your project. There will be occasions when conflicts do arise, however, as with the copyright notice in the Dos Perros application. The next section takes a closer look at the broken link and searches for a resolution.

You can use the tooltips help for an object that contains a broken link to identify the conflict. For example, placing the mouse cursor over the CPYRIGHT.HTM file displays a tooltips message that is crying out for help, as shown in Figure 18.25.

Figure 18.25.

Identifying the
problem.

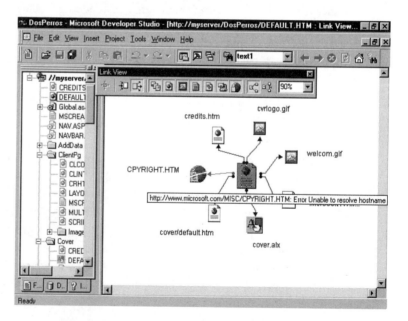

The file location information is displayed along with an error message for this object, which describes the conflict in the link relationship. The copyright notice file is located at an Internet URL address, and the user isn't logged on to the Internet to access this site. Based on this information, you can either copy the file to include it in your intranet application, or you can enable the link to be resolved at runtime when the user will be logged on to the Internet.

This example demonstrates the process to follow on those rare occasions when you have a conflict in your application. Because Visual InterDev takes a proactive approach to managing these conflicts, you can feel confident that your objects will remain in constant communication about their whereabouts, so that conflicts will be minimal.

Summary

Today's lesson demonstrated how you can take control of your projects and manage them effectively. Web-based application development can quickly get out of hand if you don't have the proper tools and methods in place to manage your projects. You have now discovered the tools that Visual InterDev includes to address the issue of site management. You also have learned about some effective methods surrounding the use of these tools. It is up to you to use them for efficient and effective management of your web sites.

The first part of today's lesson demonstrated how to get a handle on your projects by using the Link View. This powerful feature offers robust functionality for viewing and interacting with your application objects. This part of the lesson took you on a guided tour of the features of the Link View and showed you how to properly use these features to your advantage. You learned how to view the links between your objects and how to filter the information that appears in the diagram.

The lesson next explained how to leverage your current development investments for future applications. You learned how to copy your web sites and how to use this feature within the context of a single development project and across multiple projects. The Copy Web feature provides excellent support through the three key stages of your project—development, testing, and production. The lesson then shifted gears and outlined the inherent file management features of Visual InterDev.

The final lesson explained how Visual InterDev proactively manages and resolves conflicts within your application. You also learned how to use the Link View to debug conflicts that arise between objects in your application.

Q&A

Q Does the Copy Web feature provide source code control for my application?

A The Copy Web feature enables you to copy entire web sites to different locations on the same server as well as to directories on different servers. This feature really has nothing to do with source code control. Visual InterDev does support tight integration with Visual SourceSafe to provide robust source code control features for your application projects. You learn about this integration during tomorrow's lesson.

18

Q What is the main purpose of the Link View?

A The Link View provides a robust site visualization tool that enables you to oversee and manage the structure of your web site. One of the main strengths of this tool is that you can view as well as interact with your application objects, all within the confines of one integrated development environment.

Workshop

Today's workshop involves a research project. I want you to research web site management and site visualization tools on the Internet. This field is expanding at a rapid pace as the issues surrounding the proper management of a web site continue to heighten in importance. You should make a list of these tools and search for their purpose, features, strengths, and weaknesses. Then compare the purpose and qualities of these tools with the site visualization and management tools contained in Visual InterDev. In what ways are the other products weaker? In what ways are they stronger? Document answers to these questions and others that you have regarding this topic so that you can refer to them in the future.

Quiz

1. What is the difference between a primary and secondary link?
2. What is the name of the feature that enables you to view your web site?
3. Name the feature that enables you to copy an entire web site to another location.

Quiz Answers

1. A primary link defines a direct relationship between an object that has been expanded and one of its associated objects. A secondary link differs in that it represents a relationship between two or more of the associated objects.
2. Link View.
3. Copy Web.

18

Day 19

Working Effectively in Teams with Visual SourceSafe

There has been much discourse in recent years about the concepts of efficiency and effectiveness within corporate America. These terms have been loosely used and misconstrued so often that many people can't distinguish the difference between the concepts. Efficiency is the act of doing things in the right manner, while effectiveness is accomplishing the right things. Efficiency is analogous to the ship captain who, after traveling several hours, was asked by a lost crewman where the ship was going. He confidently responded, "I don't know, but we're making good time!" Effectiveness, on the other hand, involves the art of knowing where you are going, how you are going to get there, and reaching your destination.

Efficiency and effectiveness can be applied to development projects as well. You must begin with a final goal in mind and chart a course to reach this goal. The art and ability to work effectively with others is paramount to accomplishing your goal. While good interpersonal skills are a critical factor for members of any development team, that topic is for another book. Today's lesson focuses on the technical effectiveness of a project team. How can team members on an application development team use technology to effectively reach their goal? More specifically, how does Visual InterDev integrate with other products to help you accomplish effective team development? You will be able to answer both of these questions after completing today's lesson.

The lesson for today begins with an overview of two specific Visual InterDev features that facilitate effective team development. One of the features enables a development team consisting of diverse departments to work together effectively on a Web-based development project. The other major feature involves protecting the source code and files of your application.

The majority of the day is spent demonstrating how to integrate Microsoft's Visual SourceSafe with Visual InterDev. Visual SourceSafe 5.0 provides a robust set of functions that enable multiple developers to work together in harmony. By the end of the day, you will understand how to install Visual SourceSafe as well as how to unleash the power of its features within the context of your Visual InterDev projects. You also will learn about the process of reserving code and files, merging the changes of multiple team members, viewing and tracking the revisions, and rolling back to previous versions of your application.

NOTE

All references to Visual SourceSafe in this lesson represent version 5.0 of the product.

This lesson provides yet another ancillary but important advanced topic that you need to understand to develop your Web-based application effectively.

Visual InterDev Team Support Features

Effective team development tools are a pressing need for information technology managers and developers. Many IT managers will be impressed with a development tool's feature, but when the rubber hits the road, they say, "That's nice, but how will it support my team of developers?" For the past three weeks, you have learned about all of the powerful bells and whistles of Visual InterDev. Today's lesson focuses on the pressing question of how Visual InterDev supports your team of developers.

There are two main areas where Visual InterDev can enhance the effectiveness of your development efforts. First, Visual InterDev is completely compatible with Microsoft FrontPage, which you learned about on Day 5, "WYSIWYG HTML Editing with FrontPage." The compatibility of these products provides effectiveness and improves the productivity of your team members. The second method by which Visual InterDev influences your team's effectiveness is in the area of source code control. You can integrate the power of Microsoft's Visual SourceSafe with Visual InterDev to properly manage your project's file and source code. The following sections expound on these two aspects of Visual InterDev.

FrontPage and Visual InterDev

During Day 5, you discovered the implementation of the FrontPage Editor is included with Visual InterDev. You also learned how a web site development team can use the full, commercial version of FrontPage along with Visual InterDev to support different types and skills of team members. Figure 19.1 depicts this concept within the context of a sample web site development team.

Figure 19.1.

A harmonious relationship.

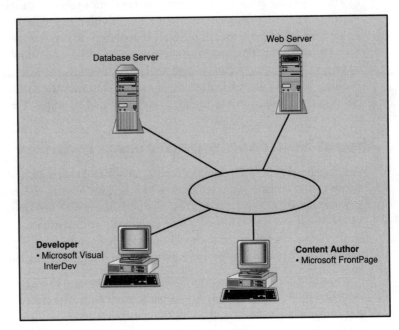

19

In this example, the development team consists of a marketing person as well as a web developer/programmer. Although your team could consist of many more types of personnel, including graphic artists and database programmers, the team has been simplified to illustrate the relationship between a web developer and a less technical marketing person. For this web site, the marketing person assumes the role of content author and uses FrontPage to develop and construct the web pages. By using FrontPage, the marketing person is removed from the intricacies of HTML and other web technologies and is able to focus on the overall design, layout, and content of the web site.

The web developer uses the more powerful Visual InterDev to build and integrate various components as well as to code the application's logic. This more technical person is familiar with HTML, VBScript, Java, ActiveX, and database programming. After the marketing team member authors the content of the web pages using FrontPage, the developer can extend them by using Visual InterDev to further develop the application, including advanced HTML, scripting logic, and database integration.

The key point in this example is that the developer can leverage the work that is performed by the FrontPage author, because the files are completely compatible. This feature enables you to assign the development tasks to the people with the right skills without having to worry about the tools that are used. The marketing person, who possesses the most knowledge on the team about the contents of the web page, can use the more simplistic FrontPage without having to learn more technical web topics. Meanwhile, the web developer, who is more intimate with the underlying technologies, can concentrate on the more technical components of the application and use the power of Visual InterDev to accomplish these tasks.

Visual SourceSafe and Visual InterDev

Another harmonious relationship consists of Visual SourceSafe and Visual InterDev. The combination of these two products provides a robust solution for source code control issues among your development team. You may be familiar with version control issues from past client-server projects. This issue only heightens in importance when considering a web project because of all the various technologies that can be used in your application. Visual InterDev addresses this issue by enabling you to integrate Visual SourceSafe into the mix.

Using Visual SourceSafe, you can control the versions and changes that are made to a Visual InterDev project. Projects that include source code control protect developers from overwriting individual module changes. These controlled projects also prevent developers from organizing different releases, or versions, of the application. Given the frequency of updates to your web site, the versioning feature can relieve many administrative nightmares. The rest of today's lesson concentrates on the integration and use of the powerful features of Visual InterDev to manage your Web-based applications effectively.

19

Integrating Visual SourceSafe with Visual InterDev

You can use the abilities of Visual SourceSafe to get a handle on the contents of your Visual InterDev project. These abilities include general library functions like check-in/check-out, version control, and differential tracking.

Visual InterDev's library functions enable you to check out a specific item in your project, like an HTML web page or ASP file, just as you would check out a book in a library. After you have finished using the object, you can check the item back in to the Visual SourceSafe database, or library.

The version control feature enables you to maintain multiple versions of your application. This feature helps you to properly manage the contents of the different versions and migrate the versions between your different environments. You also can use Visual SourceSafe to track the different versions of your files so that you can compare and contrast the changes. Based on this comparison, you can choose to merge the differences of the versions into one consolidated version, thereby resolving the conflict between the files.

The following sections explore the installation and integration of Visual SourceSafe with your Visual InterDev projects. The latter part of the day explains and demonstrates how to use the features of Visual SourceSafe.

NOTE

> Although you may not have the Visual SourceSafe product, you can still benefit from the topics that are covered in this lesson. Source code control is a major issue that you need to address for your application development teams. You may want to consider the purchase of a tool like Visual SourceSafe to address your needs in this area. At the time this book went to press, Microsoft was releasing Visual Studio 97, which includes all its development tools, including Visual InterDev, Visual J++, and Visual Basic, which comes with Visual SourceSafe. You also can purchase the product individually.

19

Installing Visual SourceSafe

This section is meant to serve as an overview of how to get up and running with Visual SourceSafe in a short amount of time so that you can place your web projects under its control. This section doesn't represent all of the nuances of the installation process and configuration parameters, but it does guide you through the process of installing the server component of Visual SourceSafe, setting up the users, and using Visual SourceSafe's features within Visual InterDev.

NOTE

This section explains the general process of integrating the two products and is not meant to cover every detail of the Visual SourceSafe installation process. Refer to the Visual SourceSafe documentation for more detail on this process.

The first step is to run the setup program for Visual SourceSafe, which displays an introductory dialog window, enabling you to enter a directory location for the product. You should choose a secure but accessible directory on the server machine that supports your development project. You will then be able to indicate the desired installation of the product, as shown in Figure 19.2.

Figure 19.2.

Choosing a configuration.

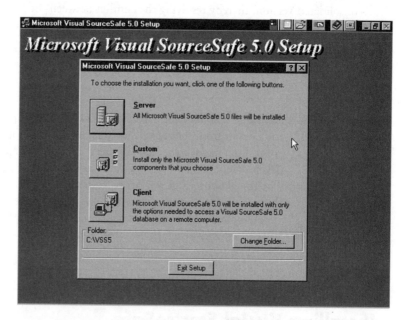

From this window, you can select the Server, Custom, or Client installation option. Server installs the product on the server, while the Client option installs the client portion of the product. You can pick the Custom option to customize which portions of the product are installed on the machine. Figure 19.3 displays the choices for the Custom option.

Figure 19.3.

Customizing the installation.

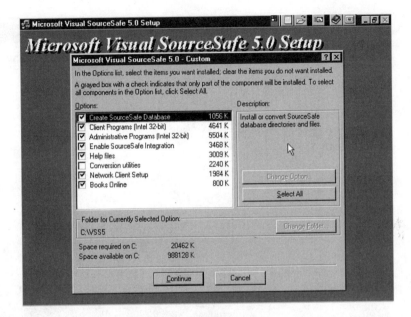

It is critical to Visual InterDev that you select the Enable SourceSafe Integration option from this dialog window. If you do so, Visual SourceSafe can be smoothly integrated with Visual InterDev, enabling you to use its features from within the Visual InterDev development environment. After you make your custom selections, you can click OK to begin the installation process for the product in the directory that you specified. You will receive a confirmation message upon completion of this process.

Setting Up the Users

Once you have installed Visual SourceSafe on the server, you need to set up access to the SourceSafe database for all of the users (developers). You can configure this access by accessing the Visual SourceSafe Administrator tool from the Windows Start menu. Upon opening this tool, you will see the main window, as depicted in Figure 19.4.

This administrator tool enables you to configure users for your SourceSafe projects as well as establish characteristics and properties for your project databases. The main window displays the users that have already been established for Visual SourceSafe access. To provide access for your individual developers, select Add User from the Users menu. The Add User dialog window will display as shown in Figure 19.5.

Figure 19.4.

The Visual SourceSafe Administrator.

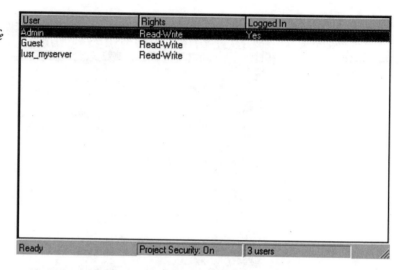

Figure 19.5.

Adding a new user.

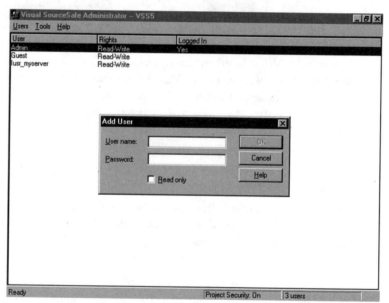

From this window, you can enter a username and password as well as specify that the person has read-only access to a project database. If you don't check the Read only box, the person will be able to read and write to the project database. After you have established the users, you are ready to use the Visual SourceSafe features from within Visual InterDev.

19

NOTE

For NT servers, the installation process should, by default, install the anonymous user account IUSR_*computername*, where *computername* is the name of the NT server machine. You can verify the name of this account by running the User Manager For Domains application that is included with Windows NT Server. If this name doesn't appear in the user list, you will need to add the anonymous account using the method as just described. You don't need to enter a password, nor do you need to check the Read only box.

Placing a Project Under Its Spell

After you install Visual SourceSafe and set up the developers, you can configure a Visual InterDev project to use its source code control capabilities. You can either open an existing project or create a new one to take advantage of these features. Both processes are examined in the following sections.

Using an Existing Project

You can enable source code control features for an existing project by opening the project within Visual InterDev and selecting Enable Web Source Control from the Project menu. A dialog window containing a confirmation message (shown in Figure 19.6) will display, explaining the process that you are initiating.

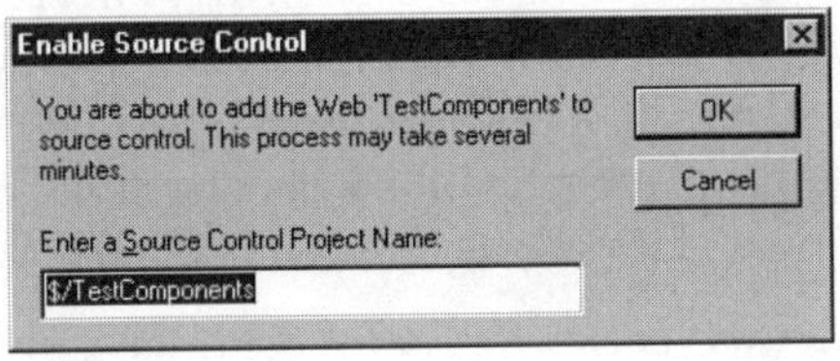

Figure 19.6.

Enabling source control for an existing project.

Enable Source Control

You are about to add the Web 'TestComponents' to source control. This process may take several minutes.

OK

Cancel

Enter a Source Control Project Name:

$/TestComponents

This dialog window displays the name for the source control project that you're establishing. This name will be used by Visual SourceSafe to establish a database entry for the project and to manage and maintain its files and components. The name consists of a $ (dollar) sign and a / (forward slash) along with the name of the Visual InterDev project. All source code control project names must contain the $/ prefix. It is recommended that you use the default name that is provided and click OK to place the project under the control of Visual SourceSafe. Once the process is complete, you will receive a confirmation message similar to the one shown in Figure 19.7.

Figure 19.7.

Confirming the process.

After the process has completed, the source control features will be in effect for your project. Enabling a project for source control affects all of the other projects within that particular web. For example, once a project for a specific web has been configured for source control, all of the other projects within that web also are enabled for this feature. After the process completes for the first project, a developer for another project within that web can open or refresh his or her project to experience the source control features.

Creating a New Project

You also can integrate source control into new Visual InterDev projects that you create. Use the Web Project Wizard to initiate the process of creating a new web. If you create a project for a new web, then you will need to select Enable Web Source Control from the Project menu once the wizard has finished in order to activate source control for the new project. If the project that you're creating is associated with an existing web that already contains source control, the newly created project will also contain this feature.

Determining the Characteristics of the Project

You can determine whether a project has been configured for source control by selecting the Project menu and looking at the text of the source code control menu item. If the menu shows Enable Web Source Control as in the previous example, then the project hasn't been enabled for source control. If the menu displays Disable Web Source Control, on the other hand, the project has been configured for source control. For example, Figure 19.8 reveals a newly created project that was associated with a web that has been enabled for source control.

This project was born with source control because it was associated with a web that had already enabled this feature. You should notice that the text of the fifth menu item reveals that the project has been placed under source control.

Another way to verify whether a web project has been enabled for source control is to right-click the name of the project in the project workspace. You can then choose Properties from the list of menu items to display the Properties window for the project. Click the Web Server tab, shown in Figure 19.9, to view properties of the project's web server.

19

Figure 19.8.

A project under source control.

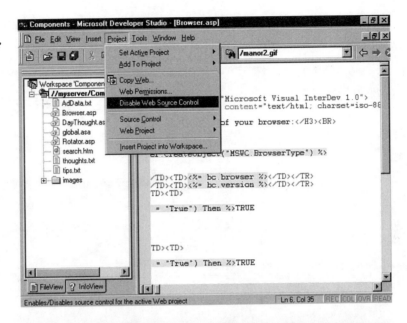

Figure 19.9.

Uncovering the properties of a project.

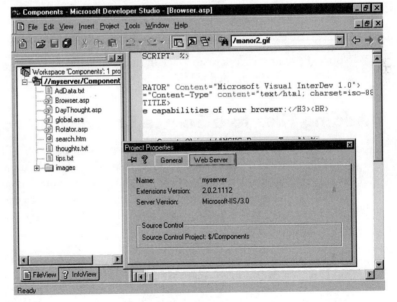

From this window you can see that source control has been enabled for this web server and project. The name of the source control project also is displayed in the middle of this window.

If you are wondering what this window looks like for a project that hasn't been enabled for source control, take a look at Figure 19.10.

Figure 19.10.

A project that is not under source control.

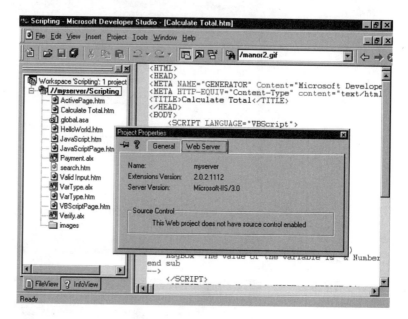

Notice the clear and concise message in the middle of this window, indicating that source control hasn't been enabled for this web server or project.

Adding Files to a Source Controlled Project

After you enable source control for an existing or new project, every file that you add or create for the project will be added to the source control database. You must ensure that you add the files through the Visual InterDev method to assume the source control characteristics instead of copying the files using the file system. To add a file to your project within Visual InterDev, you can right-click the mouse button on the project name and select Add Files to insert files into the project.

Disabling Source Control

To remove source control from a project, open the project in Visual InterDev and select Disable Web Source Control from the Project menu. This feature turns off the source control features within Visual InterDev, but it doesn't delete the Visual SourceSafe project database. If you decide to activate source control on this same project, then it is reattached to the existing Visual SourceSafe project database.

19

WARNING

Because the Visual SourceSafe database entry isn't deleted when you disable source control, you need to be careful about turning source control repeatedly on and off. If you disable source control for a project, delete some files, and then turn source control back on, the files that you delete reappear within the Visual InterDev project workspace. This scenario exists because the project workspace retrieves the entries from the Visual SourceSafe project database when source control is reenabled. To resolve this conflict, you can use Visual SourceSafe to remove the files directly from the database for this project.

Unleashing the Power of Visual SourceSafe

This section demonstrates some of the more robust features of Visual SourceSafe concerning the library functions. Visual SourceSafe and Visual InterDev combine to properly monitor and control the files contained in your project. These tools support effective team development by promoting the integration of individual components while not allowing your developers to interfere with each other's work. This uncanny ability is the measure of a tool's worth to a development team. You must be able to answer the following questions to weigh any tool's value:

19

☐ Can the tool support my team in achieving my purpose without getting in the way or hindering me along the way?

☐ Also, can the tool enhance the productivity of my team in this endeavor?

With the integration of Visual InterDev and Visual SourceSafe, you can definitely answer these questions with a resounding YES!

Using the Library Functions

You can access the check-in/check-out library functions from within the Visual InterDev development environment. This ability enables developers to exclusively reserve files contained within the web project. The developer can make any changes to the file and then check the file back in to the Visual SourceSafe project database. While the file is checked out, or reserved, other developers may be permitted to access a read-only copy of the file. When the developer is through making the changes and the updates are sent back to Visual SourceSafe, other developers can reserve a copy to make their updates. This update ability is contingent upon the access privileges that have been established for that user.

Checking Out Your Files

To check out a file within your project, open the file by double-clicking it within the Visual InterDev project workspace. Because source control has been enabled for this project, the Open File dialog window will display, as shown in Figure 19.11.

Figure 19.11.

Checking out a file.

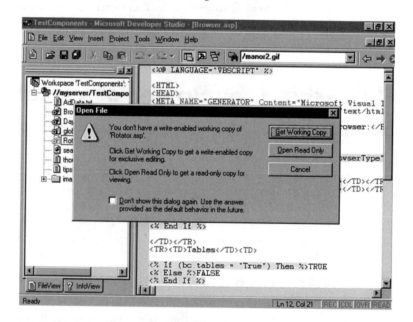

This dialog window indicates that the file is under source control and prompts you for the type of file that you want to reserve. You can choose to look over a working copy that you can fully edit, or you can retrieve a read-only copy that can be viewed but not updated.

A checkbox at the bottom of the window enables you to designate your choice on this window as the default answer every time you access this file. For example, if you have been assigned a module that is exclusively yours to develop, you may want to select this checkbox so that you won't have to see this window every time you access the file. After you make your decision, the file will open with its default editor in the mode that you specified. Figure 19.12 depicts a write-enabled file that has been opened.

19

Figure 19.12.

Editing a file.

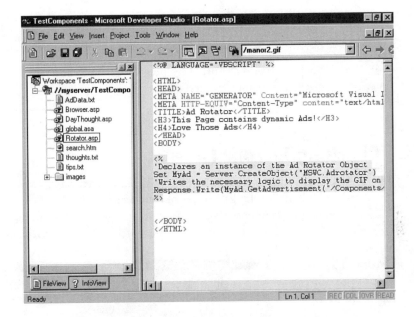

You can now make the necessary updates to the file. Notice that the file's icon is now displayed in color, because the developer checked out a working copy that can be edited. Figure 19.13 illustrates the display of a read-only working copy.

Figure 19.13.

Viewing a read-only working copy.

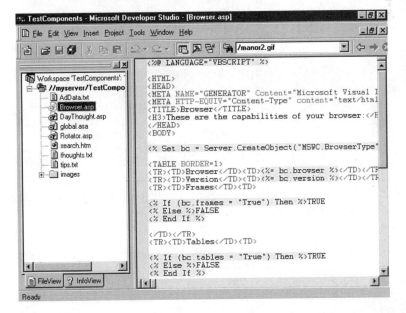

19

The icon for this file appears in gray rather than in color, indicating that the file is read-only.

 TIP

> You also can use the Open, Open With, and Get Working Copy menu commands to open the file.

Checking In Your Files

As you make changes to the file, you can perform intermittent saves to the file, which will save the file in the working directory of your client machine. When you're ready to save your changes to the server for the world to see, you can select the file in the project workspace and choose Release Working Copy, as demonstrated in Figure 19.14.

Figure 19.14.

Releasing the working copy to the server.

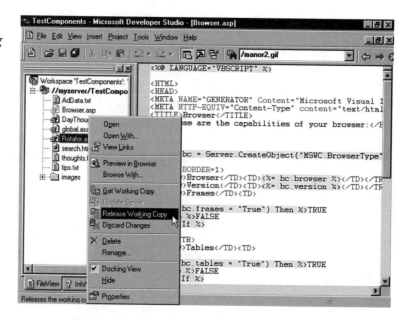

After you select this option, you will be prompted to enter a comment to document the changes that you made, as depicted in Figure 19.15.

You should enter a meaningful comment for the updates in the space provided. All too many times I have seen developers who didn't take the time to document their code. Two reasons for this scenario usually exist—job security or apathy.

19

Figure 19.15.

Documenting the change.

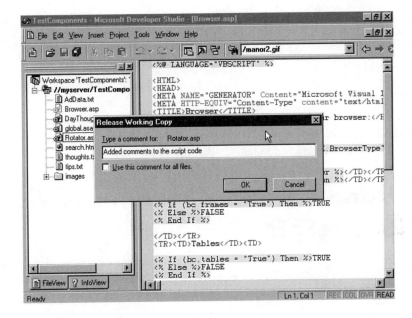

The ability to enter comments is very helpful in enabling you to document the changes in your code for future reference. There are two main benefits to tracking your changes with comments. First, if something goes wrong and the change that you made now causes the server to crash, you can use the comments to trace the problem back to the change that you made. Second, it's very helpful for other team members to understand your code, in case they wind up supporting and testing it. If the changes that you make are properly documented, the team members can better understand the code's history.

You also can choose to use the entered comment for all files that you edit. Suppose that you needed to make a change to multiple files in your project due to a common reason. By selecting this option, you wouldn't have to enter the comment for every file that you update. You can then click OK to release the working copy of the file and save the changes back to the server.

Discarding the Changes

Another option that is available from the file's shortcut menu is Discard Changes. This option enables you to ignore and discard any updates that you have made to the file. If you choose this option, the file is sent back to the server without the updates you have made. When you select this option, you are prompted with a confirmation message, as shown in Figure 19.16.

Figure 19.16.

Discarding the
changes.

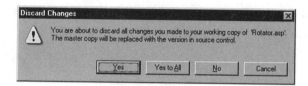

You have the option of discarding changes to this file, or you can choose to discard the updates to all of the files you have changed. Clicking No or Cancel returns you to the editor for your file, enabling you to make further updates.

Using Advanced Features of Visual SourceSafe

Visual SourceSafe offers many robust and advanced features that can be used in accordance with Visual InterDev to properly manage your web project. This section explores the Visual SourceSafe environment and provides an overview of some of the more useful features.

NOTE

This section assumes that you're using Visual SourceSafe on the server as an administrator. This section covers the use of some of the more powerful features you can use for your web project within the Visual SourceSafe environment. You will learn about a method to further integrate these features into Visual InterDev so that you can execute them from the project workspace at the end of today's lesson.

Exploring the Visual SourceSafe Environment

The Visual SourceSafe environment resembles the Windows Explorer environment and gives you easy access to the files within your web project. Figure 19.17 depicts the Visual SourceSafe Explorer.

Your projects are listed in the pane to the left, while the contents of the currently selected project are displayed on the right side of the environment. The Visual SourceSafe Explorer operates just like the Windows Explorer in that you can access and interact with folders and files on the directory tree by clicking and double-clicking the mouse buttons.

Figure 19.17 depicts a sample web project. The files that contain a red checkmark over their icon represent files that have been checked out. The name of the user who has checked out the files as well as the folder that contains the reserved files is also displayed with these files.

Figure 19.17.

Visual SourceSafe unveiled.

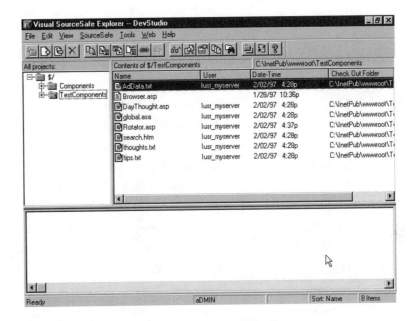

From this window, you can click the right mouse button to display the shortcut menu, as shown in Figure 19.18.

Figure 19.18.

Displaying the options of the shortcut menu.

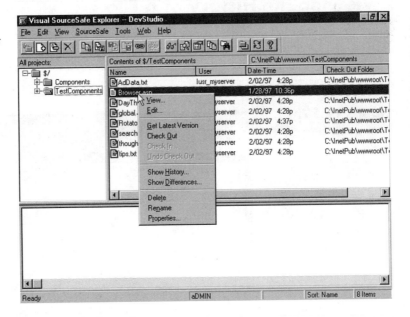

Table 19.1 describes each of the options on the shortcut menu.

Table 19.1. Shortcut menu options.

Item	Description
View	Enables you to view the file
Edit	Opens a copy in a working folder that you can edit
Get Latest Version	Retrieves the most up-to-date version of the file
Check Out	Reserves a copy of the file
Check In	Checks the file back into the project
Undo Check Out	Reverses the reservation of a file
Show History	Displays a history of updates to the file
Show Differences	Displays the differences between two or more versions of a file
Delete	Deletes the files
Rename	Renames a file
Properties	Displays the Properties window for a file

Viewing the History of a File

The Show History option is a very valuable feature that enables you to view the history of updates to a file and track the individual changes to your files and why they are made. When you select Show History for a particular file, you are presented with a window similar to the one displayed in Figure 19.19.

Figure 19.19.

Viewing the history of a file.

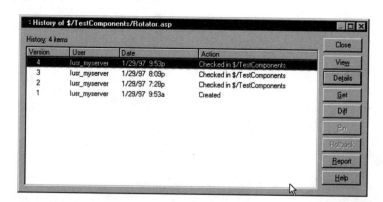

This window displays a listbox that shows the history of changes to a particular file. The first column in the listbox reveals the version number, which is automatically generated by Visual SourceSafe. The next few columns display who made the change, the date the change was made, and the action that was taken regarding the change.

From this window, you can choose to view the file as well as get a working copy of the file that you can edit. You also can see more details about a particular change that was made as well as view the differences between the different versions of the files. This window also enables you to roll back to a previous version of a file.

Seeing the Differences

Visual SourceSafe enables you to view the differences between two or more versions of a file. This feature is helpful in resolving conflicts between versions of a file and can help you roll back to a previous version of a file. To effectively use this feature, open the Show History dialog window for the desired file. Then select the versions of the file that you want to compare. You can select multiple files by using the combination of the right mouse button and the Ctrl (Control) key. Click an item in the list to select the first item. Next, press the Ctrl key and click each additional file that you want to select. After selecting all of the files that you want to compare, click the Diff push button. The Differences dialog window displays, as shown in Figure 19.20.

Figure 19.20.

Examining the capabilities.

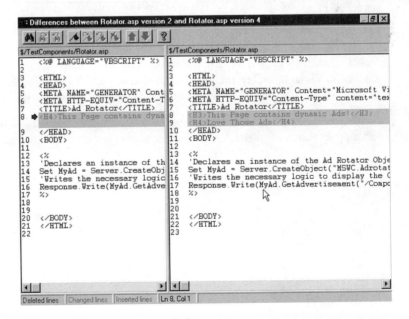

19

All of the differences between the files will be highlighted, enabling you to compare and contrast the versions. As you can see, the status bar at the bottom of the window defines the color-coded syntax contained in the files. This legend helps you to discern what has been added, changed, and deleted.

Further Integrating the Features of Visual SourceSafe

You can install a personal version of Visual SourceSafe on the machines of individual developers to enable them to further integrate the features with their development tools. Specifically, you can install Visual SourceSafe on a developer's client machine, enabling the execution of its features from within the Visual InterDev environment. To accomplish this task, run the NETSETUP program, which is a part of Visual SourceSafe. This program installs a client version of Visual SourceSafe that integrates with the server database that was previously established. The main reason that you would want to install a client version is extra features that become enabled within Visual InterDev.

Examining the Remnants of Visual SourceSafe

Once you have installed the client version of Visual SourceSafe, you can use the options associated with the Source Control menu item located under the Project menu. Figure 19.21 displays the additional SourceSafe features that are available within Visual InterDev.

As you can tell, you now have the ability to execute many of the SourceSafe features from within Visual InterDev, including an option to start Visual SourceSafe. These features give your developers a lot of power and flexibility in accomplishing their tasks.

As you can see, the combination of Visual SourceSafe and Visual InterDev provides the support you need to effectively work in harmony with your other team members.

Figure 19.21.

Examining the capabilities.

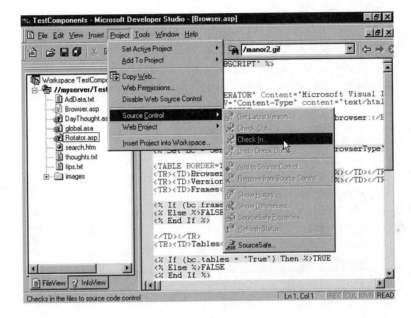

Summary

Unity in diversity is the central theme of effective team development. For an application development project to be a success, you must be able to bring together various people, processes, and technologies to work toward a common goal. You have discovered today how Visual InterDev facilitates effective team development through its integration with other tools. The harmonious relationship that exists between Visual InterDev and FrontPage brings together people of different backgrounds and skills for the good of the application. The synergy and tight integration that exists between Visual InterDev and Visual SourceSafe enables developers to achieve maximum productivity through the proper management and control of the application's files and content.

19

During the first part of the day, you learned the importance of effective team development and how Visual InterDev promotes the productivity of your team members. Specifically, the lesson explained how Visual InterDev and FrontPage can be used on your project to enable different members of your team to be productive. You also learned about the tight integration that exists between Visual InterDev and Visual SourceSafe and why source code control is important.

The lesson then demonstrated how Visual SourceSafe can be integrated with Visual InterDev. You received a personal tour through the process—from installing Visual SourceSafe to enabling source control for your Visual InterDev project. Next, the lesson provided an overview of the robust features of Visual SourceSafe. You gained an understanding of these features and learned how to take advantage of them within the Visual InterDev and Visual SourceSafe environments. Throughout the day, the lesson illustrated how the marriage of Visual InterDev and Visual SourceSafe can definitely increase the productivity and effectiveness of your development team.

This lesson has provided you with the knowledge you need to work effectively with others. There still may be interpersonal conflicts that arise during the course of your projects, but at least you won't have developers writing over each other's code.

Q&A

Q I still don't understand the difference between FrontPage and the FrontPage Editor for Visual InterDev. Does Visual InterDev include the full version of FrontPage?

A The lesson today provided insight into how you can use the full commercial version of FrontPage with Visual InterDev. The FrontPage Editor included as a part of Visual InterDev is a special implementation of the editor that comes as a part of the full version of FrontPage. While Visual InterDev is compatible with the commercial version of FrontPage and includes an implementation of one of its products, they are separate products. The results that are produced by FrontPage can be used within your Visual InterDev projects, enabling team members with different skill sets to work in congruence.

Q Should I use Visual SourceSafe to edit files contained in my Visual InterDev project?

A While this capability does exist, you should not edit your Visual InterDev project files using Visual SourceSafe. As a general rule, you should use the Visual InterDev

19

development environment and tools to make all updates to your project files. In this way, you can be assured of the results of your application. You should, however, take advantage of the integrated features that are available by integrating the two products.

Q You mentioned Visual Studio 97 during today's lesson. What is it and how does it relate to Visual InterDev?

A Visual Studio 97 provides a common integrated development environment (IDE) for all of the Visual Tools from Microsoft. This common IDE is achieved through the use of Developer Studio, which you have discovered by using Visual InterDev. Visual Studio enables you to take advantage of both client-server and Internet development tools to provide truly integrated solutions for your users. You can understand from the lesson on Day 17, "Using Active Server Components to Create Multitier Applications," how a common IDE for both client-server and Internet development tools can be very useful.

Workshop

Today's workshop extends the lesson for today by enabling you to practice using the integrated features of Visual SourceSafe. You should create a Visual InterDev project and enable the source control for the project. Once you have accomplished this step, use Visual InterDev to create some files for your project. These files can consist of HTML pages, ASP files, images, and any other item that you want to include. As you develop these components, notice the behavior of Visual InterDev as the Visual SourceSafe features are enforced. You also should make several updates to one of your web pages and then compare the differences of the versions to understand how this process works. Also, you may want to practice merging different versions of files as well as rolling back to a different version of a file. The more familiar you become with the features and process, the more productive you will be.

19

Quiz

1. What is the command that enables you to activate source control for your Visual InterDev project?

2. What happens when you disable source control for your Visual InterDev project?

3. Describe the Visual SourceSafe library functions.

Quiz Answers

1. Enable Web Source Control, found under the Project menu in Visual InterDev.

2. When you choose to disable source control for a Visual InterDev project, source control is deactivated, and your files are no longer governed by the Visual SourceSafe rules of versioning and source code control. The Visual SourceSafe database entry that contains your Visual InterDev project, however, isn't deleted.

3. The Visual SourceSafe library functions include check-in and check-out, which enable you to reserve working copies of your project files. The check-out function enables you to reserve an exclusive copy of a file which can be either read-only or read- and write-enabled. The check-in function enables you to send your file changes back to the Visual SourceSafe database where others are then free to reserve their working copy of the file. Both of these functions are available from within the Visual InterDev environment.

Day **20**

Debugging Your Applications

It seems like only yesterday that I was using Expediter to test my big-iron application on an IBM 3090. Actually, it was 8 years ago, and I have tried to forget that I ever developed character-based applications for the mainframe. The positive aspects of mainframe development were the integrated and comprehensive tools that were available for testing your application. Then, the client-server wave hit, freeing everyone from the mainframe behemoth. With this wave, new possibilities were introduced, along with new challenges. Testing and debugging an application initially felt like you were undergoing a process of cupellation to reach your final destination of a thoroughly tested application. As client-server technology has matured, the testing tools that are available have also been refined.

Now, the Web-based applications are upon us, bringing with them their own set of challenges, and, as you would expect, the testing challenge has heightened in complexity. This dilemma is in large part due to the number of technologies that can be integrated to build your application for the Web. There aren't many integrated debuggers available that you can use to test your application. Also, many books are being written about building applications for the Web without giving much thought into the debugging and testing aspects of this process. Web-based development is at the point where client-server was when it first came out. I think you will see a heightened interest in this topic in the next couple of months and years.

Today's lesson provides some considerations concerning the testing and debugging of your application. While the lesson doesn't provide the silver bullet concerning this topic, you will receive many gems of knowledge that can be applied to your Web-based application development. The first part of the lesson focuses on the types of bugs that you can possibly encounter. It's always good to know your opponent before you choose your weapon. Next, the lesson explains and demonstrates how to debug your script both on the client and the server. You also learn how to implement error-handling routines in your code to capture and how to exterminate your bugs. Examples of how Visual InterDev traps and displays errors are given. The final lesson of the day covers common considerations about testing and debugging your application.

Types of Bugs...Not That Your Code Has Any!

This section explores the types of errors and bugs that you will uncover while developing a Web-based application with Visual InterDev. This isn't to imply that your code will have bugs; but, on that rare occasion that you encounter one, you will understand how to resolve it.

Because Visual InterDev supports the use of many different technologies, the possible types of errors grow exponentially with each new component that you add to your project. Fortunately, many of the advanced objects that you will use in your project can be debugged with their own debugger. For example, if you create and use an Active Server Component built with Visual Basic, you can use Visual Basic's powerful debugger to analyze problems with your component. In general, you will face the following types of bugs at some time in your Web-based application development career:

- [ ] HTML errors
- [ ] Component errors

☐ Database errors

☐ Script errors

The following sections explore each of these error categories.

HTML Errors

HTML serves as the foundation language for constructing pages on the Web. For this reason, you will implement a good amount of HTML within your Visual InterDev project, leaving room for errors. You can use the FrontPage Editor for Visual InterDev to reduce your chance for errors, but they will invariably show up at the worst time.

One type of HTML error you may encounter involves invalid hyperlinks. This error is sometimes the result of a URL address that has been deleted, causing your link to go into a black hole, as seen in Figure 20.1.

Figure 20.1.

Where in the world has my page gone?

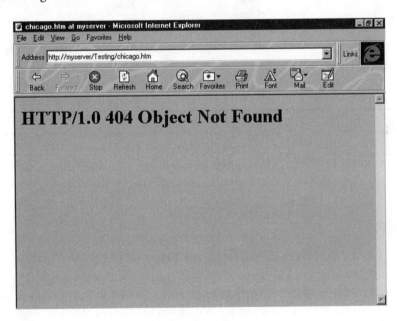

Another cause of a bad hyperlink involves a URL address whose content has changed. In this scenario, the user accesses the hyperlink expecting to go one page and ends up viewing another one. In Figure 20.2, the user has pressed a hyperlink to view a schedule of Houston Rockets basketball games, but instead travels to a schedule of the Chicago Bulls.

Figure 20.2.

*Traveling north
instead of south.*

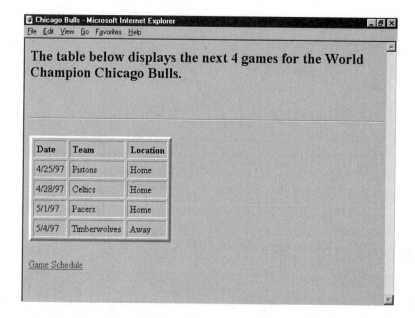

You also may encounter errors that involve forms, tables, and overall document structure. For example, your code could contain unclosed tags that will cause an error in your code. Also, your HTML may be completely valid for some browsers, but not for others. A common error for pages that consist of tables involves unclosed <TD>, <TR>, and <TH> tags. If your table contains a lot of data, it's easy to leave off a closing tag, thereby creating an error in your HTML code. Other errors include spelling and grammatical mistakes in your web page. The written communication within your web page is vital to its acceptance. Users of your web site won't have a lot of confidence in the reliability of your application if the basic text that describes a web page isn't correct.

Resolving Conflicts in Your HTML

Now that you know some of the problems you face concerning HTML, the lesson outlines some tools that can help you analyze and resolve these errors. One resolution is a tool that's available as a service on the Web called Doctor HTML. This program is a web site analysis tool that provides a pretty comprehensive review and evaluation of the web pages contained in your site. You can find this product at the following location:

```
http://imagiware.com/RxHTML/
```

You provide a URL address for your web site and indicate the kinds of tests that you want the Doctor to perform, as shown in Figure 20.3.

20

Figure 20.3.
Getting an HTML checkup.

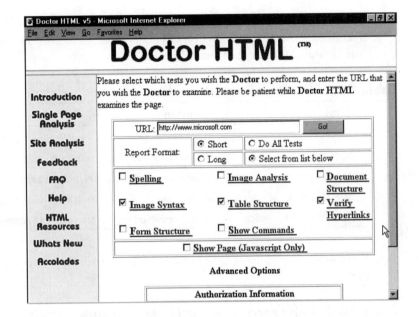

Doctor HTML provides an intuitive interface and is easy to use. As you can tell, Doctor HTML can perform several kinds of tests for your web pages, including image analysis and syntax checking, verifying the spelling, confirming the HTML syntax, analyzing document, table, and form structure, and validating hyperlinks. After the Doctor performs the checkup, you will receive a report similar to the one displayed in Figure 20.4.

Figure 20.4.
Receiving the news.

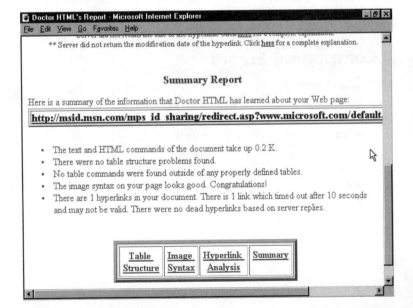

20

Doctor HTML is a good tool for debugging your HTML in several ways. The report that is returned is comprehensive yet easy to understand. Table 20.1 outlines several other tools that are available to validate your HTML.

Table 20.1. HTML validation tools.

Tool	Location
Arena Browser	`http://www.yggdrasil.com/Products/Arena/`
htmlchek	`http://uts.cc.utexas.edu/~churchh/htmlchek.html`
MOMspider	`http://www.ics.uci.edu/pub/Websoft/MOMspider/`
WebTechs Validation	`http://www.webtechs.com/html-val-svc/`
WWWeblint Service	`http://www.unipress.com/cgi-bin/WWWeblint`

You also can check the sites listed in Table 20.2 for a list of the most current HTML validation tools.

Table 20.2. Reference sites for HTML validation tools.

Topic	Location
HTML Checkers	`http://www.yahoo.com/Computers/World_Wide_Web/HTML/Validation_Checkers/`
Validation Discussion	`http://www.earth.com/bad-style/why-validate.html`
Validation Tools	`http://www.ccs.org/validate/`

Component Errors

This category involves those errors that occur while using a component such as a Java applet, an ActiveX control, or an Active Server Component program. You will invariably incorporate these objects into your application. If you encounter a problem with one of these components, you need to use the software tool that was used to create the object to debug the error. For example, if you encounter a problem with a Visual Basic Active Server Component, you can use the robust debugger included with Visual Basic 5.0 to resolve the problem. If you don't locate the problem within the Visual Basic environment, the other option is to verify that you're setting the right properties and using the object correctly within your Visual InterDev project.

Database Errors

Database errors involve problems that you encounter while trying to access your database. These errors include SQL syntax errors, logic errors, connection problems, and access errors. To resolve database errors, you tackle them in the correct order. First, you need to make sure that you can connect to the database and that you can access the desired tables and information. Next, you need to make sure that your syntax is correct for SQL statements. Then, you need to test your logic to ensure that the SQL produces accurate results. The Visual data tools provided in Visual InterDev enable you to address all of these possible problem situations.

Script Errors

The use of scripting languages like VBScript and JavaScript is increasing due to the growing number of dynamic applications that are being created. This increase again augments the chance for errors in your Visual InterDev projects. The types of script errors that you can expect to find include syntax and logic errors. Syntax errors occur when you use the wrong syntax for a scripting language command. Logic errors consist of script that doesn't provide the intended result. The majority of the lesson focuses on how to resolve these errors.

Debugging Your Script

The increased use of scripting languages to create dynamic applications has increased the aspirin intake for Web application developers. The reason for the rising number of headaches among this group is that there haven't been many sophisticated script debugging tools to hit the market. Most developers have regressed to the old trial and error method due to the lack of these tools.

This section covers the types of errors that you can expect to encounter in your scripting logic. The lesson focuses on VBScript, but the concepts apply to other scripting languages such as JavaScript. After you know what you're facing, the lesson outlines some effective methods for tackling these problems.

20

Types of Errors

The types of errors that you can expect to face concerning your scripting code consist of two main categories—syntax and logic. An error in syntax means that you used a command in the wrong manner or that your code conflicts with the rules of the VBScript run-time interpreter. The following line of code contains a VBScript syntax error:

```
Dimension MyVariable
```

This statement results in an error because the correct VBScript command hasn't been used to define this variable. Figure 20.5 depicts the error that results from this erroneous statement.

Figure 20.5.

Improper use of VBScript.

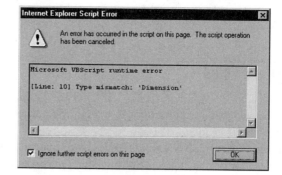

The correct syntax for this statement should be as follows:

```
Dim MyVariable
```

Other examples of syntax errors include errors where the rules of VBScript have been broken. For example, this statement results in a VBScript error:

```
Dim X, Y, Z
Y = 0
Z = X/Y
```

In this example, an error occurs as shown in Figure 20.6, because you cannot divide by zero.

Figure 20.6.

Breaking the rules.

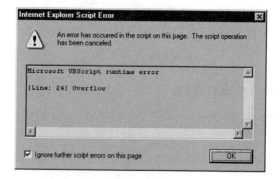

Syntax errors basically revolve around the question of validity. Is the statement valid according to the rules of VBScript?

The other category of scripting errors that you will face include logic errors. These errors involve the accuracy of your code. Is the statement reliable? Does the scripting code produce the desired results for your application? Your code can be completely valid according to the rules of VBScript but not address the needs of your application, thereby producing inaccurate results. These errors are harder to find, because the VBScript interpreter no longer provides you with any help. As far as it's concerned, the code looks great. You must decide if the logic accomplishes its intended purpose. An example of a logic error is depicted in the following lines of code:

```
Dim Discount, Price, SalePrice
Discount = .10
Price = 25
SalePrice = Price * Discount
```

This example attempts to calculate the sale price for an item. The discount for the item is 10 percent. In the code example the price is multiplied by the discount to determine the sale price. Can you identify what is wrong with this logic? If you multiply the price by the discount, you're actually calculating the discount amount to subtract from the price. When this logic is implemented, the customer receives a discount of 90 percent rather than the intended 10 percent. Your next question is, "Where do I find this store?" The line of code that calculates the sale price should actually be the following:

```
SalePrice = (Price - (Price * Discount))
```

The developer of this code was able to locate the error before the application was put into production, thereby saving his job. The method for discovering the error, however, involved a laborious process of trial and error. This programmer later learned some other methods for debugging scripting logic and is a much happier person today. Some of these methods are covered in the following sections.

Using Error Handling Routines

One option for debugging your VBScript code is to insert error-handling routines as a part of the code. VBScript includes several methods that enable you to trap errors within your script and deal with them in the proper manner. The following sections cover two of the more popular methods.

20

Resolving Errors with a Statement

The first methods involve the use of the VBScript On Error statement. This statement enables you to capture an error and enables the application to continue executing. Accomplished Visual Basic programmers may be familiar with using this method in their client-server applications. The basic syntax for the On Error statement is as follows:

```
On Error Resume Next

... Block of Code ...

On Error Resume Next
```

The On Error statement tells the VBScript interpreter to ignore the error and proceed on to the next statement as though nothing had happened. This scenario is analogous to a situation where you witness a person who has just been hit by a car. Your natural reaction is to go help the individual and call for an ambulance, but you are told to move along, because everything is fine. It's very hard to accept this statement, because everything is *not* fine.

With Visual Basic, you can both recognize the error as well as send the logic to an error-handling routine to determine the severity of the error and take the necessary actions. VBScript is limited in that you can only proceed to the next statement using this method. The next section demonstrates how to extend the effectiveness of the On Error statement to debug your code.

Resolving Errors with an Object

The On Error statement can be extended to properly handle your VBScript errors within your application by using the err object. This object is an inherent VBScript object and enables you to incorporate debugging and run-time logic into your application. Because the err object is an intrinsic object, it's freely available throughout your code without any extra effort on your part. All you need to do to use the object is to reference it after the On Error statement. Table 20.3 explains the available properties of the err object.

Table 20.3. Err **object properties.**

Property	Description
Number	Numeric error code
Description	Description of the error code
Source	Name of the program that caused the error
Helpfile	Name of a help file with more information on the error
HelpContext	ID of the topic index for the help file

You also can use two methods with the err object—Raise and Clear. The Raise method enables you to create an error within your application. Why, you ask, would you even consider creating an error in your application? This method can be used to test how your application responds to adversity. For instance, it's already been established that you don't produce bugs in your code. You, therefore, don't know how your application would respond to an error.

This situation is analogous to the basketball team that wins 20 games in a row. The coach of the team is concerned going into the playoffs, because the players haven't been tested with a trial. Now, don't get me wrong, there's nothing wrong with winning every game. Unfortunately, the undefeated season doesn't happen very often. Also, many times a team that wins several games in a row will, after a defeat, lose several games. They then have to adjust to the different feeling and take the necessary steps to get back on the winning track. Likewise, you can test your application using the Raise method to ensure that your application can handle adversity.

You use the Clear method to clear the contents of the err object. This method should only be used after an error has been detected and dealt with properly. The worst thing you can do is to clear out the err object before the application has processed the error. This situation results in disaster for your application, because it no longer knows the error it is processing or what to do next.

Listing 20.1 demonstrates an example of using the On Error statement with the err object to properly handle the bugs in your application.

Listing 20.1. Effective error handling.

```
Sub cmdSubmit_OnClick ()
On Error Resume Next
Dim SalePrice

SalePrice = (txtRetailPrice.Text - (txtRetailPrice.Text*txtDiscount.Text))

If err.number <> 0 Then
MsgBox "Error #: " & err.number & " Description: " & err.description &
"Source: " & err.Source
End If

End Sub
```

This code calculates the sale price based on the retail price and discount that the user enters on the form. The err object is used to check for a number that isn't equal to zero, which indicates an error. If an error occurs, a message box is displayed to the user, as shown in Figure 20.7.

Figure 20.7.
Displaying an error.

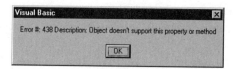

Using the Microsoft Script Debugger

At the time of press for this book, Microsoft had just come out with a debugger for testing your script code. The Microsoft Script Debugger (MSD) provides a fairly robust tool for debugging both VBScript and JScript code. This debugger is intended to be used with Internet Explorer to provide an integrated environment with which to test your script code. The following list outlines the basic features of the script debugger:

- ☐ Ability to set breakpoints in the code
- ☐ Ability to sequentially step through the code
- ☐ Integrated view of JScript and VBScript call stack
- ☐ Ability to immediately evaluate the value of a variable or expression
- ☐ Color-coded syntax
- ☐ Ability to dynamically view HTML structure of the web page
- ☐ Ability to view the HTML object model for the page

Once the script debugger is installed on your machine, you can open your web pages with Internet Explorer and choose Source from the View menu. The MSD environment is activated, displaying the code for the page in debug mode, as shown in Figure 20.8.

The MSD provides a Project Explorer that enables you to see all of the currently opened files and their contents. The Code window enables you to view and interact with the code for the page. This window enables you to set breakpoints and step through the code. You can set a breakpoint by placing your cursor on the desired line in the Code window and selecting the Debug menu, as shown in Figure 20.9.

20

Figure 20.8.

The MSD environment.

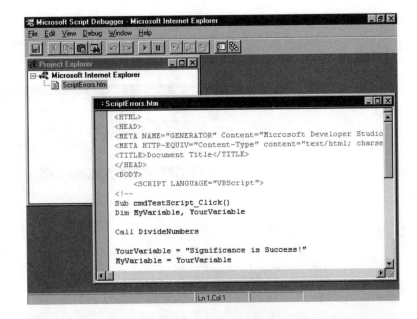

Figure 20.9.

Setting a breakpoint.

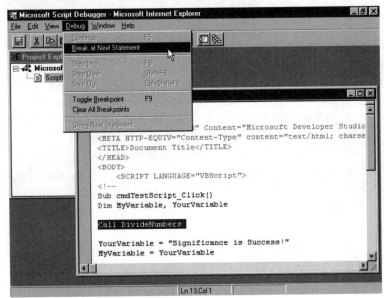

20

From this menu, you can set a breakpoint for a line of code by choosing the Break At Next Statement menu item. The line for which you have set the breakpoint will display in the Code window, as shown in Figure 20.10.

Figure 20.10.

Viewing a breakpoint.

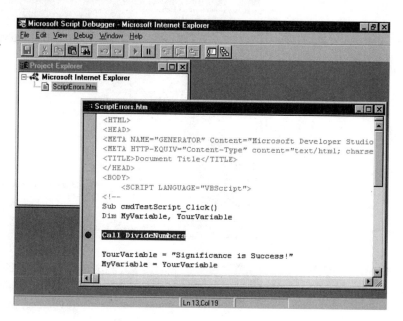

As you can see, the line of code appears highlighted in red. Also, a red circle is displayed to the left side of the code. When you view the page and execute the code, the debugger pauses at the breakpoint that you have set. You can then choose to continue executing the rest of the code. You also can choose to sequentially step into the line of code, step over the code, or step out of the code, as shown in Figure 20.11.

Besides enabling you to traverse through your code, the MSD enables you to view the value of your variables in the Immediate window. To display this window, select the View menu and choose Immediate window. The Immediate window is displayed as shown in Figure 20.12.

You can then type in a variable or expression name to evaluate. Figure 20.13 demonstrates two methods of displaying the values of a variable.

This example shows two methods for viewing the value of your variables. You can use the Debug.Write method along with its variable name to display its value, or you can use the ? (question mark) shortcut method.

Figure 20.11.

Stepping through your code.

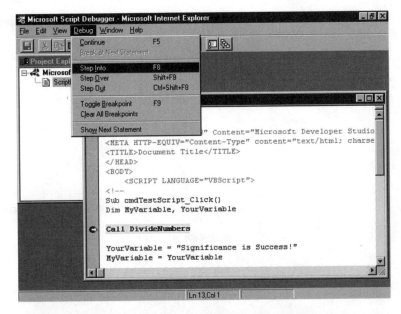

Figure 20.12.

The Immediate window.

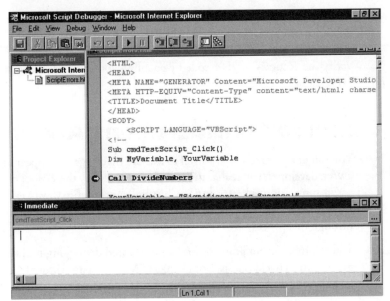

20

Figure 20.13.

Viewing the value of a variable.

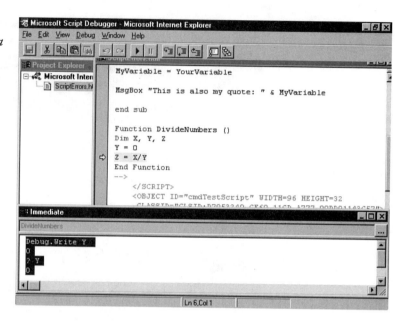

The MSD provides a significant enhancement for Internet Explorer that enables you to debug your script. The environment is very similar to the Visual Basic debugger and enables you to truly test and safeguard your code against unwanted bugs. The MSD also helps you verify the accuracy of your code by enabling you to check the values of your variables and expressions.

Common Considerations About Bugs

You might as well resolve yourself to the fact that bugs will appear in your code someday. As a Web developer, you realize the complexity of testing the various components of your Web-based application. There's no one silver bullet or surefire way to exterminate your bugs. You should use a combination of the tools and methods mentioned in this lesson to help you through this process.

You're probably not going to find an integrated debugging tool that tests your application from front to back; that is, from your HTML web page through your ActiveX controls and Java applets to your Active Server Pages and Components to your database. You need to break your application into its respective parts and test these components with the best tool or method possible. For example, use tools like Doctor HTML to evaluate your HTML. Then, test the integration of ActiveX controls and Java applets into your web pages. You can then use the tools and methods mentioned previously in today's lesson to test your scripting logic. Finally, you can use the native development environments like Visual Basic and Visual C++

for your more advanced components. You also can use the Visual data tools to test the database components of your application.

As far as integrated testing, you're the one who's going to have to pull it all together. With no integrated tool available, you will have to face this task alone. The best method for performing an integrated test of your application is to use the methods and processes that were discussed on Day 3, "Design and Development Considerations." Refer back to this lesson for a refresher on these tips and techniques regarding integration testing.

Summary

It will be very interesting to watch the emerging developments in the area of Web-based application testing. Right now, there aren't true integrated debuggers that can examine your total application. Tools like the Microsoft Script Debugger and Doctor HTML can help, but developers will be clamoring for more as the area of application development for the Web continues to grow. Just as client-server testing tools are maturing, Web-based testing tools will arrive to meet the needs of its constituents.

Today's lesson provided an overview regarding how to test your Web-based applications. First, the lesson outlined the types of bugs that you might encounter when you develop an application for the Web. You also learned about some of the tools that are available to help you exterminate these bugs. The next few lessons focused on debugging your script code, which leaves the most room for error in your application. You learned about some error handling statements and routines that you can use in your code to help take the bite out of the bugs in your application. You then discovered a new tool that has been introduced by Microsoft to help alleviate the pain of debugging script code. The lesson provided an introduction to the Microsoft Script Debugger, which enables you to step through your code and monitor its results. The final lesson for the day focused on some common considerations and concepts to ponder concerning the testing of your application.

As a Web developer, you should publicize your needs and requirements regarding testing tools to your neighborhood software vendor. Make your requests known, and they will be answered by the companies that want to remain in business.

Q&A

Q How can I expect to deliver a quality, Web-based application when there are no adequate testing tools?

A This is an excellent question with no magic answer. The tools that are emerging enable you to test different components of your application. If you think about client-server testing tools, they're still emerging and don't provide the silver bullet either. There are still times when you have to implement compartmentalized testing techniques to examine the effectiveness and accuracy of your client-server application.

The central problem is that while emerging technologies like the Web offer much more functionality than the olden days of mainframe applications, they add several extra layers of complexity. In other words, you have to pay for the added features just as you would for a new car. The best way to address the testing dilemma is to use the best tools for each type of technology contained in your application. Then, you should implement a robust testing plan for the integration of these components within your application. This plan will enable you to perform an effective, trial-and-error approach for the integration test of your application. Remember, there will always be some degree of manual testing, no matter what kind of application you are developing.

Q Can I use the methods that you have discussed in this lesson with Visual InterDev?

A Yes. All of the methods that have been covered can be used for testing your Visual InterDev application. While tools like Doctor HTML will be executed outside of the Visual InterDev environment, the Visual data tools and error handling routines can be employed within the confines of the project workspace. Also, the VBScript interpreter will run inside of the Visual InterDev environment when you preview the page with the internal browser, allowing you to receive instant feedback on the validity of your code.

Workshop

Today's workshop involves more research on the topic of Web-based testing and debugging tools. You should review the sites that have been mentioned in this lesson as well as do some searching of your own. The goal is to proactively find some methods and tools that will help you debug your application. Knowing the complexity of this task, you can be prepared by doing research up front and becoming knowledgeable about the right solutions for your needs.

Quiz

1. What are the four general categories that you will find in a Web-based application?
2. What object can be used to determine the number and description for a VBScript error?
3. What new tool from Microsoft addresses the need for debugging your script code?

Quiz Answers

1. HTML errors

   Component errors

   Database errors

   Script errors

2. Err object

3. Microsoft Script Debugger

20

Day 21

Putting It All Together: The Publishers' Paradise Case Study

The final day of your intense Visual InterDev training has arrived. It seems like only yesterday that you began this journey. You have learned a lot of material in a relatively short time. The best way to reinforce your learning is to apply it, which this lesson gives you a chance to do. Your three weeks of training ends with a case study of an application you help finish. You will be completing an intranet application for Publishers' Paradise, a large, hypothetical conglomerate that owns several publishing companies. This application gives you a chance to apply all the knowledge you've gained in the past three weeks to build a Web-based application. You should also get a feel for how the components fit together to meet users' needs. The lesson gives you a lot of the code so you can concentrate on learning how the pieces fit together, instead of worrying about strict programming.

The first part of the lesson describes the application and its purpose and explains the different components you will be working with to build the application. Next, you jump right into development by creating the client components, including HTML, ActiveX, VBScript, images, and music. You then integrate the server components into the application equation. These components include Active Server Pages and database connectivity. Next, you combine the client and the server to examine and test the results. At the end of the day, the lesson debriefs the case study. I bet you can't wait to start!

The Art of Application

Trainers agree that you must *use* the information and knowledge you gain during a course to truly lock it into long-term memory. You must apply the knowledge you learn to become proficient; in other words, true mastery comes only with practice. You have chosen to learn Visual InterDev by working through this book, so I would be remiss if I didn't give you a way to apply the knowledge before you tackle your real-world applications. During this lesson, you get to apply your knowledge and determine how much you have learned. If you discover that you need to brush up on some concept, feel free to refer to the lesson on that topic. This final examination is an open book test.

The Publishers' Paradise Case Study at a Glance

This case study involves developing an intranet application for Publishers' Paradise. As mentioned, Publishers' Paradise is one of the largest publishing conglomerates in the country. It owns several companies that publish many different types of books. This case study is a hypothetical situation, but it's meant to demonstrate the possibilities for Web-based applications.

This section reviews the application so you will understand the final product. This application is targeted at managers who are responsible for monitoring the progress and sales of books. At its core, the application enables a manager to track the sales of a company's books. The manager can also view a list of current titles and their prices. Publishers' Paradise is known for its reliability and impeccable service, which is made possible, in part, by this application.

Creating the Client Components

The Publishers' Paradise intranet application uses several different client components, including HTML web pages, scripting code, images, ActiveX controls, and music. You will be using all these components to construct the client portion of the application. Some of these pieces are given to you as part of the lesson, and others you create from scratch. Again, the goal is to reinforce your learning over the past three weeks.

NOTE

For this lesson, you need to open the project workspace in the Publishers' Paradise directory on this book's CD-ROM. This project has everything you need to complete the application. Also, this application uses a connection to the SQL Server Pubs sample database, which is also supplied on the CD-ROM.

Creating the HTML Web Pages

The first step of this case study is to create the HTML web pages that house the application's other client components. Table 21.1 lists and describes the three HTML web pages in the application.

Table 21.1. The HTML web pages.

Web Page	Description
Default.htm	Main introduction page for the application
News.htm	Contains news flashes about the company
Reports.htm	Displays a list of available reports that can be viewed

The following sections evaluate each of these web pages.

The Default Page

This page is the first, or default, page of the application. Figure 21.1 displays this page's layout.

From this page, a manager can navigate to any of the other web pages in the application. To construct this page, you need to open the web page called Default.htm that's in the PubParadise project with the FrontPage Editor for Visual InterDev. This file provides a shell you can use to further develop the web page. Once you open the file, your screen should look like the one shown in Figure 21.2.

Next, you need to create the hyperlinks for the other pages that can be accessed from this page. The names of these files were given in Table 21.1, and the files are included as part of the PubParadise project. You can easily incorporate hyperlinks to these files by using the FrontPage Editor.

21

Figure 21.1.
The default page.

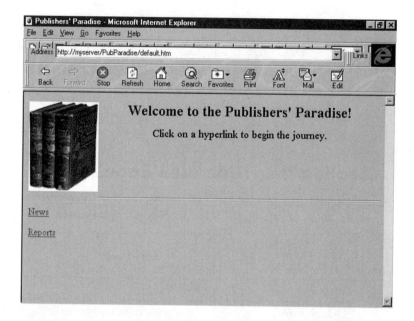

Figure 21.2.
*Opening the page
with the FrontPage
Editor.*

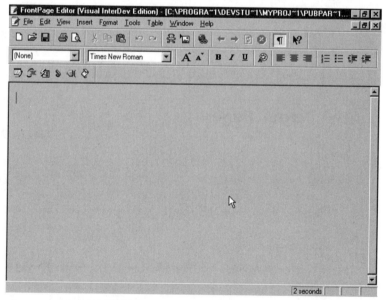

TIP

I will periodically give you tips during this lesson as a refresher to get you going in the right direction. You might want to ignore the tips and see whether you can complete the task without any help. You can then check the tip to see whether you performed the task in the same way.

The first tip is about creating hyperlinks with the FrontPage Editor. You should open the linked pages with the FrontPage Editor to make the process simpler. Next, place your cursor at the desired location in the main web page and type the text that represents and describes the link. This is the text displayed on the web page to the user. Then highlight the text and choose Hyperlink from the Insert menu. You should be able to pick the open page from a list and click OK. Figure 21.3 shows an example of this window.

Figure 21.3.

Choosing a hyperlink.

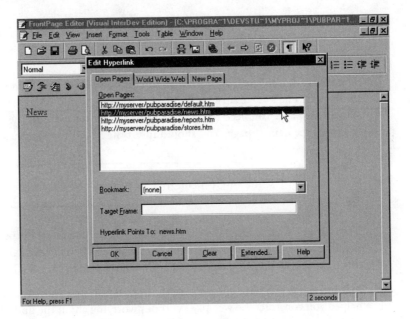

When you have finished inserting the hyperlinks, your default web page should resemble the page shown in Figure 21.4.

21

Figure 21.4.
The links revealed.

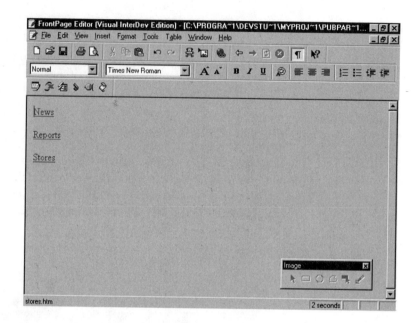

The next task is to spice up the look and behavior of this page so it seems more hospitable to the user. The PubParadise project has a GIF image and a MIDI sound file you can use to jazz up the page. You need to use the FrontPage Editor to insert the image in the top-right corner of the default page. You should insert the MIDI file as a background sound.

> **TIP**
>
> Use the Insert menu to help you perform this task.

The default page still has something missing. You need to insert the page's title and purpose, as well as a horizontal line between the header and the body of the web page. After you finish this final task, your web page should look like the one in Figure 21.5.

In a few steps, you have constructed the application's default page. The FrontPage Editor helped you construct the web page without worrying about the underlying HTML. Listing 21.1 shows you the HTML created so far, based on your design.

Listing 21.1. The default web page code.

```
<html>

<head>
<meta http-equiv="Content-Type"
```

```
content="text/html; charset=iso-8859-1">
<meta name="GENERATOR"
content="Microsoft FrontPage (Visual InterDev Edition) 2.0">
<title>Document Title</title>
<bgsound
src="file:///C:/Program%20Files/DevStudio/MyProjects/PubParadise/opening.mid"
loop="1">
</head>

<body>

<p><img
src="file:///C:/Program%20Files/DevStudio/MyProjects/PubParadise/images/
books.gif"
align="left" hspace="0" width="121" height="149"></p>

<p align="center"><font size="5"><strong>Welcome to the
Publishers' Paradise!</strong></font></p>

<p align="center"><font size="4">Click on a hyperlink to begin
the journey.</font></p>

<p> </p>

<hr>

<p><a href="news.htm">News</a></p>

<p><a href="reports.htm">Reports</a></p>

</body>
</html>
```

Figure 21.5.

*The completed
default page.*

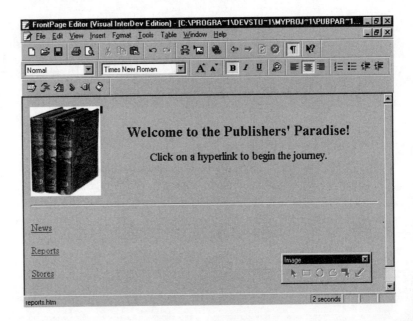

This code uses hyperlinks to serve as the main link to the other areas of the application. This page also has background music that plays when the user first gets to this page. The music is a MIDI file created with the Music Producer, and the image is a GIF file designed with the Image Composer.

The News Page

This web page has news updates for Publishers' Paradise employees; its contents have already been developed, as shown in Figure 21.6.

Figure 21.6.

The News page: Life in Paradise.

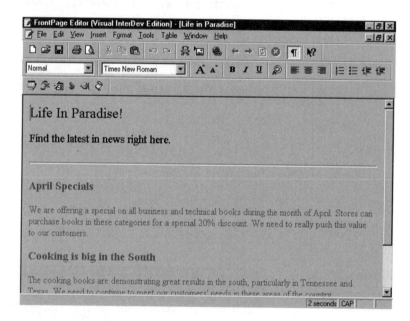

As you can see, this page offers several brief company articles; it's updated daily by the marketing department.

The Reports Page

The Reports page displays a hyperlink list of all the available reports for the application. These links are associated with their respective Active Server Pages (ASPs), which retrieve the necessary information from the database and display it in a report format. Some of these reports consist of tables, and other reports display the information in a graph. This page has also been created for you as part of the PubParadise project and is displayed in Figure 21.7.

Figure 21.7.

The Reports page.

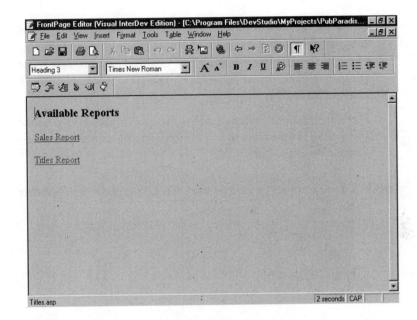

Creating the Server Components

Now that you have constructed the client portion of the application, it's time to build the server components, which include ASPs and database integration. Table 21.2 lists the ASPs included with the application.

Table 21.2. The ASP files.

ASP File	Description
Titles.asp	Report that displays all the published books
Sales.asp	Report that displays sales information for the whole company

The following sections present and explain these ASPs.

The Titles ASP

The Titles ASP enables you to view all the available books published by Publishers' Paradise. You construct this page by using the Titles.asp file contained in the project. This file is just a shell into which you insert the design-time controls for building the database query and table. You can then add the logic to display the information in the table.

21

Inserting the Data Range Controls

The first step to creating the Titles ASP is to insert the Data Range Header and Footer controls. You can choose between two methods to insert these controls. Can you remember what those methods are? Refer back to Day 14, "Extending Web Pages Through Design-Time Controls," for a reminder.

During this process, you must make some choices about the kind of data you want to retrieve and how you want to format it. Table 21.3 lists the values that you should choose for the Data Range Header control.

Table 21.3. Property table for the Data Range Header control.

Property	Value
Data Connection	Pubs
Command Type	SQL
Range Type	Table
Record Paging	Enabled
Page Size	20
Cursor Type	Keyset

After you establish these values for the properties, you need to build an SQL statement that will retrieve the Title, Type, PubDate, Price, and YTD_Sales columns from the Titles table. If you need help constructing the query, refer to the lesson on Day 9, "Using the Visual Data Tools for Maximum Productivity." After you build the query and return to the Properties window for the Data Range Header control, you need to copy all the fields you're selecting from the Titles table. You can do this by clicking the Copy Fields button.

Formatting the Results

Now that you have inserted the proper design-time controls to retrieve the data, you're ready to insert some logic to properly format the results in a table. The following lines of code need to be inserted between the Data Range Header and Footer controls:

```
<TR>
<TD> <%Response.Write DataRangeHdr1("title")%> </TD>
<TD> <%Response.Write DataRangeHdr1("type")%></TD>
<TD><%Response.Write DataRangeHdr1("pubdate") %></TD>
<TD><%Response.Write FormatCurrency(DataRangeHdr1("price"),2) %></TD>
<TD><%Response.Write DataRangeHdr1("ytd_sales") %></TD>
</TR>
```

This code example writes the individual data fields into their respective table columns for each row that's returned. The FormatCurrency function is used to format the Price field to display values with a dollar sign and two decimals. You also need to define the table width and border by entering the following lines of code at the beginning of the body section, just before the declaration for the Data Range Header control:

```
<TABLE WIDTH=100% BORDER=3>
<TR><TH>Title</TH><TH>Type</TH><TH>Published Date</TH>
<TH>Price</TH><TH>YTD Sales</TH></TR>
```

After you have entered this code, your ASP file's contents should resemble the code in Listing 21.2.

Listing 21.2. The Titles ASP code.

```
<%@ LANGUAGE="VBSCRIPT" %>

<HTML>
<HEAD>
<META NAME="GENERATOR" Content="Microsoft Visual InterDev 1.0">
<META HTTP-EQUIV="Content-Type" content="text/html; charset=iso-8859-1">
<TITLE>Book Titles Report</TITLE>
</HEAD>
<BODY>
<TABLE WIDTH=100% BORDER=3>
<TR><TH>Title</TH><TH>Type</TH><TH>Published Date</TH>
<TH>Price</TH><TH>YTD Sales</TH></TR>


<!--METADATA TYPE="DesignerControl" startspan
<OBJECT ID="DataRangeHdr1" WIDTH=151 HEIGHT=24
CLASSID="CLSID:F602E721-A281-11CF-A5B7-0080C73AAC7E">
<PARAM NAME="_Version" VALUE="65536">
<PARAM NAME="_Version" VALUE="65536">
<PARAM NAME="_ExtentX" VALUE="3986">
<PARAM NAME="_ExtentY" VALUE="635">
<PARAM NAME="_StockProps" VALUE="0">
<PARAM NAME="DataConnection" VALUE="pubs">
<PARAM NAME="CommandText" VALUE="SELECT title, type, pubdate,
price, ytd_sales FROM titles">
<PARAM NAME="CursorType" VALUE="1">
<PARAM NAME="RangeType" VALUE="2">
<PARAM NAME="PageSize" VALUE="20">
</OBJECT>
-->
<%
fHideNavBar = False
fHideNumber = False
fHideRequery = False
fHideRule = False
```

21

continues

Listing 21.2. continued

```
stQueryString = ""
fEmptyRecordset = False
fFirstPass = True
fNeedRecordset = False
fNoRecordset = False
tBarAlignment = "Left"
tHeaderName = "DataRangeHdr1"
tPageSize = 20
tPagingMove = ""
tRangeType = "Table"
tRecordsProcessed = 0
tPrevAbsolutePage = 0
intCurPos = 0
intNewPos = 0
fSupportsBookmarks = True
fMoveAbsolute = False

If Not IsEmpty(Request("DataRangeHdr1_PagingMove")) Then
tPagingMove = Trim(Request("DataRangeHdr1_PagingMove"))
End If

If IsEmpty(Session("DataRangeHdr1_Recordset")) Then
fNeedRecordset = True
Else
If Session("DataRangeHdr1_Recordset") Is Nothing Then
fNeedRecordset = True
Else
Set DataRangeHdr1 = Session("DataRangeHdr1_Recordset")
End If
End If

If fNeedRecordset Then
Set pubs = Server.CreateObject("ADODB.Connection")
pubs.ConnectionTimeout = Session("pubs_ConnectionTimeout")
pubs.CommandTimeout = Session("pubs_CommandTimeout")
pubs.Open Session("pubs_ConnectionString"),
Session("pubs_RuntimeUserName"), Session("pubs_RuntimePassword")
Set cmdTemp = Server.CreateObject("ADODB.Command")
Set DataRangeHdr1 = Server.CreateObject("ADODB.Recordset")
cmdTemp.CommandText = "SELECT title, type, pubdate, price, ytd_sales FROM
➥ titles"
cmdTemp.CommandType = 1
Set cmdTemp.ActiveConnection = pubs
DataRangeHdr1.Open cmdTemp, , 1, 1
End If
On Error Resume Next
If DataRangeHdr1.BOF And DataRangeHdr1.EOF Then fEmptyRecordset = True
On Error Goto 0
If Err Then fEmptyRecordset = True
DataRangeHdr1.PageSize = tPageSize
fSupportsBookmarks = DataRangeHdr1.Supports(8192)
```

21

```
If Not IsEmpty(Session("DataRangeHdr1_Filter")) And Not fEmptyRecordset Then
DataRangeHdr1.Filter = Session("DataRangeHdr1_Filter")
If DataRangeHdr1.BOF And DataRangeHdr1.EOF Then fEmptyRecordset = True
End If

If IsEmpty(Session("DataRangeHdr1_PageSize")) Then
Session("DataRangeHdr1_PageSize") = tPageSize
If IsEmpty(Session("DataRangeHdr1_AbsolutePage")) Then
➥Session("DataRangeHdr1_AbsolutePage") = 1

If Session("DataRangeHdr1_PageSize") <> tPageSize Then
➥tCurRec = ((Session("DataRangeHdr1_AbsolutePage") - 1) *
➥Session("DataRangeHdr1_PageSize")) + 1
tNewPage = Int(tCurRec / tPageSize)
If tCurRec Mod tPageSize <> 0 Then
tNewPage = tNewPage + 1
End If
If tNewPage = 0 Then tNewPage = 1
Session("DataRangeHdr1_PageSize") = tPageSize
Session("DataRangeHdr1_AbsolutePage") = tNewPage
End If

If fEmptyRecordset Then
fHideNavBar = True
fHideRule = True
Else
tPrevAbsolutePage = Session("DataRangeHdr1_AbsolutePage")
Select Case tPagingMove
Case ""
fMoveAbsolute = True
Case "Requery"
DataRangeHdr1.Requery
fMoveAbsolute = True
Case "<<"
Session("DataRangeHdr1_AbsolutePage") = 1
Case "<"
If Session("DataRangeHdr1_AbsolutePage") > 1 Then
Session("DataRangeHdr1_AbsolutePage") = Session("DataRangeHdr1_AbsolutePage") - 1
End If
Case ">"
If Not DataRangeHdr1.EOF Then
Session("DataRangeHdr1_AbsolutePage") = Session("DataRangeHdr1_AbsolutePage") + 1
End If
Case ">>"
If fSupportsBookmarks Then
Session("DataRangeHdr1_AbsolutePage") = DataRangeHdr1.PageCount
End If
End Select
Do
If fSupportsBookmarks Then
DataRangeHdr1.AbsolutePage = Session("DataRangeHdr1_AbsolutePage")
Else
```

continues

21

Listing 21.2. continued

```
If fNeedRecordset Or fMoveAbsolute Or DataRangeHdr1.EOF Then
DataRangeHdr1.MoveFirst
DataRangeHdr1.Move (Session("DataRangeHdr1_AbsolutePage") - 1) * tPageSize
Else
intCurPos = ((tPrevAbsolutePage - 1) * tPageSize) + tPageSize
intNewPos = ((Session("DataRangeHdr1_AbsolutePage") - 1) * tPageSize) + 1
DataRangeHdr1.Move intNewPos - intCurPos
End If
If DataRangeHdr1.BOF Then DataRangeHdr1.MoveNext
End If
If Not DataRangeHdr1.EOF Then Exit Do
Session("DataRangeHdr1_AbsolutePage") = Session("DataRangeHdr1_AbsolutePage") - 1
Loop
End If

Do
If fEmptyRecordset Then Exit Do
If tRecordsProcessed = tPageSize Then Exit Do
If Not fFirstPass Then
DataRangeHdr1.MoveNext
Else
fFirstPass = False
End If
If DataRangeHdr1.EOF Then Exit Do
tRecordsProcessed = tRecordsProcessed + 1
%>
<!--METADATA TYPE="DesignerControl" endspan-->

<TR>
<TD> <%Response.Write DataRangeHdr1("title")%> </TD>
<TD> <%Response.Write DataRangeHdr1("type")%></TD>
<TD><%Response.Write DataRangeHdr1("pubdate") %></TD>
<TD><%Response.Write FormatCurrency(DataRangeHdr1("price"),2) %></TD>
<TD><%Response.Write DataRangeHdr1("ytd_sales") %></TD>
</TR>

<!--METADATA TYPE="DesignerControl" startspan
<OBJECT ID="DataRangeFtr1" WIDTH=151 HEIGHT=24
CLASSID="CLSID:F602E722-A281-11CF-A5B7-0080C73AAC7E">
<PARAM NAME="_Version" VALUE="65536">
<PARAM NAME="_ExtentX" VALUE="3969">
<PARAM NAME="_ExtentY" VALUE="635">
<PARAM NAME="_StockProps" VALUE="0">
</OBJECT>
-->
<%
Loop
If tRangeType = "Table" Then Response.Write "</TABLE>"
If tPageSize > 0 Then
```

```asp
If Not fHideRule Then Response.Write "<HR>"
If Not fHideNavBar Then
%>
<TABLE WIDTH=100% >
<TR>
<TD WIDTH=100% >
<P ALIGN=<%= tBarAlignment %> >
<FORM <%= "ACTION=""" & Request.ServerVariables("PATH_INFO") &
stQueryString & """" %> METHOD="POST">
<INPUT TYPE="Submit" NAME="<%= tHeaderName & "_PagingMove" %>"
VALUE="   &lt;&lt;   ">
<INPUT TYPE="Submit" NAME="<%= tHeaderName & "_PagingMove" %>"
VALUE="   &lt;     ">
<INPUT TYPE="Submit" NAME="<%= tHeaderName & "_PagingMove" %>"
VALUE="    &gt;    ">
<% If fSupportsBookmarks Then %>
<INPUT TYPE="Submit" NAME="<%= tHeaderName & "_PagingMove" %>"
VALUE="   &gt;&gt;   ">
<% End If %>
<% If Not fHideRequery Then %>
<INPUT TYPE="Submit" NAME="<% =tHeaderName & "_PagingMove" %>"
VALUE=" Requery ">
<% End If %>
</FORM>
</P>
</TD>
<TD VALIGN=MIDDLE ALIGN=RIGHT>
<FONT SIZE=2>
<%
If Not fHideNumber Then
If tPageSize > 1 Then
Response.Write "<NOBR>Page: " & Session(tHeaderName & "_AbsolutePage") &
"</NOBR>"
Else
Response.Write "<NOBR>Record: " & Session(tHeaderName & "_AbsolutePage") &
"</NOBR>"
End If
End If
%>
</FONT>
</TD>
</TR>
</TABLE>
<%
End If
End If
%>
<!--METADATA TYPE="DesignerControl" endspan-->


</BODY>
</HTML>
```

21

You can preview the results by browsing the ASP web page, as illustrated in Figure 21.8.

Figure 21.8.
Viewing the titles.

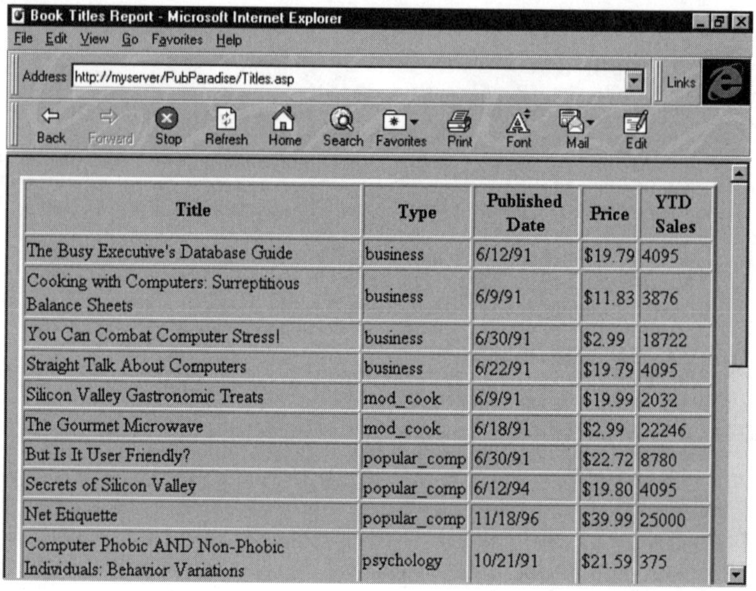

Title	Type	Published Date	Price	YTD Sales
The Busy Executive's Database Guide	business	6/12/91	$19.79	4095
Cooking with Computers: Surreptitious Balance Sheets	business	6/9/91	$11.83	3876
You Can Combat Computer Stress!	business	6/30/91	$2.99	18722
Straight Talk About Computers	business	6/22/91	$19.79	4095
Silicon Valley Gastronomic Treats	mod_cook	6/9/91	$19.99	2032
The Gourmet Microwave	mod_cook	6/18/91	$2.99	22246
But Is It User Friendly?	popular_comp	6/30/91	$22.72	8780
Secrets of Silicon Valley	popular_comp	6/12/94	$19.80	4095
Net Etiquette	popular_comp	11/18/96	$39.99	25000
Computer Phobic AND Non-Phobic Individuals: Behavior Variations	psychology	10/21/91	$21.59	375

The Sales Report

You also need to create the ASP to process the Sales report for the application. This report displays the year-to-date sales for the different types of books published by Publishers' Paradise. The ASP for this report is named Sales.asp and is located in the PubParadise project.

First, you need to open the ASP and insert the Data Range Header and Footer controls into the ASP. Next, create a query that retrieves the Type column and totals the Ytd_Sales column. The following code shows what your SQL statement should look like:

```
Select type, SUM(ytd_sales)
FROM titles
GROUP BY type
```

You should practice using the Query Designer to construct this query instead of typing the SQL statement directly. After you insert the Data Range Header and Footer controls, insert the following lines of code between the Data Range Header and Footer controls:

```
<TR>
<TD> <%Response.Write DataRangeHdr1("type")%> </TD>
<TD><%Response.Write FormatCurrency(DataRangeHdr1(1),0,,,-2) %></TD>
</TR>
```

In this code example, the FormatCurrency function is used to format the Total Sales column with a dollar sign and a comma separator. Notice the other method to refer to the second column that's returned from the database. You can access a column by referring to it either by name or by its index number.

You also need to insert the following lines of code at the top of the body section:

```
<TABLE WIDTH=100% BORDER=3>
<TR><TH>Book Type</TH><TH>Total Sales</TH></TR>
```

After you finish these tasks, your final ASP should contain the code in Listing 21.3.

Listing 21.3. The Sales ASP code.

```
<%@ LANGUAGE="VBSCRIPT" %>

<HTML>
<HEAD>
<META NAME="GENERATOR" Content="Microsoft Visual InterDev 1.0">
<META HTTP-EQUIV="Content-Type" content="text/html; charset=iso-8859-1">
<TITLE>Sales Report</TITLE>
</HEAD>
<BODY>
<TABLE WIDTH=100% BORDER=3>
<TR><TH>Book Type</TH><TH>Total Sales</TH></TR>


<!--METADATA TYPE="DesignerControl" startspan
<OBJECT ID="DataRangeHdr1" WIDTH=151 HEIGHT=24
CLASSID="CLSID:F602E721-A281-11CF-A5B7-0080C73AAC7E">
<PARAM NAME="_Version" VALUE="65536">
<PARAM NAME="_Version" VALUE="65536">
<PARAM NAME="_ExtentX" VALUE="3986">
<PARAM NAME="_ExtentY" VALUE="635">
<PARAM NAME="_StockProps" VALUE="0">
<PARAM NAME="DataConnection" VALUE="pubs">
<PARAM NAME="CommandText" VALUE="SELECT type, SUM(ytd_sales)
FROM titles GROUP BY type">
<PARAM NAME="RangeType" VALUE="2">
</OBJECT>
-->
<%
fHideNavBar = False
fHideNumber = False
fHideRequery = False
fHideRule = False
stQueryString = ""
fEmptyRecordset = False
fFirstPass = True
fNeedRecordset = False
fNoRecordset = False
```

continues

21

Listing 21.3. continued

```
tBarAlignment = "Left"
tHeaderName = "DataRangeHdr1"
tPageSize = 0
tPagingMove = ""
tRangeType = "Table"
tRecordsProcessed = 0
tPrevAbsolutePage = 0
intCurPos = 0
intNewPos = 0
fSupportsBookmarks = True
fMoveAbsolute = False

If IsEmpty(Session("DataRangeHdr1_Recordset")) Then
fNeedRecordset = True
Else
If Session("DataRangeHdr1_Recordset") Is Nothing Then
fNeedRecordset = True
Else
Set DataRangeHdr1 = Session("DataRangeHdr1_Recordset")
End If
End If

If fNeedRecordset Then
Set pubs = Server.CreateObject("ADODB.Connection")
pubs.ConnectionTimeout = Session("pubs_ConnectionTimeout")
pubs.CommandTimeout = Session("pubs_CommandTimeout")
pubs.Open Session("pubs_ConnectionString"),
Session("pubs_RuntimeUserName"), Session("pubs_RuntimePassword")
Set cmdTemp = Server.CreateObject("ADODB.Command")
Set DataRangeHdr1 = Server.CreateObject("ADODB.Recordset")
cmdTemp.CommandText = "SELECT type, SUM(ytd_sales) FROM titles GROUP BY type"
cmdTemp.CommandType = 1
Set cmdTemp.ActiveConnection = pubs
DataRangeHdr1.Open cmdTemp, , 0, 1
End If
On Error Resume Next
If DataRangeHdr1.BOF And DataRangeHdr1.EOF Then fEmptyRecordset = True
On Error Goto 0
If Err Then fEmptyRecordset = True

If Not IsEmpty(Session("DataRangeHdr1_Filter")) And Not fEmptyRecordset Then
DataRangeHdr1.Filter = Session("DataRangeHdr1_Filter")
If DataRangeHdr1.BOF And DataRangeHdr1.EOF Then fEmptyRecordset = True
End If

If fEmptyRecordset Then
fHideNavBar = True
fHideRule = True
End If

Do
If fEmptyRecordset Then Exit Do
If Not fFirstPass Then
```

```
DataRangeHdr1.MoveNext
Else
fFirstPass = False
End If
If DataRangeHdr1.EOF Then Exit Do
%>
<!--METADATA TYPE="DesignerControl" endspan-->

<TR>
<TD> <%Response.Write DataRangeHdr1("type")%> </TD>
<TD><%Response.Write FormatCurrency(DataRangeHdr1(1),0,,,-2) %></TD>
</TR>



<!--METADATA TYPE="DesignerControl" startspan
<OBJECT ID="DataRangeFtr1" WIDTH=151 HEIGHT=24
CLASSID="CLSID:F602E722-A281-11CF-A5B7-0080C73AAC7E">
<PARAM NAME="_Version" VALUE="65536">
<PARAM NAME="_ExtentX" VALUE="3969">
<PARAM NAME="_ExtentY" VALUE="635">
<PARAM NAME="_StockProps" VALUE="0">
</OBJECT>
-->
<%
Loop
If tRangeType = "Table" Then Response.Write "</TABLE>"
If tPageSize > 0 Then
If Not fHideRule Then Response.Write "<HR>"
If Not fHideNavBar Then
%>
<TABLE WIDTH=100% >
<TR>
<TD WIDTH=100% >
<P ALIGN=<%= tBarAlignment %> >
<FORM <%= "ACTION=""" & Request.ServerVariables("PATH_INFO") &
stQueryString & """" %> METHOD="POST">
<INPUT TYPE="Submit" NAME="<%= tHeaderName & "_PagingMove" %>"
VALUE="   &lt;&lt;   ">
<INPUT TYPE="Submit" NAME="<%= tHeaderName & "_PagingMove" %>"
VALUE="   &lt;   ">
<INPUT TYPE="Submit" NAME="<%= tHeaderName & "_PagingMove" %>"
VALUE="   &gt;   ">
<% If fSupportsBookmarks Then %>
<INPUT TYPE="Submit" NAME="<%= tHeaderName & "_PagingMove" %>"
VALUE="   &gt;&gt;   ">
<% End If %>
<% If Not fHideRequery Then %>
<INPUT TYPE="Submit" NAME="<% =tHeaderName & "_PagingMove" %>" VALUE="
➥Requery ">
<% End If %>
</FORM>
</P>
</TD>
<TD VALIGN=MIDDLE ALIGN=RIGHT>
```

continues

21

Listing 21.3. continued

```
<FONT SIZE=2>
<%
If Not fHideNumber Then
If tPageSize > 1 Then
Response.Write "<NOBR>Page: " & Session(tHeaderName & "_AbsolutePage") &
"</NOBR>"
Else
Response.Write "<NOBR>Record: " & Session(tHeaderName & "_AbsolutePage") &
"</NOBR>"
End If
End If
%>
</FONT>
</TD>
</TR>
</TABLE>
<%
End If
End If
%>
<!--METADATA TYPE="DesignerControl" endspan-->

</BODY>
</HTML>
```

With the code in this listing, the ASP produces a web page similar to the one in Figure 21.9.

Figure 21.9.

Viewing the sales.

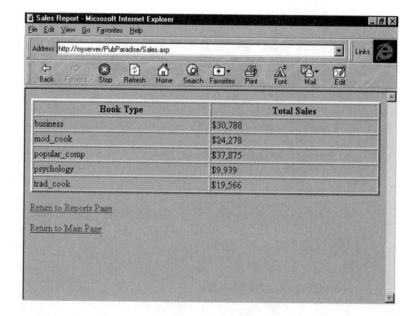

21

Case Study Review

You have now developed both the client and server portions of the application. I think you can see how these different components integrate to form a whole application. The HTML web pages in this example are used to display document and content information, supply links to other parts of the application, and provide the main default page for the application. The ASPs are used to display dynamic content that includes database integration. Given the powerful capabilities of Active Server Pages, you should use more of these pages in your future Web-based applications. I think you will see ASPs overtaking HTML pages in the not-too-distant future. The strength of ASPs comes from their ability to generate both HTML and client- and server-side script.

The lesson also demonstrates how to integrate database information into your application. The examples show you how to connect to the database, create the query, and then format the information in your web page. Try running the application now to get a feel for how the whole application works. Figures 21.10 through 21.14 illustrate the contents of the Publishers' Paradise application.

Figure 21.10.

The default page.

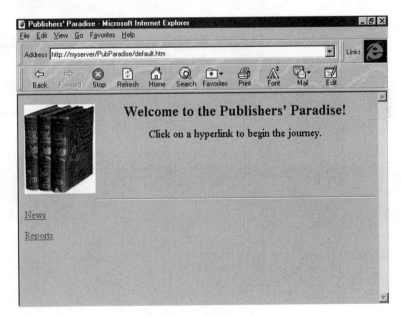

21

Figure 21.11.

The latest news.

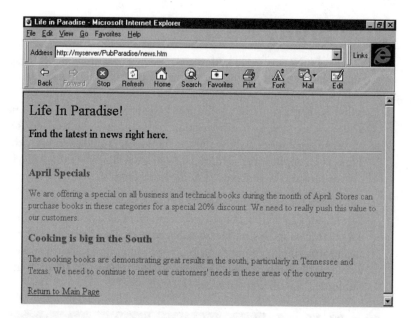

Figure 21.12.

Choosing a report.

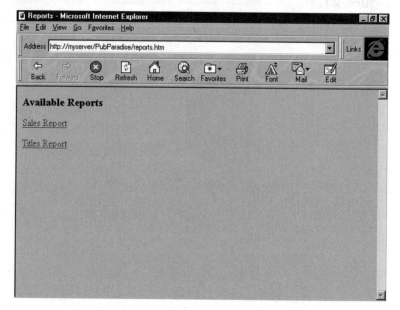

21

Figure 21.13.

Reviewing the titles.

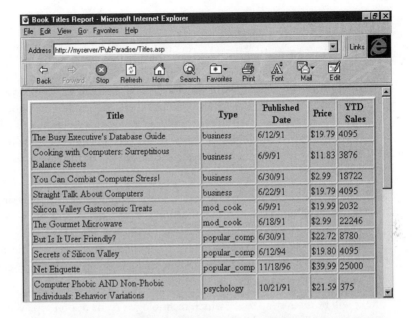

Figure 21.14.

Reviewing the sales.

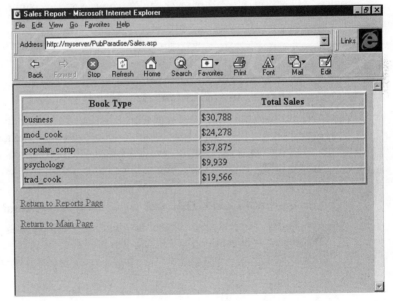

Summary

Today's lesson has demonstrated how the different components of a Visual InterDev project combine to form a Web-based application. The lesson should have given you the opportunity to apply the knowledge you gained over the past three weeks. How did you do? Were you able to recall the previous lessons you learned? You should now understand that the lessons of the past three weeks didn't focus on technology for technology's sake. Although the new and powerful technologies of the Web are technically cool, they have a more important mission as the critical tool to create the businesses of the future, as you learned in today's lesson.

The first part of the lesson gave you an overview of the Publishers' Paradise application. Next, the client components of the application were explained, and you were given a chance to test your knowledge by developing these components. Then the lesson proceeded to the server side of the equation. You were able to develop some ASP files and integrate them with a database to create a useful report. The final lesson for the day debriefed the case study and illustrated the pages in the application.

It will be interesting to see which technologies come out on top. Will it be ActiveX or Java applets? HTML or ASP? Whatever the outcome, you can count on Visual InterDev to support the winners!

Q&A

Q Are ASPs the wave of the future?

A Yes, jump on the ASP bandwagon now! Seriously, ASP offers a robust alternative to strict HTML. ASPs are HTML and more because they can generate both client- and server-side script. As you would expect, Microsoft's web site includes a heavy dose of ASPs. In the future, you will see more and more sites and Web-based applications using the power of ASPs.

Q Can I mix ASPs and HTML web pages in my application?

A Yes. Today's lesson demonstrated how HTML and ASP web pages can coexist in a Web-based application. The HTML was used for static web pages, and the ASPs were used for creating dynamic web pages that contained database integration.

Workshop

For the final workshop of this three-week journey, you should develop more web pages for the Publishers' Paradise application. You can use any of the tables in the Pubs database to support these pages. Try focusing on the concepts you might not understand as well as others. For example, you might want to create more images for the web pages, using the Image Composer to understand its capabilities. You also should practice using ASPs to deliver dynamic content from database tables. You can examine the tables and create added functions and features for the application, based on the information in the database.

Quiz

1. What design-time controls can be used to display multiple rows of data?
2. What are the main differences between HTML and ASP files?

Quiz Answers

1. The Data Range Header and Data Range Footer controls.
2. ASP files can generate HTML as well as scripting code for the client- and server-side portions of your application.

21

WEEK 3

In Review

You have now completed the third and final week of your pursuit of knowledge about the exciting new Visual InterDev. During the first and second weeks of your journey, you learned about the client and server components that can be integrated into your Web-based applications. The third week covered some advanced topics surrounding Visual InterDev and taught you how to truly integrate these components into your application. You also learned about some ancillary tools that can aid in your development.

15
16
17
18
19
20
21

Where You Have Been

The third week began with a detailed lesson that covered the integration of ActiveX controls and Java applets into your application. Next, you learned how to develop a design-time ActiveX control using the Visual Basic Control Creation Edition. The following day focused on another advanced topic as you learned how to truly integrate Active Server components into your application.

During the middle part of the week, you discovered how to properly manage your web site files using the tools included in Visual InterDev. You also learned how to integrate source code control into Visual InterDev with Microsoft Visual SourceSafe. The third week also covered the topic of debugging and presented a new script debugger from Microsoft. The final day enabled you to apply your knowledge by developing an application.

My wish for you is that you use the knowledge contained in this book to develop killer apps for the Web. These are exciting times for developers, and Visual InterDev is the perfect tool to sustain your enthusiasm. I hope you have enjoyed the journey as much as I have enjoyed presenting this dynamic and integrated tool for Web-based development. Armed with the lessons you have learned from this book and the power of Visual InterDev, you should now be prepared to untangle the technologies of the Web.

APPENDIX

A

Additional Resources

You have learned a lot of information by completing the 21 days of lessons contained in this book. The topics covered in this book have probably piqued your interest about a lot of different Web technologies. This appendix provides some additional resources that would be very good next steps for you to take in your pursuit of the killer app for the Web.

There is a wealth of information on the Web, and it's growing and changing every day. The URL addresses outlined in this appendix should provide you with additional tools and knowledge to support you in developing your Web-based applications.

Sams.net Home Page

```
http://www.mcp.com/sams
```

You can use this URL to access the home page of Macmillan Computer Publishing USA. You can then proceed to the Sams.net home page to check out updates to the information contained in this book as well as additional Internet book resources.

Microsoft Home Page

```
http://www.microsoft.com/
```

This URL address is the main home page for Microsoft. Because Visual InterDev integrates many Microsoft technologies for the Web, you can access this Web site to keep up with all of the new tools and technologies from Microsoft.

Microsoft Visual InterDev Home Page

```
http://www.microsoft.com/vinterdev/
```

This URL address is Microsoft's home page for Visual InterDev. This site includes FAQs, white papers, demos, tutorials, and links to other information concerning Visual InterDev.

Microsoft VBScript Home Page

```
http://www.microsoft.com/vbscript/
```

This site contains general information concerning VBScript.

Microsoft SiteBuilder Workshop

`http://www.microsoft.com/workshop/default.asp`

This site is an excellent resource for any Web developer. From this site, you can access information concerning every aspect of web development, from designing a web site to the site's final implementation.

Gamelan EarthWeb

`http://www-c.gamelan.com/index.shtml`

This site is an excellent resource for information about Java.

JavaSoft HomePage

`http://www.javasoft.com`

This site is another excellent resource for information on Java.

Java Boutique

`http://www.j-g.com/java/`

This site enables you to download over 100 Java applets that you can integrate into your applications.

World Wide Web Consortium

`http://www.w3.org/pub/WWW/`

You can use this site to keep up with the latest drafts on HTML specifications.

Microsoft Internet Information Server Home Page

`http://www.microsoft.com/iis/`

This URL address represents the home page for Internet Information Server (IIS). You can access a wealth of knowledge about IIS as well as Active Server Pages.

Microsoft Visual Basic Home Page for Web Developers

`http://www.microsoft.com/vbasic/icompdown/default.htm`

This web site contains information concerning Visual Basic that is targeted at web developers.

APPENDIX B

Installing Visual InterDev

This appendix provides a general overview on how to install Visual InterDev. The steps guide you through the process of installing the most common configuration of Visual InterDev—Windows 95 on the client and Windows NT on the server. The concepts described in this appendix can be applied to variations of the basic configurations.

NOTE

> If you have been participating in the public or private beta programs for Visual InterDev, Microsoft recommends that you remove all of the beta components before installing the commercial release of Visual InterDev.

Installing the Client Components

This section covers the installation of the Visual InterDev client components, which include the following:

- [ ] Microsoft Visual InterDev
- [ ] Microsoft Image Composer
- [ ] Microsoft Media Manager
- [ ] Microsoft Music Producer

NOTE

> The instructions for the client and server installation of Visual InterDev are based on Release Candidate 2 of the product. While the process should be the same for the commercial version, there may be slight variations.

Installing the Microsoft Visual InterDev Client

The following steps guide you through the process of installing the Visual InterDev client:

1. Begin the setup program for Visual InterDev by double-clicking the setup.exe program.

2. Select Visual InterDev Client under the Client Components list.

3. Click Continue on the Visual InterDev welcome screen.

4. Enter your name and organization and click OK.

5. Enter the 10-digit CD key for the product and click OK.

6. Write down the product ID number for future reference and click OK.

7. Read the license agreement and click I Agree.

8. Review the installation choices. The available options include Typical, Custom, and Compact. Choose the directory folder in which you want to install the product and click Custom installation.

9. Select the options that you want to install from the list displayed in Figure B.1.

Figure B.1.

Visual InterDev client options.

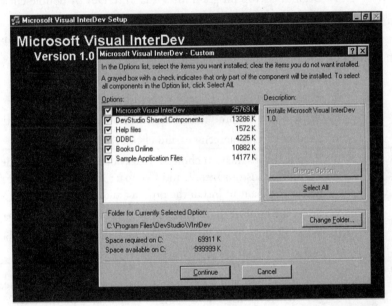

The ODBC components include drivers for SQL Server and Oracle as well as the ODBC driver manager and components. The sample applications include valuable web site samples that you can reference. You probably will want to select the Books Online option as well as the samples depending on the available disk space on your computer.

> **NOTE** You can select an item and click the Change Option button to select the items to include for an installation option. This feature is valuable when you want to perform a partial install for a certain feature.

10. Click Continue and the product is installed in the designated directory folder.

Installing the Image Composer

The following steps guide you through the process of installing the Image Composer:

1. Begin the setup program for Visual InterDev by double-clicking the setup.exe program.
2. Select Image Composer 1.0 under the Client Components list.
3. Click Continue on the Image Composer welcome screen.
4. Enter your name and organization and click OK.
5. Enter the 10-digit CD key for the product and click OK.
6. Write down the product ID number for future reference and click OK.
7. Read the license agreement and click I Agree.
8. Review the installation choices. The available options include Typical Install, Complete/Custom Install, and Compact Install. Choose the directory folder in which you want to install the product and click Complete/Custom installation.
9. Select the options that you want to install from the list displayed in Figure B.2.
10. Select all of the options except for the Photo Samples and click Continue.

> **NOTE** Unless you have an inordinate amount of disk space, you shouldn't install the Photo Samples files located on the CD. You can easily access these files from the CD when you need to integrate them into your web pages and image files.

11. Choose a program group for the application and click Continue. The product is then installed in the specified directory folder.

Figure B.2.
Image Composer options.

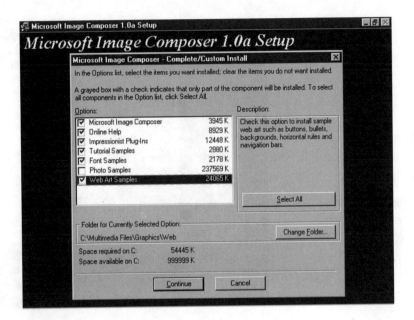

Installing the Media Manager

The following steps guide you through the process of installing the Media Manager:

1. Begin the setup program for Visual InterDev by double-clicking the setup.exe program.
2. Select Media Manager 1.0 under the Client Components list.
3. Click Continue on the Media Manager welcome screen.
4. Enter your name and organization and click OK.
5. Enter the 10-digit CD key for the product and click OK.
6. Write down the product ID number for future reference and click OK.
7. Read the license agreement and click I Agree.
8. Confirm the directory folder for the application and click OK.
9. Read the license agreement and click I Agree.
10. Choose Complete installation.
11. Choose the workgroup database for sharing media files among developers and the product files are copied to your machine. Figure B.3 displays the available options for this feature.

Figure B.3.

Media Manager options.

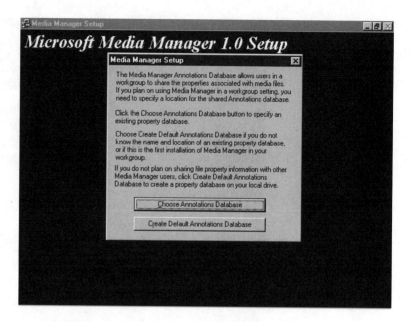

NOTE For the initial installation of the Media Manager, you should select the Create Default Annotations Database option.

12. You need to choose the Restart Windows option to complete the installation.

Installing the Music Producer

The following steps guide you through the process of installing the Music Producer:

1. Begin the setup program for Visual InterDev by double-clicking the setup.exe program.

2. Select Music Producer 1.0 under the Client Components list.

3. Click Continue on the Music Producer welcome screen.

4. Enter your name and organization and click OK.

5. Enter the 10-digit CD key for the product and click OK.

6. Write down the product ID number for future reference and click OK.

7. Read the license agreement and click I Agree.

8. Review the installation choices. The available options include Typical Install and Custom Install. Choose the directory folder in which you want to install the product and click Custom installation.

9. Select the options that you want to install from the list displayed in Figure B.4.

Figure B.4.

Music Producer options.

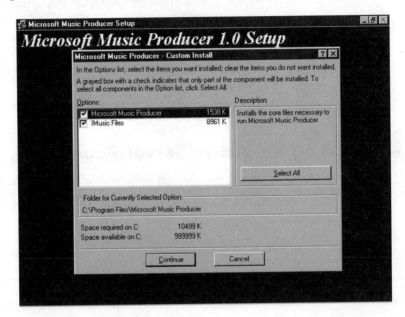

10. Select all of the options and click Continue.

11. Choose a program group for the application and click Continue. The product is then installed in the specified directory folder.

Installing the Server Components

This section covers the installation of the Visual InterDev client components, which include the following:

☐ Active Server Pages

☐ FrontPage Server Extensions

NOTE

The instructions for this section are based on a Windows NT Server installation. You also can choose to install the Personal Web Server for Windows 95. This option should be used for standalone Windows 95 development. You would typically select this option if you wanted to develop your application on a single Windows 95 machine and then deploy the application on a more robust server environment such as Windows NT. Refer to the lesson on Day 3, "Design and Development Considerations," for more information about the strengths and weaknesses of these platforms.

Installing the Active Server Pages

The following steps guide you through the process of installing the Active Server Pages:

1. Begin the setup program for Visual InterDev by double-clicking the setup.exe program.
2. Select Active Server Pages from the Server Components list.
3. Read the license agreement and click I Agree.
4. Click the Next button on the welcome screen for the Active Server Pages Wizard.

NOTE

If you're running any Internet services during the installation, the setup program prompts you to temporarily stop the services and proceed with the installation.

5. Click OK to stop the Internet services and continue with the installation.
6. Select all of the options and Click the Next button.
7. Confirm the directory folder for the installation and click the Next button to install the Active Server Pages.
8. The setup program gives you the opportunity to install the Windows NT Service Pack 1 from the Visual InterDev CD. Your NT installation must contain Service Pack 1 or higher. If you need to install the service pack, click Yes to proceed with this installation.

Installing the FrontPage Server Extensions

The following steps guide you through the process of installing the FrontPage Server Extensions:

1. Begin the setup program for Visual InterDev by double-clicking the setup.exe program.

2. Select FrontPage Server Extensions from the Server Components list.

3. Click the Next button on the welcome screen for the FrontPage Server Extensions Wizard.

4. Read the license agreement and click I Agree.

5. Confirm the directory folder for the installation and click the Next button.

6. Select the web server from the list and click the Next button.

7. Confirm the settings and click Next to install the FrontPage Server Extensions.

 NOTE

> If you're running any Internet services during the installation, the setup program prompts you to temporarily stop the services and proceed with the installation.

8. Click OK to stop the Internet services and continue with the installation. The extensions are installed in the designated directory folder.

APPENDIX

C

Visual InterDev Architecture Components Overview

Visual InterDev consists of a very robust architecture that provides many capabilities to support your application development. This appendix is provided as a supplement to the book to focus on the architecture of Visual InterDev. The information contained in this appendix presents an overview of both the development and deployment architecture to enable you to easily understand its components. In this way, you can more readily understand how to use the power and capabilities of Visual InterDev and how to formulate your team when developing a Web-based application.

Development Architecture

The first part of this appendix provides an overview of the Visual InterDev development architecture. You have already gained an understanding of how to use the features of Visual InterDev as well as the supporting technologies to build your Web-based application. Figure C.1 depicts the development environment of Visual InterDev that supports this effort.

Figure C.1.

The Visual InterDev development architecture environment.

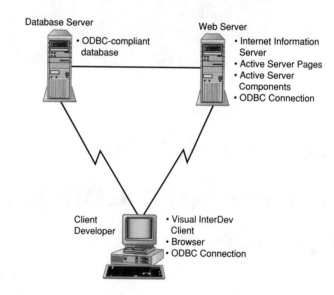

As shown in Figure C.1, the developer simultaneously connects to the database and web server during the development process. The developer uses the web server to construct and integrate HTML web pages, Active Server Pages, and Active Server Components as well as other components such as Java applets and applications. The developer uses the Visual Data

Tools contained in Visual InterDev to connect to the database server to build the database components. The web pages and application can be previewed and tested by using the browser on the client developer machine. This architecture supports a very rapid and iterative development process for your application development environment. This model changes somewhat as the process moves from development to testing, as explained in the next section.

Testing Architecture

You will want to use a slightly different model to test your Web-based application. The testing environment should simulate the production environment so that you can determine how your application will respond when it's deployed to your users. Figure C.2 illustrates the testing architecture environment for Visual InterDev.

Figure C.2.

The Visual InterDev testing architecture environment.

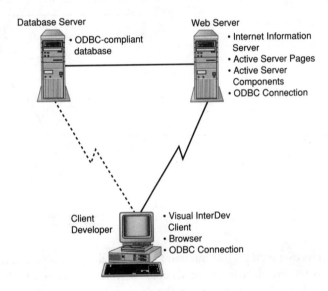

In this model, the developer tests the application without using the direct connection to the database. Instead, the developer tests the application by requesting both web pages and data through the web server. This process emulates how a user will request information from the application when it is deployed. In this way, the developer can test both the transfer of content information as well as the communication between the web server and database server. The transfer of information between the client, the web server, and the database server is crucial to the success of the application. During this phase, the direct database connection between the client machine and the database server still exists. The developer can use this connection while testing the application to make any changes to the database components or to test specific SQL statements and their results. Once the application has properly been tested, the application can be deployed.

Deployment Architecture

In this model, the user connects strictly with the web server, as shown in Figure C.3.

Figure C.3.

The Visual InterDev production architecture environment.

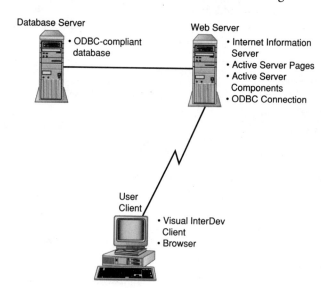

The user requests information from the web server which in turn makes the determination to retrieve data from the database server. At this point, the database connection exists between the web server and the database server. No direct connection exists between the client machine and the database server. You could say that the client machine in the deployment architecture environment lives vicariously through the web server. In this model, the browser serves as the window to your application's world.

APPENDIX

D

VBScript Language Reference

This appendix summarizes the statements, functions, and operators used in the Visual Basic Scripting Edition.

Category/ Keyword	Type	Usage
Arithmetic		
Atn	Function	Returns the arctangent of a number Atn(*number*)
Cos	Function	Returns the cosine of an angle Cos(*number*)
Exp	Function	Returns a number raised to a power Exp(*number*)
Log	Function	Returns the logarithm of a number Log(*number*)
Randomize	Statement	Primes the internal random number generator Randomize
Rnd	Function	Returns a random number Rnd
Sin	Function	Returns the sine of an angle Sin(*number*)
Sqr	Function	Returns the square root of a number Sqr(*number*)
Tan	Function	Returns the tangent of an angle Tan(*number*)
Array handling		
Dim	Statement	Declares an array Dim *arrayname([subscripts])*
Erase	Statement	Clears the contents of an array Erase *arrayname*
IsArray	Function	Returns True if *var* is an array, and False if not. IsArray(*var*)
LBound	Function	In VBScript, always returns 0 Lbound(*arrayname*)

Category/ Keyword	Type	Usage
Preserve	Statement	Copies the contents of a dynamic array to a resized dynamic array `Redim Preserve arrayname(subscripts)`
ReDim	Statement	Declares a dynamic array or redimensions a dynamic array (see `Preserve`) `ReDim arrayname()` or `ReDim arrayname([subscripts])`
UBound	Statement	Returns the largest subscript of an array `Ubound(arrayname)`

Assignment

=	Operator	Assigns a value to a variable or property `variable = value`
Set	Statement	Assigns an object reference to a variable `Set variable = object`

Comment

Rem	Statement	Declares the following line as a comment to be ignored by the language engine `Rem comment_text`

Constants/Literals

Empty	Literal	Declares a special uninitialized variable value `variable = Empty`
False	Constant	A Boolean value representing 0 `variable = False`
Nothing	Literal	Used to disassociate an object reference from a variable; used in conjunction with `Set` `Set variable = Nothing`
Null	Literal	Represents no valid data `variable = Null`
True	Constant	Boolean value representing -1 `variable = True`

continues

D

Category/ Keyword	Type	Usage
Conversions		
Abs	Function	Returns the unsigned (absolute) value of a number `Abs(number)`
Asc	Function	Returns the ANSI/ASCII code of a character `Asc(string)`
CBool	Function	Returns a Boolean subtype `Variant` value from any valid expression `CBool(expression)`
CByte	Function	Returns a Byte subtype `Variant` value from any valid expression `CByte(expression)`
CDate	Function	Returns a Date subtype `Variant` value from any valid date expression `CDate(expression)`
CDbl	Function	Returns a Double Precision subtype `Variant` value from any valid numeric expression `CDbl(expression)`
Chr	Function	Returns the character corresponding to the ANSI or ASCII code `Chr(number)`
CInt	Function	Returns an Integer subtype `Variant` value from any valid numeric expression `CInt(expression)`
CLng	Function	Returns a Long Integer subtype `Variant` value from any valid numeric expression `CLng(expression)`
CSng	Function	Returns a Single Precision subtype `Variant` value from any valid numeric expression `CSng(expression)`

Category/ Keyword	Type	Usage
CStr	Function	Returns a String subtype `Variant` value from any valid expression `CStr(expression)`
DateSerial	Function	Returns a Date subtype `Variant` value from valid year, month, and day values `DateSerial(year,month,day)`
DateValue	Function	Returns a Date subtype `Variant` value from any valid date expression `DateValue(expression)`
Hex	Function	Returns a String subtype `Variant` value representing the hexadecimal value of a number `Hex(number)`
Int	Function	Returns an Integer subtype `Variant` value rounded down from the number supplied `Int(number)`
Fix	Function	Returns an Integer subtype `Variant` value rounded up from the number supplied `Fix(number)`
Oct	Function	Returns a String subtype `Variant` value representing the octal value of a number `Hex(number)`
Sgn	Function	Returns an Integer subtype `Variant` value representing the sign of a number `Sgn(number)` values > 0 return 1 values = 0 return 0 values < 0 return -1
TimeSerial	Function	Returns a Date subtype `Variant` value from valid hour, minute, and second values `TimeSerial(hour,minute,second)`
TimeValue	Function	Returns a Date subtype `Variant` value from any valid time expression `TimeValue(expression)`

continues

Category/ Keyword	Type	Usage
Dates and Times		
Date	Function	Returns the current system date `Date()`
DateSerial	Function	Returns a Date subtype Variant value from valid year, month, and day values. `DateSerial(year,month,day)`
DateValue	Function	Returns a Date subtype Variant value from any valid date expression. `DateValue(expression)`
Day	Function	Returns an Integer subtype Variant value representing the day (1-31) from a valid date expression `Day(dateexpression)`
Hour	Function	Returns an Integer subtype Variant value representing the hour (0-23) from a valid time expression `Hour(timeexpression)`
Minute	Function	Returns an Integer subtype Variant value representing the minute (0-60) from a valid time expression `Minute(timeexpression)`
Month	Function	Returns an Integer subtype Variant value representing the month (1-12) from a valid date expression `Month(dateexpression)`
Now	Function	Returns the current date and time of the system `Now()`
Second	Function	Returns an Integer subtype Variant value representing the second (0-60) from a valid time expression `Second(timeexpression)`
Time	Function	Returns the current system time `Time()`

Category/ Keyword	Type	Usage
TimeSerial	Function	Returns a Date subtype Variant from valid hour, minute, and second values TimeSerial(*hour*,*minute*,*second*)
TimeValue	Function	Returns a Date subtype Variant value from any valid time expression TimeValue(*expression*)
Weekday	Function	Returns an Integer subtype Variant value between 1 and 7 representing the day of the week, starting at Sunday, from a date expression Weekday(*dateexpression*)
Year	Function	Returns an Integer subtype Variant value representing the year from a valid date expression Year(*dateexpression*)

Declarations

Category/ Keyword	Type	Usage
Dim	Statement	Declares a variable Dim *variable*
End	Statement	Declares the end of a Sub procedure or function End Sub End Function
Exit	Statement	Use with Do, For, Function, or Sub to prematurely exit the routine Exit Do/For/Function/Sub
Function	Statement	Declares a function and the argument list passed into the function, and declares the end of a function; also used with Exit to prematurely end a function Function *functionname*(*argumentlist*) Exit Function End Function Public *variable*

continues

Category/ Keyword	Type	Usage

Sub	Statement	Declares a custom procedure or event handler and the argument list, if any, and declares the end of a custom procedure or event handler; also used with Exit to prematurely end a custom procedure or event handler
		
		`Sub subroutinename([argumentlist])`
		`Exit Sub`
		`End Sub`

Error Handling

Category/ Keyword	Type	Usage
Clear	Method	A method of the Err object to reset the Err.Number property to 0 `Err.Clear`
Description	Property	A property of the Err object that contains a description of the last error as specified in the Err.Number property `Err.Description`
Err	Object	An object containing information about the last error `Err.property¦method`
On Error	Statement	Used in conjunction with Resume Next to continue execution with the line directly following the line in which the error occurred `On Error Resume Next`
Raise	Method	A method of the Err object used to simulate the occurrence of an error specified by number `Err.Raise(errornumber)`
Number	Property	A property of the Err object that contains the error code for the last error, or 0 if no error has occurred `Err.Number`
Source	Property	Returns the name of the object or application that raised the error `Err.Source`

Category/ Keyword	Type	Usage
Input/Output		
InputBox	Function	Displays a dialog box to allow user input `InputBox(caption[,title][,value][,x][,y])`
MsgBox	Function	Displays a dialog box `MsgBox(prompt[, definition][, title])`
Operators		
+	Operator	Addition of two numerical expressions `result = expr1 + expr2`
And	Operator	Logical conjunction operator `If expression AND expression Then`
/	Operator	Division operator `result = expression / expression`
=	Operator	Equality operator `If expression = expression Then`
Eqv	Operator	Logical equivalence operator `If expression Eqv expression Then`
^	Operator	Exponentiation operator `result = expression ^ expression`
>	Operator	Greater than comparison `If expression > expression Then`
>=	Operator	Greater than or equal to comparison `If expression >= expression Then`
Imp	Operator	Logical implication `If expression Imp expression Then`
<>	Operator	Inequality comparison `If expression <> expression Then`
\	Operator	Integer division operator `result = expression \ expression`
<	Operator	Less than comparison `If expression < expression Then`
<=	Operator	Less than or equal to comparison `If expression <= expression Then`

continues

Category/ Keyword	Type	Usage
Mod	Operator	Modulus arithmetic; returns only the remainder of a division of two numbers `result = expression mod expression`
*	Operator	Multiplication `result = expression * expression`
-	Operator	Subtraction `result = expression - expression`
Or	Operator	Logical disjunction `If expression Or expression Then`
&	Operator	Concatenation of two string values `result = string & string`
Xor	Operator	Logical exclusion `If expression Xor expression Then`

Options

Category/ Keyword	Type	Usage
Option	Statement	Forces a compile-time error if an `Explicit` undeclared variable is found `Option Explicit`

Program Flow

Category/ Keyword	Type	Usage

Call	Statement	Passes execution to a sub-routine or event handler; also can be used to replicate the actions of the user
		`Call myroutine()`
		`Call cmdbutton_OnClick()`

Do...Loop	Statement	Repeats code while a condition is met or until a condition is met
		`Do While condition`
		`...`
		`Loop`
		`or`
		`Do Until condition`
		`...`
		`Loop`
		`or`
		`Do`
		`...`
		`Loop While condition`
		`or`
		`Do`
		`...`
		`Loop Until condition`

Category/ Keyword	Type	Usage

For...Next	Statement	Repeats a block of code until the counter reaches a given number
		`For counter = lower to upper [step]`
		`...`
		`Next`

If...Then...Else	Statement	Conditional execution of code
		`If condition Then`
		`... (if condition met)`
		`Else`
		`... (if condition not met)`
		`End If`

Select Case	Statement	Selective execution of code, where *testexpression* must match *expression*
		`Select Case testexpression`
		`Case expression`
		`...`
		`Case expression`
		`...`
		`Case Else`
		`End Select`

While...Wend	Statement	Execution of a code block while a condition is met
		`While expression`
		`...`
		`Wend`

Strings

InStr	Function	Returns the starting point of one string within another string, or 0 if not found `result = InStr(start,searched,sought)`
LCase	Function	Converts a string to lowercase `result = LCase(string)`
Left	Function	Returns the *n* leftmost character of a string `result = LCase(string)`
Len	Function	Returns the length of a string `result = Len(string)`
LTrim	Function	Removes all leading spaces `result = LTrim(string)`

continues

Category/ Keyword	Type	Usage
Mid	Function	Returns a string of length L, starting at S within *string* `result = Mid(string, S, L)`
Right	Function	Returns the rightmost n character `result = Right(string, n)`
RTrim	Function	Removes all trailing spaces from a string `result = RTrim(string)`
Space	Function	Returns a string consisting of n spaces `result = Space(n)`

StrComp	Function	Returns an Integer subtype Variant representing the result of a comparison of two strings
		`result = StrComp(string1, string2)`
		`string1 < string2 returns -1`
		`string1 < string2 returns 0`
		`string1 < string2 returns 1`

String	Function	Returns a string consisting of character C, of length L `result = String(L, C)`
Trim	Function	Removes both leading and trailing spaces `result = Trim(string)`
UCase	Function	Returns a string as uppercase alphabetical characters `result = UCase(string)`

Variants

IsArray	Function	Returns True (-1) if expression is an array, and False (0) if not `result = IsArray(expression)`
IsDate	Function	Returns True (-1) if expression is a valid date and False (0) if not `result = IsDate(expression)`
IsEmpty	Function	Returns True (-1) if expression equates to an Empty subtype and False (0) if not `result = IsEmpty(expression)`

Category/ Keyword	Type	Usage
IsNull	Function	Returns True (-1) if expression equates to a Null subtype and False (0) if not *result* = IsNull(*expression*)
IsNumeric	Function	Returns True (-1) if expression is a valid numeric expression and False (0) if not *result* = IsNumeric(*expression*)
VarType	Function	Returns an integer representing the subtype of a Variant result = VarType(*expression*)

D

APPENDIX

E

JavaScript Language Reference

The first part of this reference is organized by object with properties and methods listed by the object they apply to. The second part covers independent functions in JavaScript not connected with a particular object, as well as operators in JavaScript.

The following codes are used to indicate where objects, methods, properties, and event handlers are implemented:

- ☐ C   Client JavaScript (Server JavaScript is not covered in this appendix)
- ☐ 2   Netscape Navigator 2
- ☐ 3   Netscape Navigator 3
- ☐ I   Microsoft Internet Explorer 3

The anchor Object [C | 2 | 3 | I]

The anchor object reflects an HTML anchor.

Property

☐ **name**   A string value indicating the name of the anchor. [Not 2|3]

The applet Object [C | 3]

The applet object reflects a Java applet included in a web page with the APPLET tag.

Property

☐ **name**   A string reflecting the NAME attribute of the APPLET tag.

The area Object [C | 3]

The area object reflects a clickable area defined in an imagemap. area objects appear as entries in the links array of the document object.

Properties

☐ **hash**   A string value indicating an anchor name from the URL.
☐ **host**   A string value reflecting the host and domain name portion of the URL.

- ☐ **hostname**   A string value indicating the host, domain name, and port number from the URL.
- ☐ **href**   A string value reflecting the entire URL.
- ☐ **pathname**   A string value reflecting the path portion of the URL (excluding the host, domain name, port number, and protocol).
- ☐ **port**   A string value indicating the port number from the URL.
- ☐ **protocol**   A string value indicating the protocol portion of the URL including the trailing colon.
- ☐ **search**   A string value specifying the query portion of the URL (after the question mark).
- ☐ **target**   A string value reflecting the TARGET attribute of the AREA tag.

Event Handlers

- ☐ **onMouseOut**   Specifies JavaScript code to execute when the mouse moves outside the area specified in the AREA tag.
- ☐ **onMouseOver**   Specifies JavaScript code to execute when the mouse enters the area specified in the AREA tag.

The Array Object [C|3|I]

Provides a mechanism for creating arrays and working with them. New arrays are created with *arrayName* = new Array() or *arrayName* = new Array(*arrayLength*).

Properties

- ☐ **length**   An integer value reflecting the number of elements in an array.
- ☐ **prototype**   Provides a mechanism to add properties to an Array object.

Methods

- ☐ **join(*string*)**   Returns a string containing each element of the array separated by *string*. [Not I]
- ☐ **reverse()**   Reverses the order of an array. [Not I]
- ☐ **sort(*function*)**   Sorts an array based on function which indicates a *function* defining the sort order. *function* can be omitted, in which case the sort defaults to dictionary order. [Not I]

E

The button **Object [C|2|3|1]**

The button object reflects a push button from an HTML form in JavaScript.

Properties

- ☐ **enabled**   A Boolean value indicating whether the button is enabled. [Not 2|3]
- ☐ **form**   A reference to the form object containing the button. [Not 2|3]
- ☐ **name**   A string value containing the name of the button element.
- ☐ **type**   A string value reflecting the TYPE attribute of the INPUT tag. [Not 2|1]
- ☐ **value**   A string value containing the value of the button element.

Methods

- ☐ **click()**   Emulates the action of clicking the button.
- ☐ **focus()**   Gives focus to the button. [Not 2|3]

Event Handlers

- ☐ **onClick**   Specifies JavaScript code to execute when the button is clicked.
- ☐ **onFocus**   Specifies JavaScript code to execute when the button receives focus. [Not 2|3]

The checkbox **Object [c|2|3|1]**

The checkbox object makes a checkbox in an HTML form available in JavaScript.

Properties

- ☐ **checked**   A Boolean value indicating whether the checkbox element is checked.
- ☐ **defaultChecked**   A Boolean value indicating whether the checkbox element was checked by default (that is, reflects the CHECKED attribute).
- ☐ **enabled**   A Boolean value indicating whether the checkbox is enabled. [Not 2|3]
- ☐ **form**   A reference to the form object containing the checkbox. [Not 2|3]
- ☐ **name**   A string value containing the name of the checkbox element.

☐ **type**   A string value reflecting the TYPE attribute of the INPUT tag. [Not 2|I]

☐ **value**   A string value containing the value of the checkbox element.

Methods

☐ **click()**   Emulates the action of clicking the checkbox.

☐ **focus()**   Gives focus to the checkbox. [Not 2|3]

Event Handlers

☐ **onClick**   Specifies JavaScript code to execute when the checkbox is clicked.

☐ **onFocus**   Specifies JavaScript code to execute when the checkbox receives focus. [Not 2|3]

The combo Object [C|I]

The combo object reflects a combo field into JavaScript.

Properties

☐ **enabled**   A Boolean value indicating whether the combo is enabled. [Not 2|3]

☐ **form**   A reference to the form object containing the combo. [Not 2|3]

☐ **listCount**   An integer reflecting the number of elements in the list.

☐ **listIndex**   An integer reflecting the index of the selected element in the list.

☐ **multiSelect**   A Boolean value indicating whether the combo field is in multiselect mode.

☐ **name**   A string value reflecting the name of the combo field.

☐ **value**   A string containing the value of the combo field.

Methods

☐ **addItem(*index*)**   Adds an item to the combo field before the item at *index*.

☐ **click()**   Simulates a click on the combo field.

☐ **clear()**   Clears the contents of the combo field.

☐ **focus()**   Gives focus to the combo field.

☐ **removeItem(*index*)**   Removes the item at *index* from the combo field.

Event Handlers

☐ **onClick**   Specifies JavaScript code to execute when the mouse clicks the combo field.

☐ **onFocus**   Specifies JavaScript code to execute when the combo field receives focus.

The Date Object [C|2|3|1]

The Date object provides mechanisms for working with dates and times in JavaScript. Instances of the object can be created with the syntax

newObjectName = new Date(*dateInfo*)

Where *dateInfo* is an optional specification of a particular date and can be one of the following:

"*month, day, year hours:minutes:seconds*"

year, month, day

year, month, day, hours, minutes, seconds

where the latter two options represent integer values.

If no *dateInfo* is specified, the new object will represent the current date and time.

Property

☐ **prototype**   Provides a mechanism for adding properties to a Date object. [Not 2]

Methods

☐ **getDate()**   Returns the day of the month for the current Date object as an integer from 1 to 31.

☐ **getDay()**   Returns the day of the week for the current Date object as an integer from 0 to 6 (where 0 is Sunday, 1 is Monday, and so on).

☐ **getHours()**   Returns the hour from the time in the current Date object as an integer from 0 to 23.

☐ **getMinutes()**   Returns the minutes from the time in the current Date object as an integer from 0 to 59.

☐ **getMonth()**   Returns the month for the current Date object as an integer from 0 to 11 (where 0 is January, 1 is February, and so on).

☐ **getSeconds()**   Returns the seconds from the time in the current Date object as an integer from 0 to 59.

☐ **getTime()**   Returns the time of the current Date object as an integer representing the number of milliseconds since January 1, 1970 at 00:00:00.

☐ **getTimezoneOffset()**   Returns the difference between the local time and GMT as an integer representing the number of minutes.

☐ **getYear()**   Returns the year for the current Date object as a two-digit integer representing the year minus 1900.

☐ **parse(_dateString_)**   Returns the number of milliseconds between January 1, 1970 at 00:00:00 and the date specified in _dateString_. _dateString_ should take the following format [Not I]:

Day, DD Mon YYYY HH:MM:SS TZN

Mon DD, YYYY

☐ **setDate(_dateValue_)**   Sets the day of the month for the current Date object. _dateValue_ is an integer from 1 to 31.

☐ **setHours(_hoursValue_)**   Sets the hours for the time for the current Date object. _hoursValue_ is an integer from 0 to 23.

☐ **setMinutes(_minutesValue_)**   Sets the minutes for the time for the current Date object. _minutesValue_ is an integer from 0 to 59.

☐ **setMonth(_monthValue_)**   Sets the month for the current Date object. _monthValue_ is an integer from 0 to 11 (where 0 is January, 1 is February, and so on).

☐ **setSeconds(_secondsValue_)**   Sets the seconds for the time for the current Date object. _secondsValue_ is an integer from 0 to 59.

☐ **setTime(_timeValue_)**   Sets the value for the current Date object. _timeValue_ is an integer representing the number of milliseconds since January 1, 1970 at 00:00:00.

☐ **setYear(_yearValue_)**   Sets the year for the current Date object. _yearValue_ is an integer greater than 1900.

☐ **toGMTString()**   Returns the value of the current Date object in GMT as a string using Internet conventions in the form

Day, DD Mon YYYY HH:MM:SS GMT

☐ **toLocaleString()**   Returns the value of the current Date object in the local time using local conventions.

E

☐ **UTC(*yearValue, monthValue, dateValue, hoursValue, minutesValue, secondsValue*)**   Returns the number of milliseconds since January 1, 1970 at 00:00:00 GMT. *yearValue* is an integer greater than 1900. *monthValue* is an integer from 0 to 11. *dateValue* is an integer from 1 to 31. *hoursValue* is an integer from 0 to 23. *minutesValue* and *secondsValue* are integers from 0 to 59. *hoursValue*, *minutesValue*, and *secondsValue* are optional. [Not I]

The document **Object [C|2|3||]**

The document object reflects attributes of an HTML document in JavaScript.

Properties

☐ **alinkColor**   The color of active links as a string or a hexadecimal triplet.

☐ **anchors**   Array of anchor objects in the order they appear in the HTML document. Use anchors.length to get the number of anchors in a document.

☐ **applets**   Array of applet objects in the order they appear in the HTML document. Use applets.length to get the number of applets in a document. [Not 2]

☐ **bgColor**   The color of the document's background.

☐ **cookie**   A string value containing cookie values for the current document.

☐ **embeds**   Array of plugin objects in the order they appear in the HTML document. Use embeds.length to get the number of plug-ins in a document. [Not 2|I]

☐ **fgColor**   The color of the document's foreground.

☐ **forms**   Array of form objects in the order the forms appear in the HTML file. Use forms.length to get the number of forms in a document.

☐ **images**   Array of image objects in the order they appear in the HTML document. Use images.length to get the number of images in a document. [Not 2|I]

☐ **lastModified**   String value containing the last date of modification of the document.

☐ **linkColor**   The color of links as a string or a hexadecimal triplet.

☐ **links**   Array of link objects in the order the hypertext links appear in the HTML document. Use links.length to get the number of links in a document.

☐ **location**   A string containing the URL of the current document. Use document.URL instead of document.location. This property is expected to disappear in a future release.

☐ **referrer**   A string value containing the URL of the calling document when the user follows a link.

☐ **title**   A string containing the title of the current document.

☐ **URL**   A string reflecting the URL of the current document. Use instead of `document.location`. [Not I]

☐ **vlinkColor**   The color of followed links as a string or a hexadecimal triplet.

Methods

☐ **clear()**   Clears the document window. [Not I]

☐ **close()**   Closes the current output stream.

☐ **open(*mimeType*)**   Opens a stream that allows `write()` and `writeln()` methods to write to the document window. *mimeType* is an optional string that specifies a document type supported by Navigator or a plug-in (for example, `text/html`, `image/gif`, and so on).

☐ **write()**   Writes text and HTML to the specified document.

☐ **writeln()**   Writes text and HTML to the specified document followed by a newline character.

The `FileUpload` Object [C|3]

Reflects a file upload element in an HTML form.

Properties

☐ **name**   A string value reflecting the name of the file upload element.

☐ **value**   A string value reflecting the file upload element's field.

The `form` Object [C|2|3|I]

The `form` object reflects an HTML form in JavaScript. Each HTML form in a document is reflected by a distinct instance of the `form` object.

Properties

☐ **action**   A string value specifying the URL that the form data is submitted to.

☐ **elements**   Array of objects for each form element in the order in which they appear in the form.

☐ **encoding**   String containing the MIME encoding of the form as specified in the ENCTYPE attribute.

☐ **method**   A string value containing the method of submission of form data to the server.

☐ **target**   A string value containing the name of the window to which responses to form submissions are directed.

Methods

☐ **reset()**   Resets the form. [Not 2|I]

☐ **submit()**   Submits the form.

Event Handlers

☐ **onReset**   Specifies JavaScript code to execute when the form is reset. [Not 2|I]

☐ **onSubmit**   Specifies JavaScript code to execute when the form is submitted. The code should return a true value to allow the form to be submitted. A false value prevents the form from being submitted.

The frame Object [C|2|3|I]

The frame object reflects a frame window in JavaScript.

Properties

☐ **frames**   An array of objects for each frame in a window. Frames appear in the array in the order in which they appear in the HTML source code.

☐ **onblur**   A string reflecting the onBlur event handler for the frame. New values can be assigned to this property to change the event handler. [Not 2]

☐ **onfocus**   A string reflecting the onFocus event handler for the frame. New values can be assigned to this property to change the event handler. [Not 2]

☐ **parent**   A string indicating the name of the window containing the frameset.

☐ **self**   An alternative for the name of the current window.

☐ **top**   An alternative for the name of the top-most window.

☐ **window**   An alternative for the name of the current window.

Methods

☐ **alert(*message*)**   Displays *message* in a dialog box.

☐ **blur()**   Removes focus from the frame. [Not 2]

☐ **close()**   Closes the window.

☐ **confirm(*message*)**   Displays *message* in a dialog box with OK and Cancel buttons. Returns true or false based on the button clicked by the user.

☐ **focus()**   Gives focus to the frame. [Not 2]

☐ **open(*url*, *name*, *features*)**   Opens *url* in a window named *name*. If *name* doesn't exist, a new window is created with that name. *features* is an optional string argument containing a list of features for the new window. The feature list contains any of the following name-value pairs separated by commas and without additional spaces:

toolbar=[yes,no,1,0]	Indicates whether the window should have a toolbar
location=[yes,no,1,0]	Indicates whether the window should have a location field
directories=[yes,no,1,0]	Indicates whether the window should have directory buttons
status=[yes,no,1,0]	Indicates whether the window should have a status bar
menubar=[yes,no,1,0]	Indicates whether the window should have menus
scrollbars=[yes,no,1,0]	Indicates whether the window should have scrollbars
resizable=[yes,no,1,0]	Indicates whether the window should be resizable
width=*pixels*	Indicates the width of the window in pixels
height=*pixels*	Indicates the height of the window in pixels

☐ **prompt(*message*, *response*)**   Displays *message* in a dialog box with a text entry field with the default value of *response*. The user's response in the text entry field is returned as a string.

☐ **setTimeout(*expression*, *time*)**   Evaluates *expression* after *time* where *time* is a value in milliseconds. The time-out can be named with the structure:

name = setTimeOut(*expression*, *time*)

☐ **clearTimeout(*name*)**   Cancels the time-out with the name name.

Event Handlers

- ☐ **onBlur**   Specifies JavaScript code to execute when focus is removed from a frame. [Not 2]

- ☐ **onFocus**   Specifies JavaScript code to execute when focus is moved to a frame. [Not 2]

The Function **Object [C | 3]**

The Function object provides a mechanism for indicating JavaScript code to compile as a function. The syntax to use the Function object is *functionName* = new Function(*arg1*, *arg2*, *arg3*, ..., *functionCode*). This is similar to

```
function functionName(arg1, arg2, arg3, ...) {
   functionCode
}
```

except that in the former, *functionName* is a variable with a reference to the function, and the function is evaluated each time it is used rather than being compiled once.

Properties

- ☐ **arguments**   An integer reflecting the number of arguments in a function.
- ☐ **prototype**   Provides a mechanism for adding properties to a Function object.

The hidden **Object [C | 2 | 3 | I]**

The hidden object reflects a hidden field from an HTML form in JavaScript.

Properties

- ☐ **name**   A string value containing the name of the hidden element.
- ☐ **type**   A string value reflecting the TYPE property of the INPUT tag. [Not 2|I]
- ☐ **value**   A string value containing the value of the hidden text element.

The history **Object [C | 2 | 3 | I]**

The history object allows a script to work with the Navigator browser's history list in JavaScript. For security and privacy reasons, the actual content of the list is not reflected into JavaScript.

Property

☐ **length**   An integer representing the number of items on the history list. [Not I]

Methods

☐ **back()**   Goes back to the previous document in the history list. [Not I]

☐ **forward()**   Goes forward to the next document in the history list. [Not I]

☐ **go(*location*)**   Goes to the document in the history list specified by *location*. *location* can be a string or integer value. If it is a string, it represents all or part of a URL in the history list. If it is an integer, *location* represents the relative position of the document on the history list. As an integer, *location* can be positive or negative. [Not I]

The `Image` Object [C I 3]

The `Image` object reflects an image included in an HTML document.

Properties

☐ **border**   An integer value reflecting the width of the image's border in pixels.

☐ **complete**   A Boolean value indicating whether the image has finished loading.

☐ **height**   An integer value reflecting the height of an image in pixels.

☐ **hspace**   An integer value reflecting the HSPACE attribute of the IMG tag.

☐ **lowsrc**   A string value containing the URL of the low-resolution version of the image to load.

☐ **name**   A string value indicating the name of the `Image` object.

☐ **prototype**   Provides a mechanism for adding properties to an `Image` object.

☐ **src**   A string value indicating the URL of the image.

☐ **vspace**   An integer value reflecting the VSPACE attribute of the IMG tag.

☐ **width**   An integer value indicating the width of an image in pixels.

Event Handlers

☐ **onAbort**   Specifies JavaScript code to execute if the attempt to load the image is aborted. [Not 2]

☐ **onError**   Specifies JavaScript code to execute if there is an error while loading the image. Setting this event handler to null suppresses error messages if an error does occur while loading. [Not 2]

☐ **onLoad**   Specifies JavaScript code to execute when the image finishes loading. [Not 2]

The `link` Object [C|2|3|I]

The link object reflects a hypertext link in the body of a document.

Properties

☐ **hash**   A string value containing the anchor name in the URL.

☐ **host**   A string value containing the host name and port number from the URL.

☐ **hostname**   A string value containing the domain name (or numerical IP address) from the URL.

☐ **href**   A string value containing the entire URL.

☐ **pathname**   A string value specifying the path portion of the URL.

☐ **port**   A string value containing the port number from the URL.

☐ **protocol**   A string value containing the protocol from the URL (including the colon, but not the slashes).

☐ **search**   A string value containing any information passed to a GET CGI-BIN call (that is, any information after the question mark).

☐ **target**   A string value containing the name of the window or frame specified in the TARGET attribute.

Event Handlers

☐ **moveMouse**   Specifies JavaScript code to execute when the mouse pointer moves over the link. [Not 2|3]

☐ **onClick**   Specifies JavaScript code to execute when the link is clicked.

☐ **onMouseOver**   Specifies JavaScript code to execute when the mouse pointer moves over the hypertext link.

The `location` Object [C|2|3|I]

The `location` object reflects information about the current URL.

Properties

- ☐ **hash**   A string value containing the anchor name in the URL.
- ☐ **host**   A string value containing the host name and port number from the URL.
- ☐ **hostname**   A string value containing the domain name (or numerical IP address) from the URL.
- ☐ **href**   A string value containing the entire URL.
- ☐ **pathname**   A string value specifying the path portion of the URL.
- ☐ **port**   A string value containing the port number from the URL.
- ☐ **protocol**   A string value containing the protocol from the URL (including the colon, but not the slashes).
- ☐ **search**   A string value containing any information passed to a GET CGI-BIN call (that is, any information after the question mark).

Methods

- ☐ **reload()**   Reloads the current document. [Not 2|I]
- ☐ **replace(*url*)**   Loads *url* over the current entry in the history list, making it impossible to navigate back to the previous URL with the back button. [Not 2|I]

The `Math` Object [C|2|3|I]

The `Math` object provides properties and methods for advanced mathematical calculations.

Properties

- ☐ **E**   The value of Euler's constant (roughly 2.718) used as the base for natural logarithms.
- ☐ **LN10**   The value of the natural logarithm of 10 (roughly 2.302).
- ☐ **LN2**   The value of the natural logarithm of 2 (roughly 0.693).
- ☐ **LOG10E**   The value of the base 10 logarithm of e (roughly 0.434).

E

☐ **LOG2E** The value of the base 2 logarithm of e (roughly 1.442).

☐ **PI** The value of pi—used in calculating the circumference and area of circles (roughly 3.1415).

☐ **SQRT1_2** The value of the square root of $\frac{1}{2}$ (roughly 0.707).

☐ **SQRT2** The value of the square root of 2 (roughly 1.414).

Methods

☐ **abs(*number*)** Returns the absolute value of *number*. The absolute value is the value of a number with its sign ignored, so abs(4) and abs(-4) both return 4.

☐ **acos(*number*)** Returns the arccosine of *number* in radians.

☐ **asin(*number*)** Returns the arcsine of *number* in radians.

☐ **atan(*number*)** Returns the arctangent of *number* in radians.

☐ **atan2(*number1*,*number2*)** Returns the angle of the polar coordinate corresponding to the Cartesian coordinate (*number1*, *number2*). [Not I]

☐ **ceil(*number*)** Returns the next integer greater than *number*—in other words, rounds up to the next integer.

☐ **cos(*number*)** Returns the cosine of *number* where *number* represents an angle in radians.

☐ **exp(*number*)** Returns the value of e to the power of *number*.

☐ **floor(*number*)** Returns the next integer less than *number*—in other words, rounds down to the nearest integer.

☐ **log(*number*)** Returns the natural logarithm of *number*.

☐ **max(*number1*,*number2*)** Returns the greater of *number1* and *number2*.

☐ **min(*number1*,*number2*)** Returns the smaller of *number1* and *number2*.

☐ **pow(*number1*,*number2*)** Returns the value of *number1* to the power of *number2*.

☐ **random()** Returns a random number between zero and one.

☐ **round(*number*)** Returns the closest integer to *number*—in other words rounds to the closest integer.

☐ **sin(*number*)** Returns the sine of *number*, where *number* represents an angle in radians.

☐ **sqrt(*number*)** Returns the square root of *number*.

☐ **tan(*number*)** Returns the tangent of *number*, where *number* represents an angle in radians.

The `mimeType` **Object [C|3]**

The `mimeType` object reflects a MIME type supported by the client browser.

Properties

- ☐ **type** A string value reflecting the MIME type.
- ☐ **description** A string containing a description of the MIME type.
- ☐ **enabledPlugin** A reference to a `plugin` object for the plug-in supporting the MIME type.
- ☐ **suffixes** A string containing a comma-separated list of file suffixes for the MIME type.

The `navigator` **Object [C|2|3|I]**

The `navigator` object reflects information about the version of Navigator being used.

Properties

- ☐ **appCodeName** A string value containing the code name of the client (for example, `"Mozilla"` for Netscape Navigator).
- ☐ **appName** A string value containing the name of the client (for example, `"Netscape"` for Netscape Navigator).
- ☐ **appVersion** A string value containing the version information for the client in the form

  versionNumber (platform; country)

  For instance, Navigator 2.0, beta 6 for Windows 95 (international version) would have an appVersion property with the value `"2.0b6 (Win32; I)"`.
- ☐ **mimeTypes** An array of `mimeType` objects reflecting the MIME types supported by the client browser. [Not 2|I]
- ☐ **plugins** An array of `plugin` objects reflecting the plug-ins in a document in the order of their appearance in the HTML document. [Not 2|I]
- ☐ **userAgent** A string containing the complete value of the user-agent header sent in the HTTP request. This contains all the information in `appCodeName` and `appVersion`:

  Mozilla/2.0b6 (Win32; I)

E

Method

☐ **javaEnabled()**   Returns a Boolean value indicating whether Java is enabled in the browser. [Not 2|I]

The Option **Object [C|3]**

The Option object is used to create entries in a select list using the syntax *optionName* = new Option(*optionText*, *optionValue*, *defaultSelected*, *selected*) and then *selectName*.options[*index*] = *optionName*.

Properties

☐ **defaultSelected**   A Boolean value specifying whether the option is selected by default.

☐ **index**   An integer value specifying the option's index in the select list.

☐ **prototype**   Provides a mechanism to add properties to an Option object.

☐ **selected**   A Boolean value indicating whether the option is currently selected.

☐ **text**   A string value reflecting the text displayed for the option.

☐ **value**   A string value indicating the value submitted to the server when the form is submitted.

The password **Object [C|2|3|I]**

The password object reflects a password text field from an HTML form in JavaScript.

Properties

☐ **defaultValue**   A string value containing the default value of the password element (that is, the value of the VALUE attribute).

☐ **enabled**   A Boolean value indicating whether the password field is enabled. [Not 2|3]

☐ **form**   A reference to the form object containing the password field. [Not 2|3]

☐ **name**   A string value containing the name of the password element.

☐ **value**   A string value containing the value of the password element.

Methods

☐ **focus()**   Emulates the action of focusing in the password field.

☐ **blur()**   Emulates the action of removing focus from the password field.

☐ **select()**   Emulates the action of selecting the text in the password field.

Event Handlers

☐ **onBlur**   Specifies JavaScript code to execute when the password field loses focus. [Not 2|3]

☐ **onFocus**   Specifies JavaScript code to execute when the password field receives focus. [Not 2|3]

The `plugin` Object

The `plugin` object reflects a plug-in supported by the browser.

Properties

☐ **name**   A string value reflecting the name of the plug-in.

☐ **filename**   A string value reflecting the filename of the plug-in on the system's disk.

☐ **description**   A string value containing the description supplied by the plug-in.

The `radio` Object [C|2|3|I]

The `radio` object reflects a set of radio buttons from an HTML form in JavaScript. To access individual radio buttons, use numeric indexes starting at zero. For instance, individual buttons in a set of radio buttons named `testRadio` could be referenced by `testRadio[0]`, `testRadio[1]`, and so on.

Properties

☐ **checked**   A Boolean value indicating whether a specific button is checked. Can be used to select or deselect a button.

☐ **defaultChecked**   A Boolean value indicating whether a specific button was checked by default (that is, reflects the CHECKED attribute). [Not I]

E

☐ **enabled**   A Boolean value indicating whether the radio button is enabled. [Not 2|3]

☐ **form**   A reference to the form object containing the radio button. [Not 2|3]

☐ **length**   An integer value indicating the number of radio buttons in the set. [Not I]

☐ **name**   A string value containing the name of the set of radio buttons.

☐ **value**   A string value containing the value of a specific radio button in a set (that is, reflects the VALUE attribute).

Methods

☐ **click()**   Emulates the action of clicking a radio button.

☐ **focus()**   Gives focus to the radio button. [Not 2|3]

Event Handlers

☐ **onClick**   Specifies JavaScript code to execute when a radio button is clicked.

☐ **onFocus**   Specifies JavaScript code to execute when a radio button receives focus. [Not 2|3]

The reset Object [C|2|3|I]

The reset object reflects a reset button from an HTML form in JavaScript.

Properties

☐ **enabled**   A Boolean value indicating whether the reset button is enabled. [Not 2|3]

☐ **form**   A reference to the form object containing the reset button. [Not 2|3]

☐ **name**   A string value containing the name of the reset element.

☐ **value**   A string value containing the value of the reset element.

Methods

☐ **click()**   Emulates the action of clicking the reset button.

☐ **focus()**   Specifies JavaScript code to execute when the reset button receives focus. [Not 2|3]

Event Handlers

☐ **onClick**   Specifies JavaScript code to execute when the reset button is clicked.

☐ **onFocus**   Specifies JavaScript code to execute when the reset button receives focus. [Not 2|3]

The select **Object [C|2|3]**

The select object reflects a selection list from an HTML form in JavaScript.

Properties

☐ **length**   An integer value containing the number of options in the selection list.

☐ **name**   A string value containing the name of the selection list.

☐ **options**   An array reflecting each of the options in the selection list in the order they appear. The options property has its own properties:

defaultSelected	A Boolean value indicating whether an option was selected by default (that is, reflects the SELECTED attribute).
index	An integer value reflecting the index of an option.
length	An integer value reflecting the number of options in the selection list.
name	A string value containing the name of the selection list.
selected	A Boolean value indicating whether the option is selected. Can be used to select or deselect an option.
selectedIndex	An integer value containing the index of the currently selected option.
text	A string value containing the text displayed in the selection list for a particular option.
value	A string value indicating the value for the specified option (that is, reflects the VALUE attribute).

☐ **selectedIndex**   Reflects the index of the currently selected option in the selection list.

Methods

☐ **blur()**   Removes focus from the select list. [Not 2|3]

☐ **focus()**   Gives focus to the select list. [Not 2|3]

E

Event Handlers

☐ **onBlur**   Specifies JavaScript code to execute when the selection list loses focus.

☐ **onFocus**   Specifies JavaScript code to execute when focus is given to the selection list.

☐ **onChange**   Specifies JavaScript code to execute when the selected option in the list changes.

The String Object [C | 2 | 3 | I]

The String object provides properties and methods for working with string literals and variables.

Properties

☐ **length**   An integer value containing the length of the string expressed as the number of characters in the string.

☐ **prototype**   Provides a mechanism for adding properties to a String object. [Not 2]

Methods

☐ **anchor(name)**   Returns a string containing the value of the String object surrounded by an A container tag with the NAME attribute set to name.

☐ **big()**   Returns a string containing the value of the String object surrounded by a BIG container tag.

☐ **blink()**   Returns a string containing the value of the String object surrounded by a BLINK container tag.

☐ **bold()**   Returns a string containing the value of the String object surrounded by a B container tag.

☐ **charAt(index)**   Returns the character at the location specified by index.

☐ **fixed()**   Returns a string containing the value of the String object surrounded by a FIXED container tag.

☐ **fontColor(color)**   Returns a string containing the value of the String object surrounded by a FONT container tag with the COLOR attribute set to color, where color is a color name or an RGB triplet. [Not I]

☐ **fontSize(*size*)**   Returns a string containing the value of the String object surrounded by a FONTSIZE container tag with the size set to *size*. [Not I]

☐ **indexOf(*findString,startingIndex*)**   Returns the index of the first occurrence of *findString*, starting the search at *startingIndex*, where *startingIndex* is optional—if it is not provided, the search starts at the start of the string.

☐ **italics()**   Returns a string containing the value of the String object surrounded by an I container tag.

☐ **lastIndexOf(*findString,startingIndex*)**   Returns the index of the last occurrence of *findString*. This is done by searching backward from *startingIndex*. *startingIndex* is optional and assumed to be the last character in the string if no value is provided.

☐ **link(*href*)**   Returns a string containing the value of the String object surrounded by an A container tag with the HREF attribute set to *href*.

☐ **small()**   Returns a string containing the value of the String object surrounded by a SMALL container tag.

☐ **split(*separator*)**   Returns an array of strings created by splitting the string at every occurrence of *separator*. [Not 2I]

☐ **strike()**   Returns a string containing the value of the String object surrounded by a STRIKE container tag.

☐ **sub()**   Returns a string containing the value of the String object surrounded by a SUB container tag.

☐ **substring(*firstIndex,lastIndex*)**   Returns a string equivalent to the substring starting at *firstIndex* and ending at the character before *lastIndex*. If *firstIndex* is greater than *lastIndex*, the string starts at *lastIndex* and ends at the character before *firstIndex*.

☐ **sup()**   Returns a string containing the value of the String object surrounded by a SUP container tag.

☐ **toLowerCase()**   Returns a string containing the value of the String object with all characters converted to lowercase.

☐ **toUpperCase()**   Returns a string containing the value of the String object with all characters converted to uppercase.

The submit Object [C|2|3|I]

The submit object reflects a submit button from an HTML form in JavaScript.

E

Properties

- `enabled` A Boolean value indicating whether the submit button is enabled. [Not 2|3]
- `form` A reference to the `form` object containing the submit button. [Not 2|3]
- `name` A string value containing the name of the submit button element.
- `type` A string value reflecting the `TYPE` attribute of the `INPUT` tag. [Not 2|I]
- `value` A string value containing the value of the submit button element.

Methods

- `click()` Emulates the action of clicking on the submit button.
- `focus()` Gives focus to the submit button. [Not 2|3]

Event Handlers

- `onClick` Specifies JavaScript code to execute when the submit button is clicked.
- `onFocus` Specifies JavaScript code to execute when the submit button receives focus. [Not 2|3]

The `text` Object [C|2|3|I]

The `text` object reflects a text field from an HTML form in JavaScript.

Properties

- `defaultValue` A string value containing the default value of the text element (that is, the value of the `VALUE` attribute).
- `enabled` A Boolean value indicating whether the text field is enabled. [Not 2|3]
- `form` A reference to the `form` object containing the text field. [Not 2|3]
- `name` A string value containing the name of the text element.
- `type` A string value reflecting the `TYPE` attribute of the `INPUT` tag. [Not 2|I]
- `value` A string value containing the value of the text element.

Methods

- `focus()` Emulates the action of focusing in the text field.
- `blur()` Emulates the action of removing focus from the text field.
- `select()` Emulates the action of selecting the text in the text field.

Event Handlers

- ☐ **onBlur**   Specifies JavaScript code to execute when focus is removed from the field.
- ☐ **onChange**   Specifies JavaScript code to execute when the content of the field is changed.
- ☐ **onFocus**   Specifies JavaScript code to execute when focus is given to the field.
- ☐ **onSelect**   Specifies JavaScript code to execute when the user selects some or all of the text in the field.

The textarea Object [C|2|3|I]

The textarea object reflects a multiline text field from an HTML form in JavaScript.

Properties

- ☐ **defaultValue**   A string value containing the default value of the textarea element (that is, the value of the VALUE attribute).
- ☐ **enabled**   A Boolean value indicating whether the textarea field is enabled. [Not 2|3]
- ☐ **form**   A reference to the form object containing the textarea field. [Not 2|3]
- ☐ **name**   A string value containing the name of the textarea element.
- ☐ **type**   A string value reflecting the type of the textarea object. [Not 2|I]
- ☐ **value**   A string value containing the value of the textarea element.

Methods

- ☐ **focus()**   Emulates the action of focusing in the textarea field.
- ☐ **blur()**   Emulates the action of removing focus from the textarea field.
- ☐ **select()**   Emulates the action of selecting the text in the textarea field.

Event Handlers

- ☐ **onBlur**   Specifies JavaScript code to execute when focus is removed from the field.
- ☐ **onChange**   Specifies JavaScript code to execute when the content of the field is changed.
- ☐ **onFocus**   Specifies JavaScript code to execute when focus is given to the field.
- ☐ **onSelect**   Specifies JavaScript code to execute when the user selects some or all of the text in the field.

E

The window **Object [C | 2 | 3 | I]**

The window object is the top-level object for each window or frame and is the parent object for the document, location, and history objects.

Properties

- ☐ **defaultStatus**   A string value containing the default value displayed in the status bar.

- ☐ **frames**   An array of objects for each frame in a window. Frames appear in the array in the order in which they appear in the HTML source code.

- ☐ **length**   An integer value indicating the number of frames in a parent window. [Not I]

- ☐ **name**   A string value containing the name of the window or frame.

- ☐ **opener**   A reference to the window object containing the open() method used to open the current window. [Not 2|I]

- ☐ **parent**   A string indicating the name of the window containing the frameset.

- ☐ **self**   An alternative for the name of the current window.

- ☐ **status**   Used to display a message in the status bar—this is done by assigning values to this property.

- ☐ **top**   An alternative for the name of the top-most window.

- ☐ **window**   An alternative for the name of the current window.

Methods

- ☐ **alert(message)**   Displays *message* in a dialog box.

- ☐ **blur()**   Removes focus from the window. On many systems, this sends the window to the background. [Not 2|I]

- ☐ **close()**   Closes the window. [Not I]

- ☐ **confirm(message)**   Displays *message* in a dialog box with OK and Cancel buttons. Returns true or false based on the button clicked by the user.

- ☐ **focus()**   Gives focus to the window. On many systems, this brings the window to the front. [Not 2|I]

- ☐ **navigator(url)**   Loads *url* in the window. [Not 2|3]

- ☐ **open(url,name,features)**   Opens *url* in a window named *name*. If *name* doesn't exist, a new window is created with that name. *features* is an optional string argument containing a list of features for the new window. The feature list contains any of the following name-value pairs separated by commas and without additional spaces [Not I]:

`toolbar=[yes,no,1,0]`	Indicates whether the window should have a toolbar
`location=[yes,no,1,0]`	Indicates whether the window should have a location field
`directories=[yes,no,1,0]`	Indicates whether the window should have directory buttons
`status=[yes,no,1,0]`	Indicates whether the window should have a status bar
`menubar=[yes,no,1,0]`	Indicates whether the window should have menus
`scrollbars=[yes,no,1,0]`	Indicates whether the window should have scrollbars
`resizable=[yes,no,1,0]`	Indicates whether the window should be resizable
`width=pixels`	Indicates the width of the window in pixels
`height=pixels`	Indicates the height of the window in pixels

☐ `prompt(message,response)` Displays *message* in a dialog box with a text entry field with the default value of *response*. The user's response in the text entry field is returned as a string.

☐ `setTimeout(expression,time)` Evaluates *expression* after *time*, where *time* is a value in milliseconds. The time-out can be named with the structure

`name = setTimeOut(expression,time)`

☐ `scroll(x,y)` Scrolls the window to the coordinate *x,y*. [Not 2lI]

☐ `clearTimeout(name)` Cancels the time-out with the name name.

Event Handlers

☐ `onBlur` Specifies JavaScript code to execute when focus is removed from a window. [Not 2lI]

☐ `onError` Specifies JavaScript code to execute when a JavaScript error occurs while loading a document. This can be used to intercept JavaScript errors. Setting this event handler to `null` effectively prevents JavaScript errors from being displayed to the user. [Not 2lI]

☐ `onFocus` Specifies JavaScript code to execute when the window receives focus. [Not 2lI]

□ **onLoad**   Specifies JavaScript code to execute when the window or frame finishes loading.

□ **onUnload**   Specifies JavaScript code to execute when the document in the window or frame is exited.

Independent Functions, Operators, Variables, and Literals

Independent Functions

□ **escape(*character*)**   Returns a string containing the ASCII encoding of *character* in the form %xx, where xx is the numeric encoding of the character. [C|2|3|I]

□ **eval(*expression*)**   Returns the result of evaluating *expression*, where *expression* is an arithmetic expression. [C|2|3|I]

□ **isNaN(*value*)**   Evaluates *value* to see whether it is NaN. Returns a Boolean value. [C|2|3|I] [On UNIX platforms, Not 2]

□ **parseFloat(*string*)**   Converts *string* to a floating-point number and returns the value. It continues to convert until it hits a non-numeric character and then returns the result. If the first character cannot be converted to a number, the function returns "NaN" (0 on Windows platforms). [C|2|3|I]

□ **parseInt(*string,base*)**   Converts *string* to an integer of base *base* and returns the value. It continues to convert until it hits a non-numeric character and then returns the result. If the first character cannot be converted to a number, the function returns "NaN" (0 on Windows platforms). [C|2|3|I]

□ **taint(*propertyName*)**   Adds tainting to *propertyName*. [C|3]

□ **toString()**   This is a method of all objects. It returns the object as a string or returns "[object *type*]" if no string representation exists for the object. [C|2|3]

□ **unescape(*string*)**   Returns a character based on the ASCII encoding contained in *string*. The ASCII encoding should take the form "%integer" or "hexadecimalValue". [C|2|3|I]

□ **untaint(*propertyName*)**   Removes tainting from *propertyName*. [C|3]

Operators

□ Assignment operators   Table E.1 shows the assignment operators in JavaScript. [C|2|3|I]

Table E.1. Assignment operators.

Operator	Description
=	Assigns the value of the right operand to the left operand
+=	Adds the left and right operands and assigns the result to the left operand
-=	Subtracts the right operand from the left operand and assigns the result to the left operand
*=	Multiplies the two operands and assigns the result to the left operand
/=	Divides the left operand by the right operand and assigns the value to the left operand
%=	Divides the left operand by the right operand and assigns the remainder to the left operand

☐ Arithmetic operators   Table E.2 shows the arithmetic operators in JavaScript. [C|2|3|I]

Table E.2. Arithmetic operators.

Operator	Description
+	Adds the left and right operands
-	Subtracts the right operand from the left operand
*	Multiplies the two operands
/	Divides the left operand by the right operand
%	Divides the left operand by the right operand and evaluates to the remainder
++	Increments the operand by one (can be used before or after the operand)
--	Decreases the operand by one (can be used before or after the operand)
-	Changes the sign of the operand

☐ Bitwise operators   Bitwise operators deal with their operands as binary numbers but return JavaScript numerical value (see Table E.3). [C|2|3|I]

Table E.3. Bitwise operators in JavaScript.

Operator	Description
AND (or &)	Converts operands to integers with 32 bits, pairs the corresponding bits, and returns one for each pair of ones. Returns zero for any other combination.
OR (or ¦)	Converts operands to integers with 32 bits, pairs the corresponding bits, and returns one for each pair where one of the two bits is one. Returns zero if both bits are zero.
XOR (or ^)	Converts operands to integers with 32 bits, pairs the corresponding bits, and returns one for each pair where only one bit is one. Returns zero for any other combination.
<<	Converts the left operand to an integer with 32 bits and shifts bits to the left the number of bits indicated by the right operand—bits shifted off to the left are discarded and zeros are shifted in from the right.
>>	Converts the left operand to an integer with 32 bits and shifts bits to the right the number of bits indicated by the right operand—bits shifted off to the right are discarded and copies of the left-most bit are shifted in from the left.

☐ Logical operators   Table E.4 shows the logical operators in JavaScript. [C|2|3|I]

Table E.4. Logical operators.

Operator	Description
&&	Logical AND—returns true when both operands are true; otherwise it returns false.
¦¦	Logical OR—returns true if either operand is true. It only returns false when both operands are false.
!	Logical NOT—returns true if the operand is false and false if the operand is true. This is a unary operator and it precedes the operand.

☐ Comparison operators   Table E.5 shows the comparison operators in JavaScript. [C|2|3|I]

Table E.5. Logical (comparison) operators.

Operator	Description
==	Returns true if the operands are equal
!=	Returns true if the operands are not equal
>	Returns true if the left operand is greater than the right operand
<	Returns true if the left operand is less than the right operand
>=	Returns true if the left operand is greater than or equal to the right operand
<=	Returns true if the left operand is less than or equal to the right operand

☐ Conditional operators   Conditional expressions take one form:

`(condition) ? val1 : val2`

If `condition` is true, the expression evaluates to `val1`; otherwise, it evaluates to `val2`. [C|2|3|I]

☐ String operators   The concatenation operators (+) is one of two string operators. It evaluates to a string combining the left and right operands. The concatenation assignment operator (+=) is also available. [C|2|3|I]

☐ The `typeof` operator   The `typeof` operator returns the type of its single operand. Possible types are `object`, `string`, `number`, `boolean`, `function`, and `undefined`. [C|3|I]

☐ The `void` operator   The `void` operator takes an expression as an operand but returns no value. [C|3]

☐ Operator precedence   JavaScript applies the rules of operator precedence as follows (from lowest to highest precedence):

```
comma (,)
assignment operators (= += -= *= /= %=)
conditional (? :)
logical OR (¦¦)
logical AND (&&)
bitwise OR (¦)
bitwise XOR (^)
```

bitwise AND (&)
equality (== !=)
relational (< <= > >=)
shift (<< >> >>>)
addition/subtraction (+ -)
multiply/divide/modulus (* / %)
negation/increment (! - ++ --)
call, member (() [])

APPENDIX

F

What's on the CD-ROM

On the *Teach Yourself Microsoft Visual InterDev in 21 Days* CD-ROM are the sample files that have been presented in this book, along with a wealth of other applications and utilities.

NOTE

> Please refer to the readme.wri file on the CD-ROM for the latest listing of software.

Microsoft® Visual Basic®, Control Creation Edition, System Requirements

- ☐ Personal computer with a 486 or higher processor
- ☐ Microsoft Windows® 95 or Windows NT® Workstation 4.0 or later
- ☐ 8MB of memory (12MB recommended) if running Windows 95
- ☐ 16MB (20MB recommended) if running Windows 95
- ☐ Hard-disk space:

  Typical installation: 20MB

  Minimum installation: 14MB

  CD-ROM installation: (tools run from the CD-ROM): 14MB

  Total tools and information on CD-ROM: 50 MB
- ☐ CD-ROM drive
- ☐ VGA or higher-resolution monitor (SVGA recommended)
- ☐ Microsoft Mouse or compatible pointing device

Explorer

- ☐ Microsoft Internet Explorer 3

HTML Tools

- ☐ Hot Dog 32-bit HTML editor demo
- ☐ HoTMeTaL HTML editor demo
- ☐ HTMLed HTML editor
- ☐ Spider 1.2 demo
- ☐ Web Analyzer demo

Graphics, Video, and Sound Applications

☐ Goldwave sound editor, player, and recorder
☐ MapThis imagemap utility
☐ Paint Shop Pro
☐ SnagIt screen capture utility
☐ ThumbsPlus image viewer and browser

ActiveX

☐ Microsoft ActiveX Control Pad and HTML Layout Control

Utilities

☐ Adobe Acrobat viewer
☐ WinZip for Windows NT/95
☐ WinZip Self-Extractor

About This Software

Some of the software on this CD-ROM is shareware. Shareware is not free. Please read all documentation associated with a third-party product (usually contained with files named readme.txt or license.txt) and follow all guidelines.

F

INDEX

X-Z

MACMILLAN COMPUTER PUBLISHING USA

A VIACOM COMPANY

Technical ---- Support:

If you need assistance with the information in this book or with a CD/Disk
accompanying the book, please access the Knowledge Base on our Web
site at **http://www.superlibrary.com/general/support**. Our most
Frequently Asked Questions are answered there. If you do not find the
answer to your questions on our Web site, you may contact Macmillan
Technical Support **(317) 581-3833** or e-mail us at **support@mcp.com**.

Teach Yourself Visual Basic 5 in 21 Days, Fourth Edition

Nathan Gurewich and Ori Gurewich

Using a logical, easy-to-follow approach, this international bestseller teaches readers the fundamentals of developing programs. It starts with the basics of writing a program and moves on to adding voice, music, sound, and graphics. Covers Visual Basic 5.

$29.99 USA, $42.95 CDN, ISBN 0-672-30978-5

VBScript Unleashed

Brian Johnson

In *VBScript Unleashed*, Web programming techniques are presented in a logical and easy-to-follow sequence that helps readers understand the principles involved in developing programs. The reader begins with learning the basics for writing a first program and then builds on that to add interactivity, multimedia, and more to Web page designs.

$39.99 USA, $56.95 CDN, ISBN 1-57521-124-6

Laura Lemay's Web Workshop: ActiveX and VBScript

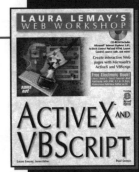

Paul Lomax and Rogers Cadenhead

ActiveX is an umbrella term for a series of Microsoft products and technologies that add activity to Web pages. Visual Basic Script is an essential element of the ActiveX family. With it, animation, multimedia, sound, graphics, and interactivity can be added to a Web site. This book is a compilation of individual workshops that show the reader how to use VBScript and other ActiveX technologies within their Web sites.

$39.99 USA, $56.95 CDN, ISBN 1-57521-207-2

Visual Basic for Applications Unleashed

Paul McFedries

Combining both power and ease of use, Visual Basic for Applications (VBA) is the common language for developing macros and applications across all Microsoft Office components. Using the format of the best-selling Unleashed series, users will master the intricacies of this popular language and exploit the full power of VBA. Covers user interface design, database programming, networking programming, Internet programming, and standalone application creation.

$49.99 USA, $70.95 CDN, ISBN 0-672-31046-5

Teach Yourself Visual J++ in 21 Days

Laura Lemay, Patrick Winters, and David Blankenbeckler

Readers will learn how to use Visual J++, Microsoft's Windows version of Java, to design and create Java applets for the World Wide Web. Visual J++ includes many new features to Java, including visual resource editing tools, source code control, syntax coloring, visual project management, and integrated bills. All of these tools are covered in detail giving readers the information they need to write professional Java applets for the Web.

$39.99 USA, $56.95 CDN, ISBN 1-57521-158-0

Visual J++ Unleashed

Bryan Morgan, et al.

Java is the hottest programming language being learned today. And Microsoft's Windows version of Java, code-named Visual J++, might prove to be even hotter as Microsoft has added several new development features, such as graphic designing, to the Java language. *Visual J++ Unleashed* shows readers how to exploit the Java development potential of Visual J++.

$49.99 USA, $70.95 CDN, ISBN 1-57521-161-0

Teach Yourself Java in 21 Days, Professional Reference Edition

Laura Lemay and Michael Morrison

Introducing the first, best, and most detailed guide to developing applications with the hot new Java language from Sun Microsystems. This book provides detailed coverage of the hottest new technology on the World Wide Web.

$59.99 USA, $84.95 CDN, ISBN 1-57521-183-1

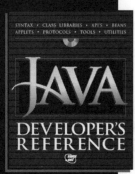

Java Developer's Reference

Mike Cohn, et al.

This is the informative, resource-packed development package for professional developers. It explains the components of the Java Development Kit (JDK) and the Java programming language. Everything needed to program Java is included within this comprehensive reference, making it the tool developers will turn to over and over again for timely, accurate information on Java and the JDK.

$59.99 USA, $84.95 CDN, ISBN 1-57521-129-7

Add to Your Sams.net Library Today
with the Best Books for Internet Technologies

ISBN	Quantity	Description of Item	Unit Cost	Total Cost
0-672-30978-5		Teach Yourself Visual Basic 5 in 21 Days, Fourth Edition	$29.99	
1-57521-124-6		VBScript Unleashed (Book/CD-ROM)	$39.99	
1-57521-207-2		Laura Lemay's Web Workshop: ActiveX and VBScript (Book/CD-ROM)	$39.99	
0-672-31046-5		Visual Basic Applications Unleashed (Book/CD-ROM)	$49.99	
1-57521-158-0		Teach Yourself Visual J++ in 21 Days (Book/CD-ROM)	$39.99	
1-57521-161-0		Visual J++ Unleashed (Book/CD-ROM)	$49.99	
1-57521-183-1		Teach Yourself Java in 21 Days, Professional Reference Edition (Book/CD-ROM)	$59.99	
1-57521-129-7		Java Developer's Reference (Book/CD-ROM)	$59.99	
		Shipping and Handling: See information below.		
		TOTAL		

Shipping and Handling: $4.00 for the first book, and $1.75 for each additional book. If you need to have it NOW, we can ship product to you in 24 hours for an additional charge of approximately $18.00, and you will receive your item overnight or in two days. Overseas shipping and handling adds $2.00. Prices subject to change. Call between 9:00 a.m. and 5:00 p.m. EST for availability and pricing information on latest editions.

201 W. 103rd Street, Indianapolis, Indiana 46290

1-800-428-5331 — Orders   1-800-835-3202 — Fax   1-800-858-7674 — Customer Service

Book ISBN 1-57521-093-2

Installing the CD-ROM

The companion CD-ROM contains all the source code and project files developed by the authors, plus an assortment of evaluation versions of third-party products. To install, please follow these steps:

Windows 95/NT 4 Installation Instructions

1. Insert the CD-ROM into your CD-ROM drive.
2. From the Windows 95/NT 4 desktop, double-click the My Computer icon.
3. Double-click the icon representing your CD-ROM drive.
4. Double-click the icon titled setup.exe to run the CD-ROM installation program.

LIMITED WARRANTY

you may install the SOFTWARE PRODUCT on a single computer provided you keep the original solely for backup or archival purposes. You may not copy the printed materials accompanying the SOFTWARE PRODUCT.

5. DUAL-MEDIA SOFTWARE. You may receive the SOFTWARE PRODUCT in more than one medium. Regardless of the type or size of medium you receive, you may use only one medium that is appropriate for your single computer. You may not use or install the other medium on another computer. You may not loan, rent, lease, or otherwise transfer the other medium to another user, except as part of the permanent transfer (as provided above) of the SOFTWARE PRODUCT.

6. U.S. GOVERNMENT RESTRICTED RIGHTS. The SOFTWARE PRODUCT and documentation are provided with RESTRICTED RIGHTS. Use, duplication, or disclosure by the Government is subject to restrictions as set forth in subparagraph (c)(1)(ii) of the Rights in Technical Data and Computer Software clause at DFARS 252.227-7013 or subparagraphs (c)(1) and (2) of the Commercial Computer Software—Restricted Rights at 48 CFR 52.227-19, as applicable. Manufacturer is Microsoft Corporation/One Microsoft Way/Redmond, WA 98052-6399.

7. EXPORT RESTRICTIONS. You agree that neither you nor your customers intend to or will, directly or indirectly, export or transmit (i) the SOFTWARE or related documentation and technical data or (ii) your software product as described in Section 1(b) of this License (or any part thereof), or process, or service that is the direct product of the SOFTWARE, to any country to which such export or transmission is restricted by any applicable U.S. regulation or statute, without the prior written consent, if required, of the Bureau of Export Administration of the U.S. Department of Commerce, or such other governmental entity as may have jurisdiction over such export or transmission.

MISCELLANEOUS

If you acquired this product in the United States, this EULA is governed by the laws of the State of Washington.

If you acquired this product in Canada, this EULA is governed by the laws of the Province of Ontario, Canada. Each of the parties hereto irrevocably attorns to the jurisdiction of the courts of the Province of Ontario and further agrees to commence any litigation which may arise hereunder in the courts located in the Judicial District of York, Province of Ontario.

If this product was acquired outside the United States, then local law may apply.

Should you have any questions concerning this EULA, or if you desire to contact Microsoft for any reason, please contact the Microsoft subsidiary serving your country, or write: Microsoft Sales Information Center/One Microsoft Way/Redmond, WA 98052-6399.

⇦ *(continued)*

d. Rental. You may not rent, lease, or lend the SOFTWARE PRODUCT.

e. Support Services. Microsoft may provide you with support services related to the SOFTWARE PRODUCT ("Support Services"). Use of Support Services is governed by the Microsoft policies and programs described in the user manual, in "online" documentation, and/or in other Microsoft-provided materials. Any supplemental software code provided to you as part of the Support Services shall be considered part of the SOFTWARE PRODUCT and subject to the terms and conditions of this EULA. With respect to technical information you provide to Microsoft as part of the Support Services, Microsoft may use such information for its business purposes, including for product support and development. Microsoft will not utilize such technical information in a form that personally identifies you.

f. Software Transfer. You may permanently transfer all of your rights under this EULA, provided you retain no copies, you transfer all of the SOFTWARE PRODUCT (including all component parts, the media and printed materials, any upgrades, this EULA, and, if applicable, the Certificate of Authenticity), and the recipient agrees to the terms of this EULA. If the SOFTWARE PRODUCT is an upgrade, any transfer must include all prior versions of the SOFTWARE PRODUCT.

g. Termination. Without prejudice to any other rights, Microsoft may terminate this EULA if you fail to comply with the terms and conditions of this EULA. In such event, you must destroy all copies of the SOFTWARE PRODUCT and all of its component parts.

3. UPGRADES. If the SOFTWARE PRODUCT is labeled as an upgrade, you must be properly licensed to use a product identified by Microsoft as being eligible for the upgrade in order to use the SOFTWARE PRODUCT. A SOFTWARE PRODUCT labeled as an upgrade replaces and/or supplements the product that formed the basis for your eligibility for the upgrade. You may use the resulting upgraded product only in accordance with the terms of this EULA. If the SOFTWARE PRODUCT is an upgrade of a component of a package of software programs that you licensed as a single product, the SOFTWARE PRODUCT may be used and transferred only as part of that single product package and may not be separated for use on more than one computer.

4. COPYRIGHT. All title and copyrights in and to the SOFTWARE PRODUCT (including but not limited to any images, photographs, animations, video, audio, music, text, and "applets" incorporated into the SOFTWARE PRODUCT), the accompanying printed materials, and any copies of the SOFTWARE PRODUCT are owned by Microsoft or its suppliers. The SOFTWARE PRODUCT is protected by copyright laws and international treaty provisions. Therefore, you must treat the SOFTWARE PRODUCT like any other copyrighted material except that

⟵ (continued)

reproduce and distribute the SAMPLE CODE, along with any modifications thereof, only in object code form provided that you comply with Section d(iii), below.

(ii) Redistributable Components. In addition to the rights granted in Section 1, Microsoft grants you a nonexclusive royalty-free right to reproduce and distribute the object code version of any portion of the SOFTWARE listed in the SOFT-WARE file REDIST.TXT ("REDISTRIBUTABLE SOFTWARE"), provided you comply with Section d(iii), below.

(iii) Redistribution Requirements. If you redistribute the SAMPLE CODE or REDISTRIBUTABLE SOFTWARE (collectively, "REDISTRIBUTABLES"), you agree to: (A) distribute the REDISTRIBUTABLES in object code only in conjunction with and as a part of a software application product developed by you that adds significant and primary functionality to the SOFTWARE and that is developed to operate on the Windows or Windows NT environment ("Application"); (B) not use Microsoft's name, logo, or trademarks to market your software application product; (C) include a valid copyright notice on your software product; (D) indemnify, hold harmless, and defend Microsoft from and against any claims or lawsuits, including attorney's fees, that arise or result from the use or distribution of your software application product; (E) not permit further distribution of the REDISTRIBUTABLES by your end user. The following exceptions apply to subsection (iii)(E), above: (1) you may permit further redistribution of the REDISTRIBUTABLES by your distributors to your end-user customers if your distributors only distribute the REDISTRIBUTABLES in conjunction with, and as part of, your Application and you and your distributors comply with all other terms of this EULA; and (2) you may permit your end users to reproduce and distribute the object code version of the files designated by ".ocx" file extensions ("Controls") only in conjunction with and as a part of an Application and/or Web page that adds significant and primary functionality to the Controls, and such end user complies with all other terms of this EULA.

2. DESCRIPTION OF OTHER RIGHTS AND LIMITATIONS.

a. Not for Resale Software. If the SOFTWARE PRODUCT is labeled "Not for Resale" or "NFR," then, notwithstanding other sections of this EULA, you may not resell, or otherwise transfer for value, the SOFTWARE PRODUCT.

b. Limitations on Reverse Engineering, Decompilation, and Disassembly. You may not reverse engineer, decompile, or disassemble the SOFTWARE PRODUCT, except and only to the extent that such activity is expressly permitted by applicable law notwithstanding this limitation.

c. Separation of Components. The SOFTWARE PRODUCT is licensed as a single product. Its component parts may not be separated for use by more than one user.

⇐ (continued)

End-User License Agreement For Microsoft® Software

Microsoft® Visual Basic®, Control Creation Edition

IMPORTANT—READ CAREFULLY: This Microsoft End-User License Agreement ("EULA") is a legal agreement between you (either an individual or a single entity) and Microsoft Corporation for the Microsoft software product identified above, which includes computer software and may include associated media, printed materials, and "online" or electronic documentation ("SOFTWARE PRODUCT"). By installing, copying, or otherwise using the SOFTWARE PRODUCT, you agree to be bound by the terms of this EULA. If you do not agree to the terms of this EULA, do not install or use the SOFTWARE PRODUCT; you may, however, return it to your place of purchase for a full refund.

Software PRODUCT LICENSE

The SOFTWARE PRODUCT is protected by copyright laws and international copyright treaties, as well as other intellectual property laws and treaties. The SOFTWARE PRODUCT is licensed, not sold.

1. GRANT OF LICENSE. This EULA grants you the following rights: Microsoft grants to you as an individual, a personal, nonexclusive license to make and use copies of the SOFTWARE for the sole purposes of designing, developing, and testing your software product(s) that are designed to operate in conjunction with any Microsoft operating system product. You may install copies of the SOFTWARE on an unlimited number of computers provided that you are the only individual using the SOFTWARE. If you are an entity, Microsoft grants you the right to designate one individual within your organization to have the right to use the SOFTWARE in the manner provided above.

b. Electronic Documents. Solely with respect to electronic documents included with the SOFTWARE, you may make an unlimited number of copies (either in hardcopy or electronic form), provided that such copies shall be used only for internal purposes and are not republished or distributed to any third party.

Redistributable Components.

(i) Sample Code. In addition to the rights granted in Section 1, Microsoft grants you the right to use and modify the source code version of those portions of the SOFTWARE designated as "Sample Code" ("SAMPLE CODE") for the sole purposes of designing, developing, and testing your software product(s), and to

⇦ (continued)